Western Australia

a Lonely Planet Australia guide

Jeff Williams

Western Australia

1st edition

Published by

Lonely Planet Publications
Head Office: PO Box 617, Hawthorn, Vic 3122, Australia
Branches: 155 Filbert St, Suite 251, Oakland, CA 94607, USA
               10 Barley Mow Passage, Chiswick, London W4 4PH, UK
               71 bis rue du Cardinal Lemoine, 75005 Paris, France

Printed by

Singapore National Printers Ltd, Singapore

Photographs by

Paul Steel (PS)
Roger Du Buisson (RDB)
Glenn Beanland (GB)
Jeff Williams (JW)
Richard Nebeský (RN)
Western Australian Tourist Commission (WATC)
Keren Flavell (KF)
Richard I'Anson (RI)
Chris Lee Ack (CLA)
Tony Wheeler (TW)

Front cover: Outcrops in the Pinnacles (Roger Du Buisson)

This Edition

April 1995

Although the authors and publisher have tried to make the information as accurate as possible, they accept no responsibility for any loss, injury or inconvenience sustained by any person using this book

National Library of Australia Cataloguing in Publication Data

Williams, Jeff, 1954 Dec. 15- .
    Western Australia.

    Includes index.
    ISBN 0 86442 268 7.

    1. Western Australia – Guidebooks. I. Title. (Series :
    Lonely Planet Australia guide).

919.410463

Jeff Williams

Jeff Williams is a Kiwi from Greymouth on New Zealand's wild west coast. He thinks he has finally found a use for his university degrees by working as a writer for Lonely Planet. When not behind his laptop computer enthusing over 'that bird', 'this mountain' or 'a great place to stay', he hikes, skis and climbs over whichever country will have him. He was co-writer of Lonely Planet's *New Zealand – a travel survival kit, Australia – a travel survival kit, Tramping in New Zealand* and a contributor to *Outback Australia*. His dream is to write a travel guide to the islands of the South Pacific, accompanied by his wife Alison and son Callum.

From the Author

A trip through the west is an undertaking of significance and the passing of the time is made better by the quality of the company. In this regard, I thank my wife Alison and my son Callum, who not only accompanied me in three and a half months but willingly participated in what some construe as work.

The Western Australian Tourism Commission in Perth was extremely helpful and Alan Morley and Rita Stinson gave much needed advice and information. Many others in tourist offices throughout the state also helped me gather information. Simply because you are not named does not mean that you have been forgotten. Thanks to Jim and Collette Truscott and their kids in Karratha for making us welcome in the Pilbara and Jim for pointing out the climbing men of the Burrup Peninsula; Helen and Albert Innes in Perth for their hospitality; Neil McLeod of Ningaloo Safari Tours in Exmouth for a great trip across Cape Range; George Swann, Broome, for showing me the waders as they arrived from Siberia; Russell Wilson for looking after matters back in the east; Stef and Angela Frodsham of East Fremantle for the tours around Freo; Pete Flavelle for keeping a weather eye on the tides, wave patterns and cloud formations near Cottesloe; and Steve Townshend and Rachel Black in Melbourne, for turning this into a book.

From the Publisher

This first edition was edited by Stephen Townshend. Rachel Black drew the maps and orchestrated the layout. A big thanks to Tom Smallman for proofing the book, Valerie Tellini for the cover design, and thanks also to Maria Nugent, Brian Nugent, Dr Malcolm Wallace, Dr David Aldous, Minetta Black and Nicole Aristidis for their invaluable advice and assistance.

Warning & Request

Things change – prices go up, schedules change, good places go bad and bad places go bankrupt – nothing stays the same. So if you find things better or worse, recently opened or long since closed, please write and tell us and help make the next edition better.

Your letters will be used to help update future editions and, where possible, important changes will also be included in a Stop Press section in reprints.

We greatly appreciate all information that is sent to us by travellers. Back at Lonely Planet we employ a hard-working readers' letters team to sort through the many letters we receive. The best ones will be rewarded with a free copy of the next edition or another Lonely Planet guide if you prefer. We give away lots of books, but, unfortunately, not every letter/postcard receives one.

Map Legend

BOUNDARIES

.... International Boundary

.... State Boundary

ROUTES

.... Freeway

.... Highway

.... Major Road

.... Unsealed Road or Track

.... City Road

.... City Street

.... Railway

.... Underground Railway

.... Tram

.... Walking Track

.... Walking Tour

.... Ferry Route

.... Cable Car or Chairlift

AREA FEATURES

.... Park, Gardens

.... National Park

.... Built-Up Area

.... Pedestrian Mall

.... Market

.... Cemetery

.... Reef

.... Beach or Desert

.... Rocks

HYDROGRAPHIC FEATURES

.... Coastline

.... River, Creek

.... Intermittent River or Creek

.... Lake, Intermittent Lake

.... Canal

.... Swamp

SYMBOLS

✪ CAPITAL		.... National Capital
◉ Capital		.... State Capital
◍ CITY		.... Major City
● City		.... City
● Town		.... Town
● Village		.... Village
■		.... Place to Stay
▼		.... Place to Eat
♟		.... Pub, Bar
✉	☎	.... Post Office, Telephone
❶	❻	.... Tourist Information, Bank
◗	Ⓟ	.... Transport, Parking
🏛	⛺	.... Museum, Youth Hostel
⌂	Å	Caravan Park, Camping Ground
† ▣ †		.... Church, Cathedral
☪ ✡		.... Mosque, Synagogue
⚊	⚊	Buddhist Temple, Hindu Temple

✚	★	.... Hospital, Police Station
✈	✝	.... Airport, Airfield
▱	✿	.... Swimming Pool, Gardens
❖	🐘	.... Shopping Centre, Zoo
⚘	⊼	... Winery or Vineyard, Picnic Site
←	A25	One Way Street, Route Number
	∴	...... Archaeological Site or Ruins
🏠	▲	.... Stately Home, Monument
🏚	▣	.... Castle, Tomb
⌒	⌂	.... Cave, Hut or Chalet
▲	☼	.... Mountain or Hill, Lookout
⚲	⤪	.... Lighthouse, Shipwreck
)(	⌔	.... Pass, Spring
		.... Ancient or City Wall
		.... Rapids, Waterfalls
		...... Cliff or Escarpment, Tunnel
		.... Railway Station

Note: not all symbols displayed above appear in this book

Contents

Introduction

Western Australia (more commonly known as WA, 'Double-U ay') is isolated by desert from Australia's population and power centres. But, paradoxically, this potential weakness has heralded a number of strengths, enhancing the feeling that WA is somehow different, almost a separate country. And let's face it, WA is also big! But we all know that size isn't everything – Australia's largest state is packed with wonders and much of its allure is the realisation that many of these are just being 'discovered'.

Chances are you will be the only person swimming in the idyllic lagoons of Ningaloo Reef on a particular day; yours will be the sole 4WD (four-wheel drive) driven into remote Rudall River National Park for some

weeks; you were one of a handful of people who camped inside a gorge in the spectacular Purnululu (Bungle Bungles) National Park in the past month; when fishing, you had a couple of hundred km of beach to yourself; and you and your partner were the only people who saw a particular huge expanse of wildflowers in bloom this year. Not only are all of the above examples possible, they'll also be the norm for some time to come.

This is a state of incredible contrasts: sophisticated cities to ghost towns, the rugged Kimberley to the billiard-table flat Nullarbor, the lush forests of the south-west to the sunbaked red and brown hues of the arid centre, and the brilliant blue waters of the oceans to the dazzling white saltpans on the fringe of civilisation. And the land, sea

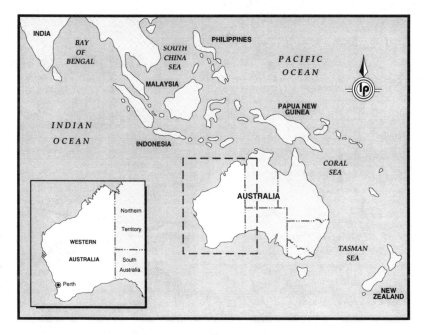

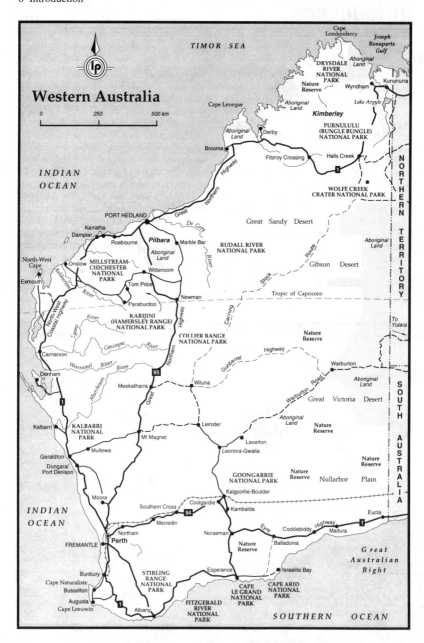

and sky are intensified by the light in a most vivid and unforgettable manner.

The only remaining frontier in non-desert Australia is in the north of the state. The Kimberley, remote, rugged and three times the size of England, has repulsed attempts at settlement and is still the least-populated area of northern Australia. To the south is the equally wild Pilbara. The spectacular Hamersley Range includes memorable views over gorges of the Karijini National Park. Sandwiched between the Kimberley and the Pilbara is the exotic town of Broome, now a major tourist Mecca.

Western Australia is the perfect ecotourism destination. Shark Bay, renowned for its friendly dolphins at Monkey Mia, has an additional wealth of flora & fauna which led to its being designated as a world heritage area. North-West Cape, with unforgettable Ningaloo Reef and the absorbing Cape Range National Park, is Australia's best ecotourism destination. The fauna seen here includes the world largest fish, the whale shark, manta rays, humpback whales, nesting turtles, plus a myriad of birds and rare marsupials.

An irresistible lure for any traveller is the wildflowers (approximately 8000 species are found in the state). The forests of the south contain mighty jarrah, karri, marri and tingle trees and more wildflowers. Birdlife and animals are prolific and the wide variety of habitats supports many species.

The regions of the Great Southern and the south-west are missed by many visitors to Australia. A pity, as they also possess a wealth of natural attractions – limestone caves, archipelagos teeming with wildlife, forests of ancient trees including the giant karri and the rare tingles, the Fitzgerald River Biosphere Reserve and the rugged Stirling and Porongurup ranges. To the north lies the goldfields region, with historic ghost towns and the frontier city of Kalgoorlie.

The hub of WA is undoubtedly its vibrant cosmopolitan capital, Perth (often called the most isolated city in the world). Perth may be isolated but it is also very classy with a complete range of accommodation, places to eat and entertainment. Not far away are historic Fremantle, Rottnest Island and a number of great surfing beaches.

Western Australia includes something for all types of traveller. So go west!

Facts about Western Australia

HISTORY

The Dreamtime

Creation stories explain the origins of Australian Aboriginal peoples, reinforcing the belief that they inhabited this continent since the beginning of time.

The creation period is often referred to as the Dreamtime. It was the time when spiritual beings (also known as ancestral spirits) travelled the land forming natural features and instituting laws and rituals. In the Kimberley, the Wandjina, Marlu the Great Kangaroo and the Maletji Dogs are all ancestral spirits. Warlu the Rainbow Snake and Mangela are ancestral spirits from the Pilbara. Other local areas have their own creation stories and ancestral spirits which are depicted in rock art – the Jaburara of the Burrup Peninsula etched the Climbing Men into the rock of Murajuga and the Ngaluma people etched images of ancestral spirits in the dolerite rocks of Depuch Island ('Womalantha' in Aboriginal), which is a site where ceremonies are performed.

But the Dreamtime is not simply the past – it is also the present and future. After creating life and everything associated with it, the ancestral spirits entered the land to dwell or formed themselves into natural features of it. This explains the strong spiritual link Aborigines have to particular tracts of land. It is possible that every major geographical feature you see in your travels in Western Australia (WA) will have special significance for them in that area. Since it is believed that ancestral spirits still live in the land, taking care of sacred sites is an essential part of maintaining life, health and social order.

However, with the arrival of Whites, the continuity of life handed down from generation to generation, since the beginning of time, was disrupted.

The Archaeological Record

It is thought that Aborigines may have landed on the northern shores of Australia some 60,000 years ago, at a time when large parts of the continental shelf were exposed.

Evidence from this period, such as camp-sites and artefacts, would now be under the sea. The expansion of polar ice caps and reduction in rainfall experienced during Pleistocene 'ice ages' would result in lower sea levels. At the end of each period of glaciation, the sea rose, inundating the continental shelf. The last rise in the sea level began about 12,000 years ago, stabilising in its present position some 6000 years ago. To a certain extent this explains the presence of flaked stone artefacts on the islands of the Archipelago of the Recherche. It is assumed many more sites would be submerged on the now inundated shelf.

If the Aborigines island-hopped from South-East Asia then it is also likely that the north-west (the present Kimberley) would have been their first landfall. They would have spread from here to all parts of the continent and, ultimately, across to Tasmania.

At Swan Bridge, near Perth, a campsite was discovered which contained stone tools and charcoal from a campfire made about 39,500 years ago. This is the oldest known site on the continent and provides the strongest proof to date that Aborigines lived in the area, or Australia for that matter, at least 40,000 years old.

In a recent discovery, fish and shellfish remains in an Aboriginal rockshelter at Mandu Mandu Creek in the Cape Range, North-West Cape, have been dated as being 34,000 years old.

Another ice-age site discovered in WA is the Devil's Lair, near Cape Leeuwin in the south-west of the state. Bone and stone tools, choppers and flakes excavated from the dry floor of this limestone cave, have been determined to be 33,000 old.

At the northern end of the Weld Ranges, near Cue in the Murchison district, the

Aborigines mined ochre which was used in ceremonies as long ago as 30,000 years. The ochre was possibly traded as far away as Queensland. This ochre mine, Wilga Mia, features in tales from the Dreamtime.

There is a great deal of evidence of a sophisticated culture further south, with examples of Aborigines' daily food-gathering. They trapped fish in the estuaries, capturing and killing now-extinct megafauna such as the large kangaroo-like creature *(Sthenurus)* and the hippopotamus-sized wombat *(Diprotodon)*. Many middens (earth closets), quarries and fishtraps remain.

The Aborigines also learnt to use the local flora in everyday life, both for food and materials for a broad range of objects. Wood was used to fashion clubs, bowls, spears and boomerangs. Slender banksia was soaked in water to make a sweet drink and the *Macrozamia* (a cycad with cones) was cooked and eaten after it too was soaked, while the small leaf clematis was roasted and pounded into a mash.

About a dozen local groups of the Nyungar people occupied the area of the Swan River Valley and it was estimated that there were over another dozen tribal groups between Geraldton and Esperance. The Aborigines travelled along *bidi* (tracks) to trade or meet for feasts and ceremonies.

Aboriginal prehistory is still being pieced together – only further archaeological discoveries and painstaking research will clarify the origins and identity of the Aborigines of the west and, indeed, Australia.

The First Foreigners

There is no doubt that the first 'outsiders' to make contact with the Aborigines were traders from the islands that are now Indonesia (who are remembered in song cycles and in paintings). Their impact, however, was likely slight and confined to coastal area.

Uncertainty surrounds the great Asian fleet under the Chinese lord Cheng Ho (Zheng He) who allegedly visited the northern Australian shores in the 15th century. A small carved figure of the Chinese god of good life, Shao Lao, was found lodged in the roots of a banyan tree near Darwin – it dated from the Ming Dynasty (1368-1644). However, no account survives of such contact.

The Europeans

The Portuguese, traversing the Indian Ocean in the 15th century, may have been the first to discover the west coast. A 16th-century book talks about a voyage to the Kimberley coast and a Portuguese map, dated 1602, indicates a landing in the region of Collier and Brunswick bays.

As early as 1606, the Dutchman Willem Jansz, sailing in the *Duyfken*, explored the western coast of Cape York. He was unaware of the significance of his discoveries and did not know that he had touched a new continent.

Another Dutchman, Henrik Brouwer, discovered a shorter route from the Cape of Good Hope to Batavia (Jakarta) in 1611. The ships would sail into the Roaring Forties in the Southern Ocean, use the tremendous winds to head east then strike north to their intended destination. These powerful winds often carried the ships too far west where they would hit the western coast of Australia.

The first known Europeans to land on or near the WA coast were Dutch. Dirk Hartog sighted land near Shark Bay on 25 October 1616. He and a party of fellow Dutch rowed ashore from the *Eendracht* and landed on the island that now bears his name. He left, at what is now called Cape Inscription – the famous pewter Hartog Plate recording the landing.

The next recorded contact was by Lenaert Jacobszoon and Willem Jansz in the *Mauritius* in 1618. They landed at Cloates Island near Exmouth and named the Willems River. The following year Houtman discovered and named the Abrolhos Islands, scene of the notorious wreck of the *Batavia* 10 years later.

In 1622, the crew of the *Leeuwin* explored the south-west coast. That same year the first English came ashore – from the crew of the *Trial* (also spelled *Tryal)*, wrecked on a reef near the Montebellos Islands.

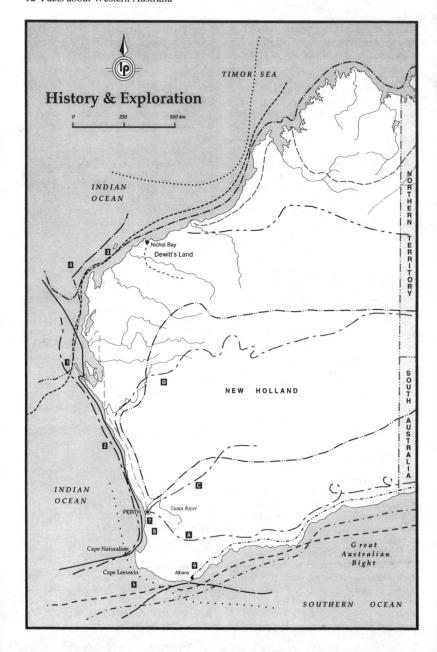

History & Exploration

0   250   500 km

TIMOR SEA

INDIAN
OCEAN

NORTHERN TERRITORY

3
4
Nichol Bay
Dewitt's Land

1
B
NEW HOLLAND

SOUTH AUSTRALIA

2
C
INDIAN
OCEAN

PERTH
7   Swan River
8
A

Cape Naturaliste
Great
Australian
Bight

Cape Leeuwin   6   Albany
5

SOUTHERN OCEAN

History & Exploration

1 Cape Inscription, Dirk Hartog Island (1616)
2 Houtman Abrolhos Islands (Houtman 1619), (*Batavia*, 1629)
3 Montebellos Islands (*Trial*, 1622)
4 Lenart Jacobszoon & Willem Jansz land on coast (*Mauritius*, 1618)

5 Leeuwin, (1622)
6 King George Sound Settlement, (*Amity*, 1826)
7 Swan River Settlement, (1829)
8 Battle of Pinjarra, (1834)

Hartog's Voyage (*Eendracht*, 1616)
Tasman's Second Voyage (1644)
de Vlamingh's Voyage (*Geelvinck*, 1696)
Thijssen's Voyage (*Gulden Zeepaard*, 1627)
de Witt's Voyage (*Vyanen*, 1628)
George Vancouver's Voyage (*Discovery, Chatham*, 1791)
French Expedition (*Recherche, L'Esperance*, 1792)
Dampier's First Voyage (*Cygnet*, 1688)
Dampier's Second Voyage (*Roebuck*, 1699)
French Expedition (*Le Géographe, Le Naturaliste*, 1801)
Matthew Flinders (*Investigator*, 1801)
Alexander Forrest (1879)
Peter Warburton (1873)
Edward John Eyre (1840-41)
George Grey (1839)
Ernest Giles, Alexander Forrest (1875-76)
John Forrest A - (1870), B - (1874), C - (1869)
A C Gregory (1855)
F T Gregory (1861)

What followed was exploration interspersed with tragedy (see under Dutch Shipwrecks in the Batavia Coast, Shark Bay & Gascoyne chapter). Francis Thijssen and Pieter Nuijts in the *Gulden Zeepaard* sighted the southern part of the continent near Cape Leeuwin and sailed a further 1600 km east across the Great Australian Bight. And the following year, Gerit Frederikszoon de Witt, in the *Vyanen*, sighted land at 21° south by accident.

The first navigator to really chart the western coast was Abel Tasman. In 1644, with the *Limmen*, *Zeemeeuw* and *Bracq*, he sailed up the north-west coast from near Exmouth Gulf, continuing further north towards the Gulf of Carpentaria.

William Dampier

The first of the English to chart the coast was William Dampier. A buccaneer and passenger of the *Cygnet*, he landed at the subsequently named Cygnet Bay (near the modern-day Dampier Peninsula) in 1688. The ship, under the command of Captain Read, was forced to spend over two months in Australian waters as it needed careening. The Aborigines encountered at Cygnet Bay were described by Read as 'the miserablest people in the world', observing that they had no houses and slept in the open.

Dampier left the *Cygnet* and returned to England in 1691 after spending more than 12 years on his first voyage. In 1697 he published an account of his voyage entitled *New Voyage Around the World*. With stature enhanced through his publication, he obtained command of the HMS *Roebuck* and embarked, in January 1699, on another voyage of discovery. In early August 1699, he found himself off the Houtman Abrolhos Islands.

Dampier, using the chart Tasman had prepared in 1644, sailed northwards. He encountered many sharks and turtles at the place he named Shark's (now Shark) Bay. Further north, the ship passed a group of small islands, which are now the Dampier Archipelago. The ship then landed at Roebuck Bay, near present-day Broome. Unfortunately, a skirmish between the sailors and local Aborigines resulted in Dampier shooting one of them. He later apologised 'for what happened'.

The lack of water and the health of his scurvy-ridden crew drove Dampier to abandon further exploration and head for Timor. By July 1700 the *Roebuck* was in Batavia and in bad need of an overhaul. The *Roebuck* sank at Ascension Island on its return voyage to England; the crew were eventually rescued in July 1701.

Willem de Vlamingh

In 1696, another group of Dutch navigators, Willem de Vlamingh in the *Geelvinck*, Gerrit Collaert in the *Nijptangh* and Cornelius de Vlamingh in the *Het Weseltje*, searched New Holland for a group of survivors from a Dutch East India Company (Verenigde Oost-Indische Compagnie) ship lost in 1694.

They sighted the coast on Christmas Day and landed on the mainland at Cottesloe Beach. Exploring parties ventured inland, saw the black swans and gave the river, on which Perth is now sited, its name. He also mistook the quokkas (small wallabies) on the island west of Perth to be rats and named the place Rottnest (or Rat's Nest).

De Vlamingh sailed north and landed on Hartog Island where he found, you guessed it, Hartog's plate, placed there in 1616. Leaving plates must have been the go in the 17th century – de Vlamingh swiped Hartog's and substituted his own. (The former is now in the Rijksmuseum in Amsterdam and the latter is in the Maritime Museum in Fremantle.) From Hartog Island, de Vlamingh continued to survey the coast and look for survivors; sailing as far north as Exmouth Gulf before heading for Batavia.

Later Exploration

Captain James Cook, aboard the *Endeavour* (1768-1771), came nowhere near the western coast of Australia, and the First Fleet, bound for Botany Bay in 1788, sailed well below the south-western coast of the continent.

In 1791, almost 100 years after de Vlamingh and Dampier, George Vancouver, in command of the *Discovery* and *Chatham*, sailed within sight of land at Cape Nuyts. He discovered and named Cape Chatham, and two days later found the harbour of King George III Sound where he formally took possession of the country for Britain. He left

the coast near Esperance and sailed to Tasmania. (He is the same person that Vancouver Island and the Canadian city are named after.)

The following year a French expedition transported by two ships – the *Recherche* and *L'Esperance* – visited the west coast looking for traces of the French explorer La Pérouse who had disappeared in 1788. The place names Esperance and Archipelago of the Recherche, relate to this visit, as does Point d'Entrecasteaux, named after the captain of the *Recherche*.

In 1800, the French navigator Nicolas Baudin set out to complete a survey of the southern coast of Australia. His two ships *Le Géographe* and *Le Naturaliste* anchored in Géographe Bay, near present-day Busselton, on 27 May 1801. They explored the coast as far as Shark Bay where, today, the naturalist of the expedition, François Péron, is remembered in the name of the cape at the tip of the peninsula.

They left for Timor in order to reprovision the expedition, returning in 1802. Baudin met Matthew Flinders – who, in 1801, passed near Cape Leeuwin in the *Investigator* on his way to Bass Strait – at Encounter Bay, near the mouth of the Murray River. Many of the place names given by the cartographer Freycinet have not survived, being replaced by the English names Flinders ascribed.

Colonisation

It was probably the exploration by French mariners such as Baudin that prompted colonists on the eastern coast of Australia to take interest in the vast west. Reports of a dry, barren land had previously discouraged attempts at settlement and it was not until 1826 that Major Edmund Lockyer, some troops and a small convict party were sent from Sydney in the brig *Amity* to establish a military outpost at King George Sound. The small outpost was never intended to be permanent and in 1831 the garrison and convicts were withdrawn.

Also in 1826, Captain James Stirling had sailed to the area of the Swan River to see if it was suitable for settlement. He was enthusiastic about its potential and pushed for the establishment of a colony when he returned to Britain in 1828. In November 1828, Captain CH Fremantle, in command of HMS *Challenger*, sailed to take possession of the territory; on 2 May 1829, at the mouth of the Swan River, he formally annexed all territory outside the colony of New South Wales for the Crown.

Stirling's proposals had received much publicity in Britain and many people flocked to take advantage of the favourable terms of settlement – one acre of land for every one shilling and sixpence (worth 15 cents today but considerably more then) of equipment, money or stock which potential settlers took with them. Stirling was appointed as Lieutenant Governor of the settlement and was provided with the 63rd Regiment along with administrators.

The *Parmelia* and *Sulphur* transports arrived in Cockburn Sound on 1 June 1829 and the new colony was officially proclaimed on 18 June. For almost two months, the settlers camped on Garden Island until a suitable site for the new colony had been determined. By the end of 1830 there were about 1500 settlers in the new colony.

The first 10 years of colonisation proved arduous. The land given the settlers was often of poor quality, food was scarce and money in short supply. In 1848 there were over 40,000 people in the colony but just over a thousand labourers. Shortages eventually lead the colony to ask the British government for help in the form of convict labour.

Aboriginal Resistance

During the long history of Aboriginal occupation of WA, hunting and gathering was done successfully in small nomadic groups, despite the often harsh environment. However, the onset of colonisation proved to have dire consequences for the local Aborigines, especially the Nyungar people of the south-west.

In 1829, the Swan River settlement was established on land known already to the Nyungar as Mooro; the site of Perth at the foot of Mt Eliza was known as Boorloo. The Aborigines, after seeing the settlers shoot their food sources such as kangaroo, took cattle and sheep in return. Under European law they were seen as thieves.

Aboriginal-European relations reached their nadir during Governor Stirling's control. The Aborigines began forming groups in order to resist the settlers during 1832-33. In October 1834, an official expedition led by Stirling, designed to eliminate resistance by the Nyungar – led by the warrior Calyute – set out for the Murray River. The Nyungar were ambushed by a force and many were killed. Two of Stirling's men were wounded and one, Captain Ellis, died later of his wounds. The Battle of Pinjarra (as it came to be known) lasted for about an hour and a half; the wounded Aborigines were hunted down and killed. About 50 were slain but Calyute survived. Nyungar resistance had effectively ended at that point and the following year the Murray leaders pledged their support to Governor Stirling.

The Convicts

The first group of convicts transported to WA at the request of the colony, arrived off Fremantle in the *Scindian* on 1 June 1850. It was at this time that transportation was ending in the eastern colonies (1840 in New South Wales and 1852 in Tasmania).

Many of the convicts were set to work constructing public buildings and roads in Perth and Fremantle. Works from this period include the gaol at Fremantle, a road linking Perth to Albany, Government House, the Perth Town Hall, the Pensioners' Barracks and a summer residence for the governor on Rottnest Island.

The colony was seen as a natural prison, where escape was made difficult by distance. The lash was employed sparingly, usually for cases of brutal assault, and chains were used around Perth and Fremantle. Convicts worked for the government until eligible for a conditional pardon or 'ticket of leave' (four years for a seven-year sentence and five years three months for a 10-year sentence) when they could do wage labour, virtually as free men, for other settlers. They were also subject to certain reporting conditions and could not return to Britain.

The first Comptroller General, Captain Edmund Henderson, oversaw the operation until 1863 (he was also largely responsible for the setting up of Scotland Yard). When an ex-Comptroller General of convicts in Tasmania and a veteran of Norfolk Island, Dr JS Hampton, arrived to take over as governor, the convicts were treated more strictly. The settlers spread out from Swan River to Champion Bay, Bunbury, Busselton and Albany, with convicts providing the labour force.

Transportation of convicts to WA had ceased by January 1868 with the 37th transport, the *Hougoumont*. Aboard were 63 Irish Fenians including the writer and editor John Boyle O'Reilly. In 1869, O'Reilly escaped from Bunbury on an American whaler. From New York he helped organise the rescue of six other Fenians – the *Catalpa* picked them up near Rockingham in 1876.

There is no denying the influence of convicts in the development of the WA colony and, in the time of transportation to the west, over 9600 were sent there. Anthony Trollope, the English novelist, visited the colony after transportation had ended and observed:

Such roads have been made as the other colonies do not possess. Public buildings have been erected, and an air of prosperity has been given to the two towns – Perth and Fremantle, the only towns in the colony – which could hardly have come to them yet but for this convict aid...

'Cinderella' Colony

In comparison to the colonies in the east, WA was much poorer, prompting the reference 'Cinderella' colony. But its apparent poverty did little to deter further exploration.

Explorers had been hard at work since the late 1830s. George Grey had walked from Shark Bay to Perth in 1839; Edward John Eyre's party had set out from South Australia in 1840, with Eyre and an Aborigine, Wylie,

reaching Albany in 1841; and in 1861 Frank T Gregory set out from Nickol Bay (near modern-day Karratha) along the Fortescue River to the Hamersley Range.

The Forrests, John and Alexander, were active explorers for 10 years from 1869 to 1879. In 1869, John led an expedition in search of Ludwig Leichhardt and got as far inland as Lake Ballard; in 1870, he and four others travelled from Perth to Adelaide (see under The Baron of Bunbury in this chapter). In 1873, a party led by Peter Warburton left Alice Springs in an attempt to cross to Perth, nearly starving to death before they reached the north-west coast near the Oakover River. In 1875-76, Alexander and Ernest Giles crossed the continent from South Australia to Perth and in 1879, Alexander, in a much-feted expedition, travelled from the De Grey River to Daly Waters in the Northern Territory.

As new regions were discovered, systems of roads, railways and telegraph lines were established to link communities. Perth was connected to the Overland Telegraph Line in 1877, providing communication to London and Adelaide.

Gold Rushes

Gold was discovered at Halls Creek in the remote Kimberley in 1885 and diggers on the Queensland fields, in 1886, made the anti-clockwise trek to the new riches. The terrain in the Kimberley was inhospitable and the track from the wharves at Wyndham and Derby the most ferocious that miners in Australia had yet negotiated.

The Pilbara was next to reveal its riches. In 1888, diggers swarmed over Pilbara Creek, fanning out through the dry gorges to Marble Bar, Nullagine and the Ashburton River. Despite the intense heat, the lure of gold proved irresistible and some diggers were rewarded with finds of huge nuggets.

Gold was found near Nannine, inland from Geraldton, in 1890. The Murchison field now bloomed and Cue, Day Dawn, Payne's Find, Lake Austin and Mount Magnet joined the huge list of gold towns in the outback.

More discoveries followed, especially

around Southern Cross in the Yilgarn. Major strikes were made in 1892 at Coolgardie and nearby Kalgoorlie, but of all the goldfield areas, Kalgoorlie remains the only large town.

Coolgardie's period of prosperity lasted only until 1905 and many other gold towns went from nothing to populations of 10,000 then back to nothing in just 10 years. However, WA profited from the gold boom for the rest of the century. It was gold that put WA on the map and finally gave it the population to make it viable in its own right, rather than just an offshoot of those colonies on the east coast.

Economic depression and unemployment often attracted fossickers back to the gullies and rivers, especially during the Great Depression. In other places mining never actually stopped – witness the Golden Mile in Kalgoorlie-Boulder.

Federation & After

The colony of WA had adopted a new constitution in 1890 and the gold discoveries had brought wealth and independence. Initially there was scepticism about whether or not the eastern colonies would care about the remote west in a federation. But when it came to vote to federate, the eastern diggers on the west's goldfields ensured a 'yes' vote. The new Australian constitution was accepted and WA retained its boundary at the 129th meridian. The first premier was the explorer Sir John Forrest (see under The Baron of Bunbury in this chapter).

Rapid expansion in primary production and a wheatbelt was established between Perth and the eastern goldfields soon after WW I. The Depression hit WA particularly hard (wheat and wool prices fell dramatically). This carried on to local manufacturing, geared to supply farmers, and many workers lost their jobs and were forced to go on the 'dole' (unemployment benefit).

During the 1930s, discussion about secession from the federation occurred, with proponents blaming the eastern states for the prevailing economic woes. Electors in the compulsory 1933 referendum voted by almost two-to-one to leave the Australian Commonwealth – only six electoral districts of 50 recorded a no majority, five in the goldfields and the Kimberley. Secession never occurred as it was deemed WA had no legal right to request legislation on the constitution. The referendum, however, was an important signal to the federal government.

Paradoxically, the state Australian Labor Party which had not supported secession, was swept into power in 1933 and remained there until the narrow Liberal-Country Party victory in 1947.

WW II

During WW II the west felt the brunt of war first-hand. The great naval engagement between the HMAS *Sydney* and the German auxiliary cruiser *Kormoran* was fought on 19 November 1941. The result was the sinking of both ships and the loss of the entire crew (645 personnel) of the *Sydney*.

Broome, Wyndham, Derby and Onslow were bombed by the Japanese in February 1942 and it is believed that the Japanese came ashore and reconnoitred part of the Kimberley. In Broome, 70 people were killed and 16 Royal Dutch Air Force flying boats destroyed while moored near the old jetty. In Wyndham, the SS *Koolama* was bombed and sunk.

Many military bases were established in the west. Fremantle became an important naval base for Allied operations in the Indian Ocean and Exmouth Gulf was the centre of Operation Potshot, an advance US submarine refuelling base.

A great number of Italian prisoners of war were allocated to work on various farms; many stayed on after the war and their descendants live in WA today.

Post-War to the Present

After the war the west began to prosper, mainly as a result of the exploitation of the state's vast mineral wealth. In 1948 iron ore was shipped from Yampi Sound and since then the state has not looked back – it is now one of the main iron-ore exporters in the world. Mines such as Tom Price, Mt

The Baron of Bunbury

John Forrest, later Lord Forrest, Baron of Bunbury, was born near Bunbury in 1847. He is the giant of WA's modern history, having achieved fame in the fields of exploration and politics. In physical appearance he was also a giant, with a huge frame, bushy whiskers and an equally dominating presence.

In 1869 he led an expedition to search for Ludwig Leichhardt's party and reached the Lake Ballard area north of modern-day Kalgoorlie. Next, in 1870, he became the first to follow the Great Australian Bight west to east when he travelled from Perth to Adelaide.

On his third expedition in 1874, he explored the hinterland from which flow the Gascoyne, Murchison, Ashburton, De Grey and Fitzroy rivers. After exploring part of the hinterland he pushed on across the Gibson Desert to the Peake telegraph station on the Adelaide to Darwin telegraph line, thus completing a more northerly west-east crossing. He published an account of his journeys, *Explorations in Australia*, in 1875.

As Commissioner of Crown Lands and Surveyor-General from 1883 to 1890, he made, in 1894, a fourth expedition to a large part of the Kimberley plateau. In 1890 Forrest entered politics as Premier of WA, heading a coalition of independent members of parliament (there were no political parties in WA at that time).

Forrest resigned from state politics in 1901 and entered the first federal parliament as Postmaster General in the first federal ministry. Later he was Minister for Defence, Minister for Home Affairs, Treasurer and, for a brief period, acting Prime Minister. His two chief political successes were the goldfields water supply scheme and the transcontinental railway. In 1918, the year of his death, he became the first Australian-born citizen to be raised to the British peerage. ∎

Newman and Goldsworthy flourished in the Pilbara and an elaborate infrastructure of transport and shipping was set up to support this massive growth. Migrants came into the state to bolster the workforce and women took a greater role in all areas of industry. In the Kimberley, the mighty Ord River Scheme was established in 1961, bringing fertility to the desert.

The state politics of the post-war years has seen three distinct periods of ascendancy by either the ALP or the conservative coalition. The ALP ran the state for six years from 1953 until 1959 when the Liberal & Country League (LCL)-Country Party (CP) coalition came to power.

Except for the three-year interruption of the Tonkin Labor government (1971-1974), the LCL-CP coalition held power from 1959 to 1983. In this time two strong Liberal leaders, David Brand and Sir Charles Court, ruled almost unopposed. Labor, led by the young and popular Brian Burke, was returned to office in 1983.

The Labor Government of the late 1980s was embroiled in a series of scandals called 'WA Inc'. The term – used loosely to describe a series of titanic collapses involving businessmen and the Labor government – led to a Royal Commission with the government suffering heavily at the hands of voters in the 1993 election. The conservative Liberal-Country Party coalition government, headed by Richard Fairfax Court, son of former premier Sir Charles Court, took reign and introduced austere economic policies. While the scandals surrounding WA Inc proved painful, they appear not to have had any effect on the state's international reputation.

Today, a larger and far more technologically advanced mineral boom forms the basis of the state's prosperity. The state was very much caught up in the rapacious 1980s with a number of high-flying entrepreneurs adding their marks to the Perth city skyline. It was the time Fremantle played host to the 1986 America's Cup (Australia was the holder after defeating the USA in 1983). Their defence, however, was unsuccessful. (see under Ruling the Waves in the Facts for the Visitor chapter.)

The display of 'paper' wealth was conspicuous and the entrepreneurs fell heavily when the economic bubble burst. A number of key players such as Laurie Connell are serving prison terms for their indiscretions during the period of WA Inc. In July 1994, former premier, Brian Burke, was sentenced to gaol for two years for rorting travel expenses. Legal actions on other prominent figures are still outstanding.

Aboriginal Protest & Land Rights

Not long after the end of WW II, in May 1946, the first real act of self-determination was enacted in the Pilbara. Then, 800 Aboriginal workers walked off their stations in the Port Hedland region in protest at their degrading conditions, 'slave wages' and the enforcement of the archaic Native Administration Act.

Led by White prospector Don McLeod and two Aborigines, Clancy McKenna and Dooley Binbin, the strikers congregated in camps. In the atmosphere of post-war security, little news of the protest was leaked to the press and Binbin and McKenna were arrested for communist subversion. When food coupons were withheld from the protesters they returned to traditional methods of food gathering.

The protest culminated with a station-to-station march in 1949 and, after protesters were arrested, the Seaman's Union banned the handling of wool from the 'slave stations'. The government conceded to the protesters demands so that the shipping ban would be lifted (shortly after, the government backed out of the deal). Meanwhile, the strikers had taken up other occupations and never returned to the stations.

Land rights became the next important issue and, in June 1966, a group at Wave Hill station (owned by the British Vestey corporation) walked off their jobs, requesting that some of their land be returned to them. It wasn't until 1973 that the federal Whitlam Labor government announced that it would buy back two cattle stations in the north-west and return them to the Aborigines. Ironically, it was part of the Wave Hill station which was returned to the traditional Gurindji owners.

In 1992 the High Court handed down the Mabo ruling. The result of a claim by Torres Strait islander, Eddy Mabo, it challenged and overturned the established concept of *terra nullius* – that Australia was empty or uninhabited on White arrival. The court's ruling – that Aborigines were the first occupants and had the right to claim land back where continuous association was demonstrated – set off a heated and deeply divided debate on land rights and mining interests within WA. The state government went so far as passing legislation which conflicted with Commonwealth legislation though little impact on new resource projects has yet been felt.

In 1993, the federal government introduced the Native Title Act, which formalised the High Court's Mabo ruling. The content of the bill had, somewhat surprisingly, been agreed upon by all the major players involved – the miners, the farmers, the government and Aborigines. Unfortunately, it appears that the present coalition government places economic development well before land rights. In 1994, it was fighting the federal government's land rights legislation in the High Court.

GEOGRAPHY

Western Australia is Australia's largest state with a size of 2,525,500 sq km. It extends 1621 km from the Indian Ocean to the 129th meridian where the Northern Territory and South Australia begin. From south to north it extends 2391 km from the Southern Ocean to the Timor Sea. The most northerly point is Cape Londonderry and the most southerly, Torbay Head.

Western Australia's geography is a little like a distorted reflection of eastern Australia except, of course, that the west is far drier than the east. The equivalent of the long fertile coastal strip on the east coast is the small south-west corner of WA. As in the east, hills rise behind the coast, but in WA they're much smaller than those of the Great Dividing Range. Further north it's dry and relatively barren. Fringing the central-west coast is the Great Sandy Desert, a very inhospitable region running right to the sea.

There are a couple of interesting variations, such as the Kimberley, in the extreme north of the state – a wild and rugged area with a convoluted coast and spectacular inland gorges. It gets good annual rainfall, but all in the 'green' season. There are small, remote patches of tropical rainforest here (see under Rainforest in this chapter).

Further south is the Pilbara, an area with more magnificent ancient rock and gorge country and the treasure-house from which the state derives its vast mineral wealth. The Pilbara has two of the state's most interesting national parks – Karijini, based in the gorges of the Hamersley Ranges; and Millstream-Chichester, interesting as an oasis in the desert. Near Karijini is Mt Meharry, WA's highest point at 1245 metres. Incidentally, the highest waterfall is King George Falls (80 metres), the highest town is Tom Price (740 metres) and the longest river the Gascoyne (865 km).

From the coast there are a number of large islands and archipelagos. Large islands include Augustus, Barrow, Bigge, Bernier and Hartog. Some of the archipelagos are Bonaparte, Buccaneer, Dampier, Houtman Abrolhos and Recherche. There are also numerous prominent peninsulas and capes that jut into the Indian Ocean – Dampier, North-West Cape, Péron and Naturaliste.

The world's largest west-coast reef, Ningaloo, stretches from North-West Cape to Coral Bay, some 260 km. This is the closest point in Australia to the continental shelf.

Away from the coast, however, most of WA seems a vast empty stretch of outback: the Nullarbor Plain in the south, the Great Sandy Desert in the north and the Gibson and Great Victoria deserts in between. There are many interesting features dotted throughout the arid regions to break the monotony, including Mt Augustus, the world's largest rock.

The south-west is much more different than the bulk of the state. The Mediterranean climate and higher rainfall has made this a much greener place with large tracts of forest (see Trees under Flora later in this chapter)

intersected by rivers and streams. The forests only occur where the rainfall exceeds 500 mm, and by far the bulk of forest is jarrah *(Eucalyptus marginata)* with nearly 15,000 sq km followed by the karri *(E. diversicolor)* with about 1500 sq km.

There are two interesting mountain ranges which punctuate the rolling, grassy plains – the Porongurups and the Stirlings. The Stirlings rise abruptly more than 1000 metres above sea level, and stretch east-west for 65 km. Prominent peaks are Bluff Knoll, Toolbrunup, Mt Trio, Mondurup and Ellen Peak, all above 800 metres. The Porongurups are 40 km south, distinguishable by their huge 1100-million-year-old granite domes. Both support unique sets of animals and plants.

The coastline in the south is exciting with numerous rugged headlands, granite boulders, rock shelves and sheltered bays.

GEOLOGY

From Perth you can look to the Darling Ranges which are, in fact, the edge of the Yilgarnia escarpment. Yilgarnia is one of the oldest lands in the world and was formed in the early stages of the Archae (a subdivision of the Pre-Cambrian), about 2600 million years ago. It was altered for about 1500 million years, covered up in many places and sank below sea level in others. The Archipelago of the Recherche is a part of Yilgarnia.

You have to proceed north of the Yilgarnia to get to the world's oldest rocks – those that are almost original crust – dated at 4.1 billion years old. These are the zircon crystals of Mt Narryer, inland from Shark Bay, formed a mere 500 million years after the earth began to coalesce.

When did life start on earth? So far WA holds the first tangible proof. In the Pilbara, fossilised stromatolites (see under Stromatolites in the Batavia Coast, Shark Bay & Gascoyne chapter), found in a layer of siltstone, have been dated at 3.5 billion years old. At sea level, in Shark Bay, stromatolites thrive in the hypersaline waters of Hamelin Pool.

Nearby, the Hamersley Ranges constitute

the backbone of the Pilbara. The rocks, which form the gorges of Karijini National Park, are over 2.5 billion years old. They originated as iron and silica-rich sediment deposits that accumulated on the sea bed. Horizontal compression forced these sediments to buckle and develop cracks, until the whole was elevated to the surface to form dry land.

The Kimberley had its origins in the Proterozoic period more than two billion years ago. Sediments referred to as the Halls Creek Group were laid down and underwent intense folding and faulting. About 150 million years later, the sediments forming the Kimberley basin were also laid down, remaining remarkably stable in spite of two mobile zones nearby. Approximately 750 and 670 million years ago the region was gripped by two severe glacial epochs.

It is in the Devonian era, 370 million years ago, that the most visible geological features were formed; this was before mammals or reptiles had evolved. In the Devonian era, a barrier reef grew south-east of Derby where the Canning Basin area was covered by a tropical sea. It is surmised that this reef, 300 km of which is exposed, could have extended some 1000 km to join with another exposed reef found in the Bonaparte Basin near Kununurra.

The limestone reefs – of which Geikie Gorge, Windjana Gorge and Tunnel Creek national parks are part – rise from 50 to 100 metres above the river valleys. Obviously the limestone was more resilient to the weathering and other geological changes which occurred.

The geological oddity of the Kimberley is the Purnululu Range. The ancient beehives, gravels and sandstones encased in silica, which make up this massif, are 350 million years old. It is believed that rivers flowing south and east from nearby formations washed sand and pebbles into the area. This gradually compacted to form sandstone which was uplifted over time and gouged out by the Wet (monsoonal rains occurring between December and April). The covering of silica (orange in colour) and lichen (green) protected the domes from complete erosion, leaving the curious beehives you see today.

East of Purnululu is the Wolf Creek meteorite crater, which is one of the best preserved craters in the world. The crater floor is 50 metres below the rim and the outer slopes are 35 metres high; it formed thousands of years ago when a meteor weighing thousands of tonnes hit the earth.

CLIMATE

Western Australia has a variety of climates as it extends from the tropical savannah in the north (the Kimberley), through the desert and semidesert of the centre to the Mediterranean climate of the south-west. The main influence of typography is a decrease in rainfall the further you get from the coast. The trade winds separate the northern south-east trade winds from the westerlies in the south.

The tropical north has hot, 'sticky' wet summers and warm dry winters. The climate is characterised by the Wet. Before the Wet there is an incredible period called the 'build-up'. The horizon is black as ominous clouds roll through the sky and there are occasional flashes of lightning. No rain falls until one day, a deluge...the Wet has started. Once the Wet begins, the roads are subject to flash flooding at any time.

Occasionally there are tropical cyclones. These usually develop well offshore and produce heavy rain, high winds and the lashing of coastal areas. Port Hedland gets a cyclone about once every two years. Cyclones produced WA's biggest wind gust (259 km/h at Mardie in 1898) and heaviest rainfall (747 mm during one day in 1975).

From May to November the nights are mostly cool and crisp and the days are sunny with blue skies.

The area of WA which could be classified as desert or semidesert is east of a line drawn roughly from Geraldton through Southern Cross to midway between Albany and Esperance, and south of a line drawn from Broome to Halls Creek. These areas have hot, dry summers and mild, dry winters. (Desert areas are those that receive less than 250 mm of rainfall each year.)

About 200 km south of Port Hedland, on

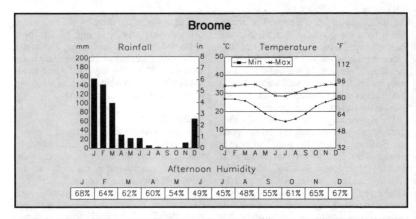

Broome

J	F	M	A	M	J	J	A	S	O	N	D
68%	64%	62%	60%	54%	49%	45%	48%	55%	61%	65%	67%

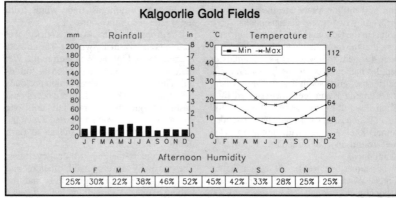

Kalgoorlie Gold Fields

J	F	M	A	M	J	J	A	S	O	N	D
25%	30%	22%	38%	46%	52%	45%	42%	33%	28%	25%	25%

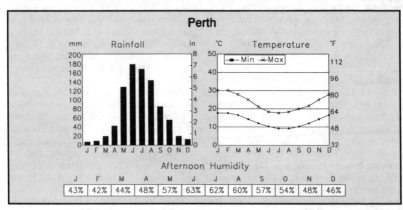

Perth

J	F	M	A	M	J	J	A	S	O	N	D
43%	42%	44%	48%	57%	63%	62%	60%	57%	54%	48%	46%

the Great Northern Highway, is Marble Bar, reputedly the hottest place in Australia. From October to March, expect daytime temperatures of 38°C and above (Australian seasons are the opposite of the northern hemisphere's and temperatures are expressed in degrees Celsius; as a rule of thumb, 20°C is about 70°F or room temperature). There was a period in the 1920s when the temperature topped 37°C for 160 consecutive days. On one occasion, in 1905, the mercury soared to 49.1°C. The highest temperature ever recorded was 50.7°C at Eucla.

The Mediterranean climate of the south has hot, dry summers and mild, wet winters. Perth, in the centre of this region, has maximum's of around 30°C from December to March, but minimum's are rarely below 10°C. February is the hottest month and July the coldest. Rainfall is lightest from November to March when it seldom rains (20 mm and below) and heaviest from May to August (120 to 200 mm). Perth's annual rainfall averages 975 mm.

Summer sees the crowds flock to Rottnest Island and the southern and northern beaches; in winter only the hardy are seen out windsurfing and surfing as the beaches are inhospitable places with strong westerlies whipping up large waves.

One peculiarity of the local weather is the 'Fremantle Doctor', a wind that blows in from the sea in the late afternoon. It is often welcomed by Western Australians as it clears away the oppressive heat.

The Great Southern area is much influenced by the prevailing winds and many storms blow in from the southern ocean. To the north, the Stirling Ranges create a weather pattern all their own. In late spring and early summer (October to December), when it begins to warm, the ranges are an ideal place to visit. Winter (June to August) in this range is cold and wet and the temperatures can drop suddenly. Hail and rain are common and snow falls on the peaks occasionally.

Average maximum and minimum temperatures for January/July and average rainfall from 1989-92 were:

Location	Temperature				Rainfall (mm)
	January		July		
Broome	33.5	31.0	27.0	17.5	567
Port Hedland	36.7	29.6	23.7	13.6	304
Learmonth	35.7	25.0	21.9	11.8	270
Carnarvon	31.5	23.9	22.3	11.0	230
Geraldton	33.3	21.2	18.6	11.3	470
Perth Airport	33.5	18.8	19.2	9.9	802
Albany	24.9	16.8	14.0	8.5	806
Narrogin	31.4	15.8	14.6	6.7	505
Esperance	25.3	18.1	15.0	8.8	620
Kalgoorlie	32.7	16.4	18.1	5.3	256

FAUNA
Animals
Australia's most distinctive fauna are the marsupials (kangaroos and koalas) and monotremes (platypuses and echidnas). Marsupials give birth to partially developed young which they suckle in a pouch. Monotremes lay eggs but also suckle their young. In all, WA has 141 native mammal species, two of which are marine mammals – the Australian sea lion and the New Zealand fur seal. Also the leopard seal, dugong, 16 species of dolphin and 19 species of whale have been recorded off the coast. Two mammals, the numbat and honey possum, have only been recorded in WA.

Good books on the subject are *Whales & Dolphins of New Zealand and Australia: An Identification Guide* by Alan N Baker (Victoria University Press, Wellington, 1990); *Whales and Whalewatching in Australia* by Mark Tucker (Australian National Parks & Wildlife Service, Canberra, 1989) and *Key Guide to Australian Mammals* by Leonard Cronin (Reed Books, Balgowlah, 1991).

The native animals you're most likely to see in the wild are wallabies, wallaroos, kangaroos and possums. However, that doesn't mean that there isn't a huge range of small, mainly nocturnal animals going about their business unobserved.

Western Australia has the country's most restricted mammal, the Shark Bay mouse *(Pseudomys praeconis)*, found only on Bernier Island near Shark Bay. Similarly, the western-barred bandicoot *(Perameles bougainville)* and banded hare-wallaby *(Lagostrophus fasciatus)* are now found only on Bernier and nearby Dorre Island.

Kangaroo

There are many other marsupial species found in WA, many of them rare and fascinating. The curious pebble-mound mouse (see under Pebble-Mound Mouse in the Coral Coast & The Pilbara chapter) and the rabbit-eared bandicoot or bilby (see under The Bilby in the Broome & The Dampier Peninsula chapter) are just two more examples.

And there are further rare and interesting species. Gilbert potoroo *(potorous tridactylus gilberti),* a sub-species of the long-nosed potoroo (kangaroo rat), was recently re-discovered in WA, after being thought extinct for 80 years.

Kangaroos The extraordinary breeding cycle of the kangaroo is well adapted to Australia's harsh, often unpredictable environment.

The young kangaroo, or joey, just millimetres long at birth, claws its way from the uterus unaided to the mother's pouch where it attaches itself to a nipple. A day or two later, the mother mates again but the new embryo does not begin to develop until the first joey has left the pouch permanently.

At this point the mother produces two types of milk – one formula to feed the joey at heel, the other for the baby in her pouch. If environmental conditions are right, the mother will then mate again. However, if food or water is scarce, the breeding cycle will be interrupted until conditions improve.

As well as many species of wallaroos and wallabies (some endangered, such as the black-footed rock and tammar), there are two main species of kangaroos in WA – the western grey *(Macropus fuliginosus)* and the red kangaroo *(Macropus rufus).*

Quokkas By far the west's most famous example of the wallaby-type of marsupial is the quokka *(Setonis brachyurus).* The quokka is mostly found on Rottnest Island (they contributed to its name, being mistaken for rats by de Vlamingh) but it also occurs in the south-east forests. It is a small robust wallaby, about a half-metre tall with a tail about 300 mm long. Its fur is grey and brown

Quokka

Honey Possum

with a reddish tinge on the upperside and a pale grey below. It can survive for a long time without water and reputedly drinks seawater.

Possums There is a wide range of possums throughout Australia – they seem to have the ability to adapt to all sorts of conditions. Apart from the common ringtail and common brushtail, a number of other species are found in WA, including the scaly-tailed possum *(Wyulda squamicaudata)* and the beautiful, 'ultra-cute' honey possum *(Tarsipes rostratus)*.

The little aboreal honey possum weighs up to 20 gm, is 40 to 90 mm high and has a prehensile tail (for wrapping around any given support) from 50 to 100 mm long. The honey possum uses its long snout and long brush-tipped tongue to dip into tubular wildflowers such as grevillea or to penetrate the stiff brushes of banksias and bottlebrushes. They are nomadic, according to the seasonal availability of favoured wildflowers.

Dunnarts These little mouse-sized creatures have pointed muzzles, and large ears and eyes. Of the 18 species known, about half are found only in the western half of the continent. These include the very rare long-tailed dunnart *(Sminthopsis longicaudata)* and sandhill dunnart *(S. psammophila)*.

They are common in the south-west of the state and species found there include the fat-tailed *(S. crassicaudata)*, little long-tailed *(S. dolichura)*, Gilbert's *(S. gilberti)*, white-tailed *(S. granulipes)*, grey-bellied *(S. griseoventer)* and the common dunnarts *(S. murina)*. It is these small innocuous species that suffer most when their habitat is slashed or burnt.

Numbats The beautifully patterned numbat or marsupial anteater *(Myrmecobius fasciatus)* is a member of the native cat family but is vastly different from other members. It has a pointed face and its tongue can extend 10 cm beyond the nose tip. It is thus ideally suited to search for termites in the fallen wandoo trees of south-west Australia; the species is extinct in the eastern states.

About the size of a rabbit (head and body 30 cm and the tail another 20 cm) it is easily recognisable by the white transverse stripes across its reddish-brown fur. There is also a dark stripe across the eye from its ear to its mouth. It is endangered because of habitat destruction and predation from foxes.

Wombats Wombats are slow, solid, powerfully built marsupials with broad heads and short, stumpy legs. The common wombat *(Vombatus ursinus)* is not found in WA but the southern hairy-nosed wombat

Wombat

(Lasiorhinus latifrons) can be found in the far east of the state around Eucla.

Koalas The koala *(Phascolarctos cinereus)* is distantly related to the wombat and found along the eastern seaboard. They can be found in WA only in special reserves such as Yanchep National Park, north of Perth. Koalas initially carry their babies in pouches, but later the larger young cling to their mothers' backs. They feed only on the leaves of certain types of eucalypt (found mainly in the forests of the Great Dividing Range) and are particularly sensitive to changes to their habitat.

Koala

Platypuses & Echidnas The platypus and the echidna are the only living representatives of the most primitive group of mammals, the monotremes.

The amphibious platypus *(Ornithorhynchus anatinus)* has a duck-like bill, webbed feet and a beaver-like body. It is not found in the wild in WA. The short-beaked echidna *(Tachyglossus aculeatus)* is a spiny anteater that hides from predators by digging into the ground and covering itself with dirt, or by rolling itself into a ball and raising its sharp quills.

Dingoes Australia's native dog *(Canis familiaris dingo)* is the dingo, domesticated by the Aborigines and a stable breed for at least 3000 years, possibly much longer. Its ancestor is the Indian wolf. After the Europeans arrived and Aborigines could no longer hunt freely, dingoes again became 'wild', and by preying on sheep they earned the wrath of graziers. These sensitive, intelligent dogs are legally considered vermin. The discovery of dingo bones has been used to verify the radiation of Aboriginal groups from the north-western corner of Australia.

Common Dolphins This dolphin *(Delphinus delphis)* is found all along the WA coast as it favours warm, temperate waters. It is dark-grey to purple-black on its upper body and white on its underside. It is easily recognised by the gold hourglass pattern on its side. The dorsal fin is sickle-shaped and it has a long, slender beak. The single calf is suckled by the mother for one to three years. Adults are from 1.7 to 2.4 metres in length.

Bottlenose Dolphins This dolphin *(Tursiops truncatus)* is found all along the WA coast as it also favours warmer waters. Dark-grey in colour, it is easily recognised as being the 'Flipper' dolphin most of us are familiar with. The dorsal fin is sickle-shaped and it has a relatively short beak in which the lower jaw extends beyond the upper jaw. The calf is suckled by the mother for 12 to 18 months. Adults are from 2.3 to four metres in length.

This is the dolphin people come to see at Monkey Mia and Bunbury but the observant visitor is likely to see it in a number of other places.

Australian Sea Lions This sea lion seal *(Neophoca cinerea)* is endemic to Australia. It is found in cool, temperate waters and rocky coastlines such as those on the south-west coast of WA. It has a bulky but streamlined body, blunt snout and dog-shaped head. The males are chocolate brown and the females range from silver-grey to fawn. They have front flippers and webbed hind legs. Males are from 1.8 to 2.3 metres and females 1.3 to 1.8 metres in length.

Dugongs This is a herbivorous aquatic mammal *(Dugong dugon)*, often known as the 'sea cow', found along the northern Australian coast from Shark Bay to the Great Barrier Reef – the Shark Bay population is estimated to be over 10,000, about 10% of the world's dugong population. It is found in shallow tropical waters and estuaries where it feeds on seagrasses, supplemented by algae. Its bulky body is grey to bronze on the upperside and lighter beneath, and it has a broad snout; males have a pair of protruding tusks. Dugongs can live for over 70 years.

Fur Seals Two types of fur seal are found in Australian waters but only one type is found in WA, the New Zealand fur seal *(Arctocephalus forsteri)*. You will likely see it sunning on offshore islands such as those in the Archipelago of the Recherche. The fur seal is smaller than the sea lion and its head has a more pointed snout with long whiskers. The seal pups congregate in pods and are suckled for about a year. Males grow from 1.5 to 2.5 metres and females 1.3 to 1.5 metres in length.

Southern Right Whales The southern right whale *(Eubalaena australis)* (so-called because it was the 'right' whale to kill), was almost hunted to the point of extinction but since the cessation of whaling, has started to return to Australian coastal waters in increasing numbers. A baleen whale, it can be seen in the waters of the Great Australian Bight and is easily recognised by its strongly down-curved mouth with long baleen plates – these filter water for planktonic krill (tiny, shrimp-like crustacean). These plates or sheafs were once used to make corsets. Its head and snout have callosities (barnacle-like protuberances); these are unique and aid in identification of individual whales. The southern right whale grows to 18 metres and travels alone or in small family groups.

Humpback Whales Now a regular visitor to the west and east coasts of Australia, this massive marine mammal *(Megaptera novae-angliae)* is a joy to behold. It breeds in winter in sub-tropical and tropical waters and in the west you are likely to see them anywhere from Cape Leeuwin to North-West Cape, even off the city of Perth, as they migrate northwards from their feeding grounds in the polar seas.

The back and sides are grey-black, the belly and throat are black and white and the baleen plates black. The body has a humpback and there are two long flippers which have a row of knobs at the front edges. The young, over four metres in length when born, are weaned at seven months but stay with the mother for two to three years. Adult humpbacks are from 14 to 19 metres in length and live for over 30 years, mating every two to three years. They are also spectacular jumpers and leapers.

Introduced Species

The Acclimatisation Society devoted itself to 'improving' the countries of the British Empire by introducing plants and animals. Unfortunately, its work proved a disastrous blunder.

Exotic animals thriving in WA include foxes, rabbits, cats, donkeys, pigs (now bristly-black razorbacks with long tusks) and goats. These species have been disastrous for the native animals, both as predators and as competitors for food and water.

Probably the biggest change to the ecosystem has been caused by another exotic animal: the sheep. To make room for sheep, wholesale clearing of the bush took place, and plains were planted with exotic grasses. Many small marsupials became extinct when their habitats changed.

And disruption of Aboriginal land-management meant that there was no longer regular burning of the bush and plains. This caused less-frequent but disastrous bushfires which fed on the accumulated growth (previously this was dependant on regular low-intensity fires for germination).

Birds

About 510 species are found in WA of which 380 are breeding species and 130 are non-breeding migratory species. Fourteen species are endemic, ie found only in this state. Over 30 species are threatened and seven of these declared in need of special protection. (See Birdwatching under Activities in the following Facts for the Visitor chapter.)

Emus The only bird larger than the emu *(Dromaius novaehollandiae)* is the African ostrich, also flightless. The emu is a shaggy-feathered bird with an often curious nature. After the female emu lays the eggs, the male hatches them and raises the young. Emus are common throughout the state.

Black Swans This is the most famous of WA's birds and very much a state symbol. The long slender-necked swan *(Cygnus atratus)* is black except for white flight quills, red eye and red beak. It is found in all water habitats where it builds its bulky nest of sticks, either as a floating island or on a small island. In Northam, on the Avon River, there is a colony of the introduced mute swan *(Cygnus olor)* which is white with a yellow bill.

Black Swan

Parrots & Cockatoos There is an amazing variety of these birds. The noisy pink-and-grey galahs *(Cacatua roseicapilla)* are among the most common, although the sulphur-crested *(C. galerita)* and pink Major

Mitchell cockatoos *(C. leadbeateri)* have to be the noisiest. Other species of cockatoo seen in the state are little corellas *(C. pastinator)*, long-billed black *(Calyptorhyncus baudinii)*, red-tailed black *(C. banksii)* and Carnabys cockatoos *(C. latirostris)*.

Lorikeets, rosellas and parrots are also numerous throughout the state. It is refreshing to see large flocks of budgerigars *(Melopsittacus undulatus)* darting about in formation and just as quickly settling on the ground, rather than the usual lone forlorn creature in a cage.

Parrots are seen just about everywhere but it is the careful observer that tells them apart – cockatiels *(Nymphicus hollandicus)* and Bourke's *(Neophema bourkii)* in the arid areas, elegant parrots *(N. elegans)* along the coast, rock parrots *(N. petrophila)* also along the coast from Esperance to Shark Bay, red-capped parrots *(Purpureicephalus spurius)* in the south-west, regents *(Polytelis anthropeplus)* throughout the goldfields, Alexandra's parrot *(P. alexandrae)* in the extremely arid centre, red-winged parrots *(Aprosmictus erythropterus)* in the Kimberley, blue bonnets *(Northiella haematogaster)* on the Nullarbor and 28s or Port Lincoln ring-necks *(Barnardius zonarius)* just about everywhere from the Pilbara south.

Visitors to the eastern states will be familiar with the ubiquitous eastern rosella *(Platycercus eximius)*. This species is not seen in the west, but in the north-east of the state, the northern rosella *(P. venustus)* is found in the hills near water. In the south-west, the western rosella *(P. icterotis)* inhabits open woodland and farmland.

Raptors (Birds of Prey) Birds that prey on other species have long been a subject of fascination for birdwatchers and species of all three families found in Australia can be observed in WA.

The osprey *(Pandion haliaetus)* is found along the coast from the Kimberley to Esperance and several nest *in* Broome; the white-bellied sea eagle *(Haliaeetus leucogaster)* is also found along the coast and you will definitely see it in the Archipelago of the

Wedge-tailed eagle

Recherche; the majestic wedge-tailed eagle *(Aquila audax)* is seen throughout the state feeding on road kills; and the brahminy kite *(Milvus indus)* is found in the north-west near coastal mudflats and mangroves.

Kookaburras A member of the kingfisher family, the kookaburra is heard as much as it is seen – you can't miss its loud, cackling laugh, usually at dawn and sunset. Kookaburras can become quite tame and pay regular visits to friendly households. In WA, the laughing kookaburra *(Dacelo novaeguineae)* is found in the south-west; in the Kimberley and the coastal centre of the state, the blue-winged kookaburra *(D. leachii)*, unfamiliar to most people in the east, can be found.

Fish
There is a bewildering variety of fish found in WA waters. They range from minute tropical fish to the world's largest, the whale shark *(Rhiniodon typus)*. Around 1040 of the 1500 or so species are tropical and the remainder either southern temperate (400 species) or freshwater (60 species).

Reptiles
There are at least 750 known species of Australian reptiles and 439 of these are found in WA. The two main deserts, the Great Sandy and Great Victoria, each support about 75 species of reptile. One of the world's rarest species, the western swamp tortoise, is found in one nature reserve near Perth.

Snakes There are a number of species of snake in WA, all protected. Many are poisonous, some deadly, but very few are at all aggressive and they'll usually get out of your way before you even realise that they are there. (See under Dangers & Annoyances in the Facts for the Visitor chapter for ways of avoiding being bitten and what to do in the unlikely event that you are.)

The best known of the local venomous species is the dugite *(Pseudonaja affinis)*, which is confined to the southernmost part of WA, including the Perth metropolitan area and Rottnest Island. The greenish-brown to greenish-grey dugites prefer sandy areas and places where house mice are plentiful.

One species of blind snake *(Rhamphotyphlops leptosoma)* is known only from the area around Kalbarri. Some other venomous snakes found in the west are the desert death adder *(Acanthopus pyrrhus)*, mulga snake *(Pseudechis australis)* and black-striped snake *(Vermicella calonota)*; the latter is believed only to occur within a 35-km radius of Perth.

Crocodiles There are two types of crocodile in Australia: the extremely dangerous saltwater crocodile *(Crocodylus porosus)*, or 'saltie' as it is known, and the less aggressive freshwater crocodile *(Crocodylus johnstoni)* or 'freshie'. These living relics were on earth 200 million years before humans.

Saltwater crocodile

Freshwater crocodile

Salties are not only confined to salt water. They inhabit estuaries, and, following floods, may be found many km from the coast. They may even be found in fresh water more than 100 km inland. Learn to tell the difference between the saltie and its less dangerous relative, as both are prolific in WA.

Freshies are smaller than salties – anything over four metres should be regarded as a saltie. Freshies are also more finely constructed and have much narrower snouts and smaller teeth. Salties, which can grow to seven metres, will attack and kill humans. Freshies, though unlikely to seek human prey, have been known to bite, and children in particular should be kept away from them.

You'll probably see many freshies (along the banks of Geikie Gorge) in the Kimberley, and there are many known haunts of the saltie along the northern coast, including the big crocs found near the outfall of the Wyndham abattoir.

Lizards There is a wide variety of lizards, from tiny skinks to prehistoric-looking goannas which can grow up to 2.5 metres long, although most species you'll meet in WA are much smaller. Goannas can run very fast and when threatened will use those big claws to climb the nearest tree – or perhaps the nearest leg! The 'racing' goanna (known as the sleek bungarra) is most often seen.

Blue-tongue lizards, slow-moving and stumpy, are children's favourites and are sometimes kept as pets. Their even slower and stumpier relations, shingle-backs, are common in the Darling Ranges near Perth and in the outback.

More fleet-footed are the frilled lizards *(Chlamydosaurus kingii)* and bizarre and ugly (or beautiful if you are of the same species) thorny or mountain devil *(Moloch horridus)*. The latter can change colour by a variation of skin pigments to match the desert sand or clay surface.

Marine Turtles These are often seen in the waters off the north-west coast of Australia. Four species can be observed coming ashore on islands and beaches to nest – green

(Chelonia mydas), loggerhead *(Caretta caretta)*, flatback *(Chelonia depressa)* and hawksbill *(Eretmochelys imbricata)*. All four species are protected; Aborigines, however, whose diet traditionally includes turtle, can hunt them. The flatback is believed to nest only on Australian coasts.

Turtles nest between September and April, although they can be seen in north-west waters throughout the year. Nesting occurs nightly during warmer summer months and the best time to observe them is two hours before or after high tide.

Turtles live a long life and are thought to be about 40 to 50 years old before they breed. The incubation temperature determines the sex of the hatchlings; outside the temperature range of 24°C to 32°C, no egg development occurs. For guidelines to watching nesting check with the nearest CALM office.

Amphibians The only amphibians that occur in Australia are frogs. Western Australia has 25 species of tree frog and 51 species of ground frog, one-third of Australia's known species.

FLORA
Trees
Trees are found all over the moist and semi-arid parts of WA but only as forests of trees in the south-west corner of the state. All the species subsequently described grow only in WA.

There are over 500 species of eucalypts (gum) trees, so-named as the flower bud has a little cap protecting the flowers (from the Greek *eucalyptus* or well-covered) in Australia. In WA's south-west, there are eucalypts, and other species of tree, that you will see nowhere else. In the Kimberley, the curiously shaped boab tree *(Adansonia gregorii)* is a characteristic feature of the landscape – for more information see under Boabs in the Kimberley chapter.

A good book to have is *Key Guide to Australian Trees* by Leonard Cronin (Reed Books, Frenchs Forest, 1988). A useful general book covering flora & fauna is the *Environmental Guide to Flora & Fauna: Australia's Outback* by Frank Haddon (Simon & Schuster, East Roseville, 1992).

Rainforest

It wasn't until 1965 that it was first realised that WA had its own patches of rainforest. These are found along the north-west coast between Broome and the Northern Territory and in parks and reserves such as Prince Regent River, Drysdale River, Point Spring, Coulomb Point and Purnululu.

The rainforests are distinguished by closed evergreen canopies and a profusion of vines and plants. Of the 20 types of rainforest found in Australia, three types occur in the Kimberley. If you can, get a copy of the Conservation and Land Management's (CALM) pamphlet *The Kimberley Rainforests*. ■

Jarrah These majestic hardwood trees *(E. marginata)* grow up to 40 metres and live up to 400 years. In coastal areas, poor soils reduce their growth to about 15 metres, and the average height in forests is closer to 30 metres. The bark has deep vertical grooves and is stringy in texture and dark-grey or reddish-brown in colour. The botanical name refers to a thick margin around the leaves. Jarrah is a popular timber and is in demand worldwide.

Karri Another giant hardwood tree, karri *(E. diversicolor)* has a pale, smooth bark which changes to the colour of pink in autumn. Reaching upwards of 90 metres in height, this is the world's third tallest hardwood tree after the Californian sequoia and Australia's mountain ash *(E. regnans)*. Karri grows in red clay loams where there is more than 750 mm of rain per year. *Diversicolor* refers to the difference between the top and underside of its leaf.

Marri This hardwood tree *(E. calophylla)* is often called redgum as it oozes drops of red gum from its grey bark. They are different from jarrah as they have a larger fruit (honkey nuts) and their branches are more widespread. In dry areas they only grow to about 10 metres but in forests they reach up to 60 metres. It grows widely throughout the south-west and along the Darling Scarp.

Tingle There are three species of this rare and restricted eucalypt (it is restricted as it is found only in a small area near Walpole-Nornalup National Park and nowhere else).

The red tingle *(E. jacksonii)* has a similar look to jarrah except that it is much larger. Its thick trunk often has spreading buttresses up to 20 metres and the tree is one of the top 10 largest living things on the planet. The term red relates to the purple colour of its timber.

Much smaller is the yellow tingle *(E. guilfoylei)* but it still has a buttressed base. Identification is difficult as the flowers and gumnuts are often over 30 metres above the ground.

The last of the tingles is Rates tingle *(E. brevistylis)*, only recently discovered northeast of Walpole. It is not easily distinguished from the red and yellow tingles.

There are a number of places where you can get close to the tingles in the Walpole-Nornalup forests, most notably the Tingle Tree Walk east of Walpole and in the aptly named Valley of the Giants.

Wandoo This tree *(E. wandoo)* is one of Australia's dense and durable hardwoods. Commonly referred to as the white gum, wandoo forms a major part of the south-west eucalypt forests. The powder-bark wandoo *(E. accedens)* is found on the hills of the wheatbelt and is distinguished from the common wandoo by the powder on its bark which rubs off easily.

Tuart Also rare and restricted is the tuart *(E. gomphocephala)* which is found between the Hill River and Busselton and is at its best in the Ludlow Forest. Its height is determined by the salt-laden winds but it can reach upwards of 40 metres. Its presence is an indication of limestone soils.

Red Flowering Gum Another rare and restricted eucalypt is the red flowering gum *(E. ficifolia)* which is found on the headland of Point Irwin, between Walpole and Peaceful Bay. It has brilliantly coloured flowers, varying from vermilion, crimson, orange and pink. It is a small tree of about five metres with a short trunk.

WILDFLOWERS

Western Australia is famed for its wildflowers, which bloom from August to October. Even some of the driest regions put on a technicolour display after just a little rainfall. It is estimated that there are more than 8000 species of flowering plants in the state.

The south-west has over 3000 species, many of which, because of the state's isolation, are unique. They're commonly known as everlastings because the petals stay attached even after the flowers have died. The flowers seem to spring up almost overnight, and transform vast areas within days.

You can find the flowers almost everywhere in the state, but the jarrah forests in the south-west are particularly rich. The coastal parks, such as Fitzgerald River and Kalbarri, also put on brilliant displays. Near Perth, the Badgingarra, Tathra, Alexander Morrison, Yanchep and John Forrest national parks are excellent prospects to see wildflowers. There's also a wildflower display in Kings Park, Perth.

The excellent *Wildflower Discovery – a Guide for the Motorist*, which details wildflower trails north and south of Perth, is available free from the Western Australia Tourism Commission (WATC) in Perth. *Discovering the Wildflowers of Western Australia* by Margaret Pieroni ($7.95) is the best of the semi-technical books with a description and illustration of over 200 plants. Probably harder to get but a valuable resource is *Flowers & Plants of Western Australia* (Rica Erickson et al, AH & AW Reed, Frenchs Forest, NSW, reprinted 1983).

SEASONS & LOCATIONS

The beauty of the wildflowers of WA cannot be overstated. No matter what time of year, there will always be the opportunity to see some species of flowering plants at their best. Undoubtedly the best time is late winter to early summer (August to November). This brief coverage does not purport to be comprehensive and a good book or a knowledgeable guide will enhance your appreciation of the many wildflowers you will encounter (see under Wildflowers in this chapter).

Once you begin to take an interest in wildflowers the same names start to crop up. Often they are the common names: gums, wattles, featherflowers, coneflowers, mulla mulla, honey myrtle and mountain bells. With a bit of practice you will soon be recognising the names of the genera (those above are *Eucalyptus, Acacia, Verticordia, Isopogon, Ptilotus, Melaleuca* and *Darwinia* which should become familiar to you).

The genus name *Caladenia* occurs often. The winter spider orchid is named *Caladenia drummondii* but the bee orchid is *Diuris laxiflora* and the elbow orchid is *Spiculaea ciliata*. With a bit of juggling, however, you will soon be recognising *Acacia gregorii* as Gregory's wattle, *Verticordia forrestii* as Forrest's featherflower and *Eucalyptus sepulcralis* as weeping gum.

In this section, genera abbreviations are used if it is obvious from the text what the genus is (blue leschenaultia – *L. biloba* for *Leschenaultia biloba* – and Stirling Range banksia – *B. solandri* for *Banksia solandri*).

To give you an indication of the number of wildflower events that are available in WA, here are some examples:

August – Mullewa Wildflower Show
September – Ravensthorpe Wildflower Show, Bindoon Wildflower Weekend, Kalgoorlie-Boulder Spring Flower Show, Augusta Annual Spring Orchid Show, Cranbrook Wildflower Display, Ongerup Wildflower Display, Nannup Wildflower Display, Albany Wildflower Festival, Busselton Wildflower Exhibition, Mingenew Wildflower Show
October – Kings Park Wildflower Festival, Kojonup Country Wildflower Festival, Walpole Orchid Show

Perth to the Jarrah Forests
(Early September to November)

The North Dandalup, south of Perth, is a great place to see Darling Range wildflowers such as colourful peas, Swan River myrtle *(Hypocalymma robustum)*, green kangaroo paw *(Anigozanthos viridis)* and golden dryandras *(D. nobilis)*.

Further inland, near Collie, expect to see the beautiful silky yellow banjine *(Pimelea sauveolens)* and the *Pimelea spectabilis*, with its large white flowers. Also found here are blue

Ashby's Banksia
(Banskia ashbyi)

Baxter's Kunzea
(Kunzea baxteri)

Black Kangaroo Paw
(Macropidia fuliginosa)

Cat's Paw
(Anigozanthos humilis)

Broad Leaf Lambstail
(Lachnostachys verbascifolia)

Christmas Tree
(Nuytsia floribunda)

Cootamundra Wattle
(Acacia baileyana)

Common Blackboy Grass Tree
(Xanthorrhoea preissii)

Cowslip Orchid
(Caladenia flava)

All photographs courtesy of Western Australian Tourist Commission

Crab-lipped Spider Orchid
(Caladenia plicata)

Dampiera
(Dampiera linearis)

Everlastings
(Helichrysum bracteatum)

Firewood Banksia
(Banksia menziesii)

Geraldton Wax Flower
(Chamelaucium uncinatum)

Karri Boronia
(Boronia gracilipes)

Lemon-flowered Gum
(Eucalyptus woodwardii)

Lesser Bottlebrush
(Callistemon phoeniceus)

Mangles' Kangaroo Paw
(Anigozanthos manglesii)

All photographs courtesy of Western Australian Tourist Commission

Oak-Leaved Dryandra
(Dryandra quercifolia)

Pear-fruited Mallee
(Eucalyptus ipyriformis)

Pincushion Hakea
(Hakea laurina)

Pink Enamel Orchid
(Elythranthera emarginata)

Pink Featherflower
(Verticordia monadelpha)

Prickly Bitter-pea
(Daviesia decurrens)

Royal Hakea
(Hakea victoria)

Scarlett Banksia
(Banksia coccinea)

Southern Cross
(Xanthosia rotundifolia)

All photographs courtesy of Western Australian Tourist Commission

Sturt's Desert Pea
(Clianthus formosus)

Swamp Bottlebrush
(Beaufortia sparsa)

Tall or Pink Boronia
(Boronia elatior)

Tree Hovea
(Hovea elliptica)

Yellow Feather Flower
(Verticordia acerosa)

White Spider Orchid
(Caladenia patersonii)

Wilson's Grenvillea
(Grenvilla wilsonii)

Wreath Lechenaultia
(Lechenaultia macrantha)

All photographs courtesy of Western Australian Tourist Commission

leschenaultia *(L. biloba)*, one of the state's many excellent flowers, and mauve pepper-and-salt *(Eriostemon spicatus)*, which is related to boronia.

In the Leeuwin-Naturaliste region there is an amazing variety of flowering plants from the swamp bottlebrush *(Beaufortia sparsa)* in Scott National Park to the common hovea *(H. trisperma)* and yellow flags *(Patersonia xanthina)* along Caves Rd. There is also the incredible flying duck orchid *(Paracaleana nigrita)* in the jarrah forests.

A number of interesting species also exist on the Swan Coastal Plain. The Yanchep rose *(Diplolaena angustifolia)* is found on sand and limestone; the rough daisybush *(Olearia rudis)* is widespread; the chenille honeymyrtle *(Melaleuca huegelii)* is common along the coast from Geraldton to Augusta; Mangle's kangaroo paw *(Anigozanthos manglesii)*, the floral emblem of WA, ranges from Shark Bay to Manjimup; Stirling's mulla mulla *(Ptilotus stirlingii)* and the snottygobble *(Persoonia saccata)* grow in sandy woodlands along the coastal plain; and the vibrant redcoat *(Utricularia menziesii)* ranges from Perth to the south coast and as far east as Esperance.

The Stirling & Porongurup Ranges (September to November)
Wildflower enthusiasts will be overwhelmed by the diversity and proliferation of flowering plants both in and around the Stirling Range and Porongurup national parks. In the Stirlings, 1500 species of flowering plants occur and around 60 are endemic.

Some 10 species of Darwinias, or mountain bells, have been identified. Near Cranbrook you can see the magnificent Cranbrook bell *(D. meeboldii)*. The lemon-yellow bell *(D. collina)* is found on Bluff Knoll, the pink mountain bell *(D. squarrosa)* occurs higher up in the range on the Bluff Knoll Trail and the large red and white Mondurup bell *(D. macrostegia)* is found on Mondurup Peak.

The Stirling Range banksia *(B. solandri)*, the stunning Stirling Range coneflower *(Isopogon baxteri)* and the mountain pea (get ready for this: *Oxylobium atropurpureum)* are also restricted to this range. There are also many black gins *(Kingia australis)*, named after the explorer Philip King, near Bluff Knoll; these examples of *Xanthorrhoea* are truly beautiful when in flower (any month).

In the vicinity of the Stirling Range caravan park are orchids and near the damp flats of the range is a good place to look for the dwarf kangaroo paw *(Anigozanthos gabrielae)*. The natural display in the Porongurups includes the tree hovea *(H. elliptica)*.

Albany Region (June to November)
The national parks of the Albany region provide much reward for the keen observer. In West Cape Howe, the coastal heath supports many species of banksias, dryandras and hakeas. The scarlet banksia *(B. coccinea)* is common in areas of deep sand, as is Baxter's banksia *(B. baxteri)*, while the red swamp banksia *(B. occidentalis)* prefers wetter areas. The insect-eating Albany pitcher plant *(Cephalotus follicularis)* is also found in this park; it is the only member of its plant family.

In William Bay National Park, west of Denmark, the five-petalled sticky tail-flower *(Anthocercis viscosa)* is found and along Ficifolia Rd, near Walpole, you may be lucky enough to see the red-flowering gum *(E. ficifolia*; see under Flora & Fauna in this chapter) in bloom.

North of Albany, on the sandy heaths, the hidden fleatherflower *(Verticordia habrantha)* flowers from September to November. The Albany cat's paw *(Anigozanthos preissii)* grows only within 50 km of Albany in sandy jarrah woodlands. A perennial favourite is the Southern Cross *(Xanthosia rotundifolia)* which is common in sandy soil from Albany to the Stirling Range.

The region is rich in orchids including the slender zebra orchid *(Caladenia cairnsiana)*, the crab-lipped spider orchid *(C. plicata)*, the clubbed spider orchid *(C. longiclavata)*, the curious hammer orchid *(Drakaea elastica)*, one of four species endemic to WA which has to be seen to be believed, the king leek orchid *(Prasophyllum regium)* and the pouched leek orchid *(P. gibbosum)*.

Bremer Bay to Esperance & Fitzgerald River Biosphere Reserve (September to November)
There are a wealth of opportunities for observing flowering plants in this expansive region. North-west of Bremer Bay, near the towns of Ongerup and Gnowangerup, in the open heath under woodland, there are pockets of the tough perennial herb pincushions *(Borya nitida)*, the barrel

coneflower *(Isopogon trilobus)*, the sprawling red combs *(Grevillea concinna)*, the ouch bush *(Daviesia pachyphylla)* and several varieties of poison bushes.

Along the Jerramungup-Ravensthorpe road is a wide road reserve which is 'chokker' (packed) with wildflowers. The ubiquitous bush cauliflowers, the robust ashy hakea *(H. cinerea)*, the Ravensthorpe bottlebrush *(B. orbifolia)* and a host of banksias are seen here.

To the south of the Jerramungup-Ravensthorpe road is the Fitzgerald River Biosphere Reserve, one of two such reserves in WA (see the Tall Trees & The Great Southern chapter for more information).

The most coveted flowers in this sensational reserve are the strange-looking royal hakea *(H. victoria)*, the only native plant in WA with variegated leaves; the pinky red pin-cushion hakea *(H. laurina)*; the creamy or orange chittick *(Lambertia inermis)*; the striking scarlet banksia; the four-winged mallee *(E. tetraptera)* and the warted yate *(E. megacornuta)*; the red or white (or combinations of both) heath leschenaultia *(L. tubiflora)*; the silky triggerplant *(Stylidium pilosum)*; the Qualup bell *(P. physodes)*, the only pimelea with a bell-like inflorescence; the thorny hovea *(H. acanthoclada)*; the weeping gum *(E. sepulcharis)*, which only grows on a few ranges at the eastern end of the Barrens Range; the Barrens clawflower *(Calothamnus validus)*; the oak-leafed dryandra *(D. quercifolia)*; Barrens leschenaultia *(L. superba)*; and the beautiful Barrens regelia *(R. velutina)* – any one of these species is reason enough to turn off the main highway.

The Ravensthorpe Range is also noted for its rare flora. Get information from the Ravensthorpe information centre then go in search of ouch bush, the rattle pea *(Daviesia oppositifolia)*, the common blue dampiera *(D. linearis)* and the cushion fan-flower *(Scaevola pulvinaris)*.

In the national parks around Esperance there are a wealth of wildflowers. In the Cape Le Grand region, look for thickets of the showy banksia *(B. speciosa)* and the spreading shrub of the teasal banksia *(B. pulchella)* in the deep sand of the sandplains. The rocky hills and heaths of Stokes National Park are great places to seek the bell-fruited mallee *(Eucalyptus pressiana)*. Other flowering plants to look out for include the nodding banksia *(B. nutans)*, the Southern Plains banksia *(B. media)*, the shining honeypot *(Dryandra obtusa)*, the coastal hakea *(H. clavata)* and the remarkable crab claws *(Stylidium macranthum)*. The stunning pink enamel orchid *(Elythranthera emarginata)* is found in a number of habitats in the Esperance region.

South-East Wheatbelt
(September to November)
A lot more than wheat, barley and oats grow in this region. The gem of the region is the Dryandra State Forest, often described as an 'ecological oasis'. Here you will spot many golden dryandras, the purple tangled grevillea *(G. flexuosa)* and pink rainbows *(Drosera menziesii)*. Orchids also abound in this forest.

Just a few of the possibilities are listed but the tourist bureaus will give out information on flowering plants around their towns. In particular, go in search of the unusual cricket ball hakea *(H. platysperma)* between Coorow and Hyden; the common cauliflower *(Verticordia brownii)* towards Lake King; the spectacular King dryandra *(D. proteoides)* on the ridges between Northam and Narrogin; red bonnets *(Burtonia hendersoni)* near Hyden; star-leaf grevillea *(G. asteriscosa)* between Kulin and Bruce Rock; cluster boronia *(B. capitata)* known only from the Pingelly region; Pritzel's featherflower *(Verticordia pritzelii)*; the widespread scarlet honeymyrtle *(Melaleuca fulgens)*; curved mulla mulla *(Ptilotus declinatus)* around Katanning; the perennial herb, downy stackhousia *(S. pubescens)*; the dark pea-bush *(Brachysema lanceolatum)* between Wagin and Bremer Bay; and the fringed mantis orchid *(Caladenia dilatata)*. If nothing else, this list will indicate what is available in a predominantly agricultural area.

North of Perth – Brand Highway & Midland Road
(Late July to end of November)
Brand Highway, north of Perth, is the place to see green kangaroo paws and red kangaroo paws *(Anigozanthos rufus)* near the Gingin cemetery, the open-branched *Dryandra kippistiana*, with many other species of dryandra in the Red Gully Reserve, and cowslip orchids *(Caladenia flava)* beside Regan's Ford. In the Badgingarra National Park grow a great profusion of wildflowers including the black kangaroo paw *(Macropidia fuliginosa)*. Not far past Badgingarra is Coomallo Creek, with 200 or more wildflowers in the vicinity – black kangaroo paws, yellow kangaroo paws

(A. pulcherrimus), scarlet (Verticordia grandis) and painted featherflowers (V. picta), the endemic Coomallo banksia (B. lanata) and the Christmas tree (Nuytsia floribunda), one of the few arborescent mistletoes in the world (it flowers between November and January).

There is an abundance of banksias including the unusual propeller banksia (B. candolleana) around Eneabba. The summer months see the superb starflower (Calytrix superba) bloom on the open sandy heaths; it has the largest flowers of any calytrix.

Mingenew, on the Midland road, is a centre of the fledgling wildflower-growing industry. This area has a large variety of wattles which shade the bright pink schoenia (S. cassiniana) and a number of everlastings. There are many wildflower drives nearby – keep an eye out for red pokers (Hakea bucculenta) growing in sand among tall scrub and prickly plume grevillea (G. annulifera), a many-branched shrub which grows on sandy heaths.

Wildflower Way
(Late July to end of November)
The displays of wildflowers that you see in this region are most likely those found in brochures – fields of everlastings (Helichrysums and Helipterums) stretching off into the distance. Well these are here, if the conditions are right, but there are many more varieties of flowering plants to be seen.

You have to head north from Perth on the Great Northern Highway to get to the famous Wildflower Way. A small deviation off the highway is Piawanning, where you can see the biggest eucalypt – the spectacular mottlecah (Eucalyptus macrocarpa).

The Wildflower Way starts at Wubin and passes through Perenjori and Morawa before it ends at Mullewa. If the rains come, this road is sandwiched between fields of everlastings which are at their best for a six to eight-week period.

Other beautiful flowers to seek out are the truly magnificent wreath leschenaultia (L. macrantha), found between Wubin and Mullewa; rose Darwinia (D. purpurea), found near granite outcrops around Mullewa; the widespread native foxglove (Pityrodia terminalis), a grey-felted perennial herb; pink spike hakea (H. coriacea) in gravelly soils between Mullewa and Southern Cross; bottlebrush grevillea (G. paradoxa) growing on heaths; and the scarlet honeymyrtle, found in gravelly soil among scrub.

If you head towards Geraldton, returning down the coast to Perth, look out for the famous Geraldton wax (Chamelaucium uncinatum), a long-time favourite in gardens.

The North-West (July to September)
Most travellers heading north beyond the spring everlastings of the Wildflower Way are probably in search of more than flowers – ecotourist attractions of a different nature are the magnets up here. There are still some great repositories of flowering plants, however, and 'spotting' these can add to the enjoyment of the journey.

The Kalbarri National Park has tremendous displays of wildflowers over a long season, July to September – banksias, grevilleas and eucalypts are abundant.

The road into Shark Bay and the North-West Coastal Highway from Shark Bay to Carnarvon, passes through a region which has a surprising number of flowering plants. Look out for bright podolepsis (P. canescans), hairy mulla mulla (Ptilotus helipteroides), tall mulla mulla (P. exaltatus), pincushion mistletoe (Amyema fitzgeraldii), the omnipresent Sturt pea (Clianthus formosus), native fuschia (Eremophila maculata), the Shark Bay poverty bush (Eremophila maitlandii), and the strange, rare, samphire bulli bulli (Tecticornia arborea).

North-West Cape (April to September)
The wildflower display in the Cape Range National Park is dependent on rainfall and, if rain falls, the best time to see it is winter and early spring.

The Cape Range grevillea (G. varifolia) is particularly beautiful as are the rock morning glory (Ipomoea costata) and the Yardie morning glory (I. yardiensis). The pretty yulbah (Erythrina vespertilio) is common in the canyons of the range; the leafless toucan flower (Brachysema macrocarpum) grows in sand or limestone; native plumbago (P. zeylanica) which grows in shaded parts of gorges, is the only species of plumbago native to Australia; white cassia (C. pruinosa) occurs on open rocky hillsides; the green birdflower (Crotalaria cunninghamii) which resembles a hummingbird in flight, is found in the coastal dunes; and mat mulla mulla *(Ptilotus axillaris)* grows in open spaces in rocky soil.

One of the most unusual (but aptly named) plants you will see is the cockroach bush *(Cassia notabilis)*. The distinctive yellow pom poms of Gregory's wattle *(Acacia gregorii)* can be found in sand or limestone country between North-West Cape and Lake Macleod.

Pilbara (April to October)

The best time to see wildflowers in the Pilbara is after the winter rain when a thin, green blanket of growth spreads across the countryside.

In disturbed soils, the popular Sturt pea, purple mulla mulla and the northern bluebell *(Trichodesma zeylanicum)* can be seen. Perennials include sennas, native fuschias, an abundance of wattles *(Acacia)* and the holly-leafed grevillea *(G. wickhamii)*.

In sandy coastal areas, the Dampier pea *(Swainsonia pterostylis)* and the coastal caper *(Capparis spinosa)* are common. The beautiful flowers of the white dragon tree *(Sesbania formosa)* are the largest of any native legume in WA; they are seen along rivers on the plains of the upper north-west.

The gorges of the Hamersley Ranges are home to many flowering plants. The striking mistletoe *(Lysiana casuarinae)* is found on many host plants; the weeping mulla mulla *(Ptilotus calostachyus)* occurs on open plains among spinifex; and the paperbark cadjeput *(Melaleuca leucadendron)*, found in many of the gorges, has terminal white 'bottlebrush-like' flowers

The Kimberley (April to November)

Not many people head to the Kimberley to see flowering plants. They usually travel this far north for the spectacular scenery. Wildflowers enthusiasts will find much to look at here at a time when the pickings are pretty slim in the rest of WA.

Two species of *Stenocarpus* with flowers similar to a grevillea, occur in the Kimberley; the little wheel bush *(S. cunninghamii)* grows among sandstone rocks in gorges. Common on rocky sandstone hills are the magnificent scarlet gum *(E. phoenicia)* and the bushy shrub Xanthostemon *(X. paradoxus)*.

Unlike the featherflowers in the south, this species occurs as a tree in the Kimberley. The tree featherflower *(Verticordia cunninghamii)* grows in sand among sandstone rocks and blooms from June to August.

There are nine orchids in the Kimberley and the most common species is *Cymbidium canaliculatum*, seen throughout the region in a number of trees. The waxy flowers of the native hoya *(H. australis)* are found where this scrambler clings to sandstone cliffs. And *Melastomas*, attractive shrubs which are found throughout the tropics, hide in shady places. ■

NATIONAL PARKS & RESERVES

Western Australia has about 60 national parks and nearly 20 forest recreation areas which are administered by CALM; overseeing almost 200,000 sq km. They cover a diverse range of landforms, marine environments and flora & fauna imaginable. Unlike other states, such as Victoria and New South Wales, they do not cover a large area of this huge state. They tend to focus on special features. Don't be perturbed, however, as exploration of these parks will be rewarded with breathtaking scenery, fascinating glimpses into ancient cultures and objects of interest at almost every turn. About 10 of

Australia's 30 most interesting features are found in this state; reasonable odds considering the state takes up one-third of continental Australia. Of course, this begs the question: what are they?

Try the Purnululu, the Devonian Reef national parks, Ningaloo Marine Reserve, Cape Range, Shark Bay World Heritage area, Karijini (Hamersley Range), Millstream-Chichester, the Montebellos, Nambung (the Pinnacles), Fitzgerald River Biosphere Reserve, Walpole-Nornalup, Leeuwin-Naturaliste and the Stirling Ranges. More than 10, there are still others worthy of top 30 status.

CALM publishes pamphlets on all of the

main parks, forests and marine reserves. In addition, it has a number of interesting publications for sale. Recommended are: *Discover Wild Places, Quiet Places* (southwest) and *North-West Bound* (Shark Bay to Wyndham).

In addition to the national parks, there are 1100 nature reserves and seven marine conservation reserves.

The main CALM office is in Perth. The address is 50 Hayman Rd (PO Box 104), Como, WA 6152 (☎ (09) 367 0333). There are a number of CALM regional offices:

Central Forest
> North Boyanup Rd, PO Box 733, Bunbury 6230 (☎ (097) 25 4300)

Goldfields
> Hannan St, PO Box 366, Kalgoorlie 6430 (☎ (090) 21 2677)

Greenough
> 7th Floor, Town Towers, PO Box 72, Geraldton (☎ (099) 21 5955)

Kimberley
> Konkerberry Drive, PO Box 942, Kununurra 6743 (☎ (091) 68 0200)

Metropolitan
> 5 The Esplanade, Mount Pleasant 6153 (☎ (09) 364 0777)

Northern Forest
> 3044 Albany Highway, Kelmscott 6111 (☎ (09) 390 5977)

Pilbara
> Welcome Rd, SGIO Building, PO Box 835, Karratha 6714 (☎ (091) 86 8288)

South Coast
> 44 Serpentine Rd, Albany 6330 (☎ (098) 41 7133)

Southern Forest
> Brain St, Manjimup 6258 (☎ (097) 71 1988)

Wheatbelt
> Hough St, PO Box 100, Narrogin 6312 (☎ (098) 81 1113)

GOVERNMENT

Western Australia is one of the six states which make up the federation together with the Australian Capital Territory and the Northern Territory.

The state is represented vice-regally by a Governor who performs official and ceremonial functions pertaining to the Crown. Western Australia contributes twelve senators to the Senate at federal

Edith Dirksey Cowan (1861-1932)

Edith Cowan was born 2 August 1861 at Glengarry, near Geraldton. A leading social reformer who was passionately interested in women's issues, she was awarded the OBE in 1920 and the following year was elected by constituents of West Perth to the Legislative Assembly. In her three-year term she highlighted the need for improved migrant welfare, sex education, infant health centres and encouraged women to enter the legal profession through her sponsorship of the Women's Legal Status Act in 1923.

After losing her seat she continued advocating women's rights until she died on 9 June 1932. (Interestingly, the first woman Cabinet Minister was also West Australian – Mrs A F G Cardell-Oliver, Member of the Legislative Assembly (MLA) for Subiaco, in the Ministry of 1947.) ∎

level (four Labor, six Liberal and two Green following the last election) and a proportional number of Members of Parliament (MPs) based on population figures. In the last federal election – March 1993 – there were 147 MPs in total and 14 came from WA (six were Labor and eight Liberal). Interestingly, two of the elected members of the Senate were Green candidates, representing environmental issues. Currently, the Greens hold the balance of power in the Senate and therefore greatly influence the passage of legislation.

The Parliament consists of two parts (Legislative Council and a Legislative Assembly). The principal minister is called the Premier. The last state election was held on 6 February 1993 and the Liberal and National parties in coalition formed the government. They held majorities in the upper (Legislative Council) and lower (Legislative Assembly) houses and the Premier, the Honourable Richard F Court, is the leader of the coalition, and Hendy Cowan is his deputy.

ECONOMY

Western Australia is fundamentally based on the production and export of mineral and agricultural products, and continues to play a crucial role in Australia's economic recovery. During the 1980s the WA economy experienced strong growth and the Gross State Production (GSP) increased over that period by 57% in contrast to the overall national growth in Gross Domestic Product (GDP) of 34%. In the period 1990-91, WA led the nation in exports with 23.7% of the Australian total. In 1991-92, mining, representing 34% of Australia's total mining output, contributed 16% to the GSP and 5% of GDP, a significant proportion. Agriculture, forestry and fisheries still contributed 12.9% of Australian output in this sector.

Within the state in 1991-92, the major exports, in terms of dollar value, were iron ore (20.1%) and gold bullion (17.6%). These were followed by petroleum and petroleum products, wheat and wool, all roughly a third of the value of gold exports. Lobsters made up 67% of the value of the state's fish catch, a dollar sum about 10% of the value of iron-ore exports.

The state still has a relatively small manufacturing sector and continues to receive more interstate imports than it exports.

Trade with Japan dominates foreign trade and was worth over $3 billion in 1990-91. Of the total of Australia's exports to certain countries, WA has the following component: China 43%, USA 26%, Japan 26% and Indonesia 24%.

Tourism is one of the real growth industries (yes you!). International tourism increased 25% in 1993-94, compared to a national growth of 15%, with the remotest corner of WA – rather than city skylines and cuddly koalas – a major lure.

POPULATION & PEOPLE

Western Australia with 1.8 million people, about a 10th of the nation's population, is very sparsely populated. Compare this to New South Wales, only a third the size of WA, which has a population approaching six million. The annual growth rate in WA is less than 2%.

There are estimated to be between 50,000 and 60,000 Aborigines in the state, about the same number before the coming of the European.

Migrants contribute to the population and it seems that a lot of British citizens never quite made it past WA on their way to Sydney or Melbourne. Perth has 170,000 of them (almost as many as Melbourne).

Ireland, South Africa and New Zealand are other English-speaking migrants and Germany, India, Greece, Italy, Poland, the Netherlands and former citizens of Yugoslavia are non-English speakers. Its proximity to Asia also means that it has a sizeable Asian population – Malaysia, Singapore and Vietnam being significant contributors. In fact Perth has more Singaporeans than either Sydney or Melbourne, both three times its size.

ARTS & CULTURE

While Perth and WA lack the supposed cultural status of, say, Melbourne and Victoria, they certainly lack nothing in regard to solid artistic and cultural bases. There is a resident symphony orchestra, a ballet company, a number of theatre companies, an impressive art gallery, the innovative Perth Institute of Contemporary Art, literary publishing houses and a string of contributors in all facets of artistic and cultural endeavour over the years. The Perth Cultural Centre, Northbridge, and the Perth Concert Hall are a focus for the arts in WA (see the Perth chapter).

You just have to look at the varied list of festivals and events to realise that the state has much to offer culturally. (See under Cultural Events in the Facts for the Visitor chapter.)

Probably the richest cultural heritage of this state is to be found amid the spinifex and rocks. Visitors to WA get the chance to witness Aboriginal culture first-hand, either in the modern communities or at traditional sites.

Aboriginal Culture

In Perth, the Museum of WA and Art Gallery of WA have comprehensive collections of Aboriginal art and culture. Other branches of the museum in Geraldton and Albany also

Aborginal rock painting

have displays covering pre-colonisation and the modern life of Aborigines. You can also see one of Australia's best collections of Aboriginal art in the Art Gallery of WA.

There is also plenty of opportunity to participate in the daily lives of Aboriginal groups in the north-west (see the Coral Coast & The Pilbara and The Kimberley chapters).

In several places there are engrossing self-guided walking trails. Some heritage trails include the Yaberoo Budjara near Yanchep, the Manjaree Track in Fremantle, the petroglyphs (rock engravings) of the Burrup Peninsula and the excellent Jaburara Trail in the range above Karratha. At Minarriny, about 80 km north of Broome, there is the Lurujarri Heritage Trail which follows part of a traditional song cycle from the Dreamtime.

Architecture
The most dominating aspect of Perth's architecture is the line of skyscrapers that tower above the Swan River. Fortunately, a few fine stone and brick buildings survive (see the Perth chapter) and, not far out of the city, there are gracious Victorian homes.

Fremantle's architectural heritage survives thanks to the efforts of residents who fought to preserve it.

The goldfields architecture, often referred to as 'Boom architecture', is the most noticeable aspect of a number of towns in the west. Nowhere is this more apparent than along Kalgoorlie's Hannan St (see under Architectural Styles in The Goldfields & Nullarbor chapter). The wealth from gold also contributed to the fine architecture seen in Gwalia, Coolgardie and Cue.

Western Australia has many examples of vernacular homes, those which show ingenious adaptation to the climate and clever use of local, available building materials. Examples are Bedamanup Homestead in Gingin, the houses of Yalgoo, the timber slab and stone cottage in West Arthur, Old Blythewood near Pinjarra, the shell-block church in Denham and the fieldstone buildings of Milligan Homestead near Kellerberrin.

One of the most famous architects in the WA was the enigmatic and controversial Monsignor John Hawes (see under Monsignor John Hawes in the Batavia Coast, Shark Bay & Gascoyne chapter).

Theatre
Theatre is alive and well in the west. For real-life soap opera you can watch the local TV news. The Perth Theatre Company (PTC), Theatre West, Black Swan, Barking Gecko and Hole in the Wall theatre companies reside in Perth. The city also has a number of venues for live theatre, the most striking being the beautiful Edwardian-style His Majesty's Theatre at 285 Hay St (for more information see the Perth chapter).

A number of playwrights were either born or began their careers in the west. The expatriate Alan Seymour gave us *One Day of the Year* (1962), an examination of the generational differences one Anzac Day. The son of Katharine Sussanah Prichard, Ric Throssell, has continued his family's literary tradition, producing a string of satires and plays with serious themes. Dorothy Hewett, known for her poetry, has written many plays.

The prolific WA writer, Jack Davis, has

had plays produced throughout Australia and, in 1986 with *The Dreamers*, became the first Aborigine to have a play performed in the UK.

The first Aboriginal stage musical came from Broome. Jimmy Chi's *Bran Nue Dae* has since been produced throughout Australia. *Sistergirl* – a tragicomedy about racial reconciliation – is the first play by WA writer Sally Morgan, and another production that has fared well throughout the country. For details of other playwrights see under Literature in this chapter.

Fine Arts

The geographical epicentre of fine arts in the west is the Perth Cultural Centre in Northbridge (see the Perth chapter) which includes the Alexander Library, WA Museum, Art Gallery of WA and Perth Institute of Contemporary Art (PICA). There are many other galleries in Perth, Fremantle and the south-west region. Obtain a copy of the *Gallery Guide* from the Art Gallery of WA as it lists all the current exhibitions at nearly 20 galleries in and around Perth.

The west has a rich tradition of fine arts with painting, indigenous art, sculpture and ceramics well represented. In the 1890s there was an influx of people who had formal training in the arts, such as the painters FM Williams, AW Bassett, George Pitt Morrison and James WR Linton. The well-known artist Daisy Rossi, whose wildflower and garden paintings were widely exhibited, was prominent during and after WW I.

The 1930s heralded a discernible change in subject matter – Aboriginal portraiture and a noticeable interest in cityscapes became serious themes. In the late 1930s, Herbert McLintock, as Max Ebert, made an impact with his figurative surrealist compositions; he later joined a group of realists in Sydney and was a war artist during WW II.

Following WW II, artists branched out from Perth in search of subject matter. Two good interpreters of the outback were the German Elise Blumann and Elizabeth Durack. Blumann painted Aborigines living on the fringe of European society and

Durack mined her familiar Kimberley for ideas.

Well-known modern WA painters have looked to the local landscape and the special light in the west for inspiration. Robert Juniper, Guy Grey Smith and George Haynes are three artists to have achieved recent success. While their art would not be considered avant-garde in the eastern states, it nonetheless reflects an inspired interpretation of the aridity and untamed nature of their surroundings. A good place to see the work of Juniper is in the Holy Trinity Church in York where his paintings and glass designs are featured. Sally Morgan, the respected WA writer, is also a nationally recognised artist and was awarded an AM (Member of the Order of Australia) in 1990.

The Art Gallery of WA in Perth has a fine collection of local and overseas art. The major attraction is a world famous indigenous collection. A local publication, *Arts Unlimited*, details happenings, exhibitions and has interviews with local artists and critiques of their work. There are numerous galleries dotted throughout Perth and the south-west.

Literature

Western Australia's literary tradition is remarkably fecund, encompassing the unpolished, rough humour of the early writers from the north-west and goldfields to sophisticated works from a string of modern writers.

By far the most prolific of WA's writers was Katharine Susannah Prichard. She wasn't born in WA but settled there in 1916. She wrote extensively on WA themes, often infusing her own communist beliefs into many of her works. *Black Opal* (1921) deals with the independent ownership of mines in the mythical town of Fallen Star Ridge; *Working Bullocks* (1926) was an account of the timber-getters in the karri forests of the south-west; *Coonardoo* (1929) examines the taboo subject of Black-White sexual relationships; and *The Roaring Nineties* (1946), *Golden Miles* (1948) and *Winged Seeds* (1950) were parts of an enormous socialist-realist trilogy about the goldfields.

Henrietta Drake-Brockman, a contemporary of Prichard's, was known mainly for her work *Men without Wives and Other Plays* (1955). Her novels include *Blue North* (1934) which is set in the pearling town of Broome and *Sheba Lane* (1936), also set in Broome, but when it is no longer a rollicking frontier town.

Two respected novelists to come out of the University of WA were Peter Cowan and Randolph Stow. Cowan has written a number of collections of short stories (*Drift, The Unploughed Land, The Empty Street, The Tins* and *Mobiles*) since the end of WWII. Most of his stories have a theme of isolation very much influenced by the WA bush. Stow was an accomplished novelist, poet and librettist. His work has deservedly won many awards and his *The Merry-Go-*

Round in the Sea (1965), a semi-autobiographical look at life through the eyes of a child in Geraldton, is one of Australia's most popular novels.

Not strictly a novel, but dramatic in its presentation, is Dame Mary Durack's saga of her own family in *Kings in Grass Castles* (1959). The sequel to this monumental work on life in the Kimberley was *Sons in the Saddle* (1983). In addition to these she wrote children's books and the novel *Keep Him My Country* (1955).

One of the great modern WA writers is English-born Elizabeth Jolley. She has won numerous writing awards for her short stories and novels. Her short fiction includes *Five Acre Virgin and Other Stories* (1976), *The Travelling Entertainer* (1979), *Woman in a Lampshade* (1983) and the novels *The*

Albert Facey

One of the great stories of a 'battler' is Albert Barnett Facey's autobiography *A Fortunate Life* (1981), which won the NSW Premier's Award for non-fiction in 1981.

Facey was born in Maidstone, Victoria, in 1894 and grew up in the Coolgardie goldfields and outback WA. His father died before he was two and his mother deserted him (and his sister and two brothers). The family was subsequently raised by his grandmother. He started work at eight and was variously employed doing station work, working on the railway, droving and boxing in an itinerant troupe.

He returned to Perth in 1915 after fighting and sustaining injury at Gallipoli (his brother Joseph was killed there). Facey married, joined the WA Tramways, then became a farmer as part of the Soldier Settlement Scheme near Wickepin (see under The Fortunate House in the Midlands, Wheatbelt & Great Northern Highway chapter). After the war he learned to read and write and eventually compiled the notes which formed the basis of his best-selling autobiography.

The Depression combined with his injuries forced him to return to Perth in 1934. He rejoined the Tramways and became active in the union. Three of his sons went off to fight in WWII and one was killed when Singapore fell. Albert died in Perth in 1982.

A Fortunate Life is a marvellous heart-wrenching story, giving an historic glimpse of the lives of ordinary Australians from the turn of the century to the 1970s. The story has subsequently been dramatised and made into a TV series. ∎

Albert Facey aged 20 (1914)

Newspaper of Claremont Street (1981), *Mrs Scobie's Riddle* (1982) and *Miss Peabody's Inheritance* (1983).

Jack Davis' *The First-Born and other Poems* (1970) was a watershed in Aboriginal literature. The work was 'discovered' almost by accident after Davis had pinned it on a board outside his office in the Perth Aboriginal Centre. He was later named Aboriginal Writer of the Year (1981) and in 1985 won the inaugural Sydney Myer Performing Arts Award.

Another outstanding talent is the Aboriginal writer, Archie Weller. His *The Day of the Dog*, tracing the fall of the traditional male role in Aboriginal society, garnered great reviews and was highly commended in the Australian/Vogel Literary Awards (1980).

Sally Morgan's autobiography, *My Place*, charted her Aboriginality and outlined her grandmother's family history. Winner of the inaugural Human Rights and Equal Opportunity Commission Humanitarian Award (1987), Morgan also received, in 1988, the WA Week Literary Award for non-fiction.

Many of the works of Dorothy Hewett (born in Perth in 1923) can be linked to the Great Southern region of the state and include the collections of poetry found in *Windmill Country* (1965), *Rapunzel in Suburbia* (1979) and plays *The Man from Mukinupin* (1980) and *The Fields of Heaven* (1982).

The young and highly successful Tim Winton, born in 1960, has written a number of novels including the immensely popular *Cloudstreet* (1991) and the recent *The Riders*. His first novel, *An Open Swimmer*, was joint winner of the Australian/Vogel Award in 1981 and his second, *Shallows* (1984), won the prestigious Miles Franklin Award. His other novels include *Scission* (1985), *In the Winter Dark* (1988), *Jesse* (1988) and *Lockie Leonard, Human Torpedo* (1990).

Magabala Books is an Aboriginal-controlled publishing house located in Broome and the first Aboriginal publishing house in Australia. Its aims are to preserve Aboriginal culture and history through the written word, and at the same time, to bridge the gap between, and promote their culture to, non-

Aborigines. Forthcoming titles include *Lori* by John Wilson and *Don't Go Around the Edges* by Daisy Utemmorah.

Music
One of the first things you should do is buy a tape of Aboriginal music to play in the car as you drive through WA. The hauntingly beautiful tones seem to vivify the landscape and allow the 'whitefella' a bit of a chance to experience the magic of the Dreamtime.

All choices of music are available in Perth. It could be listening to a pub band or enjoying a night under the stars wooed by the strings of the Western Australian Symphony Orchestra (WASO).

Classical Wine seems to be the most natural accompaniment to classical music in this state – performances at the Leeuwin Estate are extremely popular. The WASO performs regularly at the Perth Concert Hall. Under the direction of David Measham, the WASO has made many acclaimed recordings. There is also a state youth orchestra, the WAYO.

The Perth Concert Hall will have details of the annual calendar of events, which are as varied as the WASO playing pop one night to the Academy of St Martins in the Field Octet performing serious classical the next.

The west has also provided a cavalcade of composers and performers. The former group includes Janet Dobie of Armadale, George Tibbits of Boulder and Jennifer Fowler of Bunbury.

Renowned performers include the saxophonist Peter Clinch, baritones Bruce Martin (a Wagner specialist) and Greg Yurisich, soprano Glenys Fowles and mezzo-soprano Lorna Sydney. The indomitable arts administrator Herbert C ('Nugget') Coombs was born in Kalamunda.

Pop You can taste it in the air, and the flavour is decidedly sweet. Western Australia's public have begun to celebrate a music scene with a noticeable verve that is finally deserving of its quality.

It wasn't always so. While a lot of good musicians grew up in WA, they inevitably gravitated to Sydney and Melbourne, leaving the state, especially Perth, with a reputation as a 'cover city'.

In the early 1960s, a grinning, dentally-scarred Ronald ('Bon') Scott served time in a juvenile detention centre in Perth, dreaming of a song he was later to sing with the band AC/DC, *Jailbreak*. He later drifted to Melbourne where, in 1969, his group the Valentines became the first Australian band to be arrested for possession of marijuana. Bon later unleashed his raunchy vocals on an unsuspecting world as the lead singer of AC/DC and ascended (or descended) into 'rock 'n' roll heaven' after a wayward bout of heavy drinking.

In the 1980s, Dave Faulkner wandered across the Nullarbor to form the immensely successful Hoodoo Gurus; the guitarist in the Innocent Bystanders became Johnny Diesel; and a legend in the west, Dave Warner, crooned the poignant lines of *I'm Just a Suburban Boy*, summarising the ethos of Perth for those not covered wiv' glitter.

Perth also gave us the Dugites, the Scientists, Chad's Tree and The Triffids. The latter band drew rave critical reviews in the UK for their countrified rock, showcased in their album *Treeless Plain*.

These days there are plenty of venues around Perth where you can go and see any type of modern music from grunge to covers (yes, these kinds of bands still exist) of Elvis, U2 and Midnight Oil (see under Entertainment in the Perth chapter). You can find out where the action is in *Xpress* magazine, available free from record shops and pubs. There seems to be an inner city (read 'cool' scene) and a suburban pub music scene (read 'not so cool').

Jazz lovers have a number of regular venues in Perth including pubs in North Fremantle and Applecross. The WA Jazz Society meets every Monday night at the Hyde Park Hotel in Bulwer St, Perth.

An inexplicably large following is reserved for country & western music in Perth. Perhaps it is easier to understand if you are in the bush in a wheatbelt or goldfields town. In such an environment, you're likely to hear Willy Nelson, Waylon Jennings and Tammy Wynette with unfailing regularity. Maybe it has something to do with ' Western' in the title of country & western. Northam, in the Avon Valley, is the Nashville of the west and host of a well-attended festival. The annual calendar of events throughout the state will keep country & western fans yodelling, yelping and boot scooting until the wee small hours.

In the north-west you may have the opportunity to see a contemporary Aboriginal band. The Stompem Ground Festival in Broome would be the best annual collection of such musicians. The blend of traditional instruments with guitars, brass and drums has become widely accepted thanks to the international success of Yothu Yindi.

The Broome Musicians Aboriginal Corporation (BMAC) was established to promote and develop music amongst the Aboriginal community and protect musicians from the usual rip-offs associated with the industry. There is a distinctive Broome sound which combines corroboree influences, folk music from a number of sources such as Polynesia and Asia, and even Gregorian chant. There have been a succession of bands: the Broome Beats, Tombstone Shadows (aka Crossfire, aka Scrap Metal), Maja, Chocolate Solja, Black Label, Sunburn and Bingurr. In the eastern states it is hard to find any of this music so the record shops in the west are your best bet.

Cinema

The west does not have a large film industry although its location and climate would make it an ideal replacement for California, should the need ever arise.

The WA Film Commission, founded in 1978, has produced some good films but they have yet to achieve widespread exposure. Examples of their films are *Harlequin* (1980), *Roadgames* (1980) and the TV series *Falcon Island*. The strong feminist film *Shame*, directed by Steve Jodrell, is set in an isolated WA community, and examines attitudes towards rape.

The Film Corporation of WA is a private

company which has produced *Runnin' on Empty* (1982), *We of the Never Never* (1982) and *Winds of Jarrah* (1983).

The west has given us actors such as Kate Fitzpatrick, Rolf Harris, Alan Cassell, Phillip Ross and that 'cop of cops', Alwyn Kurts (immortalised as an icon in blue in TV shows such as *Cop Shop*).

A number of films concentrating on Aboriginal themes have started to filter out of the west such as *Milli Milli* by Wayne Barker and Paul Roberts.

RELIGION

A shrinking majority of people in Australia are at least nominally Christian. Most Protestant churches have merged to become the Uniting Church, although the Church of England has remained separate. The Catholic Church is popular (about a third of Christians are Catholics), with original Irish adherents boosted by the large numbers of Mediterranean immigrants.

Non-Christian minorities abound: Buddhist, Jewish and Muslim (the town of Katanning in the wheatbelt has a significant Muslim population made up of Christmas Islanders).

LANGUAGE

Any visitor from abroad who thinks Australian (that's 'strine') is simply a weird variant of English/American will soon have a few surprises. For a start many Australians speak other languages such as Italian, Lebanese, Vietnamese, Turkish or Greek.

Those who do speak the native tongue are liable to lose you in a strange collection of Australian words. Some have completely different meanings in Australia to those in English-speaking countries north of the equator; some commonly used words have been shortened almost beyond recognition. Others derive from Aboriginal languages, or from convict slang.

There is a slight regional variation in the Australian accent, while the difference between city and country speech is mainly a matter of speed. If you want to pass for a native, try speaking in a slightly nasal tone,

shortening any word of more than two syllables and then adding a vowel to the end of it. You can also make anything you can into a diminutive (even the Hell's Angels can become mere 'bikies'). And don't forget to pepper your speech with as many expletives as possible. The list that follows may help:

amber fluid – beer
arvo – afternoon
award wage – minimum pay rate

bail out – leave
bail up – hold up, rob, talk incessantly
banana bender – resident of Queensland
barbie – barbecue (bbq)
barrack – cheer on team at sporting event, support (as in 'who do you barrack for?')
battler – trier, struggler
beaut, beauty, bewdie – great, fantastic
big mobs – a large amount
bikies – motorcyclists
billabong – water hole in dried up riverbed, more correctly an ox-bow bend cut off in the dry season by receding waters
billy – tin container used to boil tea in the bush
bitumen – material used for surfacing roads
bloke – man
blowies – blow flies
bludger – lazy person, one who won't work
blue (ie have a blue) – to have an argument or fight
bluey – swag, or nickname for a red-haired person
bonzer – great, fantastic
boomer – very big, a particularly large male kangaroo
boomerang – a curved flat wooden instrument used by Aborigines for hunting
booze bus – police van used for random breath testing for alcohol
bottle shop – liquor shop
Buckley's – no chance at all
bugger off – literally 'If you don't like it here, go somewhere else!'
build-up, the – the period of atmospheric instability which precedes the Wet or a major sporting event

bull dust – fine and sometimes deep dust on outback roads, also bullshit

bunyip – Australia's yeti or bigfoot

burl – have a try (as in 'give it a burl')

bush – country, anywhere away from the city, especially in WA

bush (ie go bush) – go back to the land

bushbash – to force your way through pathless bush

bushranger – Australia's equivalent of the outlaws of the American Wild West (see under Moondyne Joe in the Around Perth chapter)

bush tucker – native foods, usually in the outback

BYO – Bring Your Own (booze to a restaurant, meat to a barbecue etc)

caaarn! – come on, traditional rallying call, especially at football games, as in 'Caaarn the Eagles!'

camp oven – large, cast-iron pot with lid, used for cooking on an open fire

cask – wine box (an Australian invention)

chook – chicken

chuck a U-ey – do a U-turn

chunder – vomit (aka technicolour yawn, liquid laugh)

clobber – clothes

cobber – mate (archaic)

cocky – small-scale farmer, cockatoo

come good – turn out all right

compo – compensation such as workers' compensation

counter meal, countery – pub meal

cow cocky – small-scale cattle farmer

crook – ill, badly made, substandard

crow eater – resident of South Australia

cut lunch – sandwiches

dag, daggy – dirty lump of wool at back end of a sheep, also an affectionate or mildly abusive term for a socially inept person

daks – trousers

damper – bush loaf made from flour and water and cooked in a camp oven

dead horse – tomato sauce

deli – delicatessen

didjeridoo – deep-toned Aboriginal wind instrument made from a long section of bamboo pipe

dill – idiot

dinkum, fair dinkum – honest, genuine

dinky-di – the real thing, typical

divvy van – police divisional van

dob in – to tell on someone

Doctor (ie the Fremantle Doctor) – an afternoon sea breeze on WA's coast

donk – car or boat engine

don't come the raw prawn – don't try and fool me

drongo – worthless person

Dry (ie the Dry) – the period of dry weather in the north-west

duco – car paint

dunny – outdoor lavatory

earbash – talk nonstop

eastern states – the rest of Australia viewed from WA

esky – large insulated box for keeping beer etc cold

fair crack of the whip! – fair go!

fair go! – give us a break!

FJ – most revered Holden car

flake – shark meat, used in fish & chips

fossick – hunt for gems or semiprecious stones

Freo – Fremantle

galah – noisy parrot, thus noisy idiot

game – brave (as in 'game as Ned Kelly')

gander – look (as in 'have a gander')

garbo – person who collects your garbage

g'day – good day, traditional Australian greeting

gibber – Aboriginal word for stony desert

give it away – give up

good on ya – well done

grazier – large-scale sheep or cattle farmer

Green – (ie the Green) the preferred name for the Wet in WA's north-west

grog – general term for alcohol

grouse – very good, unreal

heaps – lots of

hoon – idiot, hooligan

how are ya? – standard greeting, expected answer 'good, thanks, how are *you?*'
HQ – second most revered Australian car

icy-pole – frozen lolly water or ice cream on a stick

jackaroo – young male trainee on a station (farm)
jillaroo – young female trainee on a station
jocks – men's underpants
journo – journalist

kiwi – New Zealander
knock – criticise, deride
knocker – one who criticises

lair – layabout, ruffian
lairising – acting like a lair
lamington – square of sponge cake covered in chocolate icing and coconut
larrikin – a bit like a lair
lay-by – put a deposit on an article so the shop will hold it for you
lollies – sweets, candy
lurk – a scheme

manchester – household linen
mate – general term of familiarity, whether you know the person or not
middy – 285 ml beer glass
milk bar – general store
milko – milkman
mob – a kinship group of Aborigines
mozzies – mosquitoes
mulga – the bush, away from the city

never-never – remote country in the outback
no hoper – hopeless case
no worries – that's OK

ocker – an uncultivated or boorish Australian
off-sider – assistant or partner
O-S – overseas, as in 'he's gone O-S'
outback – remote part of the bush

pastoralist – large-scale grazier
pavlova – traditional Australian meringue and cream dessert, named after the Russian ballerina Anna Pavlova

perve – to gaze with lust
pineapple (rough end of) – stick (sharp end of)
piss – beer
piss turn – boozy party
pissed – drunk
pissed off – annoyed
pokies – poker machines
pom – English person
possie – advantageous position
postie – mailman
push – group or gang of people, such as shearers

ratbag – friendly term of abuse
ratshit (R-S) – lousy
rapt – delighted, enraptured
reckon! – you bet!, absolutely!
rego – registration, as in 'car rego'
ridgy-didge – original, genuine
ripper – good (also 'little ripper')
road train – semi-trailer-trailer-trailer
root – have sexual intercourse
rooted – tired
ropable – very bad-tempered or angry
Rotto – Rottnest Island
rubbish (ie to rubbish) – deride, tease

salvo – member of the Salvation Army
sandgroper – resident of WA to people in eastern states
schooner – large beer glass
sea wasp – deadly box jellyfish
sealed road – surfaced road
semi-trailer – articulated truck
session – lengthy period of heavy drinking
sheila – woman
shellacking – comprehensive defeat
she'll be right – no worries
shonky – unreliable
shoot through – leave in a hurry
shout – buy round of drinks (as in 'it's your shout')
sickie – day off work ill (or malingering)
skimpies – scantily-clad female bar staff
smoke-o – tea break
snag – sausage
spunky – good looking, attractive (as in 'what a spunk')

squatter – pioneer farmer who occupied land as a tenant of the government

squattocracy – Australian 'old money' folk, who made it by being first on the scene and grabbing the land

station – large farm

stickybeak – nosy person

stinger – box jellyfish

strides – trousers

strine – Australian slang

stubby – small bottle of beer

sunbake – sunbathe (well, the sun's hot in Australia)

surfies – surfing fanatics

swag – canvas-covered bed roll used in the outback, also a large amount

tall poppies – achievers (knockers like to cut them down)

tea – evening meal

thingo – thing (aka whatchamacallit, hooza meeboh, doo velacki, thingamajig)

tinny – can of beer

too right! – absolutely!

Top End – northern part of the Northern Territory

trucky – truck driver

true blue – dinkum

tucker – food

two-pot screamer – person unable to hold their drink

two-up – traditional heads/tails gambling game

uni – university

ute – utility, pickup truck

Wakka (ie the WACA) – Western Australian Cricket Association

wag (ie to wag) – to skip

walkabout – lengthy walk away from it all

weatherboard – wooden house

Wet (ie the Wet) – rainy season in the north

wharfie – dockworker

whinge – complain, moan

wobbly – disturbing, unpredictable behaviour (as in 'throw a wobbly')

woomera – stick used by Aborigines for throwing spears

wowser – spoilsport, puritan

yahoo – noisy and unruly person

yakka – work (from an Aboriginal language)

yobbo – uncouth, aggressive person

yonks – ages, a long time

youse – plural of you

Aboriginal Language

At the time of contact there were around 260 separate Australian languages spoken by the 600 to 700 Aboriginal language groups, and these languages were as distinct from each other as English and French. Often three or four adjacent groups would speak what amounted to dialects of the same language, but another adjacent group might speak a completely different language.

There are a number of words, however, that occur right across the continent, such as *jina* (foot) and *mala* (hand), and similarities also exist in the often complex grammatical structures.

Aboriginal Kriol is a new language which has developed since European arrival in Australia. It is spoken across northern Australia and has become the first language of many young Aborigines. It contains many English words, but the pronunciation and grammatical usage are along Aboriginal lines, the meaning is often different, and the spelling is phonetic. For example, the English sentence 'He was amazed' becomes 'I bin luk kwesjinmak' in Kriol.

There are a number of generic terms which Aborigines use to describe themselves, and these vary according to the region. The most common of these is Koori, used for the people of south-east Australia. Nunga is used to refer to the people of coastal South Australia, Murri for those from the north-east, and Nyoongah or Nyungar is used in the country's south-west.

Facts for the Visitor

VISAS & EMBASSIES

Once upon a time, Australia was fairly free and easy about who was allowed to visit the country, particularly if you were from the UK or Canada. Until recently, only New Zealanders got any sort of preferential treatment and even they will require visas after 1994.

Visa application forms are available from Australian diplomatic missions overseas or travel agents, and you can apply by mail or in person. There are several different types of visas, depending on the reason for your visit.

Australian Embassies

Australian consular offices overseas include:

Canada
    Suite 710, 50 O'Connor St, Ottawa K1P 6L2 (☎ (613) 236 0841), also in Toronto and Vancouver
China
    15 Dongzhimenwai Dajie, San Li Tun, Beijing (☎ (1) 532 2331)
Denmark
    Kristianagade 21, 2100 Copenhagen (☎ (3126 2244)
France
    4 Rue Jean Rey, Paris, 15eme (☎ (1) 40 59 33 00)
Germany
    Godesberger Allee 107, 5300 Bonn 1 (☎ (0228) 81030), also in Frankfurt and Berlin
Greece
    37 Dimitriou Soutsou St, Ambelokpi, Athens 11512 (☎ (01) 644 7303)
Hong Kong
    Harbour Centre, 24th floor, 25 Harbour Rd, Wanchai, Hong Kong Island (☎ (5) 73 1881)
India
    Australian Compound, No 1/50-G Shantipath, Chanakyapuri, New Delhi 110021 (☎ (60 1336), also in Bombay
Indonesia
    Jalan Thamrin 15, Gambir, Jakarta (☎ (21) 323109), also in Denpasar
Ireland
    Fitzwilton House, Wilton Terrace, Dublin 2 (☎ (01) 76 1517)

Italy
    Via Alessandria 215, Rome 00198 (☎ (06) 832 721) also in Milan
Japan
    2-1-14 Mita, Minato-ku, Tokyo (☎ (3) 5232 4111), also in Osaka
Malaysia
    6 Jalan Yap Kwan Seng, Kuala Lumpur 50450 (☎ (03) 242 3122)
Netherlands
    Carnegielaan 12, 2517 KH The Hague (☎ (070) 310 8200)
New Zealand
    72-78 Hobson St, Thorndon, Wellington (☎ (4) 473 6411), also in Auckland
Papua New Guinea
    Independence Drive, Waigani, Port Moresby (☎ 25 9333)
Philippines
    Bank of Philippine Islands Building, Paseo de Roxas, Makati, Manila (☎ 817 7911)
Singapore
    25 Napier Rd, Singapore 10 (☎ 737 9311)
South Africa
    4th floor, Mutual & Federal Centre, 220 Vermuelen St, Pretoria 0002 (☎ (012) 325 4315)
Sweden
    Sergels Torg 12, Stockholm C (☎ (08) 613 2900)
Switzerland
    29 Alpenstrasse, Berne (☎ (031) 43 0143), also in Geneva
Thailand
    37 South Sathorn Rd, Bangkok 10120 (☎ (2) 287 2680)
UK
    Australia House, The Strand, London WC2B 4LA (☎ (0171) 379 4334), also in Edinburgh and Manchester
USA
    1601 Massachusetts Ave NW, Washington DC 20036 (☎ (202) 797 3000), also in Los Angeles, Chicago, Honolulu, Houston, New York and San Francisco

Tourist Visas

Tourist visas are issued by Australian consular offices abroad; they are the most common and generally valid for a stay of up to six months within a 12-month period. If you intend staying less than three months, the visa is free; otherwise there is a $30 processing fee.

When you apply for a visa, present your passport and a passport photo, as well as signing an undertaking that you have an onward or return ticket and 'sufficient funds' – the latter is obviously open to interpretation.

Working Visas

Young visitors from Britain, Ireland, Canada, Holland and Japan may be eligible for a 'working holiday' visa. 'Young' is loosely interpreted as around 18 to 26, and working holiday means up to 12 months, but the emphasis is supposed to be on casual employment rather than a full-time job, so you are only supposed to work for three months. Officially this visa can only be applied for in your home country, but some travellers report that the rule can be bent.

See Work later in this chapter for details on the type of work available and where in WA.

Visa Extensions

The maximum stay given to visitors in Australia is one year, including extensions.

Visa extensions are made through Department of Immigration & Ethnic Affairs offices in Australia and, as the process takes some time, it's best to apply about a month before your visa expires. There is an application fee of $200 – and even if they turn down your application they can still keep your money! To qualify for an extension you are required to take out private medical insurance to cover the period of the extension, and have a ticket out of the country. Some offices are more strict in enforcing these conditions than others.

If you intend staying longer in Australia, the books *Tourist to Permanent Resident in Australia* and *Practical Guide to Obtaining Permanent Residence in Australia*, both published by Legal Books, might be useful.

Foreign Consulates

The principal diplomatic representations to Australia are in Canberra. There are also representatives in various other major cities including Perth, particularly from countries with major connections with Australia like the USA or UK; or in cities with important connections – Perth has a Japanese consulate, for example. There are nearly 30 countries represented in WA by consular staff or trade representatives. The important ones for travellers are:

Canada
  Honorary Consul, 11/111 St George's Terrace, Perth 6000 (☎ (09) 322 7930)
France
  Honorary Consul, 21/146 Mounts Bay Rd, Perth 6000 (☎ (09) 321 1940)
Germany
  Honorary Consul, 8th Floor, 16 St George's Terrace, Perth 6000 (☎ (09) 325 8851)
Ireland
  Honorary Consul-General, 10 Lilika Rd, City Beach 6015 (☎ (09) 385 8247)
Japan
  Consul, 21st Floor, 221 St George's Terrace, Perth 6000 (☎ (09) 321 7816)
Sweden
  Honorary Consul-General, 23 Walters Drive, Osborne Park 6017 (☎ (09) 244 3699)
Switzerland
  Honorary Consul, 5 Marie Way, Kalamunda 6076 (☎ (09) 293 2704)
UK
  Consul-General, 26th Floor, 77 St George's Terrace, Perth 6000 (☎ (09) 221 5400)
USA
  Consul-General, 16 St George's Terrace, Perth 6000 (☎ (09) 231 9400)

CUSTOMS

You can bring most articles in duty free when entering Australia, provided Australian Customs are satisfied they are for personal use and that you'll be taking them with you when you leave. There's also the usual duty-free per-person quota of one litre of alcohol, 250 cigarettes and dutiable goods up to the value of A$400.

With regard to prohibited goods, there are two areas you need to pay particular attention to. Number one is, of course, dope – Australian Customs have a positive mania about the stuff and can be extremely efficient when it comes to finding it. Unless you want to make first-hand investigations of conditions in Australian gaols (not very good), don't bring any with you. This particularly applies if you are arriving from South-East Asia or the Indian subcontinent.

Problem two is animal and plant quarantine. You will be asked to declare all goods of animal or vegetable origin – wooden spoons, straw hats, the lot – and show them to an official. The authorities are naturally keen to prevent weeds, pests or diseases getting into the country – Australia has so far managed to escape many of the agricultural pests and diseases prevalent in other parts of the world. Fresh food is also unpopular, particularly meat, sausages, fruit, vegetables and flowers. There are also restrictions on taking fruit and vegetables between states; in WA there are quarantine stations at the South Australian and Northern Territory borders.

Weapons and firearms are either prohibited or require a permit and safety testing. Other restricted goods include products (such as ivory) made from protected wildlife species, non-approved telecommunications devices and live animals.

When it is time to leave there are duty-free stores at the international airports and their associated cities. Treat them with healthy suspicion. 'Duty free' is one of the world's most overworked catch phrases, and it is often just an excuse to sell things at prices you can easily beat by a little shopping around.

MONEY
Currency
Australia's currency is the Australian dollar, which comprises 100 cents. The dollar was introduced in 1966 to replace the old system of pounds, shillings and pence. There are coins for 5c, 10c, 20c, 50c, $1 and $2, and paper notes for $5, $10, $20, $50 and $100. There are also nasty little indestructible plastic versions of the $5 and $10 notes, and these are far more common than the good old paper ones these days.

There are no notable restrictions on importing or exporting currency or travellers' cheques except that you may not take out more than A$5000 in cash without prior approval.

Exchange Rates
In recent years the Australian dollar has fluctuated quite markedly against the US dollar, but it now seems to hover around the 70c to 74c mark – a disaster for Australians travelling overseas but a real bonus for inbound visitors.

Canada	C$1	= A$1.00
Germany	DM 1	= A$0.90
Hong Kong	HK$10	= A$1.75
Japan	¥100	= A$1.40
New Zealand	NZ$1	= A$0.55
UK	UK£1	= A$2.25
USA	US$1	= A$1.35

Changing Money
Changing foreign currency or travellers' cheques is no problem at almost any bank. It's done quickly and efficiently and never involves the sort of headaches and grand production changing foreign currency in the USA always entails.

Travellers' Cheques There is a variety of ways to carry your money with you around Australia. If your stay is limited then travellers' cheques are the most straightforward and they generally enjoy a better exchange rate than foreign cash in Australia.

American Express, Thomas Cook and other well-known international brands of travellers' cheques are all widely used in Australia. A passport will usually be adequate for identification; it would be sensible to carry a driver's licence, credit cards or a plane ticket in case of problems.

Commissions and fees for changing foreign-currency travellers' cheques seem to vary from bank to bank and year to year. It's worth making a few phone calls to see which bank currently has the lowest charges. Some charge a flat fee for each transaction, which varies from $2.50 (Commonwealth Bank) to $6.50 (ANZ Bank), while others take a percentage of the amount changed – Westpac charges 1% with a minimum charge of $10.

Buying Australian dollar travellers' cheques is an option worth looking at. These can be exchanged immediately at the bank cashier's window without being converted from a foreign currency or incurring commissions, fees and exchange rate fluctuations.

Credit Cards

Credit cards are widely accepted in Australia and are an alternative to carrying large numbers of travellers' cheques. The most common credit card, however, is the Australian Bankcard system. Visa, MasterCard, Diners Club and American Express are also widely accepted.

Cash advances from credit cards are available over the counter and from many automatic teller machines (ATMs), depending on the card.

If you're planning to rent cars while travelling around Australia, a credit card makes life much simpler; they're looked upon with much greater favour by rent-a-car agencies than nasty old cash, and many agencies simply won't rent you a vehicle if you don't have a card.

Local Bank Accounts

If you're planning to stay longer than just a month or so, it's worth considering other ways of handling money that give you more flexibility and are more economical. This applies equally to Australians setting off to travel around the country.

Most travellers these days opt for an account which includes a cash card, which you can use to access your cash from ATMs found all over Australia. You put your card in the machine, key in your personal identification number (PIN) number, and then withdraw funds from your account. Westpac, ANZ, National and Commonwealth bank branches are found nationwide, and in all but the most remote town there'll be at least one agency where you can withdraw money from. In many of the really small towns in WA, the post office acts as the local bank.

ATM machines can be used day or night, and it is possible to use the machines of some other banks: Westpac ATMs accept Commonwealth Bank cards and vice versa; National Bank ATMs accept ANZ cards and

vice versa. There is a limit on how much you can withdraw from your account. This varies from bank to bank but is usually $400 to $500 per day.

Many businesses, such as service stations, supermarkets and convenience stores, are linked to the EFTPOS system (Electronic Funds Transfer at Point Of Sale), and at places with this facility you can use your bank cash card to pay for services or purchases direct, and sometimes withdraw cash as well. Bank cash cards and credit cards can also be used to make local, STD and international phone calls in special public telephones, found in most towns throughout the country.

Opening an account at an Australian bank is not all that easy these days, especially for overseas visitors. A points system operates and you need to score a minimum of 100 points before you can have the privilege of letting the bank take your money. Passports, driver's licences, birth certificates and other 'major' IDs earn you 40 points; minor ones such as credit cards get you 20 points. Just like a game show really! However, if visitors apply to open an account during the first six weeks of their visit, just showing their passport will suffice.

If you don't have an Australian Tax File Number, interest earned from your funds will be taxed at the rate of 48% and this money goes straight to my old mate, the Deputy Commissioner of Taxation. You may be able to reclaim this by filing a tax return when leaving the country if the total you have earned officially falls below the tax-free threshold (currently around $6000).

Costs

Compared to the USA, Canada and European countries, Australia is cheaper in some ways and more expensive in others. Manufactured goods tend to be more expensive: if they are imported they have all the additional costs of transport and duties, and if they're locally manufactured they suffer from the extra costs entailed in making things in comparatively small quantities. Thus you pay more for clothes, cars and other manufactured items. On the other hand, food is both high in quality and low in cost.

Accommodation is also very reasonably priced. In virtually every town where backpackers are likely to stay, there'll be a backpackers' hostel with dorm beds for $10 or less, or a caravan park with on-site vans for around $20 for two people.

The biggest cost in any trip to WA is going to be transport, simply because it's such a vast state. If there's a group of you, buying a second-hand car is probably the most economical way to go.

Tipping

In Australia, tipping isn't entrenched the way it is in the USA or Europe. It's only customary to tip in more expensive restaurants and only then if you want to. If the service has been especially good and you decide to leave a tip, 10% of the bill is the usual amount. Taxi drivers don't expect tips (of course, they don't hurl it back at you if you decide to leave the change). In contrast, just try getting out of a New York cab, or even a London one, without leaving your 10 to 15%.

WHEN TO GO

Any time is a good time to be in WA, but as you'd expect in a state this large, different parts of the country are at their best at different times.

The southern part of the state is most popular during the summer months, as it's warm enough for swimming and it's great to be outdoors. In the centre of the state it's too hot to do anything much, while in the far north, the summer is the Wet season and the heat and humidity can make life pretty uncomfortable. On the other hand, if you want to see the Kimberley green and free of dust, be treated to some spectacular electrical storms and have the best of the fishing while all the other tourists are down south, this is the time to do it.

Spring and autumn give the greatest flexibility for a short visit as you can combine highlights of the whole state while avoiding the extremes of the weather. Spring is the time for wildflowers in the west and these can be absolutely stunning after rain.

The other major consideration when travelling in WA is school holidays. Families take to the road (and air) en masse at these times and many places are booked out, prices rise and things generally get a bit crazy. Holidays vary somewhat from state to state, but in WA the main holiday period is from late December to late January; the other two-week periods are roughly mid to late April, mid to late July, and early to late October.

TOURIST OFFICES
Local Tourist Offices

The Western Australia Tourism Commission (WATC) oversees tourism in the state and has an office in Perth. It's in The Western Australian Tourist Centre (☎ (09) 483 1111), Albert Facey House in Forrest Place, on the corner of Wellington St and opposite the railway station. The office is open from 8.30 am to 5.30 pm Monday to Friday and from 9 am to 1 pm Saturday. It has a wide range of maps and brochures on Perth and the rest of WA, and an accommodation and tours reservation service. The Pinnacles Travel Centre, on the corner of Hay and Pier Sts, acts as the information office on Saturday afternoon and on Sunday until noon.

Often the best sources of information will be staff at the backpackers' hostels. They know the best tours to take, what's on, where to go, what to see and how to get there.

Interstate Tourist Offices

Each of the major states, the Northern Territory and the Australian Capital Territory have an agent of the WATC:

Australian Capital Territory
    Contal Travel, 33 Ainslie Avenue, Canberra 2608 (☎ (06) 2485214)
New South Wales
    Justravel Pty Ltd, Mezzanine Level, 231-247 Pitt St, Sydney 2000 (☎ (02) 261 2800; fax 264 1006)
Queensland
    Justravel Pty Ltd, 204 Adelaide St, Brisbane 4000 (☎ (07) 221 5022)

South Australia
> Tourism House, 88 Currie St, Adelaide 5000 (☎ (08) 211 8455)

Tasmania
> RACT, corner of Murray and Patrick Sts, Hobart 7000 (☎ (002) 38 2200; fax 34 8784)

Victoria
> Contal Travel, 253 Flinders Lane, Melbourne 3000 (☎ (03) 654 1400; fax 654 6218)

Northern Territory
> AANT, 79-81 Smith St, Darwin 0800 (☎ (089) 81 3838; fax 41 2965)

Overseas Reps

In addition to the state WATC offices, there are a number of overseas representatives including:

Germany
> Schlosstrasse 60, 51429 Bergisch Gladbach, Berlin (☎ 2204 56153; fax 2204 52556)

Indonesia
> Jl. KH Hasyim Ashari, No 33B, Jakarta (☎ 362 449; fax 231 3679)

Japan
> Landic No 2 Akasaka Building, 5th Floor, 10-9 Akasaka 2-chome, Minato-ku, Tokyo 107 (☎ 3582 2677; fax 3582 4447)

Malaysia
> 4th Floor, UBN Tower, Letterbox 51, 10 Jalan P Ramlee, Kuala Lumpur 50250 (☎ 232 5996, 232 8300; fax 232 1266)

Singapore
> Unit 03-03 Thong Sia Building, 30 Bideford Rd, Singapore 0922 (☎ 732 8187; fax 733 5491)

Taiwan
> 3F, No 101, Nanking E Rd, Section 2, Taipei (☎ 522 1280, 531 1320; fax 531 1320)

Thailand
> 6th Floor, Asia Building, 294/1 Phya Thai Rd, Bangkok 10400 (☎ 215 4686, 216 9372; fax 216 6599)

UK
> Western Australia House, 115 The Strand, London WC2R OAJ (☎ (0171) 240 2881; fax (0171) 379 9826)

USEFUL ORGANISATIONS

There are numerous organisations in WA formed for just about every conceivable purpose. If you need to find them, check with the tourist information office in Perth or delve into the Yellow Pages phone book under 'Organisations'.

Automobile Association

The Royal Automobile Club of Western Australia (RACWA) (☎ (09) 421 4444) is at 228 Adelaide Terrace. It provides pilot services to first-time visitors to the city. Its bookshop has an excellent travel section, and detailed regional maps can be obtained at its Road Travel counter. The addresses of road travel specialists in bordering states are:

South Australia
> Royal Automobile Association of South Australia (RAA), 41 Hindmarsh Square, Adelaide 5000 (☎ (08) 223 4555)

Northern Territory
> Automobile Association of the Northern Territory, 79-81 Smith St, Darwin 0800 (☎ (089) 81 3837)

Youth Hostels

The Youth Hostel Association (YHA) (☎ (09) 227 5122) has its main office at 65 Francis St in Northbridge. The helpful staff give out all sorts of information and make bookings for tours and accommodation.

English-Language Schools

If English isn't your first language and you wish to come to Australia to study it, places specialising in teaching English in WA include:

Canning College
> Marquis St, Bentley (☎ (09) 458 9644; fax 541 5143)

Phoenix English Language Academy
> 223 Vincent St, North Perth 6006 (☎ (09) 227 5538; fax 227 5540)

Tuart College
> Banksia St, Tuart Hill (☎ (09) 444 9377; fax 444 8538)

Conservation & the Environment

In spite of the lack of resources, a fair degree of political opposition and a small population base, the 'green movement' is alive and well in the west. The peak body which co-ordinates the 60 or so environmental groups is the Conservation Council of Western Australia (CCWA) (☎ (09) 220 0652), 79 Stirling St, Perth 6000. The government department charged with the care of WA's natural resources is Conservation & Land Management (CALM). Its methods of forest conservation and management are often at odds with ecological organisations. Consequently, the environmental watchdogs are very much opposed to a number of CALM's policies, especially in the south-west forests.

Other useful environmental organisations include:

Environment Centre of WA Inc
  PO Box 7375, Cloisters Square 6001; resource and information base for both the public and various organisations, publishes *What's On...Environmentally* monthly (☎ (09) 321 5942).
Friends of the Earth
  PO Box 23, Northbridge 6000; promotes the restoration, conservation and rational use of the earth's resources (☎ (09) 328 3155).
South-West Forests Defence Foundation
  PO Box 203, Nedlands 6009; organisation to prevent destruction of the beautiful native forests, especially karri, in the south-west (☎ (09) 328 3155).
Wilderness Society, The
  2nd floor, 79 Stirling St, Perth 6000; dedicated to protection of wilderness areas and publishes the monthly *Wilderness WA Newsletter* (☎ (09) 220 0667).

Disabled Travellers

The office of the Australian Council for the Rehabilitation of the Disabled (ACROD), 189 Royal St, East Perth (☎ (09) 222 2961) produces information sheets for disabled travellers, including lists of state-level organisations, specialist travel agents, wheelchair and equipment hire and access guides. It can also help with specific queries but would be grateful if enquirers could send at least the cost of postage.

People with Disabilities (WA) Inc (☎ (09) 386 6477) in Perth will also be able to help. Its freecall number outside the Perth metropolitan area is ☎ (008) 193 331 and the TTY (talking telephone) number is ☎ (09) 386 6451. Other useful organisations are:

Blind Association
  16 Sunbury Rd, Victoria Park (☎ (09) 311 8202)

Deaf Society of WA (Inc)
  16 Brentham St, Leederville (☎ (09) 443 2677; TTY 433 1960)
Paraplegic-Quadriplegic Association of WA (Inc)
  10 Selby St, Shenton Park (☎ (09) 381 0111)

In 1994 the Office of the Minister for Disability Services (WA) was conducting a ministerial review into disability services in country areas; hopefully improved services for the disabled in regional areas will be the result.

BUSINESS HOURS & HOLIDAYS
Business Hours

Most shops close at 5 or 5.30 pm weekdays, and either noon or 5 pm on Saturday. In some places Sunday trading is starting to catch on, but it's currently limited to suburban areas such as Subiaco, Northbridge and Fremantle. In most towns there is one late-shopping night each week when the doors stay open until 9 pm.

Banks are open from 9.30 am to 4 pm Monday to Thursday, and until 5 pm on Friday. Some bank agencies are open on Saturday, but generally all banks are closed on Saturday, Sunday and on public holidays. Of course there are some exceptions to WA's opening hours and all sorts of places stay open late and at weekends – particularly milk bars, convenience stores, supermarkets, delis and city bookshops.

Holidays

The Christmas holiday season is part of the long summer school vacation and the time when accommodation is booked out. There are three other shorter school-holiday periods during the year (see When to Go earlier in this chapter). The following is a list of the main national and WA public holidays:

1 January
  New Year's Day
26 January
  Australia Day
Second Monday in March
  Labour Day (WA)
Good Friday and Easter Saturday, Sunday and Monday

25 April
    ANZAC Day
First Monday in June
    Foundation Day (WA)
First Monday in October
    Queen's Birthday (WA)
25 December
    Christmas Day
26 December
    Boxing Day

CULTURAL EVENTS

Perth has a number of festivals including the big Festival of Perth in February. Migrants have added a number of festivals to the calendar also, including the Perth Italian Festival in September, an Oktoberfest in October and the Japanese-style Shinju Matsuri (Pearl) Festival in Broome. For other events in Perth throughout the year – see Festivals in the Perth chapter for details.

Both Broome in the Kimberley and York in the Avon Valley have achieved reputations as festival centres; more details on the numerous festivals and events in those towns will be given in the relevant sections. Outside Perth, WA's major annual festivals and events include the following (for more information see the relevant chapters):

January
    Lancelin to Ledge Point Sailboard Race, Mount Barker Summer Wine Festival, Esperance Oz Rock Festival & Sailboard Classic
February
    Geraldton Kite Festival & Wind on Water, Margaret River Wine & Food Festival, Great Southern Wine Festival
March
    Kalbarri Sports Fishing Classic, Bunbury Show & Aqua Festival, Leeuwin Estate Concert (Margaret River), Margaret River Surf Masters, Pemberton King Karri Karnival
April
    Apart from Fool's Day not much happens in this month, so just be careful about invitations on the 1st, Kalgoorlie Great Gold Festival, Broome Waterbirds Odyssey
May
    Broome Fringe Arts Festival, Toodyay Moondyne Festival & Colonial Fair
June
    Carnarvon Rodeo, Cossack Fair and Regatta, New Norcia Festival of Flowers

July
    Exmouth Exmo Week, Broome Aboriginal Culture & Arts Festival, Derby Boab Festival, Katanning Islamic Celebration
August
    Avon Descent, Mullewa Wildflower Show, Karratha FeNaCLNG Festival, Broome Shinju-Matsuri (Pearl) Festival, Kununurra Ord River Festival, Denmark Winter Festival
September
    York Jazz Festival, Kojonup Wildflower Festival, Ravensthorpe Wildflower Show, Stompem Ground (Broome)
October
    Chittering Sheep Dog Trials, Toodyay WA Folk Festival, Geraldton Sunshine Festival, Nannup Wildflower Display
November
    Geraldton Blessing of the Fleet, Discover Bunbury, York Flying 50 Vintage/Veteran Car Race, Margaret River Surf Classic & Show, Manjimup Timber Festival
December
    Broome Mango Festival, Derby Boxing Day Sports

POST & TELECOMMUNICATIONS
Postal Rates

Australia's postal services are relatively efficient but not too cheap. It costs 45c to send a standard letter or postcard within Australia, while aerogrammes cost 70c.

Air-mail letters/postcards cost 75/70c to New Zealand, Singapore and Malaysia, 95/90c to Hong Kong and India, $1.05/95c to the USA and Canada, and $1.20/$1 to Europe and the UK.

Post offices are open from 9 am to 5 pm Monday to Friday, but you can often get stamps from local post offices operated from newsagencies or from Australia Post shops, found in large cities, on Saturday mornings.

Receiving Mail

All post offices will hold mail for visitors and the Perth city GPO has a busy poste restante. You can also have mail sent to you at the American Express office in Perth if you have an Amex card or carry Amex travellers' cheques.

Telephone

From the year dot the Australian phone

☎ From September 1997, Perth's existing phone numbers will be prefixed by the additional digit 9 (for example, ☎ 123 4567 becomes ☎ 9123 4567). From April 1998, in regional areas, the last two digits of the current area code will be added to the existing number (for example, ☎ (012) 123 456 becomes ☎ 1212 3456). The area code for the state will be (08). ■

system was wholly owned and run by the government, but these days the market has been deregulated with a second player, Optus, now offering an alternative. The system (still run by the government-owned Telecom) is efficient and, equally important, easy to use. Local phone calls cost 40c for an unlimited amount of time. You can make local calls from gold or blue phones – often found in shops, hotels, bars etc – and from payphone booths.

It's also possible to make Subscriber Trunk Dialling (STD) calls from virtually any public phone. Many public phones accept the Telecom Phonecards, which are very convenient. The cards come in $2, $5 and $10 denominations, and are available from retail outlets such as newsagents and pharmacies which display the Phonecard logo. You keep using the card until the value has been used in calls. Otherwise, have plenty of 20c, 50c and $1 coins, and be prepared to feed them through at a fair old rate.

Some public phones are set up to take only bank cash cards or credit cards, and these too are convenient, although you need to keep an eye on how much the call is costing as it can quickly mount up. The minimum charge for a call on one of these phones is $1.20.

Many businesses and some government departments operate a toll-free service, so no matter where you are ringing from around the country, it's only the cost of a local call, or free from a public phone. These numbers have the prefix 1800 (or the old toll-free prefix 008) and they are listed wherever possible throughout the book. Phone numbers with the prefix 018 are mobile or car phones.

Many companies, such as the airlines, have six-digit numbers beginning with 13, and these are charged at the rate of a local call. Often they'll be Australia-wide numbers, but sometimes are applicable only to a specific STD district. Unfortunately there's no way of telling without actually ringing the number.

Other odd numbers you may come across are nine-digit numbers starting with 0055. These calls, usually recorded information services, are provided by private companies, and your call is charged in multiples of 25c (40c from public phones) at a rate selected by the provider (Premium 70c per minute, Value 55c per minute, Budget 35c per minute).

STD calls are cheaper at night. In ascending order of cost:

Economy	– from 6 pm Saturday to 8 am Monday; 10 pm to 8 am every night
Night	– from 6 to 10 pm Monday to Friday
Day	– from 8 am to 6 pm Monday to Saturday

From most STD phones you can also make International Subscriber Dialling (ISD) calls. Dialling ISD means you can get through to overseas numbers almost as quickly as you can locally and if your call is brief it won't cost very much.

All you do is dial 0011 for overseas, the country code (44 for the UK, 1 for the USA or Canada, 64 for New Zealand), the city code (0171 or 0181 for London, 212 for New York etc), and then the telephone number. And have a Phonecard, credit card or plenty of coins at hand. To use Optus rather than Telecom, dial 1 before the ISD country code or STD area code. This facility is only available from private phones in certain areas.

A standard call to the USA or the UK costs $2.50 a minute ($2 off peak); New Zealand is $2.10 a minute ($1.40 off peak). Off-peak times, if available, vary depending on the destination – see the front of any telephone book for more details. Saturdays is often the cheapest day to ring.

With the competition offered by Optus, Telecom often has discount specials to various destinations, although many of these are only available from private phones.

Country Direct is a service which gives travellers in Australia direct access to operators in 32 other countries. You can then make reverse-charge (collect) or credit-card calls. For a full list of the countries hooked into this system, check any local telephone book. Some of them include: Canada (☎ (0014) 881 150), Germany (☎ (0014) 881 490), Japan (☎ (0014 881 810), New Zealand (☎ (0014) 881 640) and the UK (☎ (0014) 881 440).

Western Australian Area Codes This may be a large state but the area code system is relatively simple. The north-west as far south as Onslow, has the prefix 091; from Onslow south to Dongara, it is 099; the Avon Valley, Midlands and goldfields including Esperance, is 090; Perth is 09; the south-west from the coast to a line running north just before Denmark, is 097; and the remainder including Albany and the Stirling Range region, is 098. Area codes have been included with all telephone numbers in this book.

TIME
Australia is divided into three time zones: Western Standard Time is plus eight hours from GMT/UTC, Central Standard Time is plus 9½ hours (Northern Territory, South Australia and parts of WA near the border) and Eastern Standard Time is plus 10 (Tasmania, Victoria, New South Wales, Queensland). When it's noon in WA, it's 1.30 pm in the Northern Territory and South Australia and 2 pm in the rest of the country. During the summer things get slightly screwed up as daylight saving time (when clocks are put forward an hour) does not operate in WA or Queensland, and in Tasmania it lasts for two months longer than in other states.

This time difference isn't really a problem in the south where the Nullarbor provides a good distance buffer but it is in the north, in East Kimberley, where a mere border crossing changes the time significantly.

In winter, when it is noon in Perth, it is 6 am in Paris, 5 am in London, midnight in New York and 9 pm in Los Angeles. In Auckland it would be 4 pm and in Tokyo it would be 1 pm.

ELECTRICITY
Voltage is 220-240 V and the plugs are three-pin, but not the same as British three-pin plugs. Users of electric shavers or hairdryers should note that, apart from up-market hotels, it's difficult to find converters to take either US flat two-pin plugs or the European round two-pin plugs. Adapters for British plugs can be found in good hardware shops, chemists and travel agents. You can easily bend the US plugs to a slight angle to make them fit.

WEIGHTS & MEASURES
Australia went metric in the early 1970s. Petrol and milk are sold by the litre, apples and potatoes by the kg, distance is measured by the metre or km, and speed limits are in km per hour (km/h).

For those who need help with metric, there's a conversion table at the back of this book.

BOOKS
History
A Short History of Australia by Manning Clark is a succinct, fascinating and readable history of Australia. Robert Hughes' bestseller *The Fatal Shore*, a colourful and detailed historical account of convict transportation, has a brief section on this era in WA. Geoffrey Blainey's *The Tyranny of Distance* is a captivating narrative of White settlement.

The most comprehensive history of WA is the 836-page *A New History of Western Australia*, edited by CT Stannage (UWAP, Nedlands, 1981). It has nearly 20 contributors and includes excellent coverage of the clash of White and Aboriginal cultures, colonisation, education, religion, sport, unionism and party politics. Shorter, but now dated, is Frank Crowley's *A Short History of Western Australia* (Macmillan, Melbourne, revised edition 1969).

Important historical biographies include *Alexander Forrest: His Life and Times* by

GC Bolton (MUP, Melbourne, 1958); R Duffield's *Rogue Bull: The Story of Lang Hancock, King of the Pilbara* (Collins, Sydney, 1979); Mary Durack's three family sagas *Kings in Grass Castles* (Constable, London, 1959), *Sons in the Saddle* (1983) and *To Be Heirs Forever* (Constable, London, 1976); *Thomas Peel of Swan River* by A Hasluck (OUP, Melbourne, 1965); *Bishop Salvado: Founder of New Norcia* by JT McMahon (Patersons, Perth, 1943); and *The Chief: CY O'Connor* by M Tauman (UWAP, Nedlands, 1978). Short biographies can be found in the *Dictionary of West Australians 1829-1914* compiled by R Erickson (UWAP, Nedlands, 1979, three volumes).

The best of the autobiographies is *A Fortunate Life* (1981) by AB Facey. A microcosm of life in post-federation Australia, it is Albert Facey's account of his misfortunes in what was the extraordinary life of a seemingly ordinary person (see also Albert Facey in the Facts about Western Australia chapter).

Good historical accounts of Perth include *The Beginning: European Discovery and Early Settlement of Swan River, Western Australia* by RT Appleyard & T Manford (UWAP, Nedlands, 1979); the Perth chapters in *The Origins of Australia's Capital Cities*, edited by Pamela Statham (CUP, Melbourne, 1989), are good sources of colonial history. The history of Fremantle is covered in *The Western Gateway* by JK Ewers (UWAP, Nedlands, 1971).

Australian Aboriginal Culture

There are a number of good books which examine Aboriginal culture and sacred places in Aboriginal history. The best coverage is that of Josephine Flood in her two books, *Archaeology of the Dreamtime* (Collins, Sydney, 1983) and *The Riches of Ancient Australia* (UQP, St Lucia, 1993).

The excellent *Sacred Places in Australia*, a photo-essay by James Cowan and Colin Beard (Simon & Schuster, East Roseville, 1991), reveals fascinating insights into the sacred areas of the Pilbara, Depuch Island, the Kimberley and Purnululu. More specific

to WA are *Thalu Sites of the West Pilbara* by David Daniel (WA Museum, 1990); *Devil's Lair: A Study in Prehistory* by Charles Dortch (WA Museum, 1984). The local Aboriginal language is covered in *A Nyoongar Wordlist from the South-West of Western Australia*, edited by Peter Bindon and Ross Chadwick (WA Museum, 1992).

For an understanding of Aboriginal art, delve into RM & CH Berndt's *Aboriginal Australian Art: A Visual Perspective* (Methuen, Richmond, 1988). It describes the art in its own traditional settings and helps the reader learn to 'read' what is painted, carved or etched. IM Crawford's *The Art of the Wandjina* (OUP, Melbourne, 1968) describes the fascinating paintings of the Kimberley region. Also focusing on the Kimberley is *Painting the Country: Contemporary Aboriginal Art from the Kimberley Region* (UWAP, 1989).

Many of the modern writings by Aborigines have focused on the theme of their alienation in White society. One account is *Outback Ghettos* by Patty O'Grady, which deals with the separation of Aboriginal children from their natural parents. Another is *Encounters in Place: Outsiders and Aboriginal Australians 1606-1985* by DJ Mulvaney.

Fiction & Drama

For a full description of fiction and drama see Literature and Theatre under Arts & Culture in the Facts about Western Australia chapter.

Travel Guides

There is no comprehensive guide to WA apart from this one (although in the process of researching it we met about 10 people in the lifelong process of researching 'a guide to WA'). Lonely Planet's *Australia – a travel survival kit* and *Outback Australia,* Moon's *Outback Australia Handbook* and *Rough Guide to Australia* have limited coverage of the state.

A number of guides to Perth including *Hello Perth & Fremantle, What's On This Week In...Perth & Fremantle, This Week in Perth & Fremantle, West Coast Visitors'*

Guide and the *Map of Perth & Fremantle* are available free at the tourist office, hostels and hotels.

There are a number of regional guides. Three of the best are the WATC pamphlets *Unique North*, *Golden Heartlands* and *Southern Wonders* which list accommodation and things to see.

National Parks

The national parks custodian, CALM, sells pamphlets on all of the main parks, forests and marine reserves. In addition it has a number of interesting publications for sale. Recommended are: *Discover Wild Places, Quiet Places* (south-west); *Shark Bay: Discover Monkey Mia and Other Natural Wonders; Wildflower Country* (Jurien Bay to Shark Bay and Inland to Meekatharra); *From the Range to the Reef* (Cape Range and Ningaloo) and *North-West Bound* (Shark Bay to Wyndham).

CALM also produces the excellent and informative quarterly *Landscope: WA's Conservation, Forests & Wildlife Magazine*; the cost is $5.95. Often the magazine focuses on one area, eg Shark Bay, and has comprehensive articles on certain aspects of national parks.

Activities

For bushwalkers there is *The Guide to the Bibbulman Bushwalking Track* (CALM, Como, 1988) which covers the 640-km walk from Perth to the south-west corner of the state. Lonely Planet's *Bushwalking in Australia* by John & Monica Chapman (Hawthorn, 1992, 2nd edition) has details of two two-day walks – the Stirling Range Circuit and Nuyts Wilderness.

Nat Young's *Surfing & Sailboard Guide to Australia* covers the west coast beaches as does his coffee-table publication *Atlas of Australian Surfing*.

Only the south-west of the state is covered in *Bicycle Touring in Australia* by Leigh Hemmings (Simon & Schuster, East Roseville, 1991). For more details of birdwatching and bushwalking titles, see Activities later in this chapter; for flora &

fauna titles, see that section in the Facts about Western Australia chapter.

MAPS

You can buy a range of maps from the headquarters of the RACWA (☎ (09) 421 4444), 228 Adelaide Terrace, Perth. Included are *Perth: City & Suburbs, Perth Region, Lower South-West, Geraldton Region, Kalgoorlie/Boulder Region, Esperance Region* (all 50c); and *Perth-Port Hedland* and *Port Hedland-Darwin* (both $1). UBD publishes two excellent street directories, *Perth* ($22.25) and *Western Australia: Cities and Towns* ($24), with maps of all major and minor towns – in fact, 145 towns in total.

If you need topographical maps you can get them from CALM and the Central Map Agency (☎ (09) 323 1344), Lands Administration, Cathedral Ave, Perth.

BP produce a road map *Western Australia: Wildflower State* which covers Perth and the south-west. There is also a full state coverage.

MEDIA
Newspapers & Magazines

The *West Australian* and the *Australian* are available each morning from Monday to Saturday. The Saturday *West Australian* has two supplements, *Big Weekend* and *West Magazine*. The *Weekend Australian* is also available on Sunday as is the *Sunday Times*. If you need an interstate newspaper such as the *Age*, they are usually available in the afternoon of the day of publication.

A number of the smaller towns have their own newspapers focusing on local news and events. These are useful in finding out what is going on in a local area. Publications include *Kalgoorlie Miner*, *North-West Telegraph* and *Kimberley Echo*.

International newspapers are available at the Plaza Newsagency, Plaza Arcade (off Hay St Mall) as well as the Public Library in James St.

Weekly newspapers and magazines are widely available. These include Australian editions of *Time* and *Rolling Stone*, and the national news magazine *Bulletin* incorporates an edition of the US *Newsweek*. The

British newspapers *Daily Express*, *Guardian* and the *Independent* have Australian editions and are popular in Perth because of its large ex-pat British population.

Radio

Unfortunately, WA has probably the worst radio coverage of all the states of Australia, due, most likely, to its small listener base in the country. Perth, however, is well served with both commercial and non-commercial radio and the Australian Broadcasting Corporation (ABC) does its best in the country. A handy guide to have in the country is *The Travellers Guide to ABC Radio*.

In Perth, the ABC's stations are the AM Regional 6WF (720 kHz), AM Radio National 6RN (810 kHz) and ABC Classical 97.7 FM. The popular Triple J FM can be found on 99.3 MHz in Perth. Other radio stations are Triple M FM (96.1 MHz, rock 'n' roll), 87.6 FM (tourist information for Perth), PMFM (92.9 MHz, rock 'n' roll), 6MM (1116 kHz, adult contemporary 'Hits and Memories'), 94.5 FM (music), 101 FM (community interest and music programmes) and Special Broadcasting Service (SBS) National (96.9 MHz, ethnic programmes).

Some of the Aboriginal communities have their own stations and make the best of minimal resources. Examples include Wangki Yupurnanupurru Radio Station (WYRS), which started transmission in Fitzroy Crossing in 1988 and Radio Goolari in Broome, which commenced in 1991.

A drive south from Darwin to Geraldton is heaven for any country & western fan. If you aren't a fan, pray that you pick up a Sheffield Shield broadcast or a rundown on the latest agricultural prices in lieu. If you absolutely loathe country & western, then play a tape!

TV

Perth has five TV stations. The three commercial networks are channels 7, 9 and 10. The ABC (Channel 2) is government-funded and supposedly free of bias as is SBS O-28.

The best international news service is on Channel O-28 (UHF), the Special Broadcasting Service (SBS) at 6.30 pm. Before the news it often has an excellent half-hour round-up of sports for those desperate to know the results of the hurling in Ireland, FA Cup qualifiers in the UK or NBL stats from the USA. Dateline, which follows the news, highlights current affairs. SBS screens many films that get a Palme d'Or at Cannes or make it into the Best Foreign Film category at the Oscars.

For details of the weeks programmes, get a copy of the *West Australian* on Saturday (the guide is in the *West Magazine*).

Country stations generally receive two stations: the ABC and a local commercial network, Golden West Network (GWN). A lot of places are too remote to get good reception unless they have good antennae or satellite dishes. In the country, head down the pub to watch Sky TV as it will probably be the best operating TV set in town.

FILM & PHOTOGRAPHY

If you come to WA via Hong Kong or Singapore, it's worth buying film there but otherwise Australian film prices are not too far out of line with those of the rest of the Western world. Including developing, 36-exposure Kodachrome 64 or Fujichrome 100 slide film costs around $25, but with a little shopping around you can find it for $20.

There are plenty of camera shops in the main centres and standards of camera service are high. Developing standards are also high, with many places offering one-hour developing of print film.

Photography is no problem, but in the arid areas you have to allow for the exceptional intensity of the light. Best results in the outback regions are obtained early in the morning and late in the afternoon. As the sun gets higher, colours appear washed out. You must also allow for the intensity of reflected light when taking shots of Ningaloo Reef or at other coastal locations. In the outback, especially in the summer, allow for temperature extremes and do your best to keep film as cool as possible, particularly after exposure. Other film and camera hazards are dust in the outback and humidity in the tropical region of the Kimberley.

As in any country, politeness goes a long way when taking photographs; ask before taking pictures of people. Note that many Aborigines do not like to have their photographs taken, even from a distance.

HEALTH

If you haven't visited an infected country in the past 14 days (aircraft refuelling stops do not count), no vaccinations are required for entry. Naturally, if you're going to be travelling around in outlandish places apart from Australia, a good collection of immunisations is highly advisable.

Medical care in Australia is first class and only moderately expensive. A typical visit to the doctor costs around $35. Health insurance cover is available in Australia, but there is usually a waiting period after you sign up before any claims can be made. If you have an immediate health problem, contact the casualty section at the nearest public hospital.

Travel Insurance

Even if you normally carry health or hospitalisation insurance, or live in a country where health care is provided by the government, it's still a good idea to buy some travellers' insurance that covers both health and loss of baggage.

Make sure the policy includes health care and medication in the countries you plan to visit and includes a flight home for you and anyone you're travelling with, should your condition warrant it.

Medical Kit

It's always a good idea to travel with a basic medical kit even when your destination is a country like Australia where most first-aid supplies are readily available. Some of the items that you should include are: Band-aids, a sterilised gauze bandage, elastoplast, cotton wool, a thermometer, tweezers, scissors, antibiotic cream and ointment, contraceptives (if required), an antiseptic agent, burn cream, insect repellent and multivitamins. Calamine lotion, anti-histamine cream and old-fashioned Tiger Balm are all useful for insect bites.

Don't forget any medication you're already taking, and paracetamol or aspirin (for pain and fever).

Health Precautions

Travellers from the northern hemisphere need to be aware of the intensity of the sun in Australia. Those ultra-violet rays can have you burnt to a crisp even on an overcast day, so if in doubt wear protective cream, a wide-brimmed hat and a long-sleeved shirt with a collar. Australia has a high incidence of skin cancer, a fact directly connected to exposure to the sun. Be careful.

The contraceptive pill is available on prescription only, so a visit to a doctor is necessary. Doctors are listed in the Yellow Pages phone book or you can visit the outpatients section of a public hospital. Condoms are available from chemists, many convenience stores, and vending machines in the public toilets of many hotels and universities.

HIV/AIDS The Human Immunodeficiency Virus (HIV), may develop into Acquired Immune Deficiency Syndrome (AIDS). HIV is a major problem in many countries. Any exposure to blood, blood products or bodily fluids may put the individual at risk. In many developing countries, transmission is predominantly through heterosexual sexual activity. This is quite different from industrialised countries where transmission is mostly through contact between homosexual or bisexual males or contaminated needles used by IV drug takers. Apart from abstinence, the most effective preventative is always to practise safe sex using condoms. It is impossible to detect the HIV-positive status of an otherwise healthy-looking person without a blood test.

HIV/AIDS can also be spread through infected blood transfusions; most developing countries cannot afford to screen blood for transfusions. It can also be spread by dirty needles – vaccinations, acupuncture, tattooing and ear or nose piercing can potentially be as dangerous as intravenous drug use if the equipment is not clean. If you do need an injection, ask to see the syringe unwrapped in front of you, or better still, take a needle and syringe pack with you overseas – it is a cheap insurance package against infection with HIV.

Fear of HIV infection should never preclude treatment for serious medical conditions. Although there may be a risk of infection, it is very small indeed. Local AIDS groups are:

Aids Help Line
    Monday to Friday 9 am to 10 pm (☎ (09) 227 8619 or toll free ☎ (008) 199 287)
Western Australia AIDS Council
    107 Brisbane St (PO Box T1872), Perth (☎ (09) 227 8355)

WOMEN TRAVELLERS
Western Australia is generally a safe place for women travellers, although it's probably best to avoid walking alone late at night in any of the major towns, especially central Perth and Kalgoorlie.

Female hitchers should exercise care at all times (see under Hitching in the Getting Around chapter). Some useful women's contacts in the west are:

Sexual Assault Referral Centre
    24-hour Crisis Line Perth (☎ (09) 340 1828); Country areas freecall (☎ (008) 199 888)
Single Women's Refuges 24-hours
    Nunyara (☎ (09) 328 7284); Wyn Carr House (☎ (09) 430 5756); Multicultural Service (☎ (09) 325 7716)

DANGERS & ANNOYANCES
Animal Hazards
There are a few unique and sometimes dangerous creatures, although it's unlikely that you'll come across any of them, particularly if you stick to the cities. Here's a rundown just in case.

The best known danger in the Australian outback, and the one that captures visitors' imaginations, is snakes. Although there are many venomous snakes, there are few that are aggressive, and unless you have the bad fortune to stand on one it's unlikely you'll be bitten. Some snakes, however, will attack if alarmed and sea snakes can also be dangerous.

To minimise your chances of being bitten, always wear boots, socks and long trousers when walking through undergrowth where snakes may be present. Don't put your hands into holes and crevices, and be careful when collecting firewood.

Snake bites do not cause instantaneous death and antivenenes are usually available. Keep the victim calm and still, wrap the bitten limb tightly, as you would for a sprained ankle, and then attach a splint to immobilise it. Then seek medical help, if possible bring the dead snake for identification. Don't attempt to catch the snake if there is even a remote possibility of being bitten again. Tourniquets and sucking out the poison are now comprehensively discredited.

Avoid spiders as there are a couple of really nasty ones. If bitten, seek medical attention straight away.

Leeches are common, and while they will suck your blood, they are not dangerous and are easily removed by the application of salt or heat.

The box jellyfish, also known as the sea wasp or 'stinger', is found in the north-west during summer and can be fatal. The stinging tentacles spread several metres away from the sea wasp's body; by the time you see it you're likely to have been stung. If someone is stung, they will probably run out of the sea screaming and collapse on the beach, with weals on their body as though they've been whipped – and sometimes stopping breathing.

Douse the stings with vinegar (available on many beaches or from nearby houses), do not try to remove the tentacles from the skin, and treat as for snake bite. If there's a first-aider present, they may have to apply artificial respiration until the ambulance gets there. Above all, stay out of the sea when the sea wasps are around – the locals are ignoring that lovely water for an excellent reason.

When reef walking you must always wear shoes to protect your feet against coral. There are stonefish – venomous fish that look like a flat piece of rock on the sea bed – throughout the tropical water of WA. Also watch out for the scorpion fish, which has venomous spines.

Crocodiles Up in the north-west, saltwater crocodiles can be a real danger (they have killed a number of people including travellers and locals). Be careful before diving into that inviting, cool water to find out if it's croc-free. Some local rules to remember:

- Don't launch your boat from the same spot all the time.
- Don't throw fish guts or old bait into the water.
- Camp well away from the banks.

Flies & Mosquitoes

For four to six months of the year you'll have to cope with those two banes of the Australian outdoors – the fly and the mosquito.

The flies are not too bad in the towns and cities; it's in the country that it starts getting out of hand, and the further 'out' you get the worse the flies seem to be. Flies are a real problem in north-west Australia and are responsible for much of the conjunctivitis and trachoma found in the Kimberley. Try hard to prevent flies from getting near the eyes of infants and young children. Repellents such as Aerogard and Rid go some way to deterring them, but don't let any of this stuff get near the eyes of kids.

Mosquitoes can also be a problem, especially in the warmer tropical and sub-tropical areas. Mosquitoes in the Kimberley are responsible for the transmission of a number of diseases such as Ross River virus and Australian encephalitis. Cover up bare skin and wear a mosquito repellent if you go outside at dusk.

On the Road

Cattle and kangaroos are often a hazard to the driver. A collision with one will badly damage your car and probably kill the animal. Unfortunately, other drivers are even more dangerous, particularly those who drink. Australia has its share of fatal road accidents, particularly in the countryside, so don't drink and drive and please take care. See the Getting Around chapter for more on driving hazards. And *never* lock a child in the car with the windows closed, especially in the tropics.

Cyclones

These are a feature of the weather pattern of the north-west and the northern coastal areas. A cyclone is a circular rotating storm of tropical origin in which the mean wind speed exceeds 63 km/h (gale force). Speeds of 100 km/h, however, are common and a speed of 248 km/h was recorded at Onslow in 1975. Some winds can extend up to 200 km from the centre or 'eye' of the cyclone. Heavy rain falls as the system decays which it does 24 to 48 hours after hitting land, and flooding often occurs. The cyclone season in the west is officially from 1 November to 30 April. Not being in the public service, cyclones turn up when they like.

Cyclones are erratic, so it is important to listen to ABC radio for information – a battery-powered radio is the best option as power supplies may be cut. There are also two recorded Severe Weather Service lines: Port Hedland (☎ (091) 11 554) and Perth (☎ (09) 11 542), which report the latest developments. There are three stages in the human-cyclone equation: blue – cyclone may affect the area in 48 hours; yellow – cyclone moving closer and inevitable in 12 hours; red – cyclone is imminent. The all clear is sounded when the cyclone has passed but there may still be wind and heavy rain. If you have any doubts, seek local advice.

Bushfires & Blizzards

Bushfires happen every year in Australia. Don't be the mug who starts one. In hot, dry, windy weather, be extremely careful with any naked flame – this means no cigarette butts out of car windows. On a Total Fire Ban Day (listen to the radio or watch the billboards on country roads), it is forbidden to use a camping stove in the open. The locals will not be amused if they catch you breaking this particular law; they'll happily dob you in, and the penalties are severe.

If you're unfortunate enough to find yourself driving through a bushfire, stay inside your car and try to park off the road in an open space, away from trees, until the danger's past. Lie on the floor under the dashboard, covering yourself with a wool blanket if possible. The front of the fire should pass quickly, and you will be much safer than if you were out in the open.

Bushwalkers should take local advice before setting out. On a Total Fire Ban Day, don't go – delay your trip until the weather has changed. Chances are that it will be so unpleasantly hot and windy, you'll be better off anyway in an air-con pub sipping a cool beer.

If you're out in the bush and you see smoke, even at a great distance, take it seriously. Go to the nearest open space, downhill if possible. A forested ridge is the most dangerous place to be. Bushfires move very quickly and change direction with the wind.

Having said all that, more bushwalkers die of cold than in bushfires! Even in summer, temperatures can drop below freezing at night in the mountains of the south-west.

WORK

If you come to Australia on a 12-month 'working holiday' visa, you can officially work for three out of those 12 months, but working on a regular tourist visa is strictly not on. Many travellers on tourist visas do find casual work, but with a national unemployment rate of 11% and youth unemployment as high as 40% in some areas, it is becoming more difficult to find a job – legal or otherwise.

To receive wages in Australia you must be in possession of a Tax File Number, issued by the Taxation Department. Forms are available from post offices and you'll need to show your passport and visa.

The best prospects for casual work include factories, bar work, waiting on tables or washing dishes, domestic chores at outback roadhouses, nanny work, fruit picking and collecting for charities.

With the current economic downturn in Australia, casual work has become increasingly difficult to find. Gone are the days when you could rock in to practically any town or city and find some sort of paid casual work. Many travellers who have budgeted on finding work return home early, simply because the work they hoped to find just isn't available. If you are coming to Australia with the intention of working, make sure you have enough funds to cover you for your stay, or have a contingency plan if the work is not forthcoming.

Having said that, it *is* still possible to find short-term work, it's just the opportunities are far fewer than in the past.

The Commonwealth Employment Service (CES) has over 300 offices around the country, and the staff usually have a good idea of what's available. Try the classified section of the daily papers under Situations Vacant, especially on Saturdays and Wednesdays. The CES also produce an annual agricultural joblist in *Harvest Table*. In WA the district CES offices are:

Kununurra
    Konkerberry Drive (☎ (091) 68 1211)
Albany
    265 York St (☎ (098) 41 2577)
Broome
    Corner Frederick & Weld Sts (☎ (091) 92 1501)
Geraldton
    73 Marine Terrace (☎ (099) 64 1420)
Bunbury
    Corner Spencer & Stirling Sts (☎ (097) 21 4355)
Carnarvon
    34 Stuart St (☎ (099) 41 1107)
Collie
    51 Forrest St (☎ (097) 34 1255)
Esperance
    Corner Dempster & Hicks Sts (☎ (090) 71 2422).
Kalgoorlie
    Corner Porter & Brookman Sts (☎ (090) 21 1011)
Mandurah
    39 Pinjarra Rd (☎ (09) 531 7979)
Manjimup
    Unit 6, 30 Rose St (☎ (097) 71 1088)
Merredin
    50A Barrack St (☎ (090) 41 1763)
Northam
    89 Fitzgerald St (☎ (096) 22 1511)

There are a number of employment agencies that can assist you to get work, but realise they don't do it out of the goodness of their hearts. Computer temps, word processor operators and programming contractors are seemingly always in demand. Some agencies are listed next, so best of luck.

Accountancy Placements
    28 The Esplanade, Perth (☎ (09) 322 5198)

Top: Whale tail (WATC)
Middle Left: Koala (RI)
Middle Right: Saltwater crocodile (WATC)
Bottom: Freshwater crocodiles (WATC)

Perth
Top: Perth skyline at dawn (PS)
Middle: Perth skyline (PS)
Bottom: Perth skyline at dusk (PS)

Centacom Tempstaff
68 St George's Terrace, Perth (☎ (09) 322 3344)
Hospitality Personnel
159 Adelaide Terrace, Perth (☎ (09) 221 2468)
Key People
47 Colin St, West Perth (☎ (09) 324 1275)
Medi-Temp
26 Charles St, South Perth (☎ (09) 474 2343)
Select Appointments
Level 4/81 St George's Terrace, Perth (☎ (09) 321 3133)
Staff Placement & Consulting Service
1200 Hay St, West Perth (☎ (09) 481 4262)
Templine
186 St George's Terrace, Perth (☎ (09) 322 6155)

The various backpackers' magazines, newspapers and hostels are good information sources – some local employers even advertise on their notice boards.

Think very carefully about the heavily advertised 'collecting' jobs and make sure you are satisfied that a reasonable percentage of the funds you collect gets to an actual charity. To give you an idea, most backpackers last less than a day in these jobs. Didn't you come here for a holiday?

Picking & Packing

Listed are the main harvest times and crops in WA where casual employment is a possibility. Enquire at the local CES office.

Crop	Season	Region(s)
Wildflowers	Feb-Mar,	Coorow
	Jul-Dec	Coorow
Fruit	Jun-Jul	Kununurra
Fruit	Jun-Dec	Carnarvon
Fruit	Dec-Jun	South-West
Grapes	Feb-Apr	Mt Barker, Margaret River, Swan Valley
Apples/Pears	Feb-May	Manjimup, Pemberton, Bridgetown, Donnybrook
Watermelons & Rockmelons/Vegies	May-Oct	Kununurra
Strawberries	Nov-Jan	Near Perth
Zucchini/Squash	May-Sep	Kununurra
Bananas	All Year	Kununurra

Fish Processing

Crayfish process workers are required from mid-November until the end of June. Try the CES offices in Fremantle, Mandurah, Dongara, Kalbarri and Geraldton. Scallop and prawn processors are required in Carnarvon from March to October. Unfortunately, most foreigners lucky to score a job in this industry will be serving fish to customers as a casual waiter in a pub or restaurant.

Oats, Barley & Wheat Harvesting/ Seeding

Some work is available in the wheatbelt during harvesting and seeding. Seeding occurs in the north from April to June, in the central belt from March to June and in the south from April to June. Harvesting is from October to January in the north, October to December in the central belt and November to December in the south. The main towns are Merredin, Northam, Wagin, Gnowangerup, Katanning, Williams, Narrogin, Geraldton, Bindoon, Chittering, Moora, Salmon Gums, Albany and Moora. Check at the CES offices listed earlier.

EMERGENCY

In case of a life-threatening emergency, telephone ☎ 000. This call is free from any phone, and the operator will connect you to either the police, ambulance or fire brigade. Personal emergency numbers can be found in the Perth White Pages telephone directory. Otherwise you can call the police on ☎ (09) 222 1111 in Perth and ☎ (09) 430 5244 in Fremantle.

In the more remote areas a number of travellers will be equipped with Flying Doctor emergency radios. For those crossing the Nullarbor and equipped with HF radios, the Royal Flying Doctor Base (VNZ) at Port Augusta monitors the following frequencies from 6 am to 9 pm daily: 2020, 4010, 6890 and 8165 kHz. Kalgoorlie (VJO) RFDS monitors 2020 kHz from 7.15 am to 5 pm Monday to Friday and from 9 to 10 am Saturday and Sunday. In the north-west, the Royal Flying Doctor Base (VKL) at Port Hedland monitors 4030 kHz from 7 am to 5 pm daily Monday to Friday, 8.30 to 9.30 am Saturday (but not on Sunday).

There is an interpreter service available on ☎ (09) 325 9144.

ACTIVITIES

Western Australia bills itself as the 'state of excitement' and there is little doubt that a huge range of activities exist. Bushwalking and birdwatching are both inexpensive activities that require a minimal cash outlay and there is no shortage of wilderness in which to do them. Surfers (windsurfers, bodysurfers and boardsurfers) and divers are well catered for in this state, especially around Perth and in the south-west. There are plenty of places to go horseriding, 4WD driving and cycling over the 2.5 million sq km of territory. Canoeing, sea kayaking and rafting are also popular in both the north and south of the state.

Forget snow skiing however, as 'rad' skiers from WA have to make an annual winter pilgrimage to the eastern states to do this activity.

Rockclimbing is popular in this state as are the associated activities of canyoning and abseiling. 'Spelunking', or caving, is also widely practised and WA has some of the best caves in the country including those in the south-west and Nullarbor.

Other activities include gold prospecting, fossicking for rocks and fishing. For the vast range of possibilities delve into *Perth Outdoors* (CALM, Perth, 1992).

Lots of Western Australians participate in major sports. Football is the most popular sport with over 55,000 players, and netball is next with more than 48,000. Bowls, tennis, indoor cricket, golf and cricket follow, and are popular with both women and men. Western Australians also love watching sport.

Bushwalking

There are some great bushwalks in this state, ranging from short trips in the forests of the south-west to the long Bibbulman Track or untracked coastal walks. Many involve substantial climbs and the traversing of picturesque ranges.

The beauty of WA is that the walks are in vastly different environments. There is the tropical Kimberley, the dry Pilbara with its magnificent gorges, Kalbarri and the Murchison River, the Darling Range near Perth and the great variety of the coastline and forests of the south-west.

For bushwalkers who like to have something high to climb, there is Mt Augustus, the largest rock in the world; Pyramid Hill in the Pilbara with its stunning views; the precipitous peaks of the Stirling Range and the Porongurups; and Peak Charles, Mt Ragged and Frenchmans Peak near Esperance.

There is a surfeit of spectacular coastline which is punctuated by a number of interesting walks. Of particular interest are the walks in Fitzgerald River, William Bay, Leeuwin-Naturaliste, Walpole-Nornalup and D'Entrecasteaux national parks. It is not unusual to see humpback whales at sea and wildflowers cascading down coastal tracks.

There are a number of bushwalking clubs in Perth including the Bushwalkers of WA (☎ (09) 387 6875), Western Walking Club (☎ (09) 385 8249) and Perth Bushwalkers Club (☎ (09) 362 1614).

Interesting walks in the hills around Perth include the 640-km Bibbulman Track that runs along old forest tracks between Perth and Walpole on WA's south-eastern coast. Information on this and many other tracks is available from CALM (☎ (008) 199 287), 50 Hayman Rd, Como, WA 6152.

Suitable bushwalking books, all published by CALM, are *Beating About the Bush: Discover the National Parks and Forests near Perth* (1986) by Andrew Cribb; *Family Walks in Perth Outdoors* (CALM, Perth); *Perth Outdoors: A Guide to Natural Recreation Areas In and Around Perth* (CALM, Perth, 1992); and *A Guide to the Bibbulman Track* (CALM, Perth, 1988).

Australia's *Wild* magazine has a number of articles on WA's bushwalks, including an account of an arduous trip in country near the Drysdale River in the Kimberley. There are a number of bushwalking equipment suppliers in Perth who will provide more information:

Australian Geographic Shop
  Forrest Chase, Murray St Mall, Perth 6000
  (☎ (09) 421 1781)
Mountain Designs
  31 Jarrad St, Cottesloe 6011 (☎ (09) 385 1689)
  and 862 Hay St, Perth 6000 (☎ (09) 322 4774)
Off the Edge
  437 Hay St, Subiaco, Perth 6008 (☎ (09) 321
  5259)
Paddy Pallin
  915 Hay St, Perth 6000 (☎ (09) 321 2666)
The Scout Shop & Outdoor Centre
  581 Murray St, Perth 6005 (☎ (09) 321 5259)
Wilderness Equipment
  Bayview Centre, corner Stirling Highway &
  Leura Avenue, Claremont 6010 (☎ (09) 385
  3711)

Heritage Trails Network The Heritage Trails Network, launched during Australia's Bicentenary in 1988, is an excellent series of trails covering historical, cultural or natural points of interest throughout the state. Somewhat neglected now, the trails are usually marked with interpretive displays and directional markers. Information on the Heritage Trails Network can be obtained from tourist offices or the WA Heritage Committee (☎ (09) 221 4177), 292 Hay St, East Perth. There is a *Heritage Trails in Western Australia* book published by the committee.

Birdwatching

Big statement coming up! This is the best place in Australia for birdwatching because of the variety of species and the ease with which you can observe them. Some Queenslanders may dispute this claim but I'm sticking to it. Western Australia is a birdwatchers delight, so much so, that two of the four official Royal Australian Ornithologist Union's (RAOU) observatories are located in the state (at Eyre and Broome).

You will need a *Field Guide to the Birds of Australia* (K Simpson & N Day, Viking O'Neill, 1989); *Field Guide to the Birds of Western Australia* (GM Storr & RE Johnstone, WA Museum, 1985) and *The Slater Field Guide to Australian Birds* (Peter Slater et al, Weldon, 1990) to help you make the distinction between species.

The search for the noisy scrub bird,

rainbow pitta, Gouldian finch, shy hylacola, peregrine falcon, wedge-tailed eagle, chestnut breasted quail thrush, gibber chat, western bristlebird, sandstone shrike-thrush, yellow-rumped pardalote, pink cockatoo and purple-gaped honeyeater will take you to all parts of the state and allow you to see the remarkable scenery as well. For more specific information on the range of birds to be seen in WA, see under Fauna in the Facts about Western Australia chapter or read the Birdwatching sections throughout this book.

For more details about sightings of rare and endangered birds, contact the RAOU (☎ (09) 364 6202), 218/15 Ogilvie Rd, Canning Bridge 6153, or get some current copies of *WA Birdnotes*.

Cycling

This is a very popular activity in WA. Rottnest Island is virtually free of motorised traffic and many visitors pedal their way around the island. Perth has a great path system for cyclists including the Around the Rivers ride, which is made up of 12 connected paths. For more information about practicalities, see under Bicycle in the Getting Around chapter.

Horse & Camel Trekking

The horse and camel were the animal pioneers of this country, enabling both the explorers and settlers to make inroads into the inhospitable interior. Today there are many places in the state where you can go either horse or camel trekking.

For further information, contact the local tourist offices for details of those companies taking treks. The type of trek ranges from a leisurely camel ride along Cable Beach near Broome to an overnight or moonlight horse ride in Kalbarri National Park.

The more adventurous could contemplate an overnight trip south of Wyndham in the rugged East Kimberley. There are also a number of horseriding and trekking operations in the south-west of the state. Specific information relating to trekking is given in the relevant chapters. The Canning Stock Route, by camel, even looms as a possibility!

Rockclimbing

It was widely thought, over a decade ago, that WA had the greatest remaining areas of unclimbed rock – this is still true. Most activity has been concentrated in the south-west of the state, close to Perth, but the Pilbara, North-West Cape and the Kimberley have endless climbing possibilities. The Kimberley, for instance, is twice the size of Victoria and much of it is covered with rock.

In the south-west corner of the state are Churchmans Brook and Mountain Quarry near Perth, the sea cliffs of Willyabrup, humongous West Cape Howe, the Gap, Peak Head, the Stirlings, the Porongurups and Peak Charles. Way back in 1972, the 280-metre Coercion (Grade 16), a route on Bluff Knoll, was climbed by a party of three. A 'doddle' (easy climb) by today's standards, it was fairly spectacular then.

A new wave of climbers have moved in and claimed previously unclimbed lines on many of the features. Slowly, the massive cliffs of the Pilbara, the Dampier Archipelago, North-West Cape and the Kimberley are succumbing to ascents by spider-like humans (check with local CALM officials as to where climbing is permitted).

Canyoning and abseiling, necessary skills of the exploratory climber, are becoming popular activities in their own right. The Miracle Mile canyoning trip in the Karijini (Hamersley Range) gorges with guide Dave Doust has assumed legendary status with foreign backpackers (America's *National Geographic* have even featured it). Abseiling into the Murchison gorges near Kalbarri with another guide, Gordon, has also won renown. There are many other locations for these two activities.

The Climbing Association of WA (☎ (09) 472 3919) meets the third Tuesday of every month at the Boulevard Ale House, Albany Highway, Victoria Park. The *Redpoint* climbing magazine comes out on a regular basis. For beginners, Adventure Out (☎ (09) 472 3919) conducts instructional courses at Churchman Brook, near Armadale; the cost for a two-day programme is $185. A two-day lead rockclimbing course conducted at Willyabrup, near Margaret River, costs $260.

Caving

There are plenty of opportunities for adventure caving in WA. This type of caving, which is vastly different to tours through electrically-lit 'commercial' caves, involves specialist knowledge and skill. Many of the caves are in the Leeuwin-Naturaliste karst system and a number, such as Brides and Dingo's, have to be accessed using ropes. The Cape Range National Park of North-West Cape has a number of unexplored caves (although human moles are rapidly drifting north and underground).

Again, Adventure Out (☎ (09) 472 3919) organises half-day/full-day trips to the Margaret River region for $55/90 and day trips to the Cape Range from Exmouth for $55.

Surfing

The WA coast is a Mecca for surfers from all over the world. It is the south-west, and the Margaret River area in particular, that are so well known. Yallingup and Prevelly Park both host top-level surf competitions attracting the best board riders in the world. Around Bunbury, Geraldton, Kalbarri, Carnarvon and Albany there is also good surfing. Chances are, if you are here with your board, then we don't have to tell you where to go. If you are a keen surfer and need further information, contact Terry (☎ (097) 57 2506).

Scuba Diving & Snorkelling

With over 6000 km of coastline in WA, there is plenty of 'divers-ity' for those heading underwater. Good diving areas include the large stretch of coast from Esperance to Geraldton, and between Carnarvon and Exmouth. You can also get out to the islands and reefs in small boats. The more popular diving spots include Esperance, Bremer Bay, Albany, Denmark, Windy Harbour, Margaret River, Busselton Jetty, Bunbury, Rottnest Island, Shoalwater Islands Marine Park (near Rockingham), Lancelin, Houtman Abrolhos Islands (near Geraldton), Carnarvon and all around North-West Cape (Exmouth, Coral Bay and Ningaloo Reef).

Perhaps the most spectacular underwater experience would be diving with the world's largest fish, the whale shark, or swimming with the graceful manta rays. This is possible off Ningaloo Reef and Exmouth (see Exmouth in the Coral Coast & The Pilbara chapter). There is a strong possibility you will also see green and loggerhead turtles, dolphins, dugongs and humpback whales, depending on when you visit.

Watching Marine Mammals

Although commercial operators will happily take you to spot marine mammals, most notably humpback whales and bottlenose dolphins, many are seen purely by chance. There are few other accessible places in the world where the spotting of such a variety of marine mammals is so easy. Notes on the more common marine mammals are included under the Flora & Fauna section in the Facts about Western Australia chapter.

Whales, particularly the humpback, are commonly seen (anywhere from Cape Leeuwin north to Dampier, even between Perth and Rottnest Island). Another 'watched' whale is the southern right, seen in increasing numbers off the Great Australian Bight.

Dolphins observed in the west are the common dolphin and bottlenose dolphin. The bottlenose attracts thousands of tourists to Monkey Mia on Shark Bay and to Bunbury south of Perth. You can also swim with the bottlenose off Rockingham, south of Perth. Common dolphins are likely to be seen on boat trips in places like the Archipelago of the Recherche.

Other marine mammals include the Australian sea lion at Carnac Island (opposite Perth); any one of the 10,000 dugongs that frequent Shark Bay; and New Zealand fur seals basking in a number of places along the southern coastline.

Sailing

Western Australia brought home the America's Cup for a brief period (see Ruling the Waves in this chapter). There are a number of opportunities to learn basic or advanced sailing, or just go for a sail, in and around Perth and Fremantle.

The Swan River is a great place to begin and there is a sailing school at Nedlands jetty. There is another school at Sorrento at Hillarys Boat Harbour. Fun catamarans are

---

Ruling the Waves

Probably the most coveted trophy in modern sailing is the America's Cup (or the 'Old Mug'). Beating the perennial holders (the USA) – represented by the New York Yacht Club – has always been one of sailings' greatest challenges.

In 1962, the Australian yacht, *Gretel*, undertook its country's first challenge only to be beaten by *Weatherly*. Australia mounted challenges in 1967 (*Dame Pattie*), 1970 (*Gretel II*), 1974 (*Southern Cross*), 1977 (*Australia*) and 1980 (named *Australia* also). These campaigns all proved unsuccessful.

What was thought impossible became reality in Newport, Rhode Island on 26 September 1983. *Australia II*, skippered by John Bertrand, financed by Alan Bond and designed by Ben Lexcen (who masterminded the revolutionary winged keel first displayed on the yacht), triumphed over the Dennis Conner-led *Liberty* by four races to three. It was the first time in 132 years that the America's Cup had been won by an entry outside the USA.

A number of challengers descended upon Fremantle in 1987, attempting to wrest the trophy from the Perth Yacht Club. Again, it was the USA who triumphed, defeating *Kookaburra III* in *Stars and Stripes*. Dennis Conner (who had suffered the ignominity four years earlier of being the first American to surrender the crown) skippered the victor.

The races were a catalyst for a much-needed face-lift to Fremantle, with the event enticing both yachting enthusiasts and the curious. ■

available for hire at a number of southern and northern beaches.

Fremantle is one of the six world legs in the Whitbread Around the World Yacht Race, concluding the arduous 'bash' across the Southern Ocean from Cape Town, South Africa.

Fishing
The coastal regions of WA offer some of the best fishing in the world. Some of the more popular areas include Rottnest Island, Albany, Geraldton and the Houtman Abrolhos Islands, Mackerel Islands, Shark Bay, Carnarvon and the coastline to the north, the North-West Cape and Broome.

The *Caravan, Camping & Fishing Guide to the Northwest* by Don & Lyn Yelland (Gumtree Publications, Perth, 1990) is useful and its philosophy is not to clean out the fish stocks but rather: 'To aim to catch a feed for oneself and family and, for a variety of personal reasons, to enjoy the experience along the way'.

Fishing licences (available for $10 from the Fisheries Department (☎ (09) 325 5988), 108 Adelaide Terrace, East Perth 6004, or country offices) are only required if you intend catching marron and rock lobsters or intend using a fishing net. The department publishes fishing guides including one for the environmentally sensitive Ningaloo Marine Park.

Canoeing
There is ample scope to paddle a canoe or kayak in WA. By canoe we mean the Canadian variety which is open and can take two or three people; a kayak has an enclosed cockpit.

For information contact the Amateur Canoe Association of WA (☎ (09) 368 3920), 6/42 Swanview Terrace, South Perth 6151. Other groups of paddlers include Ascot Kayak, Canning River, Darling Range, Peel Districts, South-West and Swan canoe clubs.

The most famous river is the Avon which is 'descended' by a rabble of powered and unpowered craft in the annual Avon Descent, held in August. There are many other calmer stretches of water that can be enjoyed in a canoe or kayak. Canadians are used for the trip down the Murchison River which gives access to the picturesque gorges of Kalbarri National Park. The forest-to-sea tour on the Blackwood River in the south-west is rated as one of the best trips in Australia in *Canoe Touring in Australia: Seven of the Country's Best River Journeys* by Leigh Hemmings (Simon & Schuster, East Roseville, 1993).

Kayaks and Canadians can be hired in Perth. A kayak or two-person Canadian costs about $40 for the week or $35 for a weekend and a three-person Canadian about $5 more.

The state's Department of Sport & Recreation (☎ (09) 325 5988) publishes a series of free *Canoeing Guides*; No 12 in the series, *Avon River: Northam to Toodyay*, is particularly useful. There are important safety notes on the back of the guides which all paddlers should read.

Whitewater Rafting
There are whitewater rafting trips available from Perth with Adventure Out (☎ (09) 472 3919). In summer, the Collie River is suitable for two-person rafts; and in winter the Murray River, about a 90-minute drive south of Perth, can be tackled in seven-person rafts. Other rafting places in the state are the Murchison River (after a cyclone) and the Ord River spillway near Kununurra (when water is being released from Lake Argyle).

Sea Kayaking
This adventure sport is starting to get a following in the west. Sea kayaking requires a good deal of skill and should only be undertaken with good equipment and the necessary training. In the north-west, the tidal changes are huge and there are dangers from crocodiles and sharks. Adventure Out (see under Whitewater Rafting in this section) should be able to put you in contact with like-minded enthusiasts.

Windsurfing
This is immensely popular, especially at Perth's city beaches. Scarborough on a windy day is ablaze with multi-coloured

sails and windsurfers making spectacular leaps over incoming breakers.

Beaches in the south-west, such as Mandurah, Rockingham, Busselton, Dunsborough and Bunbury are also popular. So are northern beaches – Seabird, Lancelin (probably the sailboard Mecca), Ledge Point and Geraldton. This type of craft features heavily in Geraldton's Festival of the Winds. Each year, in January, there is an ocean race from Ledge Point to Lancelin.

For more information about sailboard hire, good windsurfing locations, repairs etc, contact the tourist offices in the towns mentioned here.

HIGHLIGHTS

Western Australia certainly has highlights aplenty to match its size. All the flora & fauna superlatives are justified and it is fast becoming one of the great ecotourism destinations of the world.

Try this for a list of natural wonders. marvel at the oldest form of living mass – stromatolites – which first appeared 3.5 billion years ago; swim with the largest fish, the whale shark; 'fly' through the water with manta rays; feed bottlenose dolphins; witness the annual migration from the northern hemisphere of thousands of birds; swim with sea lions; climb one of the world's largest trees, the karri; waltz through a profusion of wildflowers at any time of the year; explore the Fitzgerald River International Biosphere Reserve with its numerous unique plant species; wade to the largest west coast coral reef in the world; watch turtles lay their eggs; follow a humpback whale as it leaps spectacularly; spot a pebble-mound mouse; and watch a rare black-footed wallaby bound up the side of a remote gorge.

But wait, there's more: touch the earth's oldest rocks; fly over the mysterious Purnululu Range; wander across an uplifted barrier reef from the Devonian era in the Kimberley; witness the awesome power of the tidal waterfalls of Talbot Bay; lose yourself in the labyrinthine Karijini (Hamersley) gorges; explore the magnificent Leeuwin-Naturaliste and Nullarbor caves; climb to the top of the ancient Stirling Range; admire the brilliant blues of the Indian and Southern oceans; descend into one the world's largest meteorite craters; or climb the world's biggest rock, Mt Augustus.

Furthermore, in the Kimberley and Pilbara, there are opportunities aplenty to experience Aboriginal culture and to observe painted and etched representations from the Dreamtime.

Other and no less spectacular highlights are Wave Rock near Hyden; the vibrant capital of Perth; historic and cosmopolitan Fremantle; get-away-from-it-all Rottnest Island; the amazing Pinnacles Desert; Kalbarri and its surrounding national park; exotic Broome; 'old' Albany; the huge mining constructions of the Pilbara; and the historic towns of the goldfields.

If it was mandatory to select three favourites – North-West Cape & Ningaloo Reef, Karijini (Hamersley Range) National Park and the Fitzgerald River Biosphere Reserve would get the nod.

ACCOMMODATION

Western Australia is well equipped with youth hostels, backpackers' hostels and caravan parks with campsites – the cheapest shelter you can find.

A typical town of more than a thousand people (say, for instance, Mullewa in the Midlands) will have a basic motel at around $35/55 for singles/doubles. An old hotel in the centre of town with rooms (shared bathrooms) would be around $25/40. A caravan park – probably with unpowered tent/powered caravan sites would be around $7/12 for two, and a nearby bed & breakfast (B&B) or guesthouse (in this case a station stay) may have budget singles for $20 and full board for $50. If the town is on a main road, it'll probably have several of each.

You'll rarely have much trouble finding *somewhere* to lay your head in WA, even when there are no hostels, although some surprisingly small and seemingly insignificant towns have backpackers' hostels these days. If there's a group of you, the rates for three or four people in a room are worth checking. Often there are larger 'family' rooms or units with two bedrooms.

The best free guide to accommodation is the *Western Australia Accommodation Listing* available from all tourist information offices. It comprehensively lists the accommodation in each town, including Perth. There are lists of accommodation options (name and telephone number only) in the excellent WATC series of WA's *Southern Wonders*, *Unique North* and *Golden Heartlands* and in a number of regional guides which extract information from that series.

There is also the giveaway backpackers' booklet *The Backpackers Guide to WA* available at hostels around the state. This has a fairly up-to-date listings of hostels, and give prices and details of each hostel.

Another source of comprehensive accommodation listings is the RACV-RAASA's annual directory *Accommodation Australia,* listing hotels, motels, holiday flats, caravan parks and even some backpackers' hostels in almost every city and town in the state. It is updated every year so prices are fairly current, and it is available from the club for $4 if you're a full or reciprocal member.

Camping & Caravanning

Camping in WA is a great (sometimes the only) accommodation option. There are many caravan parks, especially in the south-west, and you'll almost always find space available, even in peak periods. If you want to get around WA on the cheap, then camping is the way to go, with nightly costs for two of around $7 to $14.

One massive drawback is that the campsites you rent are often intended more for caravanners (house trailers for any North Americans out there) than for campers and the tent campers get little thought in these places. Fitzroy Crossing and Kalgoorlie are two notable exceptions with the best facilities for campers in the state.

Also remember that in most large towns, campsites are well away from the centre. This is not inconvenient in small towns but, in general, if you're planning to camp around WA, you really need your own transport.

This is as true for Perth as it is for any other large Australian city.

Western Australian caravan parks are generally well kept, conveniently located and excellent value. Many sites also have on-site vans which you can rent for the night. These give you the comfort of a caravan without the inconvenience of actually towing one of the cumbersome things.

On-site cabins are also widely available, and these are more like a small self-contained unit. They usually have one bedroom, or at least an area which can be screened off from the rest of the unit – just the thing if you have small kids. Cabins also have the advantage of having their own bathroom and toilet, although this is sometimes an optional extra. Many are air-con, a must in the Pilbara and Kimberley at certain times of the year. They are also much less cramped than a caravan, and the price difference is not always that great – say $25 to $30 for an on-site van, $30 to $40 for a cabin. In winter, if you're using this sort of accommodation on a regular basis, it's worth investing in a small electric heater as many vans and cabins are unheated.

Camping in the bush, either in national parks and reserves or in the open, is for many people one of the highlights of a visit to WA. In many places it is a necessity as there is no formal accommodation. In the outback you won't even need a tent – swags are the way to go, and nights spent around a campfire under the stars are unforgettable. Chances are you and your companions will be the only people for hundreds of km.

Youth Hostels

You'll find hostels all over the state, with more official hostels and backpackers' hostels popping up all the time.

YHA hostels provide basic accommodation, usually in small dormitories or bunk rooms, although more and more of them are providing twin rooms for couples. The nightly charges are cheap – usually between $8 and $15 a night. Many of the WA hostels are housed in grand old buildings and the hostel in Dunsborough must have the best views of them all.

With the increased competition from the proliferation of backpackers' hostels, many YHA hostels have done away with the old fetishes for curfews and doing chores, but still retain segregated dorms. Many even take non-YHA members, although there may be a small 'temporary membership' charge. To become a full YHA member in Australia costs $24 a year (there's also a $16 joining fee, although if you're an overseas resident joining in Australia you don't have to pay this). You can join at a state office or at any youth hostel.

Youth hostels are part of an international organisation, Hostelling International (HI, formerly known as the International Youth Hostel Federation or IYHF), so if you're already a member of the YHA in your own country, your membership entitles you to use the Australian hostels. Hostels are great places for meeting people and great travellers' centres, and in many busier hostels the foreign visitors will outnumber the Australians. The annual *YHA Accommodation Guide* booklet, which is available from any YHA office in Australia and from some YHA offices overseas, lists all the YHA hostels around Australia with useful little maps showing how to find them.

You must have a regulation sheet-cum -sleeping bag or bed linen – for hygiene reasons a regular sleeping bag will not do. If you haven't got sheets they can be rented at many hostels (usually for $3), but it's cheaper, after awhile, to have your own. YHA offices and some larger hostels sell the official YHA sheet bag.

All hostels have cooking facilities and 24-hour access, and there's usually some communal area where you can sit and talk. There are usually laundry facilities and often excellent notice boards. Many hostels have a maximum-stay period – because some hostels are permanently full it would hardly be fair for people to stay too long when others are being turned away.

Not all of the 20-plus hostels in WA are actually owned by the YHA. Some are 'associate hostels', which generally abide by hostel regulations but are owned by other organisations or individuals.

Backpackers' Hostels

In recent years the number of backpackers' hostels in WA has increased dramatically – Perth has more than any other capital city!

The standard of these hostels varies enormously. Some in Perth are rundown inner-city hotels where the owners have tried to fill empty rooms; unless recently renovated, these places are generally gloomy and depressing.

Others are former motels, so each unit, typically with four to six beds, will have fridge, TV and bathroom. When the climate allows, there's usually a pool too. The drawback with these places is that the communal areas and cooking facilities are often lacking, as motels were never originally designed for communal use.

Some hostels are purpose-built as backpackers' hostels; these are usually the best places in terms of facilities, although sometimes they are simply too big and therefore lack any personalised service. The managers often have backpackers running the places, and usually it's not too long before standards start to slip. Some of these places, particularly in Broome and in Perth, actively promote themselves as 'party' hostels, so if you want a quiet time, they're best avoided.

Prices at backpackers' hostels are generally in line with YHA hostels, typically $10 to $12, although the $8 bed is still alive and well (but perhaps not clean) in some places.

As with YHA hostels, the success of a hostel largely depends on the friendliness and willingness of the managers. One practice that many people find objectionable – in independent hostels only, since it never happens in YHAs – is the 'vetting' of Australians, who may be asked to provide a passport or double ID which they may not carry. This is a method of keeping unwanted customers out. Never hand over your driver's licence or passport as surety as this is not allowed. After all, how do you explain the lack of a driver's licence to the police if, while out sightseeing, you are pulled over?

Some places will only admit overseas backpackers. This happens mostly in cities and when it does it's because the hostel in question has had problems with locals treating the place more as a doss house than a hostel. The best you can do is persuade the desk staff that you're genuinely travelling the country, and aren't just looking for a cheap place to crash for a while.

Other backpackers' places frown upon children.

Sadly, our experience in WA, travelling with a child, was that rooms which were obviously free became mysteriously unavailable. Couple this with the fact we were Australians meant that most of our nights were spent camping in a tent or in rented cabins. After three weeks on the road (Kununurra to Broome) we gave up trying to stay in hostels!

Guesthouses & B&Bs

These are the fastest growing segment of the accommodation market. New places are opening all the time, and the network of accommodation alternatives throughout the state includes everything from rambling old guesthouses, up-market country homes and romantic escapes, to a simple bedroom in a family home. Many of these places are listed throughout the book. Tariffs cover a wide range, but are typically in the $40 to $100 (per double) bracket. Get a copy of the free pamphlet *Country & Coastal Hideaway Holidays* from the WATC or information offices.

Hotels & Pubs

For the budget traveller, hotels in WA are generally older places – newer accommodation is usually of the motel type. Every place called a hotel does not necessarily have rooms to rent, although many still do. A 'private hotel', as opposed to a 'licensed hotel', really is a hotel and does not serve alcohol. A 'guesthouse' is much the same as a 'private hotel'.

New hotels being built today are mainly of the Hilton variety. So, if you're staying in a hotel, it will normally mean an older place, often with rooms without private facilities. Unfortunately many older places are on the drab, grey and dreary side. Others, fortunately, are colourful places with lively interiors. Many hotels have backpackers' budget accommodation available for about $15 each per room. If a hotel has accommodation available, there are usually signs to let you know.

In some older towns, or in historic centres like Kalgoorlie, the old hotels can be magnificent. The rooms may be old-fashioned and unexciting, but the hotel facade and entrance area will often be quite extravagant. In the outback, the old hotels are often places of real character. And, of course, a place to meet characters. Try the Widgiemooltha, Whim Creek, the Spinifex in Derby or the Crossing Inn near Fitzroy Crossing.

Another good thing about hotels (guesthouses and private hotels, too) is that the breakfasts are usually excellent – big and 100% filling. Generally, hotels have rooms for around $20 to $30. When comparing prices, remember to check if it includes breakfast.

Motels, Serviced Apartments & Holiday Flats

If you've got transport and want a modern place with your own bathroom and other facilities, then you're moving into the motel bracket. Motels are everywhere in Australia, just like in the USA, but they're usually located away from the city centres. Prices vary and with the motels, unlike hotels, singles are often not much cheaper than doubles. The reason is quite simple – in the old hotels many of the rooms really are singles, relics of the days when single men travelled the country looking for work. In motels, the rooms are almost always doubles. You'll sometimes find motel rooms for less than $30, and in most places have little trouble finding something for $45 or less.

Holiday flats and serviced apartments are much the same thing. Basically, holiday flats are found in holiday areas, serviced apartments in cities. A holiday flat is much like a motel room but usually with kitchen or cooking facilities so you can fix your own food. They are not serviced like motels – you don't get your bed made up every morning and the cups washed out. In some holiday flats you actually have to provide your own sheets and bedding but others are operated like motel rooms with a kitchen. Most motels in WA provide at least tea/coffee-making facilities and a small fridge, but a holiday flat will also have cooking utensils, cutlery, crockery and so on.

Holiday flats are often rented on a weekly basis but even in these cases, it's worth asking if daily rates are available. Paying for a week, even if you stay only for a few days, can still be cheaper than having those days at a higher daily rate. If there's more than just two of you, another advantage of holiday flats is that you can often find them with two or more bedrooms. A two-bedroom holiday flat is priced about 1½ times the cost of a comparable single-bedroom unit.

In holiday areas like the Great Southern or Kalbarri, motels and holiday flats are one and the same thing. In big cities, on the other hand, the serviced apartments are often a little more obscure, although they may be advertised in the newspaper's classified ads.

One organisation that offers accommodation in country areas throughout the state is the Country Women's Association (CWA). It has holiday units in Albany, Busselton, Port Denison-Dongara, Esperance, Guilderton, Hopetoun, Jurien, Broome, Lancelin and Rockingham. As a general rule, a double would cost $30 for members and $5 extra for each non-member.

There are only a couple of 'Ys' (YWCA or YMCA) available in WA – Jewell House, in Goderich St and the Grand Central in Wellington St, Perth. The latter was recently refurbished, has a restaurant and cafe and is of a high standard.

Farm & Station Stays

Western Australia is a land of farms (known as 'stations' in the outback) and one of the best ways to come to grips with Australian life is to spend a few days on one. Many farms offer accommodation where you can sit back and watch how it's done, or get actively involved in the day-to-day activities.

The WATC or the WA Farm & Country Holidays Association can advise you on what's available; prices are pretty reasonable. The association puts out the accommodation guide *Farm Holidays & Country Retreats* which lists over 40 places in the south-west, a land of farms rather than of stations. The region around Margaret River is a popular location for farmstays; these are listed in *Bed & Breakfast and Farm Homestay: Augusta, Margaret River, Yallingup, Dunsborough.*

Apart from Queensland, WA is probably the best place to stay on a real station. There is a small pamphlet, *Bed & Breakfast Around the State*, which lists seven stations plus you'll find numerous pamphlets in the accommodation racks of tourist offices. The Gascoyne, Pilbara and Murchison areas are popular areas for station stays (see Station Stays in the Coral Coast & The Pilbara chapter).

Most stations will have comfortable accommodation in the main homestead or cottages, and budget accommodation in out buildings or former shearers' quarters. They will also allow caravans and campers for a reasonable site fee, but stress that they do not have the facilities of caravan parks and campsites.

There is one general book available: *The B&B, Farm & Station Stay Guide to WA* (Countrywide Publications, West Perth, $9.95).

Other Possibilities

That covers the usual conventional accommodation possibilities, but there are lots of less-conventional ones. You don't have to camp in caravan parks, for example. There are plenty of parks where you can camp for free, or roadside rest areas where short-term camping is permitted. Western Australia has thousands of sq km of bush where nobody is going to complain about you putting up a tent – or even notice you.

In Perth, if you want to stay longer, the first place to look for a shared flat or a room is the classified ad section of the daily newspaper. Wednesdays and Saturdays are the best days for these ads. Notice boards in universities, hostels, certain popular bookshops and cafes, and other contact centres are good places to look for flats/houses to share or rooms to rent.

Groups can hire houseboats for trips around the picturesque Walpole and Nornalup inlets of the south coast. A four-berth boat will cost $635, a six to eight-berth $900, and a 10-berth boat about $1280; all prices are for one week and low season.

FOOD

Perth/Fremantle has more restaurants per head of population than anywhere in Australia, but outside the metropolitan area there is nowhere near the variety except in some resort towns such as Margaret River and Broome.

There was once a time when Australia's food (mighty steaks apart) had a reputation for being mediocre. Miracles happen and Australia's miracle was immigration. The Greeks, Yugoslavs, Italians, Lebanese and many others who flooded into Australia in the 1950s and 1960s brought their cooking styles with them. Recent arrivals, such as the Vietnamese, are now ladling out their delicious pho in Perth.

You can also have excellent Greek moussaka (and a bottle of retsina to wash it down), delicious Italian saltimbocca and pastas, or good, heavy German dumplings; you can perfume the air with garlic after stumbling out of a French bistro, or try all sorts of Middle Eastern and Arab treats. The Chinese have been sweet & souring since the goldrush days, while more recently, Indian, Thai and Malaysian restaurants have been all the rage. And for cheap eats, you can't beat some of the Vietnamese places.

Australian Food

Although there is no real definition of Australian cuisine, there is certainly some excellent Australian food to try. For a start, there's the great Australian meat pie – every bit as sacred an institution as the hot dog is to a New Yorker. There are a few places that do a really good job on this classic dish, but the standard pie is an awful concoction of anonymous meat and dark gravy in a soggy pastry case. You'll have to try one though; the number consumed in Australia each year is phenomenal, and they're a real part of Australian culture.

Even more central to Australian eating habits is Vegemite. This strange, dark-coloured yeast-extract substance looks like tar and smells like, well, Vegemite – it is something only an Australian could love. Australians spread Vegemite on bread and become so addicted to it that anywhere in the world you find an Aussie, a jar of Vegemite is bound to be close at hand.

The good news about Australian food is the ingredients. There is a fine market garden industry in the state, kept rolling along by a host of migrant farmers, so nearly all the produce is grown in WA. Everybody knows about good Australian steaks ('This is cattle country, so eat beef you bastards', announce the farmers' bumper stickers), but there are lots of other things to try.

Western Australia has a superb range of seafood: fish like spangled emperor, coral trout, many species of cod, groper, pink schnapper, King George whiting, sand whiting and the esteemed barramundi, or superb lobsters and other crustaceans like Exmouth Gulf prawns.

Unique to the south-west of the state are marron or freshwater crayfish which are sensational if panfried in lemon, dill and garlic. The French settlers named the marron after a large edible chestnut which had a dark exterior, sweet taste and white flesh.

Even vegetarians get a fair go in WA; there are some excellent vegetarian restaurants and, once again, the vegetables are as fresh as you could ask for.

Places to Eat

If you want something familiar and utterly predictable, there are McDonald's, KFC, Pizza Hut and all the other well-known names (if coming from Darwin, the first of these multinational takeaways you see will be in Geraldton). There are also Chinese restaurants with bronzed 'pre-Peking' ducks in the window, Middle Eastern places where you get a decent doner kebab or shashlik, and many other places serving a particular national cuisine.

For real value for money, Australian delis are terrific and they'll put together a superb sandwich.

In the evening the best bargains can be found in the pubs. Look for 'counter meals', so called because they used to be eaten at the bar counter. Some places are still like that, while others are up-market, almost restaurant-like. Although the food is usually of the simple 'surf and turf' (fish or steak) and chips, the quality is often excellent and prices are commendably low. The best places usually have serve-yourself salad tables where you can add as much salad, French bread and dressings as you wish.

One catch with pubs serving meals is that they usually operate fairly strict hours. The evening meal time may be just 6 to 7.30 or 8 pm. Pubs doing counter meals often have a blackboard menu outside but some of the best places are quite anonymous. Counter meals vary enormously in price but in general the better class places with good serve-yourself salad tables will be in the $6 to $14 range for all the traditional dishes: steak, veal, chicken and so on.

Australians love their fish & chips just as much as the British and, as in Britain, quality can vary enormously – all the way from stodgy and horrible to really superb. Hamburger and fish & chip shops usually serve both these Aussie favourites. The west has also got the full range of takeaway foods, from Italian to Mexican, Chinese to Lebanese.

The places to avoid eating at all costs are the dreary roadhouses that punctuate the nothingness between towns. They were designed to serve fuel and the food tastes as if it has been cooked in it. Stock up with fresh produce from supermarkets in towns either side of large drives.

DRINKS
Nonalcoholic
In the nonalcoholic department, Australians knock back Coke and flavoured milk like

there's no tomorrow and there are also excellent mineral water brands. Coffee enthusiasts will be relieved to find good Italian cafes serving cappuccino and other coffees, often into the wee small hours and beyond. Fremantle's South Terrace is where you will find those who know the difference between Vittorio, Braziliano and Lavazza.

Alcoholic
Beer Each Australian state has its own beer brands and there's always someone singing the praises of each one. The Swan Brewery is the west's biggest producer of beer with the two major brands, Swan and Emu. Swan comes as Draught, Gold and Lager; Emu comes as Export and Bitter. The Swan Brewery in Canning Vale has a free tour (see the Perth chapter) and it throws in a couple of free beers.

Another smaller brewery, Matilda Bay, in North Fremantle, produces boutique beer which is popular in all states. The beers are Redback (with a light version), Fremantle Bitter and Matilda Bay Pils and Bitter. There are many small boutique breweries in various pubs and two drops worth a mention are the Perth Brass Monkey's Stout and Fremantle's Sail & Anchor Seven Sea Real Ale. For a couple of years during the yuppie era, a Redback with a slice of lemon in the neck was a popular call. Guinness is occasionally found on draught, usually in Irish pubs such as Molly O'Gradys in Perth.

A word of warning to visitors: Australian beer has a higher alcohol content than British or American beers. Standard beer is generally around 4.9% alcohol, although most breweries now produce 'lite' beers, with an alcohol content of between 2% and 3.5%.

And another warning: people who drive under the influence of alcohol and get caught lose their licences (unfortunately, drink-driving is a real problem in Australia). The maximum permissible blood-alcohol concentration level for drivers in most parts of Australia, including WA, is 0.05%.

All around Australia, beer, the containers it comes in, and the receptacles you drink it from, are called by different names. In WA, beer comes in stubbies and tinnies. Here, a 275-ml beer is a middy and a 450-ml beer is a schooner. And, no one drinks warm beer here unless their fridge has broken down or the esky is out of ice.

According to *Mark Shield's Beer Guide*, the following WA beers received a very favourable four or five stars: Brass Monkey Stout; Dogbolter; Emu Bitter; Emu Export; Emu; Redback Pils; Matilda Bay Bitter; and Swan Western Bitter.

Wine Western Australia has the perfect climate for wine producing. There are some superb vine-growing areas and best known are the Swan Valley, the Margaret River region and the area around Mt Barker. Houghton's, in the Swan Valley, produces Australia's best selling bottled white wine, White Burgundy – the one with the blue stripe. Another winery in the Swan Valley, Lamont's, is the only winery in Australia to produce all its wines in the traditional manner. Some of the Margaret River wineries, such as Cape Mentelle and Leeuwin Estate, have a strong following in the eastern states.

An even more economical way of drinking WA wines is to do it on the cheap (or free) at the wineries. In the wine-growing areas, most wineries have tastings: you just zip straight in and say what you'd like to try.

All over WA you'll find restaurants advertising that they're BYO. The initials stand for 'Bring Your Own' and it means that they're not licensed to serve alcohol but you are permitted to bring your own with you. Transform the wine which you purchased from the cellar into BYO that night!

ENTERTAINMENT

It's often hot and dusty, you've been driving for days without the whiff of a beer or the clink of a cool glass of semillon, and you have seen 2½ of the seven geological wonders of the world and sniffed more wildflowers than you care to remember. You deserve a night out in the most isolated capital city in the known universe.

Perth has plenty of diversions for those who seek them. Friday night in Northbridge is a wonder to behold, almost a non-stop frenetic party that rages until dawn. The crowds spill out of the restaurants, party in the nightclubs and swamp the many cafes along the street. Business persons in expensive suits, dags in ill-fitting, mismatched clothing, gays and lesbians, dinky-di's and the glamorous – it's all on show.

The regional centres have one or two pubs where those in the know hang out. Just ask someone at the tourist office where you should go. In most of the towns in WA you get absolutely no choice as there is only one pub (Widgiemooltha or Whim Creek for instance). You certainly would not have a problem in Kalgoorlie as the main street, Hannan St, is choking with grog shops as befits a frontier mining town.

Cinema

Although cinema took an initial hammering from the meteoric rise of the home-video market, it has bounced back as people rediscover the joys of the big screen.

The big operators such as Greater Union and Hoyts have movie theatres scattered across Perth and Fremantle has its own Coastal Cinemas. In the west you can see really big screens as drive-ins are still a feature throughout the state, thanks to the weather. There is also the Omni Cinema in West Perth with its 12,000 watts of sound! The best and oldest movie theatre in the state is Sun Pictures, Broome – even worth going to if *The Attack of the Killer Tomatoes!* is screening.

Seeing a new-release mainstream film costs around $12 ($7.50 for children under 15) in the big cities, less in country areas.

You will also find arthouse and independent cinemas in Perth. These generally screen films that aren't made for mass consumption or specialise purely in re-runs of classics and cult movies. The Lumiere, Astor and Cinema Paradiso all fall into this category.

Discos & Nightclubs

Yep, no shortage of these either, but they are confined to Perth and the larger towns. Clubs range from the exclusive 'members only' variety to barn-sized discos where anyone who wants to spend the money is welcomed with open arms. Admission charges range from around $6 to $12.

Some places have certain dress standards, but it is generally left to the discretion of the people at the door – if they don't like the look of you, bad luck. The up-market nightclubs attract an older, more sophisticated and affluent crowd, and generally have stricter dress codes, smarter decor – and higher prices.

Many suburban pubs have discos and/or live music, and these are often great places for catching live bands. Nationally well-known names or up-and-coming performers can be seen in pubs – after all, most of Australia's popular bands started out on the pub circuit in one city or another.

The best way to find out about the local scene is to get to know some locals, or travellers who have spent some time in the place. Otherwise there are often comprehensive listings in newspapers, particularly on Friday and Saturday, and in the music and entertainment magazine *Xpress*.

Spectator Sports

One of the best things about travel in this state is watching the parochial WA crowd support their local teams in national competition. Some of the places to catch all the action are listed with the following sports.

Australian Rules This game has been heartily embraced by the west. Although headquartered in Victoria, the game has achieved national status with major league teams in Adelaide, Sydney, Brisbane, Perth, Geelong and, from 1995, the Fremantle Dockers. The other teams are from the suburbs of Melbourne.

The Perth-based West Coast Eagles (drawn from the Western Australian Football League teams of Claremont, East Fremantle, East Perth, Perth, South Fremantle, Swan Districts, Subiaco and West Perth) were the first non-Victorian Australian Rules team to win a premiership in the 96-year history of the Australian Football League (formerly the

Victorian Football League). In their sixth season in the national competition they had a 28 point win over Geelong before a crowd of 95,000 at the Melbourne Cricket Ground on 26 September 1992. The score was 16.17 (113) to 12.13 (85) with WA's Peter Sumich kicking six goals and Peter Matera five. This was as audacious an act as Australia wresting the America's Cup from the New York Yacht Club.

Many of the game's illustrious players have come from the west. One such player was the Geelong ruckman Graham 'Polly' Farmer. Subject of a recent book by Stephen Hawke (son of former Prime Minister Bob Hawke), Polly was a master of the game who could handball over 30 to 40 metres, give his rovers an 'armchair ride' and grab some real 'screamers'. Other capable WA players with the 'attributes' were North Melbourne's Aboriginal Krakouer brothers, ex-Fitzroy captain Ron Alexander and Essendon Best & Fairest (three times) and 1976 Brownlow medallist, Graeme Moss.

And finally, in the Grand Final of 1994, the West Coast Eagles again performed their magic in front of 93,860 screaming fans. Much to the chagrin of east coast football supporters, the West Coast beat a lacklustre Geelong by 20-23 (143) to 8-15 (63).

Cricket In the 1991-92 cricket season, WA won the Sheffield Shield for the 13th time since being admitted to the competition in 1947-48. They beat NSW by 44 runs at the WACA. This was their 11th success since 1970-71, equalling the combined efforts of all other states in the same period. In the limited-overs competition the tables were turned and NSW beat WA by 69 runs.

Some of the greatest cricketers in the world have come out of WA. The commentators cry 'Caught Marsh, bowled Lillee' is synonymous with Australian cricketing success in the late seventies. The Fremantle Doctor (a late afternoon wind) honed the skills of the pace bowlers Graham McKenzie and Dennis Lillee and the swing bowlers Bob Massie and Terry Alderman with often devastating results. And a little known fact: the first test ever played at the WACA was in

December 1970 – older travellers will remember it well as Greg Chappell made his maiden century (108) in his first test.

Basketball There is a WA women's and a WA men's team in the national competition. Games are played at the Perth Entertainment Centre during the winter months. The Quit WAIS Breakers won the national women's title in 1992 and the Perth Wildcats (☎ (09) 324 1844) just failed in their bid to win three consecutive national titles in 1992. For women's match details, contact the WA Basketball Federation (☎ (09) 386 5525).

Other Sports The Perth Thundersticks now play in the National Hockey League after having been omitted from inaugural competition in 1991; they have already won a national final (in 1992 against the Brisbane Blades 4-3, after a sudden-death shoot out). Perth Heat participate in the national baseball league, and have held the national crown.

Motor racing is held on Sundays during March to October at Wanneroo Park Raceway, Pinjar Rd, Wanneroo. Throughout spring and summer, speedcar and motorcycle races are held on Friday nights at the Royal Agricultural Showground at Claremont.

And Perth fielded a team, the Western Reds, for the first time in the 1995 Winfield Cup rugby-league competition.

Gambling

The saying goes that Australians would bet on two flies crawling up a wall, and Western Australians are no different. In fact, in Derby, they have an annual cockroach race at the Spinifex Hotel.

Apart from flies and cockroaches, local gamblers bet on the horses (trotters and gallopers), the dogs (greyhounds) and on the football. You can bet at any Totalisator Agency Board (TAB) betting shops, found in most shopping areas and in pubs (there are over 250 in the state). Prize money is listed per $1, but the minimum bet is 50c per unit. The PubTabs usually have a Sky-TV facility

so punters can have a beer while they check out all the main races.

In the metropolitan area, the trots are held at Gloucester Park every Friday, the races (WA Turf Club) are held at Ascot (check the newspapers for dates) and the dogs chase the bunny at Cannington every Thursday and Saturday.

Those that know the difference between Fan Tan and blackjack can visit the Burswood Casino, on the Great Eastern Highway, across the river from the city (see the Perth chapter).

There are various numbers for prize games, ranging from the usual Lotto to Scratch & Win tickets.

All eyes are directed at the floor at the legalised Two-Up 'school' in the tin shed, six km north of Kalgoorlie. Two-up is a game where two pennies are tossed into the air with a wooden stick (the kip) and the result of the bet hinges on the call, either heads or tails. If you haven't played it at one of the casinos, check it out in this rustic setting; business gets underway at 1.30 pm and goes on until the light completely fades.

THINGS TO BUY

There are a number of things that you can buy in Perth and when travelling through the state. Most of what you buy can be purchased in other states as well. There are some things that you can get in the west far more easily than in eastern states – gold and Aboriginal art are good examples.

Aboriginal Art

Aboriginal art is much cheaper in the west than the eastern states. The works of some of the Kimberley artists, such as Mingi May Barnes, are exhibited in galleries throughout the world.

Aboriginal art is an integral part of ancient and modern Aboriginal culture. Artistic expression is very much linked to the Dreamtime and the same totemic images recur regardless of the medium on which they are etched or painted. The medium could be the body, a carved wooden creature, the walls of a cave or the sides of a significant rock.

In the last couple of decades, artists began to transfer their paintings to canvas, employing long-lasting acrylic paints. The traditional ground mosaics, those that are now seen on canvas, remain inanimate until the correct chants or songs imbue the image with supernatural power. The mosaics incorporate complex interweaving of the geography of the country with traditional stories. Mosaic painters may have learnt the details of at least a thousand paintings each.

Apart from canvas paintings, you will see motifs painted on carved animals (widely available in the far south-east of the state), women's utensils such as coolamons, clapping sticks, water carriers, dancing boards and didjeridoos. There are also colourful batik scarves, dilly bags and even T-shirts. Buy designs only on approved merchandise so the original painters get some benefit; there are many imitations transferred on to T-shirts overseas, so beware.

But before you buy, do some research. Some good books are: *Aboriginal Art of the Western Desert* by Geoff Bardon (Rigby, Adelaide, 1979); *Aboriginal Australian Art: A Visual Perspective* by RM & CH Berndt with John Stanton (Methuen, Melbourne, 1982); and *Windows on the Dreaming: Aboriginal Paintings in the Australian National Gallery* (ANG/Ellsyd Press, Canberra, 1989). These titles, and many others, should be available from local libraries.

Places to buy Aboriginal paintings and crafts are Warringarri Aboriginal Arts in Kununurra; Mangkaja Aboriginal Arts Centre in Fitzroy Crossing; in Broome and Derby at various places; the old gaol in Roebourne; and from outlets in Perth such as the Creative Native, 32 King St, Perth; Indigenart, 115 Hay St, Subiaco; or Ganada, Atwell Arcade, Fremantle.

Carved Emu Eggs & Boab Nuts There are a number of places, especially in the north of the state, where you can buy exquisitely carved emu eggs and boab nuts. Derby is a good place to buy carved boab nuts; enquire at the tourist office. Emu eggs are particularly beautiful and

seen in many of the galleries selling traditional Aboriginal arts and crafts.

Australiana
Australiana is rather a vague cultural term which here refers to collections of 'souvenirs'. It's the type of thing you buy for those back at home as it supposedly represents Aussie culture.

A lot of these items are neither Australian in character nor made in Australia. Some delightfully tacky souvenirs include: ashtrays embedded with New Zealand paua shell (masquerading as pearl shell) with 'Greetings from Broome' emblazoned on them; and tea towels depicting a cross between a sperm and a humpback whale (mixing teeth with baleen sheaths) with a bubble above the air spout proclaiming: 'Welcome to Rottnest Island'.

One genuine article is the neoprene or polystyrene beer-can cooler. Prized among collectors of such amber-fluid containers is the one fashioned by countless, couthless artisans at Widgiemooltha pub, between Kalgoorlie and Norseman.

You can buy seeds for all those wildflowers you saw while in the state. Check carefully to see that you can take them with you to your own country. Many of them have successfully been transplanted within Australia, in widely different climatic conditions.

Last but not least, don't forget WA wines. The state has a number of vine-growing areas – Margaret River, the Swan Valley and Mt Barker – and there are a great diversity of styles produced. In addition to the usual cabernet/shiraz, chardonnay, rhine riesling, semillon and ports, you can sample wood fermented verdelho, rouge hermitage and cabernet rosé.

Aussie Clothing
By Aussie clothing I mean the practical workwear which has become fashionable. The humble elastic-sided Blundstone work boot, which originated in Tasmania, has 'made it' in Europe and rivals the ubiquitous Doc Martens. Moleskin trousers, once a practical form of wear in the Kimberley, are popular with both men and women. Woollen

bush shirts are another handy item for the cool European and North American climates. All this can be topped off with an Akubra hat, made, of course, of rabbit fur. Concealed underneath this attire will be Holeproof socks and Bonds singlet and undies.

The Yakka and King Gee ranges of overalls, heavy-duty shirts, slacks and Bluey coarse wool jackets are also in vogue and purchased by overseas travellers.

The last item in the perfect 'get up' for the outback traveller is the swag. These canvas beds, complete with mattresses and bedding, are made in WA on a genuine station, Cane River.

Gold, Diamonds, Pearls & Opals

Gold attracted many to the colony and still remains a booming industry in parts of WA, most notably around the Golden Mile of Kalgoorlie.

The main street of Kalgoorlie has plenty of jewellery shops where you can buy jewellery which incorporates gold nuggets – earrings, bracelets and pendants. These have sometimes been tumbled to give a slightly polished appearance or are attached in a raw state. Surprisingly, they are relatively inexpensive but make sure the fittings are of good quality as well.

World famous argyle diamonds are mined at the world's largest diamond mine, south of Kununurra. The pink diamonds can be purchased from outlets in Kununurra such as Nina's Jewellery, Djaaru Gems and Kimberley Fine Diamonds, or in a number of shops in Perth.

Broome pearls are reputed to be the best, cultured from the beautiful silver-lipped oyster *(Pinotada maxima)*, and are probably the most expensive in the world. Most of the famous pearl galleries are in Broome's Chinatown.

Fashion & Clothing

The populace of Perth are snappy dressers and use the good weather as an excuse to get out and about in all their finery. The main department stores in the city are Myer, Coles and Aherns but there are boutique clothing stores everywhere – there are no less than 16 arcades in the city. Although an eastern creation, the popular Ken Done range of clothing is available in Perth along with local designs. Also a favourite are the Margaret River Surf Company designs and merchandise from the Star Surf Shop.

Handicrafts

Many of the handicrafts for sale feature local motifs such as wildflower designs or dried-and-dyed wildflower arrangements.

One favourite handicraft is carved and turned timbers from the giant forests. Popular are tables made of timber burls (unusual circular growths which occur on the tree trunk), turned wooden bowls and exquisitely carved fauna depicting southern right and humpback whales. The timber used includes local jarrah, the rare curly jarrah, sheoak, WA blackbutt, wandoo, karri, marri, coastal banksia and the grass tree *(Xanthorrhoea)*.

Esperance, Albany, Margaret River, Pemberton, Broome, Denmark, the Avo Valley and the towns of the Blackwood Valley are all renowned for the variety of locally produced crafts.

Getting There & Away

AIR

A number of overseas airlines use Perth as their gateway to Australia but, in reality, many visitors will be coming to the west after passing through the eastern states.

While most flights land in the eastern states you still have to make another giant leap across the continent to WA, involving further time and expense.

There are lots of competing airlines and a variety of air fares from Asia or Europe. Australia's current international popularity adds another problem – flights are often heavily booked. If you want to fly to Australia at a popular time of year (December to February) or on a popular route, plan well ahead.

Australia has a large number of international gateways. Sydney and Melbourne are the two busiest international airports with flights from everywhere. Perth also gets many flights from Asia and Europe and has direct flights to Asia and Africa. The other international airport in WA is Port Hedland (for Denpasar, Indonesia only).

Discount Tickets

Buying airline tickets these days is like shopping for a car, a stereo or a camera. Rule number one if you're looking for a cheap ticket is to go to an agent, not directly to the airline. The airline can usually only quote you the absolutely straight-up-and-down, by-the-rule-book regular fare. An agent, on the other hand, can offer all sorts of special deals, particularly on competitive routes.

Ideally, an airline would like to fly all their flights with every seat in use and every passenger paying the highest fare possible. Fortunately life usually isn't like that and airlines would rather have a half-price passenger than an empty seat. When faced with the problem of too many seats, they will either let agents sell them at cut prices, or occasionally make one-off special offers on particular routes – watch the travel ads in the press.

Round-The-World Tickets

Round-the-World (RTW) tickets have become very popular in the last few years and many of these will take you through Perth. The airline RTW tickets are often bargains and since Australia is pretty much the

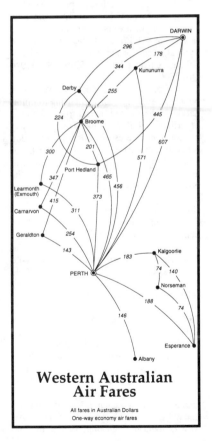

Western Australian Air Fares

All fares in Australian Dollars
One-way economy air fares

83

other side of the world from Europe or North America, it can work out no more expensive, or even cheaper, to keep going in the same direction right round the world rather than U-turn when you return. This is a good option for getting to Perth, either after entering Australia from the eastern states or using the city as the first port of call.

The official airline RTW tickets are usually put together by a combination of two airlines, and allow you to fly anywhere you want on their route systems so long as you do not backtrack. Other restrictions are that you (usually) must book the first sector in advance and cancellation penalties then apply. There may be restrictions on how many stops you are permitted and usually the tickets are valid from 90 days up to a year. Typical prices for these South Pacific RTW tickets are from £720 to £950 or US$2350 to US$2800.

An alternative type of RTW ticket is one put together by a travel agent using a combination of discounted tickets from a number of airlines. A UK agent like Trailfinders can put together interesting London-to-London RTW combinations including Perth for £790. The two main operators through Perth are Qantas and British Airways, so check the possibilities with them.

Circle Pacific Tickets

Circle Pacific fares are a similar idea to RTW tickets which use a combination of airlines to circle the Pacific – combining Australia, New Zealand, North America and Asia. These would be of little value to people trying to get to WA, as an additional costly sidetrip would be necessary.

To/From North America

There are a variety of connections across the Pacific from Los Angeles, San Francisco and Vancouver to Australia including direct flights, flights via New Zealand, island-hopping routes or more circuitous Pacific-rim routes via nations in Asia. Qantas, Air New Zealand, United and Continental all fly USA-Australia; Qantas, Air New Zealand and Canadian Airlines International fly Canada-Australia. Nearly all of these entail an additional fare for you to get to WA as the usual terminus is the east coast.

To find good fares to Australia check the travel ads in the Sunday travel sections of papers like the *Los Angeles Times*, *San Francisco Chronicle-Examiner*, *New York Times* or *Toronto Globe & Mail*. The straightforward return excursion fare from the USA west coast to Melbourne/Sydney is around US$972 and US$1260 to Perth, depending on the season. In the USA, good agents for discounted tickets are the two student travel operators, Council Travel and STA Travel, both of which have lots of offices around the country.

To/From the UK

The cheapest tickets in London are from the numerous 'bucket shops' (discount ticket agencies) which advertise in magazines and papers like *Time Out*, *City Limits*, *Southern Cross* and *TNT*. Pick up one or two of these publications and ring round a few bucket shops to find the best deal. The magazine *Business Traveller* also has a great deal of good advice on air fare bargains. Most bucket shops are trustworthy and reliable but the occasional sharp operator appears – *Time Out* and *Business Traveller* give some useful advice on precautions to take.

Trailfinders (☎ (0171) 938 3366) at 46 Earls Court Rd, London W8 and STA Travel (☎ (0171) 581 4132) at 74 Old Brompton Rd, London SW7 and 117 Euston Rd, London NW1 (☎ (0171) 465 0484) are good, reliable agents for cheap tickets.

The cheapest London to Perth bucket shop tickets are about £429 one-way or £765 return. Such prices are usually only available if you leave London in the low season – March to June. In September and mid-December, fares go up about 30% while the rest of the year they're somewhere in between (Perth is only slightly cheaper than Sydney or Melbourne). The main operators through Perth (to Europe) are Qantas via Singapore and Bangkok, and British Airways via Singapore.

Many cheap tickets allow stopovers on the

way to or from Australia. Rules regarding how many stopovers you can take, how long you can stay away, how far in advance you have to decide your return date and so on, vary from time to time and ticket to ticket. Most return tickets now allow you to stay away for any period between 14 days and one year, with stopovers permitted anywhere along your route. As usual with heavily discounted tickets, the less you pay the less you get.

From Perth you can expect to pay around A$900 one-way, and A$1400 return (low season) to London and other European capitals, with stops in Asia on the way.

To/From New Zealand

Air New Zealand and Qantas operate a network of trans-Tasman flights linking Auckland, Wellington and Christchurch in New Zealand with most major Australian gateway cities. Another flight, about the same distance, will be required to reach Perth entailing more time and expense.

From New Zealand to Sydney you're looking at around NZ$500 one-way and NZ$630 return, to Melbourne NZ$550 one-way and NZ$730 return. To Perth it's around NZ$900 one-way and NZ$1200 return.

To/From Asia

Ticket discounting is widespread in Asia, particularly in Singapore, Hong Kong, Bangkok and Penang. There are a lot of fly-by-nights in the Asian ticketing scene so a little care is required. Also the Asian routes have been caught up in the capacity shortages on flights to Australia. Flights between Hong Kong and Australia are notoriously heavily booked while flights to or from Bangkok and Singapore are often part of the longer Europe-Australia route so they are also sometimes full. Plan ahead. For more information on South-East Asian travel and on to Australia, see Lonely Planet's *South-East Asia on a shoestring*.

Typical one-way fares to WA from Asia include from Hong Kong for around HK$4600 or from Singapore for around S$670.

From Australia some typical return fares

from the west coast include Singapore $695, Kuala Lumpur $725, Bangkok $820, Hong Kong $1040 and Tokyo $1150.

The cheapest way out of Australia is take one of the flights operating between Darwin and Kupang (Timor, Indonesia); current one-way/return fares are $198/330. Flights from Port Hedland to Denpasar (Bali, Indonesia) with Garuda Indonesia are infrequent and cost approximately $624/899 for one-way/return tickets, depending on the season.

Out of Perth you could expect to pay $559/869 for one-way/return with Garuda, suggesting that flights through Port Hedland suit Pilbara locals (as there is no necessity for them to pay the extra fares to go to Perth to pick up an international flight).

Asian operators through Perth are the Indonesian airlines Sempati Air, Merpati and Garuda Indonesia, Qantas, Ansett International (to Denpasar), Thai Airways, Cathay Pacific, Royal Brunei, Malaysian Airlines and Singapore Airlines.

To/From Africa

The flight possibilities from these continents are not so varied and you're much more likely to have to pay the full fare. There is only a handful of direct flights each week between Africa and Australia and then only between Perth and Harare (Zimbabwe), Johannesburg (South Africa) and Nairobi (Kenya). A much cheaper alternative from East Africa is to fly from Nairobi to India or Pakistan and on to South-East Asia, then connect from there to Australia.

Operators on the Africa route are Air Mauritius from Nairobi via Mauritius, South African Airways from Johannesburg and Qantas from Harare. Costs for these flights are around US$650/1095 for one-way/return (February to March).

Arriving & Departing

Australia's dramatic increase in visitor arrivals has caused severe bottlenecks at the entry points, particularly at Sydney where delays on arrival or departure are frequent. An answer to this problem is to try not to arrive in Australia at Sydney. You can save yourself

---

Air Travel Glossary

Apex Apex, or 'advance purchase excursion' is a discounted ticket which must be paid for in advance. There are penalties if you wish to change it.

Baggage Allowance This will be written on your ticket: usually one 20 kg item to go in the hold, plus one item of hand luggage.

Bucket Shop An unbonded travel agency specialising in discounted airline tickets.

Bumped Just because you have a confirmed seat doesn't mean you're going to get on the plane – see Overbooking.

Cancellation Penalties If you have to cancel or change an Apex ticket there are often heavy penalties involved; insurance can sometimes be taken out against these penalties. Some airlines impose penalties on regular tickets as well, particularly against 'no show' passengers.

Check In Airlines ask you to check in a certain time ahead of the flight departure (usually 1½ hours on international flights). If you fail to check in on time and the flight is overbooked the airline can cancel your booking and give your seat to somebody else.

Confirmation Having a ticket written out with the flight and date you want doesn't mean you have a seat until the agent has checked with the airline that your status is 'OK' or confirmed. Meanwhile you could just be 'on request'.

Discounted Tickets There are two types of discounted fares – officially discounted (see Promotional Fares) and unofficially discounted. The lowest prices often impose drawbacks like flying with unpopular airlines, inconvenient schedules, or unpleasant routes and connections. A discounted ticket can save you other things than money – you may be able to pay Apex prices without the associated Apex advance booking and other requirements. Discounted tickets only exist where there is fierce competition.

Full Fares Airlines traditionally offer first class (coded F), business class (coded J) and economy class (coded Y) tickets. These days there are so many promotional and discounted fares available from the regular economy class that few passengers pay full economy fare.

Lost Tickets If you lose your airline ticket an airline will usually treat it like a travellers' cheque and, after enquiries, issue you with another one. Legally, however, an airline is entitled to treat it like cash and if you lose it then it's gone forever. Take good care of your tickets.

No Shows No shows are passengers who fail to show up for their flight, sometimes due to unexpected delays or disasters, sometimes due to simply forgetting, sometimes because they made more than one booking and didn't bother to cancel the one they didn't want. Full-fare passengers who fail to turn up are sometimes entitled to travel on a later flight. The rest of us are penalised (see Cancellation Penalties).

On Request An unconfirmed booking for a flight; see Confirmation.

Open Jaws A return ticket where you fly to one place but return from another. If available, this can save you backtracking to your arrival point.

---

a lot of time and trouble by making Perth, Brisbane, Cairns, Melbourne or another gateway city your arrival point.

For information about how to get to the city from Perth airport when you first arrive in WA, see To/From the Airport in the Perth chapter.

When you finally leave, remember to keep $25 aside for the departure tax and reserve a look of righteous indignation when you hand it over.

Domestic Flights

The major domestic carriers are Ansett (☎ 13 1300), which also flies a few international routes, and Qantas Domestic (☎ 13 1313), which is also the international flag-carrier flying as Qantas. Both fly between Perth and the other capital cities, and both have subsidiaries which fly smaller planes on shorter inter and intra-state routes.

You don't have to reconfirm domestic flights on Ansett and Qantas, but you should phone on the day of your flight to check the details. For Ansett, call ☎ 13 1515; for Qantas Domestic, call ☎ 13 1223.

Qantas operates from other interstate cities and tourist destinations to Perth but *does not* offer a service within the state. Regular one-way and return seats cost the

Overbooking Airlines hate to fly empty seats and since every flight has some passengers who fail to show up (see No Shows), airlines often book more passengers than they have seats. Usually the excess passengers balance those who fail to show up, but occasionally somebody gets bumped. If this happens guess who it is most likely to be? The passengers who check in late.

Promotional Fares Officially discounted fares like Apex fares which are available from travel agents or direct from the airline.

Reconfirmation At least 72 hours prior to departure time of an onward or return flight, you must contact the airline and 'reconfirm' that you intend to be on the flight. If you don't do this the airline can delete your name from the passenger list and you could lose your seat. You don't have to reconfirm the first flight on your itinerary or if your stopover is less than 72 hours. It doesn't hurt to reconfirm more than once.

Restrictions Discounted tickets often have various restrictions on them – advance purchase is the most usual one (see Apex). Others are restrictions on the minimum and maximum period you must be away, such as a minimum of 14 days or a maximum of one year. See Cancellation Penalties.

Standby A discounted ticket where you only fly if there is a seat free at the last moment. Standby fares are usually only available on domestic routes.

Tickets Out An entry requirement for many countries is that you have an onward or return ticket, in other words, a ticket out of the country. If you're not sure what you intend to do next, the easiest solution is to buy the cheapest onward ticket to a neighbouring country or a ticket from a reliable airline which can later be refunded if you do not use it.

Transferred Tickets Airline tickets cannot be transferred from one person to another. Travellers sometimes try to sell the return half of their ticket, but officials can ask you to prove that you are the person named on the ticket. This is unlikely to happen on domestic flights; on an international flight, tickets may be compared with passports.

Travel Agencies Travel agencies vary widely and you should ensure you use one that suits your needs. Some simply handle tours while full-service agencies handle everything from tours and tickets to car rental and hotel bookings. A good one will do all these things and can save you a lot of money but if all you want is a ticket at the lowest possible price, then you really need an agency specialising in discounted tickets. A discounted ticket agency, however, may not be useful for other things, like hotel bookings.

Travel Periods Some officially discounted fares, Apex fares in particular, vary with the time of year. There is often a low (off-peak) season and a high (peak) season. Sometimes there's an intermediate or shoulder season as well. At peak times, when everyone wants to fly, not only will the officially discounted fares be higher, so will the unofficially discounted fares or there may simply be no discounted tickets available. Usually the fare depends on your outward flight – if you depart in the high season and return in the low season, you pay the high-season fare. ∎

same as Ansett Australia although both have special deals from time to time. You have to check and book with the airlines at least 28 days in advance so you can be eligible for special fares. It would not be unusual to get a Melbourne-Perth return for $400 with 28 day's notice, $470 with three week's notice or $510 with 14 day's notice; compared with the regular return fare of $1075, this is a substantial saving.

Note that Qantas flight numbers determine which terminal to use. QF001 to QF399 operate from the Qantas International Terminal and QF400 and above operate from the Qantas Domestic Terminal. At present only a few Qantas international flights, such as QF24 and QF64, are via Perth.

Another operator into Perth is Horizon Airways (☎ (09) 277 1433). They fly from Uluru (Ayers Rock) to Perth via Kalgoorlie. All airports and domestic flights are non-smoking.

Fares Few people pay full fare on domestic travel, as the airlines offer a wide range of discounts. These come and go and there are regular 'spot specials', so keep your eyes open. Because discounting is so unpredictable, we quote full economy fares in this book.

Full-time university or higher-education

students get 25% off the regular economy fare when producing a student ID or an International Student Identity Card (ISIC) card, but you can usually find fares discounted by more than that.

There are no longer stand-by fares, but there are discount fares which allow same-day travel on certain flights, usually those which are uncomfortably early or late.

The cheapest fares are advance-purchase deals. Some advance-purchase fares offer up to 33% off one-way fares and up to 50% or more off return fares. You have to book one to four weeks ahead, and you often have to stay away for at least one Saturday night (for some reason). There are restrictions on changing flights and you can lose up to 100% of the ticket price if you cancel, although you can buy health-related cancellation insurance.

International travellers (Australians and foreigners) can get a 25% to 40% discount on Qantas or Ansett domestic flights simply by presenting their international ticket (any airline, one-way or return) when booking. It seems there is no limit to the number of domestic flights you can take, but there might be time limits, say 60 days after you arrive in Australia. Note that the discount applies only to the full economy fare, and in many cases it will be cheaper to take advantage of other discounts offered.

Economy one-way fares (not including discounts) from other parts of Australia include: Darwin $589, Melbourne $539, Adelaide $499, Sydney $601, Uluru $437, Cairns $621 and Brisbane $661.

Air Passes With so much discounting these days, air passes do not represent the value they once did, so much so that Qantas does not offer any passes.

Ansett Australia still has its Kangaroo Airpass, which gives you two options – 6000 km with two or three stopovers for $949 ($729 for children) and 10,000 km with three to seven stopovers for $1499 ($1149 for children). There are a number of restrictions on these tickets, which can be a good deal if you want to see a lot of country in a short

time. You do not need to start and finish at the same place.

Restrictions include a minimum travel time (10 nights) and a maximum (45 nights). One of the stops must be at a non-capital-city destination and be for at least four nights. All sectors must be booked when you purchase the ticket, although these can be changed without penalty unless the ticket needs rewriting, in which case there's a $50 charge. Refunds are available before travel commences, but not after you start using the ticket.

There are also special deals available only to foreign visitors. Currently, Ansett Australia's Visit Australia Pass must be bought and booked overseas, but you can alter your bookings and buy extra coupons after arrival. Four coupons (each giving a day's travel in the one direction) cost about $650 or $750 if you include Perth, and each additional coupon costs about $160, or $210 if it includes Perth.

Warning
This chapter is particularly vulnerable to change – prices for international travel are volatile, routes are introduced and cancelled, schedules change, rules are amended, special deals come and go, borders open and close. Airlines and governments seem to take a perverse pleasure in making price structures and regulations as complicated as possible and you should check directly with the airline or travel agent to make sure you understand how a fare (and ticket you may buy) works.

In addition, the travel industry is highly competitive and there are many lurks and perks. The upshot of this is that you should get opinions, quotes and advice from as many airlines and travel agents as possible before you part with your hard-earned cash. The details given in this chapter should be regarded only as pointers and cannot be any substitute for your own careful, up-to-date research.

LAND
The south-west of WA is isolated from the rest of Australia; interstate travel therefore entails a major journey. The nearest state

capital to Perth is Adelaide, 2700 km away by the shortest road route. To Melbourne it's at least 3440 km, Darwin is around 4160 km and Sydney 4200 km away. But in spite of the vast travelling distances, you can still drive across the Nullarbor Plain from the eastern states to Perth and then all the way up the Indian Ocean coast and through the Kimberley to Darwin on mainly sealed roads.

Bus

It pays to shop around for fares. Students and YHA members get discounts of at least 10% with many long-distance companies. On straight point-to-point tickets there are varying stopover deals. Some companies give one free stopover on express routes, others charge a fee, maybe $5 for each stopover. This fee might be waived if you book through certain agents, notably some of the hostels.

With Greyhound Pioneer Australia (☎ 13 2030), which consists of the former Greyhound/Pioneer and Bus Australia, major interstate routes and fares from Perth are:

Sydney via the Nullarbor – $243
Melbourne via the Nullarbor – $209
Adelaide via the Nullarbor – $180
Darwin via the North-West Coastal Highway – $330
Darwin via the Inland Route (SH 95) – $330

Bus Passes If you're planning to travel around Australia, check out Greyhound Pioneer Australia's excellent bus-pass deals – make sure you get enough time and stopovers. Greyhound Pioneer's Adelaide to Perth, Perth to Darwin via the Coastal Highway and return to Adelaide through the Centre route would be an attractive option for many people; the cost is $820 but the fare does not allow backtracking. Added to this would be the cost of a fare to Adelaide from either Sydney or Melbourne, say about $100.

There are also set-duration passes which allow travel on a set number of days during a specified period. There are no restrictions on where you can travel, and passes range from $380 for seven days of travel in one month up to $2100 for 90 days of travel in six months (what a nightmare!).

Train

There is only one interstate rail link, the famous Indian-Pacific Railway. Along with the Ghan to Alice Springs, the long Indian-Pacific run is one of Australia's great railway journeys – a 65-hour trip between the Pacific Ocean on one side of the continent and the Indian Ocean on the other. Travelling this way, you see Australia at ground level and by the end of the journey you really appreciate the immensity of the country (or, alternatively, are bored stiff).

From Sydney, you cross NSW to Broken Hill and then continue on to Adelaide and across the Nullarbor. From Port Augusta to Kalgoorlie, the seemingly endless crossing of the virtually uninhabited centre takes well over 24 hours, including the 'long straight' on the Nullarbor – at 478 km this is the longest stretch of railway line in the world. Unlike the trans-Nullarbor road, which runs south of the Nullarbor along the coast of the Great Australian Bight, the railway line crosses the Nullarbor Plain. From Kalgoorlie, it's a straightforward run into Perth.

Travel Arrangements To Perth, one-way fares from Adelaide are $337 for an economy sleeper, $566 for a 1st-class sleeper or $170 in an economy seat with no meals; from Melbourne $444 economy sleeper, $715 1st-class sleeper or $215 seat only; and Sydney $495 economy, $850 1st class or $230 seat only. Caper (advance-purchase) fares offer good reductions (around 30%).

Melbourne and Adelaide passengers connect with the Indian-Pacific at Port Pirie. Cars can be transported between Adelaide and Perth ($290) and most other major cities. This makes a good option for those not wishing to drive the Nullarbor in both directions.

The rail distance from Sydney to Perth is 3961 km. You can break your journey at any stop along the way and continue on later as long as you complete the one-way trip within two months; return tickets are valid for up to six months. Westbound, the Indian-Pacific departs Sydney on Thursday and Monday. Heading east, the train departs Perth on

---

Building the Trans-Continental Railway

The promise of a trans-continental railway link helped lure gold-rich WA into the Australian Commonwealth in 1901. Port Augusta (South Australia) and Kalgoorlie were the existing state railheads in 1907 and, that year, surveyors were sent out to map a line between those towns. In 1911 the Commonwealth legislated to fund north-south (The Ghan) and east-west (Indian-Pacific) routes across the continent; over 80 years later the former has not been completed.

The first soil was turned in Augusta in 1912 and, for five years, two self-contained gangs – a total of 3000 workers – inched towards each other. They endured sandstorms, swarms of blowflies and intense heat as they laid 2.5 million sleepers and 140,000 tonnes of rail. The soil and rock was removed with pick and shovel and the workers were supplied by packhorse and camel. The whole job was completed with a minimum of mechanical aids, one of the few machines being the Roberts track-layer.

There was no opening celebration as planned (to mark the spot where the track gangs met in the sandhills near Ooldea) as Australia was embroiled in WWI. The first Transcontinental Express pulled out of Port Augusta at 9.32 pm on 22 October 1917, heralding the start of the 'desert railway from Hell to Hallelujah'. It arrived in Kalgoorlie on 24 October at 2.50 pm (42 hours 48 minutes with time difference taken into account) after covering over 1682 km.

The participants in the building of the railway are reflected in the names of the stations along the stretch – Forrest, Deakin, Hughes, Cook, Fisher, O'Malley and Barton. Bates commemorates Daisy Bates, who devoted herself to the welfare of Aborigines and for a time lived alongside the line near Ooldea. Denman was the Governor-General who turned the first sod in 1917.

A good read is Patsy Adam Smith's *The Desert Railway* (Rigby, Adelaide, 1974) which has many photographs depicting the building of the line. The history of the line is covered exhaustively in *Road Through the Wilderness* by David Burke (NSW University Press, Sydney, 1991). ∎

Monday and Friday. Book at least a month in advance.

The main difference between economy and 1st-class sleepers is that 1st-class compartments are available as singles or twins, economy as twins only. First-class twins have showers and toilets; 1st-class singles have toilets only, with showers at the end of the carriage. In the economy-seating compartments, the showers and toilets are at the end of the carriage. Meals are included in the fare for 1st class only; economy-berth and economy-seat passengers have the option of purchasing meals from the restaurant car. First-class passengers also have a lounge compartment complete with piano.

Between Adelaide and Perth you can also travel on the weekly Trans-Australian. Fares are the same as the Indian-Pacific fares, and the trip takes 38 hours. Reservations for all services are made with Australian National in Adelaide and Port Augusta; both on ☎ 13 2232.

Car, Motorbike & Bicycle

See the Getting Around chapter for details of road rules, driving conditions and information on buying and renting vehicles.

The main road routes into WA are combinations of Highway No 1 and the North-West Coastal Highway (still part of Highway No 1); Highway 1 and State Highway 95 (Inland Route) from Darwin to Perth; and a combination of State Highway 94 and the Eyre Highway (Highway No 1) from the eastern states.

Hitching

Hitching across the Nullarbor is not advisable; waits of several days are not uncommon. Driving yourself is probably the cheapest way of getting to WA from the eastern states – if there is a group of you. You'll probably spend around $450 to $500 on fuel, travelling coast to coast; between four people that's about $125 each. Coming from Darwin, we never saw anyone, in a period of two months, hitching on main roads in the Kimberley or Pilbara but we are sure it is possible (see under Hitching in the Getting Around chapter).

Cycling the Nullarbor

The Nullarbor (Eyre Highway) is a real challenge to cyclists. They are attracted by the barrenness and distance, certainly not by the interesting scenery. As you drive across you see many of them, at all times of the year, lifting their waterbottles to their parched mouths or sheltering under a lone tree.

Excellent equipment is needed and adequate water supplies have to be carried. The cyclist should also know where all the water tanks are located. And beware the sun – adequate protection should be applied even in cloudy weather. Realise that the prevailing wind for most of the journey will be west to east, the most preferable direction to be pedalling.

Spare a thought for the first cyclist to cross the Nullarbor. Arthur Richardson set off from Coolgardie on 24 November 1896 with a small kit and water bag. Thirty-one days later he arrived in Adelaide having followed the telegraph line. Problems he encountered were the hot winds, '1000 in the shade' and 40 km of sandhills west of Madura station.

In 1900, Richardson became the first person to pedal around Australia. He left Perth on 5 June 1899 and arrived back in Perth on 4 February 1900. It was much publicised at the time as another group had left in a counter-clockwise direction from Melbourne. The epic journey is described in his *Story of a Remarkable Ride* (1900). ■

Tours

Another interesting route into WA is from Yulara near Uluru to Perth via the Warburton Rd. There are a number of escorted tours including Austracks 4WD Outback Adventures (☎ (008) 655 200); the cost for their six-day trip is $399. Also operating is Marlu Camping Safaris (☎ (09) 302 1320) who have an 11-day Red Centre tour for $720. There is no longer a bus service from Yulara to Perth via Kalgoorlie.

SEA
To/From Indonesia

A small shipping company takes passengers between Darwin and Bali on a regular basis. The vessel sails roughly twice a month in each direction, the trip takes six to seven days non-stop and the cost is A$340/300 /270 per person in two, four or eight-berth cabins. For full details contact Golden Shipping (☎ 289508; fax 287431), Denpasar, Indonesia or All Points Travel (☎ (0800) 41 0066; fax 41 1602), Anthony Plaza, Smith St Mall, Darwin, NT, Australia.

Getting Around

AIR

Western Australia is so vast (and at times so empty) that unless your time is unlimited you will probably have to fly at some point. In WA, large companies use aircraft as a shuttle service for their workers from Perth to the outback.

There are only two main domestic carriers within Australia – Qantas Domestic (which merged with Australian Airlines) and Ansett Australia – despite the fact that the airline industry is deregulated. So far deregulation has made little difference to flying within WA. Ansett Australia controls most traffic, with Skywest and local operators in spirited competition on some routes. Ansett has a comprehensive network of flights connecting Perth with regional centres. The frequency of some flights seems ridiculous given the state's small population – until you realise how many mining projects are based there.

Ansett Australia (☎ 13 1300) – formerly Ansett WA – operates regular services from Perth to the following destinations: Kalgoorlie, Geraldton, Carnarvon, Learmonth (Exmouth), Paraburdoo, Newman, Karratha, Port Hedland, Broome, Kununurra and Derby. These are linked with interstate flights to Darwin, Sydney, Adelaide, Melbourne, Uluru (Ayers Rock), Cairns and Townsville.

There are a number of other smaller operators within the state. Western Airlines operates a service from Perth to Geraldton, Kalbarri, Useless Loop and Monkey Mia.

Skywest Airlines (☎ (09) 478 9999, 13 1300) operates services from Perth to Albany, Esperance, Kalgoorlie, Laverton, Leinster, Leonora, Geraldton, Mt Magnet, Cue, Meekatharra and Wiluna. Typical one-way fares, without any discounting, are: Perth to Leinster via Kalgoorlie $246, and to Kalgoorlie via Esperance $183.

Goldfields Air Services (☎ (090) 93 2116) flies to towns such as Leonora and Laverton from Kalgoorlie. There is also a regular service to Rottnest Island (☎ (09) 478 1322): usually three flights in the morning and three in the afternoon.

Travelling from airport to town is reasonably cheap and convenient by airline bus. Quite often a taxi shared between three or more people can be cheaper than the bus. For transport to/from Perth Airport, see the Perth chapter.

BUS

Bus travel is generally the cheapest way from A to B, other than hitching of course, but the main problem is to find the best deal. A great many travellers see WA by bus because it's one of the best ways to come to grips with the state's size and variety of terrain, and because the bus companies have comprehensive route networks – far more comprehensive than the limited railway system. The buses all look pretty similar and are equipped with air-con, toilets and videos.

There is only one national bus network – Greyhound Pioneer Australia, which consists of the former separate companies Greyhound/Pioneer and Bus Australia. In fact, the buses are still in their original paint-jobs.

As well as interstate destinations, it has intrastate departures to Dongara/Port Denison ($32), Geraldton ($36), Kalbarri ($69), Shark Bay ($105), Port Hedland ($137), Exmouth ($147), Broome ($190), Derby ($209), Kununurra ($300), Meekatharra ($98), Newman ($121), Northam ($34) and Kalgoorlie ($71).

Its buses run from Perth along the coast to Darwin ($330) and Perth to Adelaide via Kalgoorlie and the Eyre Highway ($180). Greyhound Pioneer Australia is the most extensive service in the state with an interconnecting service that would allow an almost-loop trip such as Perth to Kalbarri, Monkey Mia, Exmouth and Broome, and return via the inland route. (A return fare on Greyhound is double, less 10%.)

Kalbarri, Denham (for Monkey Mia) and Tom Price are well off the main drag so there are connecting services with the Greyhound Pioneer Australia service. Kalbarri Coachlines (☎ (099) 37 1104) connects Kalbarri and the town of Ajana on the North-West Coastal Highway. Denham Seaside Tours (☎ (099) 48 1253) operates from the Overland Roadhouse, on the North-West Coastal Highway, to Denham. Tom Price Leisure Travel (☎ (091) 89 2375) operates from Tom Price and Paraburdoo to Nanutarra on the North-West Coastal Highway.

The other operator in the northern region is Dickson's Westliner (☎ (09) 250 3318). It has a daily Perth-to-Derby service ($198) via the coast and another Perth-to-Port Hedland service ($129) via the inland Great Northern Highway. The impecunious will note that these costs are a little less than Greyhound Pioneer. Westliner (☎ (09) 250 3318) does the Port Hedland to Perth run via Newman ($130; 21 hours) and the Great Northern Highway; and daily Perth to Derby ($200; 38 hours) via the coastal route. It has a 28-day West Pass for $277; some restrictions apply such as a seven stopover limit.

Westliner also has a comprehensive service to the goldfields which includes Leinster ($90), Laverton ($85) and Leonora ($77). Westliner's service to Kalgoorlie ($55), which includes towns on the Great Eastern Highway, is much cheaper than Greyhound Pioneer who concentrate on the trans-Australia route.

There are a couple of other bus services that will be of use to travellers coming to grips with the sheer size of this state. The largest operator in the mid-west and south-west is Westrail, and its buses run in conjunction with limited rail services. Westrail services York, Geraldton, Kalbarri, Esperance, Bunbury, Kalgoorlie, Margaret River, Augusta, Pemberton, Mukinbudin, Hyden, Albany and Meekatharra. Reservations are necessary on all Westrail bus/train services (☎ (09) 326 2222). It has 14 main routes, most of which originate at the East Perth Terminal (EPT):

1 Williams-Albany ($36)
2 Collie-Boyup Brook-Pemberton ($31)
3 Northam-Mullewa-Geraldton-Meekatharra ($67)
4 Geraldton ($37)
5 Northam-Narrogin-Albany ($35)
6 Esperance ($52)
7 Bunbury-Augusta ($29)
8 Bunbury-Pemberton ($31)
9 Mukinbudin ($29)
10 York-Narembeen-Kulin-Hyden-Esperance ($53)
11 Kalgoorlie Terminal-Esperance ($33)*
12 Northam-York ($90)*
13 Perth/Bunbury-Manjimup-Albany (King Karri) ($33)*
14 Albany-Esperance (price on application)*

* denotes not originating from EPT.

Concession-card holders can get a fare reduction on Westrail (pensioners, seniors, unemployed/low-income earners and students). Children under 16 travel for half fare and children under 10 may not travel unaccompanied. There is a free luggage allowance of 50 kg (two items) and bicycles or surfboards can only be accepted if room permits. Bicycles carried should be suitably packed.

South-West Coachlines (☎ (097) 54 1666; (09) 324 2333) in the Transperth bus station, Wellington St, Perth, runs bus services between Perth and the following centres in the state's south-west: Bunbury, Busselton, Augusta, Dunsborough, Nannup, Manjimup and Collie.

Kalgoorlie Express (☎ (09) 328 9199) does the Perth-to-Leinster via the goldfields run; the one-way cost is $90.

TRAIN

Western Australia's internal rail network, operated by Westrail, is limited to services between Perth and Kalgoorlie (the *Prospector*), and Perth and Bunbury in the south (the *Australind*). There are connections with Westrail's more extensive bus service (for more information see under Getting There & Away in the Perth chapter).

There is a Westrailpass which can be used

for all travel on intrastate road and rail passenger services; tickets are available for 14-day, one-month and three-month periods. For information on the Indian-Pacific see the Getting There & Away chapter.

TAXI

These are not to be used as a means of getting from A to B in WA unless you have buckets of money. They are available in most of the cities and towns where locals are heavily reliant on them as a means of beating the booze buses and police patrols. Shared among a number of people they are reasonable and a good means of getting around.

Perth has a good system of metered taxi cabs, and there are taxi ranks throughout the city and in nearby Fremantle. The two main companies are Swan Taxis (☎ (09) 322 0111, 335 3944) and Black & White or Green & Gold (☎ (09) 333 3333). A special taxi service for the disabled, officially available from 8.30 am to 4.30 pm Monday to Friday, can be booked on ☎ (09) 333 3377.

CAR

More and more travellers are finding the car the best way to see the state – with three or four of you, the costs are reasonable and the benefits many, provided you don't have a major mechanical problem. As so many travellers are buying cars these days, you may find it difficult to find people who need a lift and share costs if you buy one on your own.

Road Rules

Driving in WA holds few surprises. Australians drive on the left-hand side of the road as in the UK, Japan and most countries in Asia and the Pacific. There are a few local variations from the rules of the road as applied elsewhere in the West.

The main one is the 'give way to the right' rule. This means that if you're driving on a main road and somebody appears on a minor road on your right, you must give way to them – unless they are facing a give-way or stop sign. Most intersections are now signposted to indicate the priority road.

The general speed limit in built-up areas in WA is 60 km/h, the freeways are 90 km/h and out in country areas it's 110 km/h depending on where you are; lower limits are designated by roadside speed-limit signs. The police have radar speed traps and speed cameras and are very fond of using them in carefully hidden locations – don't exceed the speed limit as the boys and girls in blue may be waiting for you.

Australia was one of the first countries in the world to make the wearing of seat belts compulsory. All new cars in Australia are required to have seat belts back and front and if your seat has a belt then you're required to wear it – you're liable to be fined if you don't. Western Australia is the only state which does not require small children to be belted into an approved safety seat – a foolish omission which should be rectified in future.

Although overseas licences are acceptable in Australia for genuine overseas visitors, an International Driving Permit is even more acceptable.

On the Road

Western Australia is not crisscrossed by multi-lane highways. There simply is not enough traffic and the distances are too great to justify them.

In general, roads in WA are well-surfaced two-lanes on all of the main routes. You don't have to get very far off the beaten track, however, to find yourself on dirt roads, and anybody who sets out to see the state in reasonable detail will have to expect to do some dirt-road travelling. If you seriously want to explore, then you'd better plan on having a 4WD and a winch.

A few useful spare parts are worth carrying if you're travelling on highways in the Kimberley, Pilbara or remote south-eastern parts of the state. A broken fan belt can be a real nuisance if the next service station is 200 km away.

Driving standards in Australia aren't exactly the highest in the world and drink-driving is a real problem, especially in country areas. Serious attempts have been made in recent years to reduce the road toll – random breath tests are not uncommon in built-up areas. If you're caught with a blood-alcohol level of more than 0.05 (0.08 in the Northern Territory) then be prepared for a hefty fine, a court appearance and the loss of your licence. If possible, get a copy of the booklet *Drive Safe*.

Fuel Supplies Petrol is available from stations sporting the well-known international brand names. In WA, prices vary enormously from place to place. In a trip from Kununurra to Perth, expect a price variation of 35c per litre for diesel or petrol, decreasing as you get closer to major centres and increasing on lonely stretches of road.

In the outback, the price can soar and some outback service stations are not above exploiting their monopoly position, especially those between Kununurra and Geraldton where fuel transport costs feature heavily in the equation. In general, the price ranges throughout the state from 65c a litre to $1. If you have a 4WD then long-range fuel tanks assist in making large savings on fuel costs.

If travelling the Coastal route, the Great Northern Highway or the Eyre Highway (Nullarbor), realise that fuel supplies are widely spaced along the way. There is 24-hour availability at the following places (these roadhouses are under no obligation to stay open for 24 hours, so always be prepared to have to drive further). Roadhouse distances from Perth are in brackets:

North-West Coastal Highway
    Cataby (162 km), Dongara (359 km), Glenfield (436 km), Wannoo (Billabong Roadhouse) (657 km), Overlander Roadhouse (704 km), Carnarvon (905 km), Barradale (1204 km), Nanutarra Roadhouse (1275 km), Sandfire Roadhouse (1937 km)
Great Northern Highway
    Wubin (272 km), Meekatharra (765 km), Kumarina (1021 km), Auski Roadhouse (1384 km)
Eyre Highway (Nullarbor)
    Norseman (726 km), Balladonia (917 km), Caiguna (1099 km), WA/SA Border Village (1448 km), Nullarbor Roadhouse, SA (over Christmas only) (1284 km)

Driving Hazards Cattle, emus and kangaroos are two common hazards on country roads, and a collision is likely to kill the animal and seriously damage your vehicle. Kangaroos are most active around dawn and dusk, and they travel in groups. If you see one hopping across the road in front of you, slow right down – its friends are probably just behind it. Many Australians avoid travelling altogether between 5 pm and 8 am, because of the hazards posed by animals.

Finally, if one hops out in front of you (as a family of emus did to us), hit the brakes and only swerve to avoid the animal if it is safe to do so. The number of people who have been killed in accidents caused by swerving to miss an animal is high – better to damage your car and probably kill the animal than kill yourself and others with you.

At some stage you are bound to find yourself on a dirt road, eg the Stirling Ranges, Gibb River Rd and the access roads to Karijini and Millstream Chichester national parks. Driving on the dirt requires special care as a car performs differently under braking and turning when on dirt. You should under no circumstances exceed 80 km/h on dirt. If you go faster you will not have enough time to respond to a sharp turn, stock on the road or an unmarked gate or cattle grid. So take it easy. See the sights and don't break the land speed record.

Travelling in WA, especially in the north-west, means having to pass a road train. On some days you will see more road trains than cars. These articulated trucks and their loads can be up to 50 metres long, 2.5 metres wide and travel around 100 km/h. Overtaking is a tricky process and requires a clear view ahead. At times you will have to drive off the bitumen to get past. Exercise caution and remember that it is much harder for the larger road train to be kept in control than your car; basically, show some courtesy.

Flooding is a real problem up north during the Wet because of cyclonic storms. If you travel at this time, delays should be expected. You can check whether roads are open, following heavy rain, by telephoning one of the following numbers:

Perth   ☎ (09) 323 4354 or ☎ (008) 013 314
Carnarvon   ☎ (008) 013 315
Port Hedland ☎ (008) 013 316
Derby   ☎ (008) 013 317
Darwin   ☎ (089) 84 3585

Distances by Rd One thing you have to adjust to in the west is the vast distances between places. The truth is that places of interest are a bloody long way away from Perth. In researching this book we covered 16,000 km! Here are some examples of the distances from Perth to regional centres:

Albany (409 km); Augusta (320 km); Broome (2237 km); Bunbury (180 km); Carnarvon (904 km); Cervantes (245 km); Coral Bay (1131 km); Cue (650 km); Dampier (1555 km); Denham (for Monkey Mia 856 km) (831 km); Derby (2391 km); Esperance (721 km); Eucla (1436 km); Exmouth (1260 km); Fitzroy Crossing (2566 km); Geraldton (444 km); Hyden (340 km); Kalbarri (589 km); Kalgoorlie (597 km); Karratha (1535 km); Lake Argyle (3284 km); Manjimup (307 km); Marble Bar (1476 km); Margaret River (277 km); Mount Barker (360 km); Newman (1184 km); Onslow (1386 km); Pemberton (335 km); Port Hedland (1646 km); Roebourne (1560 km); Southern Cross (368 km); Tom Price (1553 km); Walpole (426 km) and Wyndham (3229 km).

Distances to eastern state capitals are:

Adelaide (2700 km); Brisbane (4357 km); Darwin (4165 km); Melbourne (3438 km); Sydney (4200 km).

Outback Travel

You can now drive around Australia on Highway 1 or through the middle all the way from Adelaide in the south to Darwin in the north almost without ever leaving sealed road, but this hasn't always been so. The Eyre Highway across the Nullarbor Desert in the south was only surfaced in the 1970s and the final stretch of Highway 1 in the Kimberley region of WA was completed in the mid-1980s. Occasionally there are sections of dirt when the road is being repaired after the Wet floods.

If you really want to see outback WA, there are still lots of roads where the official recommendation is that you report to the police before you leave one end, and again

when you arrive at the other. That way, if you fail to turn up at the other end they can start the search parties (there are at least a couple of stories each year of motorists being stranded for weeks).

Nevertheless, many of these tracks are now better kept and you don't need a 4WD or fancy expedition equipment to tackle them. You do need to be carefully prepared and to carry important spare parts, however. Backtracking 500 km to pick up some minor malfunctioning component or, much worse, to arrange a tow, is unlikely to be easy or cheap.

You will need to carry a fair amount of water in case of disaster – around 20 litres a person is sensible – stored in more than one container. Food is less important – the space might be better allocated to an extra spare tyre.

The state automobile associations can advise on preparation and supply maps and track notes. Most tracks have an ideal time of year – in the centre it's not wise to attempt the tough tracks during the heat of summer (November to March) when the dust can be severe, chances of mechanical trouble are much greater and water will be scarce and hence a breakdown more dangerous. Similarly in the north, travelling in the wet season may be impossible due to flooding and mud.

If you do run into trouble in the back of beyond, stay with your car. It's easier to spot a car than a human being from the air, and you wouldn't be able to carry your 20 litres of water very far anyway.

Make sure you practise gate etiquette. The rules are quite simple: if you find a gate open leave it open and if you find it closed make sure you close it after you have passed through. Farm owners can be understandably irate if you neglect to do this.

Some of the favourite outback tracks in the west follow.

Warburton Road/Gunbarrel Highway This route runs west from Yulara by the Aboriginal settlements of Docker River and Warburton to Laverton in WA. From there you can drive down to Kalgoorlie and on to

Perth

A: Town Hall (TW)

B: Perth buildings:
   the old & the new (PS)

C: Trains, Planes & Automobiles
   Restaurant in Northbridge (PS)

D: Hay St Mall (TW)

E: Havana Restaurant in Northbridge (PS)

F: View of South Perth (RDB)

A	B
	C
D	

Rottnest Island
A: Lighthouse in Wadjemup Hill (c.1895) (GB)
B: Quokka *(Setonix brachyurus)* (GB)
C: Old building (GB)
D: Beach in Thomson Bay (GB)

Perth. The route passes through Aboriginal reserves and permission to enter them must be obtained in advance if you want to leave the road.

A well-prepared conventional vehicle can complete this route although ground clearance can be a problem and it is very remote. From the Yulara resort at Yulara to Warburton is 567 km, and it's another 568 km from there to Laverton. It's then 361 km on sealed road to Kalgoorlie. For 300 km, near the Giles Meteorological Station, the Warburton Rd and the Gunbarrel Highway run on the same route. Taking the old Gunbarrel (to the north of the Warburton) all the way to Wiluna is a much rougher trip requiring 4WD. The Warburton Rd is now commonly referred to as the Gunbarrel – just to make life simple.

Tanami Track Turning off the Stuart Highway just north of Alice Springs, the Tanami Track goes north-west across the Tanami Desert to Halls Creek in WA. It's a popular short cut for people travelling between the centre and the Kimberley. The road has been extensively improved in recent years and conventional vehicles are quite OK although there are occasional sandy stretches on the WA section. Be warned that the Rabbit Flat Roadhouse in the middle of the desert is only open from Friday to Monday.

Canning Stock Route This old stock trail runs south-west from Halls Creek to Wiluna in WA. It crosses the Great Sandy Desert and Gibson Desert, and since the track has not been maintained for over 30 years, it's a route to be taken seriously. Like the Simpson Desert crossing you should only travel in a well-equipped party and careful navigation is required. Two good books on the route are Ronele & Eric Gard's *Canning Stock Route: A Traveller's Guide for a Journey through History* (Western Desert Guides, Wembley, 1990) and the *Australian Geographic Book of the Canning Stock Route* (Australian Geographic, Terrey Hills, 1992).

Gibb River Rd This is the short cut between Derby and Kununurra, and runs through the heart of the spectacular Kimberley in north-

ern WA. Although fairly badly corrugated in places, it can be negotiated with care by conventional vehicles in the dry season and is 720 km, compared with about 920 km via the bitumen Northern Highway. For more information see Gibb River Rd in the Kimberley chapter.

Buying a Car

If you want to explore WA by car and haven't got one or can't borrow one, then you've either got to buy or rent one. Australian cars are not cheap – another product of the small population. Locally manufactured cars are made in small, uneconomic numbers and imported cars are heavily taxed so they won't undercut the local products. If you're buying a second-hand vehicle, reliability is all important. Mechanical breakdowns in the outback can be very inconvenient (and dangerous) – the nearest mechanic can be a hell of a long way down the road.

Shopping around for a used car involves much the same rules as anywhere in the Western world but with a few local variations. First of all, used-car dealers in Australia are just like used-car dealers from Los Angeles to London – they'd sell their mother into slavery if it turned a dollar. For any given car you'll probably get it cheaper by buying privately through newspaper ads (Saturday's *West Australian*) rather than through a car dealer. Buying through a dealer does give the advantage of some sort of guarantee, but a guarantee is not much use if you're buying a car in Perth and intend setting off for Sydney next week. Used-car guarantee requirements vary from state to state – check with the RACWA in Perth.

There's much discussion amongst travellers about where is the best place to buy used cars. Popular theories exist that you can buy a car in Sydney or Melbourne, drive it to Darwin or Perth and sell it there for a profit. Or was it vice versa? It's quite possible that prices do vary but don't count on turning it to your advantage.

What is rather more certain is that the further you get from civilisation, the better it is to be in a Holden or a Ford. New cars can be a whole different ball game of course, but if you're in an older vehicle, something that's likely to have the odd hiccup from time to time, then life is much simpler if it's a car for which you can get spare parts anywhere from Kununurra to Kellerberrin. When your fancy Japanese car goes kaput near the remote Mt Augustus or Collier Range national parks, it's likely to be a month wait while the new part arrives fresh from Fukuoka. On the other hand, when your rusty old Holden goes bang there's probably another old Holden sitting in a ditch with a perfectly good widget waiting to be removed. Every scrap yard in Australia is full of good ole Holdens.

Remember that in Australia, third-party personal injury insurance is always included in the vehicle registration cost. This ensures that every vehicle (as long as it's currently registered) carries at least minimum insurance. You're wise to extend that minimum to at least third-party property insurance as well – minor collisions with Rolls Royces can be amazingly expensive.

When you come to buy or sell a car, there are usually some local regulations to be complied with. In WA a car has to have a compulsory safety check (Road Worthiness Certificate – RWC) before it can be registered in the new owner's name – usually the seller will indicate if the car already has a RWC. Stamp duty has to be paid when you buy a car and, as this is based on the purchase price, it's not unknown for buyer and seller to agree privately to understate the price! It's much easier to sell a car in the same state that it's registered in, otherwise it will have to be re-registered in the new state. It may be possible to sell a car without re-registering it, but you're likely to get a lower price.

One way of getting around the hassles of buying and selling a vehicle privately is to enter into a buy-back arrangement with a car or motorcycle dealer. However, dealers will often find ways of knocking down the price when you return the vehicle, even if a price has been agreed in writing – often by pointing out expensive repairs that allegedly will be required to gain the dreaded RWC needed to transfer the registration.

The cars on offer have often been driven around Australia a number of times, often with haphazard or minimal servicing, and are generally pretty tired. The main advantage of these schemes is that you don't have to worry about being able to sell the vehicle quickly at the end of your trip, and can usually arrange insurance, which short-term visitors may find hard to get.

A company that specialises in buy-back arrangements on cars and motorcycles, with fixed rates and no hidden extras, is Car Connection Australia. Also known as Bike Tours Australia, it has been organising adventure holidays and expeditions covering the entire continent for over 10 years, and has recently branched into this sideline venture. Its programme is basically a glorified long-term rental arrangement where you put down a deposit to the value of the vehicle and in the end you get your money back, minus the fixed 'usage' fee.

The bottom line is that a second-hand Ford station wagon or Yamaha XT600 trail bike will set you back a fixed sum of $1950 for any period up to six months; a Toyota Land Cruiser, suitable for serious outback exploration, is $3500, also for up to six months. Prices include pick-up at Melbourne Airport and a night's accommodation in Castlemaine to help you acclimatise, and you'll be sent on your way with touring maps and advice. You can also rent camping equipment (but not sleeping bags). Car Connection Australia (☎ (054) 73 4469; fax (054) 73 4520) is at RSD Lot 8, Vaughan Springs Rd, Glenluce (near Castlemaine), Victoria 3451. Information and bookings are handled by its European agent: Travel Action GmbH (☎ (49-2764) 7824; fax 7938), Einsiedeleiweg 16, 57399 Kirchhundem, Germany.

Finally, make use of the RACWA – see the Facts for the Visitor chapter for more details about this organisation. It can advise you on any local regulations you should be aware of, give general guidelines about buying a car and, most importantly, for a fee (around $70) will check over a used car and report on its condition before you agree to purchase it. It also offers car insurance to its members.

Two really useful, free publications for the do-it-yourself motorists are *Across Australia* and *Perth to Darwin* (Leisure Time Publications, Perth). They are particularly good for pointing out places of interest and include advertisements for the important road-houses. *Self Drive Tours Within WA* lists 14 of the state's most popular drives; it is available free from the WATC. Gregory's *Touring Guides* cover the Great Southern, south-east and goldfields, Mandurah and Murray and Northern Agricultural regions.

Renting a Car

If you've got the cash there are plenty of car-rental companies ready and willing to put you behind the wheel. Competition in the WA car-rental business is pretty fierce so rates tend to be variable and lots of special deals pop up and disappear again. Whatever your mode of transport, it can be very useful to have a car for local travel. Between a group it can even be economical. There are places in the state – if you haven't a car – where you'll have to choose between a tour and a rented vehicle since there is no public transport and the distances are too great for walking or even bicycles.

The three major companies are Budget, Hertz and Avis, with offices in the main towns – all three have offices in Broome, Carnarvon, Derby, Exmouth and Kununurra, for example.

The big firms have a number of advantages, however. First of all, they're the ones at the airports – Avis, Budget, Hertz and, quite often, Thrifty. If you want to pick up a car or leave a car at the airport, then they're the best ones to deal with. In some, but not all airports, other companies will also arrange to pick up or leave their cars there. It tends to depend on how convenient the airport is.

One-way rentals are generally not available into or out of the Northern Territory or WA. Special rules may also apply to one-ways into or out of other 'remote areas'.

Daily rates are about $70 a day for a small car (Ford Laser, Toyota Corolla, Nissan Pulsar), about $90 a day for a medium car

(Holden Camira, Toyota Camry, Nissan Pintara) or about $100 to $110 a day for a big car (Holden Commodore, Ford Falcon), all including insurance.

There is a whole collection of other factors to bear in mind about this rent-a-car business. For a start, if you're going to want it for a week or longer then they all have lower rates. You usually must be at least 21 to hire from most firms.

OK, that's the big hire companies. What about the rest of them? Well, some of them are still pretty big in terms of numbers of shiny new cars. There's a plethora of hire companies and lots of competition. In many cases local companies are markedly cheaper than the big boys, but in others, what looks like a cheaper rate can end up quite the opposite if you're not careful. In Perth there is a lot to choose from and this list is by no means exhaustive:

ATC Rent-a-Car
126 Adelaide Terrace, Perth (☎ (09) 325 1833)
Ace Rent-a-Car
311 Hay St, Perth (☎ (09) 221 333)
Action Hire Cars
652 Albany Highway, Victoria Park (☎ (09) 472 1722)
Apex Car Rentals
400 William St, Northbridge (☎ (09) 227 9091)
Bayswater Car Rental
160 Adelaide Terrace, Perth (☎ (09) 325 1000, 430 5300)
Carousel Rent-a-Car
1971 Albany Highway, Maddington (☎ (09) 459 9999)
Economic Car Rentals
179 William St, Northbridge (☎ (09) 227 1112)
Ezidrive Car Rentals
90 Newcastle St, Perth (☎ (09) 227 6699)
Geddes Car Rentals
36A Geddes St, Victoria Park (☎ (09) 361 7388)
Magic Car Rental
164 Leach Highway, Melville (☎ (09) 330 7000)
Network Vehicle Rentals
253 William St, Northbridge (next to Britannia YHA Hostel) (☎ (09) 227 8810); 207 Great Eastern Highway, Midland (☎ (09) 250 2216)
Perth Rent-a-Car
338 Charles St, North Perth (☎ (09) 227 8555)
Swan Car Rentals
368 Guildford Rd, Bayswater (☎ (09) 271 4813)
Thrifty Car Rental
33 Milligan St, Perth (☎ (09) 481 1999)

Topless Rentals
    58 Hunter St, Broome (☎ (091) 93 5017)

Companies are eager to get you to rent if you are restricting yourself to Perth and surrounding environs. Tell them you plan to go further afield and the daily rate zooms upwards. Mere mention of the 'bush' attracts price hikes like uncovered meat does flies.

And don't forget the 'rent-a-wreck' companies. They specialise in renting older cars – at first they really were old, and a flat rate like '$12 a day and forget the insurance' was the usual story. Now many of them have a variety of rates, typically around $35 a day. If you just want to travel around the city, or not too far out, they can be worth considering. A couple of contacts are:

Letz Rent a Car
    126 Grandstand St, Belmont (☎ (09) 478 1999)
Rent a Heap
    368 Guildford Rd, Bayswater (☎ (09) 272 2206)

4WDs A 4WD enables you to get off the beaten track and see some great wilderness and outback regions (Purnululu or the Kimberley).

Renting a 4WD vehicle is within the budget range if a few people get together. Something small like a Suzuki or similar costs around $100 per day; for a Toyota Landcruiser you're looking at around $150, which should include insurance and some free km (typically 100 km). Check the insurance conditions, especially the excess, as they can be onerous. A few places to check are:

Osborne Rentals
    528 Hannan St, Kalgoorlie (☎ (090) 21 4722)
South Perth 4WD Rentals
    80 Canning Highway, Victoria Park (☎ (09) 362 5444)
Woody's 4WD Hire
    corner of Frederick & Herbert Sts, Broome (☎ (091) 92 1791)

Campervans Brits Australia (☎ (1800) 331 454) is a company which hires fully equipped 4WD vehicles fitted out as campervans. These have proved extremely popular in WA in recent years, although they are not cheap at $155 per day for unlimited km, plus Collision Damage Waiver ($15 per day). It has offices in all the mainland capitals, so one-way rentals are also possible.

Another company which hires out camper rentals is Koala Campers (☎ (09) 478 3973); its 4WD cruiser sleeps four and is equipped with an erect rooftop camper conversion; depending on the season these vehicles cost from $175 to $195 per day. You would definitely need four passengers to make this rental worthwhile. Its camping utes are cheaper but only accommodate two persons; expect to pay from $85 to $110 per day.

MOTORCYCLE
Motorcycles are a very popular way of getting around. The climate is just about ideal for biking much of the year, and the many small trails from the road into the bush often lead to perfect spots to spend the night in the world's largest camping ground.

The long, open roads are really made for large-capacity machines above 750cc, which Australians prefer once they outgrow their 250cc learner restrictions. But that doesn't stop enterprising individuals – many of them Japanese – from tackling the length and breadth of the continent on 250cc trail bikes. Doing it on a small bike is not impossible, just tedious at times.

If you want to bring your own motorcycle into Australia you'll need a *carnet de passage*, and when you try to sell it you'll get less than the market price because of restrictive registration requirements (not so severe in WA). Shipping from just about anywhere is expensive.

However, with a little bit of time up your sleeve, getting mobile on two wheels in Australia is quite feasible, thanks largely to the chronically depressed motorcycle market. Australian newspapers and the lively local bike press have extensive classified advertisement sections where $2500 gets you something that will easily take you around the country if you know a bit about bikes.

The main drawback is that you'll have to try and sell it again afterwards.

An easier option is a buy-back arrangement with a large motorcycle dealer in a major city. They're keen to do business, and basic negotiating skills allied with a wad of cash (say, $8000) should secure an excellent second-hand bike with a written guarantee that they'll buy it back in good condition minus $1500 after your four-month, round-Australia trip. Popular brands for this sort of thing are BMWs, large-capacity, shaft-driven Japanese bikes and possibly Harley-Davidson's (very popular in Australia). The percentage drop on a 600cc trail bike (for, say, $3000) will be much greater, though the amount should be similar – if you can find a dealer willing to come to the party.

You'll need a rider's licence and a helmet. A fuel range of 350 km will cover fuel stops up the Inland Route and on Highway 1 around the coast. Beware of dehydration in the dry, hot air – force yourself to drink plenty of water, even if you don't feel thirsty.

The 'roo bars' (outsize bumpers) on interstate trucks and many outback cars warn you never to ride at night, or in the early morning and evening. Marsupials are nocturnal, sleeping in the shade during the day and feeding at night, and road ditches often provide lush grass for them to eat. Cattle and sheep also stray onto the roads at night. It's wise to stop riding by around 5 pm. Many roadhouses offer showers free of charge or for a nominal fee. They're meant for truck drivers, but other people often use them too.

It's worth carrying some spares and tools even if you don't know how to use them, because someone else often does. If you do know, you'll probably have a fair idea of what to take. The basics include: a spare tyre tube (front wheel size, which will fit on the rear but usually not vice versa); puncture repair kit with levers and a pump (or tubeless tyre repair kit with two or three carbon-dioxide cartridges); a spare tyre valve, and a valve cap that can unscrew same; the bike's standard tool kit for what it's worth (aftermarket items are better); spare throttle, clutch and brake cables; tie wire, cloth tape

('gaffer' tape) and nylon 'zip-ties'; a handful of bolts and nuts in the usual emergency sizes (M6 and M8), along with a few self-tapping screws; one or two fuses in your bike's ratings; a bar of soap for fixing tank leaks (knead to a putty with water and squeeze into the leak); and, most important of all, a workshop manual for your bike (even if you can't make sense of it, the local motorcycle mechanic can). You'll never have enough elastic straps (octopus or 'ocky' straps) to tie down your gear.

Make sure you carry water everywhere – at least two litres on major roads in WA, and much more off the beaten track. In 1993, a foreign motorcyclist headed off to do the Warburton Rd with a couple if cheap plastic containers of water which subsequently leaked. A major search ensued and the rider was lucky to be found alive.

So finally, if something does go hopelessly wrong in the back of beyond, park your bike where it's clearly visible and observe the cardinal rule: don't leave your vehicle!

BICYCLE

Whether you're hiring a bike to ride around Rottnest Island or wearing out your Bio-Ace chain-wheels on a trans-Nullarbor marathon, you'll find that WA is a great place for cycling. There are lots of bike tracks in Perth, and in the country you'll find thousands of km of good roads which carry so little traffic that the biggest hassle is waving back to the drivers. Especially appealing is that in many areas you'll ride a very long way without encountering a hill.

It's possible to plan rides of any duration and through almost any terrain. A day or two cycling around the Margaret River wineries is popular, or you could tackle the Bibbulman Walking Track over a week or so on a mountain bike.

Cycling has always been popular here, and not only as a sport: some shearers would ride for huge distances between jobs, rather than use less reliable horses. It's rare to find a town that doesn't have a shop stocking at least basic bike parts. A list of approved bike shops should be available from the Cycle Touring Association of WA, PO Box 174, Wembley WA 6014.

If you're coming specifically to cycle, it makes sense to bring your own bike. Check your airline for costs and the degree of dismantling/packing required. Within WA you can load your bike onto a bus to skip the boring bits. Bus companies require you to dismantle your bike (and some don't guarantee that it will travel on the same bus as you).

You can get by with standard road maps, but as you'll probably want to avoid both the highways and the low-grade unsealed roads, the government series is best. The 1:250,000 scale is the most suitable but you'll need a lot of maps if you're covering much territory. The next scale up, 1:1,000,000, is adequate. These, and the excellent series of RACWA maps, are available in Perth and elsewhere.

Until you get fit you should be careful to eat enough to keep you going – remember that exercise is an appetite suppressant. It's surprisingly easy to exhaust yourself and end up camping under a gum tree just 10 km short of a shower and a steak.

No matter how fit you are, water is still vital. Dehydration is no joke and can be life-threatening. It can get very hot in summer, and you should take things slowly until you're used to the heat. Cycling in 35°C-plus temperatures isn't too bad if you wear a hat and plenty of sunscreen, and drink *lots* of water.

Of course, you don't have to follow the larger roads and visit towns. It's possible to fill your mountain bike's panniers with muesli, head out into the bush, and not see anyone for weeks. Or ever again – outback travel is very risky if not properly planned. Water is the main problem in the 'dead heart', and you can't rely on it where there aren't settlements. That tank marked on your map may be dry or the water from it unfit for humans, and those station buildings probably blew away years ago. That little creek marked with a dotted blue line? Forget it – the only time it has water is when the country's flooded for hundreds of km.

Always check with locals if you're heading into remote areas, and notify the police if you're about to do something particularly adventurous. That said, you can't rely too much on local knowledge of road conditions – most people have no idea of what a heavily loaded touring bike needs. What they think of as a great road may be pedal-deep in sand or bull dust, and cyclists have happily ridden along roads that were officially flooded out.

Bicycle helmets are compulsory wear in all states and territories.

HITCHING

Hitching is never entirely safe in any country in the world, and we don't recommend it. Travellers who decide to hitch should understand that they are taking a small but potentially serious risk. However, many people do choose to hitch, and the advice that follows should help to make their journeys as fast and safe as possible.

Travel by thumb can be a good way of getting around and it is certainly interesting. Sometimes it can even be fast, but it's usually foolish to try and set yourself deadlines when travelling this way – you need luck. Successful hitching depends on several factors, all of them involves common sense.

The most important is your numbers – two people are really the ideal, any more may make things difficult. Ideally those two should comprise one male and one female – two guys hitching together can expect long waits. It is not advisable for women to hitch alone, or even in pairs.

Another major consideration is knowing when to say no. Saying no to a car-load of drunks is pretty obvious, but it can be time-saving to say no to a short ride that might take you from a good hitching point to a lousy one. Wait for the right, long ride to come along.

If you're visiting from abroad, a nice prominent flag on your pack will help, and a sign announcing your destination can also be useful. Uni and hostel notice boards are good places to look for hitching partners. Remember not to stand in the road, and step back when you see the law coming.

FERRY

There are ferry operations that you will possibly use when in WA: Transperth's from the city to South Perth and a number of operators who travel from Fremantle and Perth to Rottnest Island. For information on these services, see under Local Transport in the Perth chapter and Rottnest Island in the Around Perth chapter.

TOURS

There are all sorts of tours available in WA including some interesting camping tours, many which originate in Perth. Adventure tours include 4WD safaris – some of these go to places you simply couldn't get to on your own without large amounts of expensive equipment. The tours listed here are only a sample of what is available; check with the local tourist information office.

Australian Pacific Tours
    Bus, the 20-day Westcoaster is a Perth to Darwin trip which includes Monkey Mia, Hamersley Gorges, Broome, flight over Purnululu and Kakadu; $2265 (☎ (09) 221 1163).
Milesaway Tours
    4WD, five and eight-day trips in the south-west including Hyden, Stirling Ranges, Margaret River, Albany and Esperance; from $340 (☎ (097) 55 3574).
Overland 4WD Safaris
    4WD, five-day trip which includes Wolleen Station, Monkey Mia, Kalbarri Gorges, the Pinnacles; $399 (☎ (09) 354 4396).
Pathfinder (Ansett)
    Bus, 12-day Kimberley Top End Explorer includes Broome, Giekie Gorge, Wyndham, Lake Argyle and a flight over Purnululu; $2300 (☎ (09) 354 4396).
Travelabout
    4WD, a number of options including a 10-day Hamersley Range tour, a 16-day Purnululu-Kakadu tour and four-day Monkey Mia-Kalbarri-Pinnacles tour; $750, $1300, $280 respectively (☎ (09) 244 1200).

STUDENT TRAVEL

STA Travel is the main agent for student travellers in Australia. It has a network of travel offices around the country and apart from selling normal tickets also has special student discounts and tours. STA Travel doesn't only cater to students, it also acts as normal travel agents to the public in general. The STA Travel head office (☎ (03) 818 0645) is in Faraday St, Melbourne, but there are a number of other offices around the various cities and at the universities. The main office (☎ (09) 382 3977) in WA is at 426 Hay St, Subiaco 6008.

Perth

Population: 1,400,000

Perth is a vibrant and modern city, pleasantly sited on the Swan and Canning rivers, with the cerulean Indian Ocean to the west and the ancient Darling Ranges to the east. It's claimed to be the sunniest state capital in Australia and the most isolated capital city in the world. Of WA's 1.8 million people, almost 80% live in and around Perth – and a fair percentage of the 80% are intent on enjoying the type of easy-going lifestyle which an equable climate fosters.

The city centre, with its sterile concrete and glass skyscrapers, unfortunately dominates a site which has the potential, with its picturesque riverside location, to be stunning. These domineering edifices now hide a handful of 19th-century buildings and facades, and some beleaguered patches of greenery.

Away from this cluttered rectangle of commerce and public service, there is indeed a beautiful city, enhanced by the Indian Ocean beaches, the hillside hideaways, romantic Fremantle, cosmopolitan Subiaco and the select, comfortable suburbs which fringe the Swan River.

History

The site that is now Perth had been occupied by groups of the Nyungar tribe for thousands of years. They, and their ancestors, can be traced back some 40,000 years (verified by discoveries of stone implements near the Swan Bridge).

In December 1696, three ships in the fleet commanded by de Vlamingh – *Nijptangh*, *Geelvinck* and *Het Weseltje* – anchored off Rottnest Island. On 5 January 1697, a well-armed party landed near present-day Cottesloe Beach then marched eastwards to the Swan River near Freshwater Bay. They tried to contact some of the Nyungar to enquire about the fate of survivors of the *Ridderschap van Hollant*, lost in 1694, but were unsuccessful. They sailed north, but not

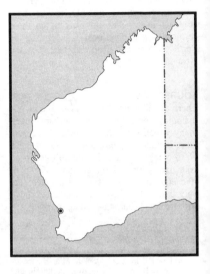

before de Vlamingh had bestowed the name 'Swan' on the river.

Perth was founded in 1829 as the Swan River Settlement, but it grew very slowly until 1850, when convicts were brought in to alleviate the labour shortage. Many of Perth's fine buildings such as Government House and Perth Town Hall were built using convict labour. Even then, Perth's development lagged behind that of the eastern cities, until the discovery of gold in the 1890s increased the population four-fold in a decade and initiated a building boom. Many of these 19th-century buildings have since disappeared amid a deluge of concrete and questionable architectural taste.

Western Australia's mineral wealth has undeniably contributed to Perth's growth, sparking further construction in the outer suburbs. A somewhat squeaky-clean, nouveau-riche image has been tainted by scandals such as WA Inc but it all seems to add to the town's frontier image.

Orientation

The city centre is fairly compact, situated on a sweep of the Swan River. The river, which borders the city centre to the south and east, links Perth to its port, Fremantle. The main shopping precinct in the city is along the Hay St and Murray St malls and the arcades that run between them. St George's Terrace is the hub of the city's business district.

The railway line bounds the city centre on the northern side. Immediately north of the railway line is Northbridge, a popular restaurant and entertainment enclave with a number of hostels and cheap accommodation. The western end of Perth rises to the pleasant Kings Park, which overlooks the city and Swan River and then further on to cosmopolitan Subiaco. Further to the west, suburbs extend as far as Scarborough and Cottesloe beaches on the Indian Ocean.

Information

Tourist Offices The Western Australian Tourist Centre (WATC) (☎ 483 1111) is in Albert Facey House in Forrest Place, on the corner of Wellington St and opposite the railway station. The centre is open from 8.30 am to 5.30 pm Monday to Friday and from 9 am to 1 pm Saturday.

It has a wide range of maps and brochures on Perth and WA, and an accommodation and tours reservation service. The Pinnacles Travel Centre, on the corner of Hay and Pier Sts, acts as the information centre on Saturday afternoon and on Sunday until noon.

A number of guides to Perth including *Hello Perth & Fremantle, What's On This Week in...Perth & Fremantle, This Week in Perth & Fremantle, West Coast Visitor's Guide* and the *Map of Perth & Fremantle* are available free at the tourist centre, hostels and hotels. There is a 24-hour tourist information line (☎ 0055 12572); the maximum call charge is $1.

Useful Organisations The Royal Automobile Club of Western Australia (RACWA) (☎ 421 4444) is at 228 Adelaide Terrace. Its bookshop has an excellent travel section, and detailed regional maps can be obtained at its Road Travel counter. The Perth Map Centre (☎ 322 5733), 891 Hay St, has the full range of maps including the excellent StreetSmart touring series.

Disabled visitors can use the services of ACROD (☎ 222 2961), 189 Royal St, East Perth. Paraquad (☎ 381 0173) will advise about accommodation with disabled access.

The YHA (☎ 227 5122) has its office at 65 Francis St in Northbridge. The staff here really care about the visitor to WA and will hunt around for the best travel bargains.

Post & Telecommunications Perth's GPO (☎ 326 5211) is in Forrest Place which runs between Wellington St and the Murray St Mall. There are phones for international calls in the foyer of the GPO. The GPO provides a post office service between 8 am and 6 pm Monday to Friday and 9 am to noon Saturday. You only have to telephone ☎ 131318 to be automatically connected to the post office nearest to where you are calling from. The STD telephone area code for Perth is 09.

Bookshops Some good city bookshops include Angus & Robertson, 199 Murray St and 625 Hay St; Dymocks, Hay St Mall; and the Down to Earth Bookshop, 790 Hay St. For a more esoteric selection try the Arcane Bookshop, 212 William St, Northbridge.

Kings Park

There are superb views across Perth and the river from this four-sq-km park, which is very much the lungs of the city centre. It includes a 17-hectare **Botanic Garden** that displays over 2000 different plant species from WA and a section of natural bushland, ie bush as it was before White settlement. In spring, there's a cultivated display of WA's famed wildflowers.

Free guided tours of Kings Park and the Botanic Garden are available all year. The park also has a number of bike tracks; bikes can be rented from Koala Bicycle Hire (☎ 321 3061) at the western side of the main car park. An information centre, situated next to the car park, is open daily from 9.30

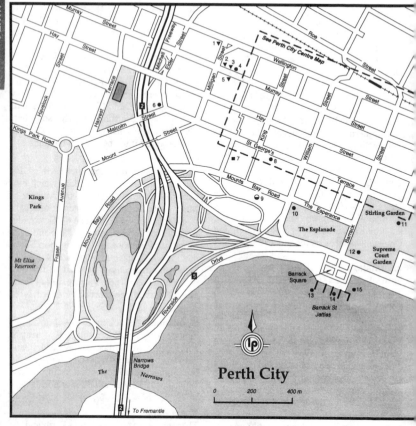

Perth City

am to 3.30 pm. The park also has a restaurant with a pleasant coffee shop.

To get there, catch bus No 33 from St George's Terrace, the Green Clipper to Kings Park entrance or walk up Mount St from the city, then cross the freeway overpass.

City Buildings

There are a few architectural remnants of yesteryear but you need the archaeological tenacity and guile of Indiana Jones to find them. The **Cloisters,** near the corner of King St and St George's Terrace, date from 1858 and are noted for their beautiful brickwork.

Originally a school, they have now been integrated into a modern office development.

On the corner of St George's Terrace and Pier St is the **Deanery,** which was built in 1859 and restored after a public appeal in 1980. It is one of the few existing cottage-style houses that survive from the period. Neither the Cloisters nor the Deanery are open to the public.

Opposite the Deanery, on St George's Terrace, is **Government House**, a Gothic-style, fantastical building built between 1859 and 1864. The grand **Palace Hotel**, at the corner of St George's Terrace and William

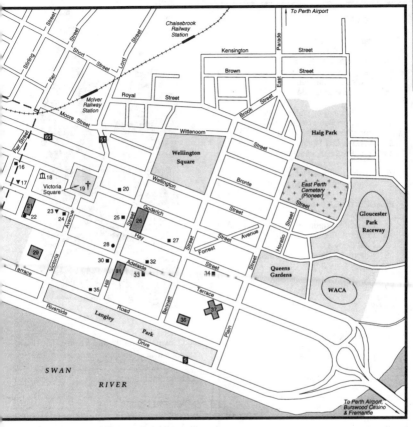

To Perth Airport

Chaisebrook
Railway
Station

Kensington   Street

Brown   Street

Royal   Street

McIver
Railway
Station

Moore Street

Wittenoom

Haig Park

■16

▼17

Victoria
Square

🏛18

19 †

■ 20

Wellington
Square

East Perth
Cemetery
(Pioneer)

Gloucester
Park
Raceway

Bronte   Street

21
22

23 ▼
24

25 ■

Goderich

26

Hay

28 ●

30 ■

81

Adelaide

33 ■

■32

Street

Forrest

34 ■

Queens
Gardens

WACA

29

27

35

Terrace

Riverside

Langley

Road

Park

Drive

37

36

SWAN

RIVER

5

To Perth Airport,
Burswood Casino
& Fremantle

St, dates back to 1895 and is now a banking chamber.

In the Stirling Gardens, off Barrack St, is the old **courthouse**, next to the Supreme Court. One of the oldest buildings in Perth, it was built in Georgian style in 1836. Other old buildings include **Perth Town Hall** on the corner of Hay and Barrack Sts (1867-70); the **Central Government Buildings** on the corner of Barrack St and St George's Terrace, which can be recognised by their patterned brick; the recently restored Edwardian **His Majesty's Theatre** (originally opened in 1904) on the corner of King and Hay Sts; the

Treasury, on the corner of Barrack St and St George's Terrace, an example of a fine colonial building dating from 1874; and the Gothic-style **Old Perth Boys' School**, 139 St George's Terrace, which was built in 1854 and now houses a National Trust gift shop.

The distinctive **Barracks Arch**, at the western end of St George's Terrace, is all that remains of a barracks built in 1863 to house the Pensioner Guards of the British Army – discharged British Army soldiers who guarded convicts.

The **Pioneer Cemetery** in Bronte St, East Perth, was used from 1830 to 1899. The

PLACES TO STAY

7 Parmelia Hilton
16 Inntown Hotel
20 YMCA Jewell House
21 Perth International Hotel
24 Chateau Commodore Hotel
25 Downtowner Lodge
27 Carlton Hotel
30 Quality Langley Hotel
31 Sheraton Perth Hotel
32 Perth Ambassador Hotel
33 Airways City Hotel
34 East Perth Backpackers'
35 City Waters Lodge
36 Perth Parkroyal Hotel
37 Hyatt Regency Perth Hotel

PLACES TO EAT

1 Firenze Restaurant, Passage to India, Orchard Village
2 Fast Eddy's
3 Katong Singapore Restaurant
5 Lenox Cafe & Bar
17 Benardi's
23 Magic Apple Wholefoods

OTHER

4 Rumours
6 Barracks Arch
8 Old Perth Boys School
9 Perth City Bus Port
10 Allan Green Plant Conservatory
11 Government House
12 Orchestral Shell
13 Transperth Ferries to South Perth
14 Ferries to Rottnest Island
15 Swan River Cruises
18 Fire Brigade Museum
19 St Mary's Catholic Cathedral
22 Ansett Airlines
26 Perth Mint
28 Royal Automobile Club of WA
29 Perth Concert Hall

Perth Town Hall

National Trust (☎ 321 6088) conducts free one-hour tours of the chapel and graves of interest (or is that places of grave interest?) every Sunday at 2 and 2.30 pm.

You can take an informative heritage day-tour of Perth which includes most of the historic buildings. Davis Tours (☎ 322 7654) depart every Monday and Friday at 9.10 am and return at 5.15 pm; the cost is $67 for adults (children $52) and morning tea and lunch are included.

Parliament House

Tours of the Parliament buildings on Harvest Terrace can be arranged from Monday to Friday through the Parliamentary Information Officer (☎ 222 7222) – you will get a more extensive tour when Parliament is not in session. You can get there on the Purple Clipper from St George's Terrace or by the Green Clipper to Harvest Terrace.

Museums

On Francis St, north across the railway lines from the city centre, is the **WA Museum**, which includes an excellent gallery of Aboriginal culture, a marine gallery with a 25-metre whale skeleton, vintage cars, a gallery of dinosaur casts and a good collection of meteorites, the largest of which is the

Mundrabilla specimen which weighs 11 tonnes. (The Australian outback is a rich source of meteorites.)

The museum complex also includes Perth's original **prison**, built in 1856 and used until 1888. Admission to the museum is free and it is open from 10.30 am to 5 pm Monday to Friday and from 1 to 5 pm Saturday and Sunday.

There are four other museums close to town. The **WA Fire Brigade Museum**, on the corner of Irwin and Murray Sts, has

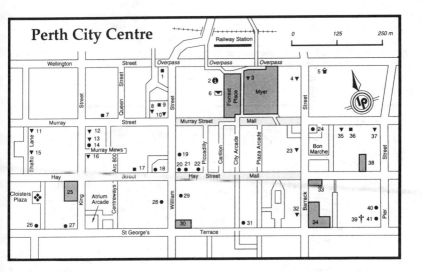

PLACES TO STAY

1 Royal Hotel
5 Grand Central YMCA
7 Quality Princes Hotel
9 Wentworth Plaza Hotel
17 Perth Townhouse Travelodge
36 Murray St International Hostel
38 Hotel Regatta

PLACES TO EAT

3 McDonalds
4 Ann's Malaysian Restaurant
10 Bobby Dazzler's
11 Iguana Cafe & Bar
12 City Hotel
13 No 44 King St
15 Buzz Bar
16 Figaro's
23 Mr Samurai
32 Granary Wholefoods
35 Jun & Tommy's Japanese Restaurant
37 Miss Maud's

OTHER

2 Western Australia Tourist Centre
6 General Post Office
8 Moon & Sixpence Bar
14 Creative Native Gallery
18 Thomas Cook
19 British Airways
20 American Express
21 Ansett Australia
22 Piccadilly Cinema
24 Cinecentre
25 His Majesty's Theatre
26 The Cloisters
27 United Airlines
28 Qantas Airlines
29 Malaysia Airlines
30 Old Palace Hotel
31 South African Airlines
33 Town Hall
34 Old Government Buildings
39 St George's Anglican Cathedral
40 Playhouse Theatre
41 The Deanery

displays on fire safety and fire-fighting equipment. It is housed in a limestone building which became the headquarters of the Perth City Fire Brigade in 1901. The museum is open Monday to Thursday from 10 am to 3 pm and admission is free.

The **Mines Department Museum**, in Plain St on the corner of Adelaide Terrace, features rocks, minerals and fossils and has occasional interest displays. It's open from 9 am to 5 pm on weekdays.

The **It's a Small World Museum**, at 12 Parliament Place, has the largest array of collectable toys, miniatures and dolls houses in the country; it is open Sunday to Friday from 10 am to 5 pm and Saturday 2 to 5 pm. The **Army Museum of WA**, on the corner of Bulwer and Lord Sts, has a display of army memorabilia; it is open 1 to 4.30 pm Sunday or at other times by arrangement (☎ 227 9269) and admission is free.

In the Social Sciences Building of the University of WA, off Hackett Drive, Nedlands, is the excellent **Berndt Museum of Anthropology**. This is one of Australia's finest collections of traditional and contem-

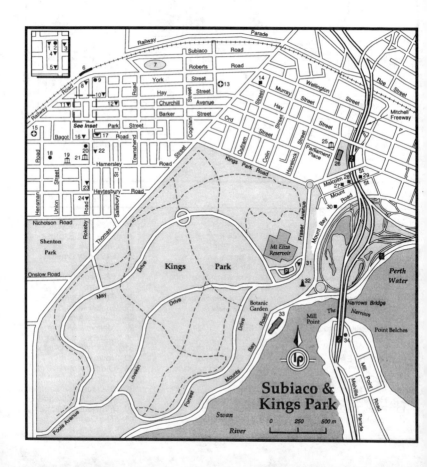

Subiaco & Kings Park

porary Australian Aboriginal art and artefacts. It combines material from Arnhem Land in the Northern Territory and the southwest, desert and Kimberley regions of WA. The museum is open from 2 to 4.30 pm

PLACES TO STAY

14   Murray Lodge Motel
27   Perth Riverview Holiday Apartments
28   Mountway Holiday Units
29   The Mount St Inn
30   Adelphi Hotel Apartments

PLACES TO EAT

1   Oriel Cafe & Brasserie
3   Subiaco Hotel
4   Witch's Cauldron Restaurant, Cafe Pizzo
5   Duck Inn Bar & Restaurant
8   Bar Bzar
10   Redd's Cafe
11   Subiaco Village Shopping Centre, Henry's Cafe & Grill
12   Subiaco Mews: Subiaco Steakhouse
16   Monet's Cafe
22   Chanterelle Restaurant
23   Bretzel Patisserie
24   The Very Serious Cafe, Little Lebanon
31   Frasers Restaurant, Kings Park Restaurant

OTHER

2   Regal Theatre
6   Subiaco Railway Station
7   Subiaco Oval
9   Subiaco Pavilion (Markets)
13   Princess Margaret Hospital
15   King Edward Women's Hospital
17   Post Office, Crossways Shopping Centre
18   Hole in the Wall Theatre
19   Museum of Childhood
20   Public Library
21   Historical Museum
25   It's a Small World Museum
26   Parliament House
28   Entrance to Kings Park
32   War Memorial
33   Old Swan Brewery
34   Old Mill

Monday and Wednesday and Friday from 10 am to 2 pm; admission is free.

Perth Zoo

Perth's popular zoo is set in attractive gardens across the river from the city at 20 Labouchere Rd, South Perth. It has a number of interesting collections including a nocturnal house which is open daily from noon to 3 pm, an Australian Wildlife Park, a numbat display and a Conservation Discovery Centre.

The zoo itself is open from 10 am to 5 pm daily and admission is $6 (children $2). You can reach the zoo on bus Nos 110 or 108 (on weekends it leaves from bus stand No 42 on St George's Terrace) or by taking the ferry across the river from Barrack St jetty.

Underwater World

One place deserving of special mention is Underwater World, north of the city, at Hillarys Boat Harbour, West Coast Drive, Hillarys. This is not your run-of-the-mill aquarium. There is an underwater tunnel aquarium displaying 2500 examples of 200 marine species including sharks and stingrays. There are also interactive displays such as a Touch Pool, Microworld and an audiovisual theatre. In season they conduct three-hour whalewatching trips to see humpbacks. Underwater World is open daily from 9 am to 5 pm and entry costs $13.50 ($6.50 for children and $33.50 for families). Watch the expressions on the faces of the children!

Art Gallery of WA

This is housed in a modern building which runs from James St through to Roe St, behind the railway station. It has a fine exhibition of European, Australian and Asian/Pacific art and a wide variety of temporary exhibitions. The gallery is open from 10 am to 5 pm daily, and admission is free except for special exhibitions.

Perth Institute of Contemporary Arts

Commonly referred to by its abbreviation PICA, this institute is at 51 James St. PICA promotes the creation, presentation and discussion of new and experimental art. The emphasis is on non-traditional media such as video, sound and performance and the aim is to induce struggling artists out of their insular garrets. PICA is open Tuesday to Sunday from 10 am to 5 pm; admission is free.

Parks & Gardens

On the Esplanade, between the city and the river, is the **Allan Green Plant Conservatory**. It houses a tropical and semitropical controlled-environment display; admission is free. Also close to the city, on the corner of St George's Terrace and Barrack St, are the **Supreme Court Gardens**, a popular place to eat lunch.

The **Queen's Gardens**, at the eastern end of Hay St, is a pleasant little park with lakes and bridges; get there on a Red Clipper bus. The lake in **Hyde Park**, Highgate, is popular for the waterbirds it attracts, and the park is the site for the annual Hyde Park Festival – catch bus No 60 from stand No 2 in Barrack St. **Lake Monger** in Wembley is another hang-out for local feathered friends, particularly the famous black swans. Get there on bus Nos 91, 92 and 95 from opposite the Wellington St bus station (stand No 49). **Bold Park**, west of the city centre, is very popular with the locals.

Beaches

Perth residents claim that the city has the best beaches and surf of any Australian city. There are calm bay beaches on the Swan River at Crawley, Peppermint Grove and Como. Or you can try a whole string of patrolled surf beaches on the Indian Ocean coast, including Perth's very popular nude beach at **Swanbourne** which is patrolled by a Surf Life Saving Club (SLSC) – take bus Nos 205 or 207 from stand No 44 on St George's Terrace.

Some of the other surf beaches include **Port** near Fremantle; **Cottesloe**, a very safe swimming beach which is patrolled by a SLSC (bus Nos 70-73 from the city busport and 207 from stand 32 on St George's Terrace); **Leighton** (bus No 103 from stand 34 on St George's Terrace); the usually safe

City Beach patrolled by a SLSC (bus No 84 from Raine Square); the normally safe **Floreat**; popular **Scarborough**, known for its beachside cafe society, but which is great for experienced surfers and sailboarders and is patrolled by a SLSC (bus Nos 268 and 269 from platform A in the Wellington St bus station); and **Trigg Island**, another surf beach that is dangerous when rough and which is prone to rips (bus No 250 from Wellington St then transfer to No 255 at Karrinyup bus station).

To the north lies a string of good beaches. **Watermans Bay, North Beach, Hamersley** and **Mettams Pool** are small, safe bays suitable for families and inexperienced swimmers. **Burns** and **Mullaloo** are both safe family beaches and **Sorrento**, south of Hillarys Boat Harbour, is patrolled by a SLSC as surf can build up during on-shore winds.

Perhaps the best beach of all is on secluded **Carnac Island**, frequented by the odd marooned human and sea lion. (See under Rottnest Island in the Around Perth chapter.)

Markets

There are many lively markets around Perth – ideal if you're into browsing and buying. The **Subiaco Pavilion**, on the corner of Roberts and Rokeby Rds near Subiaco Railway Station, is open Thursday to Sunday. On the weekends there are street markets, comprising 130 or so stalls, near Subiaco station. These are open all day on the weekend and on Monday during public holidays.

The **Wanneroo Markets** north of Perth at Prindiville Drive, Wangara, also have a large licensed food hall and a variety of stalls; it's open on Saturday and Sunday from 9 am to 6 pm.

Other markets include the historic **Fremantle Markets** (see under Fremantle in the Around Perth chapter); the weekend **Stock Rd Markets**, on the corner of Stock Rd and Spearwood Ave in Bibra Lake, south of Perth; **Gosnells Railway Markets**, corner of Albany Highway and Fremantle Rd, open Friday to Sunday; the **Canning Vale**

Markets, on the corner of Ranford and Bannister Rds, open from 7.30 am every Sunday with room for more than 1000 stalls; and the **Midland Sunday Markets**, Crescent Car Park, Midland, open from 8 am to 4 pm.

Other Attractions
Across Narrows Bridge is one of Perth's landmarks: the finely restored **Old Mill**, built in 1835. It's open in the afternoon, except Tuesday and Friday; admission is free.

Between Hay St and St George's Terrace is the narrow, touristy **London Court**, a photographer's delight. Although it looks very Tudor English, it dates from just 1937. At one end of this shopping court, St George and the dragon do battle above the clock each quarter of an hour, while at the other end knights joust on horseback. Mega-kitsch but cute.

The **Perth Mint**, at 310 Hay St, was established in 1899, and still produces Australia's gold, silver and platinum bullion coins. A variety of coins are on display including a numismatist's delight, a one-kg nugget coin. You are allowed to touch a 400-ounce gold bar worth about $200,000. The mint is open from 9 am to 4 pm weekdays and 9 am to 1 pm on Saturday; entry is free.

The **Scitech Discovery Centre** in the City West centre, corner of Sutherland St and Railway Parade, West Perth, has over 160 hands-on and large-scale exhibits and is well worth a visit. It is open daily but admission is not cheap – $10 for adults, $7 for children.

Perth Suburbs
Armadale The Pioneer World at Armadale, 27 km south-east of the city, is a working model of a 19th-century village; it's open daily from 10 am to 5 pm and admission is $8.50. You can get to Armadale on a bus from Pier St or a local train from Perth Railway Station.

The **History House Museum**, near the corner of Church Ave and Jull St, is a free museum in a 19th-century pioneer's house. **Tumbulgum Farm**, about six km south of Armadale, has a number of Australian products for sale, and puts on Aboriginal cultural and farm shows.

On Mills Rd, in Martin, try riding a miniature railway through the **Cohunu Koala Park**, while watching native animals in natural surroundings. There are also plenty of waterbirds and a large walk-in aviary at the park. Open Wednesday to Sunday (daily during school holidays) from 10 am to 5 pm, the park's about a 35-minute drive from Perth; there is an admission fee.

Up the Swan River There are many attractions up the Swan River, easily combined into a winery tour. **Tranby House,** on Maylands Peninsula, is beautifully restored. Built in 1839, it is one of the oldest houses in WA and a fine example of early colonial architecture. It's open from 2 to 5 pm Monday to Saturday and from 11 am to 1 pm and 2 to 5 pm Sunday; admission is $2 for adults ($1 for kids).

The **Rail Transport Museum** on Railway Parade, Bassendean, has locomotives and all

Old Mill, South Perth

PERTH

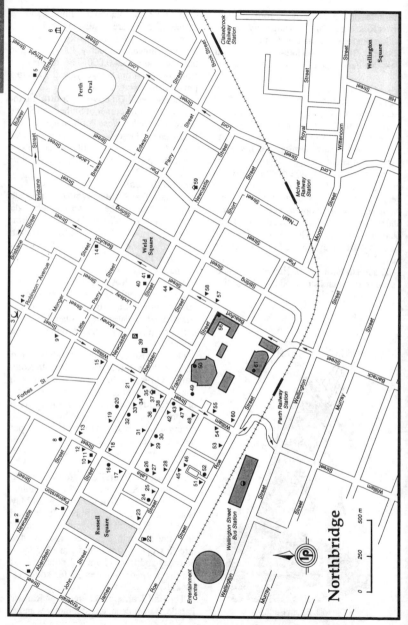

Northbridge

0   250   500 m

PLACES TO STAY

1 12.01 Central Backpackers
2 Budget Backpackers International
5 Cheviot Lodge
7 Perth Travellers Lodge
11 Backpackers International
14 North Lodge
32 Aberdeen Lodge
36 Perth City YHA Hostel
37 Brittania YHA Hostel
40 Newcastle Lodge
41 Backpackers HQ & Lone Star Tavern
59 Newcastle YHA Hostel

PLACES TO EAT

4 Kyoto Restaurant
9 City Fresh Fruit Co
10 Mintaro Restaurant
12 Monty's Burgers
13 L'Alba Cafe
15 The Moon, White Elephant Thai
    Restaurant
17 Papa Razzi, Vendetta's
18 Lake Street Cafe
19 Harry's Seafood Restaurant
21 Aberdino
22 Molly O'Grady's Pub
23 Victoria Gardens Food Hall
25 Valentino's Cafe,
27 Northbridge Pavilion Food Hall
28 The Fishy Affair
29 Simon's Seafood Restaurant
31 Marco Polo's
33 La Luna Cafe
34 Cafe Navona

35 Bar Italia
38 Fellini's Licensed Restaurant, Seoul
    Korean
42 Gabriel's Natural Food
44 Phuong Hoang Vietnamese
45 Old Shanghai Markets
46 Asian Food Court
47 Vulture's 24-Hour Restaurant
48 Brass Monkey Bar & Brasserie
51 Thai Me Down Sport
53 Oyster Bar, Baan-Thai Restaurant
54 Sylvana Pastry
55 Hare Krishna Food for Life, Ophelia's
    Cafe
57 Court Wine Bar & Cellar Restaurant
58 Eve's Place Coffee Bar, Turn 'n'
    Tender Steakhouse
60 Escargot French Restaurant

OTHER

3 Mosque
6 Army Museum
8 Arcadia Hotel
16 Havana Bar
20 Aberdeen Hotel
24 Cinema Paradiso
26 Planes, Trains & Automobiles
30 YHA Australia
39 Restaurant Parking
43 Bell Tower
49 Aqua Late Nite Bar
50 Alexander Library
52 Chinatown
56 WA Museum
61 Art Gallery of WA

sorts of railway memorabilia; it is open from 1 to 5 pm on Sunday; entry is $3.

Guildford has a number of historic buildings, including **Mechanics Hall**, in Meadow St, and the **Folk Museum & Gaol** which is open Sunday from 2 to 5 pm (March to December). **Woodbridge** in Third Ave, was built in 1855 and is a fully restored and beautifully furnished colonial mansion overlooking the river. It's open daily (closed Wednesday); there's a $2 entry fee.

In Arthur St, West Swan, is the **Caversham Wildlife Park**, which has a large collection of Australian animals and birds; it's open from 10 am to 5 pm daily.

Also in West Swan, on Lord St, is the 26 sq km **Whiteman Park**. There are picnic and barbecue facilities at Mussell Pool, the Trade Village with craft shops and displays, over 30 km of walkways and bike paths and train ($4/2 for adults/children) and tram ($2/1) rides; there is an entry fee of $3 per car.

Other Suburbs There's a real potpourri of other options; enquire at the tourist centre for opening times. In Subiaco, the **Museum of Childhood**, at 160 Hamersley Rd, houses an interesting collection. Across the Canning River towards Jandakot Airport, on Bull Creek Drive, Bull Creek, there is the excellent

Aviation Museum with a collection of aviation memorabilia. In Melville, just off the Canning Highway, is the **Wireless Hill Park & Telecommunications Museum**. The **Claremont Museum**, in the Freshwater Bay School at 66 Victoria Ave, Claremont, concentrates on local history.

In Cannington, on the road to Armadale, is **Woodloes**, a restored colonial home of 1874. The small **Liddelow Homestead** in Kenwick, has also been restored.

Adventure World, 15 km south of Perth at 179 Progress Drive, Bibra Lake, is a large amusement park open daily.

At **Cables Water Park**, at Troode St in Spearwood (just off Rockingham Rd, south of the city), cables haul skiers along the water at 20 to 50 km/h. It is open daily; an hour's skiing costs $12. If you wish to throw yourself off a 40-metre tower then head to **Bungee One** on Progress Drive, Bibra Lakes. Cowards can stay on the ground, the slightly braver can go up the tower for views and those not brave enough to jump can abseil down. Go on, jump!

Swan Valley Vineyards These are dotted along the river from Guildford to the Upper Swan River and many are open for tastings and cellar sales.

Olive Farm Wines, 77 Great Eastern Highway, South Guildford, is the oldest in the region, as it was established at the same time Perth was settled in 1829. Houghton Wines, on Dale Rd, Middle Swan, was established later but produced the first commercial vintage in 1859. Its white burgundy (the one with the blue stripe) is the biggest selling bottled white in Australia.

Lamont's Winery, on Bisdee Rd in Millendon, produces traditional, full-flavoured wines which you can enjoy with an alfresco lunch (the author's favourite).

Other wineries in the valley are Jane Brook Estate, Toodyay Rd, Middle Swan; Sandalford, West Swan Rd, Upper Caversham; Henley Park, corner West Swan Rd and Swan St, Henley; and Evans & Tate, Swan St, Henley Brook.

Organised Tours & Cruises

The WATC has the most detailed information about the many tours around Perth; it can also book them for you.

Land-Based Tours Half-day city tours of Perth and Fremantle are about $20, and for around $30 you can get tours to the Swan Valley wineries, Cohunu Wildlife Park, or Underwater World and the northern beaches.

Other day tours, to places like Avon Valley, Mandurah, New Norcia or the south

---

Perff 4 Kids

If you are travelling with kids in tow, then this section will certainly be of use. A number of the activities are covered in other parts of this chapter and include: It's a Small World (Perth), Underwater World (Hillarys), Energy Museum (Freo), Perth Zoo (South Perth), Omni Theatre (Perth), Caversham Wildlife Park (West Swan), Adventureworld (Bibra Lakes), Whiteman Park (West Swan) and the Scitech Discovery Centre (West Perth).

In addition, there are the grounds of Burswood Park where the children can run around and explore; the Dizzy Lamb Park & Koala Gardens, corner of Karaborup and Wanneroo Rds, Carabooda, where there are heaps of rides and attractions (10 am to 5 pm Sundays and public holidays, $8 for adults and $5 for children); and Heritage Mini Golf, Swan Bank Rd, Maylands (9 am to 7 pm every day, $5 for adults and $3 for children).

Other 'babysitters' are the Bavarian Castle, Village and Adventure Playground, Old Coast Rd, Halls Head; Children's Playground, May Drive, Kings Park; Enchantmentland, Great Eastern Highway, Glen Forrest; A Maze 'n' Koalas (isn't that a clever little name?), Neaves Rd, Bullsbrook; and the Cameleer Park Camel Farm and Gumnut World, both in Wanneroo.

If you want a place for the kids to play while you enjoy a glass of white wine and a plate of fish, try the *Surf Club Fish Cafe* in North Fremantle. ■

coast, range from $50 to $70. Some of the larger tour operators include Feature Tours (☎ 479 4131), Pinnacles (☎ 221 5411) and Australian Pacific Tours (☎ 221 4000).

A favourite is the free tour of the **Swan Brewery** (☎ 350 0650), 25 Baile Rd, Canning Vale. The tour takes 1½ hours (followed by a couple of beers) and departs at 10 am from Monday to Thursday and 2.30 pm on Monday to Wednesday. Remember to make reservations.

There are daily trips to the Pinnacles with Safari Treks (☎ 322 2188) for $78. Travelabout Outback Tours (☎ 242 2243) also has one-day tours to the Pinnacles. Recommended by Lonely Planet reader, Harald Berger, is Active Safaris (☎ 316 3882) which does a four-day trip to the Pinnacles, Monkey Mia and Kalbarri gorges; all for $230. All Terrain Safaris (☎ 572 3456) has a number of 4WD safaris including those to Pinnacles/Monkey Mia (four days; $279) and the north-west (14 days; $795). Safari Treks does a good half-day tour of the Swan Valley; it's not cheap at $58 but you cover a lot of territory. For $178, Sunset Coast Tours (☎ 341 5431) takes a two-night, three-day tour to Monkey Mia and the Pinnacles; accommodation is included.

A good alternative for backpackers is West Coast Experience's (☎ 561 5236) southwest tour for $145; this five-day trip goes from Perth to Margaret River, Pemberton, Walpole, Albany and back to Perth.

A recommended walking tour of Perth and surrounds is the three-hour Perth and Beyond tour through the Kings Park (☎ 483 2601); they also do specialised sports tours.

Perth Walking Tours leaves from outside the WATC in Forrest Place, revealing interesting aspects of the city you would otherwise probably miss; the two-hour tours leave at 10 am and 1 pm Monday to Saturday and cost $15. Barry Strickland (☎ 322 6751) conducts a number of informative, thematic walks through the city.

Cruises There are also a number of cruise companies that operate tours from the Barrack St jetty, including Captain Cook Cruises (☎ 325 3341) and Boat Torque (☎ 221 5844). Tours include scenic cruises of the Swan River, winery visits, trips to Fremantle and lunch and dinner cruises.

From September to May, the Transperth MV *Countess II* departs daily except Saturday at 2 pm from the Barrack St jetty. It's a three-hour cruise towards the Upper Swan River; the cost is $10. Boat Torque also has a three-hour Tranby House river cruise for $15; and Captain Cook Cruises have a three-hour Scenic River Cruise around Perth and Fremantle for $20.

Ecotourism – Marine Mammals

There are a number of activities that bring you into contact with marine mammals in and around Perth, including sea lion swimming, and dolphin and whalewatching.

Whalewatching is possible out of Perth as there are a number of operators. The trip with Mills Charters (☎ 401 0833), which runs its tours in conjunction with Underwater World (in their boats *Blue Water* and *Blue Horizon*) is very informative. The search is for the humpback whale, returning to Antarctic waters after wintering in the waters of north-west Australia. The trip leaves from Hillarys boat harbour and costs $25 and $20 for weekends and weekdays respectively (children $20 and $15). Other operators are Oceanic Cruises (☎ 430 5127) and Boat Torque (☎ 246 1039).

Spotting dolphins can be done on two-hour cruises with Rockingham Dolphins (☎ 527 1803) from Mangles Bay.

Festivals

Every year around February/March the Festival of Perth offers entertainment in the form of music, drama, dance and films. In early June, West Week is held to celebrate WA's foundation – there are historical recreations, arts & crafts events, concerts and sporting events.

The Royal Perth Show takes place every September. The Artrage festival is in October and the Northbridge Festival is hosted at the same time as the Festival of Perth.

PERTH

Places to Stay

Perth has a wide variety of accommodation catering for all tastes and price brackets. There are numerous caravan parks scattered around the metropolitan area. The main area for budget accommodation is Northbridge, while hotels, motels and holiday flats of all standards are spread throughout Perth.

Camping Perth, like many other large cities, is not well endowed with campsites convenient to the city centre. There are, however, many caravan parks in the suburbs, and many within a few km of the centre. Some of these include (distances are from the city):

Armadale Tourist Village (27 km south-east)
South-West Highway, Armadale – powered sites are $12 for two, on-site vans are $38 for two (☎ 399 6376).

Careniup Caravan Park (14 km north)
467 North Beach Rd, Gwelup – camping $13 for two, on-site vans from $29 (☎ 447 6665).

Central Caravan Park (seven km east)
34 Central Ave, Redcliffe – tent camping $12 for two, on-site vans are $35 (☎ 277 1704).

Forrestfield Caravan Park (18 km east)
351 Hawtin Rd, Forrestfield – on-site vans for $25 for two (☎ 453 6378).

Gosnells Caravan Village (21 km south-east)
2462 Albany Highway, Gosnells – tent camping $14 for two, park cabins are $35 (☎ 398 2746).

Guildford Caravan Park (19 km north-east)
372 West Swan Rd, Guildford – camping $13 for two, on-site vans from $28 (☎ 274 2828).

Kenlorn Caravan Park (nine km south-east)
229 Welshpool Rd, Queens Park – tent camping $12 for two (weekly rates available), on-site vans are $25 (☎ 356 2380).

Lakelands Village (22 km north)
289 Sydney Rd, Wanneroo – camping $12 for two, on-site vans from $80 per week (☎ 405 1212).

Midland Caravan Park (19 km east)
2 Toodyay Rd, Midland – camping $13 for two, cabins from $30 (☎ 453 6677).

Perth Tourist Caravan Park (18 km east)
Hale Rd, Forrestfield-camping $10 for two, on-site vans from $27 (☎ 453 6677).

Starhaven Caravan Park (14 km north-west)
14-20 Pearl Parade, Scarborough – camping $15 for two, on-site vans from $30 (☎ 341 1770).

Hostels There are over twenty budget hostels around Perth – most are reasonably central and many have similar names. Dorm beds range from $9 to $13 – a good rule of thumb is obviously the less you pay, the rougher the place – but $12 is about average. A twin share room is about $24 to $30; $14 each is a good average.

Northbridge The busy, friendly and slightly run-down *YHA Perth City Hostel* (☎ 328 1135), at 60 Newcastle St, is about a 15-minute walk from the city centre. *Northbridge-Francis St YHA Hostel* (☎ 328 7794), at 42-48 Francis St, in an old guesthouse near the corner of William St, has friendly hosts, bicycles for hire and a large outdoor area. Around the corner at 253 William St is the large and central *Britannia YHA Hostel* (☎ 328 6121). The better single-only rooms are at the back on the verandah; rooms near the hallways are noisy.

Budget Backpackers' International (☎ 328 9468), at 342 Newcastle St, has a comfortable lounge and good kitchen facilities. Further down Newcastle St, at No 496, is the small, new *Redbackpackers* (☎ 227 9969; (1800) 679 969); they pick up from the airport.

Rory's Backpackers (☎ 328 9958), also listed as *Backpackers Perth Inn*, at 194 Brisbane St, is further north of the city centre than other hostels. However, this clean, renovated colonial house has a pleasant garden and barbecue area. It also has a ski boat to take guests out on the water in summer.

A good alternative is the *North Lodge* (☎ 227 7588) at 225 Beaufort St. It's clean, friendly and has all the usual facilities and comfortable dorm/twin bedrooms.

Perth Travellers Lodge (☎ 328 6667) at 156-158 Aberdeen St, is actually made up of two recently renovated houses, one for males and one for females.

Aberdeen Lodge (☎ 227 6137), at 79 Aberdeen St, East Perth, is central and has four-bed dorms. Two other Aberdeen St places are the *Backpackers International* (☎ 227 9977), at the corner of Lake and Aberdeen Sts; and the impressive *12.01 Central* (☎ 227 1201), at the corner of Fitzgerald and Aberdeen Sts. In the 12.01 there are dorms and twins, and downstairs is the Whistle Stop Deli and Junction Cafe.

Also in the Northbridge area is *Cheviot Lodge* (☎ 227 6817) at 30 Bulwer St. Open 24 hours, it is close to the interstate rail terminal and provides a free pick-up service from Westrail Bus Station. There are no bunk beds. A little way from the budget strip, is the *Beatty Lodge* (☎ 227 1521), 235 Vincent St.

Other hostels are: *Backpackers HQ – Lone Star* (☎ 328 7566), on the corner of New-castle and Beaufort Sts, where most rooms have fridges, fans and balconies. Bring ear plugs as the Lone Star Bar is below. Next door is the ordinary *Newcastle Lodge* (☎ 328 5186) at 144-148 Newcastle St. Dorm beds are $8 so you get what you pay for!

Inner City Close to the city centre is the *Murray Street Hostel* (☎ 325 7627), 119 Murray St, which has all the usual facilities as well as an open-air barbecue area. The new *East Perth Backpackers'* (☎ 221 1666), 195 Hay St, has rooms from $10 per person; the rooms are clean and air-con.

Scarborough This is a good alternative to Northbridge, being close to the surf. The *Mandarin Gardens* (☎ 341 5431), at 20-28 Wheatcroft St, is the pick of the beach accommodation. It has dorm/twin rooms for $12/14. The hostel is within walking dis-tance (500 metres) of popular Scarborough Beach, has friendly hosts, a swimming pool and a sizeable recreation area. It also has self-contained flats from $50 per night.

The *Western Beach Lodge* (☎ 245 1624), 5 Westborough St, has male and female dorms. This small place is clean and airy. Also in Scarborough, the *Sunset Beach Cafe & Accommodation* (☎ 341 6655), on the corner of the Brighton and West Coast high-ways, has dorms and twin rooms – meals are also available (a 'big' breakfast is $5.90).

Y's & Guesthouses The Speer-designed *Jewell House YMCA* (☎ 325 8488), at 180 Goderich St (as Murray St becomes after Victoria Square), has 206 comfortable, clean and modern rooms; singles/doubles are

$28/36 and weekly rates are six times the daily rate. The *Grand YWCA Central* (☎ 221 2682), at 379 Wellington St, has recently been renovated. There is a great variety of accommodation; bunk beds are $15, and doubles are $40 to $50. There is also a res-taurant and cafe.

Centrally located, good value and recom-mended by readers is the *Downtowner Lodge* (☎ 325 6973), at 63 Hill St, opposite the Perth Mint. The rooms are clean and pleas-ant, and it's a very tranquil, friendly, nonsmoking place; beds are $17 in twin rooms and there are weekly rates.

Motels & Holiday Flats Perth and the sur-rounding suburbs have an abundance of motels and holiday flats (see the *Western Australia Accommodation Listing* available from the tourist office for more information). A selection follows.

City Waters Lodge (☎ 325 1566), at 118 Terrace Rd, by the river, is conveniently central and good value with cooking facili-ties, bathroom, TV and laundry; daily costs are $67/72 for singles/doubles.

North of the city centre at 166 Palmerston St are the self-contained *Brownelea Holiday Units* (☎ 328 4840) at $40 a double. The *Adelphi Hotel Apartments* (☎ 322 4666), at 130A Mounts Bay Rd, has well-equipped units for $53/65.

The *Mount St Inn* (☎ 481 0866), 24 Mount St, West Perth, is between the city and Kings Park and has magnificent views over the city and river; rooms are $97 for two. Nearby, across the overpass, are the *Mountway Holiday Units* (☎ 321 8307), at No 36; singles/doubles are $36/41. In the same vicinity is the *Perth Riverview Holiday Apartments* (☎ 321 8963), at No 42; singles/doubles are $60/65.

The *Murray Lodge Motel* (☎ 321 7441), 718 Murray St, West Perth, is an economic motel with singles/doubles for $45/53. *Kings Park Motel* (☎ 381 3488), 225 Thomas St, Subiaco, with rooms for $56/61 is similar.

Across the bridge, on the South Perth side, the *Canning Bridge Auto Lodge* (☎ 364 7742), at 891 Canning Rd, has rooms from

$55 for two. Along the Swan River are the *Swanview Motor Inn* (☎ 367 5755), 1 Preston St, in Como, with rooms for $57/60; the *Metro Inn* (☎ 367 6122), 61 Canning Highway, at $83; *The Regency Motel* (☎ 362 3000), 61-69 Great Eastern Highway, Rivervale, at $45/52; and the *All Travellers Motel* (☎ 479 4060), 169 Great Eastern Highway, Belmont, at $45/55.

There is a host of accommodation between the airport and city on the Great Eastern Highway; ask at the WATC.

Hotels There are a number of old-fashioned hotels around the centre of Perth. *Hotel Regatta* (☎ 325 5155), centrally located at 560 Hay St, has friendly staff and simple but clean singles/doubles for $35/54 with shared bathroom ($47/60 with facilities). At the back of the Wentworth Hotel is the *Royal Hotel* (☎ 481 1000), a renovated federation-style building in the city centre; it has singles/doubles from $30 to $45/$45 to $60. There are three bars and three restaurants in the complex. The *Carlton* (☎ 325 2092), 248 Hay St, provides single/double B&B for $30/50.

If you are chasing something up-market, you won't be disappointed with what's available in the centre of Perth. You could choose from any of these:

Airways City Hotel
   195 Adelaide Terrace, from $250 a double (☎ 323 7799).
Burswood Resort Hotel
   Great Eastern Highway, from $250 a double (☎ 362 7777).
Chateau Commodore Hotel
   417 Hay St, from $90 a double (☎ 325 0461).
Hyatt Regency Perth Hotel
   99 Adelaide Terrace, from $210 a double (☎ 225 1234).
Inntown Hotel
   corner of Pier and Murray Sts, $89/99 for singles/doubles (☎ 325 2133).
Parkroyal Perth Hotel
   54 Terrace Rd, from $109 a double (☎ 325 3811).
Parmelia Hilton
   Mill St, from $175 a double (☎ 322 3622).
Perth Ambassador Hotel
   196 Adelaide Terrace, from $90 a double (☎ 325 1455).

Perth International Hotel
   10 Irwin St, from $160 a double (☎ 325 0481).
Perth Townhouse Travelodge
   778 Hay St, from $155 a double (☎ 321 9141).
Quality Langley Hotel
   corner of Adelaide Terrace and Hill St, from $137.50 a double (☎ 221 1200).
Quality Princes Hotel
   334 Murray St, 196 Adelaide Terrace, from $110 a double (☎ 322 2844).
Sheraton Perth Hotel
   207 Adelaide Terrace, from $185 a double (☎ 325 0501).
Wentworth Plaza Hotel
   300 Murray St, singles/doubles for $50/75 (☎ 481 1000).

The *OBH*, or *Ocean Beach Hotel* (☎ 384 2555), is a legendary hotel right on Cottesloe Beach at the corner of Eric St and Marine Parade. Spacious rooms with fridge, TV and tea & coffee-making facilities cost from $30/40; the counter meals, like the rooms, are renowned.

The *Radisson Observation City Resort Hotel* (☎ 245 1000), The Esplanade, Scarborough, with more than 300 rooms has to be the biggest eyesore in the sandy Perth Basin with a hideous price tag to match; doubles are from $155 to $290 and suites up to $2000!

Places to Eat

Food Centres This terrific Asian idea has really taken off, and crowded food halls prove that it's a popular alternative to fast food. The *Down Under Food Hall* in the Hay St Mall, downstairs and near the corner of William St, has stalls offering Chinese, Mexican, Thai, Indian and many other types of food. This food centre is open Monday to Wednesday from 8 am to 7 pm and Thursday to Saturday from 8 am to 9 pm.

The *Carillon Food Hall*, in the Carillon Arcade on Hay St Mall, is slightly more up-market than the Down Under Food Hall and has the same international flavour with Italian, Middle Eastern and Chinese food from $5 to $7. It also has sandwich shops, a seafood stall and fast-food outlets. The Carillon Arcade is open until 9 pm every evening, although some of the food stalls do close around 7 pm.

The large *Northbridge Pavilion*, at the corner of Lake and James Sts, is another good-value international food hall with Japanese, Italian, Indian, Thai, vegetarian and Chinese food. Open from Wednesday to Sunday, it has some outdoor seating and a couple of bars; the juices at *Naturals* are truly wonderful after a tiring day.

There are three other food halls in Northbridge. Two are on James St at the back of Chinatown (the *Old Shanghai Markets* and the *Asian Food Court*) and the other, *Victoria Gardens*, is on the corner of Aberdeen St, overlooking Russell Square.

Seafood Perth is famous for its seafood restaurants. A number of frequented places are *Simon's*, 73 Francis St, *Harry's Seafood Grill & Garden Restaurant*, 94 Aberdeen St, *The Fishy Affair*, 132 James St, *Oyster Bar*, 20 Roe St, all in Northbridge; on the Nedlands Foreshore is *Jo Jo's* claiming to have the freshest seafood in town; the *Surf Club Fish Cafe*, on Port Beach in North Fremantle, is personally recommended; and *Jessica's*, 99 Adelaide Terrace, in the Hyatt Regency, is also good.

City Centre The city centre is a particularly good place for lunches and light meals. The *Magic Apple* wholefood kitchen, 445 Hay St, does delicious pitta bread sandwiches, cakes and fresh juices. The busy *Benardi's*, at 528 Hay St, has good sandwiches, quiches, home-made soups and salads. The *Hayashi Japanese Barbecue*, at 107 Pier St, has excellent-value set lunches for around $10.50 and dinner for two is about $28 each. At 117 Murray St, between Pier and Barrack Sts, is a pleasant and very reasonably priced little Japanese restaurant called *Jun & Tommy's*.

Bobby Dazzler's, at the Wentworth Plaza Hotel, prides itself on its Australian menu and is a good place for a bite and a drink. The *Granary Wholefoods*, downstairs at 37 Barrack St (south of Hay St), has an extensive range of vegetarian dishes from $4 to $6 for lunch.

Mr Samurai, in Barrack St at No 83, is one of Perth's real surprises. Open Monday to Saturday from 11 am to 6 pm (and Thursday until 8.30 pm), it serves a delicious beef or tempura with rice, okonomiyaki (Japanese-style vegetables and prawns with okonomi sauce) or fried chicken with rice. At an average of $4, this food is highly recommended.

The *Venice Cafe*, at the St George's Terrace end of the Trinity Arcade (shop No 201), is a pleasant European-style cafe with tables out the front and light meals such as lasagna, quiche, home-made pies and salad from $4 to $6. It also makes excellent coffee. Local tour gurus recommend *No 44 King Street*, in King St, for 'cuisine Yuppie'. Just around the corner at 300 Murray St is the *Moon & Sixpence Bar*, popular during lunch with the office crowd.

Perth has the usual selection of counter meals in the city centre area. *Sussella's Tavern*, in the City Arcade, off Hay St, does bistro meals from $8 to $11. The *Savoy Tavern*, under the Savoy Plaza Hotel, at 636 Hay St, has basic pub fare such as roast beef and vegetables and fish & chips for lunch.

Toward the western (Kings Park) end of the city centre, there's a string of places, including a cluster of restaurants near the Orchard Perth Hotel on the corner of Wellington and Milligan Sts. These include *Firenze* which has a $10 lunch pasta special; the popular *Fast Eddy's* on the corner of Murray and Milligan Sts; the cheap and highly recommended *Katong Singapore* at 446 Murray St, for those tantalising nyonya delights; and the new, brassy, distinctly up-market *Lenox Bar & Cafe*, at 437 Murray St.

Shafto Lane, between Murray and Hay Sts, has a number of eateries including *Henry's Cafe* for pancakes; the trendy *Iguana Cafe & Bar*, which has a bottomless wine glass between noon and 2 pm for $5; the *Manhattan Deli*, where your meal can be stone-grilled at your table; and the *Tandoor Darbar*, which specialises in balti gosht (chicken, lamb or goat).

The *Kings Park Restaurant* and *Frasers Restaurant*, atop Mt Eliza in Kings Park, have great views over the city and the river; both are good for a splurge.

Northbridge North of the city centre, the area bounded by William, Lake and Newcastle Sts, is full of ethnic restaurants to suit all tastes and budgets. William St (and the streets which run perpendicular to and west of it) is the hub – this area rivals Melbourne's Lygon and Brunswick Sts for variety and certainly for value.

The best bet is to walk around and take in the sights and smells – you will soon find something to your liking at an appropriate price and the names usually denote the flavours. The restaurants which follow represent about half of your dining choices in this area but even with such a large number, it is still prudent to book on Thursday and Friday nights.

Starting west of the railway station is Roe St with its entrance to Chinatown. On the way you will pass the award-winning *Oyster Bar*, which serves those beloved crustacea (three-course lunch is $17.50) and the *Baan-Thai*. Two ferocious guardians indicate the entrance to Chinatown. Here, at No 17, is the quaintly named *Thai me Down Sport*, open seven days for lunch and dinner for all those spicy Thai favourites. In front of this place (and actually on James St) is a bewildering array of Asian cuisine squeezed into two rambling food halls, exuding aromatic and pungent smells reminiscent of Singapore, Guangzhou and Bangkok.

There is a real cornucopia of ethnic tastes on Williams St. Heading north, you'll find *Escargot*; a couple of Asian restaurants; the moderately priced and popular *Romany*, one of the city's long-running Italian eateries; *Sylvana Pastry*, a comfortable Lebanese coffee bar with an amazing selection of those sticky Middle Eastern pastries; *Ophelia's Cafe*; and *Hare Krishna Food for Life*.

On the left-hand side – for the next five blocks of William St heading north – are the *Brass Monkey Bar & Brasserie* with a great selection of beers; *Vulture's* 24-hour restau-

rant; *Fellini's* licensed restaurant; the *Seoul Korean* which is the sole Korean; the busy *Bar Italia*, which serves excellent coffee and light meals including a good selection of pasta dishes; a string of Asian and Chinese restaurants including *The Moon* and the *White Elephant Thai Restaurant*; another Italian place, *Gioia Caffe Ristorante* (which is just west on Newcastle St); and a great place to buy something healthy, the *City Fresh Food Co*, beyond Forbes Rd.

A westerly deviation onto James St, from William St, will reveal a couple of souvlaki shops; *The Fishy Affair* (see under Seafood in this chapter); and at the far western end, a host of Italian restaurants including *Valentino's*; the new *Victoria Gardens Food Hall*; and, appropriately plonked on the corner of Milligan St, the incongruous, pastiche-Irish *Molly O'Grady's* (redeemed solely by draught Guinness on tap).

Francis St is another revelation. At its eastern end, on Beaufort St, are a couple of places such as the Macedonian *Court Wine Bar & Cellar Restaurant*; the student hangout *Eve's Place*; the *Turn 'n' Tender Steakhouse* and a little way north on Beaufort, the excellent Vietnamese restaurant *Phuong Hoang*. Still on Francis, and west off William St, are *Gabriel's Natural Food*; the reasonably priced *Marco Polo's*, for those in search of a blend of Italian and Chinese; *Simon's* (see under Seafood); and Italian places such as *Vendetta's* and *Papa Razzi*.

Also between James and Francis Sts, on Lake St, there are a number of sidewalk cafes including the eponymous *Lake Street Cafe*; as well as the *Northbridge Food Hall*.

The pickings are probably richest along Aberdeen St. The feast starts on the corner of William St with Italian fare in the form of *Aberdino's*; then continues with *Cafe Navona*, another Italian place; *La Luna Cafe*, also Italian; *Harry's* (see under Seafood); and, west of Lake St, the *Mintaro*. And notta' forget *Mamma Maria's*, at 105 Aberdeen St. This place has a pleasant ambience and a deserved reputation as one of Perth's best Italian eateries. Its main courses are priced from $11.50 and two should escape sated for just over $30. North of Mama's, on Lake St, is a great little takeaway, *Monty's Burgers*, and across the road is the respectable *L'Alba Cafe* for pasta and cappuccino. Phew!

Subiaco This enclave, known as 'Subi' boasts a number of eateries, most of which are on (or just off) Rokeby Rd. Heading north from Nicholson Rd, you'll come to *The Very Serious Cafe* (about food we hope!), *Little Lebanon* and, not far beyond, the *Bretzel Patisserie*.

Just before Bagot Rd is the expensive award-winning French restaurant *Chanterelle* and, a few steps west on Bagot, another French place, *Monet's Cafe*. At the Barker St corner is the popular *Duck Inn Bar & Restaurant* and close by on Rokeby St are the *Witch's Cauldron*, at No 89, with its renowned garlic prawns, and the *Cafe Pizzo*.

There are more places on Hay St where it intersects with Rokeby Rd. The *Subiaco Hotel*, on the east corner, faces the Art Deco *Regal Theatre* and a little further east, at No 420, is the BYO *Redd's Cafe*. Next door to the theatre is the chic *Oriel Cafe & Brasserie*. The bohemian set can be seen gazing from the window of the *Bar Bzar* on the corner of Railway Rd and Rokeby St.

The Subiaco Mews hides a few decent eateries such as the *Subiaco Steakhouse* with its reef and beef lobster & fillet for $24; the *Subiaco Village*, at the west end of Hay St, houses *Henry's Cafe & Grill* (once-known as Henry Africa's); and the Subiaco Pavilion has a food hall with 15 stalls.

Oxford St, Leederville The area of Oxford St between Vincent and Aberdeen Sts, in the suburb of Leederville, has become popular with the cappuccino-sipping set. There are a number of cafes and eateries as well as a cinema hemmed in here.

The cafes include *Villa Bianchi, Oxford 130, Fat Belly Cafe, Giardini* and the *Palermo Cafe Restaurant*. The cuisines of the world are represented in an eclectic collection of eateries: *Cosmos Kebabs, Woodstock Rock Pizzeria, Anna Vietnamese* and *Hawkers Hut Asian Food*. This enclave

is fast becoming a chic alternative to the hustle and bustle of Northbridge.

Entertainment

Perth has plenty of pubs, discos and night-clubs (see the Around Perth chapter for details of the lively night scene in Fremantle). The Thursday edition of the *West Australian* has an informative entertainment lift-out called the *Revue*. The *Xpress*, a weekly music magazine available free at record shops and other outlets, has a gig guide.

Northbridge is definitely the place to go after dark. Friday night is witness to much revelry while the city centre is dead, in spite of efforts to revitalise it.

Cinemas & Theatres The Lumiere Cinema, in the Perth Entertainment Centre; Cinema Paradiso, 164 James St, Northbridge; and the Astor, on the corner of Beaufort and Walcott Sts in Mt Lawley, usually have quality art-house films. All of the Oscar-nominated favourites are on in the Hoyts, Greater Union and Village suburban cinemas.

Popular theatres include His Majesty's Theatre on the corner of King and Hay Sts, the Regal Theatre at 474 Hay St, Subiaco and the Hole in the Wall, Subiaco Theatre Centre, 180 Hamersley Rd, Subiaco.

Other venues are the Playhouse Theatre, Pier St, Perth; the Stirling Theatre, Cedric St, Stirling; and the Effie Crump Theatre, upstairs in the old Brisbane Hotel, Beaufort St, Perth. You can enjoy anything from a production of Australian playwright David Williamson's latest work to the cardboard impersonations of Ennio Marchetto.

Sessions times and programmes for these and other city and suburban cinemas and theatres are available daily in the *West Australian*.

Concerts & Recitals The Perth Concert Hall in St George's Terrace and the large Entertainment Centre in Wellington St are venues for concerts and recitals by local and international acts. You can find out more in the Perth Theatre Trust News *Applause!* or the WASO *Concert Catalogue*, both free from the WATC. Around the time of the Festival of Perth there are a number of free concerts under the stars.

Comedy Perth has a good comedy scene although those that survive the cigarette smoke, late nights and audience abuse, generally gravitate to stand-up heaven in Melbourne. Pockets, at 44 Lake St, Northbridge, seems to be the latest venue for those with a bit of a 'rep'. Otherwise, it is 'try outs' at the Swanbourne Hotel or an international comedian at the Burswood Casino.

Pubs & Live Music Some of the popular places for live music in Northbridge are the Brass Monkey Tavern, on the corner of William and James Sts; the Aqua Late Nite Bar, 232 William St; the Aberdeen Hotel at 84 Aberdeen St and The Lone Star, corner of Beaufort and Newcastle Sts. The latter has a backpackers' night every Wednesday and live bands on the weekends.

Perth has the usual pub-rock circuit with varying cover charges depending on the gig. Popular venues include Raffles on the Canning Highway, Applecross; the Stadium inside the Herdsman Hotel; the Boulevard Alehouse, 901 Albany Highway, East Victoria Park; the Charles Hotel (for genuine r&b), 509 Charles St, North Perth; Gobbles, 613 Wellington St, Perth; and the Club Original at the Grosvenor Hotel, corner of Hill and Hay Sts, East Perth.

Discos & Nightclubs Mousse your bouffant, learn the difference between funk, acid jazz, techno and house, and prepare to sweet talk the door staff. Perth has plenty of places where you can dance into the wee small hours.

In the city centre are the Buzz Bar, Shafto Lane; Brannigan's in the Perth International Hotel, Irwin St; F Scotts at 237 Hay St; the Racquet Club, Piccadilly Square, corner of Lord and Short Sts; Club Rumours at 418 Murray St (Friday and Saturday nights); Geremiah's Niteclub in the Orchard Hotel, Milligan St; and The Loft Nightclub at 237 Hay St.

Northbridge has a few late-night venues for hard-core ravers. The Aqua has been mentioned previously; and the Hippodrome and James St Nightclub are in James St. The door staff wouldn't allow babies into the town's seemingly most popular venue, The Havana, so we observed the rich and famous carousing, from the footpath.

Gay & Lesbian Places These include the Northbridge Hotel, corner of Lake and Brisbane Sts (live music on Wednesday and Sunday); the Court Hotel, corner of Beaufort and James Sts (live music on Friday and Sunday); Connections (Connies), James St for dance music and floorshows; and DC's, Francis St, for live shows on the weekend. If you are shy of the pub scene, try the 5 & Dine Dinner Club (☎ 227 1905). Check in the *Westside Observer*, available free from the Arcane Bookshop, William St or New Editions in South Terrace, Fremantle, for venues and activities.

Spectator Sports The people of Perth, like most other Australians, are parochial in their support of local sporting teams. The West Coast Eagles, Perth's representatives in the Australian Football League (AFL), and the Perth Wildcats in the National Basketball League, regularly play interstate teams in Perth. Check the *West Australian* for game details.

The venerated shrine in Perth for interstate AFL games, and games between local clubs, is Subiaco Oval. Details of matches can be found in the sporting section of the Friday and Saturday *West Australian*.

At least one of the test matches of an international cricket series (or a one-day game of that competition) is usually played in Perth, keeping interested eastern TV viewers glued to their sets until late. Games are played at the Western Australian Cricket Association (WACA) which is close to the centre of the city.

Golf There are several world-class public golf courses in and around Perth. Golf-course builders have taken advantage of the availability of space and to good effect. Good courses include the 36-hole City of Perth Golf Complex (☎ (09) 387 7075) in Floreat; Lake Claremont Public Golf Course (☎ (09) 384 2887); the 18-hole Hamersley Public Golf Course (☎ (09) 447 7137), in Karrinyup; and the Fremantle Municipal Golf Course (☎ (09) 430 2316).

Two up-market courses are the Vines Resort in the Swan Valley, a 30-minute drive from Perth; and the Joondalup Country Club, about 30 minutes north of Perth.

Casino Perth's glitzy Burswood Casino, built on an artificial island off the Great Western Highway, is open all day, every day. Its setup seems pretty similar to other Australian casinos with gaming tables (roulette and blackjack), a two-up 'shed', Keno, poker machines and extensive off-course betting. The casino is also host to a cavalcade of prominent local and foreign entertainers.

Things to Buy

Perth has a number of excellent outlets for Aboriginal arts & crafts including the Creative Native Gallery, at 32 King St. Other local crafts can be found at the various markets around town – see under Markets in this chapter.

For camping and climbing equipment, there's Paddy Pallin, 891 Hay St and, across the road, Mountain Designs, at No 862.

Getting There & Away

Air Qantas Domestic (☎ 13 1313) and Ansett Australia (☎ 13 1300) have flights to and from Sydney, Melbourne, Cairns, Townsville, Adelaide, Darwin and Alice Springs. Some Melbourne flights go direct, and some via Adelaide or, in the case of Sydney, via Melbourne.

Discounted return airfares are presently in a state of flux, but you should be able to get return tickets between Perth and Adelaide for around $440, Melbourne $510, Sydney $540 and Brisbane $660. These fares, however, may be subject to conditions such as payment at least 21 days in advance, a minimum stay away and cancellation penal-

ties – check with the various airlines when booking flights. With the deregulation of the domestic airline industry, it is worth checking the daily newspapers for special fares.

Ansett Australia and Qantas Domestic also have flights to Perth from North Queensland via Alice Springs. Apex return fares from Alice Springs are $503, and $621 from Cairns. Darwin to Perth flights go via Alice Springs or Port Hedland – Ansett Australia fly from Darwin to Perth along the coast daily; the Apex return fare from Perth to Darwin via Alice Springs is $699.

Skywest (☎ 334 2288) on the Great Eastern Highway, fly to WA centres such as Albany, Esperance, Kalgoorlie, Geraldton, Monkey Mia and Meekatharra.

Bus Greyhound Pioneer (☎ 328 6677) operates daily bus services from Adelaide to Perth from the Westrail Centre, West Parade, East Perth (Interstate Railway Station). The journey from Perth to Darwin along the coast takes around 56 hours by bus and costs $325. Greyhound Pioneer also operates a four times weekly service to Darwin via the more direct, inland route through Newman (it saves five hours and is the same price).

Westrail operates bus services to a number of WA centres including Albany ($34), Augusta ($28), Bunbury ($17), Collie ($20), Hyden (Wave Rock) ($29; twice weekly), Esperance ($50), Geraldton ($35) and Meekatharra ($64).

Train Perth is the starting and ending point of one of the world's great railway journeys – the 65-hour trip between the Pacific Ocean and the Indian Ocean (for more information see the Getting There & Away chapter).

The only rail services within WA are the *Prospector* from Perth to Kalgoorlie and the *Australind* from Perth to Bunbury. The trains from the east coast and the WA services all run to or from the Westrail Terminal in East Perth, as do the Westrail buses. Westrail bookings can be made by phone (☎ 326 2222), or through the WATC in Forrest Place.

The *Australind* has two services every

day, except Sunday when there is only one, in both directions. These leave Perth at 10 am and 7 pm and Bunbury at 6.30 am and 3.40 pm; the trip takes two hours and 20 minutes. Towns stopped at are Armadale, Mundijong, Serpentine, North Dandalup, Pinjarra, Waroona, Yarloop, Cookernup, Harvey and Brunswick Junction.

The *Prospector* has at least one service in each direction every day and there are some other limited services during the week; the trip takes about seven hours 25 minutes. Major towns stopped at are Midland, Toodyay, Northam, Meckering, Cunderdin, Kellerberrin, Merredin and Southern Cross. From Monday to Thursday it departs in the morning at around 9.30 am (it pays to check as this is only an indication) and on Friday and Sunday the train departs at 4.10 pm from both ends; on Saturday the train departs Perth at 6 pm and Kalgoorlie at 7.15 am.

Hitching Hostel notice boards are worth checking for lifts to points around the country. If you're hitching out of Perth to the north or east, take a train to Midland. For travel south, take a train to Armadale. Trans-Nullarbor hitching is not that easy, and the fierce competition between bus companies and discounted airfares have made these forms of travel much more attractive. (See under Hitching in the Getting Around chapter.)

Getting Around

Perth has a central public transport organisation called Transperth which operates buses, trains and ferries. There are Transperth information offices (☎ 13 2213) in the Plaza Arcade (off the Hay St Mall); the City Bus Port on Mounts Bay Rd at the foot of William St; and at the Wellington St bus station. They all provide advice about getting around Perth and supply a system map and timetables. These offices are open from 6.30 am to 8 pm Monday to Friday and from 8 am to 5 pm on Saturday.

Free Transit Zone A free transit zone including all Transperth bus and trains is

provided every day within the central city area – from Northbridge in the north to the river in the south, and from Kings Park in the west to the Causeway in the east.

To/From the Airport Perth's airport is busy night and day. The city's isolation from the east coast and the airport's function as an international arrival point mean planes arrive and depart at all hours.

The domestic and international terminals are 10 km apart and taxi fares to the city are around $15 and $20 respectively. The privately run Perth Airport Bus (☎ 250 2838) meets all incoming domestic and international flights and provides transport to the city centre, hotels and hostels. Although it claims to meet all flights, some travellers have reported that sometimes it doesn't turn up – if this occurs late at night, a taxi into the city is probably your best option.

The airport bus costs $6 from the domestic terminal and $7 from the international terminal. To the airport terminals, there are scheduled runs every couple of hours from 4.45 am to 10.30 pm. Call them for hotel and hostel pick-ups and timetable information.

Alternatively, you can get into the city for about $1.90 on Transperth bus Nos 200, 201, 202, 208 and 209 to William St. It departs from the domestic terminal every hour or so (more frequently at peak times) from 5.30 am to 10 pm on weekdays and for nearly as long on Saturday; Sunday services are less frequent. It leaves from bus stand No 39, on St Georges Terrace, to the domestic terminal. Some of the backpacker places pick up at the airport (generally you stay in their accommodation that night) and offer reduced fares into the city.

Bus There are five free City Clipper services which operate every 20 minutes or so from 7 am to 6 pm Monday to Friday. The Yellow Clipper (No 1) passes every eight minutes weekdays and 15 minutes on Saturday. All clipper services, except the Blue Clipper, pass through the Wellington St bus station.

No 1 Yellow Clipper
These operate around the central area of the city.
No 2 Purple Clipper
These operate from the City Bus Port to West Perth.
No 3 Green Clipper
These travel between the Wellington St bus station and West Perth.
No 4 Blue Clipper
These run from the City Bus Port, Mounts Bay Rd, to the Esplanade along Barrack and William Sts, then down Beaufort St.
No 5 Red Clipper
These depart Wellington St bus station to East Perth, near the WACA, and return.

On regular buses, a short ride of one zone costs $1.30, two zones cost $1.90 and three zones $2.30. Zone 1 includes the city centre and the inner suburbs (including Subiaco and Claremont), and Zone 2 extends all the way to Fremantle, 20 km from the city centre. A Multirider ticket gives you 10 journeys for the price of nine.

The Perth Tram (☎ 367 9404) doesn't run on rails – it's a bus that takes you around some of Perth's main attractions (such as the city, Kings Park, Barrack St jetty and the casino) in 1½ hours for $9. The 'tram' leaves from 124 Murray St (near Barrack St) six times a day, seven days a week.

Train Transperth (☎ 13 2213) operates sub-urban train lines to Armadale, Fremantle, Midland and the northern suburb of Joondalup from around 5.20 am to midnight on weekdays with reduced services on week-ends. During the day, some of the Joondalup trains continue on to Armadale and a number of Fremantle trains run through to Midland. Free train travel is allowed between Claisebrook and City West stations.

All trains leave from the city station on Wellington St. Your rail ticket can also be used on Transperth buses and ferries within the ticket's area of validity.

Car If you are travelling by car around Perth, there are a couple of things to be wary of. Driving in the city centre takes a little bit of getting used to as some streets are one-way and many street signs are not prominent.

In the city you will have no trouble getting fuel from 7 am to 9 pm from Monday to Saturday but on Sunday it is a different story. You will have to find out which fuel outlets are rostered to be open (usually from 7 am to 10 pm). For rostering details call ☎ 11573.

Car Rental Hertz (☎ 321 7777), Budget (☎ 322 1100), Avis (☎ 325 7677) and Thrifty (☎ 481 1999) are all represented in Perth, along with many more local firms mentioned in the Getting Around chapter.

Bicycle Cycling is a great way to explore Perth. There are many bicycle routes along the river all the way to Fremantle and along the Indian Ocean coast. Get the free *Along the Coast Ride* and *Around the River Ride* booklets from the WATC in Forrest Place.

At WA Bicycle Disposal Centre (☎ 325 1176) at 47 Bennett St, East Perth, you can buy a bike knowing that you get a guaranteed buy-back price after a certain time. Ride Away (☎ 354 2393) by the city side of the Causeway also rents cycles.

Boat Transperth ferries (☎ 13 2213) cross the river every day from the Barrack St jetty to the Mends St jetty in South Perth every half an hour (more frequently at peak times) from 6.45 am to 7.15 pm for 70c. Take this ferry to get to the zoo.

The Rottnest Island Getting There & Away section has details on ferries from Perth, Hillarys and Fremantle to Rottnest. See under Organised Tours & Cruises earlier in this chapter for river cruises.

Around Perth

The area around Perth has a wealth of attractions and activities. There is the historic port city of Fremantle, the traffic-less holiday resort of Rottnest Island, the beaches and national parks to the north (including the intriguing Pinnacles Desert) and the picturesque Avon Valley.

Most of these places, with the exception of the Pinnacles, are only an hour or so away by car or ferry. The southern cities – Rockingham and Mandurah – and the South-Western Highway are covered in the South-West chapter.

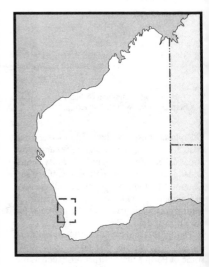

FREMANTLE

Fremantle ('Freo' to the locals), Perth's port, has a population of 25,000 and lies at the mouth of the Swan River, 19 km south-west of the city centre. Over the years, Perth has sprawled to engulf Fremantle, which is now more a suburb of the city than a town in its own right. Despite recent development, Freo has a wholly different feeling than gleaming, skyscrapered Perth. It's a place with a real sense of history and an extremely pleasant atmosphere.

The town has a number of interesting old buildings, some excellent museums and galleries, a lively produce and craft market, and a diverse range of pubs, cafes and restaurants. A visit to Fremantle will be one of the highlights of your trip to WA.

History

This region was settled many thousands of years ago by the Nyungar people. Several trails joined on the south side of the Swan River at the hub of inter-tribal trading routes; here was a natural bridge almost spanning the Swan. Known to the Aborigines as Munjaree, groups quickly occupied various parts of the area.

Fremantle's modern, European history began in 1829 when the HMS *Challenger* landed, captained by Charles Howe Freman-

tle. He took possession of 'the whole of the west coast in the name of King George IV'.

Like Perth, the settlement made little progress until taking on convict labour. These hard-worked labourers constructed most of the town's earliest buildings, some of them among the oldest and most treasured in WA. As a port, Fremantle was abysmal until the brilliant engineer CY O'Connor (see Where Water is like Gold! in The Goldfields & The Nullarbor chapter) built an artificial harbour in the 1890s.

In 1987, the city was the site of the unsuccessful defence of what was, for a brief period, one of Australia's most prized possessions – the America's Cup yachting trophy. Preparations for the influx of tourists transformed Fremantle into a more modern, colourful and expensive city. Many of the residents, however, protested that their lifestyle and the character of their community would be damaged by the development.

The Pinnacles of Nambung National Park (PS)

South-West

A: Cape Naturaliste Lighthouse (JW)
B: Sugarloaf Rock, near Cape Naturaliste (JW)
C: Jewel Cave, near Augusta (RN)
D: Cape Leeuwin Lighthouse (JW)
E: Waterwheel at Cape Leeuwin, Augusta (RN)

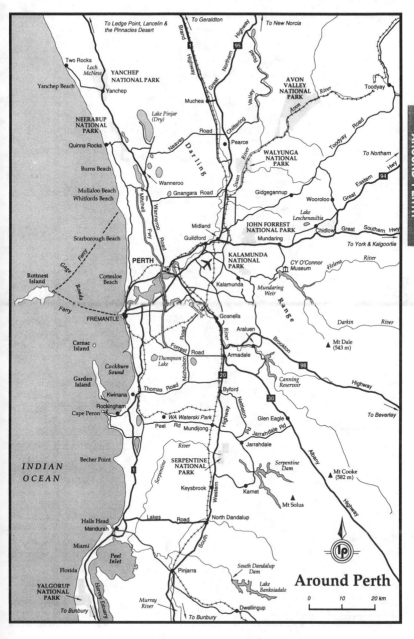

Around Perth

0   10   20 km

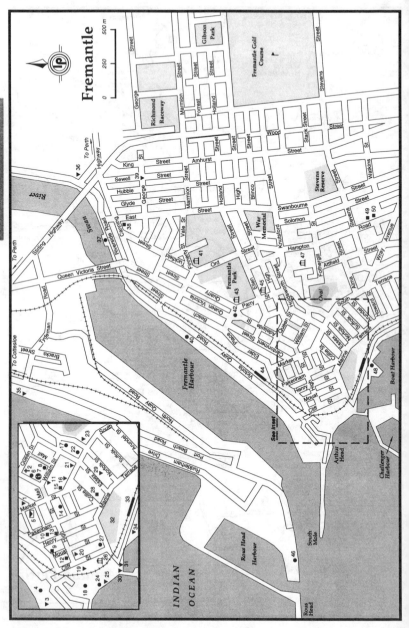

AROUND PERTH

Information

There is an information office in the Fremantle Town Hall shop (☎ 430 2346) in Kings Square, which is open Monday to Friday from 9 am to 5 pm, Saturday from 9 am to 1 pm and Sunday 10 am to 3 pm. Among the brochures are a number of guides, and information on Heritage Trails and National Trust walking tours – obtain *Manjaree Track*, *Convict Trail* and *Old Foreshore* if you can.

Fremantle Museum & Arts Centre

The museum is housed in an impressive building on Finnerty St, originally constructed by convict labourers as a lunatic asylum in the 1860s. It houses a fine collection including exhibits on Fremantle's early history, the colonisation of WA and the early whaling industry. It also tells the intriguing story of the Dutch East India Company ships which first discovered the western coast of Australia and, in several instances, were wrecked on its inhospitable shores. The museum is open from 1 to 5 pm Thursday to Sunday; admission is free.

The arts centre, which occupies one wing of the building, is open daily from 10 am to 5 pm and Wednesday evening from 7 to 9 pm; admission is free.

Maritime Museum

The Maritime Museum, on Cliff St, near the waterfront, occupies a building constructed in 1852 as a Commissariat store. The museum has a display on WA's maritime history with particular emphasis on the famous wreck of the *Batavia*. One gallery is used as a working centre where you can see the *Batavia* being preserved.

At one end of this gallery is the huge stone façade intended for an entrance to Batavia Castle. It was being carried by the *Batavia* as ballast when she sank.

Another interesting exhibit is the original **de Vlamingh plate**. When de Vlamingh retrieved Hartog's inscripted plate (see under History in the Facts about Western Australia chapter) from Hartog Island, he replaced it with another. Hartog's plate is preserved in a museum in the Netherlands.

This intriguing, not-to-be-missed museum is open Monday to Thursday from 10.30 am to 5 pm and Friday to Sunday from 1 to 5 pm; admission is free.

Fremantle Market

The colourful Fremantle Market at the corner of South Terrace and Henderson St, is a prime attraction in the area. Originally opened in 1897, the market was reopened in 1975 and draws crowds looking for anything from craft work to vegetables, jewellery and antiques; there is a also a great tavern bar where buskers often perform. The market is open from 9 am to 9 pm on Friday, from 9 am to 5 pm on Saturday, and from 10 am to 5 pm on Sunday.

Round House

On Arthur Head, at the western end of High St, near the Maritime Museum, is the Round House. Built in 1831, it's the oldest public building in WA. It actually has 12 sides and was originally a local prison (in the days before convicts were brought into WA). It was also the site of the colony's first hanging.

Later, the building was used to hold Aborigines before they were taken to Rottnest Island. Incidentally, the tunnel underneath the Round House was built by a whaling company in 1837 to provide access to Bathers Bay.

The Round House shop and information office is housed in one of the nearby pilots' cottages. The building is open from 10 am to 5 pm daily; admission is free. The site pro-

Round House

vides good views of Fremantle, especially historic High St.

Convict-Era Buildings

Many other buildings in Fremantle date from the period after 1850, when convict labour was introduced. The *Convict Trail* brochure, available from the Fremantle Town Hall shop, outlines the places of interest from this era. They include **Fremantle Prison**, one of the unlucky convicts' first building tasks.

To a certain extent, the prison with its five-metre-high walls, dominates modern Fremantle. It operated as a prison from 1855 until November 1991. The prison is open from 10 am to 6 pm daily; admission is $10.

Beside the prison gates, at 16 The Terrace, is a small **museum** on the convict era in WA.

Later Landmarks

Fremantle boomed during the WA gold rush and many buildings were constructed during, or shortly before, this period. They include **Samson House**, a well-preserved 1888 colonial home in Ellen St, which is open from 1 to 5 pm on Thursday and Sunday – tours of the house are run by volunteer guides. The fine **St John's Church** of 1882, on the corner of Adelaide and Queen Sts, contains a large stained-glass window.

Other buildings of the era include the **Fremantle Town Hall** (1887) in St John's Square; the former **German consulate building** built in 1902 at 5 Mouat St; the **Fremantle Railway Station** of 1907; and the Georgian-style **old customs house** on Cliff St. The **Victoria Grandstand** of Fremantle Oval is an example of a once popular timber and iron pavilion, complete with lace work and towers; it was opened in 1897.

The **water trough**, in the park in front of the station, has a memorial to two men who died of thirst on an outback expedition. The **Proclamation Tree**, near the corner of Adelaide and Edwards Sts, is a Moreton Bay fig, planted in 1890.

Victoria Quay Docks
From the observation tower on top of the **Port Authority Building** in Cliff St, you can enjoy a panoramic view of Fremantle harbour. You must take the escorted tours which are conducted from the foyer every weekday at 2.30 pm only.

For boat freaks and silvertails only, there is a **collection of boats** from the last 100 years, including the America's Cup winning 12-metre yacht *Australia II*, in B-Shed, Victoria Quay; admission is free. Nearby is **A-Shed**, which houses a number of art & craft outlets and a cafe.

The training ship, **STS Leeuwin II,** a 55-metre three-masted barquentine, is based at B Berth, Victoria Dock (☎ (09) 430 4105). This ship undertakes day, weekend and five-day sailing trips. There are occasionally 10-day trips – real 'eco-adventures' – to the Kimberley Coast.

Other Attractions
Fremantle is well endowed with parks, including the popular **Esplanade Reserve**, beside the picturesque fishing-boat harbour off Marine Terrace.

The city is a popular centre for craft workers of all kinds and one of the best places to find them is at the imaginative

Bannister St Workshops. The renowned potter Joan Campbell, has her **gallery** at Bathers Bay; it is reached by the underpass near the Round House.

The **Energy Museum**, at 12 Parry St, has some entertaining and educational displays tracing the development of gas and electricity. It is open from 10.30 am to 4.30 pm on weekdays and from 1 to 4.30 pm on weekends; admission is free.

Finally, there is the **Fremantle Crocodile Park**, where the reptiles have the cupidity of the 1980s entrepreneurs (yes, they're a greedy lot); admission is $8.

Organised Tours
The Fremantle Tram (☎ 339 8719) is very much like the Perth Tram and does a 45-minute historical tour of Fremantle with full commentary for $7; a harbour tour is also available for $7 and a Top of the Port tour for $10. You can combine the tour with a cruise to Perth, a tour of Perth on the Perth Tram and a return ticket to Fremantle for $34.

Places to Stay
At the corner of Cockburn and Rockingham Rds is the *Fremantle Village Caravan Park* (☎ (09) 430 4866) with ensuite sites/chalets for $15/55 for two.

The *Bundi Kudja Homestead* (☎ 335 3467), 96 Hampton Rd, has dorm beds for $11, quads for $12 and singles/twins for $16/13 per person. It is housed in former nurses' quarters built around 1896 (Bundi Kudja means 'home of good babies'). There are kitchens, plenty of facilities, a log fire, games room and TV and video lounge. The *Ocean View Lodge* (☎ (09) 336 2962), 100 Hampton Rd, has singles/twins/doubles for $15/24/27 and also weekly stay rates. There are about 200 rooms in this humongous complex which also has a gym, sauna, billiard room, swimming pool and barbecue area.

More central is the rather run-down *Roo on the Roof* (☎ (09) 335 1998), 11 Pakenham St, which offers very basic budget accommodation from $12.50 and singles from $15. *His Lordship's Larder* (☎ (09) 336 1766), on the corner of Mouat and Phillimore Sts, is a hotel with rooms for $30/50. A Backpackers hostel is supposedly being developed on High St at the Henry St corner; enquire at the tourist office. The *Newport Hotel* (☎ (09) 335 2428), 2 South Terrace, has singles/doubles for $25/45 and the *Norfolk Hotel Since 1887* (☎ (09) 335 5405), 47 South Terrace, is $55/65.

The *Flying Angel Club* (☎ (09) 335 5321), in the International Seafarers' Centre at 78 Queen Victoria St, has singles/doubles for $35/49. The fully restored *Fremantle Hotel* (☎ (09) 430 4300), 6 High St, has singles/doubles for $35 to $50/$50 to $60.

In East Fremantle, at 66 Canning Highway, is the *Tradewinds Hotel* (☎ (09) 339 2266); the river views elevate the price to $107/125 for a studio/one-bedroom apartment. The ritziest hotel in town is the four-star *Fremantle Esplanade Hotel* (☎ (09) 319 1256) on the corner of Marine Terrace and Collie St. Rooms for two are $160 and a studio will set you back $210.

For something to remind you of home, contact *Fremantle Homestays* (☎ (09) 319 1256), which can arrange B&B accommodation in houses around Fremantle from $25 to $40 a night for a single and from $50 to $75 for a double. Self-contained single and double units are also available from $200 to $250 per week.

Places to Eat

A highlight of Fremantle is the diverse range of cafes, restaurants, food halls and taverns. Many a traveller's afternoon has been whittled away sipping beer or coffee and watching life go by from kerbside tables. There is a concentration of places along South Terrace and another enclave at the west end of town near the fishing boat harbour.

South Terrace Cafes and restaurants in this area include the popular *Old Papa's – Ristorante Luigi's*, at No 17, which has coffee and gelati; the trendy *Gino's* (the place to be seen) at No 1; and the large *Miss Maud's*

at No 33. All these places can be crowded on weekends when the weather is fine.

The historic *Sail & Anchor Hotel* (formerly the Freemason's Hotel, built in 1854), at 64 South Terrace, has been impressively restored to resemble much of its former glory. It specialises in locally brewed Matilda Bay beers, and on the 1st floor is a brasserie which serves snacks and full meals.

Also in South Terrace is the *Mexican Kitchen*, next door to Old Papa's, with a range of Mexican dishes from $10 to $12. Across the road is *Pizza Bella Roma*, the *Glifada of Athens* with tasty souvlaki, and the popular and licensed *Zapata's* in Shop 30, South Terrace Piazza. A couple of affluent backpackers that we met recommended *Portfreo Cafe-Resto*, at the corner of Parry St and South Terrace, for its patisseries.

The *Up-Market Food Centre* on Henderson St, opposite the market, has stalls where you can get delicious and cheap Thai, Vietnamese, Japanese, Chinese and Italian food from $5 to $7. Open Thursday to Sunday from about noon to 9 pm, it can be very busy, especially on market days.

Fast Eddy's, similar to the one in Perth, is at 13 Essex St, not far from South Terrace. This has the best value breakfast in town with bottomless cappuccinos.

West End & Harbour The *Roma*, at 13 High St, is a reliable Freo institution, which serves home-made Italian fare including their famous chicken and spaghetti. Even the rich and famous have to queue to eat here. The nearby *Round House Cafe* is good for a cheap breakfast or a quick snack and the *Pisa Cafe*, the first place on High St, is another good breakfast place. For Vietnamese food, try the *Vung-Tau*, at 19 High St, with meals including a vegetarian menu from $6 to $9. A little out of the restaurant belt is the *Bunga Raya Satay* at 8 Cantonment St – talking of belts, tighten them as the serves here are small even though the food is good. There is also an enclave of restaurants at the east end of George St in East Fremantle.

For fish & chips *Cicerello's*, *Kailis's* or *Lombardo's*, on the Esplanade by the fishing boat harbour, are Fremantle traditions. The *Fisherman's Kitchen* is at the back of the equally popular *Sails Restaurant*, upstairs at 47 The Mews. The Fisherman's and Cicerello's have restaurants and takeaway sections.

Again, if you want value for money, then *The Sicilian*, beneath Sails Restaurant, is where you will probably end the evening – a huge plate of fish & chips and a mountain of salad costs $10.

This harbour restaurant area was quite rightly described by a couple of residents as the 'authentic and original Freo'.

Other The hipper-than-thou places are *The Left Bank Bar & Cafe*, on Riverside Rd down from the East St jetty, and the beachy, trendified *Surf Club* (which has both cheap and expensive sections) out at North Fremantle Beach.

There are typical counter meals available at the *Newcastle Club Tavern* on Market St, the *Federal Hotel* on William St and the *National Hotel* on the corner of Market and High Sts.

Entertainment
There are a number of venues around town with music and/or dancing, with the majority concentrated in the High St area.

The West End Hotel, 24 High St, has music most nights of the week and poetry on Monday night. Just across the road is the Orient, at No 39, with bands pumping up the volume to drown out the opposition. At the Newport Hotel, 2 South Terrace, there are bands most nights and weekends down the road at the Seaview Tavern, No 282.

Band names such as Mutt, The Head-cutters, Burn Baby Burn and The Hedonists typify the sounds produced at the Harbour-side Hotel, on the corner of Beach Rd and Parry St. Home of the 'big gig' is the Metropolis on South Terrace.

The Railway Hotel at 201 Queen Victoria St in North Fremantle, has r&b, rock and jazz, on alternate nights, from Thursday to Sunday.

For Latin and folk music, Fly by Night

Club, in Queen St, is frequented by some talented musicians. Tarantella, on Mouat St between High and Phillimore Sts, is an exclusive nightclub.

Getting There & Around
The train between Perth and Fremantle runs every 15 minutes or so throughout the day for around $1.90. Bus Nos 106 (bus stand No 35) and 111 (bus stand No 48) go from St George's Terrace to Fremantle via the Canning Highway; or you can take bus No 105 (bus stand No 40 on St George's Terrace), which takes a longer route south of the river. Bus Nos 103 and 104 also depart from St George's Terrace (south side) but go to Fremantle via the north side of the river.

Captain Cook cruises have daily ferries from Perth to Fremantle for around $12 one-way.

Bicycles are available for hire from Fleet Cycles (☎ (09) 430 5414), 66 Adelaide St, and Captain Munchies (☎ (09) 339 6633), 2 Beach St.

ROTTNEST ISLAND
'Rotto', as it's known by the locals, is a sandy island about 19 km off the coast of Freman-tle. It's 11 km long, five km wide and is very popular with Perth residents and visitors. The island was discovered by the Dutch explorer de Vlamingh in 1696. He named it 'Rats' Nest' because of the numerous king-size 'rats' (actually quokkas) he saw there.

What do you do on Rotto? Well, you cycle around, laze in the sun on the many superb beaches (the Basin is the most popular, while Parakeet Bay is the place for skinny dipping), climb the low hills, go fishing or boating, ride a glass-bottomed boat (Rotto has some of the southernmost coral in the world and a number of shipwrecks), swim in the crystal-clear water or go quokka spotting.

The Rottnest settlement was originally established in 1838 as a prison for Aborigi-nes from the mainland – the early colonists had lots of trouble imposing their ideas of private ownership on the nomadic Aborigi-nes. The prison was abandoned in 1903 and the island soon became an escape for Perth

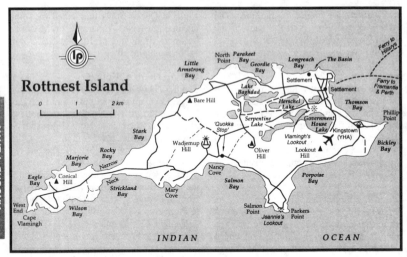

society. Only in the last 30 years, however, has it really developed as a popular day trip. The buildings of the original prison settlement are among the oldest in WA.

Information

There is an information office, open weekdays from 8.30 am to 5 pm, Saturday 9 am to 4 pm and Sunday 10 am to noon and 2.30 to 4 pm. It is just to the left of the jetty at Thomson Bay (the island's largest settlement) as you arrive. There, and at the museum, you can get useful publications, such as a walking tour of the old settlement buildings, Heritage Trail brochures, information on the various shipwrecks around the island and the *Rottnest Island Bicycle Guide* ($4). The latter has heaps of additional information on the flora & fauna of the island.

Also, grab a copy of the informative paper *Rottnest Islander* and the brochure *Rottnest: Holiday Island*. Rottnest is very popular in the summer when ferries and accommodation are both heavily booked – plan ahead.

Things To See & Do

Rottnest Museum & Old Buildings There's an excellent museum with exhibits about the island, its history, wildlife and shipwrecks. You can pick up the *Vincent Way Heritage Trail* and the *Vlamingh Memorial Heritage Trail* walking-tour leaflets ($2 and $1 respectively) here and wander around the interesting old convict-built buildings, including the octagonal 1864 'Quad' where the prison cells are now hotel rooms. The museum is open from 11 am to 4 pm.

There is also the excellent and free, one-hour tour of the old buildings which takes in Vincent Way, the Aboriginal burial ground, the sea wall and boat sheds, the picturesque chapel and the Quad. This walk commences at the visitor centre at 11.15 am and 1.30 pm daily.

You can walk to **Vlamingh's Lookout** on View Hill, not far from Thomson Bay. You pass the old cemetery on the way and at the top you get panoramic views of the island. Also of interest is the recently restored **Oliver Hill Battery**, west of Thomson Bay.

Quokka Spotting The island has a number of low-lying salt lakes – you're most likely to spot the cuddly little quokkas *(Setonix brachyurus)* around them. The quokka was one of the first marsupials spotted by

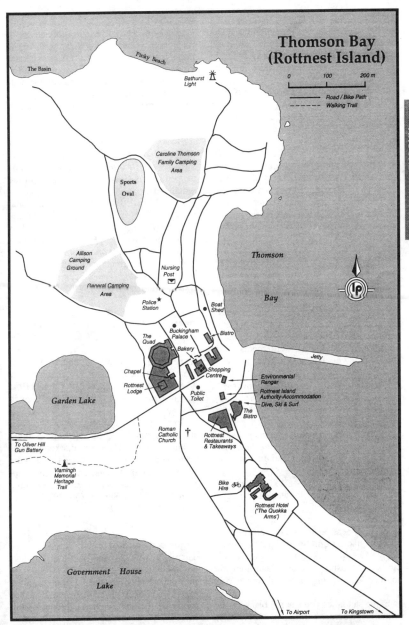

**Thomson Bay
(Rottnest Island)**

0   100   200 m

—— Road / Bike Path
---- Walking Trail

The Basin

Pinky Beach

Bathurst
Light

Caroline Thomson
Family Camping
Area

Sports
Oval

Allison
Camping
Ground

General Camping
Area

Nursing
Post

Police
Station

Boat
Shed

Thomson

Bay

Buckingham
Palace

Bistro

The
Quad

Bakery

Jetty

Chapel

Shopping
Centre

Environmental
Ranger

Rottnest
Lodge

Public
Toilet

Rottnest Island
Authority-Accommodation

Dive, Ski & Surf

The Bistro

Garden Lake

Roman
Catholic
Church

Rottnest
Restaurants
& Takeaways

To Oliver Hill
Gun Battery

Vlamingh
Memorial
Heritage
Trail

Bike
Hire

Rottnest Hotel
('The Quokka
Arms')

Government   House
Lake

To Airport   To Kingstown

Europeans and observing them has been popular ever since. De Vlamingh unflatteringly described them as 'a kind of rat as big as a common cat, whose dung is found in abundance all over the island'; thus the present name for the island.

It was known to the Aborigines as 'Quaka', Europeanised into quokka. Quokkas were once found throughout the south-west but are confined to patches of forest on the mainland and Rottnest. It is believed that there are 8000 to 12,000 on the island and you are bound to see one or two during your visit. Anniversary Park, on the right just after the last buildings of Thomson Bay (when heading to Kingstown), is a good spot to observe healthy quokkas in the wild. Just walk off the road, sit down and look out for them.

Bus tours have regular quokka-feeding points (the 'quokka stop'), where the voracious marsupials seem to appear on demand. Quokka kicking, once a popular sport on the island, is now illegal!

Birdwatching Rottnest is a great place for the avid twitcher as there are a number of habitats: coast, salt lakes, swamps, heath, woodlands and human settlements. This means that you will see a great range of species.

Coastal birds include cormorants (*Phalacrocorax*), reef heron (*Egretta sacra*), whimbrels (*Numenius phaeopus*), oystercatchers (*Haematopus*), bar-tailed godwits (*Limosa lapponica*), roseate (*Sterna dougalii*), fairy (*S. nereis*), bridled (*S. anaestheta*) and crested terns (*S. bergii*) and the majestic osprey.

There is a wedge-tailed shearwater (*Puffinus pacificus*) colony at Radar Reef at the far western end of the island and, at Phillip Point at the opposite end of the island, fairy terns nest on the sand. Parakeet Bay takes its name from the rock parrot, seen at many places on the coast feeding on sandfly larvae. The osprey are seen patrolling the southern coast from Strickland Bay to West End.

In the salt lakes you can see black swans, white-faced herons (*Ardea novaehollandiae*),

red-necked avocets (*Recurvirostra novaehollandiae*), ruddy turnstones (*Arenaria interpres*), caspian terns (*Sterna caspia*), grey-tailed tattlers (*Tringa brevipes*), stints (*Calidris*) and sandpipers (also *Calidris*). Even in Garden Lake, next to the village, you can see red-necked avocets, plovers (*Pluvialis*) and ruddy turnstones. Caspian terns have a breeding colony on Government House Lake.

Ducks and teals are found in the swamps and turtledoves (*Streptopelia*), welcome swallows (*Hirundo neoxena*) and red-capped robins (*Petroica goodenovii*) in the woodlands.

In the so-called disturbed areas are a great number of introduced birds such as the peafowl (*Pavo cristatus*) and natives such as the sacred kingfisher (*Halcyon sancta*) and rainbow bee-eater (*Merops ornatus*).

For more information, obtain *The Birdlife of Rottnest Island* (Denis Saunders & Perry de Rebeira, 1985).

Rotto Underwater The *Underwater Explorer* is a boat with windows below the waterline for viewing shipwrecks and marine life. It departs at hourly intervals from the jetty at Thomson Bay; an interesting 45-minute trip costs about $12. Contact Boat Torque Cruises (☎ (09) 221 5844) to book in advance.

Some of Rotto's **shipwrecks** are accessible to snorkellers, but getting to them requires a boat. There are marker plaques around the island telling the sad tales of how and when the ships sank. Snorkelling equipment, fishing gear and boats can be hired from Dive, Ski & Surf (☎ (09) 292 5167) at Thomson Bay.

Organised Tours
There's a two-hour and one-hour bus tour around the island for $9 and $6 respectively; they depart daily at 1 and 1.15 pm – again it is wise to book in the peak season. Both bus tours visit the island's main lighthouse. Built in 1895, it is visible 60 km out to sea.

Places to Stay

Most visitors to Rotto come only for the day but it's just as interesting staying on the island. You can camp for $12 (two people) in hired tents with rubber mattresses or get tent sites at *Rottnest Camping* (☎ (09) 372 9737). Safari cabins are also available from $25 to $66 a night, depending on the number of people. You should book in advance for a cabin or if you want to hire a tent. The set-up tents are $20 per day for four people or $10 for one person.

The *Rottnest Island Authority* (☎ (09) 372 9729) has over 260 houses and cottages for rent in Thomson Bay and the Geordie, Fays and Longreach Bay areas from $176 (bungalows) to $658 (villas) per week for four-bed accommodation. The accommodation varies widely in quality so you may need to check with the authority. Reductions of up to 25% are available in off-peak periods.

The *Kingstown Barracks Youth Hostel* (☎ (09) 372 9780), 1.2 km from the ferry terminal, is housed in an old barracks built in 1936; the cost per night is from $13 for members and $16 for nonmembers. This place has the feel and appearance of an army barracks but, fortunately these days, lacks the booming voice of a sergeant major whipping soldiers into line. Part of the complex is shared with school groups on environmental awareness courses and hot water for a shower is only a reality if you get up before 6 am. The kitchen facilities are adequate and the salvation is the nice communal lounge with its pot-belly stove.

At the top end of the scale there are a couple of good places. *The Rottnest Hotel* (☎ (09) 292 50011), the former Governor's mansion, has been converted into accommodation. All of the motel rooms have an ensuite and the single/double B&B rate is $100/130.

The *Rottnest Island Lodge* (☎ (09) 292 50011) is based on the former Quad and boy's reformatory school. These days it is run by All Seasons Hotels and is far more comfortable. The units range in price from $104 to $144 for two.

Places to Eat

The *Rottnest Family Restaurant* has a pleasant balcony overlooking Thomson Bay and serves Chinese dishes, dim sum lunches and takeaways. In the same complex, cappuccino and cakes are available from *The Bistro* and pies, pasties, salads and health foods from the *Food Hall*. *Brolley's Restaurant*, in the Rottnest Hotel, also serves light and full meals (summer only). There is the licensed *Lodge Garden Lake Restaurant* in the Rottnest Lodge; sometimes they have entertainment.

The island has a general store and a bakery that is famous for its fresh bread and pies. There's also a fast-food centre in the Thomson Bay settlement. In the Rottnest Island Lodge there is the *Governor's Bar* where they have an all-you-can-eat-meal on Tuesday, Wednesday and Thursday ($6.50). There's always the *Red Rooster*, also in the Thomson Bay shopping mall.

Geordie Bay has a licensed restaurant and coffee shop, open throughout the week during summer from 7 am to 7 pm. As this is part of the liquor store there is no shortage of things to drink. They serve Devonshire teas, fish & chips, burgers and sandwiches.

Getting There & Away

Competition, bless it, has brought prices down for the ferry trip to Rotto. Oceanic Cruises (☎ (09) 430 5127) has done some monopoly busting and its *Supercat*, which leaves the East St jetty, East Fremantle, costs only $12 (plus the $5 landing fee); the extended stay cost is $20.

Set up by rival operator, Boat Torque (☎ (09) 430 7644), is White Dolphin Cruises, which is intended to match Oceanic's prices; a same day return from the Northport Terminal is $15 and the extended stay cost is $25. There is a courtesy bus from Fremantle Railway Station to Northport, 45 minutes prior to departure.

You can also take Boat Torque's *Star Flyte* ferry from Perth's Barrack St jetty to Thomson Bay daily; it leaves Perth at 9 am and Northport, North Fremantle, at 10.15 am. The fare is $42 return from Perth and $25 from Fremantle. Boat Torque has another ferry service, *Sea Raider III*, from Hillarys Boat Harbour (north of Perth), which leaves at 8.30 am daily for $30 return. Bookings are essential at peak periods.

You can also fly to Rottnest on the Rottnest Airbus (☎ (09) 478 1322). It leaves Perth Airport four times a day, seven days a week for about $45 return; the trip takes just 15 minutes. There's a connecting bus between Rottnest Airport and Thomson Bay.

Getting Around

Bicycles are the time-honoured way of getting around the island. The number of motor vehicles is strictly limited, which makes cycling a real pleasure. Furthermore, the island is just big enough to make a day's ride good exercise. You can bring your own bike over on the ferry (free at present from East St jetty) or rent one of the hundreds available on the island from Rottnest Bike Hire (☎ (09) 372 9722) in Thomson Bay, near the hotel – a deposit of $10 is requested and helmets and locks (bicycles are often stolen) are available for hire.

Two bus services, the Bayseeker ($2) and the Settlement bus (50c), also run during the summer season – see the information office for bus timetables and departure points.

THE DARLING RANGE

The hills that surround Perth are popular for picnics, barbecues and bushwalks. There are also excellent lookouts from where you can see Perth and further down the coast. Araluen, with its waterfalls, Mundaring Weir, Gooseberry Hill and Kalamunda national parks, and Lake Leschenaultia are all of interest.

Kalamunda

The township of Kalamunda is about a 30-minute drive from Perth on the crest of the Darling Ranges. The area had its beginnings as a timber settlement in the 1860s but the clean air and magnificent bush later attracted Perth and Fremantle residents to this forest getaway. From Kalamunda, there are fine views over Perth to the coast.

The mud-brick and shingle **Stirk's Cottage**, in Kalamunda, was built in 1881. Near to town are **Gooseberry Hill**

National Park with the amazing Zig Zag Rd and **Kalamunda National Park** where you can walk, rest and picnic in beautiful surroundings. There are also a number of wineries (Hainault Vineyard, Piesse Brook Wines and Lawnbrook Estate), plant nurseries and art & craft places nearby.

South of Kalamunda, just off the Brookton Highway, is **Araluen Park**, a real gem; you get to it from Gardiner Rd, Roleystone. It was originally constructed in the 1920s by the Australian Youth League as a bush retreat but it was neglected for many years and quickly became overgrown. In recent years, the almost 'archaeological' excavations have revealed elaborate garden terraces, waterfalls and an ornamental pool, all surrounded by many species of tall trees. Well worth a visit, entry for cars/motorcycles is $5/2; there are barbecue and restaurant facilities.

Places to Stay & Eat The *Kalamunda Hotel* (☎ (09) 257 1084), 43 Railway Rd, has single/double rooms for $35/50. Numerous B&B places are tucked away in the hills and valleys. At *Looking West* (☎ (09) 454 7110), 1 Gray Rd, Gooseberry Hill, it is $70/90 for one/two persons and at the *Whistle Pipe Cottage* (☎ (09) 291 9872), 195 Orange Valley Rd, it is $30 per person.

Perth's tradition of good dining extends to the hills. If you are after coffee and a snack then try *Coffee Time*, *Village Coffee Shop*, *Barberry Cafe* and the *Kalamunda Cafe* in Kalamunda or *Le Croissant* on Gooseberry Hill Rd.

For a full meal you have the choice of the *Kalamunda Hotel* and *Williners Restaurant* on Railway Rd, *The Last Drop* and *Dons Family Restaurant* on Haynes St, the *Copperwood* on Stirk St, *The Curry Place* on Canning Rd and *Bangles Restaurant* on Mead St.

Getting There & Away Get there from Perth on bus Nos 300 or 302 via Maida Vale from bus stand No 43 in St George's Terrace; or bus Nos 292 or 305 via Wattle Grove and Lesmurdie from bus stand No 43 also.

Taking one route out and the other back makes an interesting circular tour of the hill suburbs.

Mundaring Weir

Mundaring, in the ranges only 35 km east from Perth, is the site of the Mundaring Weir – the dam built at the turn of the century to supply water to the goldfields over 500 km to the east. The reservoir has an attractive setting and is a popular excursion for Perth residents. There are also a number of walking tracks.

The **CY O'Connor Museum** has models and exhibits about the water pipeline to the goldfields – in its time one of the world's most amazing engineering feats (see Where Water is like Gold! in The Goldfields & The Nullarbor chapter). The museum is open Monday to Friday from 10.30 am to 3 pm and Saturday from 1 to 5 pm; it is closed Tuesday.

North of the Great Eastern Highway, near the village of Chidlow, is the beautiful freshwater **Lake Leschenaultia**, ideal for picnics, bushwalking and swimming; there is an entry fee of $4 per car.

The 16 sq km **John Forrest National Park**, near Mundaring, has protected areas of jarrah and marri trees, native fauna, waterfalls and a swimming pool. There is an admission fee of $5/3 for cars/motorcycles.

Places to Stay The *Mundaring Caravan Park* (☎ (09) 295 1125), two km west of town on the Great Eastern Highway, has powered sites for $6.50 for two. The *Mundaring Weir YHA Hostel* (☎ (09) 295 1809), on Mundaring Weir Rd, is eight km south of town and costs $8. The *Mundaring Weir Hotel* (☎ (09) 295 1106) is exceedingly popular with Perth escapees. Its quality units, constructed out of rammed earth, cost $60 for two (add an extra $5 on Friday nights).

The Mahogany Inn (☎ (09) 295 1118), on the corner of the Great Eastern Highway and Homestead Rd, is quite expensive at $80/160 for singles/doubles.

Walyunga National Park

The river cuts a narrow gorge through the Darling Range at Walyunga National Park in Upper Swan. This 18 sq km park is off the Great Northern Highway, 40 km north-east of Perth. There are walking tracks along the river and it's a popular picnic spot; a small entry fee for each car is charged. The bushwalks include a 5.2-km return walk to Syd's Rapids, the four-km loop Kangaroo Trail, and the 8.5-km loop Kingfisher Trail. Perhaps the best trail is the 10.6-km Echidna Loop as it has tremendous views over the Swan and Avon valleys.

The park has one of the largest known campsites of the Nyungar and it was still in use last century. The area may have been used by regional groups for more than 6000 years.

'Geoenergy' Tours

One fascinating aspect of the Darling Ranges is their geological diversity. Around Perth you can explore evidence of the break up of Gondwanaland (formerly one of two ancient supercontinents). At key sites in the Perth Basin – Yilgarn Block and Darling Ranges – you can learn about the formation of the surrounding earth with Geoenergy (☎ (09) 221 5411).

The tour starts in Perth at the Geology Museum of the University of WA, heads to 3.3 billion-year-old Toodyay sandstone, passes via the discernible rock strata of Windmill Hill cutting, pauses at the two-billion-year-old granites and gneisses of Noble Falls and ends in John Forrest National Park, on the edge of the Darling scarp. The cost is $89 and lunch is included.

North Coast

The coast north of Perth has great scenery with long sand dunes but it quickly becomes the inhospitable terrain that deterred early visitors. The north coast really begins at Yanchep and its satellite town of Two Rocks and extends up through Nambung National

Park, site of the Pinnacles, to the coastal town of Jurien.

To get to Lancelin, follow State Highway 60, which branches off to the north-west at Wanneroo. The Pinnacles are reached from the Brand Highway (National Highway No 1) which runs inland, as is Jurien. The free pamphlet *West Coast Connection* is full of information on this coastal area.

YANCHEP

The first break in Perth's northward urban sprawl is Yanchep, 51 km north of Perth, at the end of the Swan Coastal Plain. The name comes from the Aboriginal word 'Yanget' after the bulrushes at the edge of the lakes.

Yanchep National Park has natural bushland with tuart forests, some fine caves (including the limestone Crystal and Yondemp caves) and Loch McNess. The 28-km **Yaberoo Budjara Aboriginal Heritage Trail** follows a chain of lakes used by the Yaberoo people; serious walkers can obtain a brochure from the national park office. The park features such fauna as the honey possum, grey kangaroo, bandicoots, reptiles and a host of waterbirds. The national park information office (☎ (09) 561 1004) has plenty of ideas on activities in the area.

There is the Yanchep Stables (☎ (09) 561 1606) for those keen on horseriding and Blue Dolphin Dive Tours (☎ (09) 561 1106) for those wishing to explore the lagoon reefs.

Yanchep Sun City is a major marina with a modern shopping complex and Perth's only country beach resort, Club Capricorn.

On weekdays, one bus goes to Yanchep from the Wellington St Bus Station.

Places to Stay

There are a handful of places to stay, including the *Yanchep Inn* (☎ (09) 561 1001), in Yanchep National Park, which has singles/doubles from $28/45, and a motel section with rooms from $48/65. The *Yanchep Lagoon Lodge* (☎ (09) 561 1033), 11 Nautical Court, has single/double rooms for $30/50. The *Yanchep Holiday Village* (☎ (09) 561 2244), 56 St Andrews Drive, specialises in family units, accommodating

four to six persons, from $290 to $530 weekly. Similar is *Two Rocks Harbour View Apartments* (☎ (09) 561 1103), Two Rocks Rd, from $250 to $450 for two per week.

Also on Two Rocks Rd are the *Lodge Capricorn* (☎ (09) 561 1106) with doubles for $85 and *Club Capricorn* (☎ (09) 561 1106) with double chalets from $65 to $98.

GUILDERTON & SEABIRD

Some 43 km north of Yanchep is Guilderton, a popular holiday resort, at the mouth of the Moore River. The *Vergulde Draeck*, part of the Dutch East India Company fleet, ran aground near here in 1656. There is good fishing both in the Moore River and in the ocean. There is a caravan park (☎ (09) 577 1021) with tent/caravan sites for $8/10 for two and the *Sea Moore Guesthouse* (☎ (09) 577 1079).

Seabird, 36 km north of Guilderton, is a quaint fishing village. It also has a caravan park (☎ (09) 577 1038) close to a swimming area which is safe for children.

LEDGE POINT & LANCELIN

Ledge Point, 115 km from Perth, is another fishing town and a very popular holiday spot for Perth families. It is the starting point for the Ledge Point-Lancelin Sailboard Classic, held in January.

The coast road (SH 60) ends at Lancelin, a small fishing port 14 km north of Ledge Point, but coastal tracks continue north and may be passable with a 4WD. Lancelin was possibly named after PF Lancelin, a French scientific writer, by the 1801 French expedition (who passed here in the *Naturaliste* and *Geographe*). Windswept Lancelin is the finishing point of the 24-km annual sailboard race from Ledge Point. This race is now an important event on the world windsurfing calendar. Fishing, boating and swimming are options for those who have yet to stand up on a windsurfer. The information office (☎ (096) 55 1100) is open seven days from 9 am to 6 pm.

Places to Stay & Eat

There is a plethora of accommodation in

these towns but booking is strongly advised during holiday periods.

In Ledge Point, the caravan park (☎ (096) 55 1066) has caravan sites/on-site vans for $13/45 for two. Other accommodation options are the *Fern Tree Court & Gilt Dragon Villas* (☎ (096) 55 1069), on the corner of Jones St and Ammond Ave; the *Seaside Chalets* (☎ (096) 55 1524), Dewar Way; and the *Ledge Point Cottages* (☎ (096) 55 1331).

Lancelin has two caravan parks, the *North End* (☎ (096) 55 1066) and *Lancelin* (☎ (096) 55 1066), where tent/caravan sites are $10/12 for two. There are also *Campbells Cottages* (☎ (096) 55 1286); the *Lancelin Holiday Village* (☎ (096) 55 1100); a hotel/motel (☎ (096) 55 1005); *Ocean Front Flats* (☎ (096) 55 1029) and the *Windsurfer Beach Chalets* (☎ (096) 55 1563). Enquire about the much cheaper weekly rates.

The preferred hang-out in Lancelin is the *Endeavour Tavern* near the jetty. For more expensive meals, featuring the crayfish the region is famed for, try the licensed *Lancelin Island Restaurant* in the hotel on North St.

PINNACLES DESERT

The small seaport of **Cervantes**, 257 km north of Perth, was named after an American whaling ship wrecked on nearby islands. This town is the entry point for the unusual and haunting Pinnacles Desert. The Cervantes Shell service station (☎ (096) 52 7041) acts as the tourist office and books tours to the Pinnacles.

In the coastal **Nambung National Park,** the flat, sandy desert is punctured with peculiar limestone pillars, some only a few cm high and some towering up to five metres.

These pillars are calcified spires, around 30,000 years old, which have been gradually uncovered by erosion. Some have eroded into extraordinary, weird shapes. To the south of the main group is an area known as the Tombstones, where dark spires protrude from the vegetated landscape. The different colour comes from lichen, which grows on the pinnacles as they are protected from the sandblasting action of the wind. When Dutch sailors saw the pinnacles from the sea they assumed that they were the remains of an ancient city.

If possible, try to visit the Pinnacles Desert early in the morning. Not only is the light better for photography but you will avoid the crowds which tend to clutter the view, especially in peak holiday times. The park is the scene of an impressive display of **wildflowers** from August to October – look out for daisies, leschenaultia, lilies, grevillea, banksia, kangaroo paws and orchids.

Nambung may have the appearance of a desert but it still contains a wealth of fauna and the observant will spy many animal and reptile tracks. Snakes, lizards, skinks, geckos, western blue tongue's, bearded dragons, kangaroos, brush wallabies and dunnarts are all present in the park. Bird species are plentiful with many raptors, honeyeaters, emus and wrens. The Australian or kori bustard *(Ardeotis australis)* was once prolific but has been affected greatly by predation.

Check in Cervantes before attempting to drive the unsealed road into the park – if conditions are bad, a 4WD may be necessary but usually the road is OK, if somewhat bumpy, for normal vehicles. A coastal 4WD track runs north to Jurien, a crayfishing centre, and south to Lancelin. The sand dunes along the coast are spectacular.

Organised Tours

It's possible to take a half-day tour from the Cervantes Shell service station for $12 (plus a $2 park entrance fee) and save your car's suspension; it leaves daily at 1 pm (in spring there's a morning tour) and you would be wise to book. If you drive into the Pinnacles Desert yourself, there is a $3 car entrance fee. There are many tours to the Pinnacles which begin and end in Perth.

Places to Stay & Eat

Accommodation in the area includes the *Pinnacles Caravan Park* (☎ (096) 52 7060) on the beachfront with tent sites/on-site vans from $10/25 for two; *Cervantes Pinnacles Motel* (☎ (096) 52 7145), 227 Aragon St, with singles/doubles for $55/68; and *Cervantes Holiday Homes* (☎ (096) 52 7115), on the corner of Valencia Rd and Malaga Court, with self-contained units from $40 for two.

The Cervantes Shell service station sells takeaways; the *Ronsard Tavern* at 219 Cadiz St, serves counter meals; and the Cervantes Pinnacles Motel has the licensed *Europa Anchor Restaurant*.

JURIEN

This coastal town is 38 km west of the Brand Highway and 266 km north of Perth. (A coastal route runs due north from Cervantes but it is 4WD only.) Jurien, centre of a thriving crayfishing industry, is a great holiday destination for those who love boating, fishing and swimming. The **old jetty** was used in the late 1800s to load wool, from inland stations, onto boats bound for Fremantle and India. The Jurien tourist office (☎ (096) 52 1444) is in the BP service station on Bashford St.

Places to Stay

There is a caravan park (☎ (096) 52 1013) in Roberts St with sites/on-site vans for $11/25 for two. The *CWA Unit One* (☎ (096) 52 1015), 20 Padbury St, is $30 for six members and the *Jurien Bay Holiday Flats* (☎ (096) 52 1065), Grigson St, are $30 for two. The *Jurien Bay Hotel/Motel* (☎ (096) 52 1022), Padbury St, has single/double rooms for $35/40. There are a number of chalets in the town; enquire at the tourist office.

NATIONAL PARKS

In addition to Nambung, there are a number of other interesting national parks in the North Coast region. **Stockyard Gully National Park**, named after one of the stopping places used by drovers on the North Road Stock Route, is reached from the Coorow-Green Head Rd; access is by 4WD only. Some 5.6 km down Grover Rd is the ancient underground river system of Stockyard Gully tunnel, about 300 metres long (torches/flashlights are needed). Tours can be arranged through Jurien Bus & Charter Tours (☎ (096) 52 1036).

The **Drover's National Park** and **Lesueur National Park** are both north of the Jurien East Rd. The latter park is one of the most diverse and rich flora areas in WA. The Lesueur Fault, Mt Lesueur and the Cockleshell Gully formation can all be explored. Obtain a copy of a map from CALM in Cervantes which indicates the tracks you are permitted to drive on – access is restricted to prevent the spread of 'dieback' disease.

It is worth walking the 90-minute Badgingarra Trail in **Badgingarra National Park**. The park, on the west side of the Brand Highway and opposite the town of Badgingarra, was established to protect the wildflowers which grow there in great numbers.

Between the Brand Highway and State Highway 116 (Midlands Way) there are a number of national parks noted for their wildflower displays. The **Watheroo National Park** – 443 sq km of sandplain country north-east of Badgingarra – has some rare flora; the **Alexander Morrison National Park**, between Coorow and Green Head, is one of the best locations in the state to view wildflowers; and the **Tathra National Park**, east of Eneabba, has also been preserved for its important flora & fauna.

Avon Valley

The green and lush Avon Valley looks very English and proved a delight to homesick early settlers. In the spring, this area is particularly rich in wildflowers. In 1830, food shortages forced Governor Stirling to dispatch Ensign Dale to search the Darling Range for arable land – by August he had 'discovered' the Avon Valley. The valley was first settled in that year, only a year after Perth was founded, so there are many historic buildings in the area. The picturesque Avon River is very popular with canoeing enthusiasts.

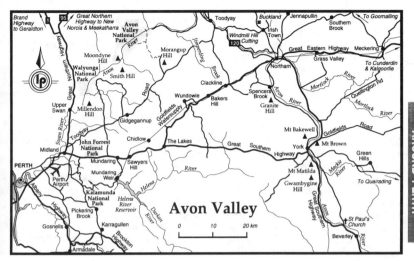

Avon Valley

GETTING THERE & AWAY

The Avon Valley towns all have bus connections to Perth; contact Westrail (☎ (09) 326 2222) for timetable details. Fares from Perth are Toodyay ($9), Northam ($10), York ($9) and Beverley ($12.50). It is also possible to take the *Prospector* from Perth to Toodyay ($9.20) and Northam ($11).

The best way to see the valley is by car as this allows you the flexibility to visit the many interesting places just outside of the towns.

TOODYAY

This charming, small town (population 800) is only 85 km north-east of Perth. There are numerous old classified and recorded buildings in this historic town, many of them built by convicts. Toodyay was declared an historic town by the National Trust in 1980.

Originally named Newcastle, the name Toodyay, from the Aboriginal 'Duidgee' ('Place of Plenty'), was applied in 1910. A big folk music festival is held here during the October long weekend.

Information

The local tourist office (☎ (09) 574 2435) is in Connor's Mill on Stirling Terrace, which also houses a working flour mill. It is open from 9 am to 5 pm, except Sunday (10 am to 5 pm).

Things to See & Do

The **Old Newcastle Gaol Museum**, on Clinton St, was built in the 1860s. Another old building is **Connors Mill**, built in 1870, as the town's third steam-driven flour mill. The **Moondyne Gallery**, on the top floor of the mill, is interesting for the story it tells of bushranger Joseph Bolitho Johns – see the Moondyne Joe aside in this chapter. There is an entrance fee for gaol and gallery. Also in town is the historic **St Stephen's Church**, built in 1862.

Some five km from the town is the oldest inland **winery** in WA, Coorinja, which began operating in the 1870s; it specialises in fortified wines, particularly port.

Downriver from Toodyay is the Avon Valley National Park and down the Perth road is the popular White Gum Flower farm, where native plants are cultivated for sale.

Avon Valley National Park

The park is 45 km from Midland and access is along Toodyay, Morangup and Quarry roads. Features of the park are the granite outcrops, transitional forests and diverse fauna. The Avon River flows through the centre of the park in winter and spring but is usually dry at other times.

This is the northern limit of the jarrah forests, and the jarrah and marri are mixed with wandoo woodland. The two species of wandoo *(Eucalyptus accedens* and *E. wandoo)* grow in the heavy, clay soils; the deep-rooted jarrah grows on the well-drained higher slopes; and the marri grows further down the slope where the soil is moist and deep.

Many bird species make use of the diverse habitats in this forest – species seen are rainbow bee-eaters, a number of honeyeaters, kingfishers and rufous treecreepers *(Climacteris rufa).* A number of animals and reptiles live in the understorey. Honey possums and western pygmy-possums *(Cercartetus concinnus)* hide among the dead leaves, and skinks and geckos are everywhere. Predators such as foxes and cats are a real problem and CALM is trying to eradicate them.

There are campsites available in the park with basic facilities such as pit toilets and barbecues. Contact the ranger (☎ (09) 574 2540); a site costs $5 for two.

Places to Stay & Eat

Toodyay Caravan Park Avon Banks (☎ (09) 574 2612), Railway Rd, on the banks of the Avon River, has tent sites/air-con on-site vans/chalets for $8/25/45; all prices are for two. It is noisy (as it is located near the railway line and road) and the tent sites are as hard as rock. The *Broadgrounds Park* (☎ (09) 574 2534), off Racecourse Rd, has unpowered/powered sites for $6/12 and on-site vans/chalets for $20/50; there is a camper's kitchen.

The old convent of *Avondown Inn* (☎ (09) 574 2995), 44 Stirling Tce, is now a budget accommodation place; singles/doubles are $18/35. There is a cottage which accommodates eight persons; this is $100 for four. Opposite is the *Freemasons Hotel* (☎ (09) 574 2201), with basic B&B from $22 to $25 per person and inexpensive counter meals. On the same street is the *Victoria Hotel/Motel* (☎ (09) 574 2206), with singles/doubles from $20/40; add $10 to the price if you want a motel unit. Counter meals are available from $7 to $9.

On Harper Rd is *Appleton House* (☎ (09) 574 2622), a luxurious B&B place where singles/doubles are $40/75. About nine km from Toodyay is *Deepdale* (☎ (09) 574 2708), an historic homestead in very pictur-

---

Moondyne Joe

Every state should have a bushranger. The west's most famous bushranger was Joseph Bolitho Johns, also known as Moondyne Joe, but he was more of a Harry Houdini than a Ned Kelly.

Transported to WA for larceny, he arrived in Fremantle in 1853 and was granted an immediate ticket of leave. In 1861 he was arrested on a charge of horse stealing, escaped from Toodyay gaol, recaptured, and sentenced to three years' imprisonment.

He subsequently achieved infamy more because of his ability to escape custody than the severity of his crimes. Between November 1865 and March 1867, he made four attempts to escape, three of them successful. He repeatedly returned to hide in the wild and inaccessible Darling Ranges while at large.

When eventually captured he was placed in a special reinforced cell with triple barred windows in Fremantle. When allowed out for exercise he (you guessed it) escaped in 1867 and headed back to the hills east of Perth. He served more time in Fremantle prison when recaptured and was conditionally pardoned in 1873. After release he worked in the Vasse district and kept his nose clean until his death in 1900.

He is reputed to have discovered the caves near Margaret River, named after him. To find out more about Moondyne Joe, visit the Moondyne Gallery in Toodyay. The Moondyne Festival is held in Toodyay in May. ■

esque surroundings; B&B singles/doubles are $45/90 and each child is charged $20.

There are a few eating places on Stirling Terrace: the *Lavender Restaurant, Emma's Restaurant* and the *Wendouree Tearooms*. O'Meara's Tavern, also on Stirling Terrace, has the *Cellar Bistro*.

NORTHAM

Northam, the major town (population 7500) of the Avon Valley, is a busy farming centre on the railway line to Kalgoorlie. The line from Perth once ended here and miners had to make the rest of the weary trek to the goldfields by road.

Northam is packed on the first weekend in August every year for the start of the gruelling 133-km Avon Descent for power boats, kayaks and canoes. The tourist office (☎ (096) 22 2100), at 138 Fitzgerald St, is open daily.

Things to See & Do

The 1836 **Morby Cottage** served as Northam's first church and school, and it now houses a museum open on Sunday; the entrance fee is $1. The **old railway station**, listed by the National Trust, has been restored and turned into a museum; it is open on Sunday from 10 am to 4 pm and admission is $2. Also of interest in town are the colony of **white swans** on the Avon River, descendants of birds introduced from England early this century.

Near Northam at Irishtown is the elegant **Buckland House** (☎ (096) 22 1130). It was built in 1874, has a fine collection of antiques and is credited with being WA's most impressive stately home. It is open by appointment only.

If you have enough funds, try **ballooning** over the Avon Valley from March to November.

Places to Stay

The *Northam Guesthouse* (☎ (096) 22 2301), 51 Wellington St, has cheap accommodation from $15 per person for the first night and $10 thereafter. On the same street, at No 426, is the *Grand Hotel* (☎ (096) 22

1024) with basic rooms and shared facilities for $20/40. The *Avon Bridge Hotel* (☎ (096) 22 1023), the oldest hotel in Northam, has singles/twins for $20/30.

The only motel in town is aptly named the *Northam* (☎ (096) 22 1755), 13 John St; singles/doubles are $46/53. The *Shamrock Hotel* at 112 Fitzgerald St, is the best in town with elegant ensuite bedrooms; a double will cost from $80 to $135.

Two excellent out-of-town choices are *Buckland Homestead* (☎ (096) 46 1200), in Irishtown, which has singles/doubles for $68/136; and the farmstay *Egoline Reflections* (☎ (096) 22 5811), on the Toodyay Rd, which has homestead rooms for $60/90 for singles/doubles.

Places to Eat

Near the tourist office are two tearooms, *Lisa's* and *Lucy's*. *Tattersalls Hotel*, at 174 Fitzgerald St, also has lunch specials and is open for breakfast from 7 to 10 am. Next to Tattersalls Hotel, *Bruno's Pizza Bar* does tasty pizza to eat in or takeaway. The *Ruen Thai*, 96 Fitzgerald St, is fast becoming popular as local palates adapt to Asian flavours. The *Whistling Kettle*, 48 Broome Terrace, overlooks the river – a great place to enjoy home-cooked food.

A good à la carte choice is *Byfield House*, out on Gordon St; it is open Wednesday to Sunday for lunch and dinner. In town, try out any of the *Shamrock Hotel's* restaurants.

YORK

The oldest inland town (population 2800) in WA, York is 97 km from Perth. York was first settled in 1831, only two years after the Swan River Colony. Settlers saw similarities in the Avon Valley to their native Yorkshire, so Governor Stirling bestowed the name York on the region's first town.

Convicts were introduced to the York region in 1851 and helped in the development of the district; the ticket-of-leave hiring depot was not closed until 1872, four years after transportation to WA had ceased. During the gold rush, York prospered as a commercial centre, equipping miners who

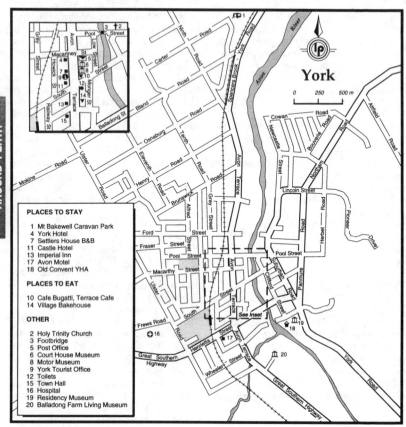

York

0   250   500 m

PLACES TO STAY

1 Mt Bakewell Caravan Park
4 York Hotel
7 Settlers House B&B
11 Castle Hotel
13 Imperial Inn
17 Avon Motel
18 Old Convent YHA

PLACES TO EAT

10 Cafe Bugatti, Terrace Cafe
14 Village Bakehouse

OTHER

2 Holy Trinity Church
3 Footbridge
5 Post Office
6 Court House Museum
8 Motor Museum
9 York Tourist Office
12 Toilets
15 Town Hall
16 Hospital
19 Residency Museum
20 Balladong Farm Living Museum

were travelling overland to Southern Cross and beyond. It is now a farming centre and a popular destination for locals looking to escape Perth for the weekend.

A stroll down the main street, with its restored old buildings, is a real step back in time. In fact, the preponderance of intact colonial and Victorian buildings has earned the National Trust classification of 'historic town'.

Orientation & Information

Most of the activity happens along Avon Terrace, very much the focal point of York.

The tourist office (☎ (096) 41 1301) is at 105 Avon Terrace; ask for a copy of the free booklet *York: The State's Festival Town*.

Things to See & Do

The excellent **Residency Museum** from the 1850s, the old **town hall**, the **Castle Hotel** (built in 1853), the old **police station, old gaol, courthouse** and **Settlers House** are all of interest. The old gaol and courthouse includes a main law court, old courtroom, prison cell block, prison exercise yard, trooper's cottage and stables with a carriage display.

The **Holy Trinity Church**, on Pool St by the Avon River, was completed in 1854. It contains glass designed by the WA artist Robert Juniper (see under Arts & Culture in the Facts about Western Australia chapter) and the high altar features his paintings. Also in the church is a rare pipe organ with eight bells. The suspension bridge near town was built in 1906 and it crosses the Avon River.

The classy **York Motor Museum** (a must for vintage-car enthusiasts) is on Avon Terrace. The cars in this museum range from an 1894 Peugeot to the Saudi Williams driven by Alan Jones, the 1980 world champion. It is open seven days from 9 am to 5 pm – entrance is $6, children $2.

On the edge of town is the **Historic Balladong Farm**, depicting life during the pioneer era and the **De Ladera Alpaca Farm**, where you can purchase those oh-so-warm and expensive jumpers.

Festivals

York is the state's festival town with no fewer than a dozen major events. The better patronised ones are the Jazz Festival in October and the Flying 50s Vintage & Veteran car race in August. Heritage Week is held in April, the agricultural show in September and car rallies in October.

Places to Stay

The only caravan park around town is *Mt Bakewell Caravan Park* (☎ (096) 41 1421) with tent sites/on-site vans at $10/30 for two.

York YHA Hostel (☎ (096) 41 1372), at 3 Brook St, in any one of three buildings that formed part of the old hospital, has dorm beds for $10; it would be good if one part was dedicated to backpackers and effort expended on that. The old section of the historic, renovated *Castle Hotel* (☎ (096) 41 1007), on Avon Terrace, is good value with singles/doubles from $25/45; the motel units are $70/95. The *Palace Hotel* (☎ (096) 41 1402), on Avon Terrace, has single/double rooms for $24/34.

There are a number of quality B&B and farmstays in the region; enquire at the tourist office. In town, *King's Head Cottage*

(☎ (096) 41 1817), 39 Avon Terrace, has single/double rooms for $35/50 and *Settlers House B&B* (☎ (096) 41 1096), 125 Avon Terrace, is $80 for two.

Places to Eat

For breakfast, go to the *Settler's House*, and for takeaways there is the *York Deli*. Try *Cafe Bugatti* for cappuccino and Italian food; its neighbour, the *Terrace Cafe*, with 'pocket-pleasing prices' for coffee; *York Village Bakehouse & Tearooms* for freshly baked bread and cakes and *Jule's Shoppe* for exquisite pasties. *Gilbert's*, in the York 'Palace' Hotel, has a range of meals and the *Castle Hotel* serves good counter meals from $9 to $13 and à la carte meals as well; you can also eat outside on the verandah cafe. All these places are on Avon Terrace.

Getting There & Away

Most people drive their own cars to York so they can take in the many heritage drives. You can also get there on the daily Westrail bus; the cost from Perth is $9.20.

BEVERLEY

South-east of York, also on the Avon River, is Beverley (population 1700), founded in 1838 and named after a town in Yorkshire. It is noted for its fine **aeronautical museum** open seven days from 10 am to 4 pm. Exhibits include a locally constructed biplane *Silver Centenary*, built between 1928 and 1930. The **grave** of a local Aborigine, Billy Noongale, who accompanied Sir John Forrest on his journey from Perth to Adelaide in 1870, is in Brooking St. The Beverley information office (☎ (096) 46 1555) is in Vincent St.

The **town hall** and **Beverley Hotel** are good examples of Art Deco architecture. The **Dead Finish Hotel** was built in 1872. With the advent of the railway, the town centre was moved closer to the station, leaving the Dead Finish isolated; it is now a museum.

The seven sq km **Avondale Discovery Farm**, six km west of Beverley, has a collection of agricultural machinery, a homestead, a workshop and stables. About 35 km south of Beverley is **Country Peak**, where you are likely to see wedge-tailed eagles.

Places to Stay & Eat

The *Beverley Caravan Park* (☎ (096) 46 1200), on Vincent St, has tent sites and on-site vans. The ordinary *Beverley Hotel* (☎ (096) 46 1190), at 137 Vincent St, has B&B for $18/35. The *Rosedale Farmstay* (☎ (096) 48 1031), on the York-Williams Rd, and *County Peak* (☎ (096) 46 4026) on the Yenyenning Lakes Rd, are both $60 per night.

Two delis, *Beverley* and *Marg's*, are both on Vincent St. The hotels serve counter meals.

NEW NORCIA

You guessed it! The small community of New Norcia is not part of the Avon Valley. But it's inclusion here is justified as it is often part of a long day trip from Perth which combines the towns of the Avon Valley.

This village, 132 km north of Perth, is decidedly incongruous – Australia's very own setting for *The Name of the Rose*. It was established as a Spanish Benedictine mission in 1846, by Dom Rosendo Salvado and Dom Jose Serra, and named after Nursia in Italy where St Benedict was born. It is still occupied by Benedictine monks who own and operate the town. It has changed little since its inception and boasts a fine collection of buildings with classic Spanish architecture – 27 of the buildings are classified by the National Trust.

The buildings which house the **museum** and **art gallery** are worth seeing for their old paintings (including works by Spanish and Italian masters), manuscripts and religious artefacts. They also house the tourist office (☎ (096) 54 8056).

There are daily tours of the monastery for $10 (children $5) which include the interior of chapels and other cloistered and secret places. Buy a snack of sourdough bread at the 150-year-old bakehouse. Search in vain for the secret recipe for the liqueur Dom Benedictine along the two-km self-guided New Norcia **heritage trail**. You can get the excellent *New Norcia Heritage Trail* brochure, which traces the development of the settlement, from the museum.

One of the interesting features of the trail is the **abbey church**, opened in 1861, and built from bush stones, mud plaster and rough-hewn tree trunks. Inside is the tomb of Dom Rosendo Salvado.

Places to Stay & Eat

Just past the museum is the historic *New Norcia Hotel* (☎ (096) 54 8034) which has interesting decor, including a grand staircase; single/double/triple rooms are $45/55/60. The Benedictine monks still live and work in New Norcia – you too can experience the monastic life by staying in the *Monastery Guesthouse* (☎ (096) 54 8018); full board is $40 per person for bed, prayer and all meals. If you don't wish to stay in the monastery, try the farmstay *Napier Downs* (☎ (096) 55 9015) in Wannamal, 15 km south of New Norcia; B&B is $100 for two.

The bread (available from the museum), known to many as the 'staff of life', is simply delicious. You can get a good home-cooked meal from *Salvado's Restaurant* in the New Norcia Roadhouse, open from 7 am to 8 pm, or from the New Norcia Hotel (if you are staying there).

The South-West

The south-western area of WA has a magnificent coastline, rugged ranges, national parks, the greenest and most fertile areas – a great contrast to the dry and barren country found in much of the state. You will find great patches of forest, the chance to whalewatch, world-famous surfing beaches, prosperous farms, the Margaret River wineries and more of the state's beautiful wildflowers.

In this chapter, the south-west includes the southern coast from Rockingham to Augusta, including a number of wineries, and part of the 'tall trees' hinterland to the east. The main town of the region is Bunbury, known for its pods of friendly dolphins.

South Coast

The coast south of Perth has a softer appearance than the often harsh landscape to the north. This is another popular resort area for Perth residents and many have holiday houses along this stretch of coast.

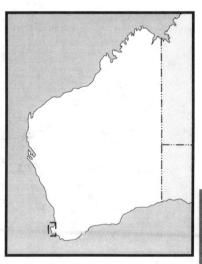

ROCKINGHAM

Rockingham (population 60,000), 47 km south of Perth, was founded in 1872 as a port, but that function, in time, was taken over by Fremantle. Today, Rockingham is a dormitory city and popular seaside resort with sheltered and ocean beaches. It also has a high proportion of British migrants in its population.

The helpful Rockingham tourist office (☎ (09) 592 3464), at 43 Kent St, is open Monday to Friday from 9 am to 5 pm and weekends from 10 am to 4 pm.

Things to See & Do

For kids there is **Marapana Wildlife World**, just south of Rockingham on Mandurah Rd. For adults there are a couple of **wineries** in the region. Baldivis Estate Winery, at 249a River Rd, Baldivis, is open from 11 am to 5 pm for cellar sales. Peel Estate, 10 km south of Rockingham on the Mandurah Rd, is open from 10 am to 5 pm.

Worshippers of the industrial revolution can visit the **Kwinana power station**, the state's second largest after Muja (see under Collie in this chapter). Tours operate daily; check by calling ☎ (09) 410 8440.

Offshore Islands

Close to Rockingham is **Penguin Island**, home to a colony of fairy penguins from late March to early December, and **Seal Island**, with its colony of sea lions. Rockingham Sea Tours (☎ (09) 528 2004) can arrange tours there – check with the tourist office. Penguin Island is closed to visitors during the breeding season from June to August.

The naval base of **Garden Island** is also nearby. It is open during daylight hours but many pleasant beaches can be reached by

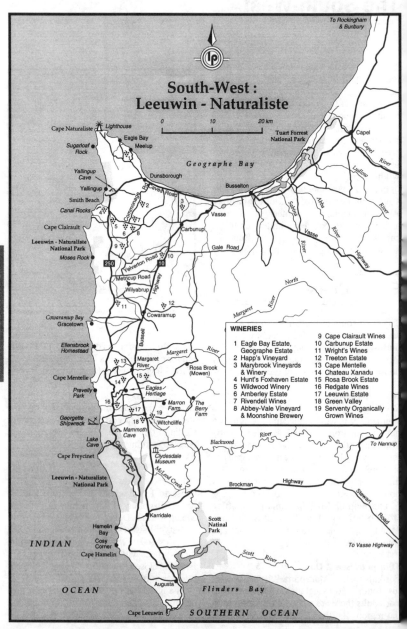

THE SOUTH-WEST

South-West :
Leeuwin - Naturaliste

0   10   20 km

WINERIES

1 Eagle Bay Estate,
   Geographe Estate
2 Happ's Vineyard
3 Marybrook Vineyards
   & Winery
4 Hunt's Foxhaven Estate
5 Wildwood Winery
6 Amberley Estate
7 Rivendell Wines
8 Abbey-Vale Vineyard
   & Moonshine Brewery

9 Cape Clairault Wines
10 Carbunup Estate
11 Wright's Wines
12 Treeton Estate
13 Cape Mentelle
14 Chateau Xanadu
15 Rosa Brook Estate
16 Redgate Wines
17 Leeuwin Estate
18 Green Valley
19 Serventy Organically
    Grown Wines

private boat. Shy tammar wallabies can occasionally be seen on the bush fringes.

One informative, laid-back trip is to **Carnac Island** with *Bellbird* Marine Discovery (☎ (09) 335 1521, (09) 335 3056). You sail out to the islands in Cockburn Sound in a small fishing boat on either a half-day or day trip. On this trip it is possible to swim with Australian sea lions *(Neophoca cinerea)* – these are much larger than fur seals and they range through the Southern and Indian oceans. The sea lions found on the island are non-mating males, barren females and juveniles.

The cost of the trip is $35 with a healthy lunch included; there are discounts for hostellers and backpackers.

Places to Stay
There are five caravan parks in the Rockingham area; enquire at the tourist office. They are the *Palm Beach* (☎ (09) 527 1515), at 37 Fisher St; the *Cee & See* (☎ (09) 527 1297), corner of Governor and Rockingham Rds; the *Holiday Village* (☎ (09) 527 4240), at Lot 51 Dixon Rd; the *Lakeside* (☎ (09) 524 1182), Mandurah Rd, Baldivis; and the *WA Waterski* (☎ (09) 524 1401), St Albans Rd, Baldivis. Sites with power are about $12 for two and on-site vans $30.

Another budget place, the *CWA Rockingham* (☎ (09) 527 9560), 108 Parkin St, is operated by a friendly couple. There are two units available, each sleeping six, from $25 per night. The *Rockingham Lodge Motel* (☎ (09) 527 1230), 20 Lake St, has singles/doubles for $28/38.

There are plenty of motels and hotels including the *Ocean Clipper Inn* (☎ (09) 527 8000), Patterson Rd, at $58/65 for singles/doubles; the *Leisure Inn* (☎ (09) 527 7777), on the corner of Read St and Simpson Avenue, at $40/50; the *Rockingham Hotel* (☎ (09) 592 1828), 26 Kent St, at $40/50 and the *Waikiki Hotel* (☎ (09) 592 1388), on the corner of Malibu and Safety Bay Rds, at $25/35.

Places to Eat
In a city of 60,000 you would expect a fair number of eateries, and Rockingham doesn't let you down. There are over 10 coffee shops and happy hunting for a cuppa will be rewarded at either the Rockingham Arcade or the city shops. The full gamut of takeaways are covered – fish & chips, burgers, chicken and pizza.

There are at least 10 Asian restaurants including the *Kinnaree Thai* in Sunray Village, *Indian Delights* at 26 Flinders Lane and the *Silver Dragon* Chinese restaurant on Rockingham Rd.

For full meals, try the local hotels. Otherwise, there is *El Roccos*, at 84 Parkin St, for good Mexican food; *The Gables*, 178 Safety Bay Rd; *La Spiaggia* at 41c Rockingham Rd; and the *Shoalwater Steakhouse* in the George 'n' Dragon Tavern in the Shoalwater shopping centre.

Getting There & Away
You can get to Rockingham on bus No 120 from Fremantle or a No 116 from bus stand No 48 in St George's Terrace, Perth.

MANDURAH
Situated on the calm Mandurah Estuary, this is yet another popular beach resort (population 29,000), 75 km south of Perth. The name comes from the Aboriginal 'mandjar', meaning 'meeting place'. Dolphins are often seen in the estuary, and the waterways in the area are noted for good fishing, prawning (March and April) and crabbing.

Things to See & Do
There is no shortage of things to do, especially during the holidays and the options available for kids will render parents penniless. There are horse, boat, camel, sailboard, jet ski, yacht and cycle rides. There is a skate arena, mini and real golf, the Castle Fun Park, Farm World, Lincoln Green archery park and the King Carnival amusement park.

Things to see in town include the restored, limestone **Hall's Cottage** (open Sunday afternoon), built in the 1830s, and the **Western Rosella Bird Park**, open daily from 9 am to 6 pm (admission is $4).

Full-day and short cruises are available on

the MV *Peel Princes* from the jetty in town. Contact the Mandurah tourist office (☎ (09) 535 1155), 5 Pinjarra Rd, for ferry schedules, maps and other information.

Prolific bird life can be seen on **Peel Inlet** and the narrow coastal salt lakes, **Clifton** and **Preston**, 20 km to the south.

Places to Stay

Mandurah is one of those places close to a major city which gets congested with holidaymakers at certain times of the year. There is a string of caravan parks around town with tent sites and on-site vans; enquire at the tourist office.

The *Brighton Hotel* (☎ (09) 535 1242), on Mandurah Terrace, is the best deal in town with B&B singles/doubles from $25/50; they also serve good counter meals. The *Mandurah Lodge* (☎ (09) 535 1265), at 52 Pinjarra Rd, has B&B for $35/60; the *Albatross Guesthouse* (☎ (09) 581 5597), 26 Hall St, is $35/70 for B&B; and the *Linksview B&B* (☎ (09) 535 7808), 52 Portmarnock Circle, Halls Head, has singles/doubles for $30/45.

Places to Eat

There are numerous places to eat around town including *Pronto's Cafe* on the corner of Pinjarra Rd and Mandurah Terrace. They have good snacks and cakes, and an all-you-can-eat pasta night on Friday for $9 – live music is often provided.

A big and tasty serve of fish & chips ($3.50) is available at *Jetty Fish & Chips* by the estuary near the end of Pinjarra Rd. Next door is *Yo-Yo's* which has a vast array of ice creams and sundaes.

If you like Chinese food try *Chow's Restaurant* in Mandurah Terrace. There are also a number of up-market choices on Mandurah Terrace: *Mandurah Terrace* for Italian, *Edward's Waterfront* at No 5, *Doddi's* at No 115 and the *Mandurah Garden* at No 124.

Getting There & Away

To get to Mandurah, catch bus No 116 from stand 48 in St George's Terrace, Perth, or bus No 117 from Fremantle. Westrail (☎ (09) 326 2477) also has a number of services which pass through Mandurah and stop at all the towns between Mandurah and Bunbury.

AUSTRALIND

Australind (population 800), yet another holiday resort, is a pleasant 11 km drive from Bunbury. The town takes its name from an 1840s plan to make it a port for trade with India. The plan never worked but the strange name (derived from Australia-India) remains.

The tiny **St Nicholas Church** (built in 1860), on Paris Rd, is just four by seven metres, and is said to be the smallest church in Australia. **Henton Cottage**, built in 1842 from local materials, has arts & crafts for sale. There is a wonderful scenic drive between Australind and Binningup along **Leschenault Inlet**, a good place to catch blue manna crabs.

Places to Stay

Australind has two caravan parks: *Leschenault Inlet* (☎ (097) 97 1095), Scenic Drive; and the *Holiday Homes* (☎ (097) 25 1206), on the Old Coast Rd.

SOUTH-WESTERN HIGHWAY

From Armadale, 29 km south of Perth, the South-Western Highway skirts the Darling Range then heads south to Bunbury via Pinjarra and Harvey.

Serpentine-Jarrahdale

This peaceful area of forest, 55 km from Perth, includes the Serpentine National Park. On Falls Rd, at the base of the national park, are the **Serpentine Falls**. There are walking tracks and picnic areas near the Serpentine Dam, on Kinsbury Drive. **Turner Cottage**, on the South-Western Highway, has been restored to its original condition.

Jarrahdale is an old mill town, established in 1871 and the old **post office** was built in 1880. Mundijong has **Tumbulgum Farm**, host venue to a farm show, Aboriginal corroboree and a place selling Aussie food. The Serpentine-Jarrahdale tourist office (☎ (09) 525 5255) is in Paterson St, Mundijong.

There is a caravan park (☎ (09) 525 2622) near Serpentine Falls; railway carriages (☎ (09) 525 5256) – popular but cold accommodation – near Whitby Falls; and railway carriages (☎ (09) 525 5780) in Jarrahdale.

North Dandalup & Dwellingup
These towns, respectively 71 km and 97 km south of Perth, are jumping-off points for the nearby forests. **Whittaker's Mill**, off Scarp Rd near North Dandalup, is a great spot for bushwalking and camping.

Destroyed by fire in 1961, Dwellingup has been rebuilt and is now a busy timber town. It is the terminus for the popular Hotham Valley Tourist Railway. The Bibbulman Track (see under Bushwalking in the Facts for the Visitor chapter) passes Dwellingup, some 500 metres to the east. Here, at Nanga Mill and Pool, is a night stopover for walkers on the track. There are a number of group camping facilities (☎ (095) 38 1001) in the Dwellingup region.

Pinjarra
Pinjarra (population 9100), 86 km south of Perth, has a number of old buildings picturesquely sited on the banks of the Murray River. The Murray tourist office (☎ (09) 531 1438), in Pinjarra, is in the historic building **Edenvale**, corner of George and Henry Sts. Behind the historic mud-brick post office is a pleasant picnic area and a **suspension bridge** – wobbly enough to test most people's coordination! **St John's Church**, built in 1861 from mud-brick, is beside the original 1862 **school house**. Picturesque **Cooper's Mill**, on Culeenup Island and only accessible by boat, was the first in the Murray region.

About four km from the town is the **Old Blythewood Homestead**, an 1859 colonial farm and a National Trust property.

Places to Stay & Eat The caravan park (☎ (09) 531 1374), 95 Pinjarra Rd, has on-site vans/cabins from $30/35. The *Pinjarra Motel* (☎ (09) 531 1811), 131 South-Western Highway, offers singles/doubles with breakfast for $40/50 and the *Exchange Hotel* (☎ (09) 531 1209), George St, has singles for $20.

The *Heritage Tearooms* serves light meals such as sandwiches and quiches for around $6. Other restaurants are the *Copper Kettle*, George St; the *River Resort Restaurant*, Murray Lakes; and the *Pinjarra Chinese Restaurant*, 55 George St.

Romance of Steam: Pinjarra to Dwellingup
Hotham Valley Tourist Railway **steam trains** run from Pinjarra to Dwellingup through blooming wildflowers and jarrah forests in winter only (August to October). You can find out the timetable for the Forest Ranger service by calling ☎ (09) 221 4444. The cost for adults is $24/30 in tourist/1st class and for children it is $11.50/19.50.

A short trip on the Etmilyn Forest Tramway, which operates Tuesday, Thursday, Saturday and Sunday, is $6/3 for adults/children. There are a number of other rail adventures offered such as three-day wheatbelt, Great Southern and Karri Forest safaris.

Waroona, Yarloop & Harvey
Originally called Drakesbrook, **Waroona** is another popular holiday spot, 112 km south of Perth. It is ideally situated with Preston and Clifton lakes to the west and the forests to the east. If you follow Preston Beach Rd from Waroona you reach **Yalgorup National Park**, which has bushwalking trails through the tuart trees. Some 13 km south of Waroona is **Yarloop** where there are restored engineering workshops dating from the steam and horsedrawn eras.

Inland from the south-west coast is the town of **Harvey**, in a bushwalking area of green hills to the north of Bunbury. This is the home of WA's Big Orange, standing 20 metres high at the Fruit Bowl on the South-Western Highway. There are dam systems and some beautiful waterfalls nearby.

The tourist office (☎ (097) 29 1122) is on the South-Western Highway. Committed vegetarians can hurl vitriol in a tour of EG

Green & Sons abattoirs (aka Harvey Beef)
(☎ (097) 29 1000).

Places to Stay There is a range of accommodation in this region. In Waroona, try the caravan village (☎ (097) 33 1518), the *Drakesbrook Guesthouse* (☎ (097) 33 1245) where B&B is $25 per person, or the *Nanga Dell Farm* (☎ (095) 538 1035), on Kyabram Rd, where a cabin is $50 for a family of four.

In Yarloop, there is the 1890 timber *Old Mill Guest House* (☎ (097) 33 5264), at 113 Railway Pde, where B&B is $25 per person.

Harvey has the *Rainbow Caravan Park* (☎ (097) 29 2239), 199 King St, where tent/caravan sites are $8/10 and on-site vans are $20 for two. The *Wagon Wheels Motel* (☎ (097) 29 1408), Uduc Rd, has singles/doubles for $45/55.

Collie

Collie, WA's only coal town, is 202 km south of Perth. It has an interesting replica of a coal mine, an historical museum and a steam locomotive museum. There is some pleasant bushwalking country around the town and plenty of wildflowers in season.

The **Wellington Forest**, near Wellington Dam and Collie, offers a great deal of 'natural' recreational activities. Walking tracks include the lengthy Bibbulman, the two-day and 24-km Lennard Circuit, the four-hour Wellington Mills and Sika circuits and the 2.5-hour Lookout Loop close to Honeymoon Pool. About 300 species of wildflowers grow in the Wellington Forest, some unique to the area.

The **Muja power station** is the state's non-nuclear answer to Three Mile Island; tours of the complex are available on Tuesday and Thursday. Far more interesting would be a **rafting** descent of the rapids of the Collie River. Book both trips at the Collie tourist office (☎ (097) 34 2051), Throssell St.

Places to Stay The *Mr Marron Holiday Village* (☎ (097) 34 2507), Porter St, has tent/caravan sites for $10/12 and on-site vans for $25 for two. As befits a mining town, there are a number of hotels offering accom-

modation – the *Victoria Hotel* (☎ (097) 34 1138), 70 Throssell St, has singles/twins for $20/40 as does the *Colliefields Hotel* (☎ (097) 34 2052), 50 Throssell St.

BUNBURY

Western Australia's second largest town (population 26,000), some 180 km south of Perth, is a port, an industrial town and a holiday resort. It is a pleasant place, worth at least a day in a trip to the south-west. Some scientific boffins actually identified Bunbury as being in a region with the 'most comfortable climatic environment for human existence'.

The town lies at the western end of Leschenault Inlet which Nicolas Baudin, commander of the *Le Geographe*, sighted in 1803 and named after his botanist Jean Batiste Leschenault. In 1836, Governor Stirling sailed south in the *Sulphur* and met Henry William Bunbury, commander of the military detachment in Pinjarra, at Port Leschenault. Stirling supposedly renamed the port Bunbury in recognition of young Bunbury's efforts in trekking overland to meet him. The real reason was probably a concerted attempt to replace the French names on the map with English ones! The first town lots were not surveyed until 1841.

Things to See & Do

The town's old buildings include **King Cottage**, which now houses a museum, the **Rose Hotel** and **St Mark's Church** built in 1842. The interesting **Arts Complex** on Wittenoom St is in a restored 1897 convent building.

The tourist office (☎ (097) 21 7922) is in the 1904 **railway station** on Carmody Place. They provide a pamphlet, *Bunbury Walk About*, which details an interesting stroll around this compact and tidy city, as well as the free *Discover Bunbury* paper.

Dolphins You don't have to go to Monkey Mia to interact with dolphins as you can also do so at the Bunbury Dolphin Trust centre on Koombana Beach. This can be a rewarding experience. Visits from a group of bottlenose

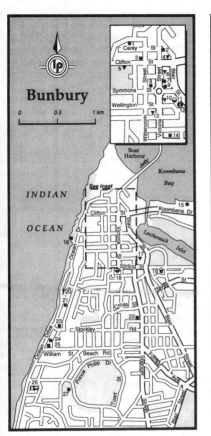

1 Lighthouse Beach Resort
2 Captain Bunbury Hotel
3 Wander Inn
4 Bakery
5 Louisa's
6 Memories of the Bond Store
7 Trafalgar's Hotel
8 Lord Forrest Hotel
9 International Food Hall
10 Cudas Café, The Rose Hotel
11 Bus Depot & Old Station Coffee Lounge
12 Information Centre
13 Benesseé, Gelaré Ice Cream
14 Prince of Wales Hotel
15 Dolphin Watch
16 Basaltic Rocks
17 Centrepoint: Johanna's, Natural Temptation
18 Post Office
19 The Residency Retreat YHA
20 Back Beach Kiosk
21 Welcome Inn
22 Admiral Motor Inn
23 Chateau La Mer
24 Ocean Drive Motel
25 Fawlty Towers
26 Punchbowl Caravan Park
27 Big Swamp Wildlife Park

THE SOUTH-WEST

dolphins *(Tursiops truncatus)* that regularly feed in the Inner Harbour, usually occur several times a day but less frequently in winter; a flag is hoisted when the dolphins are in. I rate the 'encounter' better than that at Monkey Mia, and it happens much closer to Perth!

The area, staffed during the day by helpful volunteers, was set up in 1989, and dolphins started to interact with the public in early 1990. The trust is housed in a new building near the beach. A brochure explains the simple rules of contact with dolphins; otherwise ask a ranger.

Places to Stay

There are three caravan parks in town and two out of town. Those in town are the *Bunbury Village* (☎ (097) 95 7100), Bussell Highway, with caravan sites/chalets for $12/49 for two; *Bunbury Glade* (☎ (097) 21 3800), also on Bussell Highway, with caravan sites/cabins for $12/30; and the small *Punchbowl* (☎ (097) 21 4761) on Ocean Drive with sites/on-site vans from $11/23. The *Waterloo Village* (☎ (097) 25 4434), South-Western Highway, has sites/on-site vans for $10/25 for two; and the *Riverside* (☎ (097) 25 1234), Pratt Rd, Eaton, has on-site vans/park homes for $28/35.

The Residency Retreat Hostel (☎ (097) 91 2621) is on the corner of Stirling and Moore Sts in an historic residence. Good dorm beds in this clean hostel are $15 ($12 for members) per night and there is one family room for $30.

The efficiently run and friendly *Wander Inn – Bunbury Backpackers* (☎ (097) 21 3242), closer to the city centre at 16 Clifton St (two blocks from the tourist office and the Indian Ocean), costs $12 a night for a dorm bed and $28 for a double. They will also provide free transport to the dolphins and a free trip back to Perth once a week.

The *Captain Bunbury Hotel* (☎ (097) 21 2021), on 8 Victoria St, has basic rooms for $15/25, and the *Prince of Wales* (☎ (097) 21 2016) on Stephen St has rooms for $25/45 with breakfast. The *Rose Hotel* (☎ (097) 21 4533) is a clean and lavishly restored place; singles/doubles are $31/50 with breakfast. The big hotel in town is the *Lord Forrest* (☎ (097) 21 9966), Symmons St, with singles/doubles for $135/155.

There are plenty of motels in town. The *Admiral Motor Inn* (☎ (097) 21 7322) is close to the town centre; singles/doubles are $60/70. Also close is the *Lighthouse Beach Resort* (☎ (097) 21 1311), Carey St, with rooms from $50/70; the *Clifton Beach* (☎ (097) 21 4300), voted the best motel in Australia in 1992, with rooms from $50/60; and the *Bunbury* (☎ (097) 21 7333), 45 Forrest Ave, with rooms from $40/50.

On Ocean Drive are the *Chateau La Mer* (☎ (097) 21 3166); the *Ocean Drive* (☎ (097) 21 2033); the courageously named *Fawlty Towers* (☎ (097) 21 2427); and the *Welcome Inn* (☎ (097) 21 3100); singles/doubles are about $40/55 at the first three places and from $59 to $110/$69 to $130 at the Welcome Inn.

Places to Eat

The *International Food Hall* on Symmons St is a large place with kebabs, roasts, Italian, Chinese and seafood from $5 to $7; it is open Thursday to Sunday from 11 am to 9 pm. In Victoria St is the popular *Memories of the Bond Store* which has four outlets including a brasserie. There are a number of cafes and food outlets in the Centrepoint shopping centre including *Johanna's Coffee Lounge* and *Natural Temptations*.

There are lots of cafes in the main part of town. The *Old Station Coffee Lounge* is in

Carmody Place; *Flanagan's Cafe* with a good burger selection is at 18 Wittenoom St; and *Mancini's*, *La Roma*, *Benessé*, *Gelaré Ice Cream Café* and the *Cudas Café* are all in Victoria St. The *Back Beach Kiosk* is on Ocean Drive, overlooking the sea.

Drooly's, at 70 Victoria St, does great pizzas for moderate prices. The *Rose Hotel*, on Wellington St, does good counter meals and has nine beers on tap. The *Friendship* Chinese restaurant, at 50 Victoria St, has tasty food and a varied menu; and the *China City Garden Restaurant*, 32 Wellington St, and the *Golden Flower*, 57 Victoria St, serve – guess what! Carnivorous types are drawn, salivating profusely, to the *Lump of Rump* at 119 Beach Rd.

If you are after French cuisine then hop into the *Little Frog* on Rose St which has a set menu at $20. *Louisa's*, 15 Clifton St, is an award winner – one of Bunbury's best with innovative modern cuisine. At 192 Spencer St is the licensed and BYO *Eagle Towers* which has a wide selection of seafood including dhufish, marron, blue swimmer crabs and crayfish; it is open from 6 pm Tuesday to Sunday.

Entertainment

The Forrest Drive-in & Cinema is on the Bussell Highway. There is an active pub music scene in Bunbury with musicians performing at a number of venues including Trafalgar's, the Parade, the Prince of Wales and the Burlington. The Westend Nightclub, in the Lord Forrest Hotel, and Albert's, in Albert Rd, seem to be the after-hours magnets attracting nocturnal Bunburyians.

Getting There & Around

South-West Coachlines buses travel daily between Bunbury and Perth for $16. Westrail also has daily bus ($17) and train ($17.10) services from Perth; these are one-way fares. The *Australind* takes around 2½ hours; the bus around three hours.

Bunbury City Transit (☎ (097) 911 955) covers the region around the city as far north as Australind and south to Gelorup.

BUSSELTON

Busselton (population 7700), on the shores of Geographe Bay, 230 km south of Perth, is another popular holiday resort, especially with parents in the hunt for diversions for their frenetic kids. During the holidays the population quadruples, accommodation is fully booked, and the beaches and restaurants are crowded. The Nautical Lady outdoor fun centre is one of the places that caters for children.

In 1801, a French sailor named Vasse was lost at sea in Geographe Bay during a violent storm. The names Vasse for the river and district, Geographe for the bay and Naturaliste for the cape come from this time. The town is named after the Bussell family, one of the early families of settlers in the area.

Busselton has a tourist office (☎ (097) 52 1091) in the civic centre on Southern Drive.

Things to See & Do

The town has a two-km **jetty** which was reputed to be the longest timber jetty in Australia – 'was', as a fair section of it was destroyed by Cyclone Alby in 1978.

The old **courthouse** has been restored and now houses an impressive arts centre with a gallery, a coffee shop and artists' workshops. **Wonnerup House**, 10 km east of town, is a 1859 colonial-style house lovingly restored by the National Trust.

About seven km east of Busselton is the 20 sq km **Ludlow Tuart Forest**, the only considerable natural stand of tuart in the world. Tuart has hard, coarse-grained timber, and can grow extremely large over a period of about 500 years.

Places to Stay

There is a great deal of accommodation along this popular stretch of coast; enquire at the tourist office for more information.

The most central of the many caravan parks, *Kookaburra No 1* (☎ (097) 52 1516), 66 Marine Terrace, has sites/on-site vans for $11/25 for two – accept this as an average for the other parks. The *Busselton Caravan Park* (☎ (097) 52 1175), at 163 Bussell Highway,

has extremely friendly hosts; the *Acacia* (☎ (097) 55 4034) is on the Bussell Highway near Harvest Rd; the *Amblin* (☎ (097) 55 4079) is also on the Bussell Highway; the *Lazy Days* (☎ (097) 52 1780) is at No 452; and the *Vasse Beachfront* (☎ (097) 55 4044) is, yet again, on the Bussell Highway.

The often-booked *Motel Busselton* (☎ (097) 52 1908), 90 Bussell Highway, has comfortable units from $28 per B&B double per night. *Villa Carlotta Private Hotel* (☎ (097) 54 1034), at 110 Adelaide St, is good, friendly, organises tours and has singles/doubles for $35/50 with breakfast. Another guesthouse, the *Travellers Rest* (☎ (097) 52 2290), 223 Bussell Highway, has B&B for $40/50. There are may more B&Bs; check with the tourist office.

There are a number of holiday resorts in the region with a bewildering variety of accommodation. Some examples are the *Busselton Beach Resort* (☎ (097) 52 3444), corner of Geographe Bay Rd and Guerin St, which will give rates on application; the *Broadwater Resort* (☎ (097) 54 1633), on the corner of Bussell Highway and Holgate Rd, where one/two-bedroom places are about $125/140; and the *Mandalay Holiday Resort* (☎ (097) 52 1328), 254 Geographe Bay Rd, which has park cabins/chalets/villas for $38/59/83 for two.

Places to Eat

There are lots of takeaway places along this coastal strip, catering for travellers and the hordes which descend upon the place during holiday periods. The *Pizza Bar Busselton* is in Queen St, *Red Rooster* is on the Bussell Highway and *Presto Pizza* is in the Boulevarde shopping centre.

There are a stack of more up-market places to eat in Busselton including *Michelango's* at the Riviera Motel for Italian food, the *Golden Inn* on Albert St for Chinese food, and *Tiffins* in Queen St for Indian tandoori food. Hotels such as the *Ship Hotel/Motel*, on Albert St, and the *Esplanade*, on Marine Terrace, are good for counter meals. Enjoy the succulent seafood at the BYO *Tails of the Bay*, 42 Adelaide St, or at *Albertani's*, Queen St, an Italian place which has seafood and vegetarian dishes.

Getting There & Around

To get to Busselton you can take a Westrail or South-West Coachlines bus. Geographe Bay Coachlines (☎ (097) 54 2026) conducts tours to Cape Naturaliste, Augusta, Cape Leeuwin and Margaret River.

Cape to Cape

This is an easily defined area of country – the north-west corner is Cape Naturaliste, the south-west corner Cape Leeuwin/Augusta and the centre Margaret River. The eastern boundary is fringed by jarrah and karri forest and beyond is the area of 'tall trees'. The cape region is known for its picturesque wineries, great surfing beaches and labyrinthine limestone caves. Arts & craft places are found everywhere and there are accommodation options for all travellers. The Mapanew's quarterly, *Map and Guide to the South-West Capes*, is a useful publication.

GETTING THERE & AWAY

From Bunbury, Westrail buses continue to Busselton, Yallingup, Margaret River and Augusta.

South-West Coachlines (☎ (09) 324 2333) also services the region and has daily services from Perth to Bunbury, Busselton, Dunsborough, Margaret River and Augusta.

DUNSBOROUGH

Dunsborough, just to the west of Busselton, is a pleasant little coastal town that is dependent on tourism. Like Busselton, its beaches suit families as they have shallow water for swimming. The tourist office (☎ (097) 55 3517) is in the shopping centre on Naturaliste Terrace.

Things to See & Do

The Naturaliste Rd, north-west of Dunsborough, leads to excellent beaches such as **Meelup**, **Eagle Bay** and **Bunker Bay**, some fine coastal lookouts and the tip of **Cape Naturaliste**, which has a lighthouse and some walking trails. In season you can see humpback whales, southern right whales and dolphins from the lookouts over Geographe Bay. At scenic **Sugarloaf Rock** there is the southernmost nesting colony of the rare red-tailed tropicbird *(Phaethon rubricauda)*; see The Bird has Flown – Too Far South in this chapter.

You can ride through the surrounding farms and countryside on horseback. Dunsborough Horse World (☎ (097) 55 3372) is on Mewett Rd, off Commonage Rd (near Simmo's Icecreamery) and Mirravale Riding School (☎ (097) 55 2180). It's halfway between Dunsborough and Yallingup on Biddles Rd.

Both South-West Coachlines and Westrail have daily services to Dunsborough; the one-way fare to Perth is $23.

Places to Stay

Green Acres Caravan Park (☎ (097) 55 3087), on the beachfront at Dunsborough, has caravan sites/park homes for $15/35 for two. Near Dunsborough, in Quindalup, is the well-positioned, refurbished *Dunsborough YHA Resort Hostel* (☎ (097) 55 3107) on the beachfront at 285 Geographe Bay Rd; the rate is $13 per night (dorms, twins and family) and they hire bicycles ($8 per day) and canoes and life jackets ($5 per hour).

There are a couple of up-market resorts in Dunsborough including the *Dunsborough Bay Village Resort* (☎ (097) 55 3397), on Dunn Bay Rd, with chalets for $85 for two; and the *Resort Hotel* (☎ (097) 55 3200), 536 Naturaliste Terrace, with double rooms from $65 to $95. The *Down South Private Accommodation Holiday Service* (☎ & fax (097) 54 2390) has a wide range of places on its books.

Places to Eat

The *Forum Food Centre* has a variety of eating places including a fine bakery, home of the Naturaliste-filled lamington. *Dunsborough Health Foods*, in the shopping centre, sells wholemeal salad rolls and deli-

Goldfields

Top: Warden Finnerty's Residence, Coolgardie (RN)
Bottom Left: Hair stylist, Boulder (RN)
Bottom Right: British Arms Hotel (Museum), Kalgoorlie (RN)

Goldfields
Top: Kalgoorlie Hotel (JW)
Middle: Exchange Hotel (JW)
Bottom: York Hotel (JW)

cious smoothies and juices. The *Dunsborough Bakery* has tasty pies and is reputed to be the best pastry filler around.

The *Golden Bay Chinese* restaurant is in the Dunsborough Bay Village Resort and the classy, licensed *Seymours* is in the Resort Hotel. For a Tex-Mex/cajun/creole blend, try *Texans*, open for dinner from 6 pm, Wednesday to Sunday.

On Commonage Rd is *Simmo's Icecreamery*. It is a hit with the kids as there are 20 homemade flavours available and plenty of other diversions for them once they have devoured their ice cream.

The Bird Has Flown – Too Far South

Keen birdwatchers will marvel at the sight of the red-tailed tropicbird *(Phaethon rubricauda)* soaring happily in the sea breezes above Sugarloaf Rock, south of Cape Naturaliste. Its name says it all – 'tropic' bird. The section of beaches between capes Naturaliste and Leeuwin is anything but the tropics. In fact the last time this author saw a red-tailed tropicbird was on South Plaza Island in the equatorial Galapagos!

The tropicbird is distinguished by its two long red tail streamers – almost twice its body length. It has a tern-like bill and, from a distance, could easily be mistaken for a crested tern. You'll have fun watching through binoculars as the inhabitants of this small breeding colony soar, glide, dive then swim with their disproportionately long tail feathers cocked up. They are ungainly on land and have to descend almost to the spot where they wish to nest. ∎

YALLINGUP

Yallingup, a Mecca for surfers, is surrounded by a spectacular coastline and some fine beaches. Nearby is the stunning **Yallingup Cave** which was discovered, or rather stumbled upon, in 1899. Formations include the white 'Mother of Pearl Shawl' and the equally beautiful 'Arab's Tent' and 'Oriental Shawl'. The cave is open daily from 9.30 am to 3.30 pm and you can look around by yourself or take a guided tour that also explores parts of the cave not open to most visitors.

The **Canal Rocks**, a series of rocky outcrops which form a natural canal, are off Caves Rd in the Leeuwin-Naturaliste National Park.

Surfing

Known colloquially to surfers as 'Yal's' and 'Margaret's' (when viewed from far-off Perth), the beaches between the capes offer powerful reef breaks, mainly left-handers (the direction you take after catching a wave). The wave at Margaret's has been described by surfing supremo Nat Young as 'epic' and by four-times world-surfing champion, Mark Richards, as 'one of the world's finest'.

The better locations include Rocky Point (short left-hander), The Farm and Bone Yards (right-hander), Three Bears (Papa, Mama and Baby, of course), Yallingup (breaks left and right), Injidup Car Park and Injidup Point (right-hand tube on a heavy swell; left-hander), Guillotine/Gallows (right-hander), South Point (popular break), Left-Handers (the name says it all) and Margaret River (with Southside or 'Suicides').

You can get a copy of the *Down South Surfing Guide*, free from the Dunsborough tourist office, which indicates wave size, wind direction and swell size. The Margaret River Surf Classic is held in November.

Places to Stay & Eat

The *Yallingup Beach Caravan Park* (☎ (097) 55 2164), on the beachfront at Valley Rd, has tent sites/on-site vans for $12/34; and the *Caves Caravan Park* (☎ (097) 55 2196), corner of Caves and Yallingup Beach Rds, is slightly more expensive. *Caves House Hotel* (☎ (097) 55 2131), Caves Rd, established in 1903, is one of those 'olde-worlde' lodges with ocean views and an English garden. The rooms at Caves House are not cheap at $95 for two but it's very much a 'place for lovers' – many couples honeymoon there.

There's a variety of holiday homes and cottages available; enquire at the Dunsborough or Margaret River-Augusta tourist offices.

THE SOUTH-WEST

In Yallingup, the grub, not the surf, is 'up' at the *Yallingup Store* (especially known for its burgers) or at the *Surfside Restaurant*. Indulge yourself at the fully licensed *Caves House Restaurant*; the *Brewery Brasserie* at the Moonshine Brewery; *Flutes Cafe* at the Brookland Valley winery; the *Rocks Cafe* at Canal Rocks; or the brasserie at *Wildwood Winery*, eight km south of Yallingup.

MARGARET RIVER

The attractive town of Margaret River is a popular holiday spot due to its proximity to fine surf (Margaret River Mouth, Gnarabup, Suicides and Redgate) and swimming (Prevelly and Gracetown) beaches, some of Australia's best wineries and spectacular scenery.

The Augusta-Margaret River tourist offices (☎ (097) 57 2911) has a wad of information on the area including an extensive vineyard guide; it is on the corner of the Bussell Highway and Tunbridge Rd.

Things to See & Do

There are a number of art & craft places in town including the Margaret River Pottery and Kookaburra Crafts. The National Trust property, **Ellensbrook Homestead**, the first home of the Bussell family (built in 1855), is eight km north-west of town.

Eagle Heritage, five km south of Margaret River on Boodjidup Rd, has an interesting collection of raptors in a natural setting; it is open daily from 10 am to 5 pm and costs $4.50, children $2.50.

One really interesting tour is the search for forest secrets with the **Bushtucker Lady** at Prevelly Park (☎ (097) 57 2466). This tour combines walking and canoeing up the Margaret River and teaches Aboriginal culture, bushcraft and flora & fauna. The two-hour explorations cost $12 (children $7.50).

Caves Rd, the **old coast road** between Augusta, Margaret River and Busselton is a good alternative to the direct road which runs slightly inland. The coast here has real variety – cliff faces, long beaches pounded by rolling surf, and calm, sheltered bays.

Wineries This area is famous for its wineries. You can buy a copy of the *Margaret River Regional Vineyard Guide* at tourist offices for $2.50. It lists over 35 wineries from Cape Naturaliste to Cape Leeuwin including the renowned Leeuwin Estate, Sandalford and Cape Mentelle (see the South West: Leeuwin-Naturaliste map for the location of many of the wineries).

Ellensbrook Homestead

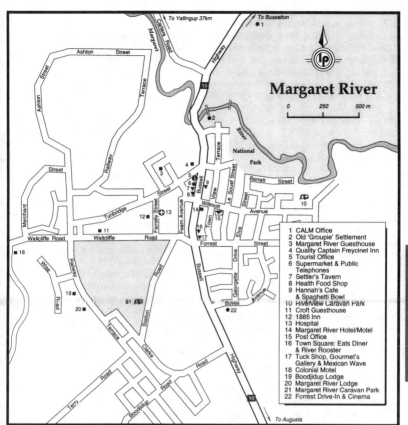

Margaret River

1 CALM Office
2 Old 'Groupie' Settlement
3 Margaret River Guesthouse
4 Quality Captain Freycinet Inn
5 Tourist Office
6 Supermarket & Public
  Telephones
7 Settler's Tavern
8 Health Food Shop
9 Hannah's Cafe
  & Spaghetti Bowl
10 Riverview Caravan Park
11 Croft Guesthouse
12 1885 Inn
13 Hospital
14 Margaret River Hotel/Motel
15 Post Office
16 Town Square: Eats Diner
   & River Rooster
17 Tuck Shop, Gourmet's
   Gallery & Mexican Wave
18 Colonial Motel
19 Boodjidup Lodge
20 Margaret River Lodge
21 Margaret River Caravan Park
22 Forrest Drive-In & Cinema

The Mediterranean climate and well-drained soils are ideal conditions for the production of wine grapes. The first grapes were only planted in 1967 and those initially established were rhine riesling and cabernet sauvignon. Since then, many varieties including pinot noir, merlot, shiraz, cabernet franc, chardonnay, sauvignon blanc, verdelho and semillon have been planted. In general, the wines are expensive but worth it. Don't expect a heavy red – these wines are produced from grapes grown in sandy soil, resulting in light textures and flavours.

Places to Stay

There are plenty of places to stay around Margaret River but unfortunately most are upwards of $50 per night. Cheap possibilities include the *Margaret River Caravan Park* (☎ (097) 57 2180), on Station Rd, which has tent sites/on-site vans for $11/30, and the *Riverview Caravan Park* (☎ (097) 57 2270) on Willmott Ave. Tenters beware of the latter unless you like sleeping on an angle. The *Gracetown Caravan Park* (☎ (097) 55 5301) is 2½ km from the beach on Cowaramup Bay Rd.

The *Margaret River Lodge* (☎ (097) 57

2532), a backpackers' hostel, is about 1½ km south-west from the town centre at 220 Railway Terrace. It's clean and modern with all the facilities; dorm beds are $11, four-bed bunkrooms from $12 each and doubles from $30 for two. Just down Railway Rd, towards town, is *Boodjidup Lodge* (☎ (097) 57 2720) with singles/doubles from $25/35.

The renovated *Margaret River Hotel/Motel* (☎ (097) 57 2655) is very central; the single/double rooms for $85/110 include a cooked breakfast. The *Quality Captain Freycinet Inn* (☎ 097) 57 2033), corner of Tunbridge St and the Bussell Highway, has single/double rooms for $81/96 and the *Colonial Motel* (☎ (097) 57 2633), on Wallcliffe Rd, is $68/79.

The *Margaret River Guesthouse* at 22 Valley Rd has single/double B&B for $40/60. If you want to splash out, the *Croft* (☎ 097) 57 2845), at 54 Wallcliffe Rd, is a comfortable guesthouse run by a very friendly couple; B&B is $65 per double. There are many other cottages, B&Bs and farmstays; enquire at the tourist offices or check the *Margaret River Regional Accommodation Guide*.

The *1885 Inn* (☎ (097) 57 3177), Farrelly St, is the place to stay if you have the money; doubles are $95 (or $105 if you want a spa in your room). The country-style *Noble Grape* (☎ (097) 55 5538), on the Bussell Highway in Cowaramup, comes highly recommended with rooms furnished with antiques; a single/double B&B is around $55/75.

Places to Eat

Among the many places to eat in Margaret River is the *Settler's Tavern*, on Bussell Highway, which has good counter meals from $10 to $12 – they also have live music occasionally. The Margaret River Hotel has counter meals in its *Rivers Bar & Bistro* and the Margaret River Guesthouse has a restaurant with a blackboard menu which reflects what is available in the district at the time.

There are a great number of eateries along the section of the Bussell Highway between the tourist offices and Wallcliffe Rd. At the southern end is the *Margaret River Tuckshop*, a bit of an institution with friendly owners, and the *Gourmet's Gallery*.

Moving north, the *River Rooster* and *Eats Diner* are in the Town Square complex. North of Willmott St is the *Spaghetti Bowl*, the *Margaret River Bakery*, *Hanna's Cafe* and *Harry's Mexican Wave*.

More expensive is the licensed *1885 Inn*, Farrelly St, for continental fare and a good selection of regional wines.

Getting There & Around

There are daily bus services between Perth and Margaret River on South-West Coachlines and Westrail (both about $26); the trip takes around five hours.

Bikes can be rented on a daily or hourly basis from Margaret River Lodge on Railway Terrace.

West Coast Experience (☎ (09) 561 5236) offer a five-day trip to the south-west region for $145, a good option for car-less budget travellers which takes in the wineries, the Bushtucker tour and the lighthouses.

AUGUSTA

A popular holiday resort, Augusta is five km north of Cape Leeuwin. It has a rugged coastline, a **lighthouse** (open daily to the public) with views extending over two oceans (the Indian and the Southern) and a salt-encrusted 1895 waterwheel. Cape Leeuwin took its name from a Dutch ship which passed here in 1622. The **Matthew Flinders memorial**, between Groper Bay and Point Matthew on the Leeuwin Rd, commemorates Flinders' mapping of the Australian coastline, which commenced at Cape Leeuwin on 6 December 1801.

The interesting **Augusta Historical Museum** on Blackwood Ave has exhibits relating to local history. The tourist offices (☎ (097) 58 1695) is in a souvenir shop at 70 Blackwood Ave.

There are some good beaches between Augusta and Margaret River to the north, including **Hamelin Bay** and **Cosy Corner.** Scenic flights over the cape are conducted by

Leeuwin Aviation; book with the Margaret River tourist office.

Places to Stay & Eat

The *Doonbanks Caravan Park* (☎ (097) 58 1517) is the most central with tent sites/on-site vans for $10/22. It's a well-run place in a good setting. Two other caravan parks in the area are *Flinders Bay* (☎ (097) 58 1380) and the *Molloy* (☎ (097) 58 4515), Kudardup. There are a number of basic campsites in the Leeuwin-Naturaliste National Park including ones on Boranup Drive and Conto's Field, near Lake Cave.

The small *Augusta Backpackers* (☎ (097) 58 1433) costs $9 per night. It is in a cottage on the corner of Bussell Highway and Blackwood Ave.

The *Augusta Hotel Motel* (☎ (097) 58 1944), Blackwood Ave, has single/double rooms from $40/45 and motel units for $75 for two; and the *Augusta Georgiana Molloy Motel* (☎ (097) 58 1255), 84 Blackwood Ave, has single/double rooms from $45 to $55/$55 to $70.

Some of the self-contained holiday flats have reasonable rates but they may have minimum-booking periods in the high season; enquire at the tourist office.

The *Augusta Hotel* does counter meals and has an à la carte restaurant, or head for *Squirrels*, next to the hotel, where you can find delicious burgers (piled high with salad), Lebanese sandwiches and various health foods. The *August Moon Chinese Restaurant* is in the Matthew Flinders shopping centre on Ellis St. And down on Albany Terrace, you can watch the Blackwood River meet the waters of Flinders Bay while drinking coffee and eating focaccia at the 'last cafe before Antarctica'.

'HIDDEN WILDERNESS' CAVES

There are a number of limestone caves between Cape Naturaliste and Cape Leeuwin. These include Jewel (the most picturesque), Lake, Mammoth and the Moondyne.

In **Mammoth Cave**, 21 km south of Margaret River, a fossilised jawbone of *Zygomaturus trilobus*, a giant wombat-like creature, can be touched. Other fossil remains have revealed a great deal about prehistoric fauna of the south-west region.

The limestone formations are reflected in the still waters of an underground stream in the **Lake Cave**, 25 km from Margaret River. The vegetated entrance to this cave is spectacular and includes a karri tree with a girth of seven metres.

Fossil remains of a Tasmanian tiger *(thylacine)* have been discovered in the **Jewel Cave**, which is eight km north of Augusta – the remains are believed to be 25,000 years old. It is the unusual formations which attract visitors underground, however, and the Jewel has a 5.9-metre straw stalactite, so far the longest seen in a 'commercial' cave.

Guided cave tours, the only way to see these caves, run daily for $7.50. Both Jewel and Mammoth are open at 9.30 and 11.30 am and 1.30 and 3 pm; Lake is open 10 am, noon, 2 pm and 3.30 pm.

Moondyne Cave, also eight km north of Augusta, was presumably discovered by and named after the bushranger Moondyne Joe (see Moondyne Joe in the Around Perth chapter). This cave is unlit and an experienced guide takes the visitor on a caving adventure; all equipment is provided on this two-hour trip which costs $18.

In all, 120 caves have been discovered between Cape Leeuwin and Cape Naturaliste but only these four, and Yallingup Cave near Busselton, are open to the public.

Between the caves is the quaint *Arumvale Siding Cafe*, which serves good nachos, Devonshire teas and a range of juices. What a great setting in the Boranup karri forest – eat, reflect and listen to the giant trees grow.

THE SOUTH-WEST

Tall Trees & the Great Southern

Some of the most impressive parts of the state are south of Perth. An area of forests south-east of Bunbury is known for its massive 'tall trees'. To the south and east of these forests is another vast area appropriately termed the Great Southern, the Rainbow Coast (Walpole to Bremer Bay) and the south-east (an area including the coastline from Cape Leeuwin east to Cape Arid, near Esperance). The scenery is magnificent, and there is a string of fascinating national parks hugging the coastline.

Tall Trees

A visit to the forests of the south-west is a must for any traveller to WA. Interspersed between the forests are many interesting towns, a variety of attractions and a host of things to do. The forests are magnificent – towering jarrah, marri, karri and tingle trees serve to protect the natural, vibrant garden beneath. Unfortunately and unbelievably, some of these forests are threatened by logging.

The area of 'tall trees' (not 'tall timber', as that predetermines their fate) is wedged between the Vasse Highway (State Highway 10) and the South-Western Highway, and includes the timber towns of Bridgetown, Manjimup, Nannup, Pemberton and Northcliffe.

DONNYBROOK

South of Bunbury, 210 km south of Perth and on the fringe of the forest region, is Donnybrook, centre of a fruit and vegetable growing area. It was given its name by five Irish settlers in 1842 as it reminded them of home, a Dublin suburb. Donnybrook's tourist office (☎ (097) 31 1720) is in the old railway station. Apple-picking work is often available in season (apparently most of the year).

The **Anchor & Hope Inn**, built in 1862 as a coaching inn has, in its time, been a community hospital; it is now a restaurant.

About 25 km to the south of Donnybrook, in Mullalyup, is the historic 1864 **Blackwood Inn**, an old stage-coach post classified by the National Trust.

Places to Stay & Eat

The *Donnybrook Hotel* (☎ (097) 31 1017) has single/double rooms for $20/35; and a motel (☎ (097) 31 1499) has units for $42/58 – all of these places are on the South-Western Highway.

The *Brook Lodge* (☎ (097) 31 1520), on Bridge St, is a private lodge with kitchen and laundry facilities. Just before the bridge leading to Brook Lodge, at 6 Bridge St, is the comfortable, rambling *Donnybrook Backpackers* (☎ (097) 31 1844); dorm beds are $11 per night or $66 per week, as are doubles and twins per person.

The *Blackwood Inn* (☎ (097) 64 1138), in

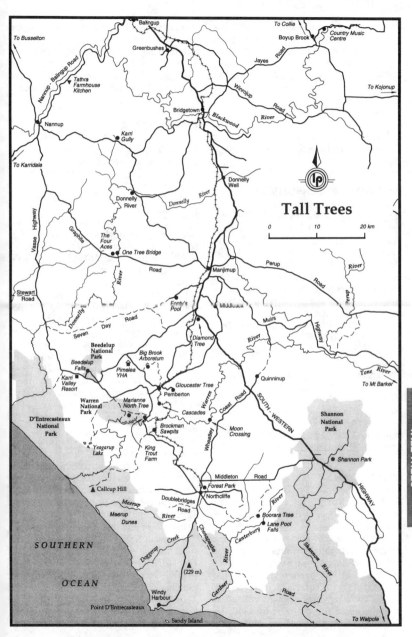

Tall Trees

Mullalyup, is the perfect winter retreat. It has spacious suites with open log fires and B&B costs $70/85 for singles/doubles.

For a snack there is the *Copper Kettle Coffee Lounge* in the Central Arcade, the fish & chip shop in Collins St and the *Pines Centre* and a bakery on the South-Western Highway. The *Anchor & Hope* is a restaurant and the *Apple Turnover* is the restaurant in the Donnybrook Hotel. There is also a classy à la carte restaurant in the Blackwood Inn in Mullalyup.

BALINGUP & GREENBUSHES

About 30 km south of Donnybrook is the art & crafts village of **Balingup**. The Balingup information office (☎ (097) 64 1018) is in the Old Cheese Factory craft centre on Nannup Rd. Other craft places include The Tinderbox for products created from herbs, Bailiwick for locally made toys and The Village Pedlars for home crafts. There are a number of farmstays in the Balingup area; contact the information office.

For a light lunch try the *Old Bakery Tearooms* on the South-Western Highway. The restaurant in the Old Cheese Factory is open for dining on Friday and Saturday nights.

Another 10 km down the South-Western Highway is **Greenbushes**, once a tin mining centre. There are two hotels in town, both on Blackwood Rd. The *Exchange* (☎ (097) 64 3509) has single/double motel units for $38/48. In the *Shamrock* (☎ (097) 64 3512), single/double rooms are $20/35.

BRIDGETOWN

This quiet country town (population 1500), on the Blackwood River and centre of the Blackwood Valley, is in an area of karri forests and farmland.

Bridgetown has some old buildings, including **Bridgedale House**, which was built of mud and clay by the area's first settler in 1862 and has been restored by the National Trust. There is a local history display and a captivating **jigsaw collection** in the tourist office (☎ (097) 61 1740) on Hampton St. As the staff are enthusiastic

volunteers, you'll have no trouble fitting the pieces together.

Interesting features of the Blackwood Valley are the burrawangs (grass trees) and large granite boulders. There's a panoramic view over the town from **Sutton's Lookout** off Philips St.

Places to Stay & Eat

The *Bridgetown Caravan Park* (☎ (097) 61 1053), South-Western Highway, has tent sites/on-site vans for $14/28 for two. The *Old Well* (☎ (097) 61 2032) on Gifford St has single/double B&Bs for $35/60. Enquire at the tourist office about the many other B&B possibilities.

The *Bridgetown Hotel* (☎ (097) 61 1034), Hampton St, has singles/doubles for $25/35; and at the *Freemasons Hotel/Motel* (☎ (097) 61 1725) rooms are $23/40 and units $45/50. The best place in town is the *Nelson House Lodge* (☎ (097) 61 1641), 38 Hampton St, in a beautifully renovated federation-style house; B&B ranges from $45 to $75 per person, depending on the standard and facilities of the room.

For snacks and takeaways there is the *Bridgetown Cafe*, the *Pottery* and *JJ's Coffee Lounge*. For an evening meal, *Buckley's Bistro*, the *Riverwood Restaurant* and the à la carte *Nelson's* are recommended. Most of these places are on Hampton St.

BOYUP BROOK

In this small town, 31 km north-east of Bridgetown, there is a flora reserve, a country & western music collection (five km from town on the Dinninup-Arthur River Rd) and a large butterfly and beetle display.

Nearby is **Norlup Pool** with glacial rock formations, and to the north, **Wilga**, which is an old timber mill with vintage engines.

After witnessing the country & western collection you will probably need to rest. The *Flax Mill Recreation Camp & Caravan Park* (☎ (097) 65 1136), Flax Mill Rd, has camping and caravan sites; the *Barracks Accommodation* (☎ (097) 65 1437), Railway Parade, is $10 per person; and there are several farmstays and B&Bs near town. For the latter, contact the tourist office on the corner of Abel & Bridge Sts (☎ (097) 65 1444).

There are a couple of delis in Boyup Brook where you can get a decent sandwich – one is in Bridge St and the other in Abel St. The *Herbs & Spices Tea House*, Abel St, serves morning and afternoon teas and the hotel is open for lunch and dinner.

NANNUP

Nannup (population 1100), 50 km west of Bridgetown, is a quiet, historical and picturesque town in the heart of forest and farmland. The tourist office (☎ (097) 56 1211), at the 1922 police station in Brockman St, is open daily from 9 am to 3 pm. They sell an excellent booklet (50c) that points out places of interest around town and details a range of scenic drives in the area, including a Blackwood River Rd drive and numerous forest drives.

Things to See & Do

There is a sawmill (one of the largest in WA), an arboretum, some fine old buildings and several craft shops. Nannup is home of the mythical **'tiger'** and along one of the scenic drives is the notice: 'No shooting or feeding of thylacines.'

Canoeing the Blackwood River The

Blackwood River begins in the salt lake system to the east of Wagin and Katanning. It then flows for over 400 km through forests and farmland and near a number of towns before emptying into the Southern Ocean east of Augusta.

It is most suited to Canadian-style canoes and these can be hired in Boyup Brook, Nannup and Bridgetown. The best time to paddle the river is in late winter and early spring when the river levels are up. There is a series of guides entitled *South-West Canoeing Guide: Blackwood River*, available from local tourist offices; carefully read the safety instructions regarding equipment and what to do in the event of a capsize.

On Wednesday and Sunday, Milesaway Tours (☎ (097) 55 3574) takes trips on the river through a section of jarrah forest; the cost is $47 (children $27) and a bush breakfast and lunch is included. If you wish to hire a canoe, expect to pay $10 an hour or $20 for a half day.

Places to Stay & Eat

The caravan park (☎ (097) 56 1211), on Brockman St near the banks of the river, has powered sites for $10 for two. There is a backpackers' lodge in Nannup; the *Black Cockatoo Hostel* (☎ (097) 56 1035), 27 Grange Rd, has singles/twins for $10/20. The centrally located and friendly *Dry Brook B&B* (☎ (097) 56 1049) has comfortable singles/doubles for $20/30 with breakfast and is highly recommended. The hotel/motel (☎ (097) 56 1080), Warren Rd, has single/ double rooms for $20/35 and motel units for $45/55. There are a great number of B&Bs, farmstays and bush cottages available; enquire at the tourist office.

The *Blackwood Cafe*, Warren Rd, has good light meals such as quiche, soup and sandwiches. It is on Warren Rd near the Nannup Hotel which has counter meals. There is also the *Farmhouse Kitchen & Tathra Wines*, on Balingup Rd, part of the scenic Nannup-Balingup tourist drive.

MANJIMUP

Manjimup (population 4900) is the commercial centre of the south-west, a major agricultural centre noted for apple-growing and wood-chipping.

Things to See & Do

The impressive **Timber Park Complex** on the corner of Rose and Edwards Sts includes various museums, old buildings and the Manjimup tourist office (☎ (097) 71 1 831), open daily from 9 am to 5 pm.

One Tree Bridge, or what's left of it after floods in 1966, is 22 km down the Graphite Rd. It was constructed from a single karri log carefully felled to span the width of the river. The **Four Aces**, 1½ km from One Tree Bridge, are four superb karri trees believed to be over 300 years old. **Fonty's Pool**, a great spot to cool off in the water during those hot summer days, is 10 km south-west of town along Seven Day Rd.

Nine km south of town, along the South-Western Highway, is the **Diamond Tree Fire Tower**. You are not allowed to climb this 51-metre karri but there is a nature trail nearby.

Perup, 50 km east of Manjimup, is the centre of a 400 sq km forest which has populations of rare mammals including the numbat, tammar wallaby, ringtail possum *(Pseudocheirus peregrinus)* and southern brown bandicoot *(Isoodon obesulus)*.

Places to Stay & Eat
The caravan park (☎ (097) 71 2093) has a hostel with dorm beds and cooking facilities for $12 per night – it can get busy in apple-picking season (March to June) when beds are $65 weekly. They also have caravan sites/on-site vans for $13/26. Two other caravan parks, *Warren Way* (☎ (097) 71 1060; two km north of town) and *Fonty's Pool* (☎ (097) 71 2105; 10 km south-west of town), also have tent sites and on-site vans.

There is a hotel on Giblett St (☎ (097) 71 1322) and three motels: the *Overlander* (☎ (097) 71 1477), *Manjimup Motor Inn* (☎ (097) 71 1900) and the *Kingsley* (☎ (097) 71 1177). The caravan park, Motor Inn and the Kingsley have facilities for the disabled. For farmstays, cottages and B&Bs contact the tourist office.

For meals, try the *Blue Marron Restaurant* which serves marron and trout, the *Country Kitchen* next to the Timber Park for Devonshire teas, the *Manjimup Hotel* for counter meals and the *Billabong Restaurant* in the Kingsley for an à la carte selection.

Getting There & Away
Westrail have a Perth to Manjimup bus service via Bunbury and Collie, and South-West Coachlines have a weekday service from Perth to Manjimup; both are about $25 one-way.

PEMBERTON
Deep in the karri forests is the delightful town of Pemberton (population 1200). The child-friendly, well-organised Karri visitor centre (☎ (097) 76 1133), Brockman St, incorporates the tourist office, pioneer museum and karri forest discovery centre.

Things to See & Do
Pemberton has some interesting **craft shops** specialising in handcrafted timber products; the **Big Brook Arboretum** which features 'big' trees from all over the world and the eastern states; the **Pemberton Sawmill** where you can go on guided tours and observe timber being sawn; the pretty **Pemberton Pool** surrounded by karri trees (ideal on a hot day); and a **trout hatchery** that supplies fish for the state's dams and rivers. Get the excellent *What to See & Do in Big Tree Country* map or the *Pemberton and Northcliffe: Kingdom of the Karri* pamphlet from the tourist office.

If you are feeling fit, you can make the scary 60-metre climb to the top of the **Gloucester Tree**, the highest fire lookout tree in the world (this is not for the faint-hearted and only one visitor in four ascends!). The view makes the climb well worthwhile. To get to the tree just follow the signs from town. The tree was named after the Duke of Gloucester who visited in 1946.

Also of interest in the area are the spectacular **Cascades** (when the water level is high), the **100-year-old forest** (once a wheat field) and the **Warren National Park** where camping is allowed in designated areas. The biggest karri, some 89 metres high, is found in Warren National Park.

Pemberton also has a burgeoning **wine industry**, with reds attracting favourable comparison to those from Burgundy in France. Check at the tourist office for a list of wineries.

The Pemberton Tramway The scenic Pemberton Tramway (☎ (097) 76 1322), one of the area's main attractions, was constructed between 1929 and 1933. It was part of the planned line between Bunbury and Albany and was in use for passengers and

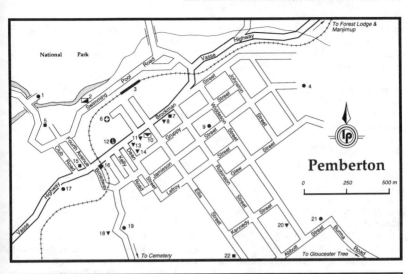

Pemberton

0   250   500 m

PLACES TO STAY

- 5 Pemberton Caravan Park
- 7 Pemberton Hotel
- 15 Warren Lodge
- 22 Gloucester Motel

PLACES TO EAT

- 8 Chloe's Kitchen
- 11 Mainstreet Cafe
- 13 Southern Chicken
- 14 Chinese Restaurant, Supermarket
- 18 Gryphon's Garden Cafe
- 20 Siver Birch Restaurant (Tammeron Lodge)

OTHER

- 1 Trout Hatchery
- 2 Swimming Pool
- 3 Pemberton Tramway
- 4 Woodcraftman's Studio
- 6 Hospital
- 9 Warren River Arts & Crafts
- 10 Post Office
- 12 Karri Visitor Centre
- 16 Pemberton Arts & Craft
- 17 Sawmill
- 19 Warren Vineyard Cellar Sales
- 21 CALM Office

TALL TREES

goods until 1986; it reopened in 1987 as the Pemberton Tramway.

Trams leave Pemberton Railway Station daily at 10.45 am and 2 pm to Warren River ($11.50) and to Northcliffe ($18) at 10.15 am Tuesday, Thursday and Friday. The route travels through lush karri and marri forests with occasional picture stops; a commentary is also provided. Be aware that the trip is incredibly noisy and only worthwhile if you don't have a car.

Beedelup National Park This enchanting forest park should not be missed. There is a short but extremely scenic walk which crosses Beedelup Brook near the **Beedelup Falls**; the bridge was built from a karri log. There is also a walk-through karri – vandals from an earlier age cut a three by four-metre hole with a chainsaw. It is sobering to think that there are over 150 tonnes of tree towering above you.

For the keen birdwatcher there are numerous

species to be found flitting in and around the tall trees. One of the most striking, the red-winged fairy wren *(Malurus elegans)*, is seen in the undergrowth of the forests.

National Park Tours Southern Forest Adventures (☎ (097) 76 1222) has 4WD tours of the forest and coastal areas around Pemberton. One half-day trip takes in karri forest as well as the spectacular Yeagarup dune systems of D'Entrecasteaux National Park; it costs $40 and includes a barbecue lunch. A two-day safari which takes in D'Entrecasteaux and the cliffs of Windy Harbour is $120. Canoeing trips on the Warren River with the same operator cost from $25.

The Hawke Forest Block
About half of this block of forest is currently threatened by logging with 80% of the logged timber destined to become wood chips. It is only a small block, situated between Warren National Park and the unique Yeagarup dune system in D'Entrecasteaux National Park. It is only a small area but it has many species of rare flora & fauna as well as virgin karri forest. It should be preserved at all cost! See it and then put some pressure on CALM to save it. ■

Places to Stay
Camping is permitted in *Warren National Park* and in some areas of the *Pemberton Forest* (☎ (097) 76 1200). The picturesque caravan park (☎ (097) 76 1300) has tent sites/on-site vans for $11/26.

Pemberton YHA Hostel (☎ (097) 76 1153), in a beautiful forest location at Pimelea, costs $9 a night (nonmembers $10); doubles in cottages are $27 and two other cottages, Pimelea and Zamia, are $55 each (maximum of five people). It's 10 km north-west of town but the hostel provides a courtesy bus to meet the Westrail bus in Pemberton – call in advance if you need transport.

In town, the centrally located *Warren Lodge* (☎ (097) 76 1105), on Brockman St, has backpackers' beds from $10 and B&B at $40 for two. It requires some work in the budget part but the B&B area is clean. The *Pemberton Hotel* (☎ (097) 76 1017) is a grand old building on Brockman St with single/double motel units for $40/55. The *Gloucester Motel* (☎ (097) 76 1266), in Ellis St, has units for $40/50.

Perth-ites flush with funds head for the *Quality Karri Valley Resort* (☎ (097) 76 2020; fax 76 2012), on the Vasse Highway. This is a very beautiful place sited at the edge of a lake and surrounded by magnificent karri forest. It is very much outside the range of a Lonely Planet writer with motel rooms for $116, and two to three-bedroom apartments for $159/180. Similar, but much cheaper, is the *Forest Lodge* (☎ (097) 76 1113), two km north of Pemberton on the Vasse Highway, which has lodge rooms for $45, an open-plan chalet for $75 and suites for $80; all prices are for two.

For more information on the plethora of farmstays, cottages and B&Bs, enquire at the Karri visitor centre.

Places to Eat
The town, for its size, has many places to eat; most have local trout and marron on their menus. The *Pemberton Patisserie* has tasty pies and cakes; *Chloe's Kitchen* has takeaways including vegetarian food; *Gryphon's Garden Cafe*, in Dickinson St, has a pleasant setting; while the *Mainstreet Cafe* on Brockman St has good, basic and cheap food such as hamburgers and Lebanese rolls. As befits the deep south, the *Southern Chicken* is on the corner of Dean and Brockman Sts.

The *Pemberton Chinese Restaurant*, next to the supermarket on Dean St, is only open Thursday to Sunday from 5 pm and has meals from $6. The *Shamrock*, on Brockman St, is a marron and steak restaurant where a three-course meal costs around $25. The *Silver Birch* at the Tammeron Motor Lodge, Widdeson St, also has great three-course meals for $25.

Getting There & Around

Westrail Perth to Pemberton buses operate daily, via Bunbury, Donnybrook and Manjimup and cost $29; the trip takes about five hours. From Albany it is three hours and the cost is $22; the service is twice weekly.

Pemberton Scenic Bus Tours does a forest industry tour Monday to Friday at 10.30 am, and a three-hour scenic bus tour Monday to Friday at 2 pm, Saturday and Sunday at 10.30 am and 2 pm.

NORTHCLIFFE

Northcliffe (population 800), 32 km south of Pemberton, has a **pioneer museum** and a **forest park** close to town with good walks through stands of grand karri, marri and jarrah trees – a brochure and map of the trails is available from the tourist office (☎ (097) 76 7203) by the museum on Wheatley Coast Rd.

The popular and picturesque **Lane Poole Falls** are 19 km south east of Northcliffe; the 2½-km track to the falls leaves from the 50-metre Boorara lookout tree. These falls slow to a trickle in the summer months.

Windy Harbour, on the coast 29 km south of Northcliffe, has prefab shacks and a sheltered beach; true to its name, it is very windy. The cliffs of magnificent **D'Entrecasteaux National Park** are accessible from here.

Places to Stay & Eat

Opposite the school, the *Northcliffe Caravan Park* (☎ (097) 76 7193) has tent sites for $5.50 (power $1 extra). *Northcliffe Hotel* (☎ (097) 76 7089), the only hotel in town, has basic accommodation for $16/30.

Out of town, *Westpool Farm* (☎ (097) 76 7179), Doublebridges Rd, and *Brook Farm* (☎ (097) 75 1014), Middleton Rd, have B&B for $22/44. At Windy Harbour, the only place to stay is the *Windy Harbour Camping Area* (☎ (097) 76 7056) where basic tent sites are $4.

The *Hollow Butt* coffee shop, on Zamia St and Wheatley Coast Rd, has light meals and cakes; avoid their soggy microwaved pies. On Wheatley Coast Rd is *Wichetty's*, named after a grub, but this grub is tasty.

Getting There & Away

The Perth-to-Albany Westrail bus goes through Northcliffe twice weekly (Wednesday and Saturday), but you need your own transport to get to Windy Harbour.

The Great Southern

This is a large area encompassing all of the south coast from Cape Leeuwin near Augusta eastwards to Esperance. It has some of the state's best coastal and mountainous national parks: d'Entrecasteaux, Walpole-Nornalup, William Bay, West Cape Howe, Fitzgerald River and Cape Le Grand national parks. The towns throughout this area all have their own distinctive character and include Denmark, 'old' Albany and Esperance.

Inland, north of Albany, are two of the best parks in Australia – the 'ecological islands' of the Stirling Ranges, which rise abruptly 1000 metres above the surrounding plains; and the karri forest and ancient granite spires of the Porongurups.

WALPOLE-NORNALUP

The South-Western Highway almost meets the coast at the twin inlets of Walpole and Nornalup.

Things to See & Do

The heavily forested **Walpole-Nornalup National Park** covers 180 sq km around Nornalup Inlet and the town of Walpole; it contains beaches, rugged coastline, inlets and the **'Valley of the Giants'**, a stand of giant karri and tingle trees, including one that soars 46 metres high.

Four species of rare eucalypts grow within four km of each other here and nowhere else in the world: red, yellow and Rates tingle (*Eucalyptus jacksonii, E. guilfoylei, E. cornuta*) and red flowering gum (*E. ficifolia*). See under Flora in the Facts for the Visitor chapter. Pleasant shady and ferny paths lead through the forest, and the area is

THE GREAT SOUTHERN

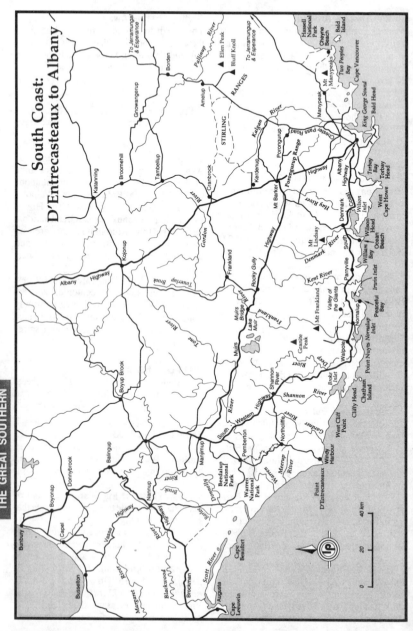

South Coast:
D'Entrecasteaux to Albany

frequented by bushwalkers. The Frankland River is popular with canoeists.

There are a number of scenic drives including the Knoll Drive, three km east of Walpole; the Valley of the Giants Rd, three km east of Nornalup; and at Mt Frankland, 29 km north of Walpole. At Mt Frankland you can climb to the summit for panoramic views or walk around the trail at its base. Opposite Knoll Drive is a road which leads to a **giant tingle tree**; the road continues from there to the Circular Pool on the Frankland River.

About 13 km west from Walpole via Crystal Springs is Mandalay Beach, where the **Mandalay**, a Norwegian barque, was wrecked in 1911. It seems to appear every 10 years out of the sands.

Details of things to see and do are available from the Walpole tourist office (☎ (098) 40 1111) at the Pioneer Cottage, in Pioneer Park, or from CALM (☎ (098) 40 1027), South Coast Highway, Walpole.

In particular, read the informative CALM publication *Finding the Magic* which costs $1.50; it includes a tree spotter's guide and the Ocean Drive is outlined in it. This includes the hauntingly beautiful **Conspicuous Cliffs** beach, which is not far from the western end of the Valley of the Giants.

Wreck of the *Mandalay*

Bushwalking One of the state's finest coastal walks, in the Nuyts Wilderness, is not far from Walpole. It combines ocean beaches, rocky headlands, idyllic estuaries and magnificent flora. There are karri and jarrah forests near Deep River, extensive heathlands on the walk to the sea and a bewildering variety of flowers, including orchids and kangaroo paw.

An easy two-day circuit walk which takes in Lost Beach and Thompson Cove is described in Lonely Planet's *Bushwalking in Australia* by John & Monica Chapman.

From the Nuyts car park to Thompson Cove is seven km and there are possible sidetrips to Crystal Lake and Mt Hopkins. The best time to do this walk is in spring as the wildflowers are prolific.

Organised Tours Karri to Coast (☎ (098) 40 1170) and Muir's Tours (☎ (098) 40 1036) run day trips around the area for $60, which includes lunch. The *Naughty Lass* (☎ (098) 40 1215) cruises the Walpole and Nornalup inlets and the river systems; morning tea is included, all for $10.

Places to Stay & Eat
There are a number of campsites in the Walpole-Nornalup National Park including tent sites at Peaceful Bay, Crystal Springs and Coalmine Beach. There are CALM huts at Fernhook Falls and Mt Frankland.

Two interesting places to stay are the *Tingle All Over Backpackers* (☎ (098) 40 1041), on the South Coast Highway in Walpole, which has dorms/twins for $12/15 per person. This is a laid-back place that is central to many of the attractions of this area – many walkers and cyclists relax here after the Bibbulman Track.

The other is the *Dingo Flat YHA Hostel* (☎ (098) 40 8073) on Dingo Flat Rd off the Valley of the Giants Rd, 18 km east of Walpole – booking is recommended. You need a car or cycle to get to this hostel, or if you ring ahead they'll pick you up at Bow Bridge (there is a public phone in the local shop). Beds are $8, the place has great char-

THE GREAT SOUTHERN

acter and there are wonderful views over the fields to the forest, especially from The Loft.

The *Walpole Hotel/Motel* (☎ (098) 40 1023) has single/double motel units for $42/50 and the *Ridgeway Guesthouse* (☎ (098) 40 1036), Walpole St near the inlet, has B&B for $60 per person.

The *Jesmond Dene Lodge* (☎ (098) 40 1107) is on the South Coast Highway in Nornalup, near the Frankland River; a unit/motel room is $40/65 for two.

There are also farmstays and cottages in the area; enquire at the tourist office. A more novel form of accommodation would be on a houseboat. Houseboat Holidays (☎ (098) 40 1310), Boronia Ave, Walpole have 10-berth houseboats for hire; again, enquire at the tourist office.

You can get counter meals at the *Walpole Hotel/Motel* and there are three street cafes – *Anne's Pantry* for cappuccino, *Golden Wattle Country Kitchen* for takeaways and the *Carragah Cafe* for light meals. Morning and afternoon teas are served at the *Thurlby Herbal Farm*, on Gardner Rd.

PEACEFUL BAY

The road to Peaceful Bay, one of those archetypal, get-away-from-it-all places, is 24 km east of Walpole. This is a beach area for those keen on fishing and swimming. There is a caravan park (☎ (098) 40 8060) with caravan sites/on-site vans for $12/20 for two, and the *Peaceful Bay Chalets* (☎ (098) 40 8169) where one-bedroom units/chalets are $40/43 for two.

DENMARK

Denmark (population 3500), or Koorabup ('place of the black swan'), was once settled by Aborigines (3000-year-old fish traps have been found in Wilson Inlet). Named by an early explorer after his friend, the town was established supplying timber for goldfield developments. About 54 km west of Albany, it has some fine beaches in the area (especially Ocean Beach for surfing) and is a good base for trips into the karri forests. Today it is an art & crafts centre with a number of fine

PLACES TO STAY

1	Riverview Cottage
10	Denmark Guesthouse, Tiger & Snake Restaurant
15	Denmark Unit Hotel
22	Rivermouth Caravan Park
23	Denmark Motel & Cottages, Thai Chinese Takeaway
24	Kon Tiki House in the Trees
25	Tree Tops Holiday Cottages
28	Wilson Inlet Caravan Park, YHA

PLACES TO EAT

5	Mary Rose
7	Scoundrel's Brasserie
8	Day Bros Bakery
11	Blue Wren Cafe
12	Bill's Bakery
13	Kettles Deli
14	Riverview Coffee Shop
19	The Denmark Chippy

OTHER

2	Hospital
3	Country Club
4	Boat Hire
6	Groundrey's Winery
9	Taxis
16	Public Toilets
17	Denmark Historical Museum
18	Denmark Tourist Office
20	Post Office
21	Mokare Heritage Trail
26	Wilson Inlet Trail
27	Walking Trail to Poisson Point

restaurants and a wealth of accommodation choices.

Things to See & Do

The Denmark tourist office (☎ (098) 48 1265), housed in an old church on Strickland St, has Heritage Trail brochures including the **Mokare Trail** (a three-km trail along the Denmark River) and the **Wilson Inlet Trail** (a six-km trail that starts from the rivermouth). They also provide a free booklet *Discover Denmark*.

There are fine views from **Mt Shadforth Lookout** while the **William Bay National**

THE GREAT SOUTHERN

Denmark

Park, 15 km west of Denmark, has fine coastal scenery of rocks and reefs. There are also scenic spots such as Greens Pool, Elephant Rocks, Madfish Bay, Tower Hill and Waterfall Beach.

Places to Stay

A popular holiday spot for locals, there is a great deal of accommodation choices. There are several caravan parks in town, the closest being the idyllic *Rivermouth Caravan Park* (☎ (098) 48 1262), one km south of the town centre on Inlet Drive; tent sites/vans are $9/18 for two. Other caravan parks in the area are *Ocean Beach* (☎ (098) 48 1105), *Wilson Inlet* (☎ (098) 48 1267) and *Rudgyard Beach* (☎ (098) 48 1169).

The *Denmark Associate YHA Hostel* at the Wilson Inlet Caravan Park, over four km south of Denmark, isn't much chop. The dingy dorm accommodation in the park's most dilapidated building is $10 per night – four or five people could band together and get something much better in town.

The *Denmark Guesthouse* (☎ (098) 48 1477, free call (1800) 671 477), on the South Coast Highway in the centre of town, remains one of the best accommodation bargains in WA. It is a friendly place with a TV lounge and clean rooms for $20/35; ensuite rooms are $32/50. (Show this book for a $5 discount.) The *Denmark Unit Hotel* (☎ (098) 48 2206), Holling Rd, has single/double rooms for $20/40 and motel units for $40/55; and the *Denmark Motel & Cottages* (☎ (098) 48 1147), two km past the Denmark Unit Hotel on Inlet Drive, has motel units for $40/50.

There are many types of farmstays, B&Bs, chalets and cottages in the Denmark area; the tourist office keeps a current list. A small selection of these with good settings are the *Kon Tiki House in the Trees* (☎ (098) 48 1265), Adams Rd, with a two-bedroom cottage for $60; the *Mount Shadforth Lodge* (☎ (098) 48 1555), Mt Shadforth Rd, for $95 for two; and the A-frame *Tree Tops Cottage* (☎ (098) 48 1265), Payne Rd, for $85 (minimum of two nights).

Places to Eat

There are three bakeries in town: *Bill's* and *Day Bros* on the South Coast Highway, and the *Denmark* on the corner of Fig Tree Square.

Beneath the Denmark Guesthouse is the *Tiger & Snake*, open from Wednesday to Sunday from 5 pm, which serves tasty and hearty servings of Indian and Chinese food ($6 and $8 for small and large servings). Just around the corner, on the South Coast Highway, is the *Blue Wren Cafe*, open from 8 am to 8 pm most days. The *Denmark Chippy* is near the corner of Walker and Strickland Sts and the *Thai Chinese Restaurant & Takeaway* is out of town on Inlet Drive.

The *Riverview Coffee Shop*, at 18 Holling Rd, has very good German food – no meal is over $10. For a quick meal or takeaway food, try *Kettles Deli* on the corner of the highway and Holling Rd. Also beside the river, *Scoundrel's Brasserie*, a BYO with blackboard menu, is open later than most places.

The *Mary Rose*, on North St next to Goundrey's Winery, is a quaint place with a pleasant balcony, which serves tasty light meals. There is a restaurant in the Mt Shadforth Lodge which serves meals incorporating local produce and they stock a variety of regional wines.

Getting There & Around

Westrail's Perth-to-Albany (via the south coast) service comes through Denmark four times a week (Tuesday, Wednesday, Thursday and Saturday) and costs $40 one way; the trip takes about seven hours. Contact the tourist office about local tours and bike hire.

THE MOUNTAIN NATIONAL PARKS

To the north-east of Denmark and almost due north of Albany are two spectacular mountainous national parks: the Stirling Ranges and the Porongurups. The best time to visit both parks is in late spring and early summer as it is beginning to warm up and the wildflowers are at their best. From June to August it is cold and wet and hail is not uncommon.

Occasionally, snow falls on the top of the ranges.

Further information on these parks can be obtained from the following CALM centres: Porongurup National Park, Bolganup Rd, RMB 1112, Mt Barker 6324; Stirling Range National Park, Chester Pass Rd, c/o Amelup via Borden 6338 and South Coast Regional Centre, 44 Serpentine Rd, Albany 6330.

CALM produces two informative booklets on this region – *Mountains of Mystery: A Natural History of the Stirling Ranges* and *Rugged Mountains Jewelled Sea: The South Coast from Eucla to Albany*.

The Porongurups

The beautiful Porongurup National Park (24 sq km) has panoramic views, beautiful scenery, large karri trees, 1100 million-year-old granite outcrops and excellent bushwalks. The range is 12 km long and 670 metres at its highest point.

In the Porongurups, karri trees grow in the deep red soil (known as karri loam) of the upper slopes. It is unusual to find such large trees growing this far east of the forests between Manjimup and Walpole, but the correct soil, combined with an annual rainfall of over 700 mm, accounts for this outlier of forest. Beneath these trees is a beautiful display of wildflowers in season.

There are a number of **bushwalking** trails. These range from the short 10-minute Tree in the Rock stroll, the intermediate Castle & Balancing Rocks (two hours) to the harder Hayward and Nancy Peaks (four hours) and excellent Devil's Slide and Marmabup Rock (three hours) walks. A scenic six-km drive along the northern edge of the park starts near the ranger's residence.

Places to Stay There is no camping in Porongurup National Park but there's a caravan park (☎ (098) 53 1057) in Porongurup township; the *Porongurup Chalets*, on the corner of Bolganup and Porongurup Rds, for $50 for four; and *Karribank Lodge* (☎ (098) 53 1022), on Main St, with singles/doubles for $25/40. There are also a number of farmstays and

B&Bs in the region which cost around $60 for two; enquire in Albany, Cranbrook or Mount Barker.

The Stirling Range

This national park (1156 sq km) consists of a single chain of peaks, 10 km wide and 65 km long. Running most of its length are isolated peaks which tower above broad valleys covered in prickly shrubs and heath. The range is also noted for its spectacular colour changes through blues, reds and purples. The range was first visited in 1832 by Ensign Dale in search of grains and, three years later, Surveyor General Roe named the range. In his diary he recorded:

The remarkable and picturesque mountains being as yet unknown collectively by any distinguishing appellation...I called them 'Stirling Range' after the Governor of the Swan River Colony, by whom they were about to undergo a closer personal examination.

Because of the combination of height and climate there are a great number of localised plants in the range. It is estimated that over 1500 species of plants occur naturally, 60 of which are endemic. The most beautiful are the Darwinias or mountain bells. Ten species of these mountain bells, which only occur above 300 metres, have been identified, and only one of them occurs outside the range. One particularly beautiful example is the Mondurup bell *(Darwinia macrostegia)*.

The bells are not the only plants with such a restricted distribution. The *Eucalyptus talyuberlup*, with its fingerlike buds, is known only from a few localities; you can see it at the beginning of the Mt Talyuberlup walk.

This park is one of the best **bushwalking** locations in the state. Keen walkers can choose from a number of high points: Toolbrunup (for views and a good climb), Bluff Knoll (at 1073 metres, the highest peak in the range), Mt Hassell, Talyuberlup, Mondurup, and Toll Peak (for the wildflowers) are popular half-day walks.

The most challenging walks are a crossing of the eastern sector of the range from Bluff Knoll to Ellen Peak which should take three

THE GREAT SOUTHERN

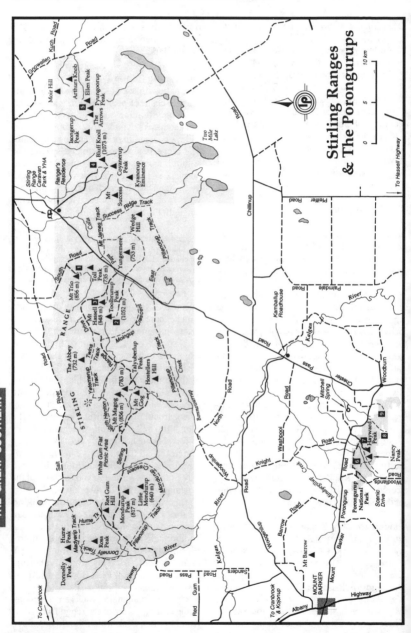

Bushwalks:

Stirlings
1 Mt Trio
2 Toolbrunup
3 Mt Hassell
4 Bluff Knoll
5 The Arrows to Ellen Peak

Porongurups
6 Marmabup Rock & Devil's Slide
7 The Pass
8 Millinup Pass
9 Castle Rock & Balancing Rock

days, or the shorter traverse from the Arrows to Ellen Peak, for which you should allow two days. The latter alternative is a loop but the former, from Bluff Knoll, would require a car shuttle. For track details see Lonely Planet's *Bushwalking in Australia* by John & Monica Chapman. Walkers must be suitably experienced and equipped as the range is subject to sudden drops in temperature, driving rain and sometimes snow.

Places to Stay You can camp in the *Stirling Range National Park* on Chester Pass Rd, near the Toolbrunup Peak turn-off; call the ranger (☎ (098) 27 9278) for details. Facilities are limited, and tent sites are $4 for two. *Stirling Range Caravan Park* (☎ (098) 27 9229), on the north boundary of the park, is also on Chester Pass Rd; there is an *Associate YHA Hostel* here with beds for $12 in self-contained rammed-earth units ($40 for four).

MOUNT BARKER

Mount Barker (population 4500), 55 km north-east of Denmark, 64 km south of the Stirling Ranges and about 20 km west of the Porongurups, is very much the centre of the Mountain National Parks region. There's a tourist office (☎ (098) 51 1163), at 57 Lowood St, open weekdays from 9 am to 5 pm, Saturday 9 am to 2 pm.

Things to See & Do
The town has been settled since the 1830s

and the old convict-built **police station and gaol** of 1868 is preserved as a museum. South-west of town on the Egerton-Warburton estate is **St Werburgh's chapel**, built between 1872 and 1873. The wrought-iron chancel screen and altar rail were shaped on the property. You can get a panoramic view of the area from the Mount Barker **Lookout**, five km south of town.

The region has a good reputation for wine making, and there are many **wineries** with cellar sales and tastings within a few km of town (see under Great Southern Wineries in this chapter).

Kendenup, 16 km north of Mount Barker, was the actual site of WA's first gold discovery, though this was considerably overshadowed by the later and much larger finds in the Kalgoorlie area. North of Mount Barker is **Cranbrook**, an access point to the Stirling Range National Park.

Great Southern Wineries There are about a dozen wineries in the Mount Barker/Porongurups area, with three near Albany and another three near Denmark. This is surprising considering the Department of Agriculture only set up an experimental vineyard, west of Mt Barker, in 1966.

Alkoomi, near Mt Frankland, has rich, full-flavoured reds; the vineyards based on the Porongurup soil produce divergent varieties such as Castle Rock liqueur muscat, Jingalla verdelho and Karrivale late-harvest riesling; and the Mt Barker vineyards boast Plantagenet fleur (light red) and pinot noir, and Karrelea Estate chaleur (a white fortified wine).

Near Denmark is the town-bound Goundrey in the historic butter factory, Karriview on Scotsdale Rd and Tingle-Wood on Glenrowan Rd. The latter produces a Red Tingle (as yet unsampled by this writer) which is a cabernet sauvignon-shiraz blend.

Most of the wineries are open daily from 10 am to 4 or 5 pm. Get a copy of the excellent free map and guide *Wines of the Great Southern Region*.

Places to Stay & Eat
The caravan park (☎ (098) 51 1619), Albany

THE GREAT SOUTHERN

Highway, has tent sites/park homes at $8.50/30 for two people. The *Plantagenet Hotel* (☎ (098) 51 1008), 9 Lowood Rd, has singles/doubles from $20/36 (in the older hotel section) and good counter meals (beaut steaks) for around $10. The *Mt Barker Hotel* (☎ (098) 51 1477), 39 Lowood Rd, has basic twin rooms at $20 per person. For those wanting to sample country air there is the 1872 stone cottage, *Abbey Holme B&B* (☎ (098) 51 1101), at the south entrance to town on the Albany Highway, for $30/55.

Getting There & Away

The Westrail, Perth-to-Albany-via-Williams bus service, stops daily in Mt Barker; the fare from Perth is $29 one-way.

ALBANY

The town of Albany (population 16,450) is the commercial centre of the southern region and the oldest European settlement in the state. It was established in 1826, three years before Perth. The area was previously occupied by Aborigines and there is much evidence, especially around Oyster Harbour, of their earlier presence.

Albany's excellent harbour, on King George Sound, meant it became a thriving whaling port. Later, when steamships started travelling between the UK and Australia, Albany was a coaling station for ships bound for the east coast. It was the gathering point for troopships of the 1st Australian Imperial Force (AIF) before they sailed for Egypt and the Gallipoli campaign.

The coastline around Albany contains some of Australia's most rugged and spectacular scenery. There are a number of pristine beaches in the area where you don't have to compete for space on the sand – try Misery, Ledge and Nanarup beaches.

Information

The informative Albany tourist office (☎ (098) 41 1088) is in Peels Place. It is open from 8.30 am to 5.30 pm Monday to Friday and from 9 am to 5 pm Saturday and Sunday. Get a copy of the free *Albany Experience*

booklet which lists accommodation, places to eat and things to do.

If you are in need of some reading material, there is a book exchange diagonally across from the tourist office. The post office is at 218 York St, most of the banks are on York St and the CALM district office is at 44 Serpentine Rd.

Old Buildings

Albany has some fine old colonial buildings – **Stirling Terrace** is noted for its Victorian shopfronts. The informative **Albany Residency Museum**, opposite the Old Gaol, was originally built in the 1850s as the home of the resident magistrate; it is open daily from 10 am to 5 pm. Displays include seafaring subjects, flora & fauna and Aboriginal artefacts. Housed in another building is 'Sea & Touch', a great hands-on experience for children and adults. Next to this museum is a full-scale replica of the **brig Amity**, the ship that brought Albany's founding party to the area; there is $2 entry fee.

The **old gaol**, built in 1851, was originally intended as a hiring depot for ticket-of-leave convicts. Most of them were in private employment by 1855 so it was closed until 1872, when it was extended and reopened as a civil gaol. Now a folk museum, it is open daily; admission is $2 (this includes entry into Patrick Taylor Cottage).

The restored **old post office**, built in 1870, now houses the Inter-Colonial Museum. It has an interesting collection of communications equipment from WA's past; admission is free.

The 1832 wattle-&-daub **Patrick Taylor Cottage** is open daily. The farm at **Strawberry Hill**, two km from town, is one of the oldest in the state, having been established in 1827 as the government farm for Albany.

Other historic buildings in town include the railway station, St John's Anglican Church and the courthouse. A guided walking-tour brochure of colonial buildings in Albany is available from the tourist office.

Views

There are fine views over the coast and inland from the twin peaks, **Mt Clarence** and

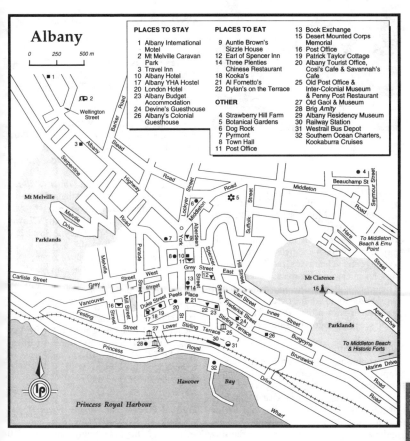

THE GREAT SOUTHERN

Mt Melville, which overlook the town. On top of Mt Clarence is the Desert Mounted Corps Memorial, originally erected in Port Said as a memorial to the events of Gallipoli. It was brought here when the Suez crisis in 1956 made colonial reminders less than popular in Egypt.

Mt Clarence can be climbed along a track accessible from the end of Grey St East; turn left, take the first turn on the right and follow the path by the water tanks. The walk is tough but the views from the top make it worthwhile. The easier way to the top is along Apex Drive.

There are also spectacular panoramic views from the lookout tower on Mt Melville; the turn-off to the tower is off Serpentine Rd.

Other Attractions

The **Princess Royal Fortress**, on Mt Adelaide, was built in 1893 – as Albany was a strategic port, its vulnerability to attack loomed as a potential threat to Australia's security. The restored buildings, gun emplacements and fine views make it well worth a visit. It is open daily from 7.30 am to 5.30 pm and costs $2.

Dog Rock

Dog Rock, a deformed and painted boulder that looks like a dog's head, is on Middleton Rd. More bizarre is **Extravaganza**, a museum with a difference, at Middleton Beach. All the exhibits in this cornucopia of trash and treasure are for sale – vintage and veteran cars, rare books, paintings, jewellery and ceramics. Strange to see a museum with greed as its central theme! Outside its doors are the ocean, the sky and the boulder-strewn bay. To get inside costs $5; to see the wonders outside costs nothing.

Whalewatching
The whalewatching season is from July to September – southern right whales are observed near the bays and coves of King George Sound. Southern Ocean Charters (☎ (098) 41 7176) takes trips out to the whales and also operate diving, fishing, underwater photography and snorkelling tours on demand. Remember that whales were still hunted here until 1979 so it will take time for numbers to increase.

Organised Tours
The *Silver Star* leaves the Emu Point jetty three times a week for a 2½-hour cruise around King George Sound; the cost is $18.50. The Kookaburra Jet (☎ (098) 42 2174) leaves from the Emu Point Marina three days a week; the two-hour cruise up Oyster Harbour and Kalgan River costs $20.

Escape Tours operate from the tourist office and have many local half and full-day tours around Albany from $22.50 to $55.

Check with the tourist office for information on these and other tours.

Places to Stay
Caravans & Camping There are caravan parks aplenty in Albany. The closest to the city centre are: *Mt Melville Caravan Park* (☎ (098) 41 4616), one km north of town on the corner of Lion and Wellington Sts; and the spotless *Middleton Beach Caravan Park* (☎ (098) 41 3593) on Middleton Rd, three km east of town. Both have caravan sites/cabins for $13/36 for two.

Other parks include the *Tourist Village* (☎ (098) 41 3752), on the Albany Highway four km north of town; *Panorama* (☎ (098) 44 4031), Frenchman Bay Rd; *Cheyne Beach* (☎ (098) 46 1247), Cheyne Beach Rd; *Happy Days* (☎ (098) 44 3267), at 21 Millbrook Rd, 10 km north of town; *Emu Beach* (☎ (098) 44 1147), Medcalf Pde, Emu Point; *King River Palms Waterfront* (☎ (098) 44 3232), 10 km north on Chester Pass Rd; *Kalgan River Chalets & Caravan Park* (☎ (098) 44 7937), north-east of Albany on Nanarup Rd near the Lower King Bridge; *Oyster Harbour* (☎ (098) 44 7164), Elizabeth St, Lower King, 10 km north-east of town; and *Rose Gardens* (☎ (098) 44 1041), Mermaid Ave, Emu Point.

Budget Places The *Albany Youth Hostel* (☎ (098) 41 3949), at 49 Duke St, is only 400 metres from the town centre, and costs $10 a night; the comments in the visitors' book are almost unanimously favourable. *Albany Budget Accommodation* (☎ (098) 41 8848), also centrally located, is on the corner of Stirling Terrace and Spencer St. It's worth going there just to check out the upstairs murals by Australian artist Jack Davies. Shared accommodation costs $12 per night, and twins/doubles are $25 for two. This place has all the necessities and they hire out mountain bikes.

The *London Hotel* (☎ (098) 41 1048), on Stirling Terrace, has entered the backpacker market; single/double rooms in bland surrounds are $18/30.

Guesthouses & B&Bs Albany also has a number of reasonably priced guesthouses and B&B places; enquire at the tourist office. A couple of places have been criticised for the snobbishness and inflexibility of the owners; we hope you select a good one.

Some of the places on the tourist office's list are: *Albany's Colonial Guesthouse* (☎ (098) 41 3704), at 136 Brunswick Rd, charges $25/38 per night including breakfast; and *Devines B&B* (☎ (098) 41 8050) at 20 Stirling Terrace is $32/50. At Middleton Beach is the *Middleton Beach Guesthouse* (☎ (098) 41 1295), 18 Adelaide Crescent; the cost is $32 to $40 per night for two. The *King River Homestead* (☎ (098) 44 7770), 64 Bushby Rd, is located in bushland overlooking the estuary. All of the rooms have a bathroom and the cost for double B&B is $55.

The *Coraki Holiday Cottages* (☎ (098) 44 7068) are about a 10-minute drive from Albany, on Lower King River Rd on the banks of Oyster Harbour. Self-contained cottages in this pretty setting are from $50 per night.

Hotels & Motels There are many hotels and motels in Albany, many of which are on the Albany Highway. The *Friendly Motel* – we like the name – (☎ (098) 41 2200), at No 234, has single/double motel units from $50 to $64/$60 to $69. The *Quality Inn* (☎ (098) 41 1177), at No 369, has rooms from $44 to $63/$50 to $73; the *Travel Inn* (☎ (098) 41 4144), at No 191, is from $69 to $79/$77 to $87; and the *Albany International* (☎ (098) 41 7399), at No 270, is from $50/60.

The town's finest (and most expensive) accommodation is *The Esplanade Hotel* (☎ (098) 42 1711), Middleton Beach; double rooms with a mountain view are $159 – add $30 to the tab for a sea view or $70 if you think you have executive status.

This a small selection of available accommodation; the tourist office has more details, especially about self-catering options.

Places to Eat

Albany You will not starve if you wander along Stirling Terrace. *Dylan's on the Terrace* at No 82 has an excellent range of light meals including hamburgers and pancakes at reasonable prices; it is open late most nights, early for breakfast and has a takeaway section.

Also on the terrace is *Kooka's*, at No 204, in a restored old house, where you can count on paying $30 for an excellent three-course meal. Other sterling choices are the *Penny Post Restaurant* in the old post office, the *Harbourfront Steakhouse & Seafood Grille* nearby, *Stirling Terrace Dine-In*, *Cafe Bizarre* and three pubs with ubiquitous counter meals. The *Royal George's* Johnny Cook's smorgasbord wins our sterling Silver Fork Award for value.

Breakfasts at the *Wildflower Cafe*, on York St, have been recommended. Also in the area is *Eatcha Heart Out* for breakfasts, and next to the tourist office is *Cosi's Cafe* for breakfasts and light lunches. Not far away at 14 Peels Place is a new restaurant, *Savannah's Cafe*, which serves African food (write and tell us about this one). There are also a couple of pizza places on York St including *Al Fornetto's* and the *Venice*. At No 280 is *Auntie Brown's Sizzle House* – they have a very good all-you-can-eat smorgasbord for just over $20.

The *Lemon Grass Thai*, at 370 Middleton Rd, has a good range of Thai food (including vegetarian meals) and *The Melting Pot*, at No 338, serves Vietnamese and Asian dishes. The *Three Plenties* Chinese Restaurant in York St does not use MSG in its dishes.

Middleton Beach & Emu Point At Middleton Beach there is the trendy *Beachside Cafe* and the *Middleton Beach Fish & Chips*, close to the Extravaganza. The latter has crisp golden chips and a diverse catch of groper, schnapper, shark and flounder to select from. The Esplanade Hotel has two swish restaurants – *Cafe Pericles* and the fully licensed *Genevieve's*.

It is the setting more than the food which attracts diners to Emu Point. Restaurants in the vicinity of the view include *Arnold's* and *Cravings*; both are BYO.

Getting There & Away

Ansett Australia and Skywest fly daily from Perth to Albany; the one-way fare on Skywest is $146 ($200 Apex return). Westrail have daily buses from Perth via various wheatbelt towns for $33, and buses four times a week via Bridgetown, Manjimup and Denmark for $43.

Getting Around

Love's run bus services around town from Monday to Friday and Saturday mornings. Buses will take you along Albany Highway from Peels Place to the roundabout; others go to Spencer Park, Middleton Beach, Emu Point and Bayonet Head.

Albany Car Rentals (☎ (098) 41 7077) has cars from $40 per day with unlimited km. Avis (☎ (098) 42 2833) and Budget (☎ (098) 41 2299) have offices in town.

You can rent bicycles from Albany Backpackers in Stirling Terrace; the cost is $10 per day.

AROUND ALBANY

South of Albany, off Frenchman Bay Rd, is a stunning stretch of coastline that includes the **Gap** and **Natural Bridge**, rugged natural rock formations surrounded by pounding seas; the **Blowholes**, especially interesting in heavy seas when air is blown with great force through the surrounding rock; the **rockclimbing** areas of Peak Head and West Cape Howe National Park; steep, rocky coves such as **Jimmy Newhill's Harbour** and **Salmon Holes**, popular with surfers (considered quite dangerous though); and **Frenchman Bay** which has a caravan park, a fine swimming beach and a grassed barbecue area with plenty of shade. This is a dangerous coastline so be aware of king waves.

Whaleworld Museum

The Whaleworld Museum, at Frenchman Bay, 21 km from Albany, is positively ghoulish. Based on the Cheynes Beach Whaling Station, which only ceased operations in November 1978, there's a rusting 'Cheynes 4' whalechaser and station impedimenta (such as whale oil tanks) to inspect. It also screens a gore-spattered film on whaling operations.

It is open daily from 9 am to 5 pm, but the $4.50 admission is considered a bit rich by some. As a keen whalewatcher, I couldn't bring myself to go inside, even though the museum houses a superb collection of marine mammal paintings by noted US artist Richard Ellis. Listen carefully and you will hear the haunting, mournful songs of the humpbacks at sea.

National Parks & Reserves

There are a number of excellent natural areas near Albany. From west to east along the coast you can explore many different habitats and see a wide variety of coastal scenery. The 17 sq km **William Bay National Park** (see under Denmark in this chapter), has coastal dunes, granite boulders, heathlands and mature karri forest.

West Cape Howe National Park, 30 km west of Albany, is a 35 sq km playground for naturalists, bushwalkers, rockclimbers and anglers. Inland, there is coastal heath, areas of lakes and swamp and karri forest. With the exception of the road to Shelley Beach, access is restricted to 4WD and walkers.

Torndirrup National Park includes the regions two very popular attractions, the Natural Bridge and the Gap, as well as the Blowholes, Jimmy Newhill's Beach and Bald Head. The views are spectacular. Whales are frequently seen from the cliffs and the park's varied vegetation provides habitats for many native animals and reptiles. Keen walkers can tackle the hard 10-km return **bushwalk** (six plus hours) over Isthmus Hill to Bald Head, the eastern extremity of the park.

Some 20 km east of Albany is **Two People's Bay**, a nature reserve of 46 sq km with a good swimming beach, scenic coastline and a small colony of the once-thought-extinct noisy scrub birds (see under Noisy Scrub Bird in this chapter). The title 'Baie des Deux Peuples' leaves you in no doubt as to who gave this place its name – there is a two-km heritage trail of that 'nom' in the reserve.

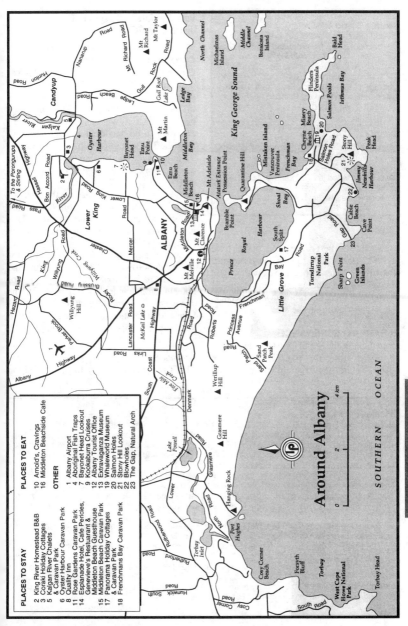

Around Albany

PLACES TO STAY

2 King River Homestead B&B
3 Coraki Holiday Cottages
5 Kalgan River Chalets
& Caravan Park
6 Oyster Harbour Caravan Park
8 Quality Inn
11 Rose Gardens Caravan Park
14 Esplanade Hotel, Cafe Pericles,
Genevieve's Restuarant &
Middleton Beach Guesthouse
15 Albany Tourist Office
17 Panorama Holiday Cottages
& Caravan Park
18 Frenchmans Bay Caravan Park

PLACES TO EAT

10 Arnold's, Cravings
16 Middleton Beachside Cafe

OTHER

1 Albany Airport
4 Aboriginal Fish Traps
7 Bayonet Head Lookout
9 Kookaburra Cruises
12 Albany Tourist Office
13 Extravaganza Museum
19 Whaleworld Museum
20 Salmon Holes
21 Stony Hill Lookout
22 Blowholes
23 The Gap, Natural Arch

Noisy Scrub Bird

This little, near-flightless bird lives up to its name as it has a powerful, ear-piercing call. The noisy scrub bird *(Atrichornus clamosus)* almost joined the thylacine to extinction. It was sighted in jarrah forest at the foot of the Darling Scarp, near Perth, in 1842, and the last recorded specimen was collected near Torbay in 1889. It was then thought extinct until rediscovered in 1961 in Two People's Bay.

In 1983, breeding pairs were transferred to similar habitats in Mt Manypeaks Nature Reserve (now part of Waychinicup National Park) to reseed populations where the bird had died out. Later, in 1987, another colony was established at Walpole-Nornalup. It is now believed that there are well over 100 breeding pairs. ■

Probably the best of the parks, but the least visited, is the 39 sq km **Waychinicup National Park** which includes Mt Manypeaks and other granite formations. At the moment there is a problem with dieback, restricting walking in the area.

ALBANY TO ESPERANCE

From Albany, the South Coast Highway runs north-east along the coast before turning inland to skirt the Fitzgerald River National Park and finally finishes in Esperance. The distance is 476 km.

Ongerup & Jerramungup

Ongerup, a small wheatbelt town 153 km north of Albany, has an annual wildflower show in September/October with hundreds of local species on show. The Ongerup-Needilup district (within 40 km of Ongerup) has over 1300 recorded species, ranging from the 30-metre-high salmon gum to small 25-mm trigger plants. Two excellent nature reserves are Cawallelup, 19 km to the south, and Vaux's Lake, 19 km north.

In Jerramungup, you can visit the interesting **Military Museum** in Tobruk Rd. All the restored vehicles are in working order. This is also where you'll find the tourist office (☎ (098) 35 1119).

There is a caravan park (☎ (098) 28 2015) and hotel (☎ (098) 28 2001) in Ongerup, and a caravan park (☎ (098) 35 1174) and motor hotel in Jerramungup (☎ (098) 35 1049). The *Jerramungup Farm B&B* (☎ (098) 35 1002) is on a 30 sq km sheep and wheat property two km south of town; singles/doubles are $35/50.

Bremer Bay

This fishing and holiday town (population

Rockclimbing

This is a highly technical and potentially dangerous sport. The moral is don't climb if you don't know how. The Great Southern is the hub of WA's climbing scene with West Cape Howe, Torndirrup, Porongurup and the Stirling Range national parks. Contact Bushed! for Adventure (☎(098) 42 2127), 334 Middleton Rd, Albany, for more advice and information. (Bushed! also offers climbing guides, abseiling, walking and canoeing trips.)

West Cape Howe is remote 'out there' climbing territory where a group size of three should be the minimum. The area has multi-pitch climbs on granite sea cliffs, all usually reached by abseil. Climbs are scaled by the level of difficulty; 30 would be regarded as suitable for the experienced climber while 10 is somewhat easier. Classics include Tombstone (20), The Elite (18) and Vulture St (17).

Torndirrup includes The Gap, Natural Bridge and Amphitheatre granite climbing areas. Most of the climbs are single pitch and classics include Horrie Cometh (17) and Surfs Up (15).

The Porongurups have a number of long climbs on weathered white granite; it is requested that you register with the CALM ranger.

Bluff Knoll in the Stirlings is the closest WA gets to offering a real mountaineering experience and has been the scene of many 'epics'. Climbs can be up to 350 metres in length involving a dozen or more pitches and as many hours to complete. Again, let the CALM ranger know of your intentions and log out when climbing has ended. ■

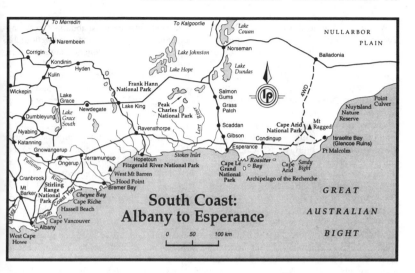

South Coast:
Albany to Esperance

200), which sits at the western end of the Great Australian Bight, is 61 km from the South Coast Highway. The BP service station (☎ (098) 37 4093), Gnombup Terrace, acts as the information office.

From June until November, Bremer Bay is a good spot to observe **southern right whales**. These whales come in to many bays in the area to give birth to their calves. Sometimes they are as close as six metres from the shore, and can be seen from many vantage points on the coastline.

The caravan park (☎ (098) 37 4018) has caravan sites/cabins for $12/30 for two and the hotel (☎ (098) 37 4133) has singles/doubles for $59/69. A nice place to stay within Fitzgerald River National Park is the historic 1858 *Quaalup Homestead* (☎ (098) 37 4124), Gardiner Rd; camping is $5, single/double units are $25/29 and homestead rooms $35/39.

Ravensthorpe

The small town of Ravensthorpe (population 380) was once the centre of the Phillips River goldfield; later, copper was also mined there. Nowadays, the area is dependent on farming. Every September a wildflower show is held

in town. The tourist office (☎ (098) 38 1163) is in Morgan St.

The ruins of a disused government smelter and the Cattlin Creek Mine (copper) are near town, and the Ravensthorpe Historical Society has a display in the **Dance Cottage**. If possible, avoid getting petrol here as it seems to be well above normal prices. About 150 km north of Ravensthorpe, the **Frank Hann National Park** has a range of typical sand-plain region flora.

West of town is the **WA time meridian**, indicated by a boulder with a plaque on it.

Places to Stay & Eat The caravan park (☎ (098) 38 1050) has tent sites/on-site vans at $8/25 for two. The *Palace Motor Hotel* (☎ (098) 38 1005), classified by the National Trust, has single/double rooms for $20/30; there are more rooms in the motel section. Tempt yourself with the sumptuous selection of cakes at *Ravy's Country Kitchen*.

Hopetoun

The fine beaches and bays around Hopetoun (population 350) are south of Ravensthorpe. It is also the eastern gateway to the Fitzgerald River National Park.

About five km north of town is **Dunn's Swamp**, an ideal location for a picnic, bushwalking and birdwatching. West of town is the landlocked **Culham Inlet**, a beaut spot for fishing (especially black bream) and east of town is the very scenic **Southern Ocean East Drive** which features beaches and the Jerdacuttup lakes.

The world's longest fence – the 1822-km long **rabbit-proof fence** – enters the sea in the south at Starvation Bay, east of Hopetoun and 40 km south of the Southern Highway. (For those who have asked, where does it start? – Eighty Mile Beach on the Indian Ocean, north of Port Hedland.)

The Hopetoun information office (☎ (098) 38 3088) is in the Blue Groper Hardware & Tackle Store, Veal St. The *Community Spirit Holiday Guide* has heaps of information on history, national parks and local pursuits.

Places to Stay & Eat A caravan park (☎ (098) 38 3096) has tent sites/on-site vans for $10/25 and the *Port Hotel* (☎ (098) 38 3053), Veal St, has singles/doubles for $20/40. The *Hopetoun Motel & Chalet Village* (☎ (098) 38 3219), Veal St, has units/chalets for $58/75. You can get a counter meal from the Port Hotel or takeaways from the BYO *Starboard Cafe*.

Fitzgerald River National Park

This 3,200 sq km park is one of two places in WA with a UNESCO Biosphere rating. The park contains a very beautiful coastline, sand plains, the rugged Barren mountain range and deep, wide river valleys.

The **bushwalking** is excellent and the wilderness route from Fitzgerald Beach to Whalebone Beach is recommended – there is no trail and no water but camping is permitted. Clean your shoes at each end of the walk to discourage the spread of dieback; also register with the ranger on Quiss Rd or Hamersley Drive. Other shorter walks in the park are East Mount Barren (three hours), Twertup 'Horri and Dorri' (two hours), West Mount Barren (one-two hours) and the Point Ann Heritage Trail (one hour).

Wildflowers are most abundant in spring but there are flowers in bloom throughout the year. This park is botanically significant in Australia with 20% of the state's described species. In the park are half the orchids in WA (over 80 species) and 70 of these occur nowhere else; 22 mammal species including honey possums, dibblers (*Parantechinus apicalis*) – highly endangered with only a few hundred left – and tammar wallabies; 200 species of birds including the ground parrot *(Pezoporus wallicus)* and western bristlebird *(Dasyornis longirostris)*; 41 reptiles and 12 frogs; and 1700 species of plants. Many of the plant species have not yet been named by botanists! To top off the list of superlatives, this is the home of the royal hakea and Qualup bell, and southern right whales are seen off-shore from August to September.

The fires of 1989, which swept through 48% of the park, have done little to diminish the magnificent display of wildflowers. Fitzgerald River is still one of the state's ecotourism highlights.

You can gain access to the park from Bremer Bay and Hopetoun or from the South Coast Highway along Devils Creek, Quiss and Hamersley Rds. There is accommodation in Bremer Bay, Quaalup (in the park) and Hopetoun. The Culham Inlet causeway, west of Hopetoun, washed away in floods in 1993, has been reopened to traffic.

ESPERANCE

Esperance (population 8500), on the coast 200 km south of Norseman, was named in 1792 when the *Recherche* and *L'Esperance* sailed into the bay to shelter from a storm. Although the first settlers came to the area in 1863, it was during the gold rush in the 1890s that the town really became established as a port. When the gold fever subsided, Esperance went into a state of suspended animation until after WW II.

In the 1950s, it was discovered that adding missing trace elements to the soil around Esperance restored fertility, and since then the town has rapidly become an agricultural centre. It has become a popular resort due to

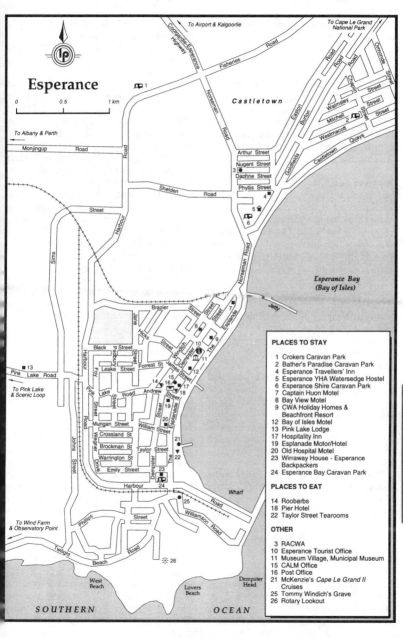

Esperance

0   0.5   1 km

To Airport & Kalgoorlie

To Cape Le Grand National Park

Fisheries

Coolgardie-Esperance Highway

Norseman

Road

Castletown

Easton

Burton

Chaplin

Walmsley

Ormonde

Street

Mitchell

Street

Westmacott

Goldfields

Castletown

Quays

To Albany & Perth

Monjingup   Road

Road

Shelden   Road

Harbour

Street

Sims

Arthur Street

Nugent Street

Daphne Street

Phyllis Street

Norseman Road

Esperance Bay (Bay of Isles)

Jetty

Brazier   Street

Jane

Hicks

Street

Street

Esplanade

Street

Black   Street

Padbury

Street

Wingold

Dempster

James Street

Forrest St

Foy

Pink

Leake   Street

Lake

Road

Andrew

Street

The Esplanade

Harbour   Road

Mungan   Street

Wegner

Crossland St

William Street

Brockman St

Taylor

Street

Warrington St

Emily   Street

Dempster

The

Harbour   Road

Johns

Street

Wharf

To Pink Lake & Scenic Loop

Twilight

Beach

Phillips

Road

Street

Williamson Road

To Wind Farm & Observatory Point

West
Beach

Lovers
Beach

Dempster
Head

SOUTHERN   *OCEAN*

PLACES TO STAY

1 Crokers Caravan Park
2 Bather's Paradise Caravan Park
4 Esperance Travellers' Inn
5 Esperance YHA Watersedge Hostel
6 Esperance Shire Caravan Park
7 Captain Huon Motel
8 Bay View Motel
9 CWA Holiday Homes & Beachfront Resort
12 Bay of Isles Motel
13 Pink Lake Lodge
17 Hospitality Inn
19 Esplanade Motor/Hotel
20 Old Hospital Motel
23 Wirraway House - Esperance Backpackers
24 Esperance Bay Caravan Park

PLACES TO EAT

14 Roobarbs
18 Pier Hotel
22 Taylor Street Tearooms

OTHER

3 RACWA
10 Esperance Tourist Office
11 Museum Village, Municipal Museum
15 CALM Office
16 Post Office
21 McKenzie's *Cape Le Grand II* Cruises
25 Tommy Windich's Grave
26 Rotary Lookout

THE GREAT SOUTHERN

its temperate climate, magnificent coastal scenery, blue waters, good fishing and sandy, dazzling beaches.

Information

The Esperance tourist office (☎ (090) 71 2330) on Dempster St, in the museum village, is open daily from 9 am to 5 pm and can book tours along the coast, to the islands and into the surrounding national parks. The post office is on the corner of Andrew and Dempster Sts.

Things to See & Do

Esperance, or the Bay of Isles, has some excellent beaches, and the seas offshore are studded with the many islands of the Archipelago of the Recherche. Distinctive Norfolk Island pines line the foreshore. The **Esperance Municipal Museum** contains the tourist office and various old buildings, including gallery, smithy's forge, cafe and craft shop.

The museum itself, between the Esplanade and Dempster St, is open daily from 1.30 to 4.30 pm and contains a Skylab display – when the USA's Skylab crashed to earth in 1979, it made its fiery re-entry right over Esperance.

The interesting 36-km **Scenic Loop Rd** has a number of highlights including the spectacular vistas from Observatory Point and the Rotary Lookout on Wireless Hill; Twilight Bay and Picnic Cove, popular swimming spots; and the Pink Lake, stained by a salt-tolerant algae called *Dunalella salina*.

There are about 100 small islands in the **Archipelago of the Recherche**. Colonies of seals, penguins and a wide variety of waterbirds live on the islands. Woody Island is a wildlife sanctuary, and there are regular trips there.

Organised Tours

Vacation Country Tours (☎ (090) 71 2227) runs a number of tours around Esperance including a town-and-coast tour for $12 and a Cape Le Grand National Park tour twice a week for $25. More adventurous alternatives

are Safari Wheels and Reels (☎ (090) 71 1564) which, as the name suggests, conduct 4WD safaris and fishing trips to secluded beaches and bays. There are also trips run by the YHA to Arid and Le Grand capes.

Tours on the waters of Esperance Bay are a must. Unfortunately, the tug *Cape Le Grand II* (McKenzies Marine, ☎ (090) 71 1772) only heads out if the right numbers front up on the jetty. Just remember, even though they advertise daily tours these tours are at the owner's convenience. McKenzies operate a daily ferry service to Woody Island in January and February.

The *Dive Master II* (☎ (090) 71 5111) *does* goes out on Tuesday and Thursday. The *Dive Master II* is the flagship of the Esperance Diving Academy which conducts dive charters, diving courses and cruises.

Expect to see New Zealand fur seals, Australian sea lions, sea eagles, Cape Barren geese *(Cereopsis novae-hollandiae)*, common dolphins and a host of other wildlife in the two-hour cruise around the Bay of Isles. Trips are weather-dependent and cost $20 (children $10).

Places to Stay

There are half a dozen caravan parks around Esperance that provide campsites and on-site accommodation; the rate for caravan sites/park homes is usually around $13/30 for two. The most central of the parks are the *Esperance Bay Caravan Park* (☎ (090) 71 2237), on the corner of the Esplanade and Harbour Rd, near the wharf; and the *Esperance Shire Caravan Park* (☎ (090) 71 1251) on the corner of Goldfields and Norseman Rds. Two others not far away are *Bathers Paradise* (☎ (090) 71 1014), on the corner of Westmacott and Chaplin Sts; and the well-kept and efficiently run *Crokers* (☎ (090) 71 4100), 629 Harbour Rd.

The large and popular *Esperance YHA Watersedge Hostel* (☎ (090) 71 1040), on Goldfields Rd, is two km north of the town centre and costs $10 per night in dorms, and singles/twins are $12. The new, purpose-built *Wirraway House Esperance Backpackers* (☎ (090) 71 4724, (018) 93

4541), 14 Emily St, has dorm rooms for $12 per night and twins/doubles for $26 for two.

The well-run *Esperance Travellers' Inn* (☎ (090) 71 1677), at the corner of Gold-fields Rd and Phyllis St two km from town, has clean rooms for $40/50 and friendly staff. In addition, the *Pink Lake Lodge* (☎ (090) 71 2075), at 85 Pink Lake Rd, has singles/ doubles from $18/30 and the *CWA Esperance* (☎ (090) 71 1364), 23 The Espla-nade, has units for around $40.

There are numerous motels with rates from about $50/65 for singles/doubles. The *Bay of Isles Motel* (☎ (090) 71 3999) is at 32 The Esplanade; the *Bay View* (☎ (090) 71 1847) is in Dempster St; the *Esperance Motor Hotel* (☎ (090) 71 1555) is in Andrew St; the *Captain Huon* (☎ (090) 71 2383) is at 5 The Esplanade; *The Old Hospital* (☎ (090) 71 3587) is at 1A William St; the *Hospitality Inn* (☎ (090) 71 1999) is also on The Espla-nade; as is the *Beachfront Resort* (☎ (090) 71 2513) at No 19.

Places to Eat

The town has a good number of cafes. Sip at *Beachfront Coffee Lounge, Taylor Street Tearooms* or the *Village Cafe*; the latter is in the museum enclave. The best known of the takeaways is *Pizza, Pasta & Rib House*, on the corner of William and Dempster Sts, but there are also a number of fish & chip places. If you like cooking fish then buy fillets of gnanagi – coat them in flour and lightly cook in butter with a sprinkling of lemon pepper.

Coffee lounges which serve meals are the *Island Fare* in the Boulevard shopping centre, *Roobarbs* at the corner of Dempster and Andrew Sts and *Captain's Cabin*, in Andrew St. The *Spice of Life*, also on Andrew St, has a varied health-food menu including zucchini slice, vegetarian pasties, Lebanese rolls chock full of salad, and fruit smoothies. *Ollies on the Esplanade* is open from 7 am until 11 pm, seven days – you can get a cappuccino, soup or three-course meal here and they don't mind kids.

The garden bistro at the *Pier Hotel* has tasty meals with an all-you-can-eat, well-stocked salad bar for around $10. There are really good counteries at the *Travellers' Inn*.

Some up-market choices are the licensed *Peaches* in the Bay of Isles Motel, *Seasons Restaurant* in the Hospitality Inn and the BYO *Gray Starling*, Dempster St.

Getting There & Around

Ansett Australia and Skywest fly daily from Perth to Esperance for $188 one-way ($252 Apex return) and Goldfields Air Services fly from Kalgoorlie via Norseman for $137 every Tuesday.

Westrail has a bus three times a week from Kalgoorlie to Esperance, an Esperance-to-Albany service and a 10-hour Perth-to-Esperance service, that runs on Monday via Jerramungup and on Wednesday and Friday via Lake Grace for $50. Greyhound Pioneer's Albany-to-Norseman-via-Esper-ance service wasn't operating when we checked; locals hope that an alternative will be found.

You can hire bicycles from the Captain Huon Motel for $10 per day, or from the Esperance YHA Watersedge Hostel.

NATIONAL PARKS

There are four national parks in the region around Esperance. The closest and most popular is **Cape Le Grand National Park**, which extends 60 km east of Esperance. The park has spectacular coastal scenery, some good white-sand beaches and excellent walking tracks. There are fine views across the park from Frenchmans Peak, at the western end of the park, and good fishing, camping and swimming at Lucky Bay and Le Grand Beach.

Just over six km east of Cape Le Grand is **Rossiter Bay**. This is where Eyre and Wylie, during their epic overland crossing in 1841, fortuitously met Captain Rossiter of the French whaler *Mississippi*.

Further east is the coastal **Cape Arid National Park**, at the start of the Great Aus-tralian Bight and on the fringes of the Nullarbor Plain. It is a rugged and isolated park with abundant flora & fauna, good bushwalking, beaches and campsites.

THE GREAT SOUTHERN

Whales and seals are regularly spotted off the coast and Cape Barren geese are often seen. Most of the park is only accessible by 4WD, although the Poison Creek and Thomas River sites are accessible in normal vehicles. To get to other popular sites such as Mount Ragged requires a 4WD.

Mt Ragged and the Russell Range were islands during the late Eocene period (40 million years ago) and there are wave-cut platforms on their upper slopes. The world's most primitive species of ant was found thriving near Mt Ragged in 1930.

Other national parks in the area include the **Stokes Inlet National Park**, 90 km west of Esperance, with an inlet, long beaches and rocky headlands backed by sand dunes and low hills; and the **Peak Charles National Park**, 130 km to the north. For information about these national parks, contact CALM (☎ (090) 71 3733) in Dempster St, Esperance.

If you are going into the national parks, take plenty of water as there is little or no fresh water in most of these areas. Also, be wary of spreading dieback and get information about its prevention from the park rangers.

Places to Stay & Eat

Limited-facility tent sites are $5 per night at *Cape Le Grand* (☎ (090) 75 9022) and free at *Cape Arid* (☎ (090) 75 0055) national

---

> **Dieback**
> Many of the national parks along the south coast (and huge areas outside the parks) are infected with dieback, a plant disease caused by the fungus *Phytophthora cinnamomi*. This microscopic fungus lives in the soil and attacks the root systems of plants causing them to rot. As a result, plants cannot take up water or nutrients through their roots and die of 'starvation'.
>
> The fungus is spread by vehicles and on the feet of bushwalkers. You can help prevent its spread by keeping to formed roads and by observing 'no go' road signs in the conservation reserves. There are also places where you are instructed to clean mud and soil from your boots before you enter reserves. The CALM rangers will provide information on the prevention and spread of the disease. ■

---

parks. Apply for permits with the ranger at the park entrances. Between the two national parks is the *Orleans Bay Caravan Park* (☎ (090) 75 0033), a good friendly place to stay; campsites/park homes are $9/30.

If heading into the national parks make sure you stock up with supplies from the supermarkets in Esperance. Just off Merivale Rd, on the way to Le Grand, is *Merivale Farm*, known throughout the free world for cakes and tempting tortes.

The Goldfields & The Nullarbor

Beyond the expansive wheatbelt lies a huge region of semi-desert and desert. Towns are few and far between, the distances are great and much of the attraction is found in the isolation of this frontier. The goldfields include the mining towns of Kalgoorlie-Boulder, Kambalda and Norseman and the many ghost towns in-between which appear and, just as quickly, fade into the spinifex. East of the goldfields is the famed Nullarbor and the sealed Eyre Highway to the eastern states.

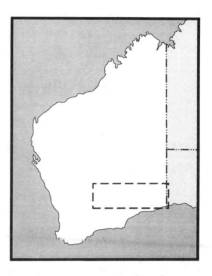

The Goldfields

Fifty years after its establishment in 1829, the WA colony was still going nowhere, so the government in Perth was delighted when gold was discovered at Southern Cross in 1887. That first strike petered out pretty quickly, but following more discoveries, WA profited from the gold boom for the rest of the century. It was gold that put WA on the map and finally gave it the population to make it viable in its own right, rather than just a distant offshoot of the east-coast colonies.

The major strikes were made in 1892 at Coolgardie and nearby Kalgoorlie, but in the whole goldfields area, Kalgoorlie is the only large town left. Coolgardie's period of prosperity lasted only until 1905 and many other gold towns went from nothing to populations of 10,000 then back to nothing in just 10 years. Nevertheless, the towns capitalised on their prosperity while it lasted, as the many magnificent public buildings grandly attest.

Life in the early goldfields was terribly hard. This area of WA is extremely dry – rainfall is erratic and never great. Even the little rain that does fall quickly disappears into the porous soil. Many early gold seekers, driven more by enthusiasm than by commonsense, died of thirst while seeking the elusive metal. Others succumbed to diseases that broke out periodically in the unhygienic shanty towns. The supply of water to the goldfields by pipeline in 1903 was a major breakthrough (see Where Water is like Gold! in this chapter) and ensured the continuation of mining.

Today, Kalgoorlie-Boulder is the main goldfields centre and mines still operate there. Elsewhere, a string of fascinating ghost and near-ghost towns, often surrounded by carpets of wildflowers, make a visit to WA's gold country a must.

COOLGARDIE

A popular pause in the long journey across the Nullarbor, and also the turn-off for Kalgoorlie, Coolgardie (population 1500) really is a ghost of its former self. You only have to glance at the huge town hall, warden's court and post office building to appreciate the size that Coolgardie once was.

A reef of gold was discovered here in

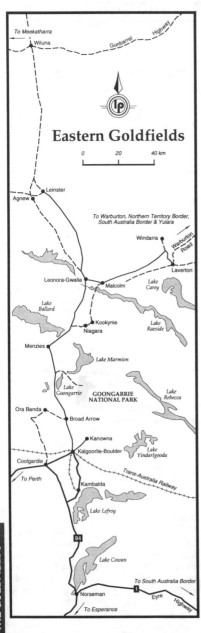

Eastern Goldfields

0   20   40 km

1892, by the prospector Arthur Bayley and his mate Bill Ford, and called 'Bayley's Reward'. By the turn of the century the population of Coolgardie had boomed to 15,000, there were two stock exchanges, six newspapers, over 20 hotels and three breweries. The gold then petered out and the town withered away just as quickly. However, there's still plenty of interest for the visitor.

The helpful Coolgardie tourist office (☎ (090) 26 6090), in the Warden's Court in Bayley St, is open daily from 9 am to 5 pm. The BP service station on the corner of Hunt St has an ATM and the post office is just around the corner.

Things to See & Do
Many historical markers, scattered in and around the town, tell of what was once there

or what the buildings were formerly used for. The **Goldfields Exhibition**, in the same building as the tourist office, is open from 9 am to 5 pm daily and has a fascinating display of goldfields memorabilia. You can even find out about US President Herbert Hoover's days on the WA goldfields. It's an interesting museum and worth the $2.50 admission fee, which includes a film.

The **railway station** in Woodward St also operates as a museum; you can learn the incredible story of the Varischetti mine rescue. In 1907, a miner was trapped 300 metres underground by floodwater and rescued by divers 10 days later.

One km west of Coolgardie is the **town cemetery**, which includes many old graves such as that of explorer Ernest Giles (1835-97) and several Afghan camel drivers. Due to the unsanitary conditions and violence in the goldfields, it's said that 'one half of the population buried the other half'. The old **pioneer cemetery**, used from 1892 to 1894, is near the old oval at the end of Forrest St.

One of Coolgardie's sights is **Ben Prior's Open Air Museum**, diagonally opposite the tourist office, but it seems a little neglected these days.

Other attractions are **Warden Finnerty's Residence**, restored by the National Trust, which is open daily except Tuesday from 1 to 4 pm and Sunday from 10 am to noon (admission $2); nearby is the lightning-dissected **Gaol Tree**, complete with leg irons.

At the **Camel Farm** (☎ (090) 26 6159), three km west of town on the Great Eastern Highway, you can take camel rides or organise longer camel treks; it is open daily 9 am to 5 pm and admission is $2 (rides are $2.50).

About 30 km south of Coolgardie is **Gnarlbine Rocks**, an important watering point for the early prospectors. The **Queen Victoria Rock Nature Reserve**, which has interesting transitional vegetation types and limited primitive camping, is a further 18 km south.

Places to Stay & Eat

The *Coolgardie Caravan Park* (☎ (090) 26 6009), 99 Bayley St, has excellent tent/caravan sites for $8/10 and on-site vans for $25. Parents with kids will appreciate the playground. The other van-choked caravan park (☎ (090) 26 6123), mistitled *The Haven*, has very poor tent sites; on-site vans are $18 to $25. The fine old *Coolgardie YHA Hostel* (☎ (090) 26 6051), at 56-60 Gnarlbine Rd, costs $10.

There are a couple of historic hotels in Bayley St with long, shady verandahs: the *Railway Lodge* (☎ (090) 26 6166) which has singles/doubles for $25/35 and the *Denver City Hotel* (☎ (090) 26 6031) with rooms for $30/45. The *Coolgardie Motor Inne* (☎ (090) 26 6002), 10 Bayley St, has good singles/doubles for $55/70; the *Coolgardie Motel* (☎ (090) 26 6080), 49 Bayley St, is $55/68; and the *Caltex Motel* (☎ (090) 26 6049), 110 Bayley St, is $40/49.

The *Denver City Hotel* does counter lunches and teas from $10, and there are a couple of roadhouses on Bayley St that do meals. The *Premier Cafe*, on Bayley St, does excellent meals for $7 and the usual snacks and takeaways. There are restaurants in the Motor Inne and Coolgardie Motel.

Getting There & Away

Greyhound Pioneer passes through Coolgardie on its Perth to Adelaide runs; the one-way fare from Perth to Coolgardie on Greyhound Pioneer is $70, to Adelaide it's $180. The local operator Goldenlines (☎ (090) 21 2655) runs two buses on weekdays from Kalgoorlie to Coolgardie; the bus departs Kalgoorlie at 7.10 am and returns at 3.45 pm and the fare is $2.75.

The *Prospector* from Perth to Kalgoorlie stops at Bonnie Vale Railway Station, 14 km away, daily except Saturday; the one-way fare from Perth is $53.60, with a meal. For bookings call the tourist office or Westrail (☎ (09) 326 2222).

KALGOORLIE-BOULDER

Kalgoorlie ('Kal' to the locals) is a real surprise – today it is a prosperous, humming metropolis (population 29,000) some 570 km from Perth. The longest lasting and most successful of WA's gold towns, it rose to prominence later than Coolgardie.

There is no doubt that this town invokes traveller ambivalence. Walk into the wrong bar and a group of dishevelled, hoary miners will turn slowly and observe you as if you were some sort of 'bad smell' that had wafted in. Don't be surprised if the lady at the bar appears somewhat *deshabille* in bra, panties, suspenders and high heels – it might be a 'skimpy' night. And if you're not in thongs, shorts and Jack Howe T-shirt you have failed to meet the 'dress-down' standards. Hey, this is Kal and that is the way it is and if you don't like it, then the standard retort would be 'bugger off!'.

In spite of the overwhelming 'macho' feel and air of crassness there is something appealing about Kal. This is Australia at its raw edge, larrikin-like, threatening and at the same time loving, sweet and sour, warts and all, that mythical Oz that permeates the alter ego of many urban dwellers.

History

In 1893, Paddy Hannan, a prospector, set out from Coolgardie for another gold strike with a couple of Irish mates but stopped at the site of Kalgoorlie and found, lying on the surface, enough gold to spark another rush.

As in so many places, the surface gold soon dried up, but at Kalgoorlie the miners went deeper and more and more gold was found. There weren't the storybook chunky nuggets of solid gold – Kalgoorlie's gold had to be extracted from the rocks by a costly and complex processes of grinding, roasting and chemical action – but there was plenty of it.

Kalgoorlie quickly reached fabled heights of prosperity, and the enormous and magnificent public buildings at the turn of the century are evidence of its fabulous wealth. After WW I, however, increasing production costs and static gold prices led to Kalgoorlie's slow but steady decline.

In 1934 there were bitter race riots in Kalgoorlie and Boulder. On 29 and 30 January, mobs of disgruntled Australians roamed the streets setting fire to foreign-owned businesses and shooting at foreigners. They were suppos-

edly upset at preference being given by shift bosses to southern European immigrants. The disturbance had died down by the time police reinforcements and volunteers arrived by train from Perth.

With the substantial increase in gold prices since the mid-1970s, mining of lower-grade deposits has become economical and Kalgoorlie is again the largest producer of gold in Australia. Large mining conglomerates have been at the forefront of new open-cut mining operations in the Golden Mile – gone are the old headframes and corrugated iron homes. Mining, pastoral development and a busy tourist trade ensure Kalgoorlie's continuing importance as an outback centre.

Orientation

Although Kalgoorlie sprang up close to Paddy Hannan's original find, the mining emphasis soon shifted a few km away to the Golden Mile, an area which was probably the wealthiest gold-mining locale for its size in

Paddy Hannan's Statue

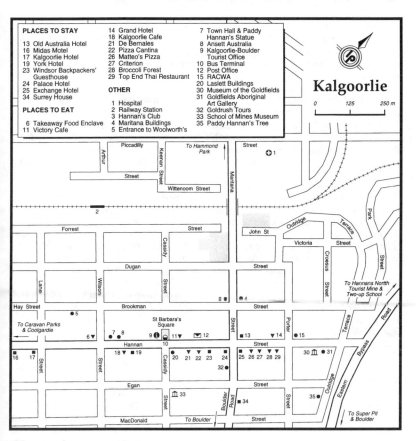

Kalgoorlie

PLACES TO STAY	14 Grand Hotel	7 Town Hall & Paddy
13 Old Australia Hotel	18 Kalgoorlie Cafe	Hannan's Statue
16 Midas Motel	21 De Bernales	8 Ansett Australia
17 Kalgoorlie Hotel	22 Pizza Cantina	9 Kalgoorlie-Boulder
19 York Hotel	26 Matteo's Pizza	Tourist Office
23 Windsor Backpackers'	27 Criterion	10 Bus Terminal
Guesthouse	28 Broccoli Forest	12 Post Office
24 Palace Hotel	29 Top End Thai Restaurant	15 RACWA
25 Exchange Hotel		20 Laslett Buildings
34 Surrey House	OTHER	30 Museum of the Goldfields
		31 Goldfields Aboriginal
PLACES TO EAT	1 Hospital	Art Gallery
	2 Railway Station	32 Goldrush Tours
6 Takeaway Food Enclave	3 Hannan's Club	33 School of Mines Museum
11 Victory Cafe	4 Maritana Buildings	35 Paddy Hannan's Tree
	5 Entrance to Woolworth's	

the world. The satellite town of Boulder developed to service this area. The two towns amalgamated in August 1989 into the City of Kalgoorlie-Boulder.

Kalgoorlie itself is a grid of broad, tree-lined streets. The main street (Hannan St), flanked by imposing public buildings, is wide enough to turn a camel train – a necessity in turn-of-the-century goldfield towns. You'll find most of the hotels, restaurants and offices on or close to Hannan St.

Information

There's a helpful tourist office (☎ (090) 21 1966, 21 1413), on the corner of Hannan and Cassidy Sts, where you can get a good free map of Kalgoorlie and friendly advice; a number of other area maps are for sale. The office is open from 8.30 am to 5 pm Monday to Friday and from 9 am to 5 pm on weekends. The daily paper in Kal is the *Kalgoorlie Miner*.

Kal can get very hot in December and January; overall the cool winter months are the best time to visit. From late August to the end of September, however, the town is packed because of wildflower tours and the local horse races, and accommodation of any type can be difficult to find.

The RACWA (☎ (090) 21 1511) is on the corner of Porter and Hannan Sts. The post office is at 204 Hannan St and the railway station is on the corner of Wilson and Hannan Sts.

Hannan's North Tourist Mine
One of Kalgoorlie's biggest attractions is the Hannan's North Tourist Mine. You can take the lift cage down into the bowels of the earth and make a tour around the drives and cross-cuts of the mine, guided by an ex-miner.

The $14 (children $7, family $36) entry fee covers the underground tour, an audio-visual presentation, a tour of the surface workings and a gold pour. Underground tours are on demand daily (more frequently during peak seasons) and the complex is open from 9.30 am to 4.30 pm. Fully enclosed shoes must be worn on underground tours and children under four are not permitted underground.

Golden Mile Loopline
You can make an interesting loop around the Golden Mile by catching the 'Rattler', a tourist train complete with commentary which makes an hour-long trip daily at 10 am (☎ (090) 21 7077). On Sunday it also goes at 11.45 am. It leaves from Boulder Railway Station, passing the old mining works. The cost is $9 for adults and $5 for children.

In the early part of this century, the Loopline was the most important urban transport for Kal and Boulder and the Golden Gate Station was once the busiest in WA.

Museum of the Goldfields
The impressive Ivanhoe mine headframe at the northern end of Hannan St marks the entrance to this excellent museum. It is open daily from 10 am to 4.30 pm (admission is free) and has a wide range of exhibits including an underground gold vault and historic photographs. A lift takes you up to a viewing point on the headframe where you can look out over the city and mines and down into delightfully untidy backyards.

Gold and sandalwood are treated in detail in this museum and there is an underground vault which features specimens from the state gold collection. The tiny **British Arms Hotel** (the narrowest hotel in Australia) is part of the museum.

Other Attractions – Kalgoorlie
The **Mt Charlotte Lookout** and the town's reservoir are only a few hundred metres from the north-eastern end of Hannan St, off the Eastern Bypass Rd. The view over the town is good but there's little to see of the reservoir, which is covered to limit evaporation. This is the reservoir, however, which is the culmination of the genius of CY O'Connor – the water in it took 10 days to get there from Mundaring Weir.

The **School of Mines Mineral Museum**, on the corner of Egan and Cassidy Sts, has a geology display including replicas of big nuggets discovered in the area. It's usually open from 9 am to 4 pm Monday to Friday.

Along Hannan St, you'll find the imposing **town hall** and the equally impressive **post office**. There's an art gallery upstairs in the decorative town hall, while outside is a replica of a statue of Paddy Hannan himself holding a water bag. The original is inside the town hall, safe from nocturnal painters.

A block back, north-west from Hannan St, is Hay St and one of Kalgoorlie's most famous 'attractions'. Although it's quietly ignored in the tourist brochures, Kal has a block-long strip of **brothels** where working ladies beckon passing men (sometimes driving past in huge bedecked rigs) to their true-blue, and pink, Aussie galvanised-iron doorways. A blind eye has been turned to this patronage for so long that it has become an accepted and historical part of the town.

Kalgoorlie also has a **two-up school** in a corrugated-iron amphitheatre six km north of town – follow the signs from Hannan St.

Two-up is a frenetic, uniquely Australian gambling game where two coins are tossed and bets are placed on the result. Amongst the gamblers' yelps, a lot of money seems to change hands. It is open from 2.30 pm until dark as the owners have lost so much moolah they can't afford to put the power on.

On Outridge Terrace is **Paddy Hannan's tree**, marking the spot where the first gold strike was made. **Hammond Park** is a small fauna reserve with a miniature Bavarian castle. It's open daily from 9 am to 5 pm. Not far away is a pleasant **arboretum**.

Architectural Styles

Kalgoorlie-Boulder boasts an interesting collection of architectural styles, many unconventional. Nowhere is this better represented than along Hannan St. Expect to see curious blends of Victorian gold boom, Edwardian, Moorish and Art Nouveau styles. The turn-of-the-century styles have melded to produce a bizarre mix of ornate facades, colonnaded footpaths, recessed verandahs, stuccoed walls and general overstatement.

Buildings to look out for in Hannan St include the Kalgoorlie Miner and Old Western Argus building (Nos 117-119); Exchange Hotel (No 135); Palace Hotel (Nos 135-139); Exchange Building (Nos 149-151); Lasletts (No 181); York Hotel (No 259) – don't miss its staircase; the town hall; and the City Markets (No 276). In Maritana St, look out for Hannan's Club and the Maritana buildings. ■

Things to See & Do – Boulder

The **Goldfields War Museum** in Burt St, Boulder, was undergoing renovation at the time of writing. The Boulder Railway Station, home to the **Eastern Goldfields Historical Society Museum**, was built in 1897. It is open from 9 am to 11.30 pm daily.

The **Super Pit** lookout, just off the Eastern Bypass near Boulder, is open from 7.30 am to 4.15 pm daily (closed when blasting is in progress).

On Hopkins St is the **Cornwall Hotel**, which was involved in the notorious Pittman and Walsh murders.

During April 1926, Detective Sergeant Pittman of the Gold Stealing Detection staff and Inspector John Walsh went missing. They were found shot, dismembered, partially burnt and dumped in a mineshaft.

The police were determined to get the killers and did, eventually, when Teddy Clarke, licensee of the Cornwall and a gold stealer, turned King's evidence. His barman Phillip Treffene and one William Coulter, a punter and backer of bookies, were found guilty of the murders and hanged at Fremantle gaol.

Organised Tours

Goldrush Tours (☎ (090) 21 2954) are the main tour operators in Kalgoorlie. Book through the tourist office or from Goldrush Tours directly at Palace Chambers, Maritana St. They have tours of Kal, Coolgardie and nearby ghost towns. There's also a gold-detector tour for avid fossickers, and August and September wildflower tours.

Starting from $25, you can see Kal and the Golden Mile mining operations from the air with Goldfields Air Services.

Keen fossickers who wish to strike it rich can purchase a **gold-fossicking** package from the tourist office. The package entitles visitors to spend from half a day to a week camping on the Boorara lease which is 18 km from Kal. Metal detectors can be hired from the tourist office.

Places to Stay

Caravans & Camping There are a number of caravan parks in Kalgoorlie. The closest to the city centre are the *Golden Village Caravan Park* (☎ (090) 21 4162), 406 Hay St, two km south-west of the railway station, which has tent sites/on-site vans for $7.50 to $15 /$25 to $46 for two; and the *Prospector Tourist Park* (☎ (090) 21 2524) on the Great Eastern Highway with tent sites/on-site vans/cabins for $13/38/45 for two. The Prospector has a pool, a grassed area for campers and a campers' kitchen – one of the best in WA, so thumbs up.

The other caravan parks are the *Kalgoorlie* (☎ (090) 21 4855), Lower Hannan St; the *Boulder Village* (☎ (090) 93 1266), Lane St, Boulder; *Kalgoorlie Village* (☎ (090) 93 2780), Burt St, Boulder; and the *Goldminer* (☎ (090) 21 3713), on the Great Eastern Highway.

Hostels The popular and central *Windsor*

Backpackers' Guesthouse (☎ (090) 21 5483), at the end of the courtyard at 147 Hannan St, is an austere, quiet place with a TV room and kitchen facilities; beds are $15/30 for shared/twins and, strangely, singles are $30. At 9 Boulder Rd is the comfortable *Surrey House* (☎ (090) 21 1340), which has backpackers' beds for $15 per night and singles/doubles for $28/40; a continental breakfast is $4.50 extra per person.

B&B One particularly interesting place to stay is the homestay (☎ (090) 91 1482) at 164 Hay St. A former brothel in the heart of Kal's rue Pigalle, rooms are $30/50 for B&B singles/doubles and there's a preferred three-night minimum. The tourist office has a list of other B&B accommodation.

Hotels & Motels There are several pleasantly old-fashioned hotels right in the centre of Kalgoorlie, including the *Palace Hotel* (☎ (090) 21 2788) on the corner of Maritana and Hannan Sts. Standard rooms cost $40/60 for singles/doubles. The *York Hotel* (☎ (090) 21 2337), 259 Hannan St, has B&B single/twins for $35/60; it is exceptionally placed in the heart of town. Other pubs are the *Kalgoorlie* (☎ (090) 21 3046), 319 Hannan St; *The Grand* (☎ (090) 21 2353), 90 Hannan St; and the *Exchange* (☎ (090) 21 2833), also on Hannan St.

There is no shortage of good-quality motels. On Hannan St there are *Hannan's View* (☎ (090) 91 3333) with singles/doubles for $60/75; the *Quality Inn* (☎ (090) 21 1433) with rooms at $68/79; the *Old Australia* (☎ (090) 21 1320) with rooms at $45/65; and the *Star and Garter* (☎ (090) 21 3004) with rooms at $60/70. Make sure you strike it rich before you try the *Hospitality Inn* (☎ (090) 21 2888), on the corner of Hannan and Throssell Sts, as singles/doubles are from $65 to $90/$80 to $105 and suites are $110 to $120.

Places to Eat

Kalgoorlie There are plenty of counter-meal pubs (where they skimp on clothing and not the servings), restaurants and cafes in Kalgoorlie, particularly along Hannan St. The *York Hotel*, on Hannan St, does solid counter meals in its Steak House from $7 to $10, and meals in the saloon bar for around $6. The *Criterion Bistro* and the *Grand Hotel* also do counter meals and usually have cheap lunch specials.

The *Exchange Hotel*, in Maritana St, and the *Palace Hotel*, on the corner of Hannan St and Boulder Rd, have restaurants with main courses from around $10, and cheaper food ($4 to $7) in the saloon bars.

The *Broccoli Forest*, at 75 Hannan St, has a lunch bar with an interesting menu – most of it vegetarian. Nearby, the *Top End Thai* restaurant, at 71 Hannan St, is good for a splurge – a wide range of prawn, curry and noodle dishes costs from $14 to $18.

On Wilson St, between Brookman and Hannan Sts, is a small enclave of takeaway places including the *Fu Wah* Chinese restaurant and *Thai Food* with small and large combination dishes from $6.50 to $8. At 90 Egan St there is the BYO *Loaded Cactus* Mexican restaurant advertising a $12.50 lunch special which includes starter, enchilada, nachos and dessert.

At 277 Hannan St is the *Kalgoorlie Cafe*, which has burger-type fast food, or there's the *Victory Cafe*, at 246 Hannan St, for an early breakfast. For pizza, try *Pizza Cantina*, 211 Hannan St, or *Matteo's* at No 123.

The more up-market *De Bernales*, 193 Hannan St, does tasty food from $12 to $16 and has a pleasant verandah opening onto Hannan St – a good place to sip a beer and watch life go by. The *Amalfi*, at 409 Hannan St in the Midas Motel, is at the top end of the dining scale; this place is à la carte and fully licensed and will cost from $25 per person.

Boulder You can get counter meals at *Tattersalls* on the corner of Bart and Lane Sts, and, opposite, at the *Albion Hotel*. You can also try the *Wah On* Chinese restaurant, 110 Burt St, next to the Goldfields War Museum, and *Peachy's* takeaway at 16 Burt St.

Things to Buy

The Goldfields Aboriginal Art Gallery, next

to the Museum of the Goldfields, has crafts for sale. Kal is a good place to buy actual gold nuggets fashioned into relatively inexpensive jewellery.

Getting There & Away
Air Ansett Australia fly from Perth to Kalgoorlie several times daily; the Apex return fare is $218, and the full return fare is $408. The Ansett Australia office (☎ (090) 91 2828), at 314 Hannan St, is near the town hall.

Skywest has two direct flights a day for $248 (Apex return) or $183 (one-way full fare) – other discounts such as a special weekend fares are also available (☎ (090) 91 1446). Goldfields Air Services (☎ (090) 93 2116) flies from Kalgoorlie to Esperance (via Norseman) every Tuesday and returns the same day; the one-way fare is $134.

Horizon (☎ 13 1313) has one flight daily from Perth to Alice Springs which stops in Kal.

Bus Greyhound Pioneer (☎ (090) 21 7100, 13 2030) buses operate through Kalgoorlie on their services from Perth to Sydney, Melbourne and Adelaide; the fare from Perth is around $71. The Kalgoorlie Express (☎ (09) 328 9199) also has a twice-weekly Perth to Kalgoorlie service which also heads north to Laverton ($43), Leinster ($49) and Leonora ($31). Check timetables carefully as some of these buses pull into Kalgoorlie at an ungodly hour of the night when everything is closed and finding a place to stay can be difficult.

Westrail (☎ (090) 21 2023) run a bus three times a week from Kal to Esperance – once via Kambalda and Norseman and twice via Coolgardie and Norseman; the trip takes 5½ hours and costs $16.30 to Norseman and $30.40 to Esperance.

Train The daily *Prospector* service from Perth takes around 7½ hours and costs $55.80, including a meal. From Perth, you can book seats at the WATC in Forrest Place or at the Westrail Terminal (☎ (09) 326 2222). It's wise to book as this service is fairly popular, particularly in the tourist season. The Indian-Pacific and Trans-Australian trains also go through Kalgoorlie.

Getting Around
Between Kalgoorlie and Boulder, there's a regular bus service (get the timetable from the tourist office). Goldenlines (☎ (090) 21 2655) travels to Boulder, either directly or via Lionel St, between 8 am and 6 pm. There are also daily buses to Kambalda and Coolgardie.

You can rent cars from Hertz (☎ (090) 91 2625), Budget (☎ (090) 93 2300) and Avis (☎ (090) 21 1722). If you want to explore further afield, you'll have to drive, hitch or take a tour as public transport is limited. A taxi to the airport costs around $8. You can hire bicycles from Johnston Cycles (☎ (090) 21 1157), 76 Boulder Rd; a deposit is required.

NORTH OF KALGOORLIE
The road north is surfaced from Kalgoorlie to the three 'Ls' – Laverton (130 km northeast), Leinster (160 km north) and Leonora-Gwalia, 240 km north. Off the main road, however, traffic is virtually nonexistent and rain can quickly close the dirt roads. There are a number of towns of interest along the way including Kanowna, Broad Arrow, Ora Banda, Menzies and Kookynie.

Kanowna
This is the most fascinating of the goldfields ghost towns in terms of history. It is just 18 km from Kalgoorlie-Boulder along a dirt road. In 1905, Kanowna had a population of 12,000, 16 hotels, two breweries, many churches and an hourly train service to Kalgoorlie. Today, apart from the railway-station platform and the odd pile of rubble, absolutely nothing remains!

Broad Arrow & Ora Banda
With a population of 20, compared with 2400 at the turn of the century, Broad Arrow is definitely a shadow of its former self. One of the town's original eight hotels still operates in a virtually unchanged condition. The

town was featured in *The Nickel Queen*, the first full-length feature film made in WA. The stone railway station featured in the film was demolished in 1973.

Ora Banda, 28 km west of the Kal-Menzies Rd, has shrunk from a population of 2000 to less than 50.

Menzies & Kookynie

Another typical goldfields town, Menzies is 132 km north of Kal. It has about 230 people today, compared with 5000 in 1900. Many early buildings remain, including the railway station with its 120-metre long platform (1898) and the imposing town hall (1896) with its clockless clocktower. The ship bringing the clock from England, the SS *Orizaba*, sank off the coast south of Rottnest Island.

There are no rivers in the area and the surrounding countryside is mostly flat with eucalypts, salmon gum and blackbutt trees. If there is adequate winter rainfall, marvellous displays of **wildflowers** can be seen from August to September.

Kookynie is a small ghost town, 69 km south-east of Leonora, surrounded by old mine workings and tailings. The *Grand Hotel* (☎ (090) 31 3010), built in 1894, has big verandahs and spacious rooms. There is also an interesting little museum in town with a collection of photographs and antique bottles. About 10 km from Kookynie is the **Niagara Dam**, built with cement carried from Coolgardie by a caravan of 400 camels.

Well worth a visit, especially in spring, is the 500 sq km **Goongarrie National Park**. It includes large areas of mulga, prolific birdlife of the arid region and wildflowers in season. The park is reached on a metal road north-east of Menzies.

Places to Stay & Eat In Menzies, the caravan park (☎ (090) 24 2041), Shenton St, has tent/caravan sites for $6/9; and the *Railway Hotel* (☎ (090) 24 2043), 22 Shenton St has singles/doubles for $28/50. Meals can be obtained from the *Caltex Roadhouse* and the hotel. Unwind with a beer (and

barbecued food) in the beer garden of the *Grand Hotel* in Kookynie.

Leonora-Gwalia

Named after the wife of a WA Governor, Leonora is 237 km north of Kalgoorlie. It has a population of 2000 and serves as the railhead for the nickel from Windarra and Leinster. Climb up to the summit of **Mt Leonora** to get a great view of the town or wander down to the **Cenotaph** to see the 1927 restored hearse. The tourist office (☎ (090) 37 6044) is in the shire offices on Power St.

In adjoining Gwalia (a ghost town), the Sons of Gwalia Goldmine, the largest in WA outside Kalgoorlie, closed in 1963 and much of the town closed with it; due to the increase in gold prices this and other mines in the area have been reopened. In the late 1890s, the mine was managed by Herbert Hoover, later to become president of the USA.

The Gwalia Historical Society is housed in the 1898 **mine office** – this fascinating local museum is open daily. Also of interest is the restored State Hotel, Patronis Guesthouse and the mine manager's house. The pamphlet *Historic Gwalia Heritage Trail* describes the places of interest to see on a fascinating one-km walk around the town.

Places to Stay The caravan park (☎ (090) 37 6568) in Rochester St has tent/caravan sites for $8/14 for two; the motel (☎ (090) 37 6181), in Tower St, has singles/doubles for $65/70; the *Whitehouse Hotel* (☎ (090) 37 6030) has singles only for $30; and the *Central Hotel* (☎ (090) 37 6042) has rooms for $30/60.

A great BB&D (bed, breakfast & dinner) place is the *Ida Valley Station* (☎ (090) 37 5918), set on a mere 'half million acres'; full board is $45 per person and a room in the shearer's quarters is $10.

Laverton

From Leonora-Gwalia, you can turn northeast to Laverton, 361 km north of Kalgoorlie, where the surfaced road ends. The population here declined from 1000 in 1910 to 200

The Gwalia Beer Strike

The Gwalia State Hotel was the first and last of the government-owned state hotels in operation in WA. Built in 1903 in an attempt to cut down the sly-grog trade, the hotel did well as salaries in Gwalia were relatively high.

In March 1919, about 50 residents voted to boycott the hotel until certain conditions were met. They wanted some control over the brands of beer offered, cleanliness and the price and size of glasses. They also wanted the manager dismissed.

It was to their credit that these thirsty workers maintained the boycott until September – the number of sly grog prosecutions in that time increased, however. During the 'strike', the hotel was used as a hospital because a serious influenza epidemic hit town (as it did in most parts of WA). ■

in 1970 when the Poseidon nickel discovery (beloved of stock-market speculators in the late 1960s and early 1970s) revived mining operations in nearby Windarra. The town now has a population of 1500 and there are many abandoned mines in the area.

From here, it is just 1710 km north-east to Alice Springs (see under Warburton Rd & Gunbarrel Highway later in this chapter).

Places to Stay The *Desert Pea Caravan Park* (☎ (090) 31 1072) is at Weld Ave. The *Desert Inn Hotel* (☎ (090) 31 1188), 2 Laver Place, has single/double hotel rooms for $50/70 and motel units for $55/75.

Leinster

North of Leonora-Gwalia, the road is now surfaced to Leinster (population 1000), another modern nickel-mining centre. **Agnew**, 23 km west of Leinster, is another old gold town that has all but disappeared. The old brick gaol at **Lawlers**, 25 km southeast of Leinster on the Agnew-Leonora Rd, is all that is left of that township.

From Leinster, it's 170 km north to Wiluna and another 180 km west to Meekatharra. The surfaced Great Northern Highway runs

765 km south-west to Perth or 860 km north to Port Hedland.

Places to Stay The caravan park (☎ (090) 37 9005) in Mansbridge Rd has powered sites at $10 for two. The *Leinster Lodge* (☎ (090) 37 9241), on the corner of Mansbridge and Agnew Rds, has single/doubles for $50/70.

Getting There & Away

Air Ansett Australia has flights from Perth to Laverton (every day except Friday and Saturday), Leinster (Monday to Thursday) and Leonora (Thursday and Friday).

Bus Westliner (☎ (09) 250 3318) has a service from Perth to Leonora, Laverton and Leinster on Friday and Sunday. The bus heads to Perth from these towns on Monday and Friday (Leinster $90, Laverton $85 and Leonora $77).

WILUNA

Remote Wiluna marks the end of civilisation eastwards until Alice Springs. As the local shire puts it: 'Wiluna is a dusty outback town that hasn't got a lot of the creature comforts. What Wiluna has got is friendly people and a real bush atmosphere.'

When gold was mined in the district, Wiluna had a population of 9000 and was a prosperous town. Today, Wiluna is an administrative centre with a mainly Aboriginal population. Just 11 km east of town is the Desert Gold **orange orchard**, proof that the desert (as it does in Israel) can bloom.

Wiluna is the starting or finishing point of two of Australia's great driving adventures – the **Canning Stock Route** and the **Gunbarrel Highway** (see under Warburton Rd & Gunbarrel Highway).

The Canning runs south-west from Halls Creek to Wiluna, crossing the Great Sandy and Gibson deserts. As the track has not been maintained for over 30 years it's a route to be taken seriously. If you intend taking this route get a copy of the *Australian Geographic Book of the Canning Stock Route* (Australian Geographic, Terrey Hills, 1992)

THE GOLDFIELDS

which contains all the maps and information you will require.

Obtain tourist information from the shire office (☎ (099) 81 7010) in Scotia St.

Places to Stay & Eat

Most visitors come in their own 4WD transport and head to the local caravan park (☎ (099) 81 7021); nonpowered/powered sites are $6/9 for two. The *Club Motel Hotel* (☎ (099) 81 7012) in Wotton St has single/double rooms (and, obviously, a captive market) for $45/65 and motel units for $80/95. Out on the Gunbarrel Highway is *Carnegie Station* (☎ (099) 63 5809) where a tent site is $8 and a basic unit $15 per person.

Counter meals are available from the *Club Hotel* which also has a licensed restaurant for evening meals. Buy provisions for the inevitable long journeys (whichever way you leave town) from the Canning Trading Company or Ngangganawili Community store; both of these places are on Wotton St.

Getting There & Away

There is one Ansett Australia flight to Wiluna on Sunday. There is no regular bus service; most people get here in their own 4WD vehicles in order to tackle one of the great outback tracks.

WARBURTON RD & GUNBARREL HIGHWAY

For those interested in an outback experience, the unsealed road from Laverton to Yulara (the tourist development near Uluru) via Cosmo Newbery Aboriginal Land and Warburton, provides a rich scenery of red sand, spinifex, mulga and desert oaks.

The road, while sandy in places, is suitable for conventional vehicles, although a 4WD would give a much smoother ride. Although this road is often mistakenly called the Gunbarrel Highway, the genuine article actually runs some distance to the north, and is very rough and only partially maintained.

You should take precautions relevant to travel in such an isolated area – tell someone (shire office or local police) of your travel plans and take adequate supplies of water, petrol, food and spare parts.

The route passes through Aboriginal land and permission to enter must be obtained in advance if you want to leave the road. Petrol is available at Laverton, Warburton (where basic supplies are also available) and Yulara. In an emergency, you may be able to get fuel at the Docker River settlement.

The longest stretch without fuel is between Laverton and **Warburton** (570 km). The *Warburton Roadhouse & Caravan Park* (☎ (089) 56 7656) has accommodation (camping and self-catering), fuel and food supplies. The Warburton township is an Aboriginal community on private land and not open to the public.

At **Giles**, 231 km north-east of Warburton and about 105 km west from the Northern Territory border, there is a meteorological station with a friendly 'Visitors Welcome' sign and a bar – it is well worth a visit. The *Warakurna Roadhouse & Caravan Park* (☎ (089) 56 7344) has accommodation, fuel and food supplies, and you can arrange tours to the meteorological station here.

Don't even consider doing this route from November to March due to the extreme heat. See the Getting Around chapter for more details. For nearly 300 km west from Giles, the Warburton Rd & Gunbarrel Highway run on the same route. Taking the old Gunbarrel Highway (to the north of the Warburton Rd) all the way to Wiluna is a much rougher and far more serious trip requiring a 4WD.

SOUTH OF KALGOORLIE
Kambalda

Kambalda (population 5000) died as a gold-mining town in 1906, but nickel was discovered there in 1966, and today it is a major mining centre. Kambalda is split into two parts, East and West, about four km apart. East was the original centre but when nickel was found in an area due for housing expansion, the mining company simply built another town away from the nickel deposits.

The tourist office (☎ (090) 27 1446), on Irish Mulga Drive, Kambalda West, provides information and a map of the area.

Kambalda is on the shores of Lake Lefroy, a large salt pan and a popular spot for **land sailing**. The yachts can travel at 100 km/h across the smooth salt lake. The first land sailors were prospectors who mounted wheels on a five-metre sailboat. The best time to see the boats in action is on Sundays from November to April.

The view from Red Hill Lookout in Kambalda East is well worth checking out. If you have binoculars you will be able to watch the land sailing from here.

Places to Stay The caravan park (☎ (090) 27 1582) in Gordon Adams Rd, Kambalda East, has powered sites/on-site vans for $12/28 for two. In Bluebush Rd, Kambalda West, there is a motor hotel (☎ (090) 27 1582) with singles/doubles for $65/75.

Norseman

To most people, Norseman (population 2500) is just a crossroads where you turn east for the trans-Nullarbor Eyre Highway journey, south to Esperance along the Leeuwin Way or north to Coolgardie and Perth. The town, however, also has gold mines, some of which are in operation. The tourist office (☎ (090) 39 1071), at 68 Roberts St, is open daily from 9 am to 5 pm. Next to the tourist office is a tourist rest park, open from 8 am to 6 pm. The **Historical & Geological Collection** in the old School of Mines has items from the gold-rush days; it's open weekdays from 10 am to 4 pm and admission is $2.

An interesting gold-mining tour is conducted by the Central Norseman Gold mining operations every weekday at 10 am and 1 pm; the 2½-hour tour costs $5 and bookings can be made at the tourist office.

You can get an excellent view of the town and the surrounding salt lakes from the **Beacon Hill Mararoa Lookout** down past the mountainous tailings. The tailings, one of which contains 4.2 million tonnes of rock, are the results of 40 years of gold mining.

Places to Stay & Eat The *Gateway Caravan Park* (☎ (090) 39 1500) has tent sites/vans/

on-site cabins for $11/26/35. The backpackers' hostel in Norseman has closed down; when it reopens is anyone's guess. The *Norseman Hotel* (☎ (090) 39 1023), on the corner of Robert St and Talbot Rd, has singles/doubles for $25/45; and at the *Railway Hotel Motel* (☎ (090) 39 1115) they are $20/30. The *Norseman Eyre Motel* (☎ (090) 39 1130) has singles/doubles for $62/69, which is the same rate as the *Great Western* (☎ (090) 39 1633).

Bits & Pizzas has a wide range of eat-in or takeaway meals, and also cooked breakfasts with the works for $7.50. The BP and Ampol roadhouses have a wide range of food including tasty fish & chips.

Getting There & Away Goldfields Air Services (☎ (090) 93 2116) flies from Kalgoorlie to Esperance via Norseman – the Kalgoorlie to Norseman sector costs $70. See the Kalgoorlie Getting There & Away section for bus information.

Around Norseman The graffiti-covered **Dundas Rocks** are huge boulders, 22 km south of Norseman. Also worth a look are the views at sunrise and sunset of the dry, expansive and spectacular **Lake Cowans**, north of Norseman.

South of Norseman, halfway along the road to Esperance, is the small township of **Salmon Gums** (population 50), named after the gum trees, prevalent in the area, which acquire a seasonal rich-pink bark in late summer and autumn.

Eyre Highway & The Nullarbor

It's a little over 2700 km between Perth and Adelaide – not much less than the distance from London to Moscow. The long and sometimes lonely Eyre Highway crosses the southern edge of the vast Nullarbor Plain. Nullarbor is bad Latin for 'no trees' but there is actually only a small stretch where you see none at all. Surprisingly, the road is flanked by trees most of the way as this coastal fringe receives regular rain, especially in winter.

The road across the Nullarbor takes its name from John Eyre, the explorer who made the first east-west crossing in 1841. It was a superhuman effort that took five months of hardship and resulted in the death of Eyre's companion, John Baxter. In 1877, a telegraph line was laid across the Nullarbor, roughly delineating the route the first road would take.

Later in the century, miners on their way to the goldfields followed the same telegraph line route across the empty plain. In 1896, the first bicycle crossing was made and in 1912 the first car was driven across, but in the next 12 years only three more cars managed to traverse the continent.

In 1941, the war inspired the building of a trans-continental highway, just as it had the Alice Springs to Darwin route. It was a rough-and-ready track when completed, and in the 1950s only a few vehicles a day made the crossing. In the 1960s, the traffic flow increased to more than 30 vehicles a day and in 1969 the WA government surfaced the road as far as the South Australian border. Finally, in 1976, the last stretch from the South Australian border was surfaced and now the Nullarbor crossing is a much easier drive, but still a long one.

The surfaced road runs close to the coast on the South Australian side. The Nullarbor region ends dramatically on the coast of the Great Australian Bight, at cliffs that drop steeply into the ocean. It's easy to see why this was a seafarer's nightmare, for a ship driven on to the coast would quickly be pounded to pieces against the cliffs, and climbing them would be a near impossibility.

The Indian-Pacific Railway runs north of the coast and actually on the Nullarbor Plain – unlike the main road, which only fringes the great plain. One stretch of the railway runs dead straight for 478 km – the longest piece of straight railway line in the world.

CROSSING THE NULLARBOR
See also the Getting There & Away chapter

for air, rail, hitching and bus information across the Nullarbor.

Information
At the western end of the highway, there's a tourist office (☎ (090) 39 1071) in Norseman. It's at 68 Roberts St, and is open daily from 9 am to 5 pm. At the eastern end, the first tourist office is in Ceduna (☎ (086) 25 2780), in Poynton St. There is a much larger facility in Port Augusta – the Wadlata Outback Centre (☎ (086) 41 0793), 41 Flinders Terrace, is also the tourist office.

All of the roadhouses have stacks of pamphlets relating to tourist sights in the area and for the towns on either side.

Books & Maps There are a number of helpful publications which cover the Nullarbor. One of the most comprehensive is the free *Across Australia*, available in Perth and Adelaide from Leisure Time Publications. The accommodation information in the WATC's *Golden Heartlands* is also useful. If you stick to the highway no special maps are required.

Car
Although the Nullarbor is no longer a torture trail where cars get shaken to bits by potholes and corrugations or where you're going to die of thirst waiting for another vehicle if you break down, it's still wise to avoid difficulties whenever possible.

The longest distance between fuel stops is about 200 km, so if you're foolish enough to run out of petrol midway, you'll have a nice long round trip to get more. Getting help for a mechanical breakdown can be equally time-consuming and very expensive, so make sure your vehicle is in good shape and that you've got plenty of petrol, good tyres and at least a basic kit of simple spare parts. Carry some drinking water (four litres per person) just in case you do have to sit it out by the roadside on a hot summer day. Remember, there are limited fresh-water facilities between Norseman and Ceduna.

There are no banking facilities between Norseman and Ceduna so take plenty of

Nullarbor

Top: Seemingly endless Eyre Highway along the Nullarbor (RN)

Middle: Eucla Telegraph station, Eyre Highway, Nullarbor (RN)

Bottom: Eerie desolation, Eyre Bird Observatory (JW)

Mid-West & Batavia Coast

A	B
C	D
E	F

A: Dominican Chapel of St Hyacinth (WATC)
B: Leaning tree, Greenough (WATC)
C: Our Lady of Mt Carmel Church, Mullewa (WATC)
D: Coastline of Kalbarri (CLA)
E: Yardie Creek Gorge, Cape Range National Park (KF)
F: Hawk's Head Lookout, Kalbarri National Park (WATC)

cash. Some roadhouses have EFTPOS and take major credit cards.

Take it easy on the Nullarbor – plenty of people try to set speed records and plenty more have made a real mess of their cars when they've run into big kangaroos, particularly at night. There are plenty of rest areas so make use of them!

Bus & Train

As the Eyre is the most important trans-continental route, there are daily scheduled bus services all the way from Perth to Adelaide with Greyhound Pioneer. There is also a rail option and this is one of the great railway journeys of the world (see under Indian-Pacific in the Getting There & Away chapter).

Bicycle

The Nullarbor (Eyre Highway) is a real challenge to cyclists. They are attracted by the barrenness and distance, certainly not by the interesting scenery. As you drive across you see many of them, at all times of the year, lifting their waterbottles to their parched mouths or sheltering under a lone tree that often enlivens the barren stretches.

Excellent equipment is needed and adequate water supplies have to be carried. The cyclist should also know where all the water tanks are located. Adequate protection (hats, lotions etc) from the sun should be used even in cloudy weather. The prevailing wind for most of the journey is west to east, the most preferable direction to be pedalling.

Spare a thought for the first cyclist to cross the Nullarbor. Arthur Richardson set off from Coolgardie on 24 November 1896 with a small kit and water bag. Thirty-one days later he arrived in Adelaide having followed the telegraph line. The biggest problems he encountered were the hot winds, '1000 in the

---

Under the Nullarbor

Beneath the uninhabited and barren landscape of the Nullarbor lies a wealth of interest. And yes, I do mean *beneath*. The Nullarbor is an ancient limestone seabed, up to 300 metres thick in places. About 20 million years ago shells and other marine organisms began to settle and some three million years ago the bed was gently raised forming a huge plateau, 700 km long and up to 300 km wide.

Within this raised plateau is Australia's largest network of caves, formed over the millennia as rain seeped through cracks in the surface limestone. The caves vary from shallow depressions to elaborate, deep caves with immense chambers. About 50 of the caves are entered via passages which begin in large sinkholes or dolines; others can only be accessed through narrow, vertical blowholes.

The best known of the caves is Koonalda in South Australia, entered through a huge sinkhole. This cave contains a large main chamber, 70 metres below the surface, which has a 45-metre-high domed ceiling. Aborigines quarried flint from this cave over 20,000 years ago and they left unexplained incisions on the main entrance passage.

More caves exist on the WA side of the border. West of Eucla are the Weebubbie and the Abrakurrie caves. The Weebubbie Cave is entered from a sinkhole and contains a beautiful white-walled chamber with a crystal-clear lake. The Abrakurrie Cave contains the largest chamber of the Nullarbor caves, 180 metres long and 45 metres wide with a 40-metre-high ceiling; it is reached by steeply sloping passage from the sinkhole entrance.

The Cocklebiddy Cave, 12 km north of the Eyre Highway, has one of the longest underwater passages known in the world. In 1984, a team of French explorers recorded the then deepest cave dive ever made. The Mullamullang Cave east of Cocklebiddy is the most extensive cave network known in Australia and contains the Salt Cellars – superb mineral formations.

All this said, *never* enter any of these caves without an experienced guide and proper equipment. Many lives have been lost (especially in Cocklebiddy Cave) and the vertical access to a number of the caves requires highly specialised equipment. Those keen to venture underground should contact CALM in Perth or the South Australia National Parks & Wildlife Service in Ceduna for more information. ■

shade' and 40 km of sandhills west of Madura station.

THE EYRE HIGHWAY

From Norseman, where the Eyre Highway begins, it's 725 km to the Western Australia/South Australia border, near Eucla, and a further 480 km to Ceduna (from an Aboriginal word meaning 'a place to sit down and rest') in South Australia. From Ceduna, it's still another 793 km to Adelaide via Port Augusta. In the immortal words of a trans-Australian truckie: 'It's a bloody long way!'.

Balladonia

From Norseman, the first settlement you reach is Balladonia, 193 km to the east. After Balladonia, near the old station, you may see the remains of old stone fences built to enclose stock. Clay saltpans are also visible in the area. **Newman's Rocks** (50 km west of Balladonia) are also worth seeing. Visits to the oil-painting gallery at the Balladonia station homestead can be arranged by phoning ☎ (090) 39 3456 between 9 am and 4.30 pm.

The *Balladonia Hotel/Motel* (☎ (090) 39 3453) has rooms from $58/66 and its dusty

caravan park has tent/caravan sites for an exorbitant $8/14. It does, however, include use of the shower facilities.

The road from Balladonia to Cocklebiddy is one of the loneliest stretches of road across the Nullarbor.

Caiguna & Cocklebiddy

The section of road from Balladonia to Caiguna includes one of the longest stretches of straight road in the world – 146.6 km. At Caiguna, the *John Eyre Motel* (☎ (090) 39 3459) has rooms for $50/65, and a caravan park with tent/caravan sites from $5/12. Caiguna is over 370 km from Norseman and a good stop. Some 10 km south of Caiguna is the memorial to John Baxter, Eyre's companion who was killed on 29 April 1841 by Aborigines.

At Cocklebiddy are the stone ruins of an Aboriginal mission. **Cocklebiddy Cave** is the largest of the Nullarbor caves. With a 4WD, you can travel south of Cocklebiddy to **Twilight Cove**, where there are 75-metre-high limestone cliffs.

The *Wedgetail Inn* (☎ (090) 39 3462) at Cocklebiddy has a marauding and contrary

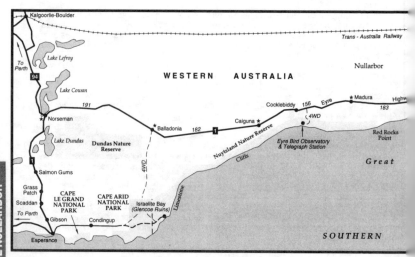

goat, extremely expensive fuel, overpriced rooms from \$58/66 and tent/caravan sites for \$6/12. Hey, it does have wedge-tailed eagles overhead!

Madura & Mundrabilla

Madura, 91 km east of Cocklebiddy, is close to the hills of the Hampton Tablelands. At one time, horses were bred here for the Indian army. You get good views over the plains from the road.

The ruins of the **Old Madura Homestead**, several km west of the new homestead by a dirt track, have some old machinery and other equipment. Caves in the area include the large **Mullamullang Caves**, north-west of Madura, with three lakes and many side passages.

The *Madura Hospitality Inn* (☎ (090) 39 3464) has rooms from \$60/70 and tent/caravan sites from \$5/12.

The Mundrabilla Roadhouse is on the lower coastal plain and has the Hampton Tablelands as a backdrop. It has a small zoo behind it, where the most notable resident is Carmel – a camel that dances for its dinner. From Mundrabilla it is 66 km to Eucla.

Mundrabilla, 116 km to the east, has the *Mundrabilla Motor Hotel* (☎ (090) 39 3465) with singles/doubles from \$45/55 and a caravan park with tent/caravan sites from \$5/10 and cabins for \$20.

Eucla & the Border

Just before the South Australia border is Eucla, which has picturesque ruins of an old **telegraph repeater and weather station**, first opened in 1877. The telegraph line now runs along the railway line, far to the north. The station, five km from the roadhouse, is gradually being engulfed by the sand dunes. Generally, the chimneys are all that is visible but about once a year, the sand dunes roll across and uncover the whole building for a few weeks. Then, as the winds change, they roll back over it for another year. You can also inspect the historic jetty, which is visible from the top of the dunes. The dunes around Eucla are a truly spectacular sight.

At Eucla, many people have their photo taken with the international sign pinpointing distances to many parts of the world. The sign is near a ferro-concrete construction of a sperm whale. At the Western Australia/

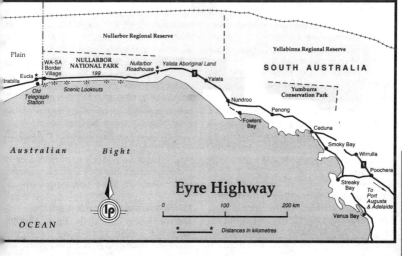

Birds of the Bight

The Eyre Bird Observatory (☎(090) 39 3450) provides accommodation by prior arrangement only. Established in 1977, it is housed in the Eyre Telegraph Station, an 1897 stone building in the Nuytsland Nature Reserve, surrounded by mallee scrubland and looking up to spectacular roving sand dunes which separate buildings from the sea. A wide range of desert flora & fauna are studied. Twitchers can expect to see many pink cockatoos, brush bronzewings and the odd furtive malleefowl. There are many raptors along all sections of the highway dispensing with road kills. By far the most spectacular is the wedge-tailed eagle. A small museum at the rear of the station has exhibits from the days of the telegraph line and of the legendary stationmaster, William Graham.

Harold Anderson, eccentric US millionaire and one-time visitor, was convinced Armageddon was nigh. He subsequently donated all the books that he thought would form the perfect account of the earth and its history to the observatory. Eyre's isolation made it just the place to sit out the firestorms and nuclear winters that would wrack the rest of the world. He returned to the USA, collated the books and dispatched them to Australia via Qantas. Not long after his return he was murdered, never to see the books on the shelves at the observatory. They are still there, alongside all the written paraphernalia an avid birder needs.

Full board is the usual arrangement; $45 per person per day (discounts for YHA and RAOU members). Return transport to the bird observatory from Cocklebiddy or the Microwave Tower can be arranged for about $25. If travelling independently, you will need a 4WD to get there, as it is about 50 km south-east of Cocklebiddy. 4WDs have to descend the escarpment and then drive through about 12 km of sand to reach the observatory. From the buildings there is a one-km walk, via the dunes, to the beach and the lonely Great Australian Bight. ■

South Australian Border Village, 13 km from Eucla, is a five-metre-high fibreglass kangaroo for connoisseurs of kitsch.

The 33 sq km **Eucla National Park** is only a 10-minute drive from the town. It features the Delisser Sandhills and the high limestone Wilson Bluff. The mallee scrub and heath of the park is typical of the coast in this region. The Eucla area also has many caves, including Weebubbie and Abrakurrie (see Under the Nullarbor in this chapter).

The *Amber Motor Hotel* (☎ (090) 39 3468) in Eucla has single/double rooms for $58/68; its Eucla Pass section has rooms for $18/30 and the tent/caravan sites are $4/10 (showers are $1). The beleaguered *WA/SA Border Village Motel* (☎ (090) 39 3474) has tent/caravan sites from $6/12, cabins from $35 a double and motel units from $60/68.

Nullarbor Roadhouse (South Australia)

Between the Western Australia/South Australia border and Nullarbor (184 km to the east), the Eyre Highway runs close to the coast and there are six spectacular lookouts over the Great Australian Bight – be sure to stop at one or two.

Around Nullarbor Roadhouse are many caves that should be explored only with extreme care (again they are recommended for experienced cave explorers only). Watch out for the many, extremely large wombat holes and poisonous snakes in the area. A dirt road leads to a beach, 30 km away – ask directions at the roadhouse.

Nullarbor National Park (5930 sq km) and Nullarbor Regional Reserve (22,000 sq km) contain part of the largest arid limestone landscape in the world. The landscape is better appreciated travelling north of the Eyre Highway along the Cook Road.

The *Nullarbor Hotel-Motel* (☎ (086) 25 6271) has tent sites from $8, backpackers' singles/twins for $15/25, units from $55/65 and a restaurant. Just look for the diminutive fibreglass model of a southern right whale.

Yalata & Nundroo (South Australia)

The road passes through the Yalata Aboriginal Reserve (6000 sq km), and Aborigines often sell boomerangs and other souvenirs by the roadside. You can also buy these in the Yalata Community Roadhouse. The *Yalata Aboriginal Community Roadhouse* (☎ (086) 25 6990) has tent sites from $3.50 and singles/doubles from $30/35; there's also a restaurant and a takeaway.

Winter and early spring is a good time to whalewatch (southern right whales) near Twin Rocks at the Head of Bight, between the Yalata and Nullarbor roadhouses. Get a $2 permit from either of the roadhouses before venturing out to the watching area.

Nundroo is the real edge of the Nullarbor. The *Nundroo Inn* (☎ (086) 25 6120) is a caravan park with tent sites and rooms. There is a licensed restaurant, takeaway food and a pool.

Penong (South Australia)
Between Nundroo and Penong is the ghost town of **Fowlers Bay**. There is good fishing here and nearby is **Mexican Hat Beach**.

You can make a short detour south of Penong to see the Pink Lake, Point Sinclair and Cactus Beach – a surf beach with left and right breaks that is a must for any serious surfer making the east-west journey.

The *Penong Hotel* (☎ (086) 25 1050) has basic singles/doubles from $20/30 and serves counter meals. The service station across the road has a restaurant and takeaways.

Eastbound from Penong to Ceduna, there are several places with petrol and other facilities. Ceduna is effectively the end of the solitary stretch from Norseman, and is equipped with supermarkets, banks and all the comforts.

ALTERNATIVE ROUTES
Esperance to Balladonia
For those travelling in the south-west of WA there is a good alternative route from Esperance. You can cut north-east to the Eyre Highway from near Cape Arid National Park utilising the 4WD-only Balladonia Rd. To get there, head out from Esperance on Fisheries Rd and when Grewer Rd comes in on the right, turn left to the north. This turns into Balladonia Rd and allows you to traverse part of Cape Arid National Park.

On this route you will pass Mt Ragged, the highest point in the Russell Range, where there is a tough walk to the top (three km return, three hours). Good topographic coverage is found in the 1:250,000 Auslig map series *Balladonia* and *Malcolm*. There is good information on the national park in the CALM pamphlet *Cape Arid and Eucla*.

You have to bring your own fuel and water, and after Orleans Bay (to the south of the route) there are no facilities until Balladonia.

North into the Nullarbor
Look at any map of the central Nullarbor and you will see few roads head south (with the exception of the rough track to the Eyre Bird Observatory described earlier in this

chapter). There are, however, a number that lead north to the trans-continental rail line and the 'real' Nullarbor.

Possibly the best detour into the Nullarbor is actually in South Australia, where you drive north through the Nullarbor National Park and the regional reserve, east along the trans-continental railway line to Ooldea and then south through Yalata Aboriginal Land to the Eyre Highway. From Eucla or the Western Australia/South Australia Border Village, it is a full day of driving, best broken into two days and 4WD is definitely recommended. Take plenty of water.

If you take two days you will need two permits: a bush camping permit for the Nullarbor Regional Reserve obtained from the South Australia National Parks & Wildlife Service (☎ (086) 25 3144) at 11 McKenzie St, in Ceduna, and a permit to cross Yalata Aboriginal Land, obtained from the Yalata Roadhouse (☎ (086) 25 6990).

It is 146 km from the Western Australia/South Australia Border Village to the Cook turn-off. If you go to a few (or all) of the Nullarbor lookouts, this stretch of sealed road will take some time. It is 107 km north to Cook where you can get fuel (phone ahead to find out opening hours of the Cook fuel depot ☎ (086) 41 8506).

Turn right and follow the rough road which parallels the trans-continental railway on its south side to Watson, passing Fisher and O'Malley stations. Then cross to the north side of the line at Watson, follow the improved road to Ooldea and then cross to the south again (the Telecom repeater station should be to your left) – it is about 141 km from Cook to Ooldea. Proceed south to the Eyre Highway (with a valid permit from the Yalata Community), crossing Ifould Lake, a large saltpan, on the way. Leave the gates in this section as you found them and remember to close the dog-barrier gate.

Midlands, Great Northern Highway & Wheatbelt

This chapter incorporates three different areas – if you look at a map they are all connected, extending from the base of the Pilbara down to the wheatbelt towns some 300 km or so below the Great Eastern Highway.

That so vast an area is covered in a small chapter suggests that there is little to see. Generally this is true, but there are some exceptions: the gold towns in the Murchison Valley, Wildflower Way and Midlands Scenic Way, the much-photographed Wave Rock and wheatbelt towns with 'real dinki-di' inhabitants are all worthwhile.

Midlands

There are two road options inland of Dongara and Geraldton and both branch off from the Great Northern Highway.

The first option, State Highway 116, is known locally as the Midlands Scenic Way. The road heads north from Bindoon and features towns such as Moora, Coorow, Carnamah (near the Yarra Yarra Lake) and Mingenew. The Midlands Rd emerges from its inland route at the coastal town of Dongara.

Towns such as Dalwallinu, Perenjori, Morawa and Mullewa are part of the second option, the Wildflower Way – famous for its brilliant spring display of wildflowers, including wreath leschenaultia, native foxgloves, everlastings and wattles (see under Wildflower Way in this chapter). This area is also a gateway to the Murchison goldfields; there are old gold-mining centres and ghost towns around Perenjori. One little-known feature of these routes are the wealth of buildings built by the enigmatic Monsignor John Hawes (see under John Hawes in the Batavia Coast, Shark Bay & Gascoyne

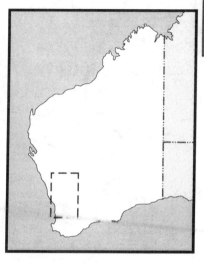

chapter). The road heads north from the town of Wubin, which is around 210 km north of where the Great Northern and North-West Coastal highways split near Muchea.

MIDLANDS SCENIC WAY
Moora
The first town of any size on your travels is Moora, 172 km north of Perth and situated on the banks of the Moore River. The Moora tourist office (☎ (096) 51 1401) is at 34 Padbury St. There is a display of crafts and artefacts (all for sale) by local Aborigines at Yuat Aboriginal Crafts, Kintore St.

Some 19 km east of town is the **Berkshire Valley Folk Museum**, in an old flour mill built in 1847. It is open from noon to 4 pm every Sunday, August to October (wildflower season), and every second Sunday, April to July. About 20 km north of Moora is Coomberdale where there is one of the largest displays of dried flowers; flowers can

MIDLANDS

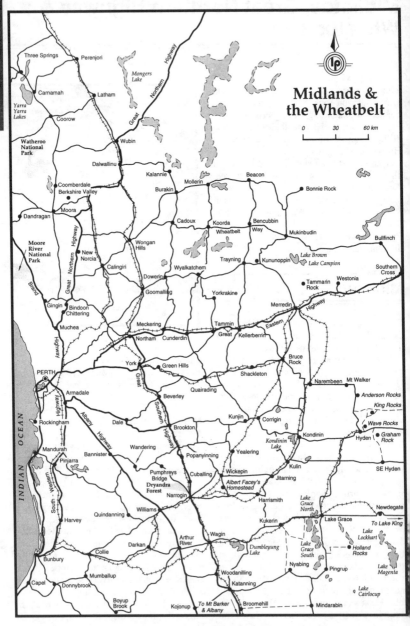

Midlands & the Wheatbelt

also be seen growing (sorry, no time lapse) and being processed for export.

The Moora heritage trail takes in a number of historic homesteads

Places to Stay & Eat The *Moora Shire Caravan Park* (☎ (096) 51 1401) is on Dandaragan St; tent/caravan sites are $8/12. The *Moora Drovers Inn* (☎ (096) 51 1108) is a restored 1909 historic building where singles/doubles are $35/45; the motel units are $40/50. The *Moora Hotel* (☎ (096) 51 1177), on the corner of Gardiner and Berkshire Valley Rds, has singles/doubles for $25/40; and the *Moora Motel* (☎ (096) 51 1247), Roberts Rd, is $48/58.

If you crave adventurous food, forget it! The cafes tried out in this town were distinctly ordinary.

Coorow

This town is in the heart of wildflower country and there are two good drives in the region; brochures are available from the shire office (☎ (099) 52 1103) in Main St. The **Darling Fault** is 12 km west of the town along Green Head Rd. To the west of this line is the Perth Basin – one of the deepest sedimentary basins in the world. About 50 km south of the town is **Watheroo National Park**, a good example of sandplain country with a number of rare species of flora.

Places to Stay *Coorow Caravan Park* (☎ (099) 52 1103), in Station St, has tent/caravan sites for $5/8.50 and there is one hotel (☎ (099) 52 1023) in Main St with pub-style accommodation at $20/40 for singles/doubles.

Carnamah & Three Springs

The town of **Carnamah** is 46 km north of Coorow. To the west of town is the **Yarra Yarra Lake**, a salt-lake system in which the water ranges in colour from blood-red to azure. Just east of town is the **MacPherson Homestead**, completed in 1880, and currently being restored.

Three Springs, close to Carnamah, is in the heart of wildflower country and the shire

office (☎ (099) 54 1001), in Railway Rd, provides details of wildflower drives.

Places to Stay *Carnamah Caravan Park* (☎ (099) 51 1055), MacPherson St, has tent/caravan sites for $6.40/8.20 and the *Carnamah Hotel/Motel* (☎ (099) 51 1023), also in MacPherson St, has single/double rooms for $25/35 and motel units for $50/60.

In Three Springs, the *BP Roadhouse Caravan Facility* (☎ (099) 54 1125), Railway Rd, has tent/caravan sites for $4/10 for two, and on-site vans at $25 for two. Also in Railway Rd is the *Commercial Hotel/Motel* (☎ (099) 54 1041), a 1928 federation-style hotel, in which rooms are $25/37 for singles/doubles and motel units $38/55.

Mingenew

This town has a small historical museum in a Roads Board office. The tourist office (☎ (099) 28 1081) is on Midlands Rd.

Some 32 km north-east of town on the gorge of the Irwin River is the coal seam discovered by the Gregory brothers in 1846.

The real attraction of this area is the carpet of **wildflowers** seen in August and September. Depot Hill National Park (14.5 km west of town on the Dongara Rd), Yandanooka and Manarra are places where you will see a great range.

Places to Stay & Eat The *Mingenew Spring Caravan Park* (☎ (099) 28 1013), in Lee Steere St, has tent/caravan sites for $6/7; and the *Commercial Hotel* (☎ (099) 28 1002), on Midlands Rd, has single/double rooms for $20/30; there is an à la carte restaurant attached to the pub. To the south of town in Yandanooka there is *Langton* (☎ (099) 72 6062), a farmstay where B&B is $25/50 for a single/double.

You can get passable food at the *Old Post Office Tearooms*, lunch and dinner from the hotel on most days, and the usual road fare from the Shell and Ampol roadhouses; all are on Midland Rd.

Not so 'Wild' Flowers

A number of enterprising farmers in the Mingenew area have combined the growing and processing of wildflowers with wheat and sheep farming. The farmers can choose from the 3600 different species of wildflower which grow freely in the region. Popular varieties are the yellow *Verticordia serrata*, white wax *(Chamelaucium alba)* and the red kangaroo paw *(Anigozanthos manglesii)* – the latter is the state's floral symbol.

The flowers are picked before they bloom and exported to Europe and Japan at a time when these parts of the world are in the depths of winter. Designer plants which suit cut-flower and pot-plant markets are even being grown in labs but nothing quite lives up to the splendour of native wildflowers in their bush setting. ■

THE WILDFLOWER WAY

For those wanting to see the famous carpet of wildflowers, mainly everlastings, from July to November, this is the area to drive through. There are many organised tours which take in the wildflowers but the best mode of transport is a car.

Dalwallinu

The name of this town, 248 km north-east of Perth and on the Great Northern Highway, means 'to rest awhile'. It is very much the start of the famed Wildflower Way and August and September are the best months to visit. There is a caravan park (☎ (096) 61 1253) and a hotel/motel (☎ (096) 61 1102) in town and *Ye Olde Convent* (☎ (096) 61 1216), on the corner of the Great Northern Highway and Kalanie Rd, is a restored guesthouse; B&B singles/doubles at the latter are $39/55.

Wubin

This is the actual junction of the Wildflower Way and the Great Northern Highway. The wildflowers seen in August and September are again the attraction. There are a number of scenic **rock formations** near the town such as Buntine, to the east, and Wubin Rocks, seven km along the Great Northern

Highway. The *Wubin Hotel/Motel* (☎ (096) 64 1040), beside the highway, has single/double accommodation for $40/60.

Perenjori

There are a number of reasons to drive the 350 km from Perth to Perenjori. Apart from wildflower displays from August to October, this town is on the fringe of mining and station country and there are some interesting drives in the region. The tourist office (☎ (099) 73 1125) is in Fowler St.

The town itself has the unusual Catholic **Church of St Joseph** designed by Monsignor John Hawes (see under Monsignor John Hawes in the Batavia Coast, Shark Bay & Gascoyne chapter). The skeletal white church with its clerestory (upper stage of main walls) of round windows seems an incongruity in this wheatbelt town.

At the rear of the tourist office is a **museum** which houses memorabilia from the early pioneering days of the district. There is a freshwater *gnamma* (waterhole), Camel Soak, 47 km east of Perenjori. These gnamma were familiar to the Aborigines and were essential stops as they journeyed between regions.

Places to Stay & Eat The *Perenjori Caravan Park* (☎ (099) 73 1002) is on Crossing Rd; tent/caravan sites are $5/10. The hotel (☎ (099) 73 1020) has single/double rooms for $25/38 and motel units for $32/45. The *York Gums Homestay* (☎ (099) 73 1125) is one km from town on the Carnamah Rd; singles/doubles are $26/44 and meals are available on request.

In town, there is the country-style *Graham's Bakery* for the usual pies, pastries and sausage rolls. The bread is baked in a 'sexagenarian' oven.

Morawa

This town has more wildflowers in its vicinity for those in search of the stamen, pistil and petal. Those undertaking the Monsignor Hawes Heritage Trail would be here to see the **Church of the Holy Cross** with its curious stone hermitage of one room (maybe the smallest presbytery in the world), used by the retiring Monsignor Hawes. The church itself is a fine piece of Spanish mission architecture, made of local stone and Cordoba tiles.

The tourist office (☎ (099) 71 1204) is at 5 Jose St and the small museum with its displays of farming machinery is on Prater St. During the wildflower season a trip out to Koolanooka Springs, 24 km east of town, is recommended.

Places to Stay The caravan park (☎ (099) 71 1380) is on White Ave and the *Morawa Motel Hotel* (☎ (099) 71 1060), at the corner of Solomon and Manning Sts, has single/double rooms for $15/30 and motel units for $40/55.

Mullewa

Again, the two main reasons for visits to this town are wildflowers and the architecture of Monsignor John Hawes. Flower lovers head for the unique wreath flower *Leschenaultia macrantha*, while those following the Monsignor Hawes Heritage Trail go to **Church of our Lady of Mt Carmel** in Doney St and the **Priest House** in Bowes St. The tourist office (☎ (099) 61 1110) is at 5 Jose St. The Wildflower Show is held in the last week of August.

At ease with his pastoral duties, Hawes put his heart and a portion of unused soul into the building. The design is Romanesque, in a style seen in old hillside churches in southern Europe. In a personal letter Hawes wrote:

I am building into these stones at Mullewa, poor little feeble church that it is, my convictions, aspirations and ideals as to what a church should be...my heart is in these stones!

Next to the church, Hawes built a house for himself and furnished the interior with jarrah pieces of his own design. It is more or less a museum honouring Hawes, although his actual buildings tell you much more about him. The house, well worth a look, is open from Monday to Friday from 10 to 11.45 am and 1.30 to 3 pm.

Just east of Mullewa, on the Mt Magnet Rd, is **Mass Rock**. Hawes used to ring a bell to let the shy Aborigines know that he was about to perform mass. Part of the rock has been flattened to serve as an altar, and although Hawes drew up plans for a Spanish mission-style archway and belltower for 'Mission Dolores', they were never built.

In the pioneer cemetery, one km north of town, there is a **headstone** to Selby John Arnold, carved by Hawes. Arnold, who died in tragic circumstances, was an altar boy to Hawes and the headstone is the result of a promise made to the boy's parents. The prolific monsignor also drew the preliminary sketches for St Mary's Agricultural School in Tardun, south-east of Mullewa.

The trail in search of the enigmatic Monsignor Hawes is one of the highlights of a visit to WA (it is around 210 km long). The juxtaposition of his curious yet functional architectural styles with the surrounding monotony of scrub and farms has to be seen to be believed.

Places to Stay The *Mullewa Caravan Park* (☎ (099) 61 1007), 1 Lovers Lane, has facilities for the disabled; tent/caravan sites for two are $7/12. The *Club Hotel* (☎ (099) 61 1131) at 30 Maitland Rd has singles/doubles for $25/40, and motel units at the *Railway Hotel/Motel* (☎ (099) 61 1050) on Grey St are $40/65.

There are three station stays in the vicinity: *Meeberrie* (☎ (099) 63 7971), *Tallering* (☎ (099) 62 3045) and *Wooleen* (☎ (099) 63 7973). Check prices with each station; usually full board is about $50 per person per day.

Yalgoo

Although not strictly part of the Wildflower Way, Yalgoo is well worth the 120-km drive east of Mullewa. In the 1890s, the town was the centre of a thriving goldfield; gold and gemstones are still found in the area. Wildflowers are also an attraction between July and September.

And guess what? The ubiquitous 'building monsignor' made it out to Yalgoo, designing and then helping to build the **Dominican Chapel of St Hyacinth**. The manual labour calloused his hands to such an extent he feared they might damage his silk vestments.

The Shire of Yalgoo office in Shamrock St is also the tourist office (☎ (099) 62 8042); they will provide a key to open the chapel. The courthouse **museum** is in Gibbons St behind the Telecom building, and the railway station is one of the few remaining buildings from the Mullewa-Meekatharra line.

Places to Stay There is a caravan park (☎ (099) 62 8042) in Stanley St; tent/caravan sites are $4/6 for two. The hotel (☎ (099) 62 8031) in Gibbons St has single/double rooms for $35/45 and motel units for $45/55. There are three station stays in the vicinity: *Barnong* (☎ (099) 63 7991), *Thundelara* (☎ (099) 63 6575) and *Yuin* (☎ (099) 63 7982). Full board for two at Thundelara is $140; at Barnong it is $50 with a bed in the shearers quarters available for $10; and at Yuin, an establishment which prefers sheep to children, it is $80 per person per night.

Great Northern Highway

Although most people heading for the Pilbara and the Kimberley travel up the coast, the Great Northern Highway is much more direct. The highway extends from Perth to Newman and then skirts the eastern edge of the Pilbara on its way to Port Hedland; the road is sealed all the way. The total distance is 1636 km – slightly longer if you plan to make the short gravel detour through Marble Bar.

The highway is one of Australia's least interesting: for much of its length it passes through country that is flat and featureless. The Murchison River goldfields and towns of Mt Magnet, Cue and Meekatharra break the monotony on the way to Newman.

The Great Northern Highway or State Highway 95, begins near Muchea, passes through Bindoon, New Norcia and Dalwallinu before heading north-east from

Wubin. It is 272 km from Perth to Wubin, then 297 km from Wubin to Mt Magnet.

GETTING THERE & AWAY
Skywest flies from Perth to Mt Magnet. One-way/return to Mt Magnet is $202/$263, Cue $214/$278 and Meekatharra $258/$335.

The Great Northern Highway is served by two bus companies: Greyhound Pioneer and Westliner. Both Greyhound and Westliner have daily services from Perth to Port Hedland which pass through Mt Magnet ($75), Cue ($80), Meekatharra ($95) and Newman ($120).

MT MAGNET
Gold was found at Mt Magnet in the late 19th century and mining is still the town's sole justification, with gold being mined at the Hill 50 mine. Mt Magnet was named after a prominent nearby hill which contained magnetic rocks. The town, however, was not developed until the gold rush. The Mt Magnet tourist office (☎ (099) 63 4172) is in Hepburn St.

You can get a panoramic view of the town and the huge open cut pits from Warramboo ('Campfire/Camping Place') Hill. About seven km north of town in an area of 'breakaways' (cliffs) are **The Granites**, a popular picnic spot where Aboriginal rock art can still be seen. Eleven km north of town are the ruins of **Lennonville**, once a busy town.

The modern magnet is often the wildflowers which carpet the landscape in spring.

Places to Stay & Eat
The *Mt Magnet Caravan Park* (☎ (099) 63 4198) has tent/caravan sites for $7/13. There are two motels in Mt Magnet in Hepburn St. The *Commercial Club* (☎ (099) 63 4021) and *Grand Hotel/Motel* (☎ (099) 63 4110) have singles/doubles for $45/70 and $50/70 respectively.

To the south-west of town is *Wogarno Outback Sheep Station* (☎ (099) 63 5846) which accepts paying humans for $60 each per night. A bed in the shearers quarters is $14. About 61 km west of Mt Magnet, on the road to Yalgoo, *Murrum Station* (☎ (099) 63 5843) has tent and caravan sites for $5 and comfortable, clean beds in the shearers' quarters for $14 per person; a hearty breakfast is $6 and dinner is $12.50.

The town does not exert much of a culinary pull. Fish & chips are fresh out of the pan at the *Golden Nugget* on Hepburn St, Chinese is available from the *Sun Ho Wan*, light meals and takeaways from *Valma's Place* and the *Crib Tin Cafe* on Main St, and counter meals from the *Mt Magnet* and *Grand* hotels. The hamburger van operates after the pubs have closed; all the locals will know where it is parked.

SANDSTONE
This town is not on the Great Northern Highway but lies 160 km east of Mt Magnet. The historic town is surrounded by a bronzed, rusty sandstone landscape, hence its name. There were four principal mines in the area during the peak mining period, 1908-1912: Oroya, WA Development, Wanderrie and Black Range. If you venture out this far make sure you obtain a copy of the *Sandstone Heritage Trail* pamphlet.

South-east of town is the basalt **London Bridge**, a rock formation over 350 million years old. On the road to the bridge, among the breakaways, is an old brewery and storage site.

Abandoned mining settlements around Sandstone include Youanmi, Montague, Paynesville, Berrigrin and Barrambie.

There is a caravan park (☎ (099) 63 5802) and the *National Hotel* (☎ (099) 63 5801) in town. The food situation is a mystery.

CUE
The tourist brochure proclaims: 'One of the most exciting places for people to visit today is Cue'. This isn't immediately apparent, but there are still some interesting old buildings of solid stone in this town, which is 80 km north of Mt Magnet. The National Trust has classified **Austin St** because of the goldfields architecture – the Cue Public Buildings, Bank of New South Wales, band rotunda and Gentlemen's Club are along this street. Away from the main street are an old gaol, historic primary school and corrugated-iron Masonic Lodge.

There are a number of ghost towns in the vicinity of Cue. The sister town of **Day Dawn** is five km to the south. It once had a population of 3000 in the heyday of the Great Fingall Mine; about all that is left standing is the Great Fingall office and the gaunt chimneys of the Cue-Day Dawn Hospital.

Other nearby ghost towns are Austin Island, Austin Mainland (20 km south on Lake Austin), the 'Dead Finish' (10 km west), Pinnacles (24 km east) and Tuckanarra (40 km north). Some 30 km west is the **Big Bell Mine**. The original town has a few remaining old buildings but access to the mine is restricted as mining has resumed.

Places to Stay & Eat
The *Cue Caravan Park* (☎ (099) 63 1107) has tent sites at $7 for two and the *Murchison Club Hotel* (☎ (099) 63 1020), in Austin St, Cue, has single/double rooms for $30/50 and motel units for $55/80. The *Dorsett Guesthouse* (☎ (099) 63 1291), 6 Austin St, is in a converted hotel (dating from 1892) and singles/doubles are $30/50; a light breakfast is included. Like a number of towns in the Murchison, there are station stays available. *Nallan Station* (☎ (099) 63 1054), 11 km north of Cue, has shearer's quarters/cottage/homestead accommodation for $12/20/60 per person; homesteaders have all meals included.

The Murchison Club Hotel has a restaurant and *RJay's Cafe* is open seven days.

WILGIE MIA & WALGA ROCK
The Murchison region has a number of significant Aboriginal sites. Two of the most celebrated are the Wilgie Mia Red Ochre Mine and Walga Rock.

Wilgie Mia is 64 km north-west of Cue via Glen Station. Red ochre has possibly been mined here by the Aborigines for more than 30,000 years. They used stone hammers and wooden wedges to remove thousands of tonnes of rock in order to get to the ochre, believed to have been traded as far away as

Queensland. There is no doubt that Wilgie Mia features a great deal in stories from the Dreamtime.

Walga Rock (also known as Walganna), about 50 km south-west of Cue via Austin Downs Station, is a rock monolith which juts 50 metres out of the surrounding scrub. It is one of the most significant Aboriginal art sites in WA. The 60-metre-long rockshelter at its base houses a gallery of desert-style paintings of lizards, birds and animals and hand stencils in red, white and yellow ochre. Not surprisingly, 'Walga' means 'ochre painting' in the Warragi language. The red ochre comes from Wilgie Mia, 65 km to the north-east.

At the northern end of the gallery, a ship, with twin masts, funnel and four wavy lines beneath, is depicted. Several theories have been advanced as to its origins, including one that it was painted by shipwrecked sailors.

MEEKATHARRA

Meekatharra (population 2000), 765 km north of Perth and 540 km north-east of Geraldton, is still a mining and administrative centre. The name is popularly understood to mean 'place of little water'. At one time it was a railhead for cattle brought down from the Northern Territory and the East Kimberley along the Canning Stock Route. There are shells of various old gold towns and workings in the area.

From Meekatharra, you can travel south via Wiluna and Leonora (see The Goldfields & The Nullarbor chapter) to the Kalgoorlie goldfields. It's over 700 km to Kal, more than half of it on unsealed road.

Places to Stay

The *Meekatharra Caravan Park* (☎ (099) 81 1253) has caravan sites/on-site vans for $12.50/27 for two, and the *Meekatharra Motel/Hotel* (☎ (099) 81 1021), on Main St, has inexpensive single/double units for $30/40. More expensive are the motel units at the *Royal Mail Hotel* (☎ (099) 81 1148), Main St, as singles/doubles are $55/70. The *Auski Inland Motel* (☎ (099) 81 1433), also on Main St, tops the range at $80/87.

If you have a delightful (or otherwise) meal in this 'place of little water', write and tell us about it.

NEWMAN

Newman (population 5500), a town which only came into existence in the 1970s, is actually in the Pilbara but is included here as it is on the Great Northern Highway. It is 414 km north of Meekatharra and 450 km south of Port Hedland, the end of the Great Northern Highway.

Newman is a modern company town built solely to service the mine. The Newman tourist office (☎ (091) 75 2888) is at the corner of Fortescue Ave and Newman Drive. The museum and art gallery, built of rammed earth and financed by BHP Iron Ore, is adjacent to the tourist office.

Near the town, the iron-ore mountain, Whaleback, is being systematically taken apart and railed to the coast some 426 km away (see under 'Company' Towns in the Pilbara chapter). Guided tours (☎ (091) 75 2888) of these operations (and the largest open-cut, iron-ore mine in the world) leave across from the tourist office at 8.30 am and 1 pm daily; safety helmets are provided and the tour is 1½ hours long.

The highlight of Newman is undoubtedly the road out of it. This is one of the most **scenic drives** in the state as the highway weaves it way through the Hamersley and Ophthalmia ranges. Wildflowers are a feature along the route from June to October.

There are Aboriginal **rock carvings** at Wanna Munna, 70 km from town, and at Punda, off the Marble Bar road. Two nearby pools of note on the Waterhole Circuit (map available from the tourist office) are **Stuarts Pool**, a difficult but adventurous trip by 4WD; and **Kalgan's Pool**, a day outing from town.

Places to Stay & Eat

There are several caravan parks in the area, the closest to town being the *Newman Caravan Park* (☎ (091) 75 1428), on Kalgan Drive; tent sites/caravan sites/on-site vans are $10/15/30 for two. Others parks are the

Capricorn Caravan Park Roadhouse (☎ (091) 75 1535) on the Great Northern Highway with caravan sites/rooms for $10/30 for two; and *Dearlove's Caravan Park* (☎ (091) 75 2802), Cowra Drive, with tent sites/caravan sites/on-site vans for $12/15/40 for two. If you are over 50 you get a discount (and will probably need it) from the *Quality Inn Newman* (☎ (091) 75 1101), Newman Drive, which has double rooms for $117.

In addition to the roadhouses there are a number of takeaway shops including the *Boulevarde Coffee Shop*, *Chicken Treat* and the *Chinese Kitchen* in the Boulevarde shopping centre. On Hilditch Avenue, choose from the *Kiwi-Inn*, *K's Pizza & Bakery* and *Coxy's Corner*. There is another Chinese takeaway, *Edens*, in the Mitre-10 complex.

Getting There & Away

Ansett Australia (☎ 13 1300) has at least one jet each day to Perth. Greyhound Pioneer (☎ (091) 75 1398) has a service from Perth to Darwin via Newman on Sunday, Wednesday, Thursday and Friday and in the other direction on Sunday, Monday, Thursday and Friday. Westliner (☎ (091) 75 2888) runs from Port Hedland to Perth on Friday and Monday and in the other direction on Thursday and Sunday.

Check carefully to see the actual day the bus passes through Newman as the trip involves vast distances. The towns which are on the Great Northern Highway are well serviced by public transport but towns to either side are accessible only if you have your own transport.

MARBLE BAR

Reputed to be the hottest place in Australia, Marble Bar (population 350) had a period in the 1920s when temperatures topped 37°C for 160 consecutive days. On one occasion, in 1905, the mercury soared to 49.1°C. From October to March, days over 40°C are common – though it is dry heat and not too unbearable.

The town, in the Pilbara but covered here as it is part of the Great Northern Highway,

is 203 km south-east of Port Hedland. It takes its name from a bar of red jasper across the Coongan River, six km west of town. The tourist office (☎ (091) 76 1166) is in the Marble Bar Travellers Stop on Halse Rd.

In town, the 1895 government buildings on the corner of Francis and Contest Sts, made of local stone, are still in use. In late winter, as the spring wildflowers begin to bloom, Marble Bar is quite a pretty place and one of the most popular towns in the Pilbara to visit.

The **Comet Gold Mine**, 10 km south of Marble Bar, is still in operation and has a mining museum and display centre; it is open daily. Coppins Gap/Doolena Gorge, about 70 km north-east of Marble Bar, is a deep cutting with impressive views, twisted bands of rock and an ideal swimming hole.

Places to Stay

The *Marble Bar Caravan Park* (☎ (091) 76 1067), on Contest St, has tent sites/on-site vans for $14/32 for two. Rooms at the *Iron Clad Hotel* (☎ (091) 76 1066), a distinctive drinking spot, range from single/double units for $25 to $40/$50 to $70; they also have backpackers' accommodation from $20. The *Marble Bar Travellers Stop* (☎ (091) 76 1166) has budget single/double rooms for $35/45 and motel units for $70/80.

Wheatbelt

East of the Darling Range and stretching north from the Albany coastal region to the areas beyond the Great Eastern Highway (the Perth to Coolgardie road) are the WA wheatlands. The area is noted for its unusual rock formations, the best known being Wave Rock, near Hyden; and for its many Aboriginal rock carvings and gnamma holes.

Some of the towns considered part of the wheatbelt have been covered in other places as they are part of a distinct and well-known route north or east. For ease of description, the wheatbelt has been divided into four areas: north-eastern wheatbelt, Great Eastern

Highway and central & southern regions. CALM produces the informative *Voices of the Bush – A Wheatbelt Heritage*.

The towns with names ending in 'up' and 'in' denote the presence of water and are Aboriginal appellations for gnamma or waterholes.

NORTH-EASTERN WHEATBELT

This vast area is north of the Great Eastern Highway (Golden Way) and east of the Great Northern Highway. It begins at the towns of Goomalling and Wongan Hills and stretches 300 km out to Mukinbudin. There are few attractions here but the odd marooned motorist may glean some satisfaction from his or her isolated circumstances.

Goomalling & Dowerin

There is a **museum** in Goomalling, 132 km north-east of Perth, which features a rare, though esoteric, windmill display. Rumour has it that Don Quixote's curiosity got the better of him and he visited here. Gnamma holes are found in Oak Park where his horse was probably watered.

Some 25 km away, in Dowerin, there is another **museum** which shows the lifestyle of early settlers. **Hagbooms Lake** is home of the Dowerin Salt Lake Sailor's Club and Easter weekend sees them speeding across it in their wheeled craft in pursuit of the Easter Cup.

There is a caravan park (☎ (096) 29 1101) in Goomalling and a hotel (☎ (096) 31 1206) in Dowerin.

Wyalkatchem

It is worth the drive to this town, 191 km north-east of Perth, just to be photographed next to the sign on the way into town. The 'town with the odd, unexplained name' has two **museums**. One has a great collection of antique farm machinery and vehicles and the other features a collection of old household items. There is a huge granite outcrop, **Uberin Rock**, 28 km north of Dowerin on the Uberin Rd. Like most towns out the back of beyond there is a nondescript caravan park

(☎ (096) 81 1166) and local hotel (☎ (096) 81 1210), with singles/doubles for $20/40.

Trayning & Nungarin

The most interesting fact about Trayning is the evolution of its name (sorry about Wyalkatchem!). In the Aboriginal language 'Duri-dring' means 'snake crawling in grass near campsite'. Over time this was transliterated into 'D'r'nin' and was, eventually, pronounced 'Trayning'. Ponder this beneath the twin ancient **granite outcrops** at Yarragin, north-east of Kununoppin. Opposite, is **Billycatting Rock**, another massive granite outcrop and a 25 sq km flora & fauna reserve. Trayning also saw the formation of the first trotting club in Australia. Every October, trotting is held in conjunction with the Gala Wool Day.

In **Nungarin** you have to make the decision whether or not to turn north to Mukinbudin or south to the Great Eastern Highway. Either toss a coin or make a decision in the Nungarin pub (☎ (090) 46 5084) which has great meals, is lovingly furnished with antiques and run by incredibly friendly people.

There are, you guessed it, a caravan park (☎ (096) 83 1001) and hotel (☎ (096) 83 1005) in Trayning.

Wongan Hills

To the Aborigines this was a place of 'whispering'. Wongan Hills is 184 km north-east of Perth and is something of a gateway to the State Highway 99 access to the north agricultural region.

Near the town are a number of **rock formations** which rise abruptly from the landscape. These all make good vantage points to observe the annual wildflower display, especially the fields of *Verticordia* seen each November. Dingo Rock is 26 km east of town, the Mt O'Brien lookout is on the Piawaning Rd, the granite rocks of the Gathercole Reserve are on Moonijin Rd and the Xmas Rock walk is just north of the Wongan Hills caravan park.

A great place to see wildflowers is Reynoldson's Flora Reserve, 15 km north of

Wongan Hills on the old Ballidu Rd. About 10 km west of town on Calingiri Rd is **Lake Ninan**, a good place to observe waterbirds. For more information contact the Wongan Hills tourist office (☎ (096) 71 1157) in the old railway station.

Places to Stay & Eat There is a caravan park (☎ (096) 71 1009) on Wongan Rd where caravan sites are $11 for two. The hotel (☎ (096) 71 1022) on Fenton St has single/double rooms for $25/38 and motel units for $48/63; and the *Wongan Hills Guesthouse* (☎ (096) 71 1015), 1 Moore St, has B&B for $25/40. The bakery at 23 Fenton Place turns out good cakes, pies and country-style bread; and the hotel has counter meals and a restaurant.

Koorda

The Aboriginal name 'Koorda' means either 'married person' or 'to separate or divide'. Koorda, 240 km north-east of Perth, is best known for its **corn dolly** workshops, held in November. A corn dolly is a dolly made of corn – believe me! To get to **Redcliffe**, an unusual geological formation near the town, enquire at the Koorda tourist office (☎ (096) 84 1219), Haig Rd.

The *Koorda Caravan Park* (☎ (096) 84 1275), Scott St, has caravan sites for $6 for two; and the hotel (☎ (096) 84 1226), Railway St, has single/double rooms for $27/40. You can get takeaway food or dine in *Helen's Kitchen* on Ninghan St.

Bencubbin & Mukinbudin

In Bencubbin, there is another one of those lovingly collected piles of trash and treasure that townsfolk have labelled the **Bates Museum**. (Flashbacks to Norman Bates' motel in *Psycho* precluded entry inside.) The shire **museum**, in the old Road Boards Building, has a piece from a meteorite found near the town.

About 12 km south-east of town are the curious **Pergandes sheepyards**, constructed of granite slabs and looking like a mini version of Stonehenge.

There are also a number of interesting

rock formations near Mukinbudin including Yanneymooning, Engolbin and Berringbooding. The town got its name from a formation called Muckenbooding, and it was later shortened to its present form.

If you get out this far you are probably going to have to stay somewhere. Bencubbin has a caravan park (☎ (096) 85 1202) and hotel (☎ (090) 85 1201), as does Mukinbudin: caravan park (☎ (090) 47 1103) and hotel (090) 47 1133). Let's face it, you didn't come all this way for nouveau cuisine – steak, peas and spud are a good compromise.

GREAT EASTERN HIGHWAY

This highway (State Highway 94), also known as the Golden Way, starts in Perth and passes through the towns of the Avon Valley before reaching the many agricultural towns on the way to Kalgoorlie. For much of its length it is paralleled by the pipes which carry water from Mundaring Reservoir to Kalgoorlie (see under Where Water is like Gold! in The Goldfields & The Nullarbor chapter).

Meckering

The small town of Meckering, 24 km west of Cunderdin, was badly damaged by an earthquake in 1968. The devastation can be seen 11 km from town on the Quellington (York) Rd.

Cunderdin

The first town of reasonable size which you reach after leaving Northam is Cunderdin, 156 km from Perth. The museum and tourist office (☎ (096) 35 1291), in Forrest St, is housed in an old pumping station used on the gold-fields water pipeline. The **Agricultural Museum** in town has exhibits relating to the 1968 earthquake as well as an interesting collection of farm machinery and equipment.

There is a caravan park (☎ (096) 35 1258) on Olympic Ave and a motor hotel (☎ (096) 35 1104), on Main St, with singles/doubles for $42/60.

WHEATBELT

Kellerberrin

Further to the east is Kellerberrin (203 km from Perth), which has an **historical museum** in the old agricultural hall (built in 1897) and a lookout on **Kellerberrin Hill**. The Milligan Homestead and outbuildings, 10 km north of town, are a fine example of vernacular architecture as they are constructed of local fieldstone.

Kokerbin Rock, 30 km south of Kellerberrin, is a prominent granite outcrop and is reputed to be the third biggest monolith in Australia. There are great views of the endless fields of wheat from its summit.

Like many towns in the area, a great attraction is the profusion of **wildflowers** in spring. Two of the best places to see them are the Durakoppin Wildlife Sanctuary, 27 km to the north, and Charles Gardner National Park, 35 km south-west.

Kellerberrin has a caravan park (☎ (090) 45 4066), motel (☎ (090) 45 4007) and hotel (☎ (090) 45 4206), with singles/doubles for $35/45 and $18/28 respectively.

Merredin

Merredin, the largest centre in the wheatbelt (population 4500), is 260 km east of Perth on the Kalgoorlie railway line and the Great Eastern Highway. It has a tourist office (☎ (090) 41 1666) on Barrack St. The 1920s railway station has been turned into a charming **museum** with a vintage 1897 locomotive and an old signal box with 95 signal switching levers. Also of note in the area is **Mangowine Homestead**, 65 km north of Merredin, restored by the National Trust.

There are several short drives in the Merredin area which allow you to view **wildflowers** in season.

There are also some interesting **rock formations** around Merredin, including Kangaroo Rock, 17 km to the south-east; Burracoppin Rock to the north; Sandford Rocks 11 km east of Westonia; and Elach Butting Rock, a Wave Rock clone, 90 km north of the Great Eastern Highway.

Places to Stay & Eat *Merredin Caravan Park* (☎ (090) 41 1535), on the Great Eastern Highway, has tent/caravan sites for $9/12 and on-site vans at $28; prices are for two people. The *Merredin Motel* (☎ (090) 41 1886), 10 Gamenya Ave, has single/double motel units for $30/45 and the *Merredin Olympic Motel* (☎ (090) 41 1588), Great Eastern Highway, has single/double rooms at $40/50. *Potts Motor Inn* (☎ (090) 41 1755), also on the Great Eastern Highway, has singles/doubles for $53/63 and the *Commercial Hotel*, Barrack St, has basic pub rooms for $20/35.

The *Commercial Hotel* does counter meals including a $2 lunch-time special, and *Jason's* Chinese restaurant, on the corner of Bates and Mitchell Sts, has takeaway or eat-in meals for around $6.

Southern Cross

Although the gold quickly gave out, Southern Cross (population 2260) was the first gold-rush town on the WA goldfields. The big rush soon moved east to Coolgardie and Kalgoorlie. Like the town itself, the streets of Southern Cross are named after the stars and constellations. The **Yilgarn History Museum** in the old courthouse has local displays; it deserves a visit. If you follow the continuation of Antares St south for three km, you will see a couple of active open-cut mines.

Situated 368 km east of Perth, this is really the end of the wheatbelt area and the start of the desert; when travelling by train the change is very noticeable. In the spring, the sandy plains around Southern Cross are carpeted with wildflowers.

Places to Stay There is a caravan park (☎ (090) 49 1212) on Coolgardie Rd which has caravan sites/on-site vans for $12/25 for two. There are two hotels in Antares St and the pick of them is the *Southern Cross Palace Hotel* (☎ (090) 49 1555), a beautifully restored place with exquisite stained-glass windows, which has rooms for $30 per person. The *Southern Cross Motel* (☎ (090) 49 1144) on Canopus St has single/double units for $51/62.

CENTRAL & SOUTHERN REGIONS

This is the area south of the Great Eastern Highway and east of the Albany Highway (State Highway 30). It stretches from Brookton/Pingelly out to Hyden/Wave Rock in the north and from Kojonup out to Grace and King lakes in the south. The considered highlight is Wave Rock but many motorists will think that this formation hardly merited the 700-km return drive from Perth. This region also includes wildflowers in season, the magnificent Dryandra Forest and the homestead of Albert Facey.

Pingelly

The name Pingelly, 120 km south-east of Perth, comes from the Aboriginal 'Pinge-culling'. There are a number of historic buildings in the town such as the courthouse which is now the museum. **Boyagin Rock Reserve**, 26 km north-west of the town, is an important remnant of natural bush on the edge of the wheatbelt. There is an annual **tulip festival** held on the fourth Sunday in August.

There is a hotel (☎ (098) 87 1001) and a motel (☎ (098) 87 1015) in the town and numerous farmstays (☎ (098) 87 1242) outside town. The hotels serve counter meals, there is a Chinese restaurant in the main street and the *Trio Cafe*, in Parade St, is open from 7 am to 8.30 pm.

Dryandra State Forest

This forest of 270 sq km and on the western edge of the central southern wheatbelt. It is a remnant of the open eucalypt woodlands which once covered much of the wheatbelt but which were cleared for agriculture. The woodlands are predominantly wandoo, powderbark and brown mallet and the plateaus have pockets of jarrah associated with *kwongan* (heath and shrublands). Marri, mallee and rock sheoak also occur.

At least 20 species of native mammal have been found in the park including the state's fauna emblem, the numbat. The small kangaroo-like woylie *(Bettongia pencillata)* and tammar *(Macropus fasciatus)* are other ground-dwelling mammals found here. It is

a great birdwatching area with over 100 species recorded and, in spring, there are many wildflowers.

There is a good five-km walk, the **Ochre Trail**, which has an ochre pit once quarried by local Nyungar Aborigines. The ochre was valued for body decoration and rock art.

Dryandra is accessible from the York-Williams Rd on the west side and the Narrogin-Wandering Rd on the east side. It is 160 km south-east of Perth and 20 km north-west of Narrogin. There is no camping in the forest but you can stay in the *Lions Dryandra Forest Settlement* (☎ (098) 83 6020) or *Bald Rock Farm* (☎ (098) 83 6063).

Narrogin

This town, 189 km south-east of Perth, is an agricultural centre in the heart of WA's richest farming land. Narrogin has a **courthouse museum** in Egerton St, an axehandle factory and a 'foxes lair' park. The steel thing at the end of the axe handle probably eliminated the fox problem and, today, the park has pygmy possums and red-tailed wambengers. There is also an old **butter factory** in Federal St; home to a collection of antiques and arts & crafts. The Narrogin tourist office (☎ (098) 81 2064), in Egerton St, has voluntary staff who really enjoy their work. Good to see! You can get the excellent pamphlets *Narrogin Heritage Trail* and *Narrogin Centenary Pathway* to help you discover the sights of this interesting town.

The Fortunate House
The Albert Facey Homestead, 39 km to the east of Narrogin, is worth a visit, especially if you have read Albert Facey's popular book *A Fortunate Life* (see under Albert Facey in the Facts about Western Australia chapter). The 86-km self-drive Albert Facey Heritage Trail begins at the homestead and visits many of the places around Wickepin which are mentioned in the book. Entrance to the homestead, which has a rambling collection of Facey memorabilia, is $2 per person. ■

Places to Stay & Eat The caravan park (☎ (098) 81 1260) has tent/caravan sites for $4/11. There are three hotels: single/double rooms at the *Cornwall* (☎ (098) 81 1877), 16 Doney St, are $20/30; at the *Hordern* (☎ (098) 81 1015), 61 Federal St, they are $25/40; and at the *Duke of York* (☎ (098) 81 1008), Federal St, you will pay $35/45. The *Narrogin Motel* (☎ (098) 81 1660), 56 Williams Rd, has twin/doubles for $46/56 and the *Wagonway Inn* (☎ (098) 81 1563), 78 Williams Rd, has singles/doubles for $50/58.

There are three farmstays near town. *Bald Rock Farm* (☎ (098) 83 6063), five km west of Yornaning, has B&B for $35 per person; *Chuckem Farm* (☎ (098) 85 9050) has B&B for $45; and *Stoke Farm* (☎ (098) 85 9018) is also $45.

As for dining, there is a great cafe in this town with a highly acceptable cappuccino. As the town's gastric tantaliser it should have been given more exposure.

Williams & West Arthur

This author would love to say that Williams was his favourite town in WA, but he can't. Named after William IV, the town doesn't assume the regal proportions of its namesake and, at best, it merits the label 'pleasant'. It has an eponymous caravan park, hotel and motel. It certainly rises above Darkan which is the most forgettable town in the whole state.

The region of West Arthur has an interesting **slab cottage**. This was built in the 1900s from timber slab and stone and is situated on the Quindanning Rd.

Quairading & Bruce Rock

If you wish to immerse yourself in agricultural delight, then the road to Quairading and Bruce Rock, 160 km and 240 km east of Perth respectively, are the places. Pigs, goats, sheep, cattle, lupins, peas, wheat and barley abound. Punctuating this sylvan scene are a number of prominent rock formations, including Kokerbin Rock (see under Kellerberrin in this chapter).

Quairading ('Home of the small bush kangaroo') has a tourist office (☎ (096) 45 1001) on Jennaberring Rd. There is a caravan park (☎ (096) 45 1001), a hotel (☎ (098) 45 1220) and a motel (☎ (098) 45 1054) in town. For those who came out here for the peace of the country, try *Quairading Farm Holidays* (☎ (096) 45 1086); B&B is $25/40 for one/two persons.

On the way to Bruce Rock you pass through Shackleton, home of the **smallest bank** in Australia, just four by three metres. Bruce Rock has a tourist office (☎ (090) 61 1169) in Johnson St, two **museums**, a caravan park (☎ (090) 61 1169), hotel (☎ (090) 61 1310) and a motel (☎ (090) 61 1174). Again, country life can be experienced at *Breakell Farm* (☎ (090) 65 1042); B&B is $35 per person.

Kulin

Only a short drive from town, along 86 Gate Rd, is the **Rabbit Proof Fence**, built during the height of the rabbit plague between 1901 and 1907. The rabbits beat the constructors of the fence to the west side so the erection of the fence was a bit of a joke.

Jilakin Rock, 16 km from Kulin, is a spectacular grey granite monolith which overlooks a lake of some 12 sq km. Near the lake's edge is a stand of jarrah trees, rare in the wheatbelt and usually associated with forests 140 km to the west. **Buckley's Breakaway**, 58 km east of Kulin, is a set of unusual kaolin formations with reddish-brown gravel caps.

Eco-hounds would probably drive further east to the **Dragon Rocks Nature Reserve**, 320 sq km, some 17 km east of Buckley's Breakaway. Over 70 species of birds including malleefowl *(Leipoa ocellata)* and the wedge-tailed eagle have been seen in the reserve. The park also boasts 10 different species of orchid. Sandplain wildflowers abound throughout the region in spring.

Kulin has a caravan park (☎ (098) 80 1220) and a hotel/motel (☎ (098) 80 1201), and nearby Kondinin has a caravan park (☎ (098) 89 1006), hotel (☎ (098) 89 1009) and motel (☎ (098) 89 1190).

Corrigin

This archetypal wheatbelt town, 68 km south of Bruce Rock and 230 km south-east of Perth, has a folk museum with a collection of farm machinery, a craft cottage and a miniature railway. The tourist office (☎ (090) 63 2203) is in Lynch St.

About five km out of town is a 'buried bone' **dog cemetery**. This homage to dogs must be one of the more bizarre sights in all of WA. Corrigin is also home to an **emu farm** and a **marron farm**. Both are open from 10 am to 4 pm every day.

Places to Stay & Eat There is a caravan park (☎ (090) 63 2203) in Kirkwood St and hotel (☎ (090) 63 2002) in Walton St. The *Windmill Motel* (☎ (090) 63 2390) on the Brookton Highway has single/double rooms for $44/54 and its guesthouse section is $30/40. There are also a couple of farmstays. *Mindalong* (☎ (090) 65 8055), on Barber Rd about 28 km west of Corrigin, is $20 per person and *Lewisdale Kelly Cottage* (☎ (090) 63 7011), Bullaring/Gorge Rock Rd, is $48 for two.

If you dine in town, insist on yabbies with your salad. The morning and afternoon teas at *The Craft Cottage*, 7 Walton St, are reasonable and the *Windmill Motel* has a BYO restaurant.

Hyden & Wave Rock

Wave Rock, 350 km south-east of Perth and four km east from the tiny town of Hyden, south of Merredin and Southern Cross, is worth the trip. It's a real surfer's delight – the perfect wave, 15 metres high and 100 metres long and frozen in solid rock marked with different colour bands. The bands are caused by the run off of waters containing carbonates and iron hydroxide.

Other interesting rock formations in the area bear names like the **Breakers, Hippo's Yawn** and the **Humps**. Hippo's Yawn is a 20-minute walk from Wave Rock, and well worth the visit. The walls of **Mulka's Cave**, 21 km from Hyden, feature Aboriginal hand paintings.

Waves Rock's image has been flashed

Wave Rock

throughout the west, serving a role that any number of alternative images would do much better. The staff at the tourist office (☎ (098) 80 5182) at the Wave Rock Wildflower Shop will certainly disagree. Wave Rock has the second biggest **lace collection** in the world (the Margaret Blackburn collection), which begs more than one question.

The area is dotted with wheat and sheep farms. At night during seeding time, huge tractors operate in all directions on the darkened landscape. Ask the farmers if you can accompany them on a few circuits of a field.

Many people stop in the area to work during the seeding and harvesting season and it is likely that you will meet an international gathering of workers at the local pub.

A Westrail bus to Hyden leaves Perth on Tuesday and returns on Thursday; it costs $29 one way and the trip takes five hours.

Places to Stay & Eat At Wave Rock, the caravan park (☎ (098) 80 5022) has unpowered/powered sites for $9/12 for two, and chalets at $45 for two. *Diep's B&B* (☎ (098) 80 5179), on Clayton St in Hyden, has B&B for around $27 per person, or there's the

Hyden Hotel Motel (☎ (098) 80 5052), on Lynch St, with singles/doubles for $48/65.

The three farmstays out here might be the best choice: *Glenorie* (☎ (098) 80 5151) is nine km north of Hyden and B&B is $25 per person; *Omeo* (☎ (098) 66 8023), 40 minutes from Hyden on the Lake Grace/Hyden Rd, is $20; and *Turromo Farms* (☎ (098) 66 8066), Hyden and Newdegate Rds, is also $20.

The food at the Hyden roadhouse isn't the best. Breakfast at the Cafe Royale, this isn't! At Wave Rock, the purveyors of food have a captive market and *you* are it – the inflated price and concomitant lack of quality are not surprising.

Wagin

Pronounced 'Way-jin' (and don't you forget it), this rural centre (population 2400) is 229 km south-east of Perth. The Wagin tourist office (☎ (098) 61 1232) is in Kitchener St. Wagin, has a 15-metre-high fibreglass ram (a tribute to the surrounding merino industry and an overwhelming sense of bad taste). There is also an **historical village** with some fine restored buildings and a vintage tractor display. There is bushwalking around **Mt Latham** ('Badjarning'), a granite rock six km to the west.

Places to Stay & Eat The caravan park (☎ (098) 61 1177), on the corner of Arthur Rd and Scadden St, has tent/caravan sites for $9/10. *Moran's Wagin Hotel* (☎ (098) 61 1017) on Tudor St is furnished with antiques and has single/double rooms for $20/32 and the *Palace Hotel* (☎ (098) 61 1003) on Tudhoe St is $20/40. The *Wagin Motel* (☎ (098) 61 1784), 57 Tudhoe St, has single/double units for $48/55. There is also the *Chameleon Coffee Lounge* on Tudhoe St.

Katanning

This town, south of Wagin and 277 km south of Perth, has a large Muslim community from Christmas Island, who worship at their own **mosque** in Andrews Rd. Other attractions include the old **flour mill** on Clive St, which houses the tourist office (☎ (098) 21 2634) and the ruins of an old winery.

The **saleyards** here are the second biggest inland saleyards in Australia (which again begs the question). Happily, we have an answer: Wagga Wagga, New South Wales, is the biggest.

There are two caravan parks, three hotels and two motels in town. The *Katanning Unit Hotel* (☎ (098) 21 1900), 43 Austral Terrace, has facilities for the disabled; B&B is $30/50 for singles/doubles.

Kojonup

This town (population 1100), 39 km south-west of Katanning and on the southernmost extremity of the wheatbelt, was established in 1837 as a military outpost to protect the mail run from Perth to Albany. The name is derived from the Aboriginal 'kodja' meaning 'stone axe'. The tourist office (☎ (098) 31 1686) is in the Old Railway Station in Benn Parade.

The **military barracks museum** still survives from the colonial era (circa 1845) and is worth a look.

Places to Stay & Eat There is a caravan park (☎ (098) 31 1127), hotel (☎ (098) 31 1028), motel (☎ (098) 31 1160) and motel/hotel (☎ (098) 31 1044) in town.

The wise would choose to stay at one of the many farmstays in the district. You could try *Jumburra* (☎ (098) 63 1021), Hall Rd, where in-house full board is $100 for the nuclear family (two adults and two children); *Kalpara Cottage*, Tenner Rd (☎ (098) 32 3016), at $25 per person; *Karana Farm* (☎ (098) 32 3072), 20 minutes west on Blackwood Rd, at $40 for two; *Kengerrup Farmstay* (☎ (098) 34 1057), off the Albany Highway, at $40 for two; and *Proandre Farmstay* (☎ (098) 32 8065), off Boscabel Rd, at $45 for a house which accommodates four people.

You can get takeaways or a meal at *Clarky's Cafe* at 124 Albany Highway, the *Golden Fleece Roadhouse* or from *Betty Travel Shop*. The two pubs, *Kojonup Top Pub* and the *Commercial*, both on the Albany Highway, serve counter meals.

Dumbleyung, Kukerin & Lake Grace

All of these towns are on State Highway 107. Dumbleyung is to the north-east of Lake Dumbleyung (where Donald Campbell broke the world speed record on water, setting 442.08 km/h in *Bluebird* in 1964). Today the lake hosts a variety of birdlife. There is a good view of the lake from Pussy Cat Hill. Surprise, there is a caravan park and hotel in Dumbleyung.

Kukerin is 39 km east of Dumbleyung. During the wildflower season there is a worthwhile drive through the Tarin Rock Nature Reserve.

Lake Grace, 345 km from Perth, takes its name from the shallow salt lake which is nine km west of town. The **Inland Mission Hospital**, built in 1925 by the famous Flynn of the Inland, has recently been restored as a hospital museum. There is a caravan park (☎ (098) 65 1263), hotel (☎ (098) 65 1219) and two motels: *Caltex Restaurant* (☎ (098) 65 1050) and *Lake Grace* (☎ (098) 65 1180). You will have no trouble locating them because, if you hit the desert, you have gone too far.

Lake King, at the end of SH 107, is where an old sand track heads off to Frank Hann and Peak Charles national parks. Lake King is a great place to see wildflowers in season. It has a caravan park (☎ (098) 74 4060) and tavern/motel (☎ (098) 74 4048).

Batavia Coast, Shark Bay & Gascoyne

This chapter covers a huge area of the WA coast and interior. It extends from Green Head/Leeman to the Gascoyne River and Carnarvon (about 600 km as the crow flies) and out to the eastern apex of Mt Augustus, 350 km from the Indian Ocean.

The Batavia Coast lies in this area and has much historical and scenic interest: the gorges of Kalbarri National Park; the world heritage area of Shark Bay with ancient stromatolites, shell beaches and the dolphins of Monkey Mia; the world's largest rock at Mt Augustus; and the rugged Kennedy Ranges in the Gascoyne.

BATAVIA COAST

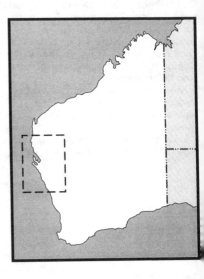

Batavia Coast

Since 1985, the strip of coast from Green Head/Leeman to Kalbarri has been referred to as the Batavia Coast, evoking the memory of the many shipwrecks which have occurred along the coast (see under Dutch Shipwrecks in this chapter), especially that of the *Batavia*.

The Batavia Coast combines rich history with many features of natural beauty. Sneak a look at the past in Greenough Hamlet, Northampton, Walkaway, the convict ruins near Port Gregory and the museums of Geraldton. There are many areas of abundant wildflowers, particularly beside the magnificent gorges of Kalbarri National Park as well as left and right of the Brand Highway. The faunal wealth of the Houtman Abrolhos, once known only as the site of shipwrecks or a place to gather crayfish (rock lobster), is finally being appreciated.

PERTH TO GERALDTON

The distance from Perth to Geraldton is 421 km. From Perth, follow the Brand Highway (National Highway No 1) through the towns of Gingin and Badgingarra, and past the turn-off to Jurien and the Pinnacles Desert

(see under North Coast in the Around Perth chapter). The towns of Green Head and Leeman can be reached from the turn-offs at Half Way Mill or Eneabba. The Brand Highway joins the Midland Rd (State Highway 116), eight km east of Dongara-Port Denison and more or less hugs the coast from there to Geraldton.

Many national parks, famed for wildflower displays, are found to the west and east of the highway. Some 58 km south of Dongara is the *Western Flora Caravan Park* (☎ (099) 55 2030), special because it is in the heart of the most diverse and dense flora region in the world. Several tracks branch out from the park into the wonderland of native plant species; a must for foreign visitors. Powered sites/on-site vans are $10/25 for two and two-room chalets with TV are $39.

GREEN HEAD & LEEMAN

Both of these places are on the coast: Green Head is 288 km north of Perth and Leeman

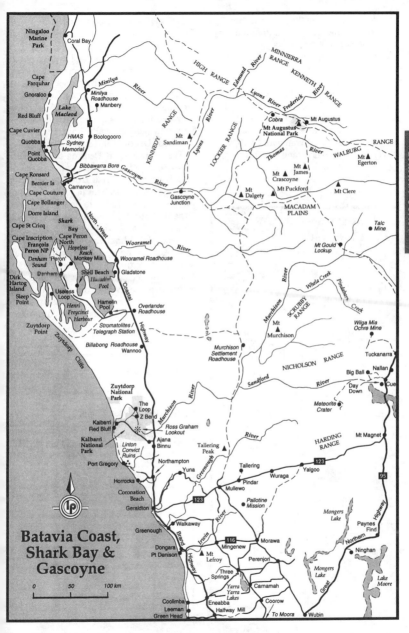

Batavia Coast, Shark Bay & Gascoyne

0   50   100 km

an additional seven km. Green Head is blessed with the beautiful **Dynamite Bay**, great for snorkelling and swimming; the idyllic bay certainly belies its combustible name.

Leeman, named after a navigator on the Dutch ship *Waeckende Boey* (sent to rescue survivors of the *Vergulde Draeck*), has a much more colourful past and now houses the workforce of a nearby mineral sands project. There is a caravan park (☎ (099) 53 1131) in Green Head and a caravan park (☎ (099) 53 1080) in Leeman.

DONGARA – PORT DENISON

The main road comes back to the coast 360 km north of Perth at Dongara. This is a pleasant little port with fine beaches, plenty of places serving crayfish and a main street lined with Moreton Bay figs. Dongara, which means the 'meeting place of seals' in Aboriginal, was first settled in 1850 and was surveyed for use as a town site in 1852. A jetty was built at nearby Port Irwin (later known as Denison) in 1860.

The Dongara-Port Denison tourist office (☎ (099) 27 1404) is in the old police station at 5 Waldeck St. **Russ Cottage**, on Point Leander Drive, was built in 1870; it is open on Sunday from 10 am to noon. The **Royal Steam Flour Mill**, easily seen from the Brand Highway, was built about 1894. Dongara's **Old East End** is a collection of four restored, stone, colonial buildings and stables dating from 1860; there is a resident blacksmith and entry to the complex is free.

Just over the Irwin River is Port Denison. The Irwin rivermouth is a great place to watch birds such as pelicans and cormorants.

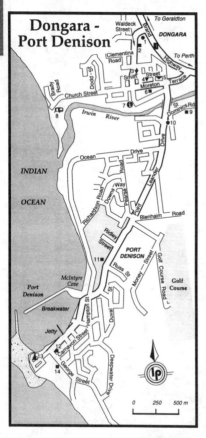

Dongara - Port Denison

PLACES TO STAY

2 Dongara Old Mill Hotel & Caravan Park
6 Dongara Motor Hotel
8 Dongara Seaspray Caravan Park
9 Priory Lodge Historic Inn
11 Dongara-Denison Strata Park
12 Dongara Marina Holiday Units
14 Port Denison Tourist Park

PLACES TO EAT

3 Bakery
4 Sea Jewels Seafood & Takeaway

OTHER

1 Old Flour Mill
5 Post Office
7 Dongara-Port Denison Tourist Office (Old Police Station)
10 Russ Cottage
13 Fisherman's Memorial & Lookout

Places to Stay & Eat

There are four caravan parks in these twin coastal towns. Two recommended ones are the *Dongara-Denison Beach* (☎ (099) 27 1131), on Denison Beach, with powered sites/on-site vans for $10/25 and the very friendly *Seaspray* (☎ (099) 27 1165), 81 Church St, with powered sites/on-site vans for $11/27. The latter is sheltered from the sea breezes by a large grassed wall. The other parks are the *Dongara Denison Strata* (☎ (099) 27 1840), Point Leander Drive; and the *Dongara Tourist* (☎ (099) 27 1210), George St.

The *Dongara Backpackers* (☎ (099) 27 1581) is at 32 Waldeck St. The *Old Mill Hotel* (☎ (099) 27 1879), on the Brand Highway by the Old Flour Mill, has single/double motel units for $45/55; the *Dongara Motor Hotel* (☎ (099) 27 1023), Moreton Terrace, has rooms for $45/55; and the *Dongara Marina Holiday Units* (☎ (099)

27 1486), 4 George St in Port Denison, are $53/58.

The *Priory Lodge Historic Inn* (☎ (099) 27 1090), 9 St Dominics Rd, is a great accommodation alternative (built in 1881) with rooms for $20 per person; and *Obawara* (☎ (099) 27 1043), five km east of Dongara, is a farm property with single B&B for $25 in the guest room and $50 for a self-contained cottage for two.

In Dongara, try *Toko's Restaurant* in Moreton Terrace. Also on Moreton Terrace, opposite the hotel, is the *Sea Jewels Seafood & Takeaway* for delicious fish & chips (and if you can afford it, crayfish). The bakery on Waldeck St is not up to much but is the place to buy a range of sticky buns. There is a barbecue area and a restaurant in the motor hotel.

GREENOUGH & WALKAWAY

Further north, about 20 km south of Geraldton (and 400 km north of Perth), is

---

Dutch Shipwrecks

During the 17th century, ships of the Dutch East India Company, sailing from Europe to Batavia (now Jakarta), would head due east from the Cape of Good Hope then beat up the WA coast to Indonesia. It only took a small miscalculation for a ship to run aground on the coast and a few did just that, usually with disastrous results. The west coast of Australia is often decidedly inhospitable and the chances of rescue at that time were remote.

Four wrecks, once belonging to the Dutch East India Company, have been located, including the *Batavia* – the earliest and, in many ways, the most interesting.

In 1629, the *Batavia* went aground on the Houtman Abrolhos Islands, off the coast of Geraldton. The survivors set up camp, sent off a rescue party to Batavia in the ship's boat and waited. It took three months for a rescue party to arrive and in that time a mutiny had taken place and more than 120 of the survivors had been murdered. The ringleaders were hanged, and two mutineers were unceremoniously dumped on the coast just south of modern-day Kalbarri.

In 1656, the *Vergulde Draeck* struck a reef about 100 km north of Perth and although a party of seven survivors made its way to Batavia, no trace, other than a few scattered coins, was found of the other survivors who had straggled ashore.

The *Zuytdorp* ran aground beneath the towering cliffs north of Kalbarri in 1712. Wine bottles, other relics and the remains of fires have been found on the cliff top. The discovery of the extremely rare Ellis van Creveld syndrome (rife in Holland at the time the ship ran aground) in children of Aboriginal descent poses the question: did the *Zuytdorp* survivors pass the gene on to Aborigines they assimilated with 300 years ago?

In 1727, the *Zeewijk* followed the ill-fated *Batavia* to destruction on the Houtman Abrolhos. Again a small party of survivors made its way to Batavia but many of the remaining sailors died before they could be rescued. Many relics from these shipwrecks, particularly the *Batavia*, can be seen today in the museums in Fremantle and Geraldton. A good account is the *Islands of Angry Ghosts* by Hugh Edwards (1966) who led the expedition which discovered the wreck of the *Batavia*. ∎

BATAVIA COAST

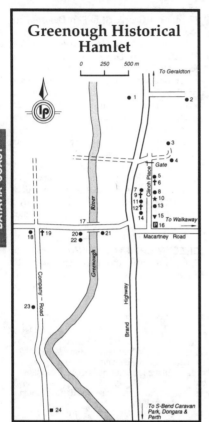

Greenough Historical Hamlet

0   250   500 m

To Geraldton

1   Leaning Trees
2   Pioneer Cemetery
3   Clinch's Mill
4   Cliff Grange
5   St Catherine's Hall
6   St Catherine's Church
7   Hackett's Cottage
8   Old Gaol & Courthouse
9   Catholic Presbytery
10 Police Station & Quarters
11 St Joseph's School
12 St Peter's Church
13 Central Greenough School
14 Dominican Convent
15 Old Store (Tearooms)
16 Parking, Public Toilets
17 Maley's Bridge
18 Gray's Store
19 Wesley Church
20 Stone Barn (Greenpough River Pottery)
21 Ahern Cottage
22 Barn Cottage
23 Nevedale Wildlife Park
24 Hampton Arms

Greenough, once a busy little mining town but now a quiet farming centre. The excellent **Greenough Historical Hamlet** contains eleven 19th-century buildings restored by the National Trust; guided tours are run daily and it is well worth a visit. The Pioneer Museum, open daily from 10 am to 4 pm, has some fine historical displays. You should allow a day to explore this area if you are staying in Geraldton for a few days. Get a copy of the *Greenough-Walkaway Heritage Trail* pamphlet from the Geraldton-Greenough tourist office.

The large stone **flour mill** was built by the Clinch family in 1858. Opposite is **Cliff Grange**, a beautifully restored nine-room National Trust property which is open to the public from 9 am to 4.30 pm Wednesday to Sunday. Out on Company Rd is the restored **Hampton Arms**, formerly a wayside inn.

Look for the flood gums in the local paddocks – the **'leaning trees'** *(Eucalyptus camaldulensis)* – deferring in the face of strong salt winds off the ocean.

It is about seven km east from Greenough Hamlet to Walkaway, another interesting old township. In the town there is the atmospheric old Walkaway Tavern and an interesting old railway station museum. Some 20 km from Walkaway is **Ellendale Pool**, a great picnic spot at the foot of cliffs which provides a welcome respite from the long grind on Highway No 1.

Places to Stay & Eat

The *Greenough Rivermouth Caravan Park* (☎ (099) 21 5845), 14 km north of Greenough Hamlet at Cape Burney, has caravan sites/

on-site vans for $10/25 for two and there is a camper's kitchen. Not far away is the *Greenough River Resort* (☎ (099) 21 8888) which has singles/doubles for $40/55.

The poorly located *S-Bend Caravan Park* (☎ (099) 26 1072), on the prominent S-bend on the Brand Highway south of Greenough, has tent sites/chalets for $8/40 for two. Pick of the accommodation is the *Hampton Arms* (☎ (099) 26 1057) on Company Rd with single/double B&B for $40/55.

There is a nice 'ye olde worlde' tearooms in the Greenough Historical Hamlet, and restaurants in the *Hampton Arms* and the *Greenough River Resort*.

GERALDTON

Geraldton (population 21,000) is the major town along the Batavia Coast and in the midwest region. It is on a spectacular stretch of coast with the magnificent coral reefs of the Houtman Abrolhos offshore.

The area has a great, Mediterranean climate with an average maximum temperature of 28.8°C and at least eight hours of sunshine per day. Most of the annual rainfall of 470 millimetres falls at night. It gets plenty of sun, but the wind drives you to distraction. In true optimistic spirit, the tourist brochures paint the wind as something of a drawcard, enabling the pursuit of such popular pastimes as windsurfing and kite flying. The Wind on Water Festival is celebrated by clusters of optimists in March.

If you are tempted by crayfish fresh from the boat then this is the place to come as the town is the centre of the multi-million dollar crayfish industry.

Orientation & Information

Geraldton stretches for nearly 10 km along the Indian Ocean coast, from the Chapman River in the north to Tarcoola Beach in the south. Located in the centre is the main part of the city and its harbour. On Marine Terrace and Chapman Rd, you will find most of the businesses and services.

The Geraldton-Greenough tourist office (☎ (099) 21 3999) is in the Bill Sewell complex on Chapman Rd, diagonally across

from the railway station and beside the Northgate shopping centre. It is open from 8.30 am to 5 pm Monday to Friday, from 9 am to 4.30 pm Saturday and 9.30 am to 4.30 pm Sunday. The main post office and many of the banks are on Chapman Rd.

If you are short of reading material, there are a couple of second-hand book stores in Geraldton: the House of Books, at 176 Marine Terrace, and the Sun City Book Exchange at No 36.

Geraldton Museum

The town's excellent museum is in two separate, but nearby, buildings on Marine Terrace. The Maritime Museum tells the story of the early wrecks and has assorted relics from the Dutch ships (see under Dutch Shipwrecks in this chapter), including items from the *Batavia* and the *Zeewijk* and the carved wooden sternpiece from the *Zuytdorp*. It was found in 1927, by a local stockman, on top of the cliffs above the point at which the ship had run aground. It was not until the 1950s that the wreckage was positively identified as that of the *Zuytdorp*.

The Old Railway Building has displays on flora & fauna and the settlement of the region by Aborigines and, later, Europeans. The museum complex is open Monday to Saturday from 10 am to 5 pm and from 1 to 5 pm on Sunday and holidays; admission is free.

St Francis Xavier Cathedral

Geraldton's St Francis Xavier Cathedral is just one of a number of buildings in Geraldton and WA's midwest designed by Monsignor John Hawes (see under Monsignor John Hawes in this chapter).

Construction of the Byzantine-style cathedral began in 1916, a year after Hawes arrived in Geraldton, but his plans were too grandiose and the partially built cathedral was not completed until 1938. This is the most striking of Hawes' Australian buildings and the interior is unlike any cathedral you may have seen!

The architecture is a blend of styles. The twin towers, with their arched openings, a large central dome similar to Brunellesci's

BATAVIA COAST

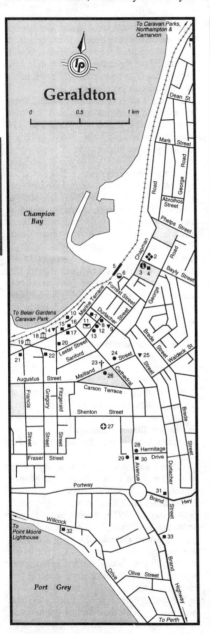

Geraldton

0   0.5   1 km

Champion
Bay

PLACES TO STAY

1   Mariner Motor Hotel
4   Batavia Backpackers
10   Ocean Centre Hotel
15   Sun City Guesthouse
16   Grantown Guesthouse
17   Victoria Hotel
20   Colonial Hotel
21   Peninsula Guesthouse & Backpackers
22   Geraldton Hotel
30   Hospitality Inn
31   Hacienda Motel
32   Ocean West Units
33   Goodwood Lodge Units

PLACES TO EAT

9   Cuisine Connection
14   Reflections
25   Los Amigos Restaurant

OTHER

2   Northgate Shopping Centre
3   Geraldton Tourist Office, Greyhound
     Pioneer
5   Railway Station
6   Westrail Bus Depot
7   RACWA
8   Geraldton Art Gallery
11   Post Office
12   Murchison Tavern
13   Ansett Australia
18   Regional Museum, Sail Inn Snack Bar
19   Geraldton Maritime Museum
23   Francis Xavier Cathedral
24   Queen's Park Theatre
26   Public Toilets
27   Hospital
28   St John of God Hospital
29   The Hermitage

famous cupola in Florence and a tower with
a coned roof, would not be out of place in the
Loire Valley. The interior is just as striking
with Romanesque columns, huge arches
beneath an octagonal dome and zebra strip-
ing on the walls. When completed, Hawes
felt that he had 'caught the rhythm of a poem
in stone'.

While he was working on the St John of
God Hospital in Cathedral Ave, Hawes lived

Monsignor John Hawes

The architect-cum-priest Monsignor John Hawes has left a magnificent legacy of buildings in the midwest. He was born in Richmond, England, in 1876. After receiving architectural training in London he converted to Anglicanism and, following his ordination in 1903, worked in the London slums as a missionary. He then went to the Bahamas where he used his architectural skill to rebuild a number of churches.

Two years later, he converted to Catholicism and went to study in Rome. He came to Australia in 1915 at the invitation of the Bishop of Geraldton and worked as a country pastor in the Murchison region. In the 24 years from 1915 until 1939 he worked tirelessly as a parish priest at Mullewa and Greenough and, as well, designed 24 buildings, 16 of which were later built.

His best works are the Church of Our Lady of Mt Carmel and the Priest House in Mullewa, the Church of the Holy Cross in Morawa, the Church of St Joseph in Perenjori and the unforgettable Cathedral of St Francis Xavier in Geraldton.

Hawes left Australia in 1939 after witnessing the opening of his controversial Geraldton cathedral the previous year. Plans for a cathedral in Perth had been rejected and the cathedral he had struggled for 22 years to build was now complete. His only regret at leaving Australia was that his fox terrier Dominie was to be left behind. He went to Cat Island in the Bahamas and lived as a hermit in a small stone building on a hilltop. He died in a Miami hospital in 1956 and his body was brought back to a tomb he had built for himself on Cat Island.

The *Monsignor Hawes Heritage Trail* pamphlet is available from the tourist office. ■

in **The Hermitage** across the road, in Onslow St. He had designed this unusual dwelling, built for him in 1937 by a local contractor, as a possible place to retire; it is open by appointment only.

Other Attractions

The **Geraldton Art Gallery**, on the corner of Chapman Rd and Durlacher St, is open daily. The **Lighthouse Keeper's Cottage** on Chapman Rd, built in 1870 and now the Geraldton Historical Society's headquarters, is open Thursday from 10 am to 4 pm. You can look out over Geraldton from the Waverley Heights Lookout, on Brede St, or watch the crayfish boats at Fisherman's Wharf, at the end of Marine Terrace. **Point Moore Lighthouse**, on Willcock Drive, in operation since 1878, is also worth a visit but you can't go inside.

The Geraldton **weekend markets** are held on Flores Rd every Friday, Saturday and Sunday; they feature art & craft and fresh produce.

Organised Tours

If you wish to go on day tours to Monkey Mia, Greenough and Dongara, and around the city, then Batavia Tours (☎ (099) 23 1006) does such trips for $180, $32 and $16 respectively. Mid-West Tours (☎ (099) 21 5089) ranges far wider to Mt Augustus, the wildflowers and the Murchison goldfields. Force 5 Charter (☎ (099) 21 6416) takes trips to the Houtman Abrolhos and Shine Aviation Services (☎ (099) 23 3600) flies over the islands (see under Houtman Abrolhos in this chapter).

Places to Stay

Camping The closest caravan parks to the city centre are *Separation Point* (☎ (099) 21 2763), on Willcock Drive, and *Belair Gardens* (☎ (099) 21 1997) at Point Moore; both have caravan sites/on-site vans for about $12/26 for two. The other parks are *Sun City* (☎ (099) 38 1655), Bosley St, Sunset Beach; *Swagman* (☎ (099) 38 1222), 10 km north of the post office at Hall Rd; and the Tarcoola (☎ (099) 21 3333), 5 Broadhead Ave, Mt Tarcoola.

Hostels The *Batavia Backpackers* (☎ (099) 64 3001), on the corner of Chapman Rd and Bayly St in the Bill Sewell complex, has good facilities and beds for $12 per night; a double is $25. At 305-311 Marine Terrace is *Peninsula Guesthouse & Backpackers*

(☎ (099) 21 4770) where singles/doubles/triples are $15/25/30; backpackers' beds are $12 and this is now officially the YHA. The *Chapman Valley Farm Backpackers* (☎ (099) 20 5160), 25 km out of town, is in an historic homestead. They can pick you up from Geraldton at 11 am; beds are $10.

Guesthouses & Hotels Geraldton has plenty of old-fashioned seaside guesthouses, particularly along Marine Terrace. The *Grantown Guesthouse* (☎ (099) 21 3275), at No 172, has singles/doubles for $22/44, including breakfast. The friendly *Sun City Guesthouse* (☎ (099) 21 2205), at No 184, offers B&B for $20/30; there is a shabby backpackers' dorm with beds at $10 and you can observe the sea from a back deck.

Cheap rooms are also available at some of the older-style hotels such as the *Colonial*, Fitzgerald St; the *Victoria*, Marine Terrace; and the *Geraldton*, Gregory St; count on about $15 to $20 per person.

Motels & Units The *Hacienda Motel* (☎ (099) 21 2155), on Durlacher St, has single/double rooms at $45/58. The *Mariner Motor Hotel* (☎ 21 2544), at 298 Chapman Rd, is cheaper at $30/40. Family units are available at both of these places. The *Quality Inn* (☎ 21 2455), on the Brand Highway, is one of those old dependables at $86 for one or two people; the car is allowed in free. Another 'chain' place (who actually owns these?) is the *Hospitality Inn* (☎ 21 1422), 169 Cathedral Ave, with singles/doubles for $65/75.

Ocean West Units (☎ (099) 21 1047), on the corner of Hadda Way and Willcock Drive at Mahomets Beach, has self-contained cottages for around $55 per double. *Goodwood Lodge Units* (☎ (099) 21 5666), at the corner of the Brand Highway and Durlacher St, also has self-contained units for $65 for two.

Places to Eat
The *Cuisine Connection*, in Durlacher St, is a food hall with Indian, Chinese and Italian food, roasts and fish & chips. The food is excellent and you should be able to get a good feed for $7. Fast-food junkies who have made the long haul from Darwin will think they have entered nirvana: *Chicken Treat*, *Hungry Jacks*, *Pizza Hut* and *Red Rooster* all occupy real estate in this town.

There are a number of small snack bars and cafes along Marine Terrace including: *Thuy's Cake Shop*, at No 202, which is open from 6 am for breakfast; and *Belvedere*, at No 149, with standard cafe food at down-to-earth prices. *Hardy's*, on Chapman Rd in the Bill Sewell complex, is also open for breakfast and lunches, including monster burgers.

The *Sail Inn Snack Bar*, by the museum on Marine Terrace, sells burgers and fish & chips; it is in a fast-food enclave which includes *Batavia Coast Fish & Chips* (which also sells pizza and chicken).

Chinese restaurants include the *Golden Coins*, on Marine Terrace; the *Manchu's Mongolian BBQ*, corner of Fitzgerald and Lester Ave; *Rose Chinese & Thai* in Forrest St; and the *Jade House* at 57 Marine Terrace. At 105 Durlacher St, *Los Amigos* is a good, licensed Mexican place. It's popular, and deservedly so. Fancier restaurants include *Reflections* on Foreshore Drive, *Fiddlers* in Marine Terrace, *Skeetas Garden Restaurant* in George Rd and the *Boatshed* in Marine Terrace for great seafood.

Occasionally a live band plays at the Geraldton Hotel in Lester Ave and, if you recently turned 20, chances are you would probably be meeting your mates at the Murchison Tavern in Chapman Rd.

Getting There & Around
Air Ansett Australia flies from Perth to Geraldton for around $158 one-way, or $189 Apex return. Skywest flies the same route; the cost is $142/190.

Bus Westrail and Greyhound Pioneer have regular services from Perth to Geraldton for around $35 one-way. Westrail services continue north-east to Meekatharra (one day per week) or north to Kalbarri (three times a week). Greyhound Pioneer continues on Highway 1 through Port Hedland and Broome to Darwin. Westrail stops at the

Shark Bay & The Gascoyne
Top: Stromatolites, Shark Bay World Heritage Area (JW)
Middle: Coastline of North Carnarvon (KF)
Bottom: The Korean Star shipwreck north of Carnarvon (KF)

Coral Coast & The Pilbara
Top: Outback near Newman in Pilbara (RI)
Bottom: Newman gums and waterhole in Pilbara (RI)

railway station, while Greyhound Pioneer stop at the Bill Sewell complex.

There is a local bus service (☎ (099) 21 1034) in Geraldton which provides access to all the nearby suburbs.

HOUTMAN ABROLHOS ISLANDS

There are 108 islands in this archipelago, about 60 km off the Geraldton coast. The island groups are Wallabi, Easter and Pelsaert and North Island stands alone at the top of the archipelago.

The beautiful but treacherous reefs surrounding the islands have claimed many shipwrecks over the years. The first to nearly run aground was Frederick de Houtman in the Dutch East India Company and it is believed that the name Abrolhos comes from the Portuguese expression 'Abri vossos olhos' ('Keep your eyes open'). The most famous wreck was that of the *Batavia* on 5 June 1629 with 300 people aboard (see under Dutch Shipwrecks in this chapter). The shelters which survived this wreck were probably the first European structures on Australian soil.

Guano (bird poo) was taken from the islands in the late 1800s and again during WWII when there were phosphate shortages. The islands are now the centre of the area's crayfish industry and about 200 boats are licensed to fish there.

The most attractive feature of the islands is the wide range of fauna. Nearly 100 species of birds, some endangered, use the islands as their home. Reptiles thrive in the harsh environment and over 20 species have been recorded. Also found on some islands are the rare tammar wallaby and the Abrolhos bush rat (subspecies of *Rattus fuscipes*).

It is below the water that the Abrolhos come into their own. The Abrolhos are the most southerly coral islands of the Indian Ocean and the Acropora family of corals, of which the well-known staghorn is a member, are found in abundance. Interwoven into this rough sea carpet are sea anemones, plate corals, the hard Tubastrea corals and seaweeds such as sargassum. One species of coral, *Gonipora pendulus*, is found only on Australia's west coast.

Getting There & Away

You are not allowed to spend the night on any of the Abrolhos Islands so all excursions are day trips. Air and diving tours to these protected and spectacular islands are available from Geraldton – check with the tourist office for details. Birdwatching tours are also conducted to the southern Abrolhos from Perth; a weekend trip, such as the 'Blizzard of Birds', with transport by Force 5 Charter (☎ (099) 21 4229) included, is about $480.

NORTHAMPTON

Northampton, with a population of 900, is 50 km north of Geraldton, and was settled soon after the establishment of the Swan River colony. Copper was discovered nearby at Wanerenooka in 1842 and lead was discovered six years later. Convicts were brought into the region to relieve labour shortages and there was a convict hiring facility established at Lynton near Port Gregory from 1853 to 1856.

The Northampton tourist office (☎ (099) 34 1488) is in the Nagle Centre on the main road. This was originally the St Mary's Convent, designed by the peripatetic Monsignor Hawes and built entirely of local stone.

The agricultural centre of Northampton has a number of historic buildings and is now making an initial foray into tourism. An early mine-manager's home, **Chiverton House**, is now a fine municipal museum ($2 entry). The stone building was constructed between 1868 and 1875. Gwalla Church **cemetery** also tells its tales of the early days.

Places to Stay & Eat

There is a caravan park (☎ (099) 34 1202) on the North-West Coastal Highway, with powered sites at $10 for two. Budget accommodation can be found in the *Nagle Centre* (☎ (099) 34 1488), which was formerly the Sacred Heart Convent. It's $12 per person in two and four-bed rooms and has all the facilities.

The *Miners Arms* (☎ (099) 34 1281) has

single/double rooms at $30/38.50 and the *Northampton Motor Hotel* (☎ (099) 34 1240) is $40/50.

You can get a coffee and a snack at the *Northampton Tourist Cafe*, takeaways from the *Northampton Roadhouse Restaurant* or counter meals from any of the hotels.

HORROCKS BEACH & PORT GREGORY

From Northampton you can head west to the coast along a very scenic road and, if conditions are right, north up the coast to Kalbarri.

Horrocks Beach, 22 km west, is a popular holiday resort with a safe, sheltered bay. This area is an angler's paradise with catches of tailor, whiting and skipjack off the beach. Boat owners can head further out in pursuit of dhufish, schnapper, cod and blue bone groper.

It is 43 km from Northampton to **Port Gregory**, the oldest port on the Midwest coast. It is named after the explorer AC Gregory, who discovered lead in the Murchison River in 1848. Today, Port Gregory supports a commercial fishing fleet and is popular as a holiday centre.

On the way to the coast you pass the numerous ruins of the **Lynton Convict Settlement**. It was established as a convict-hiring facility (for ticket-of-leave men) in 1853 and abandoned nearly four years later.

The **Hutt Lagoon**, just before Port Gregory, is a dry salt lake that sometimes looks like a small pink inland sea. The pink colour is due to naturally occurring *Beta caratine*, a dye used for food colouring.

From Port Gregory you can head north on the east side of the lagoon along the very scenic Grey Rd to Kalbarri (check to see if it is suitable for 2WD); this route takes you past all the sights of the southern part of Kalbarri National Park. Somewhere inland from here was the secessionist Hutt River Province, once a tourist destination, but now just a colourful piece of WA's history.

Places to Stay

The *Port Gregory Caravan Park* (☎ (099) 35 1052), Sandford St, and the *Horrocks*

Beach Caravan Park (☎ (099) 34 3039) have tent sites/on-site vans for $12/25 for two. The *Killara Holiday Village* at Horrocks has three to four-bed cottages at $35 per night. The *Lynton Homestead B&B* (☎ (099) 35 1040), next to the Lynton convict settlement, costs a reasonable $25 per person.

KALBARRI

Kalbarri, a popular spot with backpackers and holidaymakers, is on the coast at the mouth of the Murchison River. It has a population of 2000 and is 66 km west of the main highway. The area is appreciated for its coastline, scenic gorges and the poignant history of west coast's Dutch shipwrecks.

In 1629, two *Batavia* mutineers (Wouter Loos and Jan Pelgrom) were marooned as punishment at Wittecarra Gully, an inlet just south of the town; it is marked today by an historical cairn. The *Zuytdorp* was wrecked about 65 km north of Kalbarri in 1712. Although diving on the *Zuytdorp* is very difficult as a heavy swell and unpredictable currents batter the shoreline, divers from the Geraldton Museum did manage to raise artefacts in 1986.

The Kalbarri tourist office (☎ (099) 37 1104) on Grey St provides a wide range of tourist information and the post office is on Porter St. A number of accommodation places can arrange discounted fuel if you stay at their place; this can be quite a saving if you are driving a 'gas-guzzling' 4WD.

Things to See & Do

The **Rainbow Jungle** is an interesting rainforest and a bird park four km south of town towards Red Bluff ($4 adults, $1.50 children), and **Fantasyland** on Grey St ($3.50 adults, $1.50 children) is a collection of dolls, shells and gemstones.

Boats can be hired on the river (☎ (099) 37 1245) and tours can be made on the river's lower reaches on the *Kalbarri River Queen*. There are some excellent **surfing** breaks along the coast – **Jakes Corner**, 3½ km south of town, is reputed to be amongst the best in the state.

You can go **horseriding** through rugged bush at the Big River Ranch (☎ (099) 37 1214) or engage in a number of water-based activities with Kalbarri Boat Hire (☎ (099) 37 1245) on the foreshore opposite Murchison Caravan Park. The less energetic can feed the **pelicans** in Grey St; feeding time is 8.45 am.

Organised Tours

For tours over the Murchison River gorges take a flight with Kalbarri Air Charter. Kalbarri Coach Tours has trips to the Loop, Z-Bend and ocean gorges. It also runs a canoeing adventure tour into the gorges ($30) which takes in the Fourways gullies. The more adventurous can abseil into the gorge with Gordon the guide; for canoeing, abseiling and flights, book at the tourist office.

Kyco runs 4WD tours down the coast to Lucky Bay and Wagoe Beach. This recommended tour includes a trip along the sand beach and views of magnificent sandhills; again, book at the tourist office.

Places to Stay

Kalbarri is a popular resort and accommodation can be tight at holiday times. There's a wide selection of caravan parks, holiday units and motels.

Caravan Parks & Budget There are four caravan parks around town: the *Murchison Park* (☎ (099) 37 1005), Grey St, with powered sites for $12; the *Anchorage* (☎ (099) 37 1181), Anchorage Lane, with tent sites/on-site vans for $8/25 for two; the *Tudor* (☎ (099) 37 1077), Porter St, with on-site vans and cabins from $26 to $32 (the kids will love the mini-zoo); and *Red Bluff* (☎ (099) 37 1080), on Red Bluff Rd, four km south of town, with on-site vans/chalets at $25/30 for two.

The clean and modern *Kalbarri Backpackers* (☎ (099) 37 1430), at 2 Mortimer St, has shared accommodation from $11 and family and disabled units from $40; it has been recommended by a number of travellers and would have to be one of the best of its

type in WA. The owners organise snorkelling trips to the Blue Holes, one km south of Kalbarri. Enjoy the free beer on Friday night.

Other budget possibilities are the *Av-Er-Rest Backpackers* (☎ (099) 37 1101), on Mortimer St, and the *Murchison River Lodge* (☎ (099) 37 1584), Grey St.

Motels & Holiday Units As would be expected in a holiday destination there are plenty of holiday units/resorts. The *Kalbarri Beach Resort* (☎ (099) 37 1061), on the corner of Grey and Clotworthy Sts, has comfortable two-bedroom units from $75 to $105. Units in the *Sunsea Villas* (☎ (099) 37 1025) at 18 Grey St, the *Murchison View Apartments* (☎ (099) 37 1096) on the corner of Grey and Rushton Sts, and the *Kalbarri Reef Villas* (☎ (099) 37 1165) in Coles St are $65. The *Kalbarri Hotel/Motel* (☎ (099) 37 1000), on Grey St, is central and has comfortable singles/doubles for $45/55. Rooms are only slightly more expensive in the *Kalbarri Palm Resort* (☎ (099) 37 2333) on Porter St.

If you fancy staying in a family-owned villa then there are a number available; contact the Kalbarri Accommodation Service (☎ (099) 37 1072). For example, the *Courtis Villa* (☎ (09) 332 5073) in Kelsar Gardens costs from $40 per night.

Places to Eat

There are four cafes in town and all specialise in seafood dishes: the *Kalbarri Cafe* in the main shopping centre; the *Seabreeze*, home of the prawn roll, in the Kalbarri Arcade; *Rivers Cafe* near the jetty and the BYO *Lure 'n Line* in Grey St near the tourist office. For fish & chips try *Jonah's* in Grey St and for pizza go to *Kalbarri Pizza*. There is a bakery (hot bread shop) in the Kalbarri Arcade which serves up a range of pies, rolls and cakes. In the same arcade is a fruit & vegetable shop for the self-caterers. Nearby, at the *Gilgai Tavern*, you can get a decent counter meal for $6.

Finlay's Fresh Fish BBQ, Magee Crescent, in an old ice works, is a special place for a meal (most are less than $10). The decor

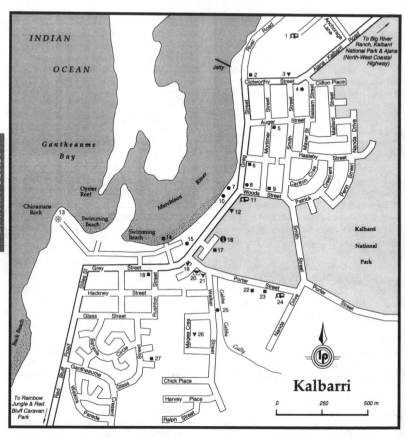

Kalbarri

is no frills but the meals and salads are filling – the atmosphere, in a word, is great.

There are three licensed restaurants in town: the *Palm* in the Palm Resort, *Echoes* in the main shopping centre and *Zuytdorp* in the Kalbarri Beach Resort; Echoes is probably the best, especially if you dine out on the balcony which overlooks the ocean.

Getting There & Around

Western Airlines has return flights from Perth on Monday, Wednesday and Friday; the one-way fare is $152 and a return is $304. Westrail buses from Perth come into Kalbarri on Monday, Wednesday and Friday ($56.50 or $113 return) returning Tuesday, Thursday and Saturday. On Monday, Thursday and Saturday there is a return shuttle into Kalbarri which connects with the Greyhound Pioneer bus at Ajana on the North-West Coastal Highway.

Bicycles can be rented from Murchison Cycles, on Porter St; if no one is there, ask at the Mini-Putt complex next door.

KALBARRI NATIONAL PARK

This national park has over 1860 sq km of bushland including some scenic gorges on

PLACES TO STAY

1 Anchorage Caravan Park
2 Kalbarri Beach Resort
5 Av-Er-Rest Backpackers
6 Kalbarri Reef Villas
9 Kalbarri Backpackers'
11 Murchison Park Caravan Park
17 Kalbarri Hotel/Motel
18 Murchison View Apartments
23 Kalbarri Palm Resort
24 Tudor Caravan Park
27 Courtis Villa

PLACES TO EAT

3 Zuytdorp Restaurant
12 Lure 'n' Line Cafe
19 Seabreeze Coffee Lounge, Kalbarri
    Hot Bread Shop, Fruit & Vegetable
    Shop
21 Gilgai Tavern, Kalbarri Cafe, Echoes
    Restaurant
26 Finlay's Fresh Fish BBQ

OTHER

4 CALM Office
7 Pelican Feeding
8 Fantasyland
10 Kalbarri Boat Hire
13 Lookout
14 *Kalbarri River Queen*
15 Children's Playground
16 Kalbarri Tourist Office, Kalbarri
    Accommodation Service, Jonah's
20 Post Office
22 Entertainment Centre (Bicycle Hire,
    Mini-Putt Golf)
25 Grey's Spring

the **Murchison River**. The Murchison starts near Peak Hill, 80 km north of Meekatharra. It once flowed over a smooth red plain of Tumblagooda sandstone but shifting of the earth's surface in the region, about two million years ago, caused the river to erode deep into the rock. This created the meandering 80-km-long gorge of the park.

From Kalbarri, it's about 40 km to the **Loop** and **Z-Bend**, two impressive gorges with steep banded cliffs. Further east along the Ajana-Kalbarri Rd are two lookouts:

Hawk's Head (a must see) and **Ross Graham** (Graham was a dedicated conservationist).

Short **walking trails** lead into the gorges from the road access points but there are also longer walks. The walk around the Loop, which begins and ends at nature's Window, takes six hours. It takes about two days to walk between Z-Bend, a narrow ravine, and the Loop. The 38-km walk from Ross Graham Lookout to the Loop requires a strenuous four days.

To the south of the town of Kalbarri there is a string of cliff faces where you can take in rugged, beautiful seascapes. These include **Red Bluff** (a red sandstone outcrop) and the banded **Rainbow Valley**. **Pot Alley**, **Eagle Gorge** and **Natural Bridge** have been sculpted by the surrounding seas. All these sights can be reached by car but the road will test your suspension in places. There is an eight-km coastal walking trail which takes from three to five hours; it is best to be dropped off at Eagle Gorge and picked up at Natural Bridge.

The park puts on a particularly fine display of wildflowers in the spring including everlastings, banksias, grevilleas, kangaroo paws, acacias and the ubiquitous *Xanthorrhoea* grass tree. More than 850 varieties of wildflower have been recorded in the park, many of which can be seen from the roads. There is also a great range of fauna. In addition to euros, rock wallabies, red and western grey kangaroos, another nine species of mammal are found. Emus are frequently spotted and over 170 species of birds have been recorded.

Shark Bay

Shark Bay World Heritage and Marine Park has some spectacular beaches, important seagrass beds, the stromatolites at Hamelin Pool and the famous dolphins of Monkey Mia. The peninsulas and nearby islands are important sanctuaries for many endangered species such as the Shark Bay mouse

(Pseudomys praeconis) and the greater stick-nest rat (see under A Story of Survival – The Stick-Nest Rat in this section). Shark Bay is undoubtedly one of Australia's best, but as yet undeveloped, ecotourism destinations and it is one of only 12 places on earth to have satisfied all four natural criteria for world heritage listing:

- Be outstanding examples representing a major stage of the earth's evolutionary history.
- Be outstanding examples representing significant ongoing geological processes, biological evolution and human interaction with the natural environment.
- Contain superlative natural phenomena, formations or features.
- Contain important and significant natural habitats where threatened species of outstanding universal value still survive.

HISTORY

Prior to colonisation, the Shark Bay region was part of the traditional lands of the Nganda and Malgana Aboriginal people. There was an abundant supply of seafood such as shellfish and turtles, and fossilised mudwhelks have been found in midden sites near Little Lagoon. More evidence of earlier Aboriginal occupation has been found near Eagle Bluff and in caves near the bluff by Monkey Mia. Some of the evidence has been dated back 22,000 years.

The first recorded landing on Australian soil by a European took place at Shark Bay in 1616 when the Dutch explorer Dirk Hartog landed on the island that now bears his name. He nailed an inscribed plate to a post on the beach but a later Dutch visitor, de Vlamingh, collected it. It's now in a museum in Amsterdam, although there's a reproduction in the Geraldton Museum.

The many French names are the legacy of the French explorers in the *Géographe* and *Naturaliste* (June 1801) but the name Bay of Sharks (now Shark Bay) was given much earlier by William Dampier in August 1699 (see under History in the Facts about Western Australia chapter). Mr Goodwin, Dampier's cook, is the first known European to be buried on Australian soil.

Shark Bay is the name loosely applied to the two fingers of land which jut into the Indian Ocean and the lagoons which surround them. Denham, the main population centre of Shark Bay, is 132 km off the main highway from the Overlander Roadhouse. Monkey Mia, on the eastern finger, is 26 km north-east of Denham on a sealed road.

BIRDWATCHING

The Shark Bay region contains a variety of habitats, making it a great location for birdwatching. In addition to being at the northern limit of the range of many birds of the south-west, it is a preferred location for birds of the arid and semi-arid zones, and for many marine birds, waterbirds and shorebirds.

At the southern end of Shark Bay look for, among others, these south-western species: blue-breasted fairy wren *(Malurus pulcherrimus)*, brown-headed honeyeater *(Melithreptus brevirostris)* and golden whistler *(Pachycephala pectoralis)*.

On the Péron Peninsula, crimson chats *(Ephthianura tricolor)*, southern whitefaces *(Aphelocephala leucopis)*, white-winged fairy wrens *(Malurus leucopterus)*, chiming wedgebills *(Psophodes occidentalis)* and rare thick-billed grass wrens *(Amytornis textilis)* may be observed. Incidentally, you will probably hear the wedgebill ask 'Did you get drunk?' before you spot it.

Marine birds are numerous and include the wedge-tailed shearwater, a number of terns and the white-bellied sea eagle. The large stands of mangroves at the north of the peninsula attract, to the southern limit of their range, the mangrove grey-fantail *(Rhipidura phasiana)* and the yellow-white-eye *(Zosterops lutea)*.

KALBARRI TO DENHAM

Between the Kalbarri turn-off and Shark Bay there is, well, not much! Aficionados of roadhouses will be delighted by the **Billabong** (☎ (099) 42 5980), a perfect architectural example of this roadside attraction, perched halfway between Geraldton and Carnarvon. Equally enthralling is the 24-hour **Overlan-**

der (☎ (099) 42 5916), near the turn-off to Shark Bay.

On the way into Denham from the highway, the first turn-off (27 km from the highway) is a six-km road to **Hamelin Pool**, a marine reserve which has the world's best known colony of **stromatolites** (see under Stromatolites in this chapter). A boardwalk is being constructed, at the time of writing, to the stromatolites.

Go into the old **Telegraph Station** (☎ (099) 42 5905), established in 1884, to get information on these unique structures. This is the only intact repeater station left in WA and served as a telephone exchange until 1977. There is camping, caravan sites and food available at Hamelin.

Just over 50 km from Hamelin is the 2000 sq km **Nanga Station**, with its old homestead building constructed of cut shell blocks. The complex has a liquor licence and is the only station licensed in Australia. There is also a small pioneer museum, BYO restaurant and a sheltered bay for swimming and fishing. Integrated into the station is the *Nanga Bay Holiday Village* (☎ (099) 48 3996) which has bunkhouse accommodation for $11 per person and cabins/motel units at $45/77 for two. Catamarans, sailboards and dinghies can be hired at the beach.

The 110-km-long stretch of **Shell Beach** is solid shells nearly 10 metres deep! In places in Shark Bay, the shells *(Fragum erugatum)* are so tightly packed that they can be cut into blocks and have been used for building construction in many parts of Shark Bay.

At **Eagle Bluff**, halfway between Nanga and Denham, there are superb views from the cliff. If you look hard enough you will see marine creatures such as manta rays frolicking in the water and white-bellied sea-eagles overhead (hence the bluff's name).

DENHAM

The name Denham comes from Captain Henry Denham who charted the waters of Shark Bay in 1858 in HMS *Herald*. He was an early graffitist, having inscribed his name into rock on the cliff face at Eagle Bluff. A

Stromatolites

The dolphins at Monkey Mia didn't solely contribute to the listing of Shark Bay as a world heritage region. Perhaps the biggest single contributor was the existence of stromatolites at Hamelin Pool. These structures are thousands of years old having evolved over 3½-billion years.

Hamelin Pool is suited to the growth of stromatolites because of the clarity and hypersalinity of the water. In essence, each stromatolite is covered in a form of cyanobacterial microbe shaped like algae which – during daily photosynthesis – wave around. At night the microbe folds over, often trapping calcium and carbonate ions dissolved in the water. The sticky chemicals they exude adds to the concretion of another layer on the surface of the stromatolite. Whew, techno-babble rules.

These are the most accessible stromatolites in the world, spectacularly set amidst the turquoise waters of Hamelin Pool. Be careful not to disturb them. ■

---

section of this rock collapsed into the sea and has been relocated to Pioneer Park in the town. Denham, once a pearling port, boasts a street paved with pearl shell. It is also the most westerly town in Australia.

These days, if it weren't for a group of friendly dolphins, Denham would probably still be a sleepy fishing village. This town has the Shark Bay tourist office (☎ (099) 48 1253) at Knight Terrace, which is open Monday to Saturday from 8.30 am to 6 pm; on Sunday it opens at 9 am. The CALM office (☎ (099) 48 1208), Knight Terrace, has a great deal of information on the World Heritage area. There is also a shell craft museum, a church and a restaurant made of shell blocks.

Things to See & Do

There is an interesting **walk** along the shore from Denham to the Town Bluff – the two rows of curved rocks are believed to be an Aboriginal fish trap. A couple of km down the road to Monkey Mia is the shallow and picturesque **Little Lagoon**. About four km from Denham on the Monkey Mia Rd is the turn-off to the fascinating, wild **François Peron National Park**.

Organised Tours

There is a wildlife cruise (weather permitting) to Steep Point on the MV *Explorer* for $50 – book at the tourist office in Denham; minimum of 10 people. Shark Bay Safari Tours (☎ (099) 48 1247) has various tours around Shark Bay and the World Heritage area; again, enquire at the tourist office. On Tuesday they go to Big Lagoon ($35) and on Wednesday they do a full-day tour to Cape Péron in François Péron National Park ($55). Every day, except Monday and Friday, the yacht *Shotover* does a morning and sunset dolphin cruise for $19.

Places to Stay

The *Denham Seaside Caravan Park* (☎ (099) 48 1242), Knight Terrace, is a friendly place on the foreshore with tent sites/on-site vans for $10/32 for two. *Shark Bay Caravan Park* (☎ (099) 48 1387) on Spaven Way and the *Blue Dolphin* (☎ (099) 48 1385) on Hamelin Rd, in Denham, are similarly priced.

Accommodation in Shark Bay can be very tight and expensive during school holidays. *Bay Lodge & Backpackers* (☎ (099) 48 1278), an associate YHA hostel in Knight Terrace, on the Denham foreshore, has a great atmosphere and is the best value in town. Bookings are recommended at this popular hostel. Beds in shared units cost $11, two bedroom self-contained units are $46 and a motel room is from $45.

There are a number of holiday cottages and villas in Shark Bay. The *Shark Bay Holiday Cottages* (☎ (099) 48 1206), Knight Terrace, has backpackers' beds for $12 in four-bed, self-contained rooms, cottages at $35 for two and three-bedroom units from $50. The *Denham Holiday Village* (☎ (09) 335 5550), on the corner of Capewell Drive and Sunter Place, has three-bedroom brick cottages and the *Denham Villas* (☎ (099) 48 1264), 4 Durlacher St, has self-contained villas; both are from $65 per night. Units in

the *Tradewinds Holiday Village* (☎ (099) 48 1222) on Knight Terrace are $70 per night.

The up-market choice is the *Heritage Resort Hotel* (☎ (099) 48 1133), also centrally located on Knight Terrace; the units are not cheap at $95/120 for singles/doubles but you get all the facilities you would expect at this price.

Shark Bay Accommodation Service (☎ (099) 48 1323) has a number of privately owned cottages and units available, usually by the week.

Places to Eat

There are a number of takeaways, a pizza place and a bakery along Knight Terrace. The other dining choices are also along Knight Terrace: the *Shark Bay Hotel* has counter meals, or there's the more expensive shell-block *Old Pearler* restaurant (main meals are from $16 to $20 and crabs and crayfish are the specialities, in season). The Heritage Resort Hotel serves bar meals and has a good à la carte restaurant which specialises in seafood dishes.

Getting There & Away

Air The airstrip between Denham and Monkey Mia has been upgraded and there are an increasing number of tour groups flying there. Check the availability of services with the WATC.

Bus North from Kalbarri, it's a fairly dull, boring and often very hot run to Carnarvon. The Overlander Roadhouse, 290 km north of Geraldton, is the turn-off to Shark Bay. Greyhound Pioneer has a connecting bus service from Denham to Overlander to connect with interstate buses on Saturday, Monday and Thursday (both north and southbound). The fare from Perth to Denham is $121. It's about $25 from Denham and Monkey Mia to the Overlander Roadhouse.

A daily local bus departs Denham (near the tourist office on Knight Terrace) at 8.45 and 3 pm for Monkey Mia and returns at 9.15 am and 3.30 pm; the fare is $7 one-way. There is an airport bus service; it is $7 one-way to Monkey Mia and $5 to Denham.

Seagrasses
You will see seagrasses, appearing as a dark shadow, in the crystal clear waters of Shark Bay and washed up on the beaches of Denham and Monkey Mia. Shark Bay is known to have 12 species of seagrass growing in 4000 of its 13,000 sq km, including the 1030-sq-km Wooramel Bank seagrass meadow, the largest in the world.

Seagrasses are not seaweeds. Seaweeds are plants without flowers or roots. In contrast, seagrasses have complex root systems, are green flowering plants and can survive in the highly saline waters of the bay. In fact, seaweeds and animals grow on the seagrasses as epiphytes. The meadows are important nurseries for small fish and act to slow water movement. They also provide the most essential part of the diet of the dugong. ∎

SHARK BAY

Hovercraft You can get to Monkey Mia from Carnarvon by hovercraft. This route is more direct than road and takes about 90 minutes less. Dolphin Express Hovercraft (☎ (099) 41 1146) does this trip for $90 return. On route you may see sharks, rays, turtles; dolphins are almost always spotted. The hovercraft leaves Carnarvon at 7 am and returns at 4 pm – bookings can be made in Carnarvon or Denham.

FRANÇOIS PÉRON NATIONAL PARK

This truly magnificent national park is appropriately named after the French naturalist who visited Shark Bay with Nicolas Baudin's *Géographe* expedition in 1801 and 1803. Baudin died of tuberculosis on the return voyage so it was left to Péron to write up the narrative and scientific accounts of the expedition in his *A Voyage of Discovery to the Southern Hemisphere* (1809).

The 400 sq km park is known for its arid scenery, tracks of wilderness and the landlocked salt lakes or *birridas*; which range from 100 metres to a km wide. At the tip of the peninsula is Cape Péron with its dramatic colour contrasts, a good place to spot passing turtles, dolphins, dugongs and manta rays.

The observant may see the rare thick-billed grass wren in the low acacia shrubland. There are many other species to observe – see under Birdwatching earlier. Several species of snake, such as the mulga and gwardar, are found in the park but perhaps the most famous of the reptiles is the thorny or mountain devil.

There are two artesian bore tanks, one which has water at 35°C and the other at a hot 43°C in the grounds of the **Péron Homestead**, itself a reminder of the peninsula's former use for sheep grazing. Campsites with limited facilities are located at Big Lagoon, Gregories, Bottle Bay, South Gregories and Herald Bight.

Always carry your own supplies of drinking water, carry out all rubbish, light fires only in the rings provided, do not collect firewood (as it provides protection for fauna), watch out for stonefish in shallow waters and keep well back from the cliffs at Cape Péron. Entry to the park is $3 for a day visit and $20 for a vehicle with four passengers for seven nights.

The road to the homestead is suitable for 2WD vehicles but a 4WD will be necessary to go any further into the park. Stick to the roads and *don't* try to cross any of the birridas – you will get bogged. For those without 4WD there is a tour option with Shark Bay Safari Tours (☎ (099) 48 1247) – see Organised Tours under Denham earlier.

MONKEY MIA

This pleasant spot with the unusual name is 26 km from Denham. Several theories exist as to how the name came about. In 1834, a schooner *Monkey* supposedly anchored in Shark Bay and 'Mia' is Aboriginal for 'house or home', hence 'home of the monkey'. This is disputed as records indicate the *Monkey* was never near the east side of the Péron Peninsula. Then there was the pearling boat which had a monkey as a mascot ('monkey' was slang at the time for Mongolian pearlers and was the colloquial expression for shepherd etc). We will probably never know for sure.

You pass the Dolphin Information Centre (☎ (099) 48 1366) just as you enter the beach viewing area; they have lots of information on the region and on the dolphins and screen a captivating 45-minute video on many aspects of Shark Bay.

The Dolphins of Monkey Mia

It's believed that bottle-nose dolphins *(Tursiops truncatus)* have been visiting Monkey Mia since the early 1960s, although it's only in the last decade or so that it's become world famous.

Monkey Mia's dolphins simply drop by to visit humans; they swim into knee-deep water and nudge up against you, even take a fish from you if it's offered. The dolphins generally come in every day during the winter months, less frequently during the summer. They may arrive singly or in groups of five or more, but as many as 13 were recorded on one occasion. They seem to come in more often in the mornings.

The entry fee to the reserve is $3 per adult and $2 for children. There are rules of good behaviour for visitors, which are sometimes ignored by eager communicators:

- Stand knee deep in water and let them approach you – don't chase or try to swim with them.
- Stroke them along their sides with the back of your hand as they swim beside you. Don't touch their fins or their blowhole.
- If you get invited to offer them fish by the ranger (feeding times and quantities are regulated) it should be whole, not gutted or filleted. They take defrosted fish only if it has completely thawed.

Places to Stay & Eat

The *Monkey Mia Dolphin Resort* has a wide range of accommodation including powered caravan sites for two for $20.50 (probably the most expensive in WA), backpacker's beds in two tented condos for $10, on-site vans for $30/50 for three/four persons respectively and motel units for $110 for two; discounts apply in the off season.

At the *Bough Shed Restaurant* in Monkey Mia, join the elite and watch the dolphins feed – a private box at Marineworld? It's expensive but there is also a more economical takeaway shop and a small grocery shop nearby.

A Story of Survival – the Stick-Nest Rat

The innocuous greater stick-nest rat *(Leporillus conditor)* seldom makes it into lists of Australian mammals these days. Its fate almost mirrors that of many now-extinct species. In a minuscule portion of geological time, some 200 years, over a dozen non-flying mammal species of the arid zone have become extinct. Introduced species such as donkeys, camels, cats, foxes and rabbits have destroyed habitat or preyed upon many native species.

The stick-nest rat builds its humble nest of intertwined sticks above ground (most of its cousins burrow) which leaves it vulnerable to trampling by roving stock.

Prior to colonisation the rat was found throughout southern Australia from the central west coast of WA to western New South Wales. It was last recorded on the mainland in the 1920s and from then on a small population of about 1000 were confined to Franklin Island in the Nuyts Archipelago, off the coast of South Australia.

A successful captive breeding programme began in South Australia in 1985 and, in 1990, 40 of the rats were fitted with radio-collars and released on Salutation Island in Shark Bay. The conditions and vegetation of the island resembled those of Franklin Island; importantly, there were no introduced predators.

At last check the rat was doing OK and even finding time to breed. Not so lucky are: the desert and pig-footed bandicoots; desert-rat kangaroo; eastern and central hare-wallabies; crescent nail-tailed wallaby; white-footed rabbit, lesser stick-nest and central rock rats; and big-eared, long-tailed and short-tailed-hopping mice. ∎

The Gascoyne

The Gascoyne region takes its name from the 764-km-long Gascoyne River, which together with its major tributary, the Lyons River, has a catchment area of nearly 70,000 sq km. Seldom does the Gascoyne River flow above ground west of the Kennedy Range.

There are a number of attractions within this vast region but a good deal of driving is necessary to get to them. North of Carnarvon is an interesting stretch of coastline with blowholes and rocky capes. To the east is the impressive north-south running Kennedy Range and the massive bulk of Mt Augustus.

CARNARVON

Carnarvon, with a population of 7500, is at the mouth of the Gascoyne River. It's noted for its tropical fruit, particularly bananas, and fine climate. It can get very hot in the middle of summer and is periodically subjected to floods and cyclones. Subsurface water, which flows even when the river is dry, is tapped to irrigate riverside plantations. Salt is produced at Lake Macleod near Carnarvon, and prawns and scallops are harvested in the area. The main street of Carnarvon is 40 metres wide, a reminder of the days when camel trains used to pass through.

The Carnarvon tourist office (☎ (099) 41 1146), on Robinson St, is open daily from 8.30 am to 5.30 pm; in the off season 9 am to 5 pm. If you are not driving the next leg of your journey you may wish to read a book – the Wise Owl Book Exchange, just past the Caltex service station (on the corner of Robinson St and Babbage Island Rd), has books for sale or to trade.

Things to See & Do

Carnarvon once had a NASA **tracking station**. It opened in 1966 and was closed in 1975; it is open daily – enquire at the tourist office. The **Fascine**, lined with palm trees, is a pleasant place for a stroll. Carnarvon's

'one mile' jetty is a popular fishing spot as is the little jetty at the prawning station. The small, furnished **Lighthouse Keeper's Cottage Museum** is beside the jetty ($1 entry).

Pelican Point, five km to the south-west, is a popular swimming and picnic spot. Other good **beaches**, also south and off the Geraldton Rd, are Bush Bay (turn-off 20 km) and New Beach (37 km).

Munro's Banana Plantation, on South River Rd, does a very informative plantation tour at 11 am and 2 pm daily (only 11 am at off-peak times). After the tour, you can indulge yourself in fantastic fresh-fruit ice cream or smoothies. They sell a banana cookbook which includes banana cures for such ills as diarrhoea, ulcers and depression.

Organised Tours

Tropical Tripper Tours and Tony's Tours (Gascoyne Lookabout Safari) depart from the tourist office and include half-day tours around town for $13 and an all-day tour that takes in Lake Macleod, Cape Cuvier, the wreck of the *Korean Star* and the blowholes for $30.

The *Dolphin Express* hovercraft runs from Carnarvon to Monkey Mia daily except Monday and Friday; the 2½-hour trip is $60 one way and $90 return. The hovercraft leaves Carnarvon at 7 am and returns at 4 pm – bookings can be made in Carnarvon or Denham.

A couple of local surfers know where the 'full bore barrels with plenty of length' are; contact West Coast Surfaris (☎ (099) 41 2496).

Places to Stay

Camping & Caravans You shouldn't have any trouble finding a caravan park in Carnarvon; the closest to the centre of town is the *Carnarvon Tourist Centre Caravan Park* (☎ (099) 41 1438), 90 Robinson St, which has tent sites/on-site vans at $12/25 for two. The *Marloo Caravan Park* (☎ (099) 41 1439), on Wise St, is well set up for campers as they have a kitchen, laundry and great

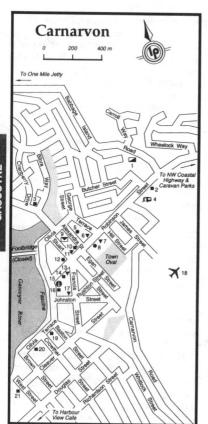

Carnarvon

0   200   400 m

To One Mile Jetty

GASCOYNE

bathroom facilities; campsites are $10 for two.

The other five caravan parks have similar rates: on Robinson St are the *Carnarvon Caravan Park & Units* (☎ (099) 41 8101), *Plantation* (☎ (099) 41 8100) and *Wintersun* (☎ (099) 41 8150); the *Norwesta* (☎ (099) 41 1277) is at 12-20 Angelo St; and the *Startrek* (☎ (099) 41 8153).

Hostels There is plenty of budget accommodation in Carnarvon. The *Carnarvon Backpackers* (☎ (099) 41 1095), an associate YHA hostel at 46 Olivia Terrace, has dorm

beds at $12. The *Backpackers' Paradise* (☎ (099) 41 2966), next to the tourist office on Robinson St, has shared accommodation, also from $12; at both there's a discount for YHA members. At the *Port Hotel* (☎ (099) 41 1704), on Robinson St, backpackers' accommodation is $10 per night.

Hotels, B&B & Motels Carnarvon has some old-fashioned hotels with old-fashioned prices. The *Port Hotel* has rooms from $25/50 in the older part of the hotel. The *Carnarvon Hotel/Motel* (☎ (099) 41 1181), Olivia Terrace, has rooms for $20/35, or for $35/55 in the newer motel section. There are self-contained units in the *Carnarvon Close* (☎ (099) 41 1317), 96 Robinson St; these are about $55 per night.

The *Gateway Motel* (☎ (099) 41 1532), on Robinson St, has rooms at $75. There are self-contained holiday units at the *Carnarvon Beach Holiday Resort* (☎ (099) 41 2226), Pelican Point, at $55 for two. The *Fascine Lodge* (☎ (099) 41 2411), 1002 David Brand Drive, and the *Hospitality Inn* (☎ (099) 41 1600), West St, cost about the same as the Gateway.

The top accommodation in Carnarvon is the Maslen family's *The Outcamp* (☎ (099) 41 2421) at 16 Olivia Tce, on the Fascine. This is a luxurious B&B in the town's best location. The cost is a mere $40 per person for the great facilities, so treat yourself.

For more information about station stays see under Station Stays in the Coral Coast & Pilbara chapter.

Places to Eat

Try *Carnarvon Fresh Seafood*, in the Boulevard Shopping Centre on Robinson St, for fish & chips and hamburgers. On the same street are *Fascine* and *Kaycee's*, both standard coffee lounges. *ChickenLand*, also on Robinson St next to the Tourist Centre Caravan Park, is a mini food hall with takeaways and pasta at reasonable prices; you can eat in or take away. Next to it is *PizzaLand*.

The *Carnarvon Bakery*, 21 Robinson St, has home-made pies and sandwiches, as does *Jenny's Hot Bread Kitchen*, on the corner of Robinson and Angelo Sts. The *Carnarvon* and *Port* hotels have good counter meals. The *Harbour View Cafe*, at the small boat harbour, is renowned for its excellent seafood and salads – read the visitors' book.

Lucki's Asian Takeaway, on Robinson St, has typical Chinese food. There is also the *Dragon Pearl* on Francis St. If you're looking for a more up-market place, you could try the Mexican-style *Red Peppers*, Robinson St ($16 for a main meal), *Sails Restaurant* in the Hospitality Inn or the excellent restaurant in the *Tropicana Tavern*.

Getting There & Around

Ansett Australia flies to Carnarvon from Perth for $254 one way ($289 Apex return). Enquire about the large range of special fares. Greyhound Pioneer and Dixon's Westliner both pass through Carnarvon on their way north or south. The one-way full fare from Perth to Carnarvon is around $100.

Bicycles are available for hire from Backpackers' Paradise (provide your own helmet). Mopeds can be hired from Jolly's Tyrepower Service in Robinson St.

NORTH COAST

About 14 km north of town, the **Bibbawarra Bore**, an artesian well sunk to a depth of 914 metres, is being developed into a spa bath. It has a continuous flow of water at 65°C. West of the bore and 22 km from Carnarvon is **Miaboolya Beach**, popular with anglers using either light or heavy line.

The spectacular **blowholes**, 70 km to the north of Carnarvon, are well worth the trip. They can be reached by the Bibbawarra Bore Track or from the North-West Coastal Highway. Water is forced through holes in the rock to a height of 20 metres. One km south of the Quobba Station homestead is the **HMAS Sydney Memorial** which commemorates the ship sunk off the coast by the German raider *Kormoran* on 19 November 1941.

Cape Cuvier, where salt is loaded for Japan, is 30 km north of the blowholes, and nearby is the *Korean Star*, grounded by Cyclone Herbie on 21 May 1988 (do not climb over the wreck as it is dangerous).

Places to Stay

There's a fine beach about one km south of the blowholes with a primitive campsite (no fresh water available) and shanty town. You can camp at *Quobba Station* for about $4.50 per person; power is limited but water is available.

KENNEDY RANGE

This spectacular eroded plateau is some 160 km east of Carnarvon; it runs north from Gascoyne Junction for 195 km and in places is 30 km wide. The southern and eastern sides have eroded forming dramatic 100-metre-high cliffs which are dissected with steep-walled canyons. The resulting mesa,

GASCOYNE

which slopes quickly on the west side, is covered with red sand dunes and spinifex.

The park was explored by the Gregory brothers in 1858 and they named the range after the then governor of WA. The many artefacts scatters attest to much earlier use by Aboriginal groups. The semi-precious coloured chert was used to make stone tools. The ranges were thoroughly explored for minerals and the mining potential was deemed low.

Some 295 species of plant have been recorded in the park and 40% of these are annual wildflowers – much of the park has not yet been explored. Euros and rock wallabies are the most visible mammals and birds are seen around the permanent waterholes. The cliff eyries are perfect vantage points for the magnificent wedge-tailed eagle.

The many marine fossils in the sandstone strata relate to the Permian period, some 250 million years ago, when the Gascoyne was a shallow ocean basin off the edge of the Australian continent. These can be seen in a number of places on the eastern escarpment.

The eastern escarpment can be reached in a 2WD vehicle but driving in the rest of the park is not recommended. If you don't fancy driving you can fly over it or get someone else to take you there. West Coast Safaris (☎ (099) 41 1146) and Kennedy Range Tours (☎ (099) 43 0550) take trips to the Kennedy Range. A three-day trip which includes the range and Mt Augustus would cost around $350. Neither fuel nor water is available in the park so you have to come with adequate supplies.

Places to Stay

Bush camping is permitted at designated sites by the eastern escarpment of the Kennedy Range, near the entry to The Temple. There is accommodation at the *Mt Sandiman Homestead* (☎ (099) 43 0546), 240 km north-east of Carnarvon via Gascoyne Junction; backpackers can stay in the old jackeroo (or jilleroo) quarters. At the *Junction Hotel* (☎ (099) 43 0504), where the Lyons River meets the Gascoyne River, single/double rooms are $35/45.

MT AUGUSTUS (BURRINGURRAH) NATIONAL PARK

Mt Augustus, in Burringurrah National Park, 450 km from Carnarvon, is the biggest rock (monadnock) in the world but certainly not the most spectacular; it is twice the size of Uluru but the partial vegetation cover makes it far less dramatic. The granite underneath the layered rocks of the mount is estimated to be 1650 million years old.

There are three main sites where Aboriginal engravings can be seen. Ooramboo has engravings on a rock face and there is a spring nearby; at Mundee the engravings are in an overhang; and at Beedoboondu, the starting point for the climb to the summit, has engraved flintstone rocks and a mostly dry waterfall.

The rock can be climbed from the car park near Beedoboondu. The excursion can take at least six hours and is 12 km return. There is a shorter walk of six km (2½ hours return) from Ooramboo which also offers elevated views.

Most visitors get to Mt Augustus via remote **Gascoyne Junction**, which is 164 km inland (east) from Carnarvon. The old pub (the Junction Hotel) is the general store and the only source of cold beer before you get to Mt Augustus or Meekatharra.

Places to Stay

Camping is not allowed in the area of Mt Augustus. There's accommodation close to Mt Augustus: *Cobra Station* (☎ (099) 43 0565), formerly the Bangemill Inn established for miners at the nearby El Dorado Goldmine, has rooms for $55 per person (or $72 with all meals); and *Mt Augustus Station/Outback Tourist Resort* (☎ (099) 43 0527), only five km from the humongous monadnock, has tent sites at $8 for two and single/double units for $28/56.

Coral Coast & The Pilbara

This chapter covers two of the most fascinating parts of Australia – the Coral Coast and the Pilbara. The Coral Coast extends from Coral Bay to Onslow and is, without doubt, one of the richest ecotourism destinations in the world. The Pilbara, composed of the oldest rocks in the world, is an ancient, arid region with a glut of natural wonders. It stretches from Onslow to north of Port Hedland and inland beyond the Karijini (Hamersley Range) National Park and several iron-ore towns.

Coral Coast

The Coral Coast is replete with wildlife, amazing vegetation, a coral reef and a perfect climate. Anyone with time should endeavour to visit, if only for a chance to observe wildlife you cannot hope to see elsewhere (see Interaction with Marine Life under Ningaloo Marine Park later). Apart from the ecotourism possibilities, this is a place to take it easy – lie on the beach and enjoy the magnificent climate, snorkel across the very accessible reef and have a meal of prawns or freshly caught fish.

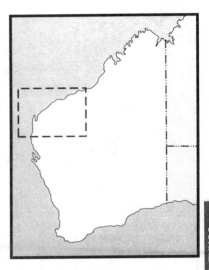

CARNARVON TO NORTH-WEST CAPE

From Carnarvon to Exmouth, via the North-West Coastal Highway, is about 370 km. It is about 145 km from Carnarvon to the first major roadhouse, at Minilya. From the roadhouse it is another eight km to the turn-off to North-West Cape, the Cape Rd.

Some 80 km up the Cape Rd is the turn-off to Coral Bay. The next major turn off is the dirt road which heads off east to Giralia Station and the North-West Coastal Highway; this is used as a short cut to North-West Cape when driving north to south.

CORAL BAY

This town, 150 km south of Exmouth and a whopping 1200 km north of Perth, is an important access point for Ningaloo Marine Park and a popular diving centre. Between April and November the temperature hovers around an equitable 28°C.

Underwater Activities

Coral Bay is at the southern base of Ningaloo Marine Park and a great place for snorkelling. The idyllic lagoon is sandwiched between the Ningaloo coral reef and the coastline and is a great spot for swimming and sunbathing. For those who love to get all their gear off, there is a secluded section of beach known as **'skinny dip corner'**.

Coral Dive (☎ (099) 42 5940) arranges scuba adventures, fills tanks and rents equipment. For those who don't wish to go underwater there are the Glass Bottom Boat and Sub-Sea Explorer (☎ (099) 42 5955) trips which leave from Coral Bay; they cost about $15. This area is also a fishing Mecca and there are a number of charter boats available for game and deep-sea fishing: contact

255

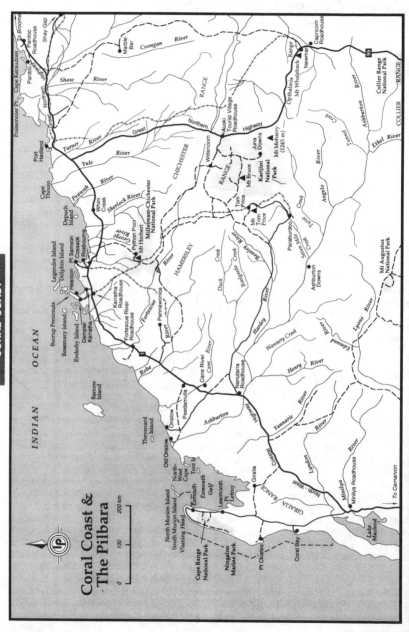

Coral Coast & The Pilbara

Station Stays

If you really want to sample a slice of genuine station life in the red sandy country, then head out to one of the station stays. On the Bullara-Giralia Rd, 43 km from the North-West Coastal Highway, is the 265,000-hectare *Giralia Station* (☎(099) 42 5937). There is a variety of accommodation here including DB&B (dinner, bed & breakfast) for $55 (bookings essential and BYO), shearers' quarters at $10, and camping and caravan sites for $5; all prices are per person. The homestead is near many features in the Pilbara and Gascoyne regions. If you want to sample activities on the station, which runs 25,000 merino sheep, just ask.

There are plenty of other places in the region. In the Kennedy Ranges there is Mt Sandiman Homestead (☎(099) 43 0546) – see under Kennedy Range in the Batavia Coast, Shark Bay & Gascoyne chapter; Manbery (☎(099) 42 5926), Gnaraloo (☎(09) 388 2881) and Boologooroo (☎(099) 42 5907) stations north of Carnarvon; Nallan Station (☎(099) 63 1054) near Cue; Mallina (☎(099) 73 2632), 98 km from Port Hedland; Wooleen Station (☎(099) 63 7973) on the Murchison River; and Cobra Station (☎(099) 43 0565) and Mt Augustus Station (☎(099) 43 0527) in the outback at the head of the Gascoyne River. Go outback! ■

Norstar (☎ (099) 42 5940) and Coral Cruiser (☎ (099) 42 5900).

Places to Stay & Eat

There are two campsites in Coral Bay. The *Peoples Park Caravan Village* (☎ (099) 42 5933) tent/caravan sites are $10/14 per double. The friendlier *Bay View Holiday Village* (☎ (099) 42 5932) in Robinson St has camp/caravan sites. There is backpackers' accommodation with kitchen facilities attached to this complex; the cost is $10 per night. The Coral Bay Hotel also offer backpackers' accommodation but some restrictions apply.

The *Coral Bay Lodge* (☎ (099) 42 5932), on the corner of Robinson and French Sts and also associated with the Bay View, has double units from $80; and the *Ningaloo Reef Resort* (☎ (099) 42 5934) has cabanas from $55 to $90 a double.

There are two places in town for a decent meal: the *Bay View Restaurant* and the *Coral Bay Hotel*. You can get basic supplies from the two caravan parks.

NORTH-WEST CAPE

North-West Cape, a finger of land jutting north into the Indian Ocean, offers a bewildering array of activities for travellers – mainly because of the excellent ecotourism opportunities at Coral Bay, Ningaloo Marine Park and Cape Range National Park.

It was once occupied by the Aborigines but about 150 years ago disease wiped their population out. In this weathered country much of the evidence of their presence has faded rapidly. The Mandu Mandu Creek Rockshelter in the Cape Range is currently being investigated; so far, evidence of the use of shellfish and fish by Aborigines has been dated over 34,000 years old.

During WW II, the area near Wapet Creek on the eastern side of the cape was used as an advance and refuelling base for US submarines; codenamed Operation Potshot, the facility was destroyed by a cyclone in 1945.

Recently the cape was again in the news because of the hush-hush US Navy communications base north of Exmouth which, fortunately, was rendered obsolete at the end of the Cold War.

The cape is a fabulous ecotourism destination with whale sharks, humpbacks, manta rays and colourful schools of fish in and around Ningaloo Reef. In addition, there are many mammals, marine and land reptiles, and abundant avifauna. If you only see one part of WA, this should be it!

NINGALOO MARINE PARK

Running alongside of the North-West Cape for 260 km, from Bundegi Reef in the northeast to Amherst Point in the south-west, is the stunning Ningaloo ('Point of Land') Reef. This miniaturised version of the Great

CORAL COAST

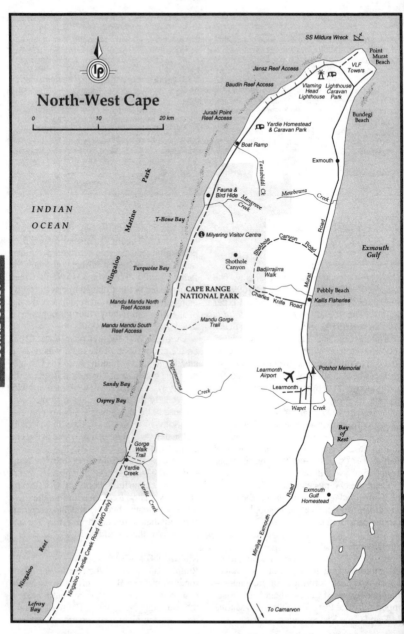

Barrier Reef is actually more accessible – in places it is less than 100 metres offshore. The lagoons enclosed by the reef vary in width from 200 metres to six km.

Within the marine park are eight sanctuary zones – no fishing, only observing. Dugongs are observed, greenback turtles lay their eggs along the cape beaches and placid whale sharks can also be seen just beyond the reef's waters.

Over 220 species of coral have been recorded in the waters of the park, ranging from the slow-growing bommies to delicate branching varieties. For eight to nine nights after the full moon in March, there is a synchronised mass spawning of coral with eggs and sperm being released into the water simultaneously. Once fertilised, the larvae drifts until it settles and begins to build a skeleton, eventually forming into juvenile coral.

Up on the arid coast of Cape Range National Park, fossil corals and fossilised shark's teeth point to an earlier location of the reef. For more information, get a copy of the CALM publication *Coral Reefs of Western Australia* ($3).

Every year, humpback whales pass close by the coast on their way north in June and July to their calving grounds, probably near the Montebello Islands. In October and November they return to Antarctica.

In November, turtles come up the beaches at night when the tide is right to lay their eggs. This usually happens from November to January near the top end of North-West Cape.

Contact the CALM office (☎ (099) 49 1676) in Thew St for more specific information. Get a copy of the excellent *Parks of the Coral Coast* pamphlet from there; special fishing regulations apply in this park. For information on local marine life, get the excellent *The Marine Fishes of North-West Australia* by Gerald Allen & Roger Swainston (Perth, 1988).

It would be environmentally suicidal to allow oil drilling anywhere in the North-West Cape region. The WA Government legislated in 1994 to prevent drilling in the marine park – we can only hope this decision remains the status quo.

Interaction with Marine Life

Whale-shark *(Rhiniodon typus)* observing goes on from late-March to the end of May. The largest number of whale sharks are seen off the Tantabiddi and Mangrove Bay areas. The season begins at the time of coral spawning and there is a plankton bloom at the same time. The best way to see them is by licensed charter vessel (after they have been initially spotted by aircraft). About 12 boats were allowed to take trips out to them in 1993, some of these were not local. Exmouth Diving Centre provide full equipment and daily refreshment for $299. This company has a 100% encounter success rate. Contact the Exmouth Diving Centre (☎ (099) 49 1201) about the wide range of diving possibilities.

It is not guaranteed that you will see manta rays every day. Enquire at the dive centre as they will know where they are if their spotter plane has been out recently. Manta rays are seen from July to November. You can fly underwater with them as part of a normal

CORAL COAST

Whale Sharks
Sharks have always been the subject of morbid fascination for visitors to Australia, especially the deadly great white which frequents the Southern Ocean. However the largest of the sharks (and indeed all fish), the whale shark, is a gentle giant. One of the few places in the world where you can see this leviathan is off Ningaloo Reef, near Exmouth. To swim with them is to participate in one of the natural wonders of the world. The best time to visit is at the end of summer.

The whale shark weighs up to 40,000 kg, is up to 18 metres long and drifts slowly across ocean currents filtering water for the plankton and small fish they feed on. They also eat an awful lot of rubbish. In the stomach of one a wallet, boot, bucket and part of an oar were discovered. The whale shark's scientific name 'rhini-odon' means 'file tooth', referring to the shark's 300 or more bands of minute teeth. ■

dive charter; this costs $25 per dive and daily rental of equipment is $50.

The dive centre organises trips to the Muiron Islands, 10 km north-east of the cape, on demand. These islands are a breeding sanctuary for three species of turtle: green, loggerhead and hawksbill. During dives it is possible to hand feed the 1.5-metre-long potato cod *(Epinephalus tukula)* at the 'cod house'. See all the marine attractions as you gain an accredited diving qualification.

EXMOUTH

Exmouth (population 2500) was established in 1967 largely as a service centre for the US navy communications base. It now provides a good focus for the many great activities in the area. On no account should it be allowed to become a supply and administrative centre for multi-national oil companies drilling in and around Ningaloo Marine Park! (Hang out locals, the world will come to you eventually.) The well-organised Exmouth tourist office (☎ (099) 49 1176), on Thew St, has a video display. It is open daily from 9 am to 5 pm. The CALM office is in the same complex.

Things to See & Do

There's a shell museum on Pellew St and the town beach at the end of Warne St is quite popular. About 13 km south of town is **Pebbly Beach**, a safe swimming beach covered in colourful pebbles. The wreck of the **SS Mildura**, beached in 1907, and the **Vlaming Head Lighthouse** are north of town and have sensational views.

Part of North-West Cape is rendered ugly by 13 low-frequency transmitter stations. Twelve are higher than the Eiffel Tower, which serve to support the 13th, which is 396 metres high – the tallest structure in the southern hemisphere.

Organised Tours

There is a host of tours in the area ranging from gulf and gorge safaris to reef and fishing tours. Perhaps the most informative is Neil Mcleod's Ningaloo Safari Tours

(☎ (099) 49 1550); the full-day safari, called 'Over the Top' (10 hours, $75) has been recommended by many travellers.

At Exmouth Backpackers' (☎ (099) 49 1101) you can arrange a four-day trip to Karijini National Park for $300; everything supplied. During the season they do turtle tours, walks in Yardie Creek and abseiling and rockclimbing with the group Adventure Out. Peter Turner, manager of the backpackers', tends to make sure you get out on a trip regardless of numbers.

Near the Walkabout Cafe you will find the Coral Coast Tourist Centre (☎ (099) 49 1625) which incorporates West Coast Safaris and the semi-submersible Ningaloo Coral Explorer which operates over Bundegi Reef. Exmouth Air Charters (☎ (099) 49 2182) conducts scenic flights.

Places to Stay

The accommodation in and around Exmouth can be quite expensive. There are a number of caravan parks around town. At the *Exmouth Caravan Park* (☎ (099) 49 1331), Lefroy St, tent and caravan sites are $12 a double; it is a bit run down. The *Norcape Lodge Caravan Park* (☎ (099) 49 1908), Truscott Crescent, has tent/caravan sites for $12/15. At Vlaming Head, the *Lighthouse Caravan Park* (☎ (099) 49 1478) has on-site vans for $30. There is a good surfing nearby.

The *Exmouth Cape Tourist Village* (☎ (099) 49 1101), on the corner of Truscott Crescent and Murat Rd, has tent sites/on-site vans/chalets at $11/32/58 for two and the town's only backpackers' for $12 per night; they also have a very cold swimming pool.

The *Potshot Hotel Resort* (☎ (099) 49 1200), Murat Rd, has self-contained units from $90 a double and single/double hotel rooms for $40/50. *Norcape Lodge* (☎ (099) 49 1334), in Truscott Crescent, has single/double rooms for $40/50 and the *Argosy Court Holiday Units* (☎ (099) 49 1177) in Murat Rd has two-bedroom units at $70 for five people.

At Minilya Bridge, seven km south of where the road to Exmouth forks away from the North-West Coastal Highway, is the

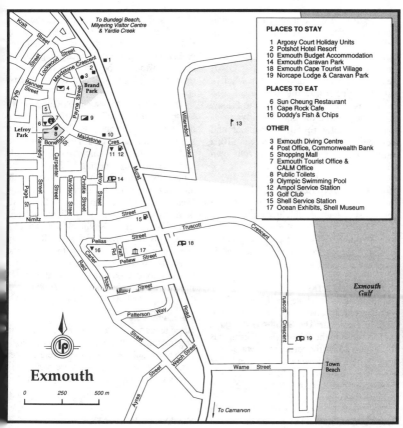

Exmouth

0   250   500 m

To Bundegi Beach,
Milyering Visitor Centre
& Yardie Creek

To Camarvon

Exmouth
Gulf

Town
Beach

PLACES TO STAY

1   Argosy Court Holiday Units
2   Potshot Hotel Resort
10 Exmouth Budget Accommodation
14 Exmouth Caravan Park
18 Exmouth Cape Tourist Village
19 Norcape Lodge & Caravan Park

PLACES TO EAT

6   Sun Cheung Restaurant
11 Cape Rock Cafe
16 Doddy's Fish & Chips

OTHER

3   Exmouth Diving Centre
4   Post Office, Commonwealth Bank
5   Shopping Mall
7   Exmouth Tourist Office &
    CALM Office
8   Public Toilets
9   Olympic Swimming Pool
12 Ampol Service Station
13 Golf Club
15 Shell Service Station
17 Ocean Exhibits, Shell Museum

CORAL COAST

Swagman Caravan Facility. It has typical roadhouse fare and units for $25/35.

Places to Eat

The number of places is growing rapidly in response to increased tourism. There are a number of takeaway shops in the main shopping area of town including *So and So's Pizza*, *Shell's Coffee Bar*, *Judy's Fast Food* and the *Walkabout Cafe*. The *Cape Rock Cafe* is on the corner of Lefroy St and Maidstone Crescent.

Fish & chips are a regional speciality – in town go to *Doddy's* and out of town try *MG*

Kailis' prawn palace, 25 km south, open May to November. At the latter, the annual prawn catch is as much as a million kg – perhaps that explains why there are so many Porsches in the township. The *Sun Cheung* Chinese restaurant is next door to the tourist office. Two hotels, the *Potshot Hotel* and *Norcape Lodge*, have buffet and à la carte meals.

Getting There & Away

Ansett Australia has a jet service once daily between Perth and Exmouth for $349 Apex return ($311 one-way), except Saturday.

Three times a week there is a Greyhound Pioneer service to Exmouth from Perth (Sunday, Tuesday and Friday). From Exmouth to Perth, services are Saturday, Monday and Thursday; the cost is $147. Westliner buses also pass through Minilya daily on their Perth-Derby run.

There is a shuttle bus, Monday to Friday, which goes from Exmouth to Minilya roadhouse to meet Greyhound Pioneer and Westliner buses. The cost one way is $10; a good option if you don't have your own vehicle.

CAPE RANGE NATIONAL PARK
The 510 sq km park, which runs down the west coast of the cape, includes the modern Milyering visitor's centre, a wide variety of flora & fauna, 50 km of good swimming beaches, gorges (including scenic Yardie Creek) and rugged scenery.

Things to See & Do
The impressive Shothole and Charles Knife gorges are, respectively, 16 km and 23 km south of Exmouth. The **Shothole Gorge** is not like those in the Pilbara. Weathering has not occurred with permanent water but through periodic downpours and wind. The wind is a feature of the climate here as it blows continually across the cape, usually from west to east.

The view from above **Charles Knife Gorge** is memorable. In front are the eroded limestone walls of the gorge and far beyond, the azure waters of Exmouth Gulf. The two gorges are connected by the four-km **Badgirragirra Walk**.

There is a 4WD-only track which crosses the range near Learmonth. It is not recommended you take the drive yourself as it is easy to get lost. About half way along this 45-km track is **Owl's Roost Cave**, which you descend into by climbing down a wild fig root. Along the sandy track are flowering shrubs and trees including species of wattle, grevillea and banksia. The view as you come down from the range to Ningaloo Reef near Osprey Bay, is nothing short of stunning.

The Milyering visitor centre (☎ (099) 49 2808) is 52 km from Exmouth on the west coast. Built in rammed-earth style, it is solar powered and has waste disposal. A comprehensive display of the area's natural and cultural history can be seen here. It is usually open from 10 am to 4 pm during tourist season.

The saltwater **Yardie Creek Gorge** is 40 km to the south of Milyering. Here, the deep blue waters of the gorge are held back by a sand bar. You can easily see the black-footed wallaby on the multi-coloured canyon walls and a number of species of birds in and around the water. One-hour long boat tours are conducted up the gorge on Monday, Wednesday and Saturday and cost $15 (children $8). A trip up the gorge is included as part of Neil McLeod's Ningaloo Safari.

Suitably equipped (4WD) vehicles can continue south to Coral Bay following the coast. The road is signposted and there is a turn-off to the picturesque Point Cloates lighthouse.

Places to Stay
Basic tent and caravan sites are available in larger camps in the park (☎ (099) 49 1676) at $5 per double per night (there were 97 sites available in 1994). Make sure you bring plenty of water; there are no supplies within the park.

MINILYA TO KARRATHA
From Minilya it is about 110 km north to the dirt road that heads west to Giralia Station, used as a short-cut to the cape when driving the North-West Coastal Highway from north to south. (You may have missed it but about 50 km north of Minilya you crossed the Tropic of Capricorn.) The Yannarie River crossing is 41 km north of the Giralia Station turn-off but the Barradale Roadhouse, not far from the bridge, has been closed.

Don't despair as it is only another 70 km to *Nanutarra Roadhouse* (☎ (099) 43 0521) on the Ashburton River, which is some 2 hours. There is a caravan park with tent/powered sites/air-con cabins at $6/12/35 for two; there is also a licensed restaurant

Importantly, there is a qualified motor mechanic on duty.

There is a turn east to the company mining towns of the Pilbara (Tom Price and Paraburdoo) and Karijini (Hamersley Range) National Park after Nanutarra. North of this, perhaps 35 km, is the westward road to Onslow and not far beyond, the eastwards turn off to Cane River Station. This station manufactures the ubiquitous canvas swags you see unfurled at many campsites.

Some 78 km from the Onslow junction is another eastward road to Pannawonica, a mining town 46 km off the highway. From this road junction it is another 41 km up the highway to the *Fortescue River Roadhouse* (☎ (091) 84 5126), the last of the roadhouses before Karratha and some 545 km north of Carnarvon; powered sites/rooms are $15/35 for two.

All in all, it's a bloody long way between drinks.

ONSLOW

The original Onslow, near the mouth of the Ashburton River, came into being in 1883 and was named after the then Chief Justice of WA. It was the centre for pearling, mining and pastoral industries.

Old Onslow was abandoned in 1925 and relocated to Beadon Bay. The 'new' town (population 600), 81 km from the North-West Coastal Highway, has the dubious distinction of being the southernmost WA town to be bombed in WW II (in 1943). It was later used as a base by the British, in the 1950s, for nuclear testing in the Montebello Islands.

Onslow is often hit by cyclones and, in 1963, one flattened the town. Today, Onslow is the mainland base for offshore oil exploration and production, and a supply base for Barrow Island (80 km to the north) and the Saladin Islands. Many people visit Onslow in winter for the fishing; the daily temperatures are between 25°C and 30°C during this time.

Montebello Islands

The Montebellos are a group of more than 100 flat limestone islands which are off the north-west coast of WA between Onslow and Karratha. They range in size from Hermite, at 1000 hectares, the largest, to small islets and rocks of about one hectare. In 1992 they were gazetted as a conservation park administered by CALM.

In 1622, the survivors of the shipwreck of the *Tryal* camped here before setting off north to the East Indies. The islands were named by the French explorer Baudin in 1801 after the battle of Monte Bello. The pearlers who came next were responsible for the introduction of the black rat and the cat which ensured the extinction on the island of the golden bandicoot and the spectacled hare-wallaby.

My, oh my, isn't nature resilient. In 1952 the British, in an operation codenamed Hurricane, detonated an atomic weapon mounted on HMS *Plym* anchored in Main Bay off Trimouille Island. Two further atomic tests were carried out in 1956, on Alpha and Trimouille Islands.

Some 40 years later we can finally step ashore and get close to a real 'ground zero', the point of detonation of an atomic weapon. I wonder how long the radiation warning signs last before being souvenired by collectors of the macabre. 'Ladies and gentlemen, your guide today is Dr Strangelove and he would like to show you a number of mutating species of fish and a coral reef that *always* glows in the dark.'

As I said, nature is resilient. The islands have thriving populations of both land and marine fauna and more than 100 plant species, including a stand of mangroves. The legless lizard *Aprasia rostrata* is found only on Hermite Island. (Was it legless before or after 1952?) Two species of marine turtle are known to nest on the islands, as are a number of seabirds. Vignerons will love the names applied to many of the bays; hock, champagne, burgundy, claret and moselle, for example.

Beautiful mountains the islands are not. They are, rather, silent witnesses to the awesome destructive power of 'Energy equals mass times the speed of light squared' and the miraculous, recuperative powers of nature. ∎

Information

The Onslow tourist office (☎ (091) 84 6001) is in the shire of Ashburton building on Second Ave.

Things to See & Do

Located on Second Ave is the Onslow Goods Shed **museum** which displays items of historical interest.

There is good swimming and fishing in the area; anglers head for the Beadon Creek Groyne and Four Mile Creek or out to sea for deep-sea fishing. The **Old Onslow ruins**, 48 km from town, include a gaol and a post office; worth a look if you are in the area.

Places to Stay & Eat

The *Ocean View Caravan Park* (☎ (091) 84 6053) on Second Ave, has tent sites/on-site vans at $14/30 for two; and the new *Beadon Bay Village* (☎ (091) 84 6042), on Beadon Creek Rd, has powered sites at $14 for two. The *Beadon Bay Hotel* (☎ (091) 84 6002), Second Ave, has rooms for $45/55 and the motel units are $70/80 for singles/doubles. The *Onslow Sun Chalets* (☎ (091) 84 6058) are on Second Ave; the beach units are $65/75/85 for singles/doubles/triples.

While haute cuisine is not one of Onslow's strong points – there is a bakery, fish shop and the *Main Street Cafe* – the opportunity to DIY is immense. In the waters off Onslow are at least a dozen varieties of table fish, so bait your hook and then cook your own catch. Fancy coral trout, mud crab or red emperor washed down with a Margaret River semillon? Then you must bring the semillon!

Getting There & Away

You really need your own transport to get in and out of Onslow. The Greyhound Pioneer and Westliner buses will drop you at the junction of the Onslow Rd and the North-West Coastal Highway but you have to hitch the 81 km to town; it costs about $105 from Perth to the turn-off.

DIRECTION & MACKEREL ISLANDS

Offshore, 11km and 22 km respectively from Onslow, are Direction & Mackerel Islands

(☎ (09) 388 2020; fax 388 1978). The tariff of $540 to $620/$1080 to $1240 for single/double full board for the week includes boat transfers to the six-km by 1.5-km coral atoll of Thevenard in the Mackerel Islands.

Crayfish and oysters are rife for those who know where to look, as are Spanish mackerel, schnapper, groper and red emperor for the keen fishing enthusiast. They didn't tell you about the huge oil tanks that dominate the island. Just ignore them, they are included in the price.

Direction Island has only one furnished cabin which sleeps eight; its pricing structure is a mystery known only to its Perth-based owner. Listening to all the money talk may be worthwhile as Direction has its own reef on one side and a beach on the other. One major plus, the islands support many species of birdlife including the majestic osprey.

The Pilbara

The Pilbara (meaning 'freshwater fish'), which contains some of the hottest country on earth, is the iron-ore and natural-gas-producing area accounting for much of WA's prosperity. Gigantic machines are used to tear the dusty red ranges apart. It's isolated, harsh and fabulously wealthy. The Pilbara towns are almost all company towns: either mining centres where the ore is wrenched from the earth or ports from which it's shipped abroad. Exceptions are the mystical islands of the Dampier Archipelago, the beautiful gorges of Karijini (Hamersley Range) National Park and earlier historic centres like Marble Bar and Cossack.

If you are travelling away from the main coastal highway in this area in your own vehicle, always carry a lot of extra water – 20 litres per person is a sensible amount – and check that you have enough fuel to get to the next petrol station. If travelling into remote areas, make sure you tell someone your travel plans, and don't leave your vehicle if you are stranded.

KARRATHA

Karratha ('good country'), the commercial centre for the area, is on Nickol Bay and some 1535 km from Perth. It is the fastest growing town (population 10,800) in the Pilbara and was developed due to the rapid expansion of the Hamersley Iron and Woodside LNG projects.

The rich town is now the hub of the coastal Pilbara. Ask the average householder how much they pay for air-conditioning and you will realise that Karratha gets hot in summer; winter is the best time to visit the Pilbara.

Information

The new Karratha & Districts tourist office (☎ (091) 44 4600), on Karratha Rd just before you reach the T-intersection of Dampier and Millstream Rds, has heaps of information on what to see and do in the Pilbara. CALM's north-west regional office is in the SGIO building, Welcome Rd, and the staff here are most helpful considering they are, daily, juggling issues of conservation and development whilst continually being prodded by their Perth overlords.

Travellers coming from the north will revel in the offerings at Karratha's shopping complex in Welcome Rd. There is a Coles, K-Mart, Woolworths, Treasureway and over 50 other speciality shops. Sounds funny to cover this in a guidebook? Wait and see!

Things to See & Do

There are good views from the lookout at **TV Hill**, and **Miaree Pool**, 35 km to the south-west, is scenic and a good place to cool off. The Karratha **salt flats** are a great place to go birdwatching; dawn and dusk are the best viewing times.

Jaburara Heritage Trail The area around town is replete with evidence of Aboriginal occupation: carvings, grindstones, etchings and middens are all located on the 3.5-km Jaburara Heritage Trail which starts near the tourist office. Jaburara (pronounced 'Yabura') is the name of the former Aboriginal inhabitants of the Karratha region. At first glance the trail looks like a huge pile of rocks sticking out of the spinifex; don't be fooled as it is an enlightening journey into the past.

The Aboriginal carvings found along the ridge, which depict various life forms and totemic themes, were carved with chert and dolerite tools; these carvings are estimated to be 5000 to 6000 years old. There are also a number of artefact scatters of stone material and shell middens. Flat rocks adjacent to one of the creeks on the trail were used for grinding spinifex and other seeds.

Most interesting, however, are the **talu sites**, or spiritual repositories, which are represented predominantly by physical features. The major talu site here is the large dolerite rock outcrop known as Warramurrangka, the giant flying fox.

It is likely that you will see the euro (wallaroo) on the trail. The short-beaked echidna (spiny anteater or 'biggada' to the Aborigines) is another common animal in the region. You may see evidence of the pebble-mound mouse but it is unlikely that you will see this diminutive creature (see under Pebble-Mound Mouse in this chapter). Reptiles include the ring-tailed dragon (*Amphibolurus caudicinctus*) and Australia's largest lizard, the perentie (*Varanus giganteus*). The *Terminalia canescens*, a tree that grows in the creek beds here, is a reminder of a former and much different tropical climate.

Tackle this walk in the early morning as climbing these hills at midday is an effort. The walk will be made all the more rewarding if you take a copy of *Jaburara Heritage Trail* with you ($1.50).

Pebble-Mound Mouse

This mouse *(Pseudomys chapmani)*, which is unique to the Pilbara, is a recent discovery. It is found living between clumps of spinifex in shallow burrows upon which it heaps a relatively flat mound of pebbles.

The carefully selected pebbles are small but the actual mound can be up to 50 cm high. The pebbles are meticulously placed around the entrance of the burrow to provide insulation and moisture. ■

THE PILBARA

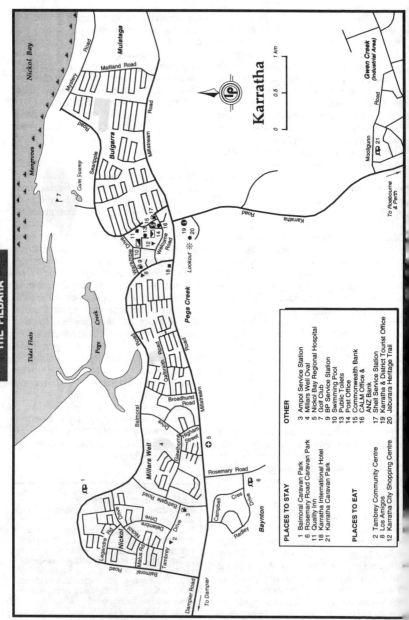

Karratha

1 km

0   0.5

PLACES TO STAY

1 Balmoral Caravan Park
6 Rosemary Road Caravan Park
11 Quality Inn
18 Karratha International Hotel
21 Karratha Caravan Park

PLACES TO EAT

2 Tambrey Community Centre
8 Los Amigos
12 Karratha City Shopping Centre

OTHER

3 Ampol Service Station
4 Millars Well Oval
5 Nickol Bay Regional Hospital
7 Golf Club
9 BP Service Station
10 Swimming Pool
13 Public Toilets
14 Post Office
15 Commonwealth Bank
16 CALM Office &
   ANZ Bank
17 Shell Service Station
19 Karratha & District Tourist Office
20 Jaburara Heritage Trail

Festivals
The Fe-NaCl-NG Festival (pronounced
'fernarkling') is held in August each year.
The title of the festival combines the chemical abbreviations of the region's main natural
resources – iron, salt and natural gas.

Places to Stay
There are three caravan parks in Karratha:
Fleetwood's Balmoral Rd (☎ (091) 85 3628)
and *Fleetwood's Rosemary Rd* (☎ (091) 85
1855) have powered sites at $15 for two; and
Karratha Caravan Park (☎ (091) 85 1012),
Mooligunn Rd, has powered sites/on-site
vans for $15/38 for two.

The up-market choices are expensive. The
Karratha International Hotel (☎(091) 85
3111), on the corner of Millstream and Hillview
Rds, is $110/125 for singles/ doubles and the
Quality Inn (☎ (091) 85 1155), Searipple Rd,
is $102/112. Both of these places have swim-
ming pools, although the kid-friendly
Tambrey Community Centre (no accommodation) is the best place for a dip.

Places to Eat
On Balmoral Rd in Karratha, *Los Amigos*,
opposite the BP station, has Mexican food
(Wednesday is 'el cheapo' night with four
courses for $11.50). The *Universal* on the
same road prepares good Chinese food.

For a snack, there are a number of cafes
and takeaway places in the Karratha shopping centre, including *Adriennes Cafe*,
Paradiso Pizza, *West Siam* and *Wendy's
Super Sundae*.

A little out of town, the *Tambrey Community Centre* has a tavern and serves good
counter meals, and the Karratha International has the licensed *Finches Restaurant*.

Getting There & Away
By far the most convenient way is by air and
Ansett Australia has daily jet services. There
are a couple of bus services which drop off
in Karratha; Greyhound Pioneer (☎ 13 2030)
and Westliner (☎ (09) 250 3318) have daily
services (about $110 from Perth); they both
use the Shell Roadhouse on Searipple Rd as

their depot. Most people coming to Karratha,
however, arrive by car.

DAMPIER
Dampier (population 2000), 20 km from
Karratha, is on King Bay and faces the other
41 islands of the Dampier Archipelago
(named after the explorer William Dampier
who passed in 1699).

Dampier is a Hamersley Iron town and the
port for Tom Price and Paraburdoo iron-ore
operations. Gas from the huge natural-gas
fields of the North-West Shelf is piped
ashore nearby on the Burrup Peninsula.
From there, it is piped to Perth and the
Pilbara, or liquefied as part of the huge
Woodside Petroleum project and exported to
Japan and South Korea.

Dampier has mild, sunny winters with the
temperatures in the high 20's but in summer
it is very hot.

Information
The information office is in the King Bay
Holiday Village (☎ (091) 83 1440), The
Esplanade. If you need permits to drive along
Hamersley Iron's service road to Karijini
National Park, they are obtained from the
security office at their depot on Dampier Rd.

Things to See & Do
An inspection of the port facilities can be
arranged (☎ (091) 44 4600). The William
Dampier Lookout provides a fine view over
the harbour and the **Woodside LNG
Visitors' Centre** (☎ (091) 83 8100) is open
weekdays 9 am to 4.30 pm during the tourist
season.

Train enthusiasts are well catered for in
this region. There is the Pilbara Railways
Historical Society **museum**, 10 km before
Dampier on the Dampier Rd, which features
the *Pendennis Castle*, supposedly the fastest
steam engine in the world. The museum is
open on Sunday from 10 am until noon; trips
along the Hamersley Iron railway are periodically organised by the society (☎ (091) 85
2894).

Nearby **Hearson's Cove** is a popular
beach and picnic area, as is **Dampier Beach**.

The explorer FT Gregory landed at Hearson's Cove in 1861 – it was his positive reports that led to settlement of the region.

The **Burrup Peninsula** has some 10,000 Aboriginal rock engravings depicting fish, turtles, euros, wallabies and a Tasmanian tiger. It is one of the most prolific sites for prehistoric rock art in the world. Particularly fascinating are the 'climbing figures', a short walk off the road near the North-West Shelf Project's onshore treatment plant. As you look back from the cluster of ancient rocks, the retorts, storage tanks and other impedimenta of the modern age, block the view of the sea which the ancient carvers would once have seen.

The Dampier Archipelago is renowned as a game-fishing Mecca and each year during the Fe-NaCl-NG Festival, it hosts the Dampier Classic.

Dampier Archipelago National Park The Dampier Archipelago of over 40 islands was formed some 6000 to 8000 years ago when rising sea levels flooded coastal valleys. The islands are in a 45-km radius of the town of Dampier and it is 20 minutes by boat to the nearest island and about two hours from the farthest.

The islands have seen the coming and going of pearling, attempts at pastoralism and whaling. For about three years in the late 1800s there was a whaling station on Malus Island which processed humpback whales, harpooned from longboats.

The relative isolation of the islands from predators has meant there are a number of nesting colonies of birds such as fairy and bridled terns, and four species of turtle use the beaches for egg-laying. A number of mammal species, including the Rothschild's rock wallaby (*Petrogale rothschildi*), inhabit the islands.

Access to all the islands is by boat from the ramps at Dampier, Samson, Wickham, Cossack and Nickol Bay (Karratha). In winter, a Coral Coast Tours charter boat (☎ (091) 83 1077) cruises the archipelago. CALM have produced a good pamphlet, *The Dampier Archipelago: Islands in the Sun*, free from their offices.

Depuch Island, accessible by boat from a road that heads north from Whim Creek, is a mystical, spiritual place with many pteroglyphs. Check with CALM in Karratha about access conditions to the island.

Places to Stay & Eat

Apart from the transit caravan park (☎ (091) 83 1109) on The Esplanade, which has tent/powered sites for $7/14 for two, there is no longer budget accommodation in Dampier. The *King Bay Holiday Village* (☎ (091) 83 1440) on The Esplanade, has expensive units at $79 for a double. (In one publication it is described as 'uncharismatic' and I would have to agree.) They do, however, have bicycles for hire. Also in Dampier is the *Mermaid Hotel* (☎ (091) 83 1222), The Esplanade, which has comfortable singles/doubles for $75/85.

The *Captain's Galley*, also on The Esplanade and overlooking Hampton Harbour, is good for fish & chips. There is a Chinese restaurant in the shopping centre and the *Harbour Lights* restaurant is part of the King Bay Holiday complex.

ROEBOURNE AREA

The Roebourne and district area is a busy little enclave of historic towns and modern port facilities. Wickham is the port for the iron ore produced at Tom Price and Pannawonica, Point Samson is a great fishing spot and Cossack is a very picturesque and historic town. This area holds the beginnings of European settlement of the north-west.

Aboriginal History

Aborigines have occupied the area around Roebourne for at least 20,000 years, according to radio-carbon dating of recovered artefacts. The Ngaluma people inhabited the flood country from the Maitland River to Peewah River, which covers about 6400 sq km. There were three divisions of this grouping: two were west and east of the Harding

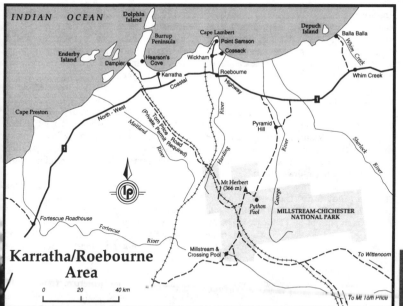

Karratha/Roebourne Area

River and the other occupied the Burrup Peninsula and were known as the Jaburara.

Numerous shell middens remain, including a number just on the outskirts of Karratha. The Ngaluma constructed spinifex fishing nets and etched symbolic motifs into thousands of rocks. When the first settlers came, they employed the Aborigines as labourers and shepherds and paid them with goods. Introduced diseases, such as smallpox and measles, soon took their toll.

For a while there was an uneasy peace between the two groups. There were a number of massacres and in one clash in 1868, known as the Flying Foam massacre, between 40 and 60 Aborigines were killed as a retaliatory measure to the spearing of four people. The Aborigines who remained were forced into working on pastoral leases, some were even forced to dive for pearl shells.

In the 1930s, several neighbouring Aboriginal tribes – the Gurruma, Injibandi,

Banjima and Marduthunia – were moved into reserves in Roebourne and Onslow, in an effort to reduce administrative costs. The main groups found today in the Roebourne area are Injibandi and Ngaluma. The Jaburara are gone but their curious etchings survive.

Information

The Roebourne District tourist office (☎ (091) 82 1060) is in the Old Gaol, Queen St, Roebourne. If in Cossack, the Heritage Council officials will help. For information about activities in Point Samson go to the fisheries building (☎ (091) 87 1414) in Point Samson Rd. There is a laundromat in the Victoria Hotel-Mt Welcome Motel complex in Roebourne and a good supermarket in Wickham. If possible, get a copy of the *Emma Withnell Heritage Trail* brochure; it outlines a 52-km walk/drive which includes Cossack, Roebourne, Wickham and Point Samson.

Roebourne

Roebourne (population 1700), 39 km from Karratha, is the oldest existing town in the Pilbara. It has a history of grazing, gold and copper mining, and was once the capital of the north-west. It is the oldest town between Port Gregory, near Geraldton, and Palmerston and there are still some fine old buildings to be seen. These include an **old gaol**, the **1888 Union Bank**, a **church** built in 1894 and the **Victoria Hotel** which is the last of the five original pubs. The town was once connected to Cossack, 13 km away on the coast, by a horse-drawn tram.

Places to Stay & Eat There is the *Harding River Caravan Park* (☎ (091) 82 1063) with tent/caravan sites at $8/11 for two. The *Mt Welcome Motel*, in Roe St, is the main accommodation with singles/doubles for $40/60; backpackers can stay here in the motel units for $12 per person.

The *Roebourne Diner*, good for eat in and takeaway, and the more up-market *Poinciana Room* are in the Victoria Hotel-Mt Welcome Motel. Also on Roe St is a snack bar, open seven days, and the BP Roadhouse for takeaways and supplies.

Cossack

This is a fascinating town with many intact early buildings. It was originally known as Tien Tsin Harbour after the barque which carried the first settlers (Walter Padbury and his party) there in 1863. It was given its present name when the HMS *Cossack*, with Governor Weld aboard, visited the town in 1871.

Cossack was a bustling town and the main port for the district in the mid to late 19th century. Cossack's boom was short lived and Point Samson soon supplanted it as the chief port for the area. The sturdy old buildings date from 1870 to 1898, and much of the ghost town has been restored as a continuing 1988 bicentennial project.

The town now includes an **art gallery** in the post office (built in 1884), **museum** in the 1895 stone-brick courthouse and budget accommodation in the police barracks (built

in 1897). Other buildings in the town are Galbraith's store (1891), the bakehouse, a custom house/bond store (1896), the post & telegraph building (1884), schoolhouse (1897) and mining Registrar's quarters and mercantile store (1895).

Beyond town, there's a **pioneer cemetery** with a small Japanese section dating from the old pearl diving days. In fact, this is where pearling actually began; it later moved on to Broome in the 1890s. There are a couple of good lookouts and excellent beaches in the area; the cooler, drier months are best for a visit.

Obtain *Cossack Historic Walk* ($1.50) and *Cossack: The First Port in the North-West* (50c) when you get to the town. All proceeds go towards restoration of the town.

The Staircase to the Moon, viewed from Reader's Point Lookout, is legendary. It comes across an average of 50 km of marsh and lasts for ages. For trivia buffs, all seven of the species of mangrove found in the Pilbara occur near the Cossack boat ramp. There is a great swimming spot at Settler's Beach.

Places to Stay *Cossack Backpackers* (☎ (091) 82 1190) is one of those gems of the road. In the old police barracks you can truly get away from it all. The dorm rooms are $9, there is a kitchen, refrigerators and hot and cold shower. There is also a small shop nearby. For $136, two persons get two night's accommodation and use of a 3.8 metre powerboat. As there are no places to eat, bring your own food from Wickham, six km away. If you ring in advance the proprietors will pick you up from the bus depot in Wickham. They do two runs each day. Brian, the custodian of Cossack, is one of the characters of the Pilbara – ask him about the early days.

Wickham & Point Samson

Wickham is a Robe River Iron town, handling their ore-exporting facilities 10 km away at Cape Lambert, where the jetty is three km long (one of the highest and longest open ocean wharves in Australia). Ore is railed there from the mining operations inland at Pannawonica.

Point Samson, beyond Wickham, took the place of Cossack when the old port silted up. In turn, it has been replaced by the modern port facilities of Dampier and Cape Lambert. The name comes from Michael Samson, who accompanied Walter Padbury, the first settler, on his 1863 journey.

There are good beaches at Point Samson and at nearby **Honeymoon Cove**. You can explore **Samson Reef** at low tide for coral and oysters. If you have any queries about the area, the friendly people at Point Samson Fisheries (☎ (091) 87 1414) will answer them.

Places to Stay & Eat In Wickham, the *Wickham Hotel* (☎ (091) 87 1204), on Wickham Drive, has singles/doubles for $70/80. *Samson Accommodation* (☎ (091) 87 1052), at 56 Samson Rd, Point Samson, has budget rooms for $37 for two and units at $72/82 for doubles/triples. The *Solveig Caravan Park* (☎ (091) 87 1414), Samson Rd, has tent/powered caravan sites for $13/15 for two.

It's also worth detouring to Point Samson for the seafood. *Trawlers* is a licensed restaurant overlooking the pier. Underneath, in the same building, is *Moby's Kitchen*, where you can get excellent fish, chips & salad. It is a popular place for locals (from Wickham, Roebourne and Karratha) to head to on weekends.

WHIM CREEK
The site of the first significant Pilbara mineral find was at Whim Creek, 80 km east of Roebourne. It once had a copper mine and all that is left is the great, old *Whim Creek Hotel* (☎ (091) 76 4953) which has accommodation and a restaurant; tent and caravan sites are free, backpackers' accommodation is $10 per person and single/double rooms are $30/35.

COMPANY' TOWNS
The Pilbara is the home of the company town. For a start there needs to be a salary earner in the family to at least pay the air-con bill. It was big companies that built most of the towns as dormitories for their workers and supply/administrative bases for their mining projects.

Dampier, Karratha, Shay Gap, Newman, Paraburdoo, Pannawonica and Tom Price all owe their existence to big mining companies. They invariably have a variety of sports facilities which always fall second in popularity behind the tavern or worker's club. Sky TV, dirt-bike racing, stock cars, takeaway food and 'eclectic' videos are the stock in trade of these communities.

Tom Price
This iron-ore town, south-west of Wittenoom, is the 'big daddy' of the Pilbara's company towns and belongs to Hamersley Iron. Built in 1962, it is even named after a mining expert, Thomas Moore Price of the giant US Kaiser Steel Corporation. The umbilical cord of the town is the railway line to Dampier, on the coast.

Check with Hamersley Iron (☎ (091) 89 2375) in Tom Price about inspecting the open-cut mine works – if nothing else, the scale of it will impress you. Conducted weekdays only, the tours cost a hefty $9 (they should pay you).

Mt Nameless (1128 metres), four km west of Tom Price, is the highest accessible mountain in the state. It offers good views of the area especially at sunset.

Places to Stay & Eat The *Tom Price Caravan Park* (☎ (091) 89 1515) has tent/powered sites for $10/13 for two and on-site vans at $35 for two. *Hillview Lodge* (☎ (091)89 1625), Stadium Rd, has expensive singles/doubles for $85/95. The *Tom Price Hotel* (☎ (091)89 1101) is also expensive with single/double units for $75/85.

The *Red Emperor* cafe and the *Milk Bar Tom Price & Chinese takeaway* (their title) in the shopping mall, provide reasonable food and the *Tom Price Hotel* has standard counter meals. Self-caterers can buy their ingredients from Charlie Carters in Central Rd.

THE PILBARA

Paraburdoo

This Hamersley Iron town, some 79 km south of Tom Price, was built in 1970 to service local iron-ore operations. In the local Aboriginal language, 'Piru-Pardu', loosely translated means 'meat feathers' after the abundance of sulphur-crested cockatoos in the area. Paraburdoo's airport is the closest commercial airport to Karijini National Park. The tourist office (☎ (091) 89 5374) is part of the Paraburdoo Caravan Park.

Each Thursday at 12.40 pm there are mine tours; book these on ☎ (091) 89 5200. About six km south of town is the **Radio Hill Lookout** (Mt Paraburdoo). There are a number of swimming holes and springs near town such as Kelly's Pool, Ratty Springs, Howie's Hole, Nanjilgardy Pool and Palm Springs. Barlow's Bridge, a picnic spot, is 63 km north-east of town.

Places to Stay & Eat The cheap option is the *Paraburdoo Caravan Park* (☎ (091) 89 5374) on Camp Rd; tent/caravan sites are $6/12 and units are $25/40 for singles/doubles. At the corner of Rocklea and Tom Price Rds is the *Paraburdoo Hotel*; there is a choice of 'old' rooms at $76/85 for singles/doubles and 'new' rooms at $94/105. There is a licensed restaurant in the Paraburdoo Hotel and a Charlie Carters store in Ashburton Ave, for those doing their own cooking.

Pannawonica

This is definitely a 'company town', built to house workers from the Robe River Iron Associates open-cut mining operations. It is 46 km off the North-West Coastal Highway on the way to Millstream-Chichester National Park. There is a tavern and hotel (☎ (091) 84 1073) in Pannawonica Drive; B&B is $65/75 for singles/doubles. If you wish to see iron ore loaded into trucks and transferred to another form of transport (still awake!) then ring Pannawonica Mine Tours (☎ (091) 84 1142), 24 hours in advance.

Getting There & Away

Air Ansett Australia flies from Perth to Newman ($312 one way/$357 Apex return),

Paraburdoo ($288/$318) and Port Hedland ($373/$424).

Bus Westliner and Greyhound Pioneer has limited services to some of the company towns. Greyhound Pioneer has a Perth to Tom Price service on Tuesday and a Tom Price to Perth service on Thursday. Both of these pass through Paraburdoo. There is also an Exmouth to Tom Price service on Wednesday which returns on Thursday, also passing through Paraburdoo. For Pannawonica, you get dropped off at the North-West Coastal Highway by both bus companies.

MILLSTREAM-CHICHESTER NATIONAL PARK

The impressive 2000 sq km Millstream-Chichester National Park lies 150 km south of Roebourne. It is reached by gravel road from the North-West Coastal Highway; the signposted turn-off is 27 km past Roebourne. The main feature passed is **Pyramid Hill**, a volcanic remnant some 1800 million years old. It is comprised of reddish breccia and tuff.

Millstream-Chichester includes a number of freshwater pools formed by a spring from the underflow of the Fortescue River. **Python Pool**, different from the rest of Millstream, is a deep waterhole at the base of a cliff. It was once an oasis for Afghani-camel drivers and still makes a good place for a swim.

The road which heads over the Chichester Range is sealed for a good deal of the climb and descent. At the top of the range is **Mt Herbert** (366 metres), a good lookout and starting point for the Chichester Range Camel Trail, an eight-km, two-hour walk through a rugged part of the range and via McKenzie Spring down to Python Pool. From the lookout you are able to see what constitutes most of the park – clay tablelands, basalt ranges and a cloak of pin-cushion spinifex.

The main part of the park is centred around Millstream Homestead and access is via a 30-km loop road which is 11.5 km off the

Broome
Top: Rock detail at Gantheaume Point (RI)
Bottom: Red, craggy cliffs at Gantheaume Point (RI)

Kimberley
Boab at sunset in Kununurra (RI)

Hamersley Iron Rd. The **Chinderwarriner Pool**, near the visitor centre in Millstream, is another pleasant oasis with pools, palms (including the unique Millstream palm – *Livistona alfredii*) and lilies; it is well worth a visit.

The lush environment is a haven for birds and other fauna such as flying foxes and kangaroos. Over 20 species of dragonfly and damselfly have been recorded around the pool. The old homestead has been converted into an information centre with a wealth of detail on the Millstream ecosystems and lifestyle of the Yinjibarndi people.

The park also has a number of walking and driving trails including the Homestead Walk, the 6.8-km Murlunmunyjurna Trail and Cliff Lookout Drive (six km).

Places to Stay & Eat
There are basic campsites (☎ (091) 84 5144) at Snake Creek (near Python Pool), Crossing Pool and Deep Reach; tent sites are $5 for two and $3 for each extra adult. You cannot buy food out here; stock up at the supermarkets in Karratha before tackling the interior Pilbara.

KARIJINI (HAMERSLEY RANGE) NATIONAL PARK
This national park, second largest in the state after Rudall River, contains rugged scenery which has few equals in Australia. It is about five hours from Roebourne and 3½ hours from Port Hedland. If you are in the Pilbara do not, on any account, miss the gorge country.

The traditional owners of the region are the Panyjima, Innawonga and Kurrama Aboriginal people. The name of the park was changed to Karijini to recognise the significance of these people, who have lived here for at least 20,000 years.

The national park office (☎ (091) 89 8157) is not far from the junction of Juna Downs and Mount Bruce Rds, in the southeast corner of the park. It seems the isolation suits the rangers who remain virtually invisible, melting into the spinifex at the first sign of tourists. If you need any information, head for the information shelters or get a copy of the pamphlet *Karijini National Park: Visitor and Walk Trail Guide*.

Flora & Fauna
The park is rich in wildlife and you may encounter euros, red kangaroos and the rare Rothschild's rock wallaby when driving. You may even see the Pilbara ningaui *(Ningaui timeealeyi)* – pronounced 'ningowie' – an almost mythological creature which comes out at night to hunt for food. Reptiles love this environment and many species are seen, especially in the gorges. Birds are also attracted to the semipermanent pools in the gorges or the nesting eyries along the cliffs.

One of the great features of the park is the profusion of wildflowers which vary with the seasons. There always seems to be something in flower. In the cooler months, look for yellow flowering sennas (cassias) and acacias, mulla-mullas and bluebells.

The Gorges
Wittenoom township is at the northern end of Karijini (Hamersley Range) and the infamous gorge, **Wittenoom**, is immediately south of the town. A surfaced road runs the 13 km to this gorge, passing old asbestos mines and a number of smaller gorges and pretty pools.

Like other gorges in central Australia, those of Karijini are spectacular both in their sheer rocky faces and their varied colours. In the early spring, the park is often carpeted with colourful wildflowers.

Travel down the Newman road, 24 km from Wittenoom, and there's a turn-off to the **Yampire Gorge** where blue veins of asbestos can be seen in the rock. Fig Tree Soak, in the gorge, was once used by Afghani-camel drivers as a watering point. Look carefully at the bird life around the fig tree, if you are lucky you will see a spotted bowerbird *(Chlamydera maculata)* feeding on the ripe figs.

The road continues through Yampire Gorge to **Dales Gorge**. Not far along the road is a turn-off to a big termite mound. On

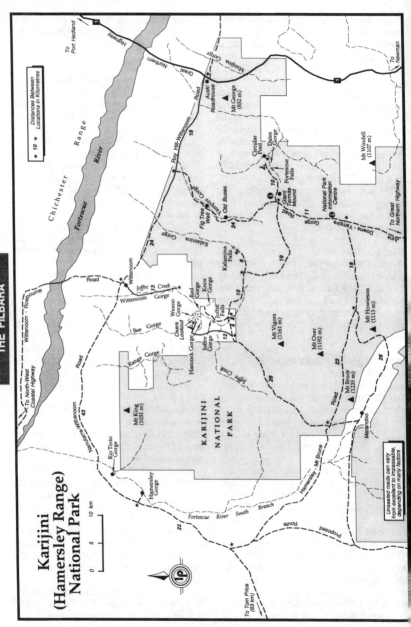

Karijini (Hamersley Range) National Park

THE PILBARA

this same route, you can get to **Circular Pool** and a nearby lookout and by a footpath to the bottom of the **Fortescue Falls**. The three-hour return walk from Circular Pool along Dales Gorge to the falls is recommended; you will be surprised by the permanent water in the gorge. The Joffre Falls road leads to **Knox Gorge**; nearby is a 1½-km return walk to Red Gorge lookout. This walk is noted for the termite mounds and the rock piles of the pebble-mound mouse.

From the Joffre Falls turn-off, it is 16 km to the spectacular Oxer Lookout at the junction of the **Red, Weano, Joffre** and **Hancock** gorges. The stack of superlatives hardly does the gorges justice – you really have to be there. If you wish to get down into the gorge proper, take the steps down to Handrail Pool (turn to the right at the bottom) in Weano Gorge.

Following the main road to Tom Price, you pass through the small **Rio Tinto Gorge**, 43 km from Wittenoom, and just beyond this is the **Hamersley Gorge**, only four km from the road. The Hamersley is a captivating sight from the lookout as the awesome power of the earth's forces are reflected in the folded ribbons of rock.

Mt Meharry (1245 metres), the highest mountain in WA, is near the south-east border of Karijini National Park. The second tallest peak is **Mt Bruce** (Punurrunha), 36 km west of the ranger station. There is a route up the scree slope on its north face and the trip is about four hours return; attempt this walk only in the early morning to avoid the inevitable heat and take plenty of water.

Organised Tours

There are a number of tour operators in the area, including Dave's Gorge Tours (☎ (091) 89 7026) which have been recommended by travellers with rave reviews to the tune of 'it's the best experience that I've had'. The one-day circuit tour costs $45 (bring your own lunch) and the famed 'Miracle Mile' (see under 'Miracle Mile' & Knox Slide in this chapter) costs $45 ($50 if you are not staying in the hostel).

Design-a-Tour (☎ (091) 89 7059) has one-day tours of Karijini and the gorges for $55, including lunch (an extra $10 for pick up from the Auski Roadhouse). Pilbara Adventure Tours (☎ (091) 73 2544), based in Port Hedland, goes to Karijini, as well as Marble Bar and Rudall River National Park.

Snappy Gum Safaris (☎ (091) 85 1278) runs tours to Karijini but mainly concentrates on Millstream-Chichester National Park and the Burrup Peninsula.

THE PILBARA

'Miracle Mile' & Knox Slide

If you want a totally different impression of the awesome scenery in Karijini, try the 'Miracle Mile' (MM) & Knox Slide with local identity Dave Doust.

The MM starts in Wittenoom early in the morning. You first go to Oxer's Lookout, then to Hancock Gorge where the adventure starts. You descend a steep track into the gorge and follow it down to where it narrows, allowing bridging on either wall of the gorge. At Kermit's Pool there is time for a swim before you climb around a waterfall using Oxer's Handle (find out for yourself what this is). Negotiate the next narrow ledge without using your hands at the next spot. It gets worse. Down the harrowing and frighteningly steep Hade's Stairs and around the corner to the end of Hancock Gorge.

Prepare to get wet – the next stage is a swim across Junction Pool. Here you can partake of some Cadjeput courage and fling yourself from a tree. Climbing starts again as you head up the 100-Foot Waterfall into Weano Gorge. This is not for the faint-hearted. Next (it goes on!), the side of Deep Pool is negotiated by a goat track. Into the water again through two pools into Handrail Pool and the MM is over. It is, unsurprisingly, one of the best experiences of most participant's lives.

In the afternoon you can continue into Knox Pool. This includes the Knox Slide. Sit on your bum, slide down a rock then drop seven metres into a deep, cold pool. You paid for it! Usually there are no complaints. How do you get out – only Dave knows the secret. ■

Places to Stay & Eat

There are several basic campsites within the Karijini including Dales Gorge, Weano Gorge and the Joffre Intersection ($5 for a tent site for two, extra adult $3); contact the rangers (☎ (091) 89 8157) for information.

Places outside the park are the towns of Tom Price, Newman and Wittenoom (see those sections). The *Auski Tourist Village Roadhouse* (☎ (091) 76 6988), at the junction of the Great Northern Highway and Wittenoom Rd, has shady, grassed tent/caravan sites for $8/13. There is a restaurant here and all types of fuel are available. Why Auski? Because it was set up by Aussies and Kiwis. Food items are expensive in Wittenoom so it is best to bring your own.

WITTENOOM

Wittenoom (population 50), 288 km southeast of Roebourne, is the tourist centre of gorge country. It had an earlier history as an asbestos-mining town but mining finally halted in 1966; it is the magnificent gorges of Karijini National Park which now draw people here.

A large number of people who worked in the milling of the blue asbestos have subsequently died from mesothelioma, caused by the inhalation of fibrous asbestos dust. The streets of Wittenoom and the nearby airstrip were once paved with asbestos tailings and the residents would have breathed it in daily. As a result, the health authorities in Perth don't want to know about this place. The remaining, stoic locals believe that Perth officials want to see their town and the blue asbestos piles bulldozed under a huge mound of dirt.

A huge blow to the town was the closing of the Fortescue Hotel as it took away the social focus. The visage of Charlie Chaplin, slowly peeling off the wall of the abandoned picture theatre, is distinctly mournful. The epitaph, 'Died of the Dust', on one of the graves in the local cemetery reinforces the general air of malaise and the voices of the ghosts are heard shouting above the afternoon wind.

To the seasoned traveller there is, however, an irresistible appeal about this place. Perhaps it unlocks all those hidden images of western moviedom: rolling tumbleweeds, lone gunslingers, scowling Jack Palance-types and cowering townsfolk.

The tourist office is in the Ashburton shire offices on Third Ave (☎ (091) 89 7011). The alternative tourist office (☎ (091) 89 7096) is in the Gem Shop in Sixth Avenue, open from 8 am to 6 pm; this also serves as the propaganda headquarters for the diehard population. There are no banking facilities so bring plenty of cash to pay for supplies and tours.

Warning

Even after 25 years, there is a health risk from airborne asbestos fibres. Avoid disturbing asbestos tailings in the area and keep your car windows closed on windy days. If you are concerned then seek expert medical advice before going to Wittenoom.

Places to Stay & Eat

The *Gorges Caravan Park* (☎ (091) 89 7075), Second Ave, has tent sites/on-site vans from $9/27 for two.

Wittenoom Bungarra Bivouac Hostel (☎ (091) 89 7026), at 71 Fifth Ave, has beds at $7 per night – incidentally, a bungarra is a big goanna. Another budget place is the *Old Convent* (☎ (091) 89 7060), Gregory St, which has an elongated dorm in the front verandah for $8 per person and double rooms at $30 for two. Spare a thought for the pious who suffered this accommodation. *Nomad Heights* (☎ (091) 89 7068), on First Ave, is a small arid/tropical permaculture farm; the cost is $6 per night.

The *Fortescue Hotel* (☎ (091) 89 7055), on Gregory St, is the classic 'pub with no beer' as it is closed until further notice. *Wittenoom Holiday Homes* (☎ (091) 89 7096), on Fifth Ave, has self-contained cottages at $45 to $55 for a double.

At present you have to bring your own food with you as there are no restaurants in town. You can get basic supplies at the Gorges Caravan Park or at the local store.

Getting There & Away

There is a Monday and Friday bus service to Wittenoom from Karratha operated by Snappy Gum Safaris (☎ (091) 85 1278). You can reach Wittenoom directly from Port Hedland (307 km via the Great Northern Highway), from near Roebourne (311 km off the North-West Coastal Highway) or from the Nanutarra turn-off (377 km off the North-West Coastal Highway). Remember many of the roads in the Pilbara are unsealed or require a permit.

PORT HEDLAND

This port, billed as the 'port of big ships', handles a massive tonnage and is the place from which Pilbara's iron ore is shipped overseas. The town itself (population 13,100) is built on an island connected to the mainland by causeways and the main highway into Port Hedland enters along a three-km causeway. The satellite community of South Hedland was established with a planned population of 40,000 and is where many of Port Hedland's inhabitants live.

Even before the Marble Bar gold rush of the 1880s, the town had been important. It became a grazing centre in 1864 and during the 1870s, a fleet of 150 pearling luggers had been based there. By 1946, however, the population had dwindled to a mere 150. Iron-ore mining operations in the Pilbara ensured a rebirth of the port's importance. The port now has the greatest export tonnage of any in Australia and is the only facility capable of handling two ships in excess of 250,000 tonnes at one time.

The port is on a mangrove-fringed inlet – there are plenty of fish, crabs, oysters and birds around. The port and iron-ore eyesores are feted at the expense of the prolific natural wonders in the area.

Information

The sleepy tourist office (☎ (091) 73 1711), which has a small art gallery and showers ($1.50), is at 13 Wedge St, across from the post office. It's open from 8.30 am to 5 pm during the week and from 8.30 to 4.30 on weekends. It provides an excellent map of the town. You have to give the staff a guernsey for their enthusiasm – few other tourism employees have to promote a town caked in red dust with a port area that at night looks like the opening scenes from *Bladerunner*!

Things to See & Do

You can visit the wharf area or view it from the 26-metre **observation tower** behind the tourist office (you have to sign a waiver to climb it and you'll need closed-in shoes). Below are huge ore carriers, stockpiles of ore and a town encrusted in red Pilbara dust. The iron-ore trains are up to 2.8 km in length. From Monday to Friday, at 9 and 11 am, there is a 'mind-numbing' 1½-hour BHP Iron Ore and Port Tour which leaves from the tourist office (adults $8, children $2).

Pretty Pool, seven km east of the town centre on the waterfront, is a safe tidal pool where shell collectors will have fun – beware of stonefish. Visits can also be made to the **Royal Flying Doctor base**, Richardson St, at 11.15 am on weekdays. There are **Aboriginal peteroglyphs** (rock engravings), including turtles and a whale, near the BHP main gate at Two-Mile Ridge.

There are four excellent heritage trails in the area. The pamphlets *Old Port Hedland & Port Trail* (1.8-km walk) and *Sutherland Trail & Out and About Trail* are available from the tourist office ($1 each).

Whale & Turtle Watching These eco-paupers receive little publicity in a town where red dust and iron ore are sovereign. We have a sneaking suspicion as to which one will bring in the tourist dollar in the future. What a dichotomy – natural attractions alongside huge piles of ore, long trains and huge ships.

The **flatback turtle** nests between October and March on some of the nearby beaches, including Munda, Cooke Point, Cemetery Beach and Pretty Pool. Nesting density is low on city beaches with only a few turtles nesting each night. At Munda, up to 20 turtles may nest in a night. Enquire at the tourist office about organised tours during the nesting season.

THE PILBARA

THE PILBARA

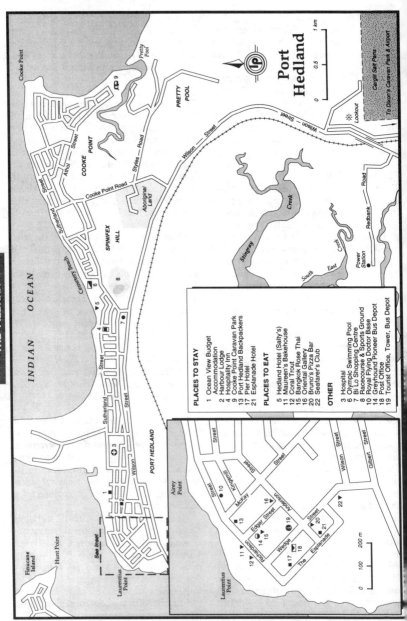

PLACES TO STAY
1 Ocean View Budget
   Accommodation
2 Harbour Lodge
4 Hospitality Inn
9 Cooke Point Caravan Park
13 Port Hedland Backpackers
21 Pier Hotel
21 Esplanade Hotel

PLACES TO EAT
5 Hedland Hotel (Salty's)
11 Maureen's Bakehouse
12 Coral Trout
15 Bangkok Rose Thai
16 Oriental Gallery
20 Bruno's Pizza Bar
22 Seafarer's Club

OTHER
3 Hospital
6 Olympic Swimming Pool
7 Bi Lo Shopping Centre
8 Racecourse & Sports Ground
10 Royal Flying Doctor Base
14 Greyhound Pioneer Bus Depot
18 Post Office
19 Tourist Office, Tower, Bus Depot

Whalewatching trips are operated by Port Hedland Fishing Charters (☎ (091) 73 2937) in their boat, the *Chatham Belle*. These take six to eight hours, leave on weekends only and cost $60 per person (lunch is $10 extra); trips are dependent on tides. The whale observed is the majestic humpback, often in pods of five to six.

Places to Stay

Camping & Caravanning You can camp by the airport at *Dixon's Caravan Park* (☎ (091) 72 2525). Tent sites are $12 for two and backpackers' rooms are $12 per person. The park has a pool and a great recreation room with cooking facilities, tape deck and TV. More convenient, but looking like a snippet out of TS Eliot's *Wasteland*, is the *Cooke Point Caravan Park* (☎ (091) 73 1271), on Athol St, which is also adjacent to Pretty Pool; dusty powered sites/on site vans are $16/35 for two. *South Hedland Caravan Park* (☎ (091) 72 1197), on Hamilton Rd, is the third park in the area and has on-site vans for $42/47 for one/two people.

Budget Accommodation The dusty *Port Hedland Backpackers* (☎ (091) 73 2198) is at 20 Richardson St between Edgar and McKay Sts. The homely atmosphere and friendly hosts make up for the lack of luxuries. Dorm beds cost from $10 a night and the place has kitchen and much-needed laundry facilities. The *Ocean View* (☎ (091) 73 2418), in Kingsmill St, has singles/doubles for $35/45; there are some backpackers' rooms for $15. The *Pier Hotel* (☎ (091) 73 1488), on the Esplanade, also has $15 beds for backpackers. Similar in price is the *Harbour Lodge* (☎ (091) 73 2996), at 11 Edgar St, which has a fully equipped kitchen.

Hotels & Motels On the corner of Anderson St, there's the *Esplanade Hotel* (☎ (091) 73 1798) which has rooms from $40 per person. The *Hedland Hotel* (☎ (091) 73 1511), on the corner of Lukis and McGregor Sts, has singles/doubles for the widely varying price range of $40 to $80/$70 to $90. The usual

cost for rooms at the *Pier Hotel* (see under Budget Accommodation earlier) is $60/80 for B&B singles/doubles.

There is a motel in South Hedland (☎ (091) 72 2222), 200 metres south of the post office in Court Place, with singles/doubles for $72/82. The most expensive motel is the *Hospitality Inn* (☎ (091) 73 1044), Webster St, with singles and doubles from $95 to $110. The *Quality Inn* (☎ (091) 72 1222), on the North-West Coastal Highway, opposite the airport, has singles/doubles for between $75 to $97.

Places to Eat

The *Pier* and the *Esplanade* hotels do counter meals at lunch time; about $8 to $9 per person. The air-con *Hedland Hotel* does excellent-value counter meals; counter teas are available only on Friday and Saturday nights, until 8 pm.

There are plenty of supermarkets if you want to fix your own food and also a number of coffee bars and other places where you can get a pie or pastie. *Maureen's Bakehouse*, on Richardson St, has been heartily recommended for its homemade salad rolls. Nearby is the *Coral Trout* with a BYO restaurant and takeaway section where you can get fish & chips; the mackerel here is superb.

The *Oriental Gallery*, on the corner of Edgar and Anderson Sts, does a good-value weekday lunch. In addition to the Oriental Gallery there are three other Asian restaurants in town: *Bangkok Rose, Dynasty Gardens* and *Golden Crown*. Up in Cooke Point, on Keesing St, is *Tammi's*, one of the more expensive options in town. The *Cooke Point Recreation Club* has a bistro which is open for lunch and dinner, and a pizza bar.

Getting There & Away

Air Ansett Australia has flights on Saturday and Sunday from Port Hedland to Darwin ($445 one way/$489 return). There are a number of connections daily to Perth ($373/$424) and also frequent flights to and from Broome ($201/$229), Derby ($224/$249), Geraldton ($318/$349), Karratha ($147/$169) and other northern centres. Garuda and Qantas operate flights every Saturday between Port Hedland and Bali.

Ansett Australia (☎ (091) 73 1777) is in the Boulevard shopping centre (better known as the Bi Lo centre) on Wilson St.

Bus It's 230 km from Karratha to Port Hedland and a further 604 km to Broome. Greyhound Pioneer has services from Perth to Port Hedland and north to Broome and Darwin. The office is in The Homestead, Throssell St, in South Hedland.

Apart from the coastal route, Greyhound Pioneer has another service that takes the inland route from Perth to Port Hedland via Newman four times weekly. Dixon's Westliner does this same route Monday and Friday south to Perth, and Thursday and Sunday return. Fares from Port Hedland are $124 to Perth, $55 to Broome, $38 to Karratha and $184 to Darwin.

Getting Around

The airport is 13 km from town; the only way to get there is by taxi, which costs $15. There's a Hedland Bus Lines service (☎ (091) 72 1394) between Port Hedland and South Hedland; it takes 40 minutes to an hour and operates Monday to Saturday ($2). You can hire cars at the airport from the usual operators. The Backpackers' Hostel lends its bikes out to responsible users.

COLLIER RANGE & RUDALL RIVER (KARLAMILYI) NATIONAL PARKS

Two of the most isolated and interesting of the state's national parks are found in the Pilbara. Both parks are true wilderness areas, accessible only by 4WD. Travellers have to be self-sufficient with fuel, water, food and first-aid equipment and seek permission from property owners before using station roads.

The Collier Range is the more easily accessible as the Great Northern Highway bisects it near the Kumarina Roadhouse, 256 km north of Meekatharra. Here, at the upper reaches of the Ashburton and Gascoyne rivers, the ranges vary from low hills to high ridges bounded by cliffs.

In the far west of the park near Coobarra there are sand dunes, then come spinifex plains and, in the north-east, mulga, which is seasonally interspersed with mulla mulla.

Even more remote is the Rudall River (Karlamilyi) National Park, a breathtakingly beautiful desert region of 15,000 sq km, which is accessible only by experienced drivers with 4WD vehicles. The best time to visit is July and August when daytime temperatures are tolerable – in the desert the nights can be exceptionally cold.

The park is reached via two routes. The first is from Marble Bar along the Telfer Rd to the northern park boundary, about 420 km. (Permission to use this route must be obtained from the Newmont Holdings' Perth office.) The second route is from Newman via Balfour Downs on the Tannawanna Track to the southern boundary, about 260 km. To give you an indication of the area you are entering, the Canning Stock Route skirts the park to the east and No 24 Well to the south-east.

The Martu Aboriginal people still live in this area and, as recently as the 1980s, established the Punmu and Parnngurr communities in the park.

Plateaus of sandstone and quartzite carved by glaciers 280 million years ago, sandplains covered with spinifex and desert oak, dunes and salt lakes, are all features of the landscape. Wattles and hakeas line some watercourses and eucalypts are found by the Rudall River. Over 70 species of birds have been recorded and the rabbit-eared bandicoot (also dalgyte or bilby – see under Bilby in the Broome & The Dampier Peninsula chapter) may still exist in the area.

At least two vehicles, equipped with Royal Flying Doctor Service radios, are needed for this trip and visitors must be *totally* self-sufficient. There are absolutely no facilities in this park.

Broome & The Dampier Peninsula

The Pilbara and the Kimberley are separated by the westerly edge of the Great Sandy Desert which extends all the way from the Northern Territory to the Indian Ocean. From the time you cross the De Grey River, there is almost nothing until you reach Broome, an isolated town which has become something of a traveller's haunt. Broome is nestled on the north side of Roebuck Bay and to the north is the Dampier Peninsula, home to many Aboriginal communities.

PORT HEDLAND TO BROOME

It is 604 km from Port Hedland to Broome on what is probably Australia's most boring stretch of highway. Consequently, it proves to be a difficult day's drive. Get a copy of the handy booklet, *Port Hedland to Broome*, from the tourist office.

About 84 km from Port Hedland is the **De Grey River**, where several bird species can be spotted from the pleasant picnic area. Just over 20 km beyond that is the turn off to Goldsworthy and **Shay Gap**, mining towns. Goldsworthy has now been dismantled and operations ceased. It is now hard to believe there was once a sizeable town on the site. Shay Gap has taken over and is a 'closed' company town run by Goldsworthy Mining.

Near the Pardoo Roadhouse (154 km) is the turn-off to **Cape Keraudren**, where there is great fishing and picturesque tidal creeks; caravan sites, from April to October, are $5. Pardoo Station (133 km) has station stays and comes recommended by a number of backpackers; camp/caravan sites are $7/9.

Many shells are washed ashore on the magnificent stretch of **Eighty Mile Beach**, 245 km from Port Hedland; this is a great place to stay and backpackers' beds are $10 per person, and tent/powered van sites are $12/15 for two. The **Sandfire Roadhouse** (295 km) is very much an enforced fuel stop for most – pack sandwiches rather than eat the dull, expensive food sold here.

On the other hand, **Port Smith** (477 km),

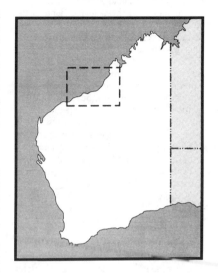

situated on a tidal lagoon and 23 km off the highway, comes recommended; campsites are $5 per person. Fishing is popular, with threadfin salmon, mangrove jack, trevally and whiting being the usual catches.

BROOME

For many travellers, Broome is Australia's archetypal getaway: palm-fringed beaches, clear, blue waters and a relaxed atmosphere. But it is also noted for its Chinatown and the influences of early Japanese pearlers.

History

The Roebuck Bay region was known to the local Aborigines of the Djuleun tribes as 'Nileribanjen'. The surrounding mudflats and shallows were rich in shellfish, fish and mudcrabs and the Djuleun traded spears and pearl shell; the latter eventually contributed to the end of their traditional way of life.

In 1864, a syndicate was formed to investigate the story of a convict that had found gold at Camden Harbour, near Kuri Bay, in 1856. Many eager pastoralists backed this expedition and, when gold was not found, a number of them put together another expedition to introduce sheep in the 'land in the vicinity of Roebuck Bay which would bear favourable comparison with some of the best runs in Victoria'.

The Aboriginal inhabitants of Roebuck Bay resented the intrusion of the pastoralists, especially their fencing of traditional waterholes. In November 1864, three members of the pastoralists' expedition were murdered by Aborigines which resulted in open conflict. The pastoralists withdrew in 1867 only to be replaced by pearlers, working north from Cossack, in the 1870s.

Pearling in the sea off Broome started in earnest in the 1880s and peaked in the early 1900s when the town's 400 pearling luggers, worked by 3000 men, supplied 80% of the world's mother-of-pearl. Today only a handful of boats operate. Pearl diving was a very unsafe occupation, as Broome's Japanese cemetery attests. The divers were from various Asian countries. The rivalries between the different nationalities were always intense and sometimes took an ugly turn.

The town was gazetted in 1883 and named after the then governor, Sir Frederick Napier Broome. It still remained very much a shanty town until the submarine telegraph cable was laid from Cable Bay, west of Broome, to Java in 1889. This kept the pearling industry in close touch with price fluctuations and the industry began to expand rapidly.

In the first decade of the 20th century, Broome produced some 80% of the world's mother-of-pearl shell. However, it slowly declined in importance and it was not until the 1950s that it was revived, but on a much smaller scale.

When Japan entered WW II in 1941, the 500 Japanese in Broome were interned for the duration of the war. On 3 March 1942, following the bombing of Darwin in February, the Japanese bombed Broome. A number of flying boats were destroyed and about 70 Dutch refugees were killed. Many of the pearl luggers anchored in the harbour were destroyed by the Australian army as part of its 'scorched earth' policy, which left nothing of use for the Japanese if they invaded.

The main industry is beef and Broome's modern meatworks can process 40,000 head during the season. Vegetarians, don't despair! Today, tourism is the other major industry and Broome's attractions and festivals bring hordes of visitors. Fortunately, the Aboriginal community is playing a major part in this cultural renaissance.

The pamphlet *Broome Heritage Trail* has historical and current accounts of the region.

Orientation

The two centres of Broome's development and growth are the southern portion of town, in the area surrounding the corner of Dampier Terrace and Saville St, and Chinatown. The museum is in the south area, as is the modern Seaview shopping plaza opposite.

Information

Broome tourist office (☎ (091) 92 2222) is just across the sports field from Chinatown. It's open daily from 9 am to 5 pm (April to November), and in the interim from 9 am to 5 pm Monday to Friday and then 9 am to 1 pm on weekends. It publishes a very useful fortnightly guide to what's happening in and around Broome, a *Town Map & Information Guide* and a *Broome Holiday Planner*. Also get a copy of the free *Broome or Bust!* pamphlet, aimed at budget tourists.

Chinatown

The term 'Chinatown' is used to refer to the old part of town, although there is really only one block or so that is multicultural and historic. Some of the plain and simple wooden buildings that line Carnarvon St still house Chinese merchants, but most are now restaurants, pearl dealers and tourist shops. The bars on the windows aren't there to deter outlaws but to minimise cyclone damage.

The Carnarvon St phone booth sign is in English, Chinese, Arabic, Japanese and Malay. There is a street statue of three men

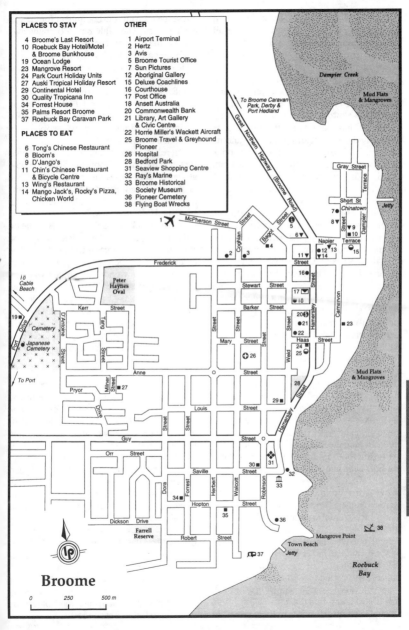

PLACES TO STAY

4 Broome's Last Resort
10 Roebuck Bay Hotel/Motel
   & Broome Bunkhouse
19 Ocean Lodge
23 Mangrove Resort
24 Park Court Holiday Units
27 Auski Tropical Holiday Resort
29 Continental Hotel
30 Quality Tropicana Inn
34 Forrest House
35 Palms Resort Broome
37 Roebuck Bay Caravan Park

PLACES TO EAT

6 Tong's Chinese Restaurant
8 Bloom's
9 D'Jango's
11 Chin's Chinese Restaurant
   & Bicycle Centre
13 Wing's Restaurant
14 Mango Jack's, Rocky's Pizza,
   Chicken World

OTHER

1 Airport Terminal
2 Hertz
3 Avis
5 Broome Tourist Office
7 Sun Pictures
12 Aboriginal Gallery
15 Deluxe Coachlines
16 Courthouse
17 Post Office
18 Ansett Australia
20 Commonwealth Bank
21 Library, Art Gallery
   & Civic Centre
22 Horrie Miller's Wackett Aircraft
25 Broome Travel & Greyhound
   Pioneer
26 Hospital
28 Bedford Park
31 Seaview Shopping Centre
32 Ray's Marine
33 Broome Historical
   Society Museum
36 Pioneer Cemetery
38 Flying Boat Wrecks

Broome

0   250   500 m

BROOME

in Carnarvon St: Hiroshi Iwaki, Tokuichi Kuribayashi and Keith Dureau who were all involved in the cultured pearl industry.

Pearling

A pearling lugger can occasionally be seen at Streeters jetty off Dampier Terrace, and there are cruises from May to October ($40).

Broome Historical Society Museum, on Saville St, has exhibits on Broome and its history and on the pearling industry and its dangers. It's in the old customs house and is open Monday to Friday from 10 am to 4 pm, and Saturday and Sunday from 10 am to 1 pm (April to November); reduced hours from November to May.

Mother-of-pearl has long been a Broome speciality. Between Carnarvon St and Dampier Terrace in Chinatown are a number of **pearl shops**. The main places are Paspaley Pearling Company in Short St; Broome Pearls, The Pearl Emporium and Linney's Pearls in Dampier Terrace; and Anastasia's Pearl Gallery in Carnarvon St. There is also the Shell House in Guy St, in the south-west section of town.

The **Japanese Cemetery**, near Cable Beach Rd, testifies to the dangers that accompanied pearl diving when equipment was primitive and knowledge of diving techniques limited. In 1914, 33 divers died of the bends, while in 1908 a cyclone killed 150 sailors caught at sea. The Japanese section of the cemetery is one of the largest and most interesting and was extensively renovated in 1983. Behind the neat Japanese section is the interesting but run-down allotment containing European and Aboriginal graves.

Other Attractions

Across Napier Terrace from Chinatown is Wing's Restaurant with a magnificent **boab tree** beside it. There's another boab tree behind, outside what used to be the old police lock-up, with a rather sad little tale on a plaque at its base. The tree was planted by a police officer when his son (later killed in France in WW I) was born in 1898. The boab tree is still doing fine.

The 1888 **courthouse** was once used to house the transmitting equipment for the old cable station. The cable ran to Banyuwangi in Java, the ferry port across from Bali.

Further along Weld St, by the library and civic centre, is a **Wackett aircraft** that used to belong to Horrie Miller, founder of MacRobertson Miller Airlines, once Ansett WA, now Ansett Australia. The plane is hidden away in a modern but absurdly designed building that most people pass without a second glance.

There's a **pioneer cemetery** near Town Beach at the end of Robinson St. In the bay, at the entrance to Dampier Creek, there's a landmark called **Buccaneer Rock**, dedicated to Captain William Dampier and his ship, the HMS *Roebuck*.

If you're lucky enough to be in Broome on a cloudless night when there is a full moon, you can witness the **Staircase to the Moon**. The reflections of the moon from the rippling mudflats creates a wonderful golden-stairway effect, best seen from the town beach. The effect is most dramatic about two days after full moon, as the moon rises after the sky has had a chance to darken. A lively evening market is held on this evening, and the town takes on a carnival air. Check with the tourist office for exact dates and times.

Organised Tours

There are a number of tours to make in and around Broome. The *Spirit of Broome* (☎ (091) 93 5025) is a small hovercraft which makes daily one-hour flights around Roebuck Bay ($45), stopping at various points of interest.

You can twilight cruise in an original pearl lugger *The Dampier*, in the replica lugger *The Willie* or the magnificent yacht *Starsand*; all cost $40 and provide beer, wine and nibblies.

There are also some good guided **bushwalks**. Paul Foulkes (☎ (091) 92 1371) concentrates on environmental features close to Broome, such as the palaeontologically important dinosaur footprints ($10), the mangroves ($20), remnant rainforest ($20), a hidden valley ($20) and the coast from Broome to Cable Beach ($50).

Other unusual options include Harley Davidson motorcycle tours with the incomparable Norm; enquire at the tourist office.

Festivals

Broome is somewhat of a festival centre. Some of the many excuses to party include:

March
  Chinatown Street Party The Chinatown Progress Committee organises a street party and the whole multicultural population of Broome turns out. There are many local wares for sale, foodstalls and heaps of entertainment.
April
  Dragon Boat Classic Dragon boat paddlers from all over Australia meet annually for this carnival. For two days the town puts on entertainment for the racers.
June
  Broome Fringe Arts Festival Local artists get together and highlight the 'fringe arts'. There are markets, displays of Aboriginal art, poetry workshops and quiet, contemplative celebrations of the 'different'.
August-September
  Shinju Matsuri (Festival of the Pearl) This excellent festival commemorates the early pearling years and the town's multicultural heritage. When the festival is on, the town population swells and accommodation is hard to find, so book ahead. Many traditional Japanese ceremonies are featured, including the Bon Festival. It's worth trying to juggle your itinerary to be in Broome at this time. It concludes with a beach concert and a huge fireworks display. Don't miss the dragon boat races.
September
  Stompem Ground If you want to listen to great music, witness colourful dance and take in ancient culture, then come to Stompem Ground, the celebration of Aboriginal culture by the Broome Musicians Aboriginal Corporation. Hail the Bran Nue Dae with the Kimberley's original people.
November
  Mango Festival The town celebrates that sticky-sweet fruit loved by some but deplored by mothers with small children. Events include mango tasting, mardi gras and the Great Chefs of Broome Cook Off.

Places to Stay

Camping Camping in Broome is not particularly cheap. The *Roebuck Bay Caravan Park* (☎ (091) 92 1366) is conveniently central; unpowered/powered sites are $14/17.50 for two. *Lambs Vacation Village* (☎ (091) 92 1057), Port Drive, has powered sites/cabins for $15/60 for two. *Broome Caravan Park* (☎ (091) 92 1776), on the Great Northern Highway, four km from town, has tent sites and on-site vans for $10/35 for two.

Budget Cheap beds in Broome are scarce and there are three hostel choices. On Bagot St, close to the centre and just a short stagger from the airport, is *Broome's Last Resort* (☎ (091) 93 5000). It's adequate and has a pool, large kitchen and courtesy bus. The accommodation is not cheap – dorm beds are $12 and twins/doubles are $36 for two, all with shared facilities. One plus, they offer excellent camping tours into the Kimberley (see under Devonian Reef National Parks in The Kimberley chapter).

Also close to the centre is the *Broome Bunkhouse* (☎ (091) 92 1221), part of the Roebuck Bay Hotel/Motel, on Napier Terrace. Accommodation is rock-bottom, with beds in 20-bed dorms for $12 and four-bed units for $48. The mattresses look as though they saw service on the Western Front in WW I and if there's a band playing at the pub you have the equivalent of pre-dawn artillery fire. All in all, a most likely place for setting an episode of *Blackadder Goes Forth*. At the time of writing, Broome Backpackers had reopened at Cable Beach (see Around Broome).

Also, at the time of writing, the *Palms Resort Broome* (☎ (091) 92 1898), on the corner of Hopton and Herbert Sts, was offering fully self-contained, air-con motel units/apartments for $15/22 per person. Backpackers would also be allowed access to the resorts other facilities, including swimming pools and barbecue areas. If this offer stands this will be the best value in town for the budget conscious.

See also under Broome Birdwatching in this chapter for my pick of the budget accommodation – this option, however, only suits those with their own car.

BROOME

Hotels, Motels & Resorts During school holidays and other peak times, getting accommodation can be extremely difficult, so book ahead if possible.

The once legendary *Roebuck Bay Hotel Motel* (☎ (091) 92 1221), on the corner of Carnarvon St and Napier Terrace, Chinatown, has a bunkhouse, as well as motel units; singles/doubles are $63/75. The pool is its saving grace.

The *Continental Hotel* (☎ (091) 92 1002) is a modern place on Weld St, at the corner of Louis St, with single/double rooms from $105/115. The *Mangrove Resort* (☎ (091) 92 1303), between the Continental and Chinatown, is a good place to 'see a bad moon arising' but it's not cheap: $105 to $120 for doubles. *Forrest House* (☎ (091) 93 5067), at 59 Forrest St, has small single/twin rooms with fan for $30/50 including breakfast (from November to March, expect to save about $5 on these prices).

The *Palms Resort Broome* (see under Budget earlier) has studio units ($99 to $165 for doubles) and the *Auski Tropical Holiday Resort* (☎ (091) 92 1183) in Milner St, has a swimming pool and all mod cons ($80/90 for singles/doubles). The *Park Court Holiday Units* (☎ (091) 93 5887), Haas St, contains nine two-bedroom units with all facilities; these are $500 to $600 per week, depending on the season.

The *Quality Tropicana Inn* (☎ (091) 92 2583), at the corner of Saville and Robinson Sts, has great gardens and reasonable air-con rooms for $86; there is also a licensed restaurant and bars attached to the hotel. One new place is the *Ocean Lodge* (☎ (091) 93 7700), on Cable Beach Rd near the Port Drive turn-off. It has backpackers' rooms for $12 per person and twin rooms for $60. On Saturday evening they have an Aussie tucker night.

Places to Eat
Light Meals & Fast Food Finding a place to stay in Broome may be a hassle but eating out is no sweat at all. *D'jangos*, on Carnarvon St, has good, healthy food such as vegetarian pasta, and excellent smoothies. Lots of people end up there for coffee after the movies at Sun Pictures. *Bloom's*, across the road, serves a very generous cappuccino and has excellent croissants.

Mango Jack's, on Hamersley St, has hamburgers and also dispenses the usual sandwiches and fish & chips. In the same shopping centre as Mango Jack's, there's a *Chicken World* and *Rocky's Pizza*, which turns out distinctly average pizzas. Another pizza place is *JK's Pizzas & Burgers*, Napier Terrace, which is open from 8 pm until late.

There's an average, pricey bakery in Chinatown, on the corner of Carnarvon and Short Sts. The Seaview shopping centre also has a bakery, as well as Broome's biggest supermarket, Charlie Carters. The *Icecreamery*, in Carnarvon St, is, unsurprisingly, busy.

Pubs & Restaurants The Roebuck Bay Hotel/Motel has *Pearlers Restaurant*, an alfresco dining area and the *Black Pearl*. The Palms Resort has the *Satay Hut*.

Chin's restaurant, on Hamersley St near Mango Jack's, has a variety of dishes from all over Asia. Prices range from $7 to $12. There's a popular takeaway section.

Other Chinese specialists are *Wing's*, on Napier Terrace; *Tong's*, near the corner of Napier Terrace and the Great Northern Highway; *Son Ming* on Carnarvon St; and *Murray's Asian Affair*, on Dampier Terrace.

Annelies is a Swiss restaurant on Napier Terrace near the Roebuck; reports from locals are all good. The *Tea House*, situated in a mud-brick building with an outdoor dining area, is at the end of Saville St. It has a great variety of Thai seafood dishes and BYO is permitted.

Other more expensive places include some of the restaurants in the resorts and motels. The Continental Hotel has both a good bistro and a decent restaurant, the *Port Light*. The latter serves delectable meals in the $12 to $18 range. The Mangrove reputedly has the best seafood restaurant in town, *Charters*.

Entertainment
Sun Pictures, at 27 Carnarvon St in Chinatown, is an open-air cinema dating from

---

Sun Pictures

Opened in 1916, Sun Pictures is believed to be the world's oldest operating picture garden. The silent movies were accompanied by music played by 'Fairy', the pianist, and the Cummin-Wilson RCA projector was adapted for sound in 1933 – the first 'talkie' screened was the musical comedy *Monte Carlo*, starring Nelson Eddy and Jeanette MacDonald. There is nothing quite like watching a movie while lying back in a deck chair under the stars on a balmy tropical evening. The snack bar still serves that old favourite of Aussie kids and adults – the 'chocolate bomb'.

There is a display of old projectors used in the early years of operation, in the foyer. The history of the theatre, *Reflections of the Sun*, by Maria Mann, is available from Sun Pictures for $5. ■

1916. It has a programme of recent releases and is probably the oldest running picture garden in the world. Watching the 'flicks' here, at least once, is a must for visitors to Broome.

Despite an attempt to improve its appearance, the Roebuck Bay Hotel still rocks along – just stand clear of the occasional fight.

Nightclubs in town include BTs, the Nippon Inn in Dampier Terrace and Tokyo Joe's in Napier Terrace.

Getting There & Away

Air Ansett Australia flies to Broome regularly on its Perth to Darwin route. From Perth the fare is $469/523 one way/Apex return; from Darwin $344/379; from Kununurra $255/289 and from Port Hedland $201/229. Ansett's office (☎ (091) 93 5444) is on the corner of Barker and Weld Sts.

Bus Greyhound Pioneer operates through Broome on its Perth-to-Darwin route. Typical fares from Broome include $185 to Perth, $62 to Port Hedland, $22 to Derby and $160 to Darwin. Its office (☎ (091) 92 1561) is at Broome Travel on Hamersley St.

Getting Around

To/From the Airport There are taxis to take you from the airport to your hotel. However, the airport is so close to the centre that backpackers staying at the Last Resort, or close by, may well decide to walk.

Bus There's an hourly Broome Coachlines bus (☎ (091) 92 1068) between the town and Cable Beach. The one-way fare is $2 or you can get 10 fares for $15. The bus goes to a variety of accommodation in town.

Bicycle Cycling is the best way to see the area. There are a number of places that hire bicycles for $6 to $12 a day, including the backpackers' places. The Broome Cycle Centre, on the corner of Hamersley and Frederick Sts, hires bikes, does repairs and gives good advice. Broome is an easy area to ride around; it's flat and you'll usually have no problem riding to Cable Beach (about seven km) as long as it's not too windy. Stay on the roads, though, or your tyres might be punctured by thorns.

Car Rental Hertz and Avis have rent-a-car desks at the airport but there are better deals available if you just want something for bopping around town or to the beach. Suzuki jeeps are popular. Topless Rentals (☎ (091) 93 5017), on Hunter St, and Woody's (☎ (091) 92 1791), Napier Terrace, are local operations.

AROUND BROOME
Cable Beach

Six km from town is Cable Beach, the most popular swimming beach in Broome. It's a classic beach – white sand and turquoise water as far as the eye can see. The beach takes its name from the cable which once linked Broome and Indonesia. You can hire surfboards and other equipment from Broome Surf Cat Hire (☎ (091) 93 5551). Parasailing ($35 to $40) is always popular;

BROOME

the operators are to the right of the rocks on Cable Beach.

The northern side beyond the rock is a popular nude-bathing area. You can also take vehicles (other than motorbikes) onto this part of the beach, although at high tide, access is limited because of the rocks, so take care not to get stranded. Take caution if swimming between November and March as stingers are present.

Two companies, Red Sun and Ships of the Desert, operate **camel rides** along the beach. The best time is at sunset. The cost is $20 per hour; book at the tourist office.

Also on Cable Beach Rd is the **Broome Crocodile Park**. It's open seven days from 10 am to 5 pm, May to November; reduced hours for the rest of the year. There are daily guided tours at 3 pm weekdays; admission is $9 (children $5, family $22).

Gantheaume Point

The long sweep of Cable Beach eventually ends at Gantheaume Point, seven km south of Broome. The red, craggy cliffs have been eroded into curious shapes. At extremely low tides, **dinosaur tracks**, made 120 million years ago by a carnivorous species, are exposed. At other times you can inspect cement casts of the footprints on the cliff top. **Anastasia's Pool**, an artificial rock pool believed to have been built by a former lighthouse keeper for his crippled wife, is on the north side of the point; it fills at high tide.

Willie Creek Pearl Farm is 35 km north of Broome, off the Cape Leveque Rd. It offers a rare chance to see a working pearl farm and is worth the trip (cost of entrance is $12.50). The farm produces cultured pearls from the silver-lipped oyster (*Pinotada maxima*). The road is open only to 4WD vehicles in the Wet, but to all vehicles in the Dry. There are daily tours from Broome ($40) with Broome Coachlines (☎ (091) 92 1068).

Places to Stay & Eat

Cable Beach Caravan Park (☎ (091) 92 2066) is at the beach, and has tent sites from $15. The well-positioned, quiet *Broome*

Backpackers (☎ (091) 93 5000), Lullfitz Drive, Cable Beach, had just re-opened at the time of writing, with twins at $32 for two; enquire at the Last Resort in Broome about its current status.

The very up-market *Cable Beach Club* (☎ (091) 92 0400) is a beautifully designed place covering a large area, although it's not right on the beach. This place was set up by the English millionaire Lord McAlpine and is priced to attract more of his ilk; a studio is $173 and one/two bedroom apartments are $225/298 per night. The Wonderful World of Birds, once part of the Cable Beach Club complex, has closed down.

The resort has an incredibly expensive restaurant, but also the much cheaper *Lord Mac's*. It's a good vantage point for the sunset but, unfortunately, not for the food. For an intimate breakfast, try *Carol's Munchies*, which overlooks beautiful Cable Beach; it is open seven days.

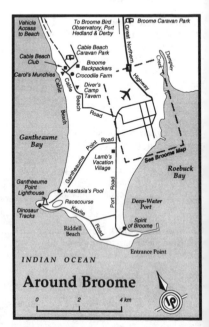

Around Broome

INDIAN OCEAN

imberley
urnululu (Bungle Bungles) National Park (RI)

Kimberley
Top: Lake Argyle (RI)
Bottom: Boabs *(Adansonia gregorii)* (RI)

DAMPIER PENINSULA

It's about 200 km from the turn-off, nine km out of Broome, to the Cape Leveque lighthouse at the tip of the Dampier Peninsula. This area features spectacular red pindan cliffs, expansive blue water and is a flora & fauna paradise. The peninsula is also a great spot for watching humpback whales.

Originally the peninsula was inhabited by the Bardi people and during the early pearling days, a number of Aborigines dived for pearl shell. The communities now welcome visitors and offer bush-tucker walks and mud-crabbing tours.

The **Lurujarri Heritage Trail** starts at Minarriny, about 80 km north of Broome; seek access details and a booklet from the Broome tourist office. The trail follows part of an Aboriginal song cycle which originates from the Dreamtime.

Also north of Broome, on the western coast of Dampier Peninsula, is **Coulomb Point Nature Reserve**. This conservation area was set up to protect the unique pindan vegetation of the peninsula and may still harbour the endangered rabbit-eared bandicoot *(Macrotus lagotis)* or bilby.

Some 96 km from Broome is the *County Downs Homestead* (☎ (091) 92 4911) which has campsites, showers and ablution blocks. The **Beagle Bay Aboriginal Community** (☎ (091) 92 4913) is a welcome diversion and has a beautiful church in the middle of a green, built by Pallotine monks and completed in 1918. Inside is an altar stunningly decorated with mother-of-pearl. A fee of $5 is charged for entry into the community and you must contact the office on arrival; petrol and diesel are available seven days.

Just before Cape Leveque is **Lombadina Aboriginal Community** (☎ (091) 92 4942), which has a church built from corrugated iron on the outside, lined with paper bark and supported by mangrove timber. There are a number of carved artefacts for sale including trochus shell, ebony carvings and pearl-shell jewellery. One-day and overnight mud-crabbing and traditional fishing tours are available; contact the Broome tourist office

for details. Petrol (no unleaded) and diesel are available every day except Sunday.

Cape Leveque, about 200 km from Broome, has a lighthouse and two wonderful beaches. Beyond it is **One Arm Point**, another Aboriginal community (☎ (091) 92 4930). Take note that while you can look around or purchase goods, communities won't want you to stay on their land. Permission to visit other areas must be obtained in advance. Check with the Broome tourist office about road conditions before setting out.

There is accommodation at *Kooljaman* (☎ (091) 92 4970), ranging from backpackers' accommodation ($10), a self-contained unit, chalets, bark huts and camping. Bush-tucker and mud-crabbing tours are available. All types of vehicle fuel, except LPG, can be purchased here.

Organised Tours

Halls Creek and Purnululu (Bungle Bungles) Tours (☎ (091) 68 6217), Over the Top Safaris (☎ (091) 93 7700), Flaktrak (☎ (091)

The Bilby
The rare rabbit-eared bandicoot *(Macrotus lagotis)* dalgyte, or bilby, is found in the northern desert regions of WA. Endangered by predation and habitat destruction, this rabbit-sized marsupial ranges from the Northern Territory to the Indian Ocean.

The bilby has adapted remarkably to its desert environment as it has a narrow head with large rabbit ears and pointed snout and thus acute senses of smell and hearing. It has very poor eyesight but this is not a problem as it is strictly nocturnal, spending the hot desert days inside its burrow (which is up to three metres below ground) and it only comes out in search of food after midnight. Its food consists of ants, termites, larvae and seeds and it seem to survive without drinking.

Male dominance is achieved without aggression. Litters of up to three newborn attach themselves firmly to the females teats for over two months before they leave the pouch. ∎

92 1487) and Pearl Coast 4WD (☎ (091) 93 5786) all operate tours to the peninsula.

Broome Birdwatching

The RAOU Broome Bird Observatory, 18 km from Broome on Roebuck Bay, is a twitcher's delight, and is rated as one of the top four non-breeding grounds for migrant Arctic waders. Officially opened in 1990, it is one of four such observatories in Australia – the others are Rotamah Island in Victoria, the Barren Grounds in New South Wales, and Eyre in WA. Each year, Roebuck Bay receives 150,000 migrants from the northern hemisphere. The observatory (☎ (091) 93 5600) is a good base from which to seek out birds in a variety of habitats – mangroves, salt marshes, plains, pindan woodland, tidal flats and beaches. Please ring beforehand to find out the best viewing times. Over 250 species of birds have been spotted in the region, with migratory waders (shorebirds) seen there in abundance as well as over 20 species of raptors, including the white-breasted sea eagle, osprey and the rare grey falcon.

The RAOU organise one to three-hour tours to see birds of the bush, shore and mangroves. In October you can take a walk to see the waders which have just arrived from Siberia; the cost for the one-hour walk is $8 and binoculars are provided. If you are around at the time of banding you can join in and help.

The observatory is not signposted along Crab Creek Rd, but there is a dry weather track off the Great Northern Highway about 3½ km north of town. You can camp near the observatory for $8 for one ($12 for two;

power $1 extra), or there are twin units for $36, and a five-bed, self-contained chalet for $50 for two ($10 each extra person).

George Swann of Kimberley Birdwatching (☎ (091) 92 1246) takes trips around town, out to Roebuck Bay, Crab Creek and the local sewage plant. He is almost guaranteed to correctly identify any species of wader you care to point out. To the uninitiated, the waders on the beach look pretty much the same. But if you wish to distinguish between the eastern curlew, sanderling, sandpiper, Asian dowitcher, greenshank, Mongolian plover, red-capped plover and whimbrel you will not be disappointed.

State-of-the-art watching equipment is provided, including tripod-mounted telescopes. Based on a minimum of four persons, the cost of a three-hour shorebird trip is $38, a five-hour Broome environs trip is $64 and an eight-hour creek tour is $100.

There are also tours to the Dampier Peninsula ($370) where you will likely see the rare Gouldian finch and rose-crowned fruit dove; tours to Eighty-Mile Beach and Anna Plains ($350); to Bell Gorge ($550) and other gorges of the Kimberley; and to the Drysdale River and Mitchell Plateau ($960), where the search for the endemic black grass wren, rainbow pitta and partridge pigeons is on in earnest.

In the process of researching this book the author had the opportunity of being in Broome at the time migratory birds began arriving from the northern hemisphere. The Broome experience proved one of the highlights of years of travel.

The Kimberley

The rugged Kimberley, at the northern end of WA, is one of Australia's last frontiers. Despite enormous advances in the past decade, this is still a little-travelled and very remote area of great rivers and magnificent scenery. The Kimberley suffers from climatic extremes – heavy rains in the Wet followed by searing heat in the Dry – but the irrigation projects in the north-east have made great changes to the economic life of the region.

Nevertheless, rivers and creeks can rise rapidly following heavy rainfall and become impassable torrents within 15 minutes (see under Cyclones in the Facts for the Visitor chapter). Unless it's a very brief storm, it's quite likely that the watercourses will remain impassable for some days. The Fitzroy River can become so swollen at times that after two or three days' rain it grows from its normal 100-metre width to a spectacular torrent more than 10 km wide. River and creek crossings on the Great Northern Highway on both sides of Halls Creek become impassable every Wet. Highway 1 through the Kimberley is sealed most of the way, but there are several notorious crossings which are still only fords, not all-weather bridges.

The best time to visit is between April and September. By October it's already getting hot (35°C), and later in the year daily temperatures of more than 40°C are common until it starts to rain. On the other hand, the Wet is a spectacular time to visit – ethereal thunderstorms, lightning, flowing waterfalls and a swathe of rejuvenated landscape.

Kimberley attractions include the spectacular gorges on the Fitzroy River, the huge Wolfe Creek meteorite crater, the Gibb River and Kalumburu roads, the tidal waterfalls of Talbot Bay and Purnululu (Bungle Bungles) National Park.

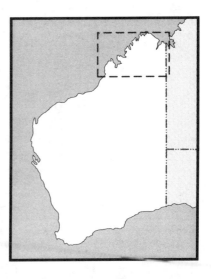

Books & Maps

The most descriptive book of the Kimberley is the excellent *The Kimberley: Horizons of Stone* (Hodder & Stoughton, Rydalmere, 1992) by Alisdair McGregor & Quentin Chester. Modern and thorough coverage is given in the *Australian Geographic Book of the Kimberley* by David McGonigal (Australian Geographic, Terrey Hills, 1990). This book includes an excellent touring map.

West Kimberley

The West Kimberley is a vast area that includes Broome out to Fitzroy Crossing, the Devonian Reef national parks, the Gibb River and Kalumburu roads and the remote north-west coast. The main town of the region is Derby. Broome, on the border of the Kimberley and Pilbara, is treated in a separate chapter.

291

The Kimberley

DERBY

Derby (population 5000), only 220 km from Broome, is a major administrative centre for the west Kimberley and a good point from which to travel to the spectacular gorges in the region.

The area has been occupied by Aborigines for many thousands of years and there is much evidence of their art and signs of habitation around Derby. In 1883, Derby was officially proclaimed a townsite and the first wooden jetty was built two years later. The Australian Aerial Medical Service (later to become the Royal Flying Doctor Service) started operation at Derby airport in 1934, largely funded by donations from Victoria. In 1942, Derby was one of the Australian towns bombed by the Japanese.

It is part of the largest shire in Australia – 102,706 sq km– with over 45% of the shire population comprising Aborigines. Mowajum ('settled at last'), on the outskirts of Derby, was one of the first independent Aboriginal communities established in the Kimberley.

Derby has the second highest tidal range in the world; the highest astronomical tide is 10.8 metres and the lowest astronomical tide is 0.3 metres, exceeded only by the Bay of Fundy in Nova Scotia, Canada (14.5 metres).

The road beyond Derby continues to Fitzroy Crossing (256 km) and Halls Creek (288 km further on). Alternatively, there's the much wilder Gibb River Rd. Derby is on King Sound, north of the mouth of the Fitzroy, the mighty river that drains the west Kimberley region.

Information

The tourist office (☎ (091) 91 1426; fax 91 1609), at 1 Clarendon St, is open from 8.30 am to 4.30 pm Monday to Friday and 8 to 11.30 am on Saturday. In the tourist season it is open seven days.

Things to See & Do

Derby has a cultural centre and a botanic garden. There's a small museum and art gallery in **Wharfinger's House**, at the end of Loch St. Built in the 1920s, this has been restored as an example of early housing in the area. In the gardens, outside the shire buildings in Stanley Square, are the anchor and propeller of the **SS Colac**, which ran aground south of Derby in 1910. Incidentally, the shire buildings are constructed of Jowlaenga sandstone. The original **old Derby gaol**, constructed in the late 1880s, is next to the present Derby police station. The **Royal Flying Doctor Service** building, in Clarendon St, is open for inspection.

Derby's lofty **wharf** has not been used since 1983 for shipping, but it provides a handy fishing spot for the locals. The whole town is surrounded by huge expanses of mud flats, baked hard in the Dry. The mud flats are occasionally flooded by king tides.

The **Prison Tree**, near the airport, seven km south of town, is a huge boab tree with a hollow trunk 14 metres around. It is said to have been used as a temporary lock-up years ago. Nearby is **Myall's Bore**, a 120-metre long cattle trough filled from a 322-metre deep artesian bore.

Organised Tours

From Derby there are flights over King Sound to **Koolan** and **Cockatoo Islands**,

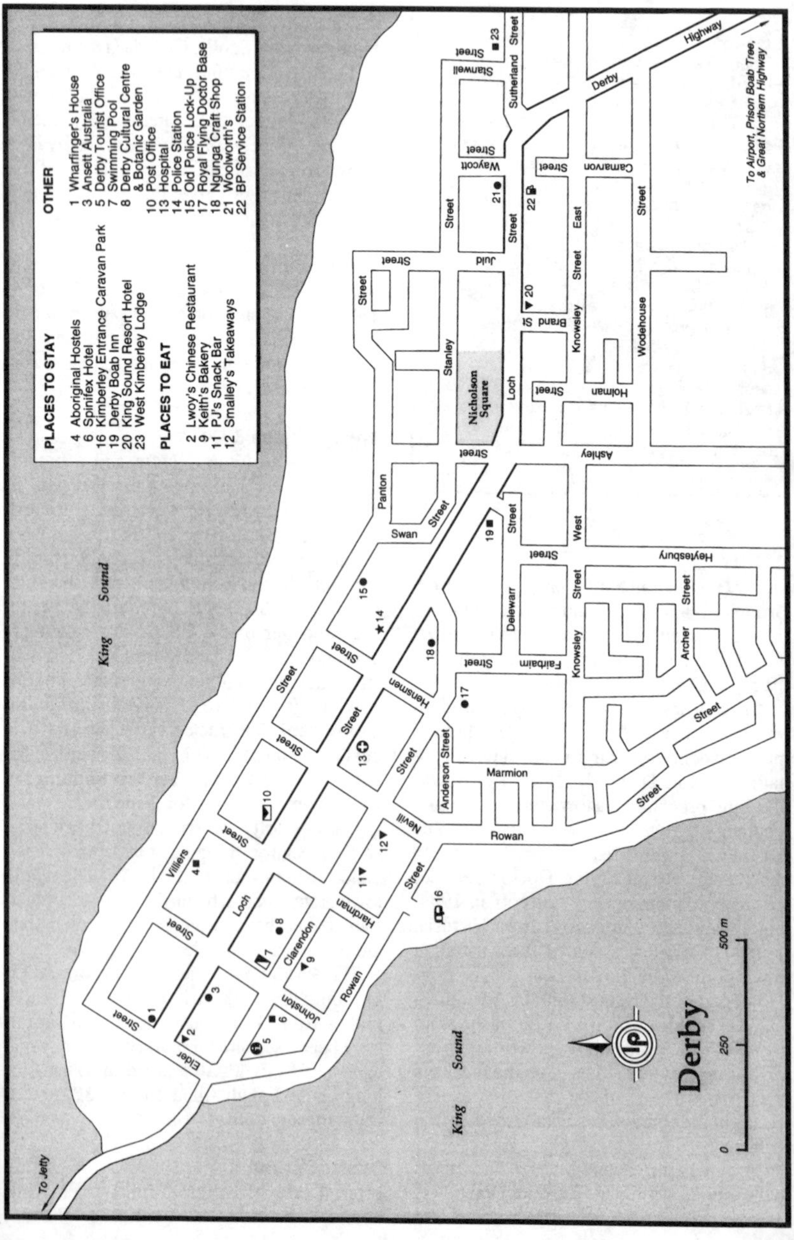

PLACES TO STAY
4 Aboriginal Hostels
6 Spinifex Hotel
16 Kimberley Entrance Caravan Park
19 Derby Boab Inn
20 King Sound Resort Hotel
23 West Kimberley Lodge
PLACES TO EAT
2 Lwoy's Chinese Restaurant
9 Keith's Bakery
11 PJ's Snack Bar
12 Smalley's Takeaways
OTHER
1 Wharfinger's House
3 Ansett Australia
5 Derby Tourist Office
7 Swimming Pool
8 Derby Cultural Centre & Botanic Garden
10 Post Office
13 Hospital
14 Police Station
15 Old Police Lock-Up
17 Royal Flying Doctor Base
18 Ngunga Craft Shop
21 Woolworth's
22 BP Service Station
King Sound
King Sound
To Jetty
To Airport, Prison Boab Tree, & Great Northern Highway
Derby Highway
Elder Street
Villiers Street
Loch Street
Clarendon Street
Johnston Street
Rowan Street
Hardman Street
Nevill Street
Hensman Street
Anderson Street
Marmion Street
Panton Street
Swan Street
Stanley Street
Nicholson Square
Delewarr Street
Fairbairn Street
Knowsley Street
Archer Street
West Street
Heytesbury Street
Ashley Street
Holman Street
Knowsley Street East
Brand St
Wodehouse Street
Judd Street
Waycott Street
Camarvon Street
Stanwell Street
Sutherland Street
Derby
0
250
500 m

THE KIMBERLEY

both owned by BHP. You can't go there unless invited by a resident, but scenic flights are available to the adjoining islands of the **Buccaneer Archipelago**. Aerial Enterprises (☎ (091) 91 1132) and Derby Air Services (☎ (091) 93 1375) provide these two-hour flights for about $110 to the Buccaneer Archipelago; there must be a minimum of four passengers.

Buccaneer Sea Safaris (☎ (091) 91 1991) does extended tours up the Kimberley coast (including the horizontal falls of Talbot Bay – see Tidal Waterfalls later in this chapter) in a large aluminium mono-hull. Bush Track Safaris (☎ (091) 91 1547) operates four to 10-day tours into the remote Walcott Inlet area.

Places to Stay

The Kimberley Entrance Caravan Park (☎ (091) 93 1055), Rowan St, has unpowered/powered campsites for $10/14 for two and on-site vans for $30 a double. It is a nice place with free barbecues. *Aboriginal Hostels Ltd* (☎ (091) 91 1867), at 233-235 Villiers St, charges $10 per person; a two-course dinner here typically costs $7.

West Kimberley Lodge (☎ (091) 91 1031), at the edge of town, on the corner of Sutherland and Stanwell Sts, has twin rooms for $45. There are a couple of regular hotels in Derby. The *Spinifex Hotel* (☎ (091) 91 1233), on Clarendon St, has rooms at $35/45 and there are backpackers' triple rooms in the bunkhouse for $10 per person. This place needs considerable cleaning up as the backpackers' facilities are pretty basic.

The *Derby Boab Inn* (☎ (091) 91 1044), on Loch St, is rather more motel-like; singles/doubles are $45/55. The *King Sound Tourist Resort* (☎ (091) 93 1044), in Loch St, is the up-market place in this 'down-market town' with singles/doubles for $85/96.

Places to Eat

Keith's Bakery near the tourist office, is good for lunch and has an excellent selection of sandwiches. *Griffo's Takeaway*, open late, is another place for a quick meal as is *Smalley's Takeaways* in Clarendon St.

The *Spinifex Hotel*, *Derby Boab Inn* and the *King Sound Tourist Resort* all do counter meals. At the Boab, there's a wide choice of

---

Tidal Waterfalls

The Kimberley coastline is made up of sheer sandstone cliffs and basalt promontories with deep indentations made by inlets and bays. It is one of the remotest coasts in the world, mainly inaccessible from the land, and it is certainly one of the most treacherous. The tidal variation is enormous, fluctuating up to 10 metres, and the region is often hit by fierce cyclonic storms. It is as if nature has constructed its own fortified Maginot Line to keep its beauty and wonders secret.

One of the most remarkable features of this coastline are the spectacular tidal 'waterfalls' which are not actual waterfalls but immense tidal currents which hurtle through the narrow coastal gorges. The speed that they attain, from 20 to 30 knots in places, gives the impression of a waterfall flowing horizontally.

The waterfalls are spectacular at Talbot Bay, north of King Sound. At the south end of the bay, two constricted gorges, both about 30 metres high and constructed of very hard sandstone, protect the Inner and Outer bays (flooded valleys). The high tide fills both bays with water and, when the tide is outgoing, the water in the bays is released. The narrow gorges restrict the outflow, resulting in a vertical difference of one metre between the first bay and the open sea of Talbot Bay, and of two metres between the first and second bays. Water then thunders through both the outer 70-metre-long gorge and the more impressive 100-metre-long inner gorge.

The Aborigines of the now-extinct Meda tribe and the Worora people knew the waterfalls as 'Wolbunum' and once had a system of bidi (tracks) running to these valleys where food was abundant. Nowadays, many people see the waterfalls from the air but occasionally someone will brave the waterfalls in a powerful motor boat in the critical still minutes of the massive tidal change. The landward journey to the falls is considered extremely difficult, as harsh terrain, lack of water and the tangle of vegetation all combine to impede progress. ∎

good food at $10 to $15. The specials at the Spinifex are $5.50.

At the end of Loch St there's *Lwoy's Chinese Restaurant*. And at the jetty is *Wharf's Restaurant & Takeaways* which has a BYO section; seafood is their speciality.

Bands can usually be heard at the local hotels on Thursday, Friday and Saturday. If you are lucky you may be able to make it to one of the legendary impromptu 'marsh parties' when barbecues are set up, great quantities of beer are consumed and a band plays into the wee small hours.

Getting There & Away
Air Ansett Australia will whisk you to Port Hedland ($224 one way/$249 Apex return), Perth ($456/$502) or to Darwin ($296/$329). Ansett's office (☎ (091) 91 1266) is at 14 Loch St.

Bus Greyhound Pioneer stops in Derby at the tourist office. Typical fares are $25 to Broome, $102 to Kununurra, $209 to Perth and $143 to Darwin. Westliner also operates the coastal route to Derby; from Broome it is $22, Port Hedland $81 and from Perth $198.

GIBB RIVER RD
This road was constructed to transport cattle from surrounding stations to the ports of Wyndham and Derby. At 667 km, from Derby to the junction of the Great Northern Highway between Wyndham and Kununurra, it's more direct by several hundred km than the Great Northern Highway (Fitzroy Crossing and Halls Creek) route.

It's almost all dirt, although it doesn't require a 4WD when it has been recently graded (not always the case). The road is impassable in the Wet and you are strongly advised not to attempt it from December to April. The best time to attempt it is from May to November; for up-to-date information on conditions, ring the Main Roads Department (☎ (091) 91 1133) or the 24-hours number (☎ (008) 13 317). There are a number of rules to observe in this area (and, indeed, in all off-road areas):

Camping
- Camping is only allowed in designated areas.
- Don't camp in river beds as they are subject to flash floods.
- When entering private property, get permission from the station owner first.
- Take extreme care to prevent bushfires and use only gas stoves for cooking.
- Don't use soap in creeks or rivers.
- Carry out all rubbish (don't bury it).
- Cash (not credit card) is the only means of transaction along the road.

Driving
- If your vehicle breaks down, stay with it and conserve water.
- Be prepared to stop for stray cattle or wildlife such as emus and kangaroos, especially at night.
- If approaching or overtaking a road train, realise that it needs to stay on the road.
- Not all roads are for public access – if you do drive onto private land, seek permission.

Fuel is available at Mt House and Mt Barnett, and Durack River (Jack's Waterhole) and Home Valley stations. The distances mentioned are from Derby.

The Kimberley gorges are the major reason for taking this route. You could also make a sidetrip to the Windjana and Tunnel Creek gorges (see under Devonian Reef National Parks in this chapter). Get a copy of *The Gibb River and Kalumburu Roads Travellers Guide* from the tourist office.

There's no public transport along the Gibb River Rd – in fact there's very little traffic of any sort, so don't bother trying to hitch!

Derby to Mt Barnett Station
From Derby the bitumen extends 62 km. It's 119 km to the Windjana Gorge (21 km) and Tunnel Creek (51 km) turn-off and you can continue down that turn-off to the Great Northern Highway near Fitzroy Crossing (see under Devonian Reef National Parks).

The Lennard River bridge is crossed at 122 km and at 145 km you pass through the Yamarra Gap in the Leopold Ranges. The country is rugged, punctuated by huge granite outcrops. At 181 km is the Inglis Gap, where the road descends into the Broome Valley. The road passes Mt Bell (also known as Elephant Hill), one of the highest points in the range.

At 190 km is the turn-off to the **Lennard River Gorge**, eight km off the road along a 4WD-only track. This gorge is five km long and has a waterfall just north of its entrance; the nearby pool is great for a quick, refreshing dip.

The signposted turn-off to **Mt House Station** (☎ (091) 91 4649) is at 246 km. The station, nestled below the odd-shaped Mt House, about 10 km down a side road, has fuel, stores and accommodation (by prior arrangement). Accommodation in the station homestead, with shared facilities, is $20 per person.

The turn-off to **Adcock Gorge** is at 267 km. This gorge is five km off the road and is good for swimming. It has great rocks for jumping or diving off, although you should check for rocks beneath the water before doing so. If the waterfall is not flowing too fiercely, climb up above it for a good view of the surrounding country. You can camp at Adcock Gorge although the site is rocky and there's little shade.

Horseshoe-shaped **Galvans Gorge** is less than a km off the road, at the 286 km mark. The small campsite here has some good shade trees, and the gorge itself has a swimming hole. The rock paintings here include a Wandjina head.

The distance from Derby to Mt Barnett Station is 306 km.

Mt Barnett Station & Manning Gorge

The Mt Barnett Station (☎ (091) 91 7007) is at the 315-km point and is owned and run by the Aboriginal Kupingarri community. There's a roadhouse (ice is available) and a small general store, open seven days from 7 am to 6 pm, May to October. It's also the access point for Manning Gorge, which lies seven km off the road along an easy dirt track. There's an entry fee of $4 per person and this covers camping.

The campsite is by the waterhole, but the best part of the gorge is about a 1¼-hour walk along the far bank – walk around the right of the waterhole to pick up the track,

which is marked with empty drink cans strung up in trees. It's a strenuous walk and, because the track runs inland from the gorge, you should carry some drinking water.

After the hot and sweaty walk, you are rewarded with this most beautiful gorge. It has a waterfall and some high rocks for daredevils.

Mt Barnett Station to Wyndham/ Kununurra Rd

There is a turn-off to the **Barnett River Gorge**, after Mt Barnett, at 328 km. This is another good swimming spot, three km down a side road. If you scan the lower level of the cliff face on the far side you should be able to spot a number of Aboriginal paintings.

The **Mt Elizabeth Station** (☎ (091) 91 4644) lies 30 km off the road at the 338-km mark. Homestead accommodation is available but this must be arranged in advance ($60 per person for BB&D). The cost for camping is $5 per adult and $1 for each chid under 15.

At 419 km you come to the turn-off to the spectacular **Mitchell Plateau** (162 km) and the **Kalumburu Aboriginal Mission** (267 km). This is remote, 4WD-only territory and should not be undertaken without adequate preparation; an entry permit is required (see under Kalumburu Rd later in this chapter).

There's magnificent scenery between the Kalumburu turn-off and Jack's (Joe's) Waterhole on **Durack River Station** (☎ (091) 61 4324) at 542 km. There is no camping at Campbell Creek (463 km), Dawn Creek (490 km) and the Durack River (514 km).

Jack's Waterhole is eight km down a side road and apart from fuel, there's also homestead accommodation or camping here. The owners, the Sinnamon family, run a number of tours from Durack River Station to Oomaloo Falls and Durack Falls. Camping is $5 per adult and $1 per child, and twin-share accommodation is $25 per night; breakfast is $8, lunch $10 and dinner $12.

At 599 km you get some excellent views of the Cockburn Ranges to the south, the

Cambridge Gulf and the twin rivers (the Pentecost and the Durack). Shortly after (two km or so) is the turn-off to **Home Valley Station** (☎ (091) 61 4322), which has camping ($5 for adults and $1 for children) and homestead accommodation for $60 BB&D. They also conduct 4WD tours from the station.

The large **Pentecost River** is forded at 610 km, and this crossing can be dodgy if there's water in the river. During the Dry it poses no problems. There is no camping and if you're fishing, beware of saltwater crocodiles.

El Questro is another station offering a variety of accommodation and riverside camping ($5 per person); it lies 16 km off the road at the 634-km mark. This is also the access point for the **Chamberlain Gorge**, **Moonshine Gorge** and **El Questro Gorge**. The latter has 60-metre towering escarpments with only nine metres between faces.

The last attraction on the road is **Emma Gorge** at 645 km. The pleasant campsite lies two km off the road and from here it's about a 40-minute walk to the spectacular gorge. Near the gorge is great wilderness cabin accommodation (run by El Questro; singles/twins $40/70), a licensed restaurant, bar and swimming pool. This gorge is close enough to Kununurra to make it a popular weekend escape for residents of that town.

At 650 km you cross King River (no camping) and at 667 km you finally hit the bitumen road; Wyndham lies 48 km to the north, while it's 52 km east to Kununurra.

All up, the distance from Mt Barnett Station to Wyndham/Kununurra Rd is 361 km.

KALUMBURU RD

This is a natural earth road which traverses extremely rocky terrain in a very isolated area. Distances in the description are given from the junction of the Gibb River and Kalumburu roads, where the road commences. The junction is 419 km from Derby or 250 km from the Great Northern Highway between Wyndham and Kununurra.

Permits

It is necessary to obtain a permit before entering the Kalumburu Reserve. Permits can be obtained by writing to the Permits Office, Aboriginal Affairs Planning Authority, PO Box 628, West Perth 6005 or calling ☎ (091) 61 4300 or ☎ 483 1222.

Gibb River Rd to Mitchell Plateau

The Gibb River is crossed at three km and Plain Creek at 16 km. The first fuel is at the **Drysdale River Homestead** (☎ (091) 61 4322) at 58 km; the homestead is one km down a side road. You can also buy supplies and trailers and caravans can be left at the homestead for a $2 per day ($10 per week) charge.

At 62 km you can turn off to the **Miner's Pool** picnic area. It is 3.5 km to the river and the last 200 metres is slow going; there is an entrance fee of $2 per adult and $1 for children. Nearby are the Drysdale Cattle Yards (watch out for wild cattle) and the Drysdale River Crossing.

The road passes a couple of entrances to stations in the next 100 km until it reaches the Mitchell Plateau turn-off at 162 km. From this junction it is 70 km along the Mitchell Plateau Road to the turn-off to the spectacular multi-tiered **Mitchell Falls**, 12 km down a side road. The plateau is also known for its ancient, tall fan palms (*Livistonia eastonii*), remnant rainforests, Wandjina paintings, the King Edward River and the Surveyor's Pool.

As this is a remote area, be sure to bring a large swag of basic necessities. In the Dry the falls are like any other with water falling from the centre of the terraces. In the Wet they are vastly different – the muddied water stretches from escarpment to escarpment and thunders down the completely submerged terraces.

Mitchell Plateau to Kalumburu

From the Mitchell Plateau turn-off, the road heads north-east towards Kalumburu, crossing the Carson River at 247 km. A km further is a road to the east to Carson River Homestead on the fringe of the Drysdale River National Park.

The **Kalumburu Mission** (☎ (091) 61 4333) and Aboriginal community (☎ (091) 61 4300) are at 267 km, about five km from the mouth of the King Edward River and King Edward Gorge. The picturesque mission is set among giant mango trees and coconut palms, and there is accommodation (campsites are $5 per person per day), a store, and food and fuel is available, Monday to Friday from 7 am to 4 pm.

There is lots to do here and fishing and trekking trips are offered at reasonable rates; scenic flights over the area are also available.

The distance between Mitchell Plateau and Kalumburu is 105 km.

Drysdale River National Park

Very few people get into Drysdale River, WA's most northern national park, which is 150 km west of Wyndham. Apart from being one of the most remote parks in Australia – it has no road access – it is also the largest park in the Kimberley with an area of 4000 sq km. Furthermore, it is also the home of the mysterious, ancient Bradshaw art figures and the more recent Wandjina art figures (see under Kimberley Art in this chapter).

Included in the park are open woodlands, rugged gorge, waterfalls (Morgan and Solea) and the wide, meandering Drysdale River. Rainforest, thought not to exist in WA until 1965, is found in pockets along the Carson Escarpment and in a number of the gorges.

The flora & fauna are diverse. Over 600 plant species have been found in the park, a number of them unique. And of the 25 fern species, half are found only in the one gorge – Worriga. Mammals include the sugar glider, water rat, a species of planigale, the short-eared rock wallaby and plenty of bats.

Kimberley Art

The Kimberley is one of the greatest ancient art galleries in the world. Many antiquated paintings remain as a testimony to one of the richest periods of cultural achievement in Aboriginal history. The indigenous art found in the overhanging rock shelters has wrongly been attributed to space travellers, early European explorers and latter day visitors. The truth is, the ancient Bradshaw figures and the more recent Wandjina are integral parts of Aboriginal culture.

In 1838, the explorer George Grey, travelling in the Glenelg river region, was probably the first European to see the Wandjina paintings. These large mouthless figures in headdresses are among the most famous of Aboriginal paintings.

The Wandjina have a lot in common with the Lightning Brothers paintings of the Victoria River in the Northern Territory (and the lightning figures in the Kimberley) in both style and tradition. Wandjina paintings are believed to be the shadows of ancestors, imprinted on the rock as they pass by. Each Wandjina site has a living custodian and, to ensure good relations between Wandjina and people, the images should be retouched annually.

The major Wandjina site is Panda-Goornnya in the Drysdale River region. Other important areas in the Kimberley are the Sale, King Edward and Glenelg rivers, the Napier, Carr Boyd and Oscar ranges and Kalumburu.

The Bradshaw figures take their name from the first European to describe them – Joseph Bradshaw – who explored the area in 1891. He said: 'The bodies and limbs were attenuated and represented as having numerous tassel-shaped adornments appended to the hair, neck, waist, arms and legs, but the most remarkable fact in connection with these drawings is that wherever a profile face is shown, the features are of a most pronounced aquiline type, quite different from those of any native we encountered.'

The Bradshaws were there long before the Wandjinas, possibly 10,000 to 20,000 years ago, and their significance to the Aborigines has been long forgotten. These exquisite paintings are consistent from shelter to shelter as if painted by artists of the same 'school'. The Bradshaw figures are now all that we have left of one particular culture that flourished many thousands of years ago. They are found in shelters in the Drysdale River, often in the same place as Wandjina figures. Who knows how many have been painted over or weathered away? ■

Some of the frogs and reptiles are known only from this park.

A permit is necessary to enter this national park and it is obtainable from CALM offices in Derby or Kununurra.

Organised Tours

Kununurra's Desert Inn and Kununurra Backpackers run five-day camping trips along the Gibb River Rd for $395 and these are excellent value. Desert Inn operates a two-day camping and walking tour to El Questro on demand ($150). Kimberley Wilderness Safaris has a Gibb River Rd Gorge Wanderer camping trip (five days; $545) which leaves from Broome and an accommodated Gibb River Rd tour (five days; $850) which leaves from Kununurra.

There are guided trips to the Mitchell Plateau, about 500 km north-west of Kununurra. Highlights include the waterfalls, Surveyor's Pool, the fan palm and ancient Wandjina art sites. Kimberley Wilderness Adventures, departing from Kununurra, has a Mitchell Plateau Explorer camping trip (six days; $655) and accommodated trip (five days; $850).

DEVONIAN REEF NATIONAL PARKS

The West Kimberley boasts three national parks, based on gorges which were once part of a western coral 'great barrier reef' in the Devonian era, 350 million years ago (see under Geology in the Facts about Western Australia chapter). The geological mysteries of this region are unravelled in the CALM pamphlet *Geology of Windjana Gorge, Geikie Gorge and Tunnel Creek National Parks* (Geological Survey of WA, 1985) by Phillip Playford.

Geikie Gorge

The magnificent Geikie Gorge, named after the British geologist Sir Archibald Geikie, is just 18 km north of Fitzroy Crossing. Part of the gorge, on the Fitzroy River, is in a small national park only eight km by three km. During the Wet, the river rises nearly 17 metres and in the Dry the river stops flowing, leaving only a series of waterholes.

The vegetation around this beautiful gorge is dense and there is also much wildlife, including the freshwater crocodile. Sawfish and stingrays, usually only found in or close to the sea, can also be seen in the river. Euros and the rare black-footed wallaby live in the gorge. Visitors are not permitted to go anywhere except along the prescribed part of the west bank, where there is an excellent 1½-km walking track.

During the April to November Dry there's a 1½-hour boat trip up the river at 9 am and 3 pm. It costs $12 and covers 16 km of the gorge (children $2). There's a weekday bus (☎ (091) 91 5155) to Geikie from Fitzroy Crossing at 8 am which connects with the morning trip. It costs $8 return (children $5).

You can go to the gorge with Darlngunaya Aboriginal guides who show you a lot more than rocks and the water. These Bunuba people reveal secrets of bush tucker, stories of the region and Aboriginal culture. The trip, which includes transport to the gorge, a river excursion and lunch beside the Fitzroy River, costs $60.

Alternatively, fly over the gorge with Geikie Air Charter (☎ (091) 91 5068) for about $50.

Windjana Gorge & Tunnel Creek

You can visit the spectacular formations of Windjana Gorge and Tunnel Creek from the Gibb River Rd, or make a detour on the Leopold Station Rd off the main highway between Fitzroy Crossing and Derby, which adds about 40 km to the distance.

The near vertical walls at the Windjana Gorge soar 90 metres above the Lennard River which rushes through in the Wet, but becomes just a series of pools in the Dry. Don't be surprised if the deafening screech of corellas and the persistent horseflies will keep you out of the gorge during the middle of the day.

Geologists are really excited by the 3.5-km long Windjana Gorge as the various deposits of an ancient reef complex are well exposed here. Fossil bones of a giant crocodile, seven metres in length, have been found in the gorge, as have bones of the extinct giant marsupial *Diprotodon*. Nightly camping fees for this gorge are $5 per person (children $1).

Three km from the river are the ruins of **Lillimilura**, an early homestead and then, from 1893, a police station. It features in the following story.

Windjana Gorge, Tunnel Creek and Lillimilura were the scene of the adventures of an Aboriginal tracker called Jundumarra or 'Pigeon'. In November 1894, Pigeon shot two police colleagues and then led a band of dissident Aborigines, skilfully evading search parties for over two years. In the meantime he killed another four men, but in early 1897, Pigeon was trapped and killed in Tunnel Creek. He and his small band had hidden in many of the seemingly inaccessible gullies of the adjoining Napier Range. Get hold of a copy of the *Pigeon Heritage Trail* from the Derby or Broome tourist office ($1.50).

Tunnel Creek is a 750-metre-long tunnel cut by the creek right through a spur of the Napier Range. The tunnel is three to 15 metres wide and you can walk all the way along it. You'll need a good light and sturdy shoes; be prepared to wade through very cold chest-deep water in places. Don't attempt it during the Wet, as the creek may flood suddenly. Halfway through, a collapse has created a shaft to the top of the range.

Near the north entrance to the tunnel, cave paintings are evident and at the other entrance is the black dolerite and basalt fashioned by the Aborigines into stone axes. A cave near the tunnel was used as a hideout for the Aboriginal tracker Pigeon between 1894 and 1897.

Broome's Last Resort (☎ (091) 93 5000) operates popular two-day trips combining Windjana and Tunnel Creek with Geikie Gorge, a good way of seeing three sites in one trip; cost $168. (There have been several recommendations for these tours.) From Fitzroy Crossing there are day trips out to Tunnel Creek and Windjana Gorge with Kimberley Safaris (☎ (091) 91 1426).

FITZROY CROSSING

Aboriginal groups have lived in this area for many thousands of years and the Bunuba

people still live near the Fitzroy River banks. A tiny settlement (population 430) where the road crosses the Fitzroy River, this is another place from which to get to the gorges and waterholes of the area. The old townsite is on Russ St, north-east of the present town. The **Crossing Inn**, near Brooking Creek, established as a shanty inn by Joseph Blythe in the 1890s, is the oldest pub in the Kimberley and still has lively nights. In the cemetery on Sandford Rd are the graves of many early European pioneers.

The Fitzroy River flows for 750 km through the hills and plains of the King Leopold and Mueller ranges. It is believed to be the biggest river in Australia when it is flooding as it is well over 10 km wide.

Places to Stay & Eat

Tarunda Caravan Park (☎ (091) 91 5004), in town, is a reasonable if dusty place, where powered campsites cost $12 for two. The *Fitzroy Crossing Caravan Park* (☎ (091) 91 5080), by the river crossing, has campsites at $10 for two with power $3 extra, cabins for $30 a double and very ordinary motel rooms for $73 a double. This place can get pretty noisy as there is a rather colourful, if a little unsavoury, bar next door.

The *Fitzroy River Lodge & Caravan Park* (☎ (091) 91 5141), two km east of town on the banks of the Fitzroy River, is the pick of the bunch and probably the best campsite along the Kununurra-Perth stretch. A campsite is $13 for two (power $2 extra) and you are allowed to use the pool for free. Air-con safari tents cost $60/73 for singles/doubles, while motel units cost $80/95.

In the Old Post Office on Geikie Gorge Rd, about four km from town, you'll find *Darlngunaya Backpackers* (☎ (091) 91 5140); dorm beds are $10. All backpackers get picked up and returned to the bus stop at the roadhouse (at some ungodly hour of the night).

It is cheaper to prepare food for yourself in this town. If your margarine is runny and the cheese you bought the day before is off, then *The Homestead* in the Fitzroy River Lodge does reasonable meals.

THE KIMBERLEY

East Kimberley

The East Kimberley is roughly the area east of Fitzroy Crossing out to the Northern Territory border. It includes Halls Creek; Mirima (Hidden Valley), Wolfe Creek Crater and the Purnululu national parks; Lake Argyle; and the towns of Wyndham and Kununurra. The hub of the region is Kununurra, a relatively new town in the heart of the Ord River Valley.

HALLS CREEK

The area around the new town of Halls Creek (population 1200), in the centre of the Kimberley and on the edge of the Great Sandy Desert, was traditionally the land of the Jaru and Kija people. The graziers took over in the 1870s and virtually used these people as slave labour on the stations. When the stations were sold, about a hundred years later, the Aboriginal people drifted to the nearby town.

Nights are often noisy and interrupted by shouting, fighting and the din from smashing bottles. Dawn brings with it the scene of an uncontrolled, nocturnal rampage with scattered debris and human bodies lying where they fell. Halls Creek is about as close as you get to an example of Australia's real shame and something should be done about it – pronto!

The region was the site of the 1885 gold rush, the first in WA. The gold soon petered out and today the town is a cattle centre, 15 km from the original site where some crumbling remains can still be seen.

Although Halls Creek is a comfortable enough little place, just remember it sits on the edge of a distinctly inhospitable stretch of country.

Things to See & Do

There's an Aboriginal art shop in the town where you can see carvers at work making high-quality artefacts. Outside the shire offices, on Thomas St, there is a statue of **Russian Jack**, a character of the 1885 gold rush.

The goldfields and the rushes threw up many heroes: successful speculators, the lucky who found nuggets or struck it rich, Peter Lalor and the diggers of Eureka Stockade, the knucklemen, the Mountain Maid and the extremely odd and unusual.

Russian Jack was the Kimberley's hero, renowned for his feats of strength and endurance. He is believed to have carried a sick friend over 300 km in his rough-and-ready wheelbarrow. He had originally pushed his barrow, with its two-metre Derbyshafts and extra wide wheel for the sandy tracks, all the way from Derby loaded with food, tools, blankets and water.

His loyalty to his mates and the job became legendary. One day he fell to the bottom of an open pit at Mt Morgan (WA), about 23 metres down. After laying there injured for three days his only comment when they pulled him out was 'I've missed a shift'.

Five km east of Halls Creek and about 1½ km off the road, there's a natural **China Wall** – so called because it resembles the Great Wall of China. This sub-vertical quartz vein with a block type formation is short but very picturesquely situated; it is located off Duncan Rd.

Halls Creek **Old Town** is a great place for fossicking. All that remains of the once bustling mining town of 3000 people are the ant-bed and spinifex walls of the old post office, the cemetery and a huge broken bottle pile where a pub once stood. 'Old Town' is the general term for the hilly area behind Halls Creek and gold might be found anywhere there.

You can swim in **Caroline Pool, Sawpit Gorge** and **Palm Springs**. Palm Springs, a popular picnic and camping spot, is a natural spring located where the Black Elvire River crosses Duncan Rd; it once supported a market garden which supplied vegetables to the area. Caroline Pool is a natural waterhole situated off Duncan Rd near Old Halls Creek and Sawpit Gorge is a popular fishing and swimming spot on the Black Elvire River.

Places to Stay

Halls Creek Caravan Park (☎ (091) 68 6169), on Roberta Ave towards the airport, has tent/caravan sites for $10/12 for two, and on-site vans at $38 per double (the latter are usually filled by workers); the pool is a good place to escape the oppressive heat.

Opposite is the *Kimberley Hotel* (☎ (091) 68 6101), which has a variety of rooms from $60/73 for singles/doubles. It has a number of rooms set aside for backpackers; the cost is $15 per night. This hotel best exhibits the rough and the smooth sides of this frontier town with what seems to be an 'Aborigines only' and a more exclusive 'Whites only' bar.

The *Shell Roadhouse* (☎ (091) 68 6060), with cabins at $55 for a double, and the *Halls Creek Motel* (☎ (091) 68 6001), with singles/doubles for $$55/72 (both on the Great Northern Highway) are other options.

Places to Eat

The *Kimberley Hotel* has a 'segregated' bar with standard counter meals at $10. You can eat outside at the tables on the grass; inside there's a surprisingly swish restaurant with smorgasbord meals at $14. The *Swagman* and *Poinciana* roadhouses both have takeaway and restaurant facilities.

Getting There & Away

It's 371 km north-east to Kununurra, 555 km west to Derby. Greyhound Pioneer passes through Halls Creek early in the morning (northbound) and late at night (southbound).

WOLFE CREEK METEORITE CRATER

The 835-metre-wide and 50-metre-deep Wolfe Creek Meteorite Crater (14 sq km) is the second largest in the world with fragments of the impacting meteorite being retrieved. It is estimated to be about two million years old. To the Aborigines, the crater is 'Kandimalal', a place where one of the snakes emerged from the ground.

Why the 'e' in 'Wolfe' when most maps don't have it? It was discovered in 1986 that the Halls Creek storekeeper and digger whom they named the crater after was one Robert Tennant Stow Wolfe.

The turn-off to the crater (the Tanami Desert Rd) is 18 km out of Halls Creek towards Fitzroy Crossing and from there it's

112 km by unsealed road to the south. It's easily accessible without 4WD in the Dry season from May to November; check with the Halls Creek shire office. You can camp (free) and get some limited supplies at the nearby Carranya Station Homestead, seven km south of the crater (☎ (091) 68 0200).

You can walk, Neil Armstrong-like, for about 200 metres along a track on the steep crater lip. Loose rocks make it unsafe, so take care. There is an information shelter and tables at the crater. The trees in the centre have only been growing since 1983, the year for the longest Wet on record.

If you can't handle one more outback road you can fly over the crater from Halls Creek for $90 with these local flight operators: Oasis Air (☎ (091) 68 6088), Kingfisher Aviation (☎ (091) 68 6162) and Crocodile Air (☎ (091) 68 6250).

HALLS CREEK TO KUNUNURRA

It is 359 km from Halls Creek to Kununurra on what is a pretty nondescript piece of highway. The lone vestige of civilisation passed through is **Turkey Creek**, which wouldn't even be mentioned if it wasn't close to one of the natural wonders of the world, Purnululu.

Turkey Creek (aka 'Warmun'), 163 km of Halls Creek, has a caravan park and roadhouse (☎ (091) 68 7882). A tent/caravan site is $10/15 for two, and motel units are $45/55. Not far south of Turkey Creek is *Bedford Downs* (☎ (091) 67 8829) where full board is $200 for three days and two nights and $50 per day thereafter. If you're desperate, grab some food from the roadhouse; your best bet is to bring fresh stuff from either Derby or Kununurra.

PURNULULU (BUNGLE BUNGLES)

I'm sure 'bungle' means superlative and 'bungle bungle' means superlatives. The 350-million-year-old Purnululu (formerly the Bungle Bungles) are an amazing spectacle which shouldn't be missed: impressive rounded rock towers, striped like tigers in alternate bands of orange (silica) and blackish-green (lichen) – truly one of Australia's natural wonders. The whole massif is a plateau which is more than 200 metres above the surrounding plain and at its edges are the curious beehive domes.

Traditionally the land of the Kija and Jaru people, who still live in settlements in the East Kimberley, there is much Aboriginal art and a number of burial sites in the area. The area was not 'discovered' by tourists until filmed by a Channel 9 television crew in 1982; in 1990 it was estimated that over 7000 people drove in to see the beehive domes.

The national park of 3000 sq km is 165 km (four hours) from Halls Creek and 305 km (five hours) from Kununurra. The range is hard to get to and access is limited to 4WDs with good clearance; no caravans or trailers are permitted. Visitors are asked to stay on authorised tracks as new tracks quickly erode in the Green season. The park is officially closed from January to March and this period is extended if the weather is unfavourable.

All visitors to the park are charged an entry fee of $20 for each vehicle with up to four people and $3 for each additional person; this covers seven nights in the park.

Things to See & Do

There is much to see once you have made the long trip to the park. It will all be a little bewildering unless you have information to interpret what you are looking at. Australian Geographic's *The Kimberley* contains a good deal of information.

Walking is the only means of access into the gorges so this is the main activity in the park. **Echidna Chasm** in the north or **Cathedral Gorge** in the south are only about a one-hour walk from the car parks at the road's end. However, the soaring **Piccaninny Gorge** is an 18-km round trip that takes eight to 10 hours return to walk.

The restricted gorges in the northern part of the park can only be seen from the air. They too are a spectacular sight, choked in fan palms. In fact, some of the plants in the park are so newly discovered that they have not yet been named. Most of the park is undulating plain which supports spinifex

and other grasses, acacia and grevillea shrubland and eucalypt woodlands. The Kimberley's southerly patches of rainforest are found around Osmond Creek (see under Rainforests in the Facts about Western Australia chapter). About 130 bird species have been recorded in the park, the most visible being spinifex pigeons *(Geophaps plumifera)* and flocks of budgerigars.

Because of the fragile nature of the rock formations you are not allowed to climb them (see under Geology in the Facts about Western Australia chapter).

Scenic Flights

As the range is so vast, flights and helicopter rides prove to be money well spent. The chopper rides cost $115 for a 45-minute flight from Bellburn campsite, or $125 in a faster helicopter from Turkey Creek Roadhouse, on the main highway. This latter flight is a popular option for people without a 4WD. Flights from Kununurra are $135 and they overfly Lake Argyle and the Argyle Diamond mine. Out of Halls Creek, the flights to Purnululu are only $100.

As the range is so vast, flights and helicopter rides over Purnululu are very popular, and rightly so. The chopper rides, operated by Heliwork WA (part of Slingair), are by far the more impressive of the two options, as you fly right in, among and over the deep, narrow gorges, while the light planes have to remain above 700 metres.

Operators of aerial tours of Purnululu and other Kimberley highlights, are:

Alligator Airways
    Fights from Kununurra over Lake Argyle, Argyle diamond mine and Purnululu (☎ (091) 68 1333)
Crocodile Air
    Flights from halls Creek over Purnululu and Wolfe Creek Crater (☎ (091) 68 6250)
East Kimberley Air Charter
    Flights from Kununurra over Purnululu (☎ (091) 69 1258)
Kingfisher Aviation
    Flights from Halls Creek and Kununurra over Purnululu, Wolfe Creek Crater and Prince Regent/Mt Barnett (☎ (091) 68 6162)

Oasis Air
    Flights from Halls Creek over Purnululu and
    Wolfe Creek (☎ (091) 686462)
Slingair
    Flights from Kununurra over Purnululu, Lake
    Argyle, Prince Regent and a full Kimberley pan-
    orama (☎ (091) 69 1300)

Places to Stay

From the main highway it's 55 km to Three Ways. It's another 20 minutes north to *Kurrajong Campsite* and 45 minutes south to *Bellburn Creek Campsite*. Bellburn Creek Campsite is mainly for the Fly/Drive visitors and licensed tour operators. Kurrajong Campsite, for casual visitors, has long-drop toilets and supplied drinking water. There is a small fee for overnight camping.

Fires are forbidden, so you'll need to have your own gas cooking equipment. There is no rubbish disposal so take all of your rubbish out of the park.

Getting There & Away

The turn-off to the single access track to the park, known as Spring Creek Track, is 110 km north of Halls Creek and 50 km south of Turkey Creek (Warnum). This 4WD-only track traverses rugged country with numerous creek crossings. From the Three Ways intersection it is 15 km to the Bellburn Creek campsite (30-45 minutes); 21 km to the Echidna Chasm car park (45 minutes); seven km to Kurrajong campsite (20 minutes); and 25 km to the Piccaninny Creek car park (one hour). Although it's only 53 km to Three Ways, in the park, from the Halls Creek to Kununurra road turn-off, the stretch takes two hours to drive.

The best option if you don't have a 4WD is to take one of the tours from Kununurra. Kununurra Backpackers has popular two-day trips ($168), while East Kimberley Tours charges much the same if you are staying at the Desert Inn Backpackers. The three-day option, which includes a lot more walking, is $240; a four-day trip is $350.

WYNDHAM

We haven't met anyone who thought the sidetrip to Wyndham (population 1500), the most northerly town and harbour in WA, was actually worth the effort – they mustn't have been avid birdwatchers.

Wyndham, a sprawling frontier town, is suffering from Kununurra's boom in popularity but its **Five Rivers Lookout** on top of Mt Bastion (380 metres) is still a must. From there you can see the King, Pentecost, Durack, Forest and Ord rivers enter the Cambridge Gulf. It's particularly good at sunrise and sunset.

There are paintings of great antiquity in the Wyndham region, evidence of the Aboriginal culture which thrived here for thousands of years. In 1819, Lieutenant Phillip Parker King in the *Mermaid*, sailed into the inlet where the town now stands; he named Cambridge Gulf after the Duke of Cambridge.

Wyndham was the starting point for two record breaking flights to England in 1931 and the finish of an England to Australia flight in 1933. It was also bombed by the Japanese in WW II and the wreck of the SS *Koolama*, sunk during a raid, lies at the bottom of the gulf, not far from the wharf.

Things to See & Do

A number of historic buildings survive in the old town (the port post office, Durack's store, the old Court House and Anthon's Landing) and these form part of the **heritage trail**; get a copy of the brochure from the tourist office (☎ (091) 61 1054) in the Old Port Post Office, O'Donnell St, Wyndham Port.

When the tide is right you can go down to the water's edge and observe (from a distance) large saltwater **crocodiles**. Failing this, you can see an 18-metre ferro-concrete saltwater crocodile at the entrance to town.

Near the town there's a rather desolate and decrepit little **cemetery** where Afghan camel drivers were buried last century. Near the Moochalabra Dam, south of Wyndham, there are Aboriginal paintings of spiritual figures and animals and another prison boab tree. The **Grotto** is a good swimming hole just off the Wyndham to Kununurra road. **Crocodile Hole** is further off the road and has a small population of freshwater crocodiles.

Not far from Wyndham is a protected bird sanctuary – **Marlgu Billabong** on Parry's Creek – where you will see many bird species including the black-necked stork or jabiru *(Ephippiorhynchus asiaticus)*, brolga *(Grus rubicundus)*, magpie geese *(Anseranas semipalmata)*, sarus cranes *(Grus antigone)*, pygmy-geese *(Nettapus pulchellus)*, pelicans *(Pelecanus conspicilattus)* and many varieties of duck. The **Moochalabra Dam** is a popular fishing and picnic spot about 25 km away.

Places to Stay & Eat
Three Mile Caravan Park (☎ (091) 61 1064), which boasts the 'largest boab tree in captivity', has tent/powered caravan sites for $10/12 a double. The *Wyndham Roadhouse* (☎ (091) 61 1290), on the Great Northern Highway, advertises budget accommodation at $15/25 for singles/doubles. The better rooms in the *Wyndham Town Hotel* (☎ (091) 61 1003), on O'Donnell St, cost $65/75 for singles/doubles. Try the *Wyndham Community Club* (☎ (091) 61 1130) for cheaper but more basic rooms ($45/55 for singles/doubles).

There is a local bakery, *Supa Fresh Hot Bread*, on the Great Northern Highway, a coffee lounge in the Tuckerbox Store, a liquor store and a restaurant in Wyndham. Face it, you didn't drive all this way for the cordon-bleu cookery.

KUNUNURRA
In the Miriwoong language the region is known as 'gananoorrang' – Kununurra is the European translation of this. As in most parts of the rugged Kimberley, the Aborigines have occupied the area for thousands of years. Nearby Hidden Valley is of great significance to the Aboriginal people and has examples of ancient rock art and axe grooves.

Founded in the 1960s, the town of Kununurra (population 4500) is in the centre of the Ord River irrigation scheme and is quite a modern and bustling little town. In the past it was just a stopover on the main highway and there was little incentive to linger. Much of the history features in Mary Durack's *Kings in Grass Castles* and *Sons in the Saddle*. That has all changed in recent years with the increase in tourism and there are now enough recreational activities, most of them water-based, to keep you busy for a week.

The town is also a popular place to look for work. The main picking season starts in May and ends about September. Ask at the Desert Inn, Kununurra Backpackers or the tourist office.

Information
The excellent Kununurra tourist office (☎ (091) 68 1177), on Coolibah Drive, has information on the town and the Kimberley. It's open from 8 am to 5 pm daily. There's a 1½-hour time change between Kununurra and Katherine in the Northern Territory.

Things to See & Do
The **Waringarri Aboriginal Arts Centre** is on Speargrass Rd, at the turn-off to Kelly's Knob. You can admire the Aboriginal art of the east Kimberley and this is as good a place as any in WA to buy art and carvings. There are good views of the irrigated fields from **Kelly's Knob Lookout**, close to the centre of town. During the Wet, distant thunderstorms can be spectacular when viewed from there, although caution is needed as the Knob itself is frequently struck by lightning.

Lake Kununurra (also called the Diversion Dam), an artificial lake beside the town, has plentiful birdlife and several swimming spots. There's good fishing below the Lower Dam (watch for crocodiles) and also on the Ord River at **Ivanhoe Crossing**. If you're swimming there, be careful. **Hidden Valley**, only a couple of km from the centre of town, is a superb national park (see under Mirima (Hidden Valley) National Park in this chapter).

There are a number of unusual **rock formations** close to town. The Sleeping Buddha, also known as Carlton Ridge or the Sleeping Mummy, is near the Ord River.

Kununurra

0   125   250 m

PLACES TO STAY

2 Hidden Valley Caravan Park
4 Kununurra Backpackers
5 Coolibah Caravan Park
6 Raintree Lodge YHA
11 Desert Inn Backpackers
17 Country Club Private Hotel
18 Kimberley Court
19 Town Caravan Park
21 Hotel Kununurra
22 Motor Inn
23 Kimberleyland Caravan Park

PLACES TO EAT

9 Salad Bowl
10 Gulliver's Tavern
12 Chicken Treat
13 Valentines & Kimbercrust Bakery
16 Three Star Cafe & Laundromat

OTHER

1 Waringarri Aboriginal Arts Centre
3 Aboriginal Medical Centre
7 Swimming Pool
8 Kununurra Tourist Office
14 Post Office
15 Coolibah Travel Centre
20 Australian Coachlines Bus Depot

THE KIMBERLEY

From a distance it looks like a person lying down. When viewed from the river it looks like an elephant's head with trunk and ears, hence another name, Elephant Rock.

The **Packsaddle Plains**, six km out of town, has a zebra rock gallery and a small wildlife park. Further along this road is **Packsaddle Falls**, popular for swimming.

About 250 km south of Kununurra is the huge **Argyle Diamond Mine**, the world's largest, which produces around 35% of the world's diamonds, although most are only of industrial quality. The ones that get diamond merchants De Beer's excited, are the extremely rare and valuable pink diamonds, the fine whites, champagne and cognac specimens. Belray's six-hour On-Site Tour (☎ (091) 68 1014) includes a flight over Purnululu, a 4WD bus trip up the East Ridge Rd to overlook the mine pit, a tour round the $430 million process plant and a chance to look in the Diamond Viewing Room; the cost is equivalent to the purchase of a very small diamond, about $260 per person.

Mirima (Hidden Valley) National Park This national park with a steep gorge, some great views and a few short walking tracks, covers an area of 18 sq km. It is a rugged area of 300 million-year-old sandstone hills and valleys, often described as a 'mini Purnululu'. Mirima is the name given to the park by the Miriwoong people and the shelter and permanent water meant that it was a popular meeting place and corroboree ground.

Within the park you will see small boabs growing out of the valley walls. Given the size of boab fruit and seeds, it is believed that rock wallabies have carried them high up in their droppings. Other vegetation which thrives in the Hidden Valley are woollybutt and long-fruited bloodwood.

Three short walking trails within the park are the Lily Pool (100 metres return) where there are stone axe grooves; Wuttuwutubin ('short and narrow', 500 metres return) which enters a steep-sided gorge; and Didbagirring (one km return) which affords great views over Kununurra and the banded rock formations of the park.

Other Activities Canoe trips on the Ord River, between Lake Argyle and the Diversion Dam, are very popular amongst travellers. A recommended operation, Kimberley Canoeing Experience (☎ (008) 805 010), has three-day self-guided tours for $80, with all gear supplied, including transport to the dam. They also run half-day guided trips which feature wildlife and birdwatching.

Kununurra Backpackers has one hour white-water trips on the Lake Argyle spillway from the end of the Wet onwards. They're $20, or $35 if you need transport to and from Kununurra.

Barramundi is the major fishing attraction, but other fish are also caught. Half-day boat trips operated by Ultimate Adventures (☎ (091) 68 1610) and Kimberley Sport Fishing (☎ (091) 68 2752) cost $65 and up. Triple J (☎ (091) 68 2682) operates high-speed boats along the Ord between Lake Argyle and Kununurra. These are a real thrill and pass through beautiful scenery. The cost is from $65 to $85 (with lunch), including bus from Kununurra. Other operators on Lake Kununurra are the *Lakeside Lady* and Triangle Tours ($35).

Kununurra Backpackers run an exciting trip into Andy's Chasm in the Wet and early Dry – hydroslide, ooze through rock squeezes, jump into the abyss, survive and enjoy – all for $30.

Organised Tours & Flights
Flights over Purnululu are popular and cost $135 a person (discounts apply). They take about two hours and also fly over lake Argyle, the Argyle and Bow River diamond projects and the irrigation area north of the town. Contact Alligator Airways (☎ (091) 68 1333) or Slingair (☎ (091) 69 1300) in Kununurra; Heliwork WA (☎ (091) 68 1811), Turkey Creek; or Ord Air Charters (☎ (091) 61 1335), Wyndham (for more operators to Purnululu, see under that heading in this chapter).

Places to Stay
Camping & Caravans There are a number of caravan parks, a couple of them by Lake

Kununurra, with tent/powered caravan sites from $10/14. *Town Caravan Park* (☎ (091) 68 1763) is on Bloodwood Drive and has on-site vans for $45; *Coolibah Caravan Park* (☎ (091) 68 1653) is on the corner of Ivanhoe and Coolibah Rds; *Hidden Valley Caravan Park* (☎ (091) 68 1790) is on Weaber Plain Rd; *Kimberleyland* (☎ (091) 68 1280), with its swimming pool, is on the lake's edge near town; and *Kona Lakeside Caravan Park* (☎ (091) 68 1031), the pick of the parks, is about a km from town, also on the lake. Kona is a great place for birdwatchers and it is likely that you will see the comb-crested jacana *(Irediparra gallinacea)* darting around on lilies beside the lake.

Hostels There are three hostels in town. With the opening of the backpackers' places, the associate YHA *Raintree Lodge* (☎ (091) 68 1372), on Coolibah Drive, where dorm beds are $10, doesn't get much business. The *Desert Inn Backpackers* (☎ (091) 68 2702) is on Tristania St, right opposite Gulliver's Tavern in the centre of town; dorm beds are $12 and twins are $28 for two. This purpose-built complex has full facilities including a spa pool. It's also a friendly and popular place.

At 112 Nutwood Crescent is *Kununurra Backpackers* (☎ (091) 68 1711). It's in a couple of adjacent houses about five minutes' walk from the centre of town; doubles are $26 to $32. The shaded pool is a big drawcard but kids are looked upon as a bit of a liability.

The *Country Club Private Hotel* (☎ (091) 68 1024), also on Coolibah Drive, has some cheap beds for $10, but no cooking facilities.

Hotels, Guesthouses & Motels Hotel accommodation is expensive with quite a variation between low and high season tariffs. The *Country Club Private Hotel* (☎ (091) 68 1024) is the cheapest, but at $50/60 a single/double for small air-con rooms with no facilities, even it is grossly overpriced; it does have a pool though. Another place is the *Kimberley Court* (☎ (091) 68 1411), on the corner of River Fig Ave and Erythrina St; B&B singles/twins are $74/84. The *Hotel Kununurra* (☎ (091) 68 1344), Messmate Way, is the town's main hotel. It has a motel section with standard rooms at $74 and deluxe rooms at $93.

The *Quality Inn* (☎ (091) 64 2622), at the corner of Duncan Highway, has high season rates of $111 for all rooms. Luxurious surroundings can be found at the *Kununurra Lakeside Resort*, Casuarina Way, where deluxe singles/doubles are $95/102. There is also a swimming pool, a necessity in the heat.

The Bush Camp This is a real opportunity to see a great part of Australia, the idyllic Lower Ord River, and stay in safari-style accommodation reminiscent of the great national parks of Kenya. *The Bush Camp* (☎ (091) 69 1214; fax 69 1371) is 50 km from Kununurra and can only be reached if you have a permit. Guided barramundi fishing and birdwatching are the two attractions here. Like the Kenyan safari camps, this style of accommodation is not cheap: an overnight stay is $100 and a weekend costs $320.

Places to Eat

The *Three Star Cafe*, on Banksia St, offers takeaway tucker and light meals; *Valentines Pizzeria* and the *Kimbercrust Bakery*, both on Cottontree Ave, are open seven days. The *Salad Bowl* on Coolibah Drive serves good salads, perfect accompaniments to their hamburgers; and the *Chicken Treat* on Coolibah Drive, opposite the tourist office, treats as their name suggests.

Standard counter meals are available at the *Hotel Kununurra* for $10 and there's a more expensive dining room. *Gulliver's Tavern*, on the corner of Konkerberry Drive and Cottontree Ave, is a popular drinking place, and, although counter meals are poor value, its George Room is quite good. The licensed *Chopsticks Restaurant* at the Country Club Private Hotel is about the best in town; main courses cost around $15. *Ivanhoe's Gallery Restaurant* in the Quality Inn is also good.

Getting There & Away

Air Ansett Australia (☎ (091) 68 1444) will fly you to Broome for ($255 one way/$289 return), Darwin ($178/$199) and Perth ($571/$640). Their office is in the Charlie Carter shopping complex.

Ansett will fly you between Kununurra and Darwin or Darwin to Broome for 50% of normal fare on presentation of authorised discount cards. Note that there is a one-way fare from Darwin to Kununurra on Wednesday ($102 all season).

Bus Greyhound Pioneer travel through on the Darwin to Perth route. Typical fares from Kununurra are $78 to Derby, $47 to Halls Creek, $43 to Katherine and $85 to Darwin.

LAKE ARGYLE

Created by the Ord River Dam, Lake Argyle is the second biggest storage reservoir in Australia, holding nine times as much water as Sydney Harbour. There are 96 islands in this huge, inland sea.

Prior to its construction, there was too much water in the wet season and not enough in the dry. By providing a regular water supply the dam has encouraged agriculture on a massive scale.

At the lake there's a **pioneer museum** in the old Argyle Homestead. The reconstructed homestead of the Durack family was moved here when its original site was flooded. The *Lake Argyle Inn & Tourist Village* (☎ (091) 68 7360), Parker Rd, has expensive rooms ($65 for a single/double, $15 each extra person) and a campsite.

Boats depart from there for the huge lake each morning and afternoon. Downstream of the lake is now green farmland. Encircling these flat lands are the small reddish mountains typical of the region. There are two cruises: Lake Argyle Cruises (☎ (091) 68 7360) has the *Bowerbird* for the two-hour cruise ($22) and the *Silver Cobbler* for the half-day cruise ($67). There is ample opportunity to observe the birdlife of the lake on the longer cruise and keen anglers get the chance to go fishing.

Index

314 Index

Guides to the Pacific

Australia – a travel survival kit
The complete low-down on Down Under – home of Ayers Rock, the Great Barrier Reef, extraordinary animals, cosmopolitan cities, rainforests, beaches ... and Lonely Planet!

Bushwalking in Australia
Two experienced and respected walkers give details of the best walks in every state, covering many different terrains and climates.

Bushwalking in Papua New Guinea
The best way to get to know Papua New Guinea is from the ground up – and bushwalking is the best way to travel around the rugged and varied landscape of this island.

Islands of Australia's Great Barrier Reef – Australia guide
The Great Barrier Reef is one of the wonders of the world – and one of the great travel destinations. Whether you're looking for the best snorkelling, the liveliest nightlife or a secluded island hideaway, this guide has all the facts you'll need.

Melbourne – city guide
From historic houses to fascinating churches and from glorious parks to tapas bars, cafés and bistros, Melbourne is a dream for gourmets and a paradise for sightseers.

New South Wales & the ACT
Ancient aboriginal sites, pristine surf beaches, kangaroos bounding across desert dunes, lyre-birds dancing in rainforest, picturesque country pubs, weather-beaten drovers and friendly small-town people, along with Australia's largest and liveliest metropolis (and the host city of the year 2000 Olympic Games) – all this and more can be found in New South Wales and the ACT.

Sydney – city guide
From the Opera House to the surf; all you need to know in a handy pocket-sized format.

Outback Australia
The outback conjures up images of endless stretches of dead straight roads, the rich red of the desert and the resourcefulness and resilience of the inhabitants. A visit to Australia would not be complete without visiting the outback to see the beauty and vastness of this ancient country.

Victoria – Australia guide
From old gold rush towns to cosmopolitan Melbourne and from remote mountains to the most popular surf beaches, Victoria is packed with attractions and activities for everyone.

Fiji – a travel survival kit
Whether you prefer to stay in camping grounds, international hotels, or something in-between, this comprehensive guide will help you to enjoy the beautiful Fijian archipelago.

Hawaii – a travel survival kit
Share in the delights of this island paradise – and avoid some of its high prices – with this practical guide. It covers all of Hawaii's well-known attractions, plus plenty of uncrowded sights and activities.

Micronesia – a travel survival kit
The glorious beaches, lagoons and reefs of these 2100 islands would dazzle even the most jaded traveller. This guide has all the details on island-hopping across the Micronesian archipelago.

New Caledonia – a travel survival kit
This guide shows how to discover all that the idyllic islands of New Caledonia have to offer – from French colonial culture to traditional Melanesian life.

New Zealand – a travel survival kit
This practical guide will help you discover the very best New Zealand has to offer: Maori dances and feasts, some of the most spectacular scenery in the world, and every outdoor activity imaginable.

Tramping in New Zealand
Call it tramping, hiking, walking, bushwalking or trekking – travelling by foot is the best way to explore New Zealand's natural beauty. Detailed descriptions of over 40 walks of varying length and difficulty.

Papua New Guinea – a travel survival kit
With its coastal cities, villages perched beside mighty rivers, palm-fringed beaches and rushing mountain streams, Papua New Guinea promises memorable travel.

Rarotonga & the Cook Islands – a travel survival kit
Rarotonga and the Cook Islands have history, beauty and magic to rival the better-known islands of Hawaii and Tahiti, but the world has virtually passed them by.

Samoa – a travel survival kit
Two remarkably different countries, Western Samoa and American Samoa offer some wonderful island escapes, and Polynesian culture at its best.

Solomon Islands – a travel survival kit
The Solomon Islands are the best-kept secret of the Pacific. Discover remote tropical islands, jungle-covered volcanoes and traditional Melanesian villages with this detailed guide.

Tahiti & French Polynesia – a travel survival kit
Tahiti's idyllic beauty has seduced sailors, artists and travellers for generations. The latest edition of this book provides full details on the main island of Tahiti, the Tuamotos, Marquesas and other island groups. Invaluable information for independent travellers and package tourists alike.

Tonga – a travel survival kit
The only South Pacific country never to be colonised by Europeans, Tonga has also been ignored by tourists. The people of this far-flung island group offer some of the most sincere and unconditional hospitality in the world.

Vanuatu – a travel survival kit
Discover superb beaches, lush rainforests, dazzling coral reefs and traditional Melanesian customs in this glorious Pacific Ocean archipelago.

Also available:
Pidgin phrasebook & **Australian** phrasebook.

Lonely Planet Guidebooks

Lonely Planet guidebooks cover every accessible part of Asia as well as Australia, the Pacific, South America, Africa, the Middle East, Europe and parts of North America. There are five series: *travel survival kits*, covering a country for a range of budgets; *shoestring guides* with compact information for low-budget travel in a major region; *walking guides*; *city guides* and *phrasebooks*.

Australia & the Pacific
Australia
Australian phrasebook
Bushwalking in Australia
Islands of Australia's Great Barrier Reef
Outback Australia
Fiji
Fijian phrasebook
Melbourne city guide
Micronesia
New Caledonia
New South Wales
New Zealand
Tramping in New Zealand
Papua New Guinea
Bushwalking in Papua New Guinea
Papua New Guinea phrasebook
Rarotonga & the Cook Islands
Samoa
Solomon Islands
Sydney city guide
Tahiti & French Polynesia
Tonga
Vanuatu
Victoria
Western Australia

South-East Asia
Bali & Lombok
Bangkok city guide
Cambodia
Indonesia
Indonesia phrasebook
Laos
Malaysia, Singapore & Brunei
Myanmar (Burma)
Burmese phrasebook
Philippines
Pilipino phrasebook
Singapore city guide
South-East Asia on a shoestring
Thailand
Thai phrasebook
Vietnam
Vietnamese phrasebook

Middle East
Arab Gulf States
Egypt & the Sudan
Arabic (Egyptian) phrasebook
Iran
Israel
Jordan & Syria
Middle East
Turkey
Turkish phrasebook
Trekking in Turkey
Yemen

North-East Asia
China
Beijing city guide
Cantonese phrasebook
Mandarin Chinese phrasebook
Hong Kong, Macau & Canton
Japan
Japanese phrasebook
Korea
Korean phrasebook
Mongolia
North-East Asia on a shoestring
Seoul city guide
Taiwan
Tibet
Tibet phrasebook
Tokyo city guide

Indian Ocean
Madagascar & Comoros
Maldives & Islands of the East Indian Ocean
Mauritius, Réunion & Seychelles

Mail Order

Lonely Planet guidebooks are distributed worldwide. They are also available by mail order from Lonely Planet, so if you have difficulty finding a title please write to us. US and Canadian residents should write to Embarcadero West, 155 Filbert St, Suite 251, Oakland CA 94607, USA ; European residents should write to 10 Barley Mow Passage, Chiswick, London W4 4PH; and residents of other countries to PO Box 617, Hawthorn, Victoria 3122, Australia.

Indian Subcontinent
Bangladesh
India
Hindi/Urdu phrasebook
Trekking in the Indian Himalaya
Karakoram Highway
Kashmir, Ladakh & Zanskar
Nepal
Trekking in the Nepal Himalaya
Nepali phrasebook
Pakistan
Sri Lanka
Sri Lanka phrasebook

Africa
Africa on a shoestring
Central Africa
East Africa
Trekking in East Africa
Kenya
Swahili phrasebook
Morocco
Arabic (Moroccan) phrasebook
South Africa, Lesotho & Swaziland
Zimbabwe, Botswana & Namibia
West Africa

Central America & the Caribbean
Baja California
Central America on a shoestring
Costa Rica
Eastern Caribbean
Guatemala, Belize & Yucatán: La Ruta Maya
Mexico

North America
Alaska
Canada
Hawaii

South America
Argentina, Uruguay & Paraguay
Bolivia
Brazil
Brazilian phrasebook
Chile & Easter Island
Colombia
Ecuador & the Galápagos Islands
Latin American Spanish phrasebook
Peru
Quechua phrasebook
South America on a shoestring
Trekking in the Patagonian Andes
Venezuela

Europe
Baltic States & Kaliningrad
Central Europe on a shoestring
Central Europe phrasebook
Czech & Slovak Republics
Dublin city guide
Eastern Europe on a shoestring
Eastern Europe phrasebook
Finland
France
Greece
Hungary
Iceland, Greenland & the Faroe Islands
Ireland
Italy
Mediterranean Europe on a shoestring
Mediterranean Europe phrasebook
Poland
Prague city guide
Scandinavian & Baltic Europe on a shoestring
Scandinavian Europe phrasebook
Switzerland
Trekking in Spain
Trekking in Greece
USSR
Russian phrasebook
Vienna city guide
Western Europe on a shoestring
Western Europe phrasebook

The Lonely Planet Story

Lonely Planet published its first book in 1973 in response to the numerous 'How did you do it?' questions Maureen and Tony Wheeler were asked after driving, bussing, hitching, sailing and railing their way from England to Australia.

Written at a kitchen table and hand collated, trimmed and stapled, *Across Asia on the Cheap* became an instant local bestseller, inspiring thoughts of another book.

Eighteen months in South-East Asia resulted in their second guide, *South-East Asia on a shoestring*, which they put together in a backstreet Chinese hotel in Singapore in 1975. The 'yellow bible' as it quickly became known to backpackers around the world, soon became *the* guide to the region. It has sold well over half a million copies and is now in its 8th edition, still retaining its familiar yellow cover.

Today there are over 140 Lonely Planet titles in print – books that have that same adventurous approach to travel as those early guides; books that 'assume you know how to get your luggage off the carousel' as one reviewer put it.

Although Lonely Planet initially specialised in guides to Asia, they now cover most regions of the world, including the Pacific, South America, Africa, the Middle East and Europe. The list of *walking guides* and *phrasebooks* (for 'unusual' languages such as Quechua, Swahili, Nepali and Egyptian Arabic) is also growing rapidly.

The emphasis continues to be on travel for independent travellers. Tony and Maureen still travel for several months of each year and play an active part in the writing, updating and quality control of Lonely Planet's guides.

They have been joined by over 50 authors, 110 staff – mainly editors, cartographers & designers – at our office in Melbourne, Australia, at our US office in Oakland, California and at our European office in Paris; another five at our office in London handle sales for Britain, Europe and Africa. Travellers themselves also make a valuable contribution to the guides through the feedback we receive in thousands of letters each year.

The people at Lonely Planet strongly believe that travellers can make a positive contribution to the countries they visit, both through their appreciation of the countries' culture, wildlife and natural features, and through the money they spend. In addition, the company makes a direct contribution to the countries and regions it covers. Since 1986 a percentage of the income from each book has been donated to ventures such as famine relief in Africa; aid projects in India; agricultural projects in Central America; Greenpeace's efforts to halt French nuclear testing in the Pacific; and Amnesty International. In 1994 over $100,000 was donated to such causes.

Lonely Planet's basic travel philosophy is summed up in Tony Wheeler's comment, 'Don't worry about whether your trip will work out. Just go!'.